We Are the American People

Our Nation's History Through Its Documents, Volume I

William D. Young
Maple Woods Community College

Greg Sanford
Lyle Gibson
Penn Valley Community College

KENDALL/HUNT PUBLISHING COMPANY
4050 Westmark Drive   Dubuque, Iowa 52002

Contents

**Chapter 4   The American Revolution: Traitors in an Evil Rebellion
or Simple Citizens Defending Their Rights?** **79**

**Chapter 5   Protecting Our Rights or Stealing Our Liberties: Debates on
the Ratifying of the Constitution** **119**

Preface

Almost every college history instructor has heard one of the following from students: "Why should I study history, it is so boring" or "History is just about old dead people that I don't have anything in common with." The students reflect the comment made in Jane Austen's novel *Northanger Abbey* that they read history only a little because "...it tells me little that does not either vex or weary me. The quarrels of popes and kings, with wars and pestilences, and in every page; the men all so good for nothing, and hardly any women at all." Historians today write accurately, with the intent to present a story that both informs and entertains. But to reach out to students, to take their minds beyond entertainment, to the realm of critical thinking that is necessary for good citizens in a democracy, requires more than clear prose.

Based on our combined sixty-plus years of teaching experience, we created *We Are the American People: Our Nation's History Through Its Documents* to supplement the usual text and lectures in a United States history survey course. The survey course, in fact any good United States history course, should provide insights and basic background on our historic past, encourage further exploration by students, and promote critical thinking. Too often the survey fails to accomplish any of these goals, because instructors are forced to use a panoramic approach. Forced to sprint across hundreds of years in two, sixteen-week courses professors paint a picture of our past with broad strokes, seldom having time for detailed work.

As attempts to remedy this, instructors assign student book critiques, create special in-class projects and group discussions, and use handouts of articles or primary documents. We believe that using primary documents is one of the best ways to do this: it's even essential. We also believe that this new primary documents reader provides an excellent way to incorporate documents into your classes.

First, this is an exciting collection of documents, which will make history classes come alive. We want this collection to let you smell the gunpowder from battles, hear the laughter of children, listen to the cries of workers, and feel the frustrations of people from all classes. Americans who face anxiety over moving can identify with the stories of traveling west into unknown areas; those arguing over critical decisions at work can identify with the intensive debates over using the atomic bomb. These documents personalize American history. They help students connect with the past as they discover that earlier Americans had worries, hopes and dreams similar to their own. This is part of learning to "think historically." History is more than just retelling the past in a chronological fashion. Students, just as historians do, must put themselves in the mindset and time of earlier Americans, understand their crisis and conflicts, and how they handled the challenges of their time. At the same time this means learning to separate fact from opinion, determine the reliability of past accounts, and understand how the events and people of our nation's past influence us today.

Second, we wanted to give instructors one of the widest possible ranges of documents. In our own classes we have often thought, "I wish I could use several readers. Then I could have the students read all the documents I wanted." To address this issue we have included materials from the entire spectrum of social and political history, from a diverse variety of people, from different ethnic groups, classes, races, regions and nationalities. "Old chestnuts" like Winthrop's sermon on the *Arabella* are here, as well as women's diaries, political speeches, first-hand accounts of slavery and business promotions.

Third, college accreditation is now tied closely to assessment of student learning. This volume specifically addresses the issues of critical thinking that so many colleges and universities, like the Metropolitan Community Colleges where we teach, identify as a learning priority. MCC has employed several standardized instruments like the Watson Glaser *Appraisal of Critical Thinking,* the Cornell *X Critical Thinking Test,* and the *Collegiate Assessment of Academic Proficiency* to evaluate the critical thinking skills of their students. The authors have also used some of these reader materials in embedded assessments to refine their understanding of students' critical thinking abilities. The presentation of materials in these volumes and the formulation of questions about the readings represent a response to student needs identified by these studies.

Further, they are using the texts to monitor their students' progress with critical thinking in general and to assess their inference skills in particular.

Fourth, this book will help students recognize issues from past points of view and learn to understand the past on its own terms. Doing these things help students think critically. We believe students learn the best, and learn to think critically, when they read specific historical content, examining the materials from the living past. This does not mean believing blindly anything put in print in texts placed before them, but questioning where and how historians reach their conclusions. Part of the critical thinking process requires students to confront the issues, themes and cultural debates from the past that often continue to this very day. These themes should be considered in every United States history course, since we have debated their meanings even before becoming independent.

Work and economic issues are a good example. How should work be rewarded, and who should determine the division of goods and services? Should everyone be rewarded equally for similar work? Does the value of goods derive from the labor producing them? How important is labor? Is there an absolute conflict between labor and capital? Does technology always improve the lives of citizens, whether they are housewives, farmers, or industrial workers? Is there true equality of opportunity in the nation, or has there been at any time? Why is this concept so important in our national history?

Human needs are important as well. What role do families, organizations, and communities play in United States history? Are they all part of what Americans define as the "good life"? Do men and women have the same needs, enjoy the same opportunities and rewards, or share the same experiences in our history? What do different groups of immigrants, ethnic and religious minorities, or anyone else have to do to belong in approved society? How do we determine what is more important, individual greed and accomplishment or the welfare and health of the entire community? How do we define community in the United States? Who gets to create and monitor these definitions and peoples behavior?

What is the relationship between individuals, citizenship, and the state? What are the origins of our government, why was it formed and who formed it? Where does the government derive its power to rule? What rights do citizens have, and how do we know this? Do all Americans enjoy these same rights throughout time, and if not, why not? What is the relationship between liberty and order, between natural rights and property rights in United States history? If the government is supposed to provide order and justice for citizens, does this mean the same for everyone in society? (i.e. slaves, women, white males, religious minorities, workers, students and the poor.) When, and on what grounds should the people challenge the authority of the government? What is the importance of security in national history, and how should this issue be defined? What is the proper role of the government in creating and preserving all types of security?

What does all of this mean to me? How am I affected by America's past, by government actions and individual accomplishments, by both virtuous citizens and evildoers? How does the past explain the United States today? How do political and business leaders misuse and abuse history for their own purposes? What is my own "sense of history"; how do I create my own perspective of the past? Where do my personal views and experiences intersect with the public history that academics teach? When I evaluate historical events, do I interpret them based on my gender, my class, my race or ethnicity?

To the Instructor

How often do students tell you that history is their worst or least favorite subject, that back in high school the coach taught it by reading out of the book while drinking coffee, or that they were taught to prepare for standardized state exams? We hear that from freshmen, who describe high school history as nothing more than memorizing names, dates and treaties. As historians we know that is learning trivia, not real history. College history classes examine why and how events happened, how they affected the nation and its people, rather than simply repeating what happened. History is learning how to put information in proper perspective, to use documents and historic accounts to understand the past.

Each chapter of this reader is organized around an issue or event in United States history. Unlike some readers we chose not to focus simply on problems in our past. For example, Chapter 5 examines the struggle to ratify the Constitution, focusing on the arguments and tactics used by both sides. Students learn that not everyone embraced the document, and that its ratification was not a sure thing. Chapter 7 examines the impact of the market economy on local communities, on workers, and on American society. We create a balance sheet of positive and negative impacts for students to consider. Chapter 16 considers the reality of urban life in the late Nineteenth and early Twentieth centuries. Cities might have meant opportunities for millions, but also meant unsafe living and working conditions, costing people their lives. In chapter 21 we take a closer look at the Cold War. Different views of the Marshall Plan, of Truman's firing of General MacArthur, and of McCarthyism force students to realize there is often not one simple answer or truth to the past.

Every chapter begins with an introduction to the topic, providing historical background and introducing the historical arguments over the issue. This is followed by clues on how to consider the evidence in the readings. Each document has its own introduction, with additional background on the material, the writer/speaker, and additional questions to help students focus on key issues.

At the end of each chapter is a worksheet, with a series of questions requiring students to apply the information in the documents. History students must learn to apply their own insights to questions, utilize data to support arguments, and compare materials in the reader to determine historical accuracy. This means cultivating critical thinking skills through open-ended questions requiring students to synthesize the documents before them with other knowledge and personal opinions. These worksheets are perforated so students may complete them and turn them in as assignments.

We included many different types of evidence in this book. Instructors who want a variety of materials will find presidential addresses, Congressional debates and hearings, personal diaries, formal speeches, musical lyrics, folk tales, advertisements, court cases, memoirs, personal letters, oral interviews, newspaper accounts, and wartime propaganda. You will hear from religious and secular leaders, from the rich and the poor, from slaveowners and slaves, from our friends and our enemies, from land-hungry whites and Native Americans, from men and women, from business and labor, from those who favor a strong government and those who oppose it, from Yankees and Confederates. Some of the documents are important classics, such as John Winthrop's sermon on the *Arabella*, the Declaration of Independence, Ida B. Wells's anti-lynching articles, and Roosevelt's "Day of Infamy" speech. Other selections have not been included in readers before, and should be a refreshing look at new material. We made sure the documents vary in length as well. Sometimes small snippets suffice, but other times instructors want (and students need) complete documents to understand the author's intent. Because the documents often assume conflicting positions, students are forced to think like historians. Our nation's past is full of conflict: our ancestors did not agree on everything, so students can try to understand what they disagreed on and why. Common assumptions and popular myths that students grew up with are challenged as well. For example, while we take the Constitution for granted today, its passage was not a sure thing, nor was support for the new government anywhere unanimous.

This reader and its contents may be used in a variety of ways. These documents can be the basis for classroom discussion and group projects. The authors write specific questions for their examinations and require students to use the documents to answer the questions. Instructors can compare materials in different chapters, to trace the development of attitudes across time. For example, does the obligation of all citizens to the health and well being of their community demonstrated in Chapter 2 continue throughout the rest of Volume I? Are there similarities in the attitudes expressed before the American Revolution in Chapter 4 and during the Civil War in Chapter 12? Do the conservative concerns in Chapter 18 on the 1920s resemble conservative concerns in Chapter 21 on the 1950s? If you want other suggestions feel free to contact the authors. We have suggestions for additional documents to use as well.

To the Student

What do you do in class when you need information, or do not understand something? You usually raise your hand and ask a question. Critical thinking is about asking questions, about not accepting statements and information blindly, but to question and evaluate what is presented. That is what historians do when they look at documents; they ask questions for the document to answer. You already do this too. Your class syllabus is a document. It contains key information about your course, insights into your instructors thinking and values, and his expectations for you and the timing of the current semester. Ten instructors may teach the same course, and every syllabus will be different. The course is the same, but uses different ideas on how and what to teach. Learning to read any historical document is like reading your syllabus. It is important to ask the right questions and reach the correct conclusions, even in the face of conflicting arguments. What types of questions should you ask about each document? Consider the following:

- Who wrote the document? This means the name of the person and their position, because their experiences and position in life affect the point-of-view expressed in the document. A slave and his owner will obviously view slavery differently, as will a factory owner and his employees. So consider what social status, specific group, religion, or gender influences the information in the document. Everyone is molded by their past experiences, their relationships with others, their occupation, and their class status. Also important to your understanding is the background information on the period covered in the module, information gained from your textbook and instructor. This will help you know how reliable a source the author of the document is, and how biased their opinions might be.

- Who is the intended audience? Every document has a specific audience, and determining who the audience is also lets you understand the document better. Was this intended as a private letter between friends, with no holds or secrets between them? Was it private and personal, as in a diary? Was the document intended for public consumption, such as an editorial, letter to the editor, speech, autobiography, or pamphlet? What story are they trying to tell? Sometimes the audience influences how the story is told. The writer includes certain details to inflame the audience, or leaves out bits of information he/she assumes the audience already knows. Knowing who the audience is helps you understand why the document was written, and also helps explain the form the document took, i.e. poem, diary etc. Was it intended to help win an election, or perhaps arouse the population into righteous indignation? Would all people accept or respond to the arguments the same way as the intended audience?

- You also need to go beyond the facts you can observe from the document if you are going to think critically like a historian; you must learn to distinguish between fact and opinion. Assuming the document intended to sway an audience at the other end, can you believe the information presented? Is the letter, diary etc. believable? Can you accept the claims of slaveowners that slavery is the best life for African Americans? Can you accept the claims of Joseph McCarthy that over 200 communists are working in the State Department in 1950? Has the document been altered from its original form, so you are reading an altered version?

- What does the document tell you about American society at that time period? Documents reveal the way their authors think about politics, class structure, immigration and other issues. Does the choice of words reveal certain attitudes or biases? Are there covert messages being spread with the overt ones? Do you think the attitudes expressed in the document, or the lifestyle described, reflect the views and lives of everyone in American society at that time? Is the author really an eyewitness to the events he/she describe? Always keep in mind that many events are linked together.

- What do these documents mean to you, a United States history student in the Twenty-first Century? What do these documents tell you about whom we are as a nation today, where our values and ideas come from? How much have we changed? What events from the past directly affect you today? Using the skills you honed comparing arguments in the chapters, can you dissect political arguments and advertisements today?

Finally, remember that this is your book, and it is speaking to you. Write in the book. Take possession of the pages and the documents included. As you question the documents, the author's ideas, or the editor's introductions, write the questions in the margins so you don't forget them. As you come across key ideas in the book, note them in the margin, so you can easily refer back to them when answering the worksheet questions, or reference them for tests and discussions. Always be sure to ask yourself, how and why I reached my own conclusions. That too is part of "thinking historically."

Acknowledgements

An enormous amount of time and labor went into preparing this reader. The authors wish to thank the following people, without whom we never could have completed the book.

William D. Young: I must begin by thanking my wife Michelle and sons, Benjamin and Michael. Once again they served as sounding boards for ideas, read documents as I acquired them, and waited patiently as I took over the work space in two rooms. Michelle has supported me through five such projects now, and is the steadiest support in my life. At Maple Woods Community College librarian Patricia M. Eklund pursued documents for me from across the country, with a smile on her face (and I suspect a song in her heart.) The chairman of the Social Sciences division, Paul Long, provided as much support and encouragement as anyone can. Our discussions about historical thinking v. philosophical ideas while team teaching the honors program were a great help. He is the ultimate example of academic peer and good friend. Steve Jansen, a.k.a. "Mr. History" in Lawrence, Kansas, helped me hunt down certain documents on the 1850s and 1860s. As a lifetime advocate of using documents to teach students, as well as the model for combining enthusiasm for local history with professional standards, his comments were always appreciated. My co-authors are special people, friends and scholars. Greg and I have known each other for almost thirty years. His dedication to teaching, knowledge of technology and philosophy, and deep-seated cynicism are greatly appreciated. Lyle willingly joined us on the project, despite this being his first year in the district. At times he must have felt we threw him into the deep end of the pool, but his scholarship and teaching enthusiasm are evident in the book. I could not ask for better co-authors, academic peers, or friends.

Greg Sanford: Completing a volume like this gives a person the chance to reflect upon and appreciate the special people who inhabit their world. Let me begin by thanking my wife Amy who is my inspiration. Without her insights and patient support, this work would not have been completed. I would also like to thank Bill Young for envisioning this project, giving me the opportunity to work on it, and counseling me about how to do this sort of thing. Lyle Gibson has my deepest appreciation as a great co-worker, colleague, and sounding board. We are both privileged to work with a Chair who has created an environment that nurtures special projects. I would like to thank Karen Curls as well for taking a personal interest in the work, listening to my concerns, and providing sage advice throughout the project. I owe a special debt of gratitude to Terry Davin who helped launch this project through his concern for knowing what it is students actually learn. Our discussions about assessment and work on it are some of the reasons for this volume. A special thanks to Charles VanMiddlesworth for his constant designing, enjoying and conducting assessment.

Lyle Gibson: This work entailed the assistance, encouragement, and patience of a formidable number of people, and it would be impossible for me to thank all of them, but I do wish to express my gratitude to some of them. First I would like to thank my wife Cynthia. She has been at my side for eight years, inspiring me to reach greater heights. Next I would like to thank my two children, Camron James and Cynae Elizabeth. Everything that I do, I do it all for you. I also want to thank Bill Young and Greg Sanford for inviting me to participate in this project. Our time spent completing this work has been educational—thank you both for your votes of confidence. Special thanks go to Karen Curls, chair of the Social Sciences Division at Penn Valley Community College, Dorether M. Welch and Cebra Sims; your words of encouragement and guidance helped me to mature professionally. More important, I thank my parents Urel and Elizabeth Gibson for believing in me—you are the best parents in the world. Special gratitude goes to Mary Burtzloff, archivist at the national Archives and Records Administration, Kansas City, Missouri, for providing me with primary documents that aided my research in this project.

All of us want to thank our students, without whom this project would not be possible. They stimulate us, frustrate us, and ask the darndest questions, which in turn inspire us. They also help us learn what works in the classroom. We also thank our editor, Eric Klosterman of Kendall Hunt for his interest in, and perseverance in pushing this work through to its conclusion. His unceasing reminders that we had to finish the book to really enjoy using it helped us along. Special thanks to Angela Puls of Kendall Hunt for her assistance in finishing both volumes. We never imagined anyone could have such patience and understanding as deadlines passed us by.

We may be reached at:

Professor William D. Young
Social Science Division
Maple Woods Community College
2601 N.E. Barry Road
Kansas City, MO 64156
William.Young@kcmetro.edu

Professor Greg Sanford and Professor Lyle Gibson
Social Science Division
Penn Valley Community College
3201 Southwest Trafficway
Kansas City, MO 64111
Greg.Sanford@kcmetro.edu
Lyle.Gibson@kcmetro.edu

Native America Through European Eyes: Strange and Disgusting Savages or Honest, Spiritual People?

The European explorers who crossed the Atlantic Ocean to the Americas encountered Indian peoples who already had long histories on this continent. For thousands of years the American Indians explored, trapped, and cultivated the land, and created diverse societies, complex religions, and a multitude of political systems. They cultivated new crops or adapted existing plants across the continents, built irrigation systems and check-dams to increase production in the arid Southwest, and created homes from whatever building materials existed. The American Indians developed hunting and fishing techniques to take advantage of what nature offered. When the European explorers and settlers arrived, the existing Americans were everywhere. Their hunting and trapping skills promoted the European economy; they served as guides, interpreters, and warriors in Europe's colonial wars, and ensured the survival of every colony.

The European newcomers were not always sure what to expect from the American Indians, or even how to describe them. Some believed they were little more than bloodthirsty savages, roaming the land like barbarians of ancient days, prepared to rob, kill, and take your scalp. Were they new and frightful versions of the Huns and Visigoths? Did they look human, or were they covered in fur and have just one eye in the center of their forehead? However, European writers promoting settlement preferred to describe them as trusting, child-like creatures, free from the worst corruptions of civilization. They were "noble allies" when they fought on your side in colonial wars, and European writers appreciated and lauded their martial abilities. If local American Indians were your partners in the fur trade, they were not threatening at all. Few European writers cared about the history of Native America, dismissing all events occurring before European arrival as **prehistory**.

The Indian peoples were as varied as the Europeans who encountered them. From the Catawbas in the Carolinas, the Cherokee in Tennessee, the Shawnees in Kentucky, the Iroquois in New York, the Wampanoags in New England, to the Navahos across the Southwest, native cultures, languages, and lifestyles were as diverse as the land they lived in. Most American Indians in the eastern woodlands were hunters and farmers. Corn was the mainstay of farming across the eastern half of North America, but wide varieties of beans, squash, and other foods were cultivated as well. Elsewhere in the Americas, natives were cultivating some of the world's most important agricultural products, including chocolate, cotton, potatoes, tobacco, and quinine. They used plants for medicines, flavoring, dyes, and smoking. Each diversified economy maximized the foods available to them without destroying the basic ecosystem they lived in.

When Europeans arrived in the New World they ignored most native accomplishments, judging the American Indians according to their own European definitions of civilization. Europeans commonly viewed as "barbaric" anything not done their way, and language was usually the first difference noted by explorers. Do they speak a recognizable language [English, Spanish, French, Latin or Dutch], or do they grunt and make animal noises? If they don't speak your language then they might not have your real religion or morality. Are they Christians, or are they heathens with no religion? Is there a viable political structure, or just anarchy? Are the customs, morals, dress styles, and daily behavior barbarous, or civilized like those in Europe? What technological advances have they made? Do they have a written language and literature? Assuming their own way of life to be superior, European newcomers judged American Indian culture by their own standards and customs. Not prepared to evaluate accurately what they encountered, European writers were often critical and judgmental in their descriptions of native lifestyles. However, historian James Axtell reminds us that, while their interpretations of native behavior may be suspect, European descriptions of their behavior and lifestyles are very useful to us.

Gender roles are a good place to consider cultural misunderstandings. In Europe there were patriarchal guidelines for almost every aspect of life. Men owned most of the land and every other form of moveable property as well. Men controlled public access and activities of women, and governmental decisions and participation were usually limited to men only. Family inheritances, family histories, and the family name all passed down the male side of the family. European males felt a great need to exercise absolute authority over everything, especially in their own households. In contrast, most (but not all) American Indian societies were matrilineal in culture; family history and descent were traced through the woman's side of the family tree. While tribes and clans owned land, it was allocated to families, and farmed almost exclusively by women. In a clearly defined division of labor, men cleared the land of trees, and then women planted, weeded, and harvested, while the men hunted and fished to supplement the crops. Control of food production and storage gave native women enormous political and social power. American Indian women participated widely in government as well, with power to call for or against wars, as well as to elect officials. European males believed Indian males were lazy for making their women work in fields; natives believed the European men were too feminine for doing women's work!

Both natives and Europeans fought, but disagreed over the goals and proper conduct of warfare. In Europe you fought to a finish on the battlefield, killing as many of your enemy as possible. Wartime slaughter could include women and children, to eliminate enemies in the future. Many wars were fought in the name of religion, killing your opponents in the name of God because they worshiped the wrong way. American Indians were appalled at this waste of life. Their battles were more often raids for honor or control of territory. The goal of "mourning wars" was acquiring captives, which you took back home for adoption into the clan to replace lost population. Other captives were subject to ritual torture or human sacrifice, behavior that European observers marked as savage. Natives would gradually adopt European ways, as settlers funneled guns and other weapons to chosen chiefs, who became clients and did their bidding in wars and trade struggles.

Each side found the others religious beliefs strange or even horrifying. European explorers were not sure where the Indians came from or even if they were human, because there was no mention of them in the Bible. Were they even human, or just animals without souls, as the Catholic theologian Juan Gines de Sepulveda insisted? (This interpretation was used as grounds for their extermination.) Were the natives Satan worshipers? The Mesoamerican Indians' practice of human sacrifices and ritual cannibalism, and their displays of skull racks and snake motifs on their buildings, led to this conclusion-and once again justified genocide by the Spanish. Issuing proclamations in Spanish that demanded the natives accept the Catholic faith (and Spanish rule), they then attacked any natives who did not understand or show acceptance of their declaration. Many English settlers felt that the ritual torture by some North American Indians justified their extermination. Perhaps natives were simply idolaters and simple ignorant heathens. The American Indians believed that every part of the world is sacred, that all parts of the earth have spiritual power. The spirits lived in the earth, the sky, the water, and everywhere else, and you must maintain a positive relationship with the inhabitants of the entire world. To the Christians of Europe, this was all wrong. But native peoples found Europeans' Christianity and practices contradictory or worse. The Spanish Inquisition's burning of heretics by the thousands looked like human sacrifices. The practice of Mass and the Eucharist puzzled American Indians as well. It seemed that Christians would eat their own god, but unfairly object to human sacrifices made to native gods. Both European and native cultures were very religious. Indian creation myths show how people and societies share a need to explain human existence and understand the world around them.

Conflict also arose as settlers from European nations with growing populations coveted Indian lands that both sides needed for their survival. Embracing the concept of private property and land ownership, they dismissed the native methods of land use and temporary abandonment as "nomadic." The natives had built no permanent public buildings, roads, or settlements. According to European legal tradition, nomads could not own land; therefore, European newcomers could take it over. Once in their possession, it would not be returned or shared with the Indians. Nor did European settlers accept the native methods of crop rotation and living within the means of the ecosystem. The earth was supposed to submit to them; all plants and animals were under their control. Thus, trees would be cut down because they were in the way and represented savagery rather than civilization, and the same crops would be planted until the soil wore out.

So what is the definition of civilization? To the peoples of Europe, technological advances in weapons, sailing ships, and astronomy all indicated they were superior to the native residents of North America. Also important was the European view of non-literate societies. Because Europeans valued the written word, any culture without established methods of writing and recording was inferior. When negotiating treaties with local Indians, the final written document was always considered more important than the discussions and oratory beforehand. But story-telling is important in all non-literate societies, as a way to preserve tribal identities and family histories, as well as pass along essential knowledge for survival from one generation to another. Public speaking was an important part of native American life. One did not order your people around, but used your oratorical skills to persuade them to follow you. Histories often had moral stories, and made your people look good in the end. American Indians referred to themselves as "true men" or the "original people," while describing their enemies as "bark-eaters" or "rattlesnakes."

European arrival devastated American Indian communities. In 1492 native peoples were among the healthiest in the world, free from most infectious diseases. The most devastating agents of change were new germs and viruses that spread through Indian populations with little or no immunity. Endemic diseases like tuberculosis, measles, yellow fever, diphtheria, and especially smallpox became New World epidemics, decimating the people. Entire tribes were wiped out, while others lost between 50 and 90 percent of their populations. This biological disaster shredded the fabric and traditions of native America. Elders died without passing along accumulated knowledge, wars increased to replace population losses, and the Indian people became increasingly dependent on trade with the European newcomers instead of surviving on their own. Cultural survival and adaptation became an issue that native Americans still face today. Smallpox would haunt North America for four hundred years.

Considering the Evidence in the Readings

In the material you are about to read you cannot make an accurate judgement on what all native American societies were like. In the variety of materials ahead you are examining what a variety of European explorers perceived Indian society to be, and then you will determine how or what standards they used to reach their conclusions.

This chapter contains several different types of evidence. There are several native creation stories, and one speech by Powhatan. Be sure to consider whether these accounts were recorded accurately, since European settlers wrote all down years later. Not all interpreters and translators were competent, sober, or impartial. Even if they were, remember that the translator is attempting to convert Indian cultural concepts into something that European readers can understand. What might be lost or altered in the translation?

The remaining evidence comes from European visitors. Keep in mind the European views of their own superiority, and what they believed made them superior. Most selections are written descriptions of first encounters with groups of natives. As you read the accounts, what images of the New World form in your thoughts?

Documents 1.1 A Maidu Account of the Beginning of the World

California was home to a large and diverse number of American Indians. Numbering as many as 300,000 and speaking more than 65 different languages, the California Indians were more diverse than their European counterparts. The Maidu, who lived in central California, had a lifestyle based on fishing for trout and salmon, catching waterfowl, and gathering plants such as acorns and yampa. Their Kuksu religion initiated male members of the tribe into secret ceremonial societies, believed these members were temporarily transformed into spirit beings, and believed that sometime in the future the sacred order that existed at creation would be restored. The Spanish arrival in California exposed the Maidu and other tribes to killer diseases and forced conversion to Christianity. The Indian population dropped 50 percent to 150,000 by 1845. Following the discovery of gold, another 100,000 died in just ten years. By the beginning of the twentieth century the Maidu numbered fewer than 300. The following is their explanation of the world's beginning. Remember that all people have origin stories, explaining how the world began, as well as the trials and joys of living in it. They assure people they have a reason for being, who they are, and how they came to be. They identify the sources of good and evil. How did the Maidu come into being? What are the origins of the sun, the moon, and the stars? What role do animals play in creation, and what is their relationship with humankind?

All the earth was covered with water, and everything was dark in the beginning. There was no sun, no moon, no stars. Then one day a raft appeared, floating on the water. In it was Turtle. Down from the sky a rope of feathers come and dangled near the bow of the raft, and then a being, who shone like the sun, descended. He was Earth Initiate. When he reached the end of the rope he tied it to the bow of the raft, and stepped in. His face was covered, so that Turtle was not able to see it. In fact, no one has ever seen his face uncovered. Earth Initiate sat down and for a long time said nothing.

"Where do you come from?" Turtle asked at last.

"I come from above," Earth Initiate said.

Then Turtle asked: "Brother, can you not make for me some good dry land, so that I may sometimes come up out of the water?"

Earth Initiate did not answer at once, and Turtle asked, "Are there going to be any people in the world?"

After thinking for a while, Earth Initiate said, "Yes."

"How long before you are going to make people?" Turtle asked.

"I don't know," Earth Initiate answered. "You want to have some dry land: well, how am I going to get any earth to make it of?"

"If you will tie a stone about my left arm I will dive for some," Turtle answered.

So Earth Initiate did as Turtle asked. Reaching around he took the end of a rope from somewhere and tied it to Turtle.

"If the rope is not long enough I will jerk it once, and then you must haul me up; if it is long enough I will give two jerks and then you must pull me quickly, as I shall have all the earth that I can carry."

Turtle was gone for six years, and when he came up he was covered with green slime, he had been down so long. He returned with only a very little earth under his nails. The rest had all washed away.

Earth Initiate scraped the earth out from under Turtle's nails, and put it in the palm of his hand and rolled it about until it was round and about the size of a small pebble. This he laid on the stem of the raft, and went away and left it. Three times he returned to look at it, and the third time found that it had grown very large. The fourth time he looked at it, it was as big as the world, the raft was on ground, and all around were mountains.

When Turtle knew the raft was on ground, he said: "I cannot stay in the dark all the time. Can't you make a light so that I can see?"

"Let's get out of the raft, and then we will see what we can do," Earth Initiate replied.

As they got out Earth Initiate said: "Look that way, to the east! I am going to tell my sister to come up."

Then it began to grow light, and day began to break, and the sun came up.

"Which way is the sun going to travel?" Turtle asked.

"I will tell her to go this way, and go down there," Earth Initiate answered.

After the sun went down it grew very dark.

"I will tell my brother to come up," said Earth Initiate.

Then the moon rose.

"How do you like it?" Earth Initiate asked Turtle.

"It is very good," Turtle answered. "Is that all you are going to do for us?"

"No, I am going to do more yet."

Then he called the stars each by name and they came out.

Then he made a tree, which had twelve different kinds of acorns growing on it. . . . For two days they sat under this tree, and then both set off to see the world which Earth Initiate had made. Turtle was not able to keep up with Earth Initiate. All he could see of him was a ball of fire flashing about under the ground and the water. When they returned from going around the world Earth Initiate called the birds from the air, and made the trees, and then the animals.

Some time after this he said: "I am going to make people."

So he took dark, red earth and mixed it with water, and made two figures, one a man and one a woman. He lay down and placed the man on his right side and the woman on his left. Thus he lay all afternoon and night. Early in the morning the woman began to tickle him in the side. Earth Initiate kept very, very still and did not laugh. Soon after he got up, he put a piece of wood into the ground, and fire burst out.

The two people Earth Initiate made were very white. Their eyes were pink, their hair was black, their teeth shone brightly, and they were very handsome. He named the man Kuksu, and the woman Morning Star Woman. . . .

Document 1.2 The Iroquois Explain How the World Begins on a Turtle's Back

Historians and anthropologists have a special fondness for the Iroquois, dating back to Father Joseph F. Lafitau's book-length account of their lives in 1724. European explorers and settlers entering upstate New York were amazed by the political unity and democratic practices of the Hodenosaunee (People of the Longhouse) who controlled the region from the Hudson River to Lake Erie, and whose influence was felt from the Atlantic to the Great Lakes. The Iroquois nation played a decisive role in United States history, from shaping the colonial empires of the Dutch, French, and English to their participation in the American Revolution. The Iroquois were farmers, and cultivating food was the primary activity for women. They planted at least 15 different varieties of maize, together with beans and squash. The Iroquois believed that when the spirits of these three plants combined they became the Three Sisters, and influenced fertility and the success of crops. Deprived of their lands in the United States by broken treaties and swindles, ravaged by disease and warfare, today most of the 90,000 Iroquois live in Canada. As you read their creation story, identify the explanation of how the Iroquois came to be. What other important origins are explained in this account? What is the relationship between the people, the earth, the plants, and the animals?

In the beginning there was no world, no land, no creatures of the kind that are around us now, and there were no men. But there was a great ocean which occupied space as far as anyone could see. Above the ocean was a great void of air. And in the air there lived the birds of the sea; in the ocean lived the fish and the creatures of the deep. Far above this unpeopled world, there was a Sky-World. Here lived gods who were like people—like Iroquois.

In the Sky-World there was a man who had a wife, and the wife was expecting a child. The woman became hungry for all kinds of strange delicacies, as women do when they are with child. She kept her husband busy almost to distraction finding delicious things for her to eat.

In the middle of the Sky-World there grew a Great Tree which was not like any of the trees that we know. It was tremendous; it had grown there forever. It had enormous roots that spread out from the floor of the Sky-World. And on its branches there were many different kinds of leaves and different kinds of fruits and flowers. The tree was not supposed to be marked or mutilated by any of the beings who dwelt in the Sky-World. It was a sacred tree that stood at the center of the universe.

The woman decided that she wanted some bark from one of the roots of the Great Tree—perhaps as a food or as a medicine, we don't know. She told her husband this. He didn't like the idea. He knew it was wrong. But she insisted, and he gave in. So he dug a hole among the roots of this great sky tree, and he bared some of its roots. But the floor of the Sky-World wasn't very thick, and he broke a hole through it. He was terrified, for he had never expected to find empty space underneath the world.

But his wife was filled with curiosity. He wouldn't get any of the roots for her, so she set out to do it herself. She bent over and she looked down, and she saw the ocean far below. She leaned down and stuck her head through the hole and looked all around. No one knows just what happened next. Some say she slipped. Some say that her husband, fed up with all the demands she had made on him, pushed her.

So she fell through the hole. As she fell, she frantically grabbed at its edges, but her hands slipped. However, between her fingers there clung bits of things that were growing on the floor of the Sky-World and bits of the root tips of the Great Tree. And so she began to fall toward the great ocean far below.

The birds of the sea saw the woman falling, and they immediately consulted with each other as to what they could do to help her. Flying wingtip to wingtip they made a great feathery raft in the sky to support her, and thus they broke her fall. But of course it was not possible for them to carry the woman very long. Some of the other birds of the sky flew down to the surface of the ocean and called up the ocean creatures to see what they could do to help. The great sea turtle came and agreed to receive her on his back. The birds placed her gently on the shell of the turtle, and now the turtle floated about on the huge ocean with the woman safely on his back.

The beings up in the Sky-World paid no attention to this. They knew what was happening, but they chose to ignore it.

When the woman recovered from her shock and terror, she looked around her. All that she could see were the birds and the sea creatures and the sky and the ocean.

And the woman said to herself that she would die. But the creatures of the sea came to her and said that they would try to help her and asked her what they could do. She told them that if they could get some soil, she could plant the roots stuck between her fingers, and from them plants would grow. The sea animals said perhaps there was dirt at the bottom of the ocean, but no one had ever been down there so they could not be sure.

If there was dirt at the bottom of the ocean, it was far, far below the surface in the cold deeps. But the animals said they would try to get some. One by one the diving birds and animals tried and failed. They went to the limits of their endurance, but they could not get to the bottom of the ocean. Finally, the muskrat said he would try. He dived and disappeared. All the creatures waited, holding their breath, but he did not return. After a long time, this little body floated up to the surface of the ocean, a tiny crumb of earth clutched in his paw. He seemed to be dead. They pulled him up on the turtle's back and they sang and prayed over him and breathed air into his mouth, and finally, he stirred. Thus it was the muskrat, the Earth-Diver, who brought from the bottom of the ocean the soil from which the earth was to grow.

The woman took the tiny clod of dirt and placed it on the middle of the great sea turtle's back. Then the woman began to walk in a circle around it, moving in the direction that the sun goes. The earth began to grow. When the earth was big enough, she planted the roots she had clutched between her fingers when she fell from the Sky-World. Thus the plants grew on the earth.

To keep the earth growing, the woman walked as the sun goes, moving in the direction that the people still move in the dance rituals. She gathered roots and plants to eat and built herself a little hut. After a while, the woman's time came, and she was delivered of a daughter. The woman and her daughter kept walking in a circle around the earth, so that the earth and plants would continue to grow. They lived on the plants and roots they gathered. The girl grew up with her mother, cut off forever from the Sky-World above, knowing only the birds and the creatures of the sea, seeing no other beings like herself.

One day, when the girl had grown to womanhood, a man appeared. No one knows for sure who this man was. He had something to do with the gods above. Perhaps he was the West Wind. As the girl looked at him, she was filled with terror, and amazement, and warmth, and she fainted dead away. As she lay on the ground, the man reached into his quiver, and he took out two arrows, one sharp and one blunt, and he laid them across the body of the girl, and quietly went away.

When the girl awoke from her faint, she and her mother continued to walk around the earth. After a while, they knew that the girl was to bear a child. They did not know it, but the girl was to bear twins.

Within the girl's body, the twins began to argue and quarrel with one another. There could be no peace between them. As the time approached for them to be born, the twins fought about their birth. The right-handed twin wanted to be born in the normal way, as all children are born. But the left-handed twin said no. He said he saw light in another direction, and said he would be born that way. The right-handed twin beseeched him not to, saying that he would kill their mother. But the left-handed twin was stubborn. He went in the direction where he saw light. But he could not be born through his mother's mouth or her nose. He was born through her left armpit, and killed her. And meanwhile, the right-handed twin was born in the normal way, as all children are born.

The twins met in the world outside, and the right-handed twin accused his brother of murdering their mother. But the grandmother told them to stop their quarreling. They buried their mother. And from her grave grew the plants which the people still use. From her head grew the corn, the beans, and the squash—"our supporters, the three sisters." And from her heart grew the sacred tobacco, which the people still use in the ceremonies and by whose upward-floating smoke they send thanks. The women call her "our mother," and they dance and sing in the rituals so that the corn, the beans, and the squash may grow to feed the people.

But the conflict of the twins did not end at the grave of their mother. And, strangely enough, the grandmother favored the left-handed twin.

The right-handed twin was angry, and he grew more angry as he thought how his brother had killed their mother. The right-handed twin was the one who did everything just as he should. He said what he meant, and he meant what he said. He always told the truth, and he always tried to accomplish what seemed to be right and reasonable. The left-handed twin never said what he meant or meant what he said. He always lied, and he always did things backward. You could never tell what he was trying to do because he always made it look as if he were doing the opposite. He was the devious one.

These two brothers, as they grew up, represented two ways of the world which are in all people. The Indians did not call these the right and the wrong.

They called them the straight mind and the crooked mind, the upright man and the devious man, the right and the left.

The twins had creative powers. They took clay and modeled it into animals, and they gave these animals life. And in this they contended with one another. The right-handed twin made the deer, and the left-handed twin made the mountain lion which kills the deer. But the right-handed twin knew there would always be more deer than mountain lions. And he made another animal. He made the ground squirrel. The left-handed twin saw that the mountain lion could not get to the ground squirrel, who digs a hole, so he made the weasel. And although the weasel can go into the ground squirrel's hole and kill him, there are lots of ground squirrels, and not so many weasels. Next the right-handed twin decided he would make an animal that the weasel could not kill, so he made the porcupine. But the left-handed twin made the bear, who flips the porcupine over on his back and tears out his belly.

And the right-handed twin made berries and fruits of other kinds for his creatures to live on. The left-handed twin made briars and poison ivy, and the poisonous plants like the baneberry and the dogberry, and the suicide root with which people kill themselves when they go out of their minds. And the left-handed twin made medicines, for good and for evil, for doctoring and for witchcraft.

And finally, the right-handed twin made man. The people do not know just how much the left-handed twin had to do with making man. Man was made of clay, like pottery, and baked in the fire.

The world the twins made was a balanced and orderly world, and this was good. The plant-eating animals created by the right-handed twin would eat up all the vegetation if their number was not kept down by the meat-eating animals which the left-handed twin created. But if these carnivorous animals ate too many other animals, then they would starve, for they would run out of meat. So the right- and the left-handed twins built balance into the world.

As the twins became men full grown, they still contested with one another. No one had won, and no one had lost. And they knew that the conflict was becoming sharper and sharper and one of them would have to vanquish the other.

And so they came to the duel. They started with gambling. They took a wooden bowl, and in it they put wild plum pits. One side of the pits was burned black, and by tossing the pits in the bowl, and betting on how these would fall, they gambled against one another, as the people still do in the New Year's rites.

All through the morning they gambled at this game, and all through the afternoon, and the sun went down. And when the sun went down, the game was done, and neither one had won.

So they went on to battle one another at the lacrosse game. And they contested all day, and the sun went down, and the game was done. And neither had won.

And now they battled with clubs. and they fought all day, and the sun went down, and the fight was done. But neither had won.

And they went from one duel to another to see which one would succumb. Each one knew in his deepest mind that there was something, somewhere, that would vanquish the other. But what was it? Where to find it?

Each knew somewhere in his mind what it was that was his own weak point. They talked about this as they contested in these duels, day after day, and somehow the deep mind of each entered into the other. And the deep mind of the right-handed twin lied to his brother, and the deep mind of the left-handed twin told the truth.

On the last day of the duel, as they stood, they at last knew how the right-handed twin was to kill his brother. Each selected his weapon. The left-handed twin chose a mere stick that would do him no good. But the right-handed twin picked out the deer antler, and with one touch he destroyed his brother. And the left-handed twin died, but he died and he didn't die. The right-handed twin picked up the body and cast it off the edge of the earth. And some place below the world, the left-handed twin still lives and reigns.

When the sun rises from the east and travels in a huge arc along the sky dome, which rests like a great upside-down cup on the saucer of the earth, the people are in the daylight realm of the right-handed twin. But when the sun slips down in the west at nightfall and the dome lifts to let it escape at the western rim,

the, people are again in the domain of the left-handed twin—the fearful realm of night.

Having killed his brother, the right-handed twin returned home to his grandmother. And she met him in anger. She threw the food out of the cabin onto the ground, and said that he was a murderer, for he had killed his brother. He grew angry and told her she had always helped his brother, who had killed their mother. In his anger, he grabbed her by the throat and cut her head off. Her body he threw into the ocean, and her head, into the sky. There "Our Grandmother, the Moon," still keeps watch at night over the realm of her favorite grandson.

The right-handed twin has many names. One of them is Sapling. It means smooth, young, green and fresh and innocent, straightforward, straight-growing, soft and pliable, teachable and trainable. These are the old ways of describing him. But since he has gone away, he has other names. He is called "He Holds Up the Skies," "Master of Life," and "Great Creator."

The left-handed twin also has many names. One of them is Flint. He is called the devious one, the one covered with boils, Old Warty. He is stubborn. He is thought of as being dark in color.

These two beings rule the world and keep an eye on the affairs of men. The right-handed twin, the Master of Life, lives in the Sky-World. He is content with the world he helped to create and with his favorite creatures, the humans. The scent of sacred tobacco rising from the earth comes gloriously to his nostrils.

In the world below lives the left-handed twin. He knows the world of men, and he finds contentment in it. He hears the sounds of warfare and torture, and he finds them good.

In the daytime, the people have rituals which honor the right-handed twin. Through the daytime rituals they thank the Master of Life. In the nighttime, the people dance and sing for the left-handed twin.

Document 1.3 The Creation as Told in Genesis

The biblical story of creation, although more familiar to most students than native American accounts, still addresses many of the same basic questions all early people wanted answered. Where do we and other living things come from? Why are we here? In Genesis, as in the other two accounts, a strong connection is made between humankind and the earth, to the task of cultivating and caring for the land. Different views of the relationship between humankind and the planet should be clear to you. Be sure to look for these and other issues, including the relationship of humans to animals, as well as why women are created. How does the Genesis account compare with the first two you read?

The Creation of the World

In the beginning of creation, when God made heaven and earth, the earth was without form and void, with darkness over the face of the abyss, and a mighty wind that swept over the surface of the waters. God said, "Let there be light," and there was light; and God saw that the light was good, and he separated light from darkness. He called the light day, and the darkness night. So evening came, and morning came, the first day.

God said, "Let there be a vault between the waters, to separate water from water." So God made the vault, and separated the water under the vault from the water above it, and so it was; and God called the vault heaven. Evening came, and morning came, a second day.

God said, "Let the waters under heaven be gathered into one place, so that dry land may appear"; and so it was. God called the dry land earth, and the gathering of the waters he called seas; and God saw that it was good.

Then God said, "Let the earth produce fresh growth, let there be on the earth plants bearing seed, fruit-trees bearing fruit each with seed according to its kind." So it was; the earth yielded fresh growth, plants bearing seed to their kind and trees bearing fruit each with seed according to its kind; and God saw that it was good. Evening came, and morning came, a third day.

God said, "Let there be lights in the vault of heaven to separate day from night, and let them serve as signs both for festivals and for seasons and years. Let them also shine in the vault of heaven to give light on earth." So it was; God made the two great lights, the greater to govern the day and the lesser to govern the night; and with them he made the stars. God put these lights in the vault of heaven to give light on earth, to govern day and night, and to separate light from darkness; and God saw that it was good. Evening came, and morning came, a fourth day.

God said, "Let the waters teem with countless living creatures, and let birds fly above the earth across the vault of heaven." God then created the great sea-monsters and all living creatures that move and swarm in the waters, according to their kind, and every kind of bird; and God saw that it was good. So he blessed them and said, "Be fruitful and increase, fill the waters of the seas; and let the birds increase on land." Evening came, and morning came, a fifth day.

God said, "Let the earth bring forth living creatures, according to their kind: cattle, reptiles, and wild animals, all according to their kind." So it was; God made wild animals, cattle, and all reptiles, each according to its kind; and he saw that it was good. Then God said, "Let us make man in our image and likeness to rule the fish in the sea, the birds of heaven, the cattle, all wild animals on earth, and all reptiles that crawl upon the earth." So God created man in his own image; in the image of God he created him; male and female he created them. God blessed them and said to them, "Be fruitful and increase, fill the earth and subdue it, rule over the fish in the sea, the birds of heaven, and every living thing that moves upon the earth." God also said, "I give you all plants that bear seed everywhere on earth, and every tree bearing fruit which yields seed: they shall be yours for food. All green plants I give for food to the wild animals, to all the birds of heaven, and to all reptiles on earth, every living creature." So it was; and God saw all that he had made, and it was very good. Evening came, and morning came, a sixth day.

Thus heaven and earth were completed with all their mighty throng. On the sixth day God completed all the work he had been doing, and on the seventh day he ceased from all his work. God blessed the seventh day and made it holy, because on that day he ceased from all the work he had set himself to do.

This is the story of the making of heaven and earth when they were created.

The Beginnings of History

When the LORD God made earth and heaven, there was neither shrub nor plant growing wild upon the earth, because the LORD God had sent no rain on the earth; nor was there any man to till the ground. A flood used to rise out of the earth and water all the surface of the ground. Then the LORD God formed a man from the dust of the ground, and breathed into his nostrils the breath of life. Thus the man became a living creature. Then the LORD God planted a garden

From *The Oxford Study Bible:* Revised English Bible, edited by Jack Suggs, et al. Used by permission of Oxford University Press, Inc.

in Eden away to the east, and there he put the man whom he had formed. The LORD God made trees spring from the ground, all trees pleasant to look at and good for food; and in the middle of the garden he set the tree of life and the tree of the knowledge of good and evil.

There was a river flowing from Eden to water the garden, and when it left the garden it branched into four streams. The name of the first is Pishon, that is the river which encircles all the land of Havilah, where the gold is. The gold of that land is good; bdellium and cornelians are also to be found there. The name of the second river is Gihon; this is the one which encircles all the land of Cush. The name of the third is Tigris; this is the river which runs east of Asshur. The fourth river is the Euphrates.

The LORD God took the man and put him in the garden of Eden to till it and care for it. He told the man, "You may eat from every tree in the garden, but not from the tree of the knowledge of good and evil; for on the day that you eat from it, you will certainly die." Then the LORD God said, "It is not good for the man to be alone. I will provide a partner for him." So God formed out of the ground all the wild animals and all the birds of heaven. He brought them to the man to see what he would call them, and whatever the man called each living creature, that was its name. Thus the man gave names to all cattle, to the birds of heaven, and to every wild animal; but for the man himself no partner had yet been found. And so the LORD God put the man into a trance, and while he slept, he took one of his ribs and closed the flesh over the place. The Lord God then built up the rib, which he had taken out of the man, into a woman. He brought her to the man, and the man said:

'Now this, at last—
bone from my bones,
flesh from my flesh!—
this shall be called woman,
for from man was this taken.'

That is why a man leaves his father and mother and is united to his wife, and the two become one flesh. Now they were both naked, the man and his wife, but they had no feeling of shame towards one another.

Documents 1.4 Christopher Columbus: Journal Excerpts, First Voyage, 1492

More than 500 years ago King Ferdinand and Queen Isabella of Spain, flush with victory after driving the Moorish Muslims from their homes in the Iberian Peninsula, supplied an ambitious sailor named Christopher Columbus with three ships and an elaborate title in return for 90 percent of all the wealth he came across. Sailing west in hopes of reaching the East Indies off the coast of Asia, Columbus and his men shocked the natives of the Caribbean islands with both their arrival and their appearance. Columbus called the natives "indios" because he believed (to his dying day) that his ships had reached islands off the coast of India, achieving his goal of finding an all-water route to the Far East. Calling all natives Indians suggests a monolithic culture, which reinforces European ideas of supremacy. He kept a diary to document his travels to the Orient, and used it to note the places and people he encountered. Columbus presented this diary to Queen Isabella, who returned a copy to Columbus. She lost the original, and his grandson lost the copy before it could be published. Luckily, Bartolome' de Las Casas was allowed to peruse and make extensive copies of the contents during the 1530s, while working on his *History of the Indies*. This is how the words of Christopher Columbus reach us today. How did Columbus believe the Native Americans compared with Europeans? What specific traits did he notice, both good and bad? What does he use as his basis for judging the local people, both on their own lives and as possible value for Spain? Could the fact that Columbus does not understand their language affect his understanding of their views?

Thursday, 11 October. Steered west-southwest; and encountered a heavier sea than they had met with before in the whole voyage. Saw pardelas and a green rush near the vessel. The crew of the Pinta saw a cane and a log; they also picked up a stick which appeared to have been carved with an iron tool, a piece of cane, a plant which grows on land, and a board. The crew of the Nina saw other signs of land, and a stalk loaded with rose berries. These signs encouraged them, and they all grew cheerful. Sailed this day till sunset, twenty-seven leagues.

Presently they descried people, naked, and the Admiral landed in the boat, which was armed, along with Martin Alonzo Pinzon, and Vincent Yanez his brother, captain of the Nina. The Admiral bore the royal standard, and the two captains each a banner of the Green Cross, which all the ships had carried; this contained the initials of the names of the King and Queen each side of the cross, and a crown over each letter. Arrived on shore, they saw trees very green, many streams of water, and diverse sorts of fruits. The Admiral called upon the two Captains, and the rest of the crew who landed, as also to Rodrigo de Escovedo notary of the fleet, and Rodrigo Sanchez, of Segovia, to bear witness that he before all others took possession (as in fact he did) of that island for the King and Queen his sovereigns, making the requisite declarations, which are more at large set down here in writing. Numbers of the people of the island straightway collected together. Here follow the precise words of the Admiral: "As I saw that they were very friendly to us, and perceived that they could be much more easily converted to our holy faith by gentle means than by force, I presented them with some red caps, and strings of beads to wear upon the neck, and many other trifles of small value, wherewith they were much delighted, and became wonderfully attached to us. Afterwards they came swimming to the boats, bringing parrots, balls of cotton thread, javelins, and many other things which they exchanged for articles we gave them, such as glass beads, and hawk's bells; which trade was carried on with the utmost good will. But they seemed on the whole to me, to be a very poor people. They all go completely naked, even the women, though I saw but one girl. All whom I saw were young, not above thirty years of age, well made, with fine shapes and faces; their hair short, and coarse like that of a horse's tail, combed toward the forehead, except a small portion which they suffer to hang down behind, and never cut. Some paint themselves with black, which makes them appear like those of the Canaries, neither black nor white; others with white, others with red, and others with such colors as they can find. Some paint the face, and some the whole body; others only the eyes, and others the nose. Weapons they have none, nor are acquainted with them, for I showed them swords which they grasped by the blades, and cut themselves through ignorance. They have no iron, their javelins being without it, and nothing more than sticks, though some have fish-bones or other things at the ends. They are all of a good size and stature, and handsomely formed. I saw some with scars of wounds upon their bodies, and demanded by signs the cause of them; they answered me in the same way, that there came people from the other islands in the neighborhood who endeavored to make prisoners of them, and they defended themselves. I thought then, and still believe, that these were from the continent. It appears to me, that the people are ingenious, and would be good servants and I am of opinion that they would very readily become Christians, as they appear to have no religion. They very quickly learn such words as are spoken to them. If it please our Lord, I intend at my return to carry home six of them to your Highnesses, that they may learn our language. I saw no beasts in the island, nor any sort of animals except parrots." These are the words of the Admiral.

Saturday, 13 October. "At daybreak great multitudes of men came to the shore, all young and of fine shapes, very handsome; their hair not curled but straight and coarse like horse-hair, and all with foreheads and heads much broader than any people I had hitherto seen; their eyes were large and very beautiful; they were not black, but the color of the inhabitants of the Canaries, which is a very natural circumstance, they being in the same latitude with the island of Ferro in the Canaries. They were straight-limbed without exception, and not with prominent bellies but handsomely shaped. They came to the ship in canoes, made of a single trunk of a tree, wrought in a wonderful manner considering the country; some of them large enough to contain forty or forty-five men, others of different sizes down to those fitted to hold but a single person. They rowed with an oar like a baker's peel, and wonderfully swift. If they happen to upset,

From *Diary of Christopher Columbus's First Voyage to America*, 1492–1493, translated and edited by Oliver C. Dunn and James E. Kelley, Jr. Published by the University of Oklahoma Press, 1989. Reprinted by permission.

they all jump into the sea, and swim till they have righted their canoe and emptied it with the calabashes they carry with them. They came loaded with balls of cotton, parrots, javelins, and other things too numerous to mention; these they exchanged for whatever we chose to give them. I was very attentive to them, and strove to learn if they had any gold. Seeing some of them with little bits of this metal hanging at their noses, I gathered from them by signs that by going southward or steering round the island in that direction, there would be found a king who possessed large vessels of gold, and in great quantities. I endeavored to procure them to lead the way thither, but found they were unacquainted with the route. I determined to stay here till the evening of the next day, and then sail for the southwest; for according to what I could learn from them, there was land at the south as well as at the southwest and northwest and those from the northwest came many times and fought with them and proceeded on to the southwest in search of gold and precious stones. This is a large and level island, with trees extremely flourishing, and streams of water; there is a large lake in the middle of the island, but no mountains: the whole is completely covered with verdure and delightful to behold. The natives are an inoffensive people, and so desirous to possess any thing they saw with us, that they kept swimming off to the ships with whatever they could find, and readily bartered for any article we saw fit to give them in return, even such as broken platters and fragments of glass. I saw in this manner sixteen balls of cotton thread which weighed above twenty-five pounds, given for three Portuguese ceutis. This traffic I forbade, and suffered no one to take their cotton from them, unless I should order it to be procured for your Highnesses, if proper quantities could be met with. It grows in this island, but from my short stay here I could not satisfy myself fully concerning it; the gold, also, which they wear in their noses, is found here, but not to lose time, I am determined to proceed onward and ascertain whether I can reach Cipango. At night they all went on shore with their canoes.

Wednesday, 17 October. At noon set sail from the village where we had anchored and watered. Kept on our course to sail round the island; the wind southwest and south. My intention was to follow the coast of the island to the southeast as it runs in that direction, being informed by the Indians I have on board, besides another whom I met with here, that in such a course I should meet with the island which they call Samoet, where gold is found. I was further informed by Martin Alonzo Pinzon, captain of the Pinta, on board of which I had sent three of the Indians, that he had been assured by one of them I might sail round the island much sooner by the northwest. Seeing that the wind would not enable me to proceed in the direction I first contemplated, and finding it favorable for the one thus recommended me, I steered to the northwest and arriving at the extremity of the island at two leagues' distance, I discovered a remarkable haven with two entrances, formed by an island at its mouth, both very narrow, the inside capacious enough for a hundred ships, were there sufficient depth of water. I thought it advisable to examine it, and therefore anchored outside, and went with the boats to sound it, but found the water shallow. As I had first imagined it to be the mouth of a river, I had directed the casks to be carried ashore for water, which being done we discovered eight or ten men who straightway came up to us, and directed us to a village in the neighborhood; I accordingly dispatched the crews thither in quest of water, part of them armed, and the rest with the casks, and the place being at some distance it detained me here a couple of hours. In the meantime I strayed about among the groves, which present the most enchanting sight ever witnessed, a degree of verdure prevailing like that of May in Andalusia, the trees as different from those of our country as day is from night, and the same may be said of the fruit, the weeds, the stones and everything else. A few of the trees, however, seemed to be of a species similar to some that are to be found in Castile, though still with a great dissimilarity, but the others so unlike, that it is impossible to find any resemblance in them to those of our land. The natives we found like those already described, as to personal appearance and manners, and naked like the rest. Whatever they possessed, they bartered for what we chose to give them. I saw a boy of the crew purchasing javelins of them with bits of platters and broken glass. Those who went for water informed me that they had entered their houses and found them very clean and neat, with beds and coverings of cotton nets. Their houses are all built in the shape of tents, with very high chimneys. None of the villages which I saw contained more than twelve or fifteen of them. Here it was remarked that the married women wore cotton breeches, but the younger females were without them, except a few who were as old as eighteen years. Dogs were seen of a large and small size, and one of the men had hanging at his nose a piece of gold half as big as a castellailo, with letters upon it. I endeavored to purchase it of them in order to ascertain what sort of money it was but they refused to part with it.

Document 1.5 Father Paul LeJeune Describes the Matagnais
Document 1.6 Unknown Jesuits' Comparison of French and Native Lifestyles

Jesuit missionaries traveled to Canada to convert the Indians to Christianity. They learned native languages and lived with the natives year-round, alternately pushing conversion and changes in native lifestyles. The Jesuits criticized native festivals, sexual habits, and gender relations, but allowed the Indians to become Christians without totally abandoning their traditional lifestyles. Jesuits were more successful than other European groups because they adapted to the Indian ways of life, and did not molest their women or steal their land. They diligently sent lengthy reports to their superiors in Quebec and Paris, where the Jesuit order published the accounts covering the years from 1632 to 1673. These reports were edited and translated into 71 volumes by American historian Reuben Gold Thwaites at the beginning of the twentieth century. Both accounts below come from the Thwaites volumes. Keeping in mind that the Jesuits still judged the native Americans by their own definitions of work and morality, what did the Fathers believe are the Indians' greatest vices? What are their greatest virtues? What parts of American Indian culture will they never understand?

Chapter IV. On the Belief, Superstitions, and Errors of the Montagnais Savages

I have already reported that the Savages believe that a certain one named Atahocam had created the world, and that one named Messou had restored it. I have questioned upon this subject the famous Sorcerer and the old man with whom I passed the Winter; they answered that they did not know who was the first Author of the world,—that it was perhaps Atahocam, but that was not certain; that they only spoke of Atahocam as one speaks of a thing so far distant that nothing sure can be known about it. . . .

As to the Messou, they hold that he restored the world, which was destroyed in the flood; whence it appears that they have some tradition of that great universal deluge which happened in the time of Noë.

They also say that all animals, of every species, have an elder brother, who is, as it were, the source and origin of all individuals, and this elder brother is wonderfully great and powerful. . . . Now these elders of all the animals are the juniors of the Messou. Behold him well related, this worthy restorer of the Universe, he is elder brother to all beasts. If any one,

when asleep, sees the elder or progenitor of some animals, he will have a fortunate chase; if he sees the elder of the Beavers, he will take Beavers; if he sees the elder of the Elk, he will take Elks, possessing the juniors through the favor of their senior whom he has seen in the dream. . . .

Their Religion, or rather their superstition, consists besides in praying; but O, my God, what prayers they make! In the morning, when the little children come out from their Cabins, they shout, *Cacouakhi, Pakhais Amisconakhi, Pakhais Mousouakhi, Pakhais,* "Come Porcupines; come, Beavers; come, Elk"; and this is all of their prayers.

When the Savages sneeze, and sometimes even at other times, during the Winter, they cry out in a loud voice *Etouctaian miraounam an Mirouscamikhi,* "I shall be very glad to see the Spring."

At other times, I have heard them pray for the Spring, or for deliverance from evils and other similar things; and they express all these things in the form of desires, crying out as loudly as they can, "I would be very glad if this day would continue, if the wind would change," etc. I could not say to whom these wishes are addressed, for they themselves do not know, at least those whom I have asked have not been able to enlighten me. . . .

From *The Jesuit Relations and Allied Documents,* 1899.

These are some of their superstitions. How much dust there is in their eyes, and how much trouble there will be to remove it that they may see the beautiful light of truth! I believe, nevertheless, that anyone who knew their language perfectly, in order to give them good reasons promptly, would soon make them laugh at their own stupidity; for sometimes I have made them ashamed and confused, although I speak almost entirely by my hands, I mean by signs. . . .

Chapter V. On the Good Things Which Are Found among the Savages

If we begin with physical advantages, I will say that they possess these in abundance. They are tall, erect, strong, well proportioned, agile; and there is nothing effeminate in their appearance. Those little Fops that are seen elsewhere are only caricatures of men, compared with our Savages. I almost believed, heretofore, that the Pictures of the Roman Emperors represented the ideal of the painters rather than men who had ever existed, so strong and powerful are their heads; but I see here upon the shoulders of these people the heads of Julius Caesar, of Pompey, of Augustus, of Otho, and of others, that I have seen in France, drawn upon paper, or in relief on medallions.

As to the mind of the Savage, it is of good quality. I believe that souls are all made from the same stock, and that they do not materially differ, hence, these barbarians having well formed bodies, and organs well regulated and well arranged, their minds ought to work with ease. Education and instruction alone are lacking. Their soul is a soil which is naturally good, but loaded down with all the evils that a land abandoned since the birth of the world can produce. I naturally compare our Savages with certain villagers, because both are usually without education, though our Peasants are superior in this regard; and yet I have not seen any one thus far, of those who have come to this country, who does not confess and frankly admit that the Savages are more intelligent than our ordinary peasants.

Moreover, if it is a great blessing to be free from a great evil, our Savages are happy; for the two tyrants who provide hell and torture for many of our Europeans, do not reign in their great forests, —I mean ambition and avarice. As they have neither political organization, nor offices, nor dignities, nor any authority, for they only obey their Chief through good will toward him, therefore they never kill each other to acquire these honors. Also, as they are contented with a mere living, not one of them gives himself to the Devil to acquire wealth.

They make a pretence of never getting angry, not because of the beauty of this virtue, for which they have not even a name, but for their own contentment and happiness, I mean, to avoid the bitterness caused by anger. The Sorcerer said to me one day, speaking of one of our Frenchmen, "He has no sense, he gets angry; as for me, nothing can disturb me; let hunger oppress me, let my nearest relation pass to the other life, let the Hiroquois, our enemies, massacre our people, I never get angry." What he says is not an article of faith; for, as he is more haughty than any other Savage, so I have seen him oftener out of humor than any of them; it is true also that he often restrains and governs himself by force, especially when I expose his foolishness. I have only heard one Savage pronounce this word, *Ninichcatihin,* "I am angry," and he only said it once. But I noticed that they kept their eyes on him, for when these Barbarians are angry, they are dangerous and unrestrained.

Whoever professes not to get angry, ought also to make a profession of patience; the Savages surpass us to such an extent, in this respect, that we ought to be ashamed. I saw them, in their hardships and in their labors, suffer with cheerfulness. My host, wondering at the great number of people who I told him were in France, asked me if the men were good, if they did not become angry, if they were patient. I have never seen such patience as is shown by a sick Savage. You may yell, storm, jump, dance, and he will scarcely ever complain. I found myself, with them, threatened with great suffering; they said to me, "We shall be sometimes two days, sometimes three, without eating, for lack of food; take courage, *Chihiné,* let thy soul be strong to endure suffering and hardship; keep thyself from being sad, otherwise thou wilt be sick; see how we do not cease to laugh, although we have little to eat." One thing alone casts them down,—it is when they see death, for they fear this beyond measure; take away this apprehension from the Savages, and they will endure all kinds of degradation and discomfort, and all kinds of trials and suffering very patiently. . . .

They are very much attached to each other, and agree admirably. You do not see any disputes, quarrels, enmities, or reproaches among them. Men leave the arrangement of the household to the women, without interfering with them; they cut, and decide, and give away as they please, without making the husband angry. . . .

Chapter VI. On Their Vices and Their Imperfections

The Savages, being filled with errors, are also haughty and proud. Humility is born of truth, vanity of error and falsehood. They are void of the knowledge of truth, and are in consequence, mainly occupied with thought of themselves. They imagine that they ought by right of birth, to enjoy the liberty of Wild ass colts, rendering no homage to any one whomsoever, except when they like. They have reproached me a hundred times because we fear our Captains, while they laugh at and make sport of theirs. All the authority of their chief is in his tongue's end; for he is powerful in so far as he is eloquent; and, even if he kills himself talking and haranguing, he will not be obeyed unless he pleases the Savages. . . .

I have shown in my former letters how vindictive the Savages are toward their enemies, with what fury and cruelty they treat them, eating them after they have made them suffer all that an incarnate fiend could invent. This fury is common to the women as well as to the men, and they even surpass the latter in this respect. I have said that they eat the lice they find upon themselves, not that they like the taste of them, but because they want to bite those that bite them.

These people are very little moved by compassion. When any one is sick in their Cabins, they ordinarily do not cease to cry and storm, and make as much noise as if everybody were in good health. They do not know what it is to take care of a poor invalid, and to give him the food which is good for him; if he asks for something to drink, it is given to him, if he asks for something to eat, it is given to him, but otherwise he is neglected; to coax him with love and gentleness, is a language which they do not understand. As long as a patient can eat, they will carry or drag him with them; if he stops eating, they believe that it is all over with him and kill him, as much to free him from the sufferings that he is enduring, as to relieve themselves of the trouble of taking him with them when they go to some other place. I have both admired and pitied the patience of the invalids whom I have seen among them.

The Savages are slanderous beyond all belief; I say, also among themselves, for they do not even spare their nearest relations, and with it all they are deceitful. For, if one speaks ill of another, they all jeer with loud laughter; if the other appears upon the scene, the first one will show him as much affection and treat him with as much love, as if he had elevated him to the third heaven by his praise. The reason of this is, it seems to me, that their slanders and derision do not come from malicious hearts or from infected mouths, but from a mind which says what it thinks in order to give itself free scope, and which seeks gratification from everything, even from slander and mockery. Hence they are not troubled even if they are told that others are making sport of them, or have injured their reputation. All they usually answer to such talk is, mama irinisiou, "He has no sense, he does not know what he is talking about"; and at the first opportunity they will pay their slanderer in the same coin, returning him the like.

Lying is as natural to Savages as talking, not among themselves, but to strangers. Hence it can be said that fear and hope, in one word, interest, is the measure of their fidelity. I would not be willing to trust them, except as they would fear to be punished if they had failed in their duty, or hoped to be rewarded if they were faithful to it. They do not know what it is to keep a secret, to keep their word, and to love with constancy,—especially those who are not of their nation, for they are harmonious among themselves, and their slanders and raillery do not disturb their peace and friendly intercourse. . . .

Chapter XII. What One Must Suffer in Wintering with the Savages

In order to have some conception of the beauty of this edifice, its construction must be described. I shall speak from knowledge, for I have often helped to build it. Now, when we arrived at the place where we were to camp, the women, armed with axes, went here and there in the great forests, cutting the framework of the hostelry where we were to lodge; meantime the men, having drawn the plan thereof, cleared away the snow with their snowshoes, or with shovels which they make and carry expressly for this purpose. Imagine now a great ring or square in the snow, two, three or four feet deep, according to the weather or the place where they encamp. This depth of snow makes a white wall for us, which surrounds us on all sides, except the end where it is broken through to form the floor. The framework having been brought, which consists of twenty or thirty poles, more or less, according to the size of the cabin, it is planted, not upon the ground but upon the snow; then they throw upon these poles, which converge a little at the top, two or three rolls of bark sewed together, beginning at the bottom, and behold, the house is made. The ground inside, as well as the wall of snow which extends all around the cabin, is covered with little branches of fir; and, as a finishing touch, a wretched skin is fastened to two poles to serve as a door, the doorposts being the snow itself. . . .

You cannot stand upright in this house, as much on account of its low roof as the suffocating smoke; and consequently you must always lie down, or sit flat upon the ground, the usual posture of the savages. When you go out, the cold, the snow, and the danger of getting lost in these great woods drive you in again more quickly than the wind, and keep you a prisoner in a dungeon which has neither lock nor key.

This prison, in addition to the uncomfortable position that one must occupy upon a bed of earth, has four other great discomforts,—cold, heat, smoke, and dogs. As to the cold, you have the snow at your head with only a pine branch between, often nothing but your hat, and the winds are free to enter in a thousand places. . . . When I lay down at night I could study through this opening both the Stars and the Moon as easily as if I had been in the open fields.

Nevertheless, the cold did not annoy me as much as the heat from the fire. A little place like their cabins is easily heated by a good fire, which sometimes roasted and broiled me on all sides, for the cabin was so narrow that I could not protect myself against the heat. You cannot move to right or left, for the Savages, your neighbors, are at your elbows; you cannot withdraw to the rear, for you encounter the wall of snow, or the bark of the cabin which shuts you in. I did not know what position to take. Had I stretched myself out, the place was so narrow that my legs would have been halfway in the fire; to roll myself up in a ball, and crouch down in their way, was a position I could not retain as long as they could; my clothes were all scorched and burned. You will ask me perhaps if the snow at our backs did not melt under so much heat. I answer, "no"; that if sometimes the heat softened it in the least, the cold immediately turned it into ice. I will say, however, that both the cold and the heat are endurable, and that some remedy may be found for these two evils.

But, as to the smoke, I confess to you that it is martyrdom. It almost killed me, and made me weep continually, although I had neither grief nor sadness in my heart. It sometimes grounded all of us who were in the cabin; that is, it caused us to place our mouths against the earth in order to breathe. For, although the Savages were accustomed to this torment, yet occasionally it became so dense that they, as well as I, were compelled to prostrate themselves, and as it were to eat the earth, so as not to drink the smoke. I have sometimes remained several hours in this position, especially during the most severe cold and when it snowed; for it was then the smoke assailed us with the greatest fury, seizing us by the throat, nose, and eyes. . . .

As to the dogs, which I have mentioned as one of the discomforts of the Savages' houses, I do not know that I ought to blame them, for they have sometimes rendered me good service. . . . These poor beasts, not being able to live outdoors, came and lay down sometimes upon my shoulders, sometimes upon my feet, and as I only had one blanket to serve both as covering and mattress, I was not sorry for this protection, willingly restoring to them a part of the heat which I drew from them. It is true that, as they were large and numerous, they occasionally crowded and annoyed me so much, that in giving me a little heat they robbed me of my sleep, so that I very often drove them away. . . .

Jesuit Comparison of French and Native Life (1657–1658)

In Europe, the seam of stockings is behind the leg. . . Among the Savages it is otherwise; the seam of stockings worn by men is between the legs, and here they fasten little ornaments—made of porcupine quills, stained scarlet, and in the form of fringe or of spangles which meet when they walk, and make . . . a pretty effect, not easily described. The women wear this ornamentation on the outer side of the leg.

In France, patterns and raised shoes are considered the most beautiful. . . . The Savages' shoes are as flat as tennis-shoes, but much wider, especially in winter, when they stuff and line them amply to keep away the cold.

Shirts are in Europe worn next to the skin, under the other garments. The Savages wear them usually over their dress, to shield it from snow and rain. . . .

The end of a shirt protruding from under the coat is an indecorous thing; but not so in Canadas. You will see Savages dressed in French attire, with worsted stockings and a cloak, but without any breeches; while before and . . . behind are seen two large shirt-flaps hanging down below the cloak. . . . That fashion seems all the more tasteful in their eyes because they regard our breeches as an encumbrance. . . .

Politeness and propriety have taught us to carry handkerchiefs. In this matter the Savages charge us with filthiness—because, they say, we place what is unclean in a fine white piece of linen, and put it away in our pockets as something very precious, while they throw it upon the ground. . . .

Most Europeans sit on raised seats, using round or square tables. The Savages eat from the ground. . . .

In France, food and drink are taken together. The Algonquins follow quite the contrary custom in their feasts, first eating what is served them, and then drinking, without touching food again. . . .

We wash meat to cleanse it of blood and impurities; the Savages do not wash it, for fear of losing its blood and a part of its fat. . . . We usually begin the dinner with soup, which is the last dish among the Savages, the broth of the pot serving them for drink. Bread is eaten here with the meat and other courses; if you give some to a Savage, he will make a separate course of it and very often eat it last. Yet they are gradually adapting themselves to our way.

In most parts of Europe, when any one makes a call he is invited to drink; among the Savages he is invited to eat. . . .

When the Savages are not hunting or on a journey, their usual posture is to recline or sit on the ground. They cannot remain standing, maintaining that their legs become swollen immediately. Seats higher than the ground they dislike; the French, on the contrary, use chairs, benches, or stools, leaving the ground and litter to the animals.

A good dancer in France does not move . . . his arms much, and holds his body erect, moving his feet so nimbly that, you would say, he spurns the ground and wishes to stay in the air. The Savages, on the contrary, bend over in their dances, thrusting out their arms and moving them violently as if they were kneading bread, while they strike the ground with their feet so vigorously that one would say they are determined to make it tremble, or to bury themselves in it up to the neck. . . .

In France, children are carried on the arm, or clasped to the breast; in Canadas, the mothers bear them behind their backs. In France, they are kept as well covered as possible. . . . The cradle, in France, is left at home; there the women carry it with their children; it is composed merely of a cedar board, on which the poor little one is bound like a bundle.

. . . In France, a Workman does not expect his pay until he completes his task; the Savages ask it in advance. . . .

Europeans have no hesitation about telling their names and conditions, but you embarrass a Savage by asking him his name; if you do ask him, he will say that he does not know, and will make a sign to some one else to tell it. . . .

In France, when a father gives his daughter in marriage, he allows her a dowry. There, it is given to the girl's father.

In Europe, the children inherit from their parents; among the Hurons the nephews, sons of the father's sister, are their uncle's heirs; and the Savage's small belongings will be given to the friends of the deceased, rather than to his children. . . . In France, the man usually takes to his house the woman whom he marries; there, the man goes to the woman's house to dwell.

In France, if any one fall into a fit of anger, or harbor some evil purpose, or meditate some harm, he is reviled, threatened, and punished; there, they give him presents, to soothe his ill-humor, cure his mental ailment, and put good thoughts into his head again. This custom, in the sincerity of their actions, is not a bad one; for if he who is angry, or is devising some ill . . . to resent an offense, touch this present, his anger and his evil purpose are immediately effaced from his mind.

In a large part of Europe, ceremonies and compliments are indulged in to such an excess as to drive out sincerity. There, quite on the contrary, sincerity is entirely naked. . . .

In Europe, we unclothe the dead as much as we can, leaving them only what is necessary to veil them and hide them from our eyes. The Savages, however, give them all that they can, anointing and attiring them as if for their wedding, and burying them with all their favorite belongings.

The French are stretched lengthwise in their graves, while the Savages, . . . in burying their dead make them take in the grave the position which they held in their mothers' wombs. In some parts of France, the dead are placed with their heads turned toward the East; the Savages make them face the West.

Document 1.7 Joseph-Francois Lafitau Compares American Natives to Primitive Societies

As the Jesuit fathers traveled along the St. Lawrence River, they settled among native peoples from the Atlantic all the way to the Great Lakes. They studied native beliefs, their lifestyles, and their family life. While not approving of all native habits, they accepted slow change and conversion. Father Joseph-Francois Lafitau lived among the Iroquois. What comparisons does he make between the farm work required of Iroquois women and French women?

━━━━━━━━━━━━━━━━

The Indian women as well as the Amazons, the Thracian, Scythian and Spanish women and those of the other barbarian races of antiquity, work the fields as women do today in Gascony, Beam and Breese where we often see them running the plough while their husbands ply the distaff. The grain which they sow is maize, otherwise known as Indian or Turkish or Spanish wheat. It is the basis of the food of almost all the sedentary nations from one end of America to the other. . . .

Cultivation of the Fields

In Canada, the moment that the snows are melted the Indian women begin their work. They do not sow in autumn either because maize is one of the seeds which they call summer crops, *aestiva*, as are sesame, millet, panic-grass and the other vegetables or because, like wheat, it is that kind of grain called by Theophrastus and Pliny *trimester* (three months grain) since only three months pass between the sowing and the harvesting. Indeed, it seems that no single species should, perhaps, be considered unusual for this reason for the customs in New France show us, quite to the contrary, that all species of grain or French wheat, are usually sown only in the months of April and May and harvested in July and August. In Florida and the more southern countries the maize is sown and garnered twice a year.

The first work done in the fields is gathering and burning the stubble. Then the ground is ploughed to make it ready to receive the grain which they are (going) to throw there. They do not use the plough (for this), any more than they do a number of other

farming implements whose use is unknown to them and unnecessary for them. All that they need is a piece of bent wood three fingers wide, attached to a long handle which serves them to hoe the earth and stir it lightly.

The fields which they are to sow are not arranged in headlands and furrows as they are in Europe, but in little round hillcock three feet in diameter. They make nine holes in each of these mounds. They cast into each hole a grain of Indian corn which they cover over carefully.

Work Party

All the women of the village join together for the heavy work. They make numerous different bands according to the different quarters where they have their fields and pass from one field to the other helping each other. This can be done with less difficulty and the more quickly in that the fields are not separated by hedges and ditches. All together these (fields) give the appearance of only a single form where there are no disputes over boundaries because every one knows how to recognize them clearly.

The mistress of the field where they are working distributes to each one of the workers the grain or seed for sowing which they receive in little *mannes*— of baskets four of five fingers high and as wide, so that they can calculate the number of grains given out.

Beside maize, they sow horse beans or little lima beans, pumpkins of a species different from those of France, watermelons and great sunflowers. They sow the lima beans next to the grains of their Indian corn, the cane or stalk of which serves them (the lima bean

Joseph-Francios Lafitau, *Customs of the American Indians Compared with the Customs of Primitive Times*, ed. And trans. William N. Fenton and Elizabeth I. Moore, 2 volumes (Toronto: the Champlain Society, 1974–1977) 2:47, 54–56.

plants) as support as the elm does to the vine. They prepare special fields for their pumpkins and melons, but before sowing them in these fields, they plant the seeds in a preparation of black, light soil between two sheets of bark and place them above their hearths where they germinate.

They keep their fields very clean. They are careful to pull up the grass in them until harvest time. There is also a set time for this (task) when they work all in common. Then each one carried with her a bundle of little sticks a foot or a foot and a half long, with her individual mark and gaily decorated with vermillion. They use these to make their accomplishments and to make their work show up.

When harvest time has come, they gather Indian corn which they pull off with the leaves around the ears so that they form the husk. These husks, strongly attached as they are serve for braiding them in bunches or in strings as is done with onions.

The festival of binding together corn shocks is doubtless one of those which the ancients called *Cereales*—which they celebrated in honour of Ceres. It takes place at night in the fields and is the only occasion when the men, who do no work either in the fields or with the harvest, are called upon by the women to help. I do not know whether or not there is some remnant of a religious cult in this (ceremony). I have not tried to learn its peculiar features. It appears, however, that this custom may have been originally due to religion. I speak here only of the North American custom. I do not know enough about what is done elsewhere to speak about it. The authors who have written about the Southern Americans limit themselves to saying, in general, that the men would be considered to have demeaned themselves if they even barely touched this task or anything else (that is) set aside as women's work.

Document 1.8 A Dutch View of the Mohawk Indians in New Netherlands

In the first part of the seventeenth century the Dutch had one of the most powerful navies in the world, and their merchants traded all over the globe. Always in search of profits, the Dutch built Fort Orange, at the site of present-day Albany, to control the fur trade with the local Indians. In 1624 the Dutch West India Company established the colony of New Netherlands on Manhattan Island, and began full-scale trade with the native Americans in the area. The senior Dutch Reformed Minister in the colony, Johannes Megapolensis, attempted to impose his will on the churches in the colony and force the native Americans to convert. A true European bigot, convinced of Dutch superiority to the "savages," he compiled notes and observations about the local people, which he sent home to the Netherlands to help recruit additional Dutch settlers. How does he describe the natives and their customs? How do they compare with the Dutch? What does he find good about them, and where can they improve?

The country here is in general like that in Germany. The land is good, and fruitful in everything which supplies human needs, except clothes, linen, woollen, stockings, shoes, etc., which are all dear here. The country is very mountainous, partly soil, partly rocks, and with elevations so exceeding high that they appear to almost touch the clouds. Thereon grow the finest fir trees the eye ever saw. There are also in this country oaks, alders, beeches, elms, willows, etc. In the forests, and here and there along the water side, and on the islands, there grows an abundance of chestnuts, plums, hazel nuts, large walnuts of several sorts, and of as good a taste as in the Netherlands, but they have a somewhat harder shell. The ground on the hills is covered with bushes of bilberries or blueberries; the ground in the flat land near the rivers is covered with strawberries, which grow here so plentifully in the fields, that one can lie down and eat them. Grapevines also grow here naturally in great abundance along the roads, paths, and creeks, and

From *Narrative of New Netherland* 1609–1644, Barnes and Noble, 1909.

wherever you may turn you find them. . . . If people would cultivate the vines they might have as good wine here as they have in Germany or France. I had myself last harvest a boat-load of grapes and pressed them. As long as the wine was new it tasted better than any French or Rhenish Must, . . . They (the women) are obliged to cut wood, to travel three or four leagues with the child; in short, they walk, they stand, they work, as if they had not lain in, and we cannot see that they suffer any injury by it; and we sometimes try to persuade our wives to lie-in so, and that the way of lying-in in Holland is a mere fiddle-faddle. The men have great authority over their concubines, so that if they do anything which does not please and raises their passion, they take an axe and knock them in the head, and there is an end of it. The women are obliged to prepare the land, to mow, to plant, and do everything; the men do nothing, but hunt, fish, and make war upon their enemies. They are very cruel towards their enemies in time of war; for they first bite off the nails of the fingers of their captives, and cut off some joints, and sometimes even whole fingers; after that, the captives are forced to sing and dance before them stark naked; and finally, they roast their prisoners dead before a slow fire for some days, and then eat them up. The common people eat the arms, buttocks and trunk, but the chiefs eat the head and the heart.

Our Mahakas carry on great wars against the Indians of Canada, on the River Saint Lawrence, and take many captives, . . . They spare all the children from ten to twelve years old, and all the women whom they take in war, unless the women are very old, and then they kill them too. Though they are so very cruel to their enemies, they are very friendly to us, and we have no dread of them. We go with them into the woods, we meet with each other, sometimes at an hour or two's walk from any houses, and think no more about it than as if we met with a Christian. . . . Their bread is Indian corn beaten to pieces between two stones, of which they make a cake, and bake it in the ashes: their other victuals are venison, turkies, hares, bears, wild cats, their own dogs, etc. The fish they cook just as they get them out of the water without cleansing; also the entrails of deer with all their contents, which they cook a little; and if the intestines are then too tough, they take one end in their months and the other in their hand and between hand and mouth they separate and eat them. So they do commonly with the flesh, for they carve a little piece and lay it on the fire, as long as one would need to walk from his house to church, then it is done; and then they bite into it so that the blood runs along their mouths. . . . It is natural to them to have no beards; not one in an hundred any hair about his mouth.

They have also naturally a very high opinion of themselves; they say, *Ihy Othkon*, ("I am the Devil") by which they mean that they are superior folks. In order to praise themselves and their people, whenever we tell them they are very expert at catching deer, or doing this and that, they say *Tkoschs ko, aguweechon Kajingahaga kouaane Jountuckcha Othkon*; that is, "Really all the Mohawks are very cunning devils." They make their houses of the bark of trees, very close and warm, and kindle their fire in the middle of them. They also make of the peeling and bark of trees, canoes or small boats, which will carry four, five and six persons. . . . Their weapons in war were formerly a bow and arrow, with a stone axe and mallet; but now they get from our people guns, swords, iron axes and mallets. Their money consists of certain little bones, made of shells or cockles, which are found on the seabeach; a hole is drilled through the middle of the little bones, and these they string upon thread, or they make of them belts as broad as a hand, or broader, and hang them on their necks, or around their bodies. They have also several holes in their ears, and there they likewise hang some. They value these little bones as highly as many Christians do gold, silver and pearls; but they do not like our money, and esteem it no better than iron. . . .

They are entire strangers to all religion, but they have a *Tharonhijouaagon*, whom they also otherwise call *Athzoockkuatoriaho*,) that is, a Genius, whom they esteem in the place of God; but they do not serve him or make offerings to him. They worship and present offerings to the Devil, whom they call *Otskon*, or *Aireskuoni*. If they have any bad luck in war, they catch a bear, which they cut in pieces, and roast, and that they offer up to their *Aireskuoni*, saying in substance, the following words: "Oh! great and mighty Aireskuoni, we confess that we have offended against thee, inasmuch as we have not killed and eaten our captive enemies;—forgive us this. We promise that we will kill and eat all the captives we shall hereafter take as certainly as we have killed, and now eat this bear." Also when the weather is very hot, and there comes a cooling breeze, they cry out directly, *Asoronusi, asoronusi, Otskon aworouhsi reinnuha*; that is, "I thank thee, I thank thee, devil, I thank thee, little uncle!" If they are sick, or have a pain or soreness anywhere in their limbs, and I ask them what ails them they say that the Devil sits in their body, or in the sore places, and bites them there; so that they attribute to the Devil at once the accidents which befall them; they have otherwise no religion. When we pray they laugh at us. Some of them despise it entirely; and some, when we tell them what we do when we pray, stand astonished. When we deliver a sermon, sometimes ten or twelve of them, more or less, will attend, each having a long tobacco pipe, made by himself, in his mouth, and will stand awhile and look, and afterwards ask me what I am doing and what I want, that stand there alone and make so many words, while none of the rest may speak. I tell them that I am admonishing the Christians, that they must not steal, nor commit lewdness, nor get drunk, nor commit murder, and that they too ought not to do these things; and that I intend in process of time to preach the same to them and come to them in their own country and castles (about three days' journey from here, further inland), when I am acquainted with their language. . . .

The other day an old woman came to our house, and told my people that her forefathers had told her "that *Tharonhij-Jagon*, that is God, once went walking with his brother, and a dispute arose between them, and God killed his brother." I suppose this fable took its rise from Cain and Abel. They have a droll theory of the Creation, for they think that a pregnant woman fell down from heaven, and that a tortoise, (tortoises are plenty and large here, in this country, two, three and four feet long, some with two heads, very mischievous and addicted to biting) took this pregnant woman on its back, because every place was covered with water, and that the woman sat upon the tortoise, groped with her hands in the water, and scraped together some of the earth, whence it finally happened that the earth was raised above the water. They think that there are more worlds than one, and that we came from another world. . . .

The government among them consists of the oldest, the most intelligent, the most eloquent and most warlike men. These commonly resolve, and then the young and warlike men execute. But if the common people do not approve of the resolution, it is left entirely to the judgment of the mob. The chiefs are generally the poorest among them, for instead of their receiving from the common people as among Christians, they are obliged to give to the mob; especially when any one is killed in war, they give great presents to the next of kin of the deceased; and if they take any prisoners they present them to that family of which one has been killed, and the prisoner is then adopted by the family into the place of the deceased person. There is no punishment here for murder and other villainies, but every one is his own avenger. The friends of the deceased revenge themselves upon the murder until peace is made by presents to the next of kin. But although they are so cruel, and live without laws or any punishments for evil doers, yet there are not half so many villainies or murders committed amongst them as amongst Christians.

Document 1.9 Captain John Smith Describes the Native Inhabitants of Virginia

John Smith was born in 1580, the son of a farmer who was not quite prosperous. In 1595 he was apprenticed to a merchant, but after his father died the following year he turned the farm over to others to manage, broke his apprenticeship, and escaped to the Continent of Europe in search of adventure. He served as a mercenary, fighting the Spanish, the Turks, and pirates. He was captured and sold into slavery, escaped, served as a pirate himself, and experienced other adventures, before becoming an integral part of the Virginia colony from 1607 to 1609. Smith wrote his *General History of Virginia* to glorify himself and solicit monetary support for New England colonization. He spends considerable time describing the Indians of Virginia and their leader Powhatan. Smith admires their pride and dignity, and admits their way of life can even appeal to a civilized Christian. He admits that Powhatan brought the Virginia colonists "corn when we rather expected he would destroy us." But there is more to his description. What terms does he use to describe the natives of Virginia, and what does he find most admirable about them? How does he describe their physical appearance, and their lifestyles? What does he criticize, and is this done to make himself look better?

The land is not populous, for the men be few; their far greater number is of women and children. Within sixty miles of Jamestown there are about some five thousand people, but of able men fit for their wars scarce fifteen hundred. To nourish so many together they have yet no means, because they make so small a benefit of their land, be it never so fertile.

Some being very great, as the Susquehannocks, others very little, as the Wighcocomocos; but generally tall and straight, of a comely proportion, and of a color brown when they are of any age, but they are born white. Their hair is generally black, but few have any beards. The men wear half their beards [heads] shaven, the other half long; for barbers they use their women, who with two shells will grate away the hair, of any fashion they please. The women['s heads] are cut in many fashions, agreeable to their years, but ever some part remaineth long.

They are very strong, of an able body and full of agility, able to endure to lie in the woods under a tree by the fire in the worst of winter, or in the weeds and grass in ambuscado in the summer.

They are inconstant in everything but what fear constraineth them to keep. Crafty, timorous, quick of apprehension, and very ingenuous. Some are of disposition fearful, some bold, some cautelous [deceitful], all savage. They are covetous of copper, beads, and such like trash. They are soon moved to anger, and so malicious that they seldom forget an injury. They seldom steal one from another, lest their conjurers should reveal it and so they be pursued and punished. That they are thus feared is certain, but that any can reveal their offenses by conjuration I am doubtful. Their women are careful not to be suspected of dishonesty without the leave of their husbands.

Each household knoweth their own lands and gardens, and most live off their own labors.

For their apparel they are sometimes covered with the skins of wild beasts, which in winter are dressed with the hair but in summer without. The better sort use large mantles of deerskins, not much differing in fashion from the Irish mantles—some embroidered with white beads, some with copper, others painted after their manner. But the common sort have scarce to cover their nakedness but with grass, the leaves of trees, or such like. We have seen some use mantles made of turkey feathers, so prettily wrought and woven with threads that nothing could

be discerned but the feathers. But the women are always covered about their middle with a skin, and very shamefast to be seen bare.

They adorn themselves most with copper beads and paintings. Their women, some have their legs, hands, breasts, and face cunningly embroidered with diverse works, as beasts, serpents, artificially wrought into their flesh with black spots. In each ear commonly they have three great holes, whereat they hang chains, bracelets, or copper. Some of their men wear in those holes a small green and yellow colored snake near half a yard in length, which, crawling and lapping herself about his neck, oftentimes familiarly would kiss his lips. Others wear a dead rat tied by the tail. Some on their heads wear the wing of a bird or some large feather with a rattle. Those rattles are somewhat like the shape of a rapier but less, which they take from the tail of a snake. Many have the whole skin of a hawk or some strange fowl stuffed with wings abroad, others a broad piece of copper, and some the hand of their enemy dried. Their heads and shoulders are painted red with the root puccoon [bloodroot] brayed to powder, mixed with oil; this they hold in summer to preserve them from the heat, and in winter from the cold. Many other forms of paintings they use, but he is the most gallant that is the most monstrous to behold.

Their buildings and habitations are for the most part by the rivers, or not far distant from some fresh spring. Their houses are built like our arbors, of small young sprigs bowed and tied and so close covered with mats or the barks of trees very handsomely that notwithstanding either wind, rain, or weather, they are as warm as stoves but very smoky; yet at the top of the house there is a hole made for the smoke to go into right over the fire.

Against the fire they lie on little hurdles of reeds covered with a mat, borne from the ground a foot and more by a hurdle of wood. On these round about the house they lie heads and points one by th'other against the fire, some covered with mats, some with skins, and some stark naked lie on the ground, from six to twenty in a house.

Their houses are in the midst of their fields or gardens, which are small plots of ground—some twenty acres, some forty, some one hundred, some two hundred, some more, some less. In some places from two to fifty of those houses [lie] together or but a little separated by groves of trees. Near their

---

From *Captain Smith's History of Virginia*, first published, 1624.

habitations is little small wood or old trees on the ground by reason of their burning of them for fire. So that a man may gallop a horse amongst those woods any way but where the creeks or rivers shall hinder.

Men, women, and children have their several names according to the several humors of their parents. Their women (they say) are easily delivered of child, yet do they love children very dearly. To make them hardy, in the coldest mornings they wash them in the rivers, and by painting and ointments so tan their skins that after a year or two no weather will hurt them.

The men bestow their time in fishing, hunting, wars, and such man-like exercises, scorning to be seen in any woman-like exercise, which is the cause that the women be very painful [toiling] and the men often idle. The women and children do the rest of the work. They make mats, baskets, pots, mortars, pound their corn, make their bread, prepare their victuals, plant their corn, gather their corn, bear all kind of burdens, and such like.

Their fire they kindle presently by chafing a dry pointed stick in a hole of a little square piece of wood, that firing itself will so fire moss, leaves, or any such like dry thing that will quickly burn.

In March and April they live much upon their fishing weirs, and feed on fish, turkeys, and squirrels. In May and June they plant their fields and live most off acorns, walnuts, and fish. But to amend their diet, some disperse themselves in small companies and live upon fish, beasts, crabs, oysters, land tortoises, strawberries, mulberries, and such like. In June, July, and August they feed upon the roots of tuckahoe, berries, fish, and green wheat.

In their hunting and fishing they take extreme pains; Yet it being their ordinary exercise from their infancy, they esteem it a pleasure and are very proud to be expert therein. And by their continual ranging and travel they know all the advantages and places most frequented with deer, beasts, fish, fowl, roots, and berries. At their huntings they leave their habitations and reduce themselves into companies, as the Tartars do, and go to the most desert places [treeless plains] with their families, where they spend their time in hunting and fowling up towards the mountains, by the heads of their rivers, where there is plenty of game. For betwixt the rivers the grounds are so narrow that little cometh here which they devour not. It is a marvel they can so directly pass these deserts some three or four days' journey without habitation. Their hunting houses are like unto arbors covered with mats. These their women bear after them, with corn, acorns, mortars, and all bag and baggage they use. When they come to the place of exercise, every man doth his best to show his dexterity, for by their excelling in those qualities they get their wives. Forty yards will they shoot level [accurately] or very near the mark, and one hundred and twenty is their best at random.

At their huntings in the deserts they are commonly two or three hundred together. Having found the deer, they environ them with many fires, and betwixt the fires they place themselves. And some take their stands in the midsts. The deer being thus feared by the fires and their voices, they chase them so long within that circle that many times they kill six, eight, ten, or fifteen at a hunting. They use also to drive them into some narrow point of land when they find that advantage, and so force them into the river, where with their boats they have ambuscados to kill them. When they have shot a deer by land, they follow him like bloodhounds by the blood and strain, and oftentimes so take them. Hares, partridges, turkeys, or eggs, fat or lean, young or old, they devour all they can catch in their power.

Document 1.10 Thomas Morton Apprises the Indians of New England

Thomas Morton established a settlement at Mount Wollaston, Massachusetts, outside the control of the Pilgrims at Plymouth. He called it Merrymount, and revived pagan May Day rituals, where Indians and settlers danced and drank around a maypole, working themselves into a sexual frenzy. He was popular with the local Indians, who preferred to trade with him instead of the Plymouth settlement. These actions all made him unpopular with the Pilgrim leaders, as did the rumor he was selling guns to the Indians; the legendary Captain Miles Standish was sent to destroy Merrymount and ship Morton out of the colony. Morton later published his version of the actions, titled *The New English Canaan*, where the innocent, open, and honest

Indians compared favorably with the hypocritical bigots known as the Pilgrims. What does Morton describe as the native Americans' best qualities? Do they have any faults, and if so what? How does he compare them with their English neighbors? Who is more "Christian-like" in their actions and attitudes?

Of Their Houses and Habitations

The Natives of New England are accustomed to build them houses much like the wild Irish; they gather Poles in the woodes and put the great end of them in the ground, placing them in forme of a circle or circumference, and, bendinge the topps of them in forme of an Arch, they bind them together with the Barke of Walnut trees, which is wondrous tough, so that they make the same round on the Topp for the smoke of their fire to ascend and pass through; . . . The fire is alwayes made in the midst of the house, with winde falls commonly: yet some times they fell a tree that groweth near the house, and, by drawing in the end thereof, maintaine the fire on both sides, burning the tree by Degrees shorter and shorter, untill it be all consumed; for it burneth night and day. Their lodging is made in three places of the house about the fire; they lie upon plankes, commonly about a foote or 18 inches above the ground, raised upon railes that are borne up upon forks; they lay mats under them, and Coats of Deares skinnes, otters, beavers, Racoons, and of Beares hides, all which they have dressed and converted into good leather, with the haire on, for their coverings: and in this manner they liee as warme as they desire. . . . for they are willing that any shall eat with them. Nay, if any one that shall come into their houses and there fall a sleepe, when they see him disposed to lie downe, they will spread a matt for him of their owne accord, and lay a roll of skinnes for a boulster, and let him lie. If he sleepe untill their meate be dished up, they will set a wooden bowl of meate by him that sleepeth, and wake him saying, Cattup keene Meckin: That is, If you be hungry, there is meat for you, where if you will eat you may. Such is their Humanity.

Likewise, when they are minded to remove, they carry away the mats with them; other materials the place adjoining will yield. They use not to winter and summer in one place, for that would be a reason to make fuel scarce; but, after the manner of the gentry of Civilized natives, remove for their pleasures; some times to their hunting places, where they remaine keeping good hospitality for that season; and sometimes to their fishing places, where they abide for that season likewise; and at the spring, when fish comes in plentifully, they have meetinges from severall places, where they exercise themselves in gaming and playing of jugling trickes and all manner of Revelles, which they are delighted in; [so] that it is admirable to behold what pastime they use of severall kindes; every one striving to surpass each other. After this manner they spend their time. . . .

Of Their Reverence, and Respect to Age

It is a thing to be admired, and indeede made a president, that a Nation yet uncivilized should more respect age than some nations civilized, since there are so many precepts both of divine and humane writers extant to instruct more Civil Nations: in that particular, wherein they excel, the younger are always obedient unto the elder people, and at their commands in every respect without grumbling; in all councels, (as therein they are circumspect to do their actions by advise and councell, and not rashly or inconsiderately) the younger mens opinion shall be heard, but the old mens opinion and councell embraced and followed: besides, as the elder feede and provide for the younger in infancy, doe the younger, after being growne to years of manhood, provide for those that be aged; . . .

Of Their Petty Conjuring Tricks

If we doe not judge amiss of these Salvages in accounting them witches, yet out of all question we may be bold to conclude them to be but weake witches, such of them as we call by the names of Powahs: some correspondency they have with the Devil out of all doubt, as by some of their actions, in

---

From *Old South Leaflets*, 1883.

which they glory, is manifested. Papasiquineo, that Sachem or Sagamore, is a Powah of greate estimation amongst all kinde of Salvages there: he is at their Revels (which is the time when a great company of Salvages meete from severall parts of the Country, in amity with their neighbours) hath advanced his honor in his feats or juggling tricks (as I may right term them) to the admiration of the spectators, whom he endevoured to persuade that he would goe under water to the further side of a river, too broad for any man to undertake with a breath, which thing he performed by swimming over, and deluding the company with casting a mist before their eyes that see him enter in and come out, but no part of the way he has been seen: likewise by our English, in the heat of all summer to make Ice appear in a bowl of faire water; first, having the water set before him, he hath begun his incantation according to their usuall custom, and before the same has been ended a thick Cloud has darkened the aire and, on a sudden, a thunder clap hath been heard that has amazed the natives; in an instant he hath showed a firm piece of Ice to float in the midst of the bowl in the presence of the vulgar people, which doubtless was done by the agility of Satan, his consort.

And by meanes of these sleights, and such like trivial things as these, they gaine such estimation amongst the rest of the Salvages that it is thought a very impious matter for any man to derogate from the words of these Powahs. In so much as he that should slight them, is thought to commit a crime no less heinous amongst them as sacrilege is with us, . . .

Of Their Acknowlegement of the Creation, and the Immortality of the Soul

Although these Salvages are found to be without Religion, Law, and King (as Sir William Alexander hath well observed,) yet are they not altogether without the knowledge of God (historically); for they have it amongst them by tradition that God made one man and one woman, and bade them live together and get children, kill deer, beasts, birds, fish and fowle, and what they would at their pleasure; and that their posterity was full of evil, and made God so angry that he let in the Sea upon them, and drowned the greatest part of them, that were naughty men, (the Lord destroyed so;) and they went to Sanaconquam, who feeds upon them (pointing to the Center of the Earth, where they imagine is the habitation of the Devill:) the other, (which were not destroyed,) increased the

world, and when they died (because they were good) went to the house of Kytan [*the word Morton records for the supreme good Spirit or God*], pointing to the setting of the sun; where they eate all manner of dainties, and never take pains (as now) to provide it.

Kytan makes provision (they say) and saves them that labour; and there they shall live with him forever, void of care. And they are persuaded that Kytan is he that makes corne growe, trees growe, and all manner of fruits. . . .

I asked him [*an Indian who had lived in Morton's house*] who was a good man; his answer was, he that would not lie, nor steal.

These, with them, are all the capital crimes that can be imagined; all other are nothing in respect of those; and he that is free from these must live with Kytan for ever, in all manner of pleasure. . . .

Of Their Custom in Burning the Country, and the Reason Thereof

The Salvages are accustomed to set fire of the Country in all places where they come, and to burne it twice a year, viz.: at the Spring, and the fall of the leaf. The reason that moves them to doe so, is because it would other wise be so overgrown with underweeds that it would be all a coppice wood, and the people would not be able in any wise to pass through the Country out of a beaten path.

The burning of the grass destroys the underwoods, and so scorcheth the elder trees that it shrinks them, and hinders their growth very much: so that he that will looke to finde large trees and good timber, must [look] . . . to finde them on the upland ground. . . .

And least their firing of the Country in this manner should be an occasion of damnifying us, and endangering our habitations, we ourselves have used carefully about the same times to observe the winds, and fire the grounds about our owne habitations; to prevent the Damage that might happen by any neglect thereof, if the fire should come near those houses in our absence.

For, when the fire is once kindled, it dilates and spreads itself as well against, as with the wind; burning continually night and day, untill a shower of rain falls to quench it.

And this custom of firing the Country is the meanes to make it passable, and by that meanes the trees growe here and there as in our parks: and makes the Country very beautifull and commodious.

Of Their Inclination to Drunkenness

Although Drunkenness be justly termed a vice which the Salvages are ignorant of, yet the benefit is very great that comes to the planters by the sale of strong liquor to the Salvages, who are much taken with the delight of it; for they will pawn their wits, to purchase the acquaintance of it. Yet in all the commerce that I had with them, I never proffered them any such thing; nay, I would hardly let any of them have a dram, unless he were a Sachem, or a Winnaytue, that is a rich man. . . . But they say if I come to the Northern parts of the Country I shall have no trade, if I will not supply them with lusty liquors: it is the life of the trade in all those parts: for it so happened that thus a Salvage desperately killed himself, when he was drunk, a gun being charged and the cock up, he sets the mouth to his breast, and, putting back the trigger with his foote, shot himself dead.

That the Salvages Live a Contended Life

Now since it is but food and rayment that men that live needeth, (though not all alike,) why should not the Natives of New England be said to live richly, having no want of either? Cloaths are the badge of sin; and the more variety of fashions is but the greater abuse of the Creature: the beasts of the forrest there doe serve to furnish them at any time when they please: fish and flesh they have in greate abundance, which they both roast and boil. . . .

I must needs commend them in this particular, that, though they buy many commodities of our Nation, yet they keepe but few, and those of speciall use.

They love not to be cumbered with many utensils, and although every proprietor knowes his owne, yet all things, (so long as they will last), are used in common amongst them: A bisket cake given to one, that one breakes it equally into so many parts as there be persons in his company, and distributes it. Plato's Commonwealth is so much practised by these people.

According to humane reason, guided only by the light of nature, these people leades the more happy and freer life, being void of care, which torments the mindes of so many Christians: They are not delighted in baubles, but in usefull things. . . .

I have observed that they will not be troubled with superfluous commodities. Such things as they finde they are taught by necessity to make use of, they will make choice of, and seeke to purchase with industry. So that, in respect that their life is so void of care, and they are so loving also that they make use of those things they enjoy, (the wife only excepted,) as common goods, and are therein so compassionate that, rather than one should starve through want, they would starve all. Thus doe they pass away the time merrily, not regarding our pomp, (which they see dayly before their faces,) but are better content with their owne, which some men esteem so meanely of.

Document 1.11 Chief Powhatan Addresses Captain John Smith

Powhatan was the leader of an Indian confederacy in Virginia that the English settlers first encountered. Courtesy of the Disney Company and John Smith's own accounts, he is best known as the father of Pocahontas, but was actually the leader of a powerful empire that could have eliminated the Jamestown colony if he chose. English behavior warranted destruction. After an attack on a village in 1610 that killed 65 natives, the English returned to Jamestown in small boats with the wife and children of the local leader as captives. On the way back, they threw the children overboard and shot them as they swam to shore. This is a record of one of Powhatan's speeches to Captain John Smith. What are his major points and concerns? How do Indian and European values compare here, especially when discussing private property and war?

Captaine Smith, you may understand that I having seene the death of all my people thrice, and not any one living of these three generations but my selfe; I know the difference of Peace and Warre better than any in my Country. But now I am old and ere long must die, my brethren, namely Opitchapam, Opechancanough, and Kekataugh, my two sisters, — and their two daughters, are distinctly each others successors. I wish their experience no less then mine, and your love to them no lesse then mine to you. But this bruit from Nandsamund, that you are come to destroy my Country, so much affrighteth all my people as they dare not visit you. What will it availe you to take that by force you may quickly have by love, or to destroy them that provide you food. What can you get by warre, when we can hide our provisions and fly to the woods? whereby you must famish by wronging us your friends. And why are you thus jealous of our loves seeing us unarmed, and both doe, and are willing still to feede you, with that you cannot get but by our labours? Thinke you I am so simple, not to know it is better to eat good meate, lye well, and sleepe quietly with my women and children, laugh and be merry with you, have copper, hatchets, or what I want being your friend: then be forced to flie from all, to lie cold in the woods, feede upon Acornes, rootes, and such trash, and be so hunted by you, that I can neither rest, eate, nor sleepe; but my tyred men must watch, and if a twig but breake, every one cryeth there commeth Captaine Smith: then must I fly I know not whether—and thus with miserable feare, end my miserable life, leaving my pleasures to such youths as you, which through your rash unadvisednesse may quickly as miserably end, for want of that, you never know where to finde. Let this therefore assure you of our loves, and every yeare our friendly trade shall furnish you with Corne; and now also, if you would come in friendly manner to see us, and not thus with your guns and swords as to invade your foes.

Chapter 1 Worksheet and Questions

1. List the descriptions the European visitors used to describe American Indians' political and religious practices. After each description, be sure to explain why you think the author chose those terms, and what it says about his attitude toward the native culture.

    _____

    _____

    _____

    _____

    _____

    _____

2. How did the European observers describe American Indians' social practices, including the role of women and families in society, eating habits, and other behaviors? Explain why you think the authors chose these phrases, and how they reflect their attitudes toward native culture.

    _____

    _____

    _____

    _____

    _____

    _____

3. Create a list of what the European authors described as Indian vices and virtues. These can include behaviors or character traits such as cunning, deceitful, intelligent, honest, etc. Why did they choose to describe them in this way? How do they justify their statements?

    _____

    _____

    _____

    _____

    _____

    _____

4. European observers often showed a great interest in the physical appearances of American Indians they encountered. What phrases and terms are used to describe the natives in these encounters? Were these positive or negative impressions? What comparisons are made with European styles and appearances?

_____

_____

_____

_____

_____

_____

_____

_____

5. Some historians explain Indian-European relations as an inevitable clash of cultures, and claim that no one is to blame for the conflicts that arose, and thus anything that happened to American Indians is justified and excusable. Do you agree? Based on your reading, is the near genocide and extermination of native cultures and peoples justified?

_____

_____

_____

_____

_____

_____

_____

_____

_____

Justifying the "New England Way": The Puritans in Their Own Words

The word "Puritan" triggers reactions and evokes stereotypes for most Americans. Some people visualize drab, colorless figures at the Thanksgiving dinner in Plymouth, others saintly heroes and moral athletes kneeling in prayer. Perhaps you recoil over the evil paranoia of the Salem Witchcraft trials, or the idea of religious bigotry and intolerance. It was one of their contemporary critics in the 1560s, William Bradshaw, who coined the word **Puritan** to describe the religious movement's objectives, and the name stuck. Bradshaw and others saw the Puritans as little more than a group of religious malcontents and troublemakers, who allowed no beautiful images in their churches and no organ music in their services. Later American writers like Nathaniel Hawthorne (*The Scarlet Letter*) and H.L. Mencken took pleasure in describing the Puritans as liberty-hating bigots, narrow-minded busybodies opposed to all forms of pleasure and creative thought. Those opposed to Prohibition during the 1920s used the term to describe supporters of the law, painting them as killjoys, damning everyone they disagreed with. But who were the Puritans, and what did they really stand for?

The origins of Puritanism go back to John Calvin, who stressed the importance of God's grace and predestination. (This is the doctrine that God determined who would be saved for eternity and who would be damned back at creation, and individual believers can never know for sure what their status is.) Through moral living, devout prayer, and heeding the message in sermons and the Bible, one could prepare for the possibility of salvation. But those God chose for salvation—known as the elect—had to try and live a perfect faith and life, search their souls for proof of God's grace, and agonize over not knowing. In England the Puritans were one of many radical Protestant sects wanting to completely purge the Church of England of any remaining Roman Catholic rituals and errors of doctrine. They desired simplified religious practices, which they claimed would return them to the origins of Christianity. But even the Puritans were never sure, nor in agreement, about how to proceed against the state church. Some wanted to abolish certain ceremonies and sacraments; others wanted no more than original prayers rather than a formal liturgy out of a book. Those who became known as the Separatists urged complete separation from the impure church state in England. Most English Puritans avoided this extreme, planning instead to institute reforms while staying linked to the Anglican Church.

Setting the Puritans apart from the state church was their emphasis on congregational independence. Each congregation, made up of the elect, would choose its own minister, elders, and teachers, without any instructions from a central church administration. The minister was a learned preacher of the Holy Word, not a figure of government authority. This independence undermined the Anglican hierarchy of bishops and state-supported appointments of ministers. Puritans also tried to set a high moral standard for their neighbors, while attacking Anglican Church elders and nobles guilty of vulgar lives and actions. Puritan ministers used their pulpits to attack high church and royal officials for what they perceived to be "Popish" practices. Such attacks invited harsh responses from the government, which relied on the Church to reinforce loyalty to the Crown and hence the nation. Sporadically the Crown and the Archbishop of Canterbury would drive Puritan ministers from their pulpits, threatening them with jail if they did not silence their criticisms of the Anglican Church. However, there was never any sustained persecution or refusal of the right to worship.

The first group of Puritans to reach the New World, known as the Pilgrims, were Separatists. They hold a special place in American history because of their struggles to reach and survive in America, as well as the popular story of the first Thanksgiving. They chose Plymouth because the farmlands were already cleared (courtesy of American Indians killed by European diseases). Before they landed, the Pilgrims bound Puritan and non-Puritan alike into a government based on consent of the governed, in a document known as the Mayflower Compact. But the major settlement of New England and the development of the "New England Way" came with the Great Migration from 1629 to 1640, when over 9,000 settlers settled in New England. Led by John Winthrop, these Puritans fused civil and religious functions in the name of preserving order in a godly community. Order was important. They believed England was falling into unregenerate Catholicism; although they left their home, they had a mission to save the Church of England and the nation itself. These immigrants were also cutting many family and community ties, which could also lead to a loss of order and proper behavior. The Puritans believed they were in America on a special mission, that they were chosen by God for an errand into the wilderness, to establish the first truly godly colony as an example for England to follow.

If they created this Christian Commonwealth in Massachusetts, and if their new community was to prosper, then each member must live a certain kind of life dedicated to God and the common good. The Puritans certainly felt blessed compared to other English colonies: only one ship sank out of the 198 crossing the Atlantic during the 1630s, and fewer than 5 percent of the colonists died of disease while making the long crossing. They justified the seizure of New England with Genesis 1:28, claiming they were just following orders to "subdue" the earth.

Traveling across the Atlantic to the New World, creating a perfect community, and maintaining this Holy Commonwealth would be difficult and would require many individual sacrifices. Fleeing the imposed orthodoxy of the Anglican Church and arbitrary government, the Puritans rejected political freedom and religious toleration for those who disagreed with them in New England. In the name of preserving the community, and of maintaining their covenant with God, they limited voting to church members, demanded hard work and proper behavior from everyone, and punished believers and non-believers alike for moral laxity and extravagance. Puritans believed all of the social and economic problems in England were caused by unruly citizens and corrupt leaders. They, the godly Puritans, were superior to all of the ungodly political and religious leaders back in England. Since a majority of settlers in New England were not Puritans, the "Puritan way" was imposed on a great many people. All religious dissenters must be kept under control or expelled from the colonies. Puritans believed that to be tolerant of other beliefs was to be untrue to your own.

It is important to remember that the Puritans took these actions because of their sense of mission. They did what they believed they needed to do to create the godly community, and save themselves, their families, and eventually England. Keep that sense of mission in mind as you read the materials in this chapter.

Considering the Evidence in the Readings

In this chapter you are going to try to determine who the Puritans are from their own words. The Puritans left behind a large number of diaries, sermons, and other documents, describing their goals and sense of mission, and ways to accomplish both. You can see what they believed to be important and how they planned to achieve their objectives. So determine who the Puritans believed they were, what their mission in the New World was, and how they should accomplish it. What do they see as the ideal relationship among people, religion, and government? How do they explain the importance of community, and what measures are taken to support and protect this community? How do Puritans justify actions that we would view as arbitrary and unfair today?

Document 2.1 William Bradford, the Mayflower Compact, November 11, 1620

When the group of Separatists known to United States history as the Pilgrims arrived off of the Massachusetts coast in November 1620, they were outside any established authority. Only one third of the settlers were Separatists; the rest the Pilgrims referred to as "Strangers." Puritan leaders feared that uncontrolled individualism and personal rights would weaken the colony and lead to its demise. To insure that everyone worked together for the community's survival, including the non-Puritans in the colony, the settlers on board the ship *Mayflower* created and signed the following document. Bradford would be governor of Plymouth for 33 of the next 35 years. In his *Of Plymouth Plantation*, Bradford wrote that this document was to overcome the appearance of faction and make sure the colonists "combine together in one body...." Do you think this agreement would achieve that goal? What exactly does this document do?

In the name of God, Amen.

We whose names are underwritten, the loyal subjects of our dread sovereign Lord, King James, by the grace of God, of Great Britain, France nd Ireland king, defender of the faith, etc., having undertaken, for the glory of God, and advancement of the Christian faith, and honor of our king and country, a voyage to plant the first colony in the Northern parts of Virginia, do by these presents solemnly and mutually in the presence of God, and one of another, covenant and combine ourselves together into civil body politic, for our better ordering and preservation and furtherance of the ends aforesaid; and by virtue hereof to enact, constitute, and frame such just and equal laws, ordinances, acts, constitutions, and offices, from time to time, as shall be thought most meet and convenient for the general good of the colony, unto which we promise all due submission and obedience.

In witness whereof we have hereunder subscribed our names at Cape-Cod the 11 of November, in the year of the reign of our sovereign lord, King James, of England, France, and Ireland the eighteenth, and of Scotland the fifty-fourth. Anno Domine 1620

Document 2.2 John Winthrop, "A Modell of Christian Charity," 1630

The Plymouth colony was a decade old when a very large Puritan fleet carrying John Winthrop and over one thousand settlers arrived. Their arrival heralded a new government for English settlements in New England, and the creation of the first public guidelines for shaping lives and communities in the Puritan world. On the voyage over, John Winthrop delivered this lay sermon to the travelers on board the *Arabella*. What does it declare the Puritans' intentions for the New World to be? Look for the social, economic, and political guidelines for Puritan life. What does Winthrop mean when he says they will be a "City Upon a Hill"? What responsibilities come with this assignment?

From *The Mayflower Compact*, November 11, 1620 by William Bradford.

God Almightie in his most holy and wise providence hath soe disposed of the Condicion of mankinde, as in all times some must be rich some poore, some highe and eminent in power and dignities; others meane and in subieccion.

The Reason Hereof

1. REAS: *First*, to hold conformity with the rest of his workes, being delighted to shewe forthe the glory of his wisdome in the variety and difference of the Creatures and the glory of his power, in ordering all these differences for the preservacion and good of the whole, and the glory of his greatnes that as it is the glory of princes to have many officers, soe this great King will haue many Stewards counting himselfe more honoured in despenceing his guifts to man by man, then if hee did it by his owne immediate hand.

2. REAS: *Secondly*, That he might haue the more occasion to manifest the worke of his Spirit: first, vpon the wicked in moderateing and restraineing them: soe that the riche and mighty should not eate vpp the poore, not the poore, and dispised rise vpp against theire superiours, and shake off theire yoake, 2ly in the regenerate in exerciscing his graces in them, as in the greate ones, theire loue mercy, gentleness temperance etc., in the poore and inferiour sorte, theire faithe patience, obedience etc:

3. REAS: *Thirdly*, That every man might haue need of other, and from hence they might be all knitt more nearly together in the Bond of brotherly affeccion: from hence it appeares plainely that noe man is made more Honourable then another or more wealthy etc., out of any perticuler and singuler respect to himselfe but for the glory of his Creator and the Common good of the Creature, Man; Therefore God still reserues the propperty of these guifts to himselfe as Ezek: 16, 17, he there calls wealthe his gold and his silver etc. Prov: 3, 9, he clarifies theire seruice as his due honour the Lord with thy riches etc. All men being thus (by divine providence) rancked into two sortes, riche and poore; vnder the first, are comprehended all such as are able to liue comfortably by theire owne meanes duely improued; and all others are poore according to the former distribution. There are two rules whereby wee are to walke one towardes another: JUSTICE and MERCY. These are allwayes distinguised in theire Act and in theire obiect, yet may they both concurre in the same

Subiect in eache respect; as sometimes there may be an occasion of showing mercy to a rich man, in some sudden danger of distresses and allsoe doeing of meere Justice to a poor man in regard of some perticuler contract etc. There is likewise a double Lawe by which wee are regulated in our conversacion one towardes another: in both the former respects, the lawe of nature and the lawe of grace, or the morrall lawe or the lawe of the gospell, to omitt the rule of justice as not propperly belonging to this purpose otherwise then it may fall into consideracion in some perticuler Cases: By the first of these lawes man as he was enabled soe withall [is] commaunded to loue his neighbour as himselfe vpon this ground stands all the precepts the morall law, which concernes our dealings with men. To apply this to the works of mercy this lawe requires two things first that every man afford his help to another in every want or distresse. Secondly, That hee performe this out of the same affeccion, which makes him carefull of his own good according to that of our Saviour Math: [7.12] Whatsoever ye would that men should doe to you. This was practised by Abraham and Lott in entertaineing the Angells and the old man of Gibea.

The Lawe of Grace or the Gospell hath some difference from the former as in these respectes first the lawe of nature was giuen to man in the estate of innocency: this of the gospell in the estate of regeneracy: 2ly, the former propounds one man to another, as the same fleshe and Image of god, this as a brother in Christ allsoe, and in the Communion of the same spirit and soe teacheth vs to put a difference betweene Christians and others. Doe good to all especially to the household of faith; vpon this gound the Israelites were to putt a difference betweene the brethren of such as were strangers though not of the Canaanites. 3ly. The Lawe of nature could giue noe rules for dealeing with enemies for all are to be considered as freinds in the estae of innocency, but the Gospell commaunds loue to an enemy, proofe. If thine Enemie hunger feed him; Loue your Enemies doe good to them that hate you Math: 5.44.

This Lawe of the Gospell propoundes likewise a difference of seasons and occasions there is a time when a Christian must sell all and giue to the poore as they did in the Apostles times. There is a tyme allsoe when a Christian (though they giue not all yet) must giue beyond theire abillily, as they of Macedonia. Cor: 2.6, likewise community of perills calls for

From *The Winthrop Papers*, Volume 2.

extraordinary liberallity and soe doth Community in some speciall seruice for the Churche. Lastly, when there is noe means whereby our Christian brother may be releiued in this distresse, wee must help him beyoond our ability, rather than tempt God, in putting him vpon help by miraculous or extraordinary meanes.

This duty of mercy is exercised in the kindes, Giueing, lending, and forgiueing.

QUEST. What rule shall a man observe in giueing in respect of the measure?

ANS. If the time and occasion be ordinary he is to giue out of his aboundance—let him lay aside, as god hath blessed him. If the time and occasion be extraordinary he must be ruled by them; takeing this withall, That then a man cannot likely doe too much especially, if he may leaue himselfe and his family vnder probable meanes of comfortable subsistance.

OBIECTION. A man must lay vpp for posterity, the fathers lay vpp for posterity and children and he is worse than an Infidell that prouideth not for his owne.

ANS: For the first, it is plaine, that it being spoken by way of Comparison it must be meant of the ordinary and vsuall course of fathers and cannot extend to times and occasions extraordinary; for the other place the Apostle speakes against such as walked inordinately, and it is without question, that he is worse then an Infidell whoe throughe his owne Sloathe and voluptuousnes shall neglect to prouide for his family.

OBJECTION. The wise mans Eies are in his head (saith Salomon) and foreseeth the plague, therefore wee must forecast and lay vpp against euill times when hee or his may stand in need of all he can gather.

ANS: This very Argument Salomon vseth to perswade to liberallity. Eccle: [11.1] cast thy bread vpon the waters etc.: for thou knowest not what euill may come vpon the land Luke 16. make you freinds of the riches of Iniquity; you will aske how this shall be? very well, for first he that giues to the poore lends to the lord, and he will repay euen in this life an hundred fold to him or his. The righteous is every mercifull and lendeth and his seed enjoyeth the blessing; and besides wee know what advantage it will be to vs in the day of account, when many such Witnesses shall stand forthe for vs to witnesse the improuement of our Tallent. And I would knowe of those whoe pleade soe much for layeing vp for time to come, whether they hold that to be Gospell Math: 16.19. Lay not vpp for yourselues Treasures vpon Earth etc. if they acknowledge it what extent will they allowe it; if onely

to those primitiue times lett them consider the reason wherevpon our Saviour groundes it, the first is that they are subiect to the moathe, the rust, the Theife. Secondly, They will steale away the hearte, where the treasure is there will the heart be alsoe. The reasons are of like force at all times therefore the exhortacion must be generall and perpetuall which [applies] allwayes in respect of the loue and affeccion to riches and in regard of the things themselues when any speciall seruice for the churche or perticuler distresse of our brother doe call for the vse of them; otherwise it is not onely lawfull but necessary to lay vpp as Joseph did to haue ready vppon such occasions, as the Lord (whose stewards wee are of them) shall call for them from vs; Christ giues vs an instance of the first, when hee sent his disciples for the Asse, and bidds them answer the owner thus, the Lord hath need of him; soe when the Tabernacle was to be builte his [servant] sends to his people to call for their silver and gold etc.; and yeildes them noe other reason but that it was for his worke, when Elisha comes to the widowe of Sareptah and finds her prepareing to make ready her pittance for herself and family, he bids her first provide for him, he challengeth first gods parte which shee must first giue before shee must serue her owne family, all these teach vs that the lord lookes that when hee is pleased to call for his right in any thing wee haue, our owne Interest wee haue must stand aside, till his turne be serued, for the other wee need looke noe further then to that of John 1. he whoe hath this worlds goodes and seeth his brother to neede, and shutts vpp his Compassion from him, how dwelleth the loue of god in him, which comes punctually to this Conclusion: if thy brother be in want and thou canst help him, thou needst not make doubt, what thou shouldst doe, if thou louest god thou must help him.

QUEST: What rule must wee obserue in lending?

ANS: Thou must obserue whether thy brother hath present or probable, or possible meanes of repayeing thee, if ther be none of these, thou must giue him according to his necessity, rather then lend as hee requires; if he hath present meanes of repayeing thee, thou art to looke at him, not as an Act of mercy, but by way of Commerce, wherein thou arte to walke by the rule of Justice, but, if his meanes of repayeing thee be onely probable or possible then is hee an obiect of thy mercy thou must lend him, though there be danger of looseing it Deut: 15.7. If any of thy brethren be poore etc. thou shalt lend him sufficient that men might not shift off this duty by the apparent hazzard, he tells them that though the Yeare of Jubile were at hand (when he must remitt it, if hee were not able to repay it before) yet he must lend him and that chearefully: it may not greiue thee to giue him (saith hee) and because some might obiect, why soe I should soone impouerishe my selfe and my family, he adds with all thy Worke etc. for our Saviour Math: 5.42. From him that would borrow of thee turne not away.

QUEST: What rule must wee obserue in forgiueing?

ANS: Whether thou didst lend by way of Commerce or in mercy, if he haue noething to pay thee [thou] must forgiue him (except in cause where thou hast a surety or a lawfull pleadge) Deut. 15.2. Every seaventh yeare the Creditor was to quitt that which hee lent to his brother if hee were poore as appeares ver: 8[4]: saue when there shall be noe poore with thee. In all these and like Cases Christ was a generall rule Math: 7.22. Whatsoever ye would that men should doe to you doe yee the same to them allsoe.

QUEST: What rule must wee obserue and walke by in cause of Community of perill?

ANS: The same as before, but with more enlargement towardes others and lesse respect towards our selues, and our owne right hence it was that in the primitiue Churche they sold all had all things in Common, neither did any man say that that which he possessed was his owne likewise in theire returne out of the Captiuity, because worke was greate for the resoreing of the church and the danger of enemies was Common to all Nehemiah exhortes the Jewes to liberallity and readines in remitting theire debtes to theire brethren, and disposeth liberally of his owne to such as wanted and stands not vpon his owne due, which hee might haue demaunded of them, thus did some of our forefathers in times of persecucion here in England, and soe did many of the faithfull in other Churches whereof wee keepe an honourable remembrance of them, and it is to be obserued that both in Scriptures and latter stories of the Churches that such as haue beene most bountifull to the poore Saintes especially in these extraordinary times and occasions god hath left them highly Commended to posterity, as Zacheus, Cornelius, Dorcas, Bishop Hooper, the Cuttler of Brussells and divers others obserue againe that the scripture giues noe causion to restraine any from being over liberall this way; but all men to the liberall and cherefull practise hereof by the sweetest promises as to instance one for many, Isaiah 58.6: Is not this the fast that I haue chosen to loose the bonds of wickednes, to take off the heavy burdens to lett the oppressed goe free and to breake every Yoake, to deale thy bread to the hungry and to bring the poore that wander into thy house, when thou seest the naked to cover them etc. then shall thy light breake forthe as the morneing, and thy healthe shall growe speedily, thy righteousnes shall goe before thee, and the glory of the lord shall embrace thee, then thou shalt call and the lord shall Answer thee etc. 2.10: If Thou power out thy soule to the hungry, then shall thy light spring out in darknes, and the lord shall guide thee continually, and satisfie thy Soule in drought, and make fatt thy bones, thou shalt be like a watered Garden, and they shall be of thee that shall build the old wast places etc. on the contrary most heavy cursses are layd vpon such as are straightened towards the Lord and his people Judg: 5.[23] Cursse ye Meroshe because the[y] came not to help the Lord etc. Pro: [21.13] Hee whoe shutteth his eares from hearing the cry of the poore, he shall cry and shall not be heard: Math: 25.[41] Goe ye curssed into everlasting fire etc. [42.] I was hungry and ye fedd mee not. Cor: 2.9 16.[6.] He that soweth spareingly shall reape spareingly.

Haueing allready set forth the practise of mercy according to the rule of gods lawe, it will be vsefull to lay open the groundes of it alsoe being the other parte of the Commaundement and that is the affeccion from which this exercise of mercy must arise, the Apostle tells vs that this loue is the fulfilling of the lawe, not that it is enough to loue our brother and soe noe further but in regard of the excellency of his partes giueing any motion to the other as the Soule to the body and the power it hath to sett all the faculties on worke in the outward exercise of this duty as when wee bid one make the clocke strike he doth not lay hand on the hammer which is the immediate instrument of the sound but sets on worke the first mouer or maine wheele, knoeing that will certainely produce the sound which hee intends; soe the way to drawe men to the workes of mercy is not by force of Argument from the goodnes or necessity of the worke, for though this course may enforce a rationall minde to some present Act of mercy as is frequent in experience, yet it cannot worke such a habit in a Soule as shall make it prompt vpon all occasions to produce the same effect but by frameing these affeccions of loue in the hearte which will as natiuely bring forthe the other, as any cause doth produce the effect.

The diffinition which the Scripture giues vs of loue is this Loue is the bond of perfection. First, it is a bond, or ligament. 2ly, it makes the worke perfect. There is noe body but consists of partes and that which knitts these partes together giues the body its perfeccion, because it makes each parte soe contiguous to other as thereby they doe mutually participate with each other, both in strengthe and infirmity in pleasure and paine, to instance in the most perfect of all bodies, Christ and his church make one body: the severall partes of this body considered aparte before they were vnited were as disproportionate and as much disordering as soe many contrary quallities or elements but when christ comes and by his spirit and loue knittes all these partes to himselfe and each to other, it is become the most perfect and best proportioned body in the world Eph: 4.16. "Christ by whome all the body being knitt together by every ioynt for the furniture thereof according to the effectuall power which is in the measure of every perfeccion of partes a glorious body without spott or wrinckle the ligaments hereof being Christ or his louc for Christ is loue" 1 John: 4.8. Soe this definition is right Loue is the bond of perfection.

From hence wee may frame these Conclusions.

1 first all true Christians are of one body in Christ 1. Cor. 12.12. 13.17.[27.] Ye are the body of Christ and members of [your?] parte.

2ly. The ligaments of this body which knitt together are loue.

3ly. Noe body can be perfect which wants its propper ligaments.

4ly. All the partes of this body being thus vnited are made soe contiguous in a speciall relacion as they must needes partake of each others strength and infirmity, ioy, and sorrowe, weale and woe. 1 Cor: 12.26. If one member suffers all suffer with it, if one be in honour, all reioyce with it.

5ly. This sensiblenes and Sympathy of each others Condicions will necessarily infuse into each parte a natiue desire and endeavour, to strengthen defend preserue and comfort the other.

To insist a little on this Conclusion being the product of all the former the truthe herof will appear both by precept and patterne 1. John. 3.10. yee ought to lay downe your liues for the brethren Gal: 6.2. beare ye one anothers burthens and soe fulfill the lawe of Christ.

For patterns wee haue that first of our Saviour whoe out of his good will in obedience to his father, becomeing a parte of this body, and being knitt with it in the bond of loue, found such a natiue sensiblenes of our infirmities and sorrowes as hee willingly yeilded himselfe to deathe to ease the infirmities of the rest of his body and soe heale theire sorrowes: from the like Sympathy of partes did the Apostles and many thousand of the Saintes lay downe theire liues for Christ againe, the like wee may see in the members of this body among themselues. 1. Rom. 9 Paule could haue beene contented to haue beene seperated from Christ that the Jewes might not be cutt off from

the body: It is very obseruable which hee professeth of his affectionate part[ak]eing with every member: whoe is weake (saith hee) and I am not weake? whoe is offended and I burne not; and againe. 2 Cor: 7.13. therefore wee are comforted because yee were comforted. of Epaphroditus he speaketh Phil: 2.30. that he regarded not his own life to [do] him seruice soe Phebe, and others are called the seruantes of the Churche, now it is apparant that they serued not for wages or by Constrainte but out of loue, the like wee shall finde in the histories of the churche in all ages the sweete Sympathie of affeccions which was in the members of this body one towardes another, theire chearfullnes in serueing and suffering together how liberall they were without repineing harbourers without grudgeing and helpfull without reproacheing and all from hance they had feruent loue amongst them which onely make[s] the practise of mercy constant and easie.

The next consideration is how this loue comes to be wrought; Adam in his first estate was a perfect modell of mankinde in all theire generacions, and in him this loue was perfected in regard of the habit, but Adam Rent himselfe from his Creator, rent all his posterity allsoe one from another, whence it comes that every man is borne with this principle in him, to loue and seeke himselfe onely and thus a man continueth till Christ comes and takes possession of the soule, and infuseth another principle loue to God and our brother. And this latter haueing continuall supply from Christ, as the head and roote by which hee is vnited get the predominency in the soule, soe by little and little expells the former 1 John 4.7. loue cometh of god and every one that loueth is borne of god, soe that this loue is the fruite of the new birthe, and none can haue it but the new Creature, now when this quality is thus formed in the soules of men it workes like the Spirit vpon the drie bones Ezek. 37.[7] bone came to bone, it gathers together the scattered bones or perfect old man Adam and knitts them into one body againe in Christ whereby a man is become againe a liueing soule.

The third Consideracion is concerning the exercice of this loue, which is twofold, inward or outward, the outward hath beene handled in the former preface of this discourse, for vnfolding the other wee must take in our way that maxime of philosophy, Simile simili gaudet or like will to like; for as it is things which are carued with disafeccion to eache other, the ground of it is from a dissimilitude or [blank] ariseing from the contrary or different nature of the things themselves, soe the ground of loue is an apprehension of some resemblance in the things loued to that which affected it, this is the cause why the Lord loues the Creature, soe farre as it hath any of his image in it, he loues his elect because they are like himselfe, he beholds them in his beloued sonne: soe a mother loues her childe, because shee throughly conceiues a resemblance of herselfe in it. Thus it is betweene the members of Christ, each discernes by the work of the spirit his owne image and resemblance in another, and therfor cannot but loue him as he loues himselfe: Now when the soule which is of a sociable nature findes any thing like to it selfe, it is like Adam when Eue was brought to him, shee must haue it one with herselfe this is fleshe (saith shee) and bone of my bone shee conceiues a greate delighte in it, therefore shee desires nearenes and familiarity with it: shee hath a greate propensity to doe it good and receiues such content in it, as feareing the miscarriage of her beloued shee bestowes it in the inmost closett of her heart, shee will not endure that it shall want any good which shee can giue it, if by occasion shee be withdrawne from the Company of it, shee is still lookeing towardes the place where shee left her beloued, if shee heare it groane shee is with it presently, if shee find it sadd and disconsolate shee sighes and mournes with it, shee hath noe such ioy, as to see her beloued merry and thriueing, if shee see it wronged, shee cannot beare it without passion, shee setts noe boundes of her affeccions, nor hath any thought of reward, shee fineds recompence enoughe in the exercise of her loue towardes it, wee may see this Acted to life in Jonathan and David. Jonathan a valient man endued with the spirit of Christ, soe soone as hee Discovers the same spirit in David had presently his hearte knitt to him by this linement of loue, soe that it is said he loued him as his owne soule, he takes soe great pleasure in him that hee stripps himselfe to adorne his beloued, his fathers kingdome was not soe precious to him as his beloued David. David shall haue it with all his hearte, himselfe desires noe more but that hee may be neare to him to reioyce in his good hee chooseth to converse with him in the wildernesse even to the hazzard of his owne life, rather then with the greate Courtiers in his fathers pallace; when hee sees danger towards him, hee spares neither care paines, nor perill to divert it, when injury was offered his beloued David, hee could not beare it, though from his owne father, and when they must parte for a Season onely, they thought theire heartes would haue broake for sorrowe, had not theire affeccions found vent by aboundance of Teares: other instance might be brought to shewe the nature of this affeccion as of Ruthe and Naomi and many others, but this truthe is cleared enough. If any shall object that it is not possible that loue should be bred or vpheld without hope of requitall, it is graunted but that is not our cause, for this loue is allwayes vnder reward it never giues, but it allwayes receiues with advantage: first, in regard that among the members of the same body, loue and affection are reciprocall in a most equall and sweete kinde of Commerce. 2ly [3ly], in regard of the pleasure and content that the exercise of loue carries with it as wee may see in the naturall body the mouth is at all the paines to receiue, and mince the foode which serues for the nourishment of all the other partes of the body, yet it hath noe cause to complaine; for first, the other parties send backe by secret passages a due proporcion of the same nourishment in a better forme for the strengthening and comforteing the mouthe. 2ly the labour of the mouthe is accompanied with such pleasure and content as farre exceedes the paines it takes: soe is it in all the labour of loue, among christians, the partie loueing, reapes loue againe as was shewed before, which the soule covetts more then all the wealthe in the world. 2ly [4ly]. noething yeildes more pleasure and content to the soule then when it findes that which it may loue fervently, for to loue and liue beloued is the soules paradice, both heare and in heaven: In the State of Wedlock there be many comfortes to beare out the troubles of that Condicion; but let such as haue tryed the most, say if there be any sweetnes in that Condicion comparable to the exercise of mutuall loue.

From the former Consideracions ariseth these Conclusions.

1 First, This loue among Christians is a reall thing not Imaginarie.

2ly. This loue is as absolutely necessary to the being of the body of Christ, as the sinewes and other ligaments of a naturall body are to the being of that body.

3ly. This loue is a divine spirituall nature free, actiue strong Couragious permanent vnder valueing all things beneather its propper obiect, and of all the graces this makes vs nearer to resemble the virtues of our heavenly father.

4ly. It restes in the loue and wellfare of its beloued, for the full and certaine knowledge of these truthes concerning the nature vse, [and] excellency of this grace, that which the holy ghost hath left recorded 1. Cor. 13. may giue full satisfaccion which is needfull for every true member of this louely body of the Lord Jesus, to worke vpon theire heartes, by prayer meditacion continuall exercise at least of the speciall [power] of this grace till Christ be formed in them and they in him all in eache other knitt together by this bond of loue.

It rests now to make some applicacion of this discourse by the present designe which gaue the occasion of writeing of it. Herein are 4 things to be propounded: first the persons, 2ly, the worke, 3ly, the end, 4ly the meanes.

1. For the persons, wee are a Company professing our selues fellow members of Christ, in which respect onely though wee were absent from eache other many miles, and had our imploymentes as farre distant, yet wee ought to account our selues knitt together by this bond of loue, and liue in the excercise of it, if wee would have comforte of our being in Christ, this was notorious in the practise of the Christians in former times, as is testified of the Waldenses from the mouth of one of the adversaries Aeneas Syluius, mutuo [solent amare] pene antequam norint, they vse to loue any of theire owne religion even before they were acquainted with them.

2ly. For the worke wee haue in hand, it is by a mutuall consent through a speciall overruleing providence, and a more then an ordinary approbation of the Churches of Christ to seeke out a place of Cohabitation and Consorteshipp vnder a due forme of Government both ciuill and ecclesiasticall. In such cases as this the care of the publique must oversway all private respects, by which not onely conscience, but meare Ciuill policy doth binde vs; for it is a true rule that perticuler estates cannott subsist in the ruine of the publique.

3ly. The end is to improue our liues to doe more seruice to the Lord the comforte and encrease of the body of christe whereof wee are members that our selues and posterity may be the better preserued from the Common corrupcions of this euill world to serue the Lord and worke out our Salvacion vnder the power and purity of his holy Ordinances.

4ly for the meanes whereby this must bee effected, they are 2 fold, a Conformity with the worke and end wee aime at, these wee see are extraordinary, therefore wee must not content our selues with vsuall ordinary meanes whatsoever wee did or ought to haue done when wee liued in England, the same must wee doe and more allsoe where we goe: That which the most in theire Churches maineteine as a truthe in profession onely, wee must bring into familiar and constatnt practise, as in this duty of loue wee must loue brotherly without dissimulation, wee must loue one another with a pure hearte feruently wee must beare one anothers burthens, wee must not looke onely on our owne things, but allsoe on the things of our brethren, neither must wee think that the loard will beare with such faileings at our hands as hee

dothe from those among whome wee haue liued, and that for 3 Reasons.

1. In regard of the more neare bond of mariage, betweene him and vs, wherein he hath taken vs to be his after a most strickt and peculiar manner which will make him the more Jealous of our love and obedience soe he tells the people of Israell, you onely haue I knowne of all the families of the Earthe therefore will I punishe you for your Transgressions.

2ly, because the lord will be sanctified in them that come neare him. Wee know that there were many that corrupted the seruice of the Lord some setting vpp Alters before his owne, others offering both strange fire and strange Sacrifices allsoe; yet there came noe fire from heaven, or other sudden Judgement vpon them as did vpon Nadab and Abihu whoe yet wee may thinke did not sinne presumptuously.

3ly When God giues a speciall Commission he lookes to haue it stricktly obserued in every Article, when hee gaue Saule a Commission to destroy Amaleck hee indented with him vpon certaine Articles and because hee failed in one of the least, and that vpon a faire pretence, it lost him the kingdome, which should haue beene his reward, if hee had obserued his Commission: Thus stands the cause beween God and vs, wee are entered into Covenant with him for this worke, wee haue taken out a Commission, the Lord hath giuven vs leaue to drawe our owne Articles wee haue professed to enterprise these Accions vpon these and these ends, wee haue herevpon besought him of favour and blessing: Now if the Lord shall please to heare vs, and bring vs in peace to the place wee desire, then hath hee ratified this Covenant and sealed our Commission, [and] will expect a strickt performance of the Articles contined in it, but if wee shall neglect the observacion of these Articles which are the ends wee haue propounded, and dissembling with our God, shall fall to embrace this present world and prosecute our carnall intencions, seekeing great things for our selues and our posterity, the Lord will surely breake out in wrathe against vs be revenged of such a periured people and make vs knowe the price of the breache of such a Covenant.

Now the onely way to avoyde this shipwracke and to provide for our posterity is to followe the Counsell of Micah, to doe Justly, to loue mercy, to walk humbly with our God, for this end, wee must be knitt together in this worke as one man, wee must entertaine each other in brotherly Affeccion, wee must be willing to abridge our selues of our superfluities, for the supply of others necessities, wee must vphold a familiar Commerce together in all meekenes, gentlenes, patience and liberallity, wee must delight in eache other, make others Condicions our owne reioyce together, mourne together, labour, and suffer together, allwayes haueing before our eyes our Commission and Community in the worke, our Community as members of the same body, soe shall wee keepe the vnitie of the spirit in the bond of peace, the Lord will be our God and delight to dwell among vs, as his owne people and will commaund a blessing vpon vs in all our wayes, soe that wee shall see much more of his wisdome power goodnes and truthe then formely wee haue beene acquainted with, wee shall finde that the God of Israell is among vs, when tenn of vs shall be able to resist a thousand of our enemies, when hee shall make vs a prayse and glory, that men shall say of succeeding plantacions: the lord make it like that of New England: for wee must Consider that wee shall be as a Citty vpon a Hill, the eies of all people are vppon vs; soe that if wee shall deale falsely with our god in this worke wee haue vndertaken and soe cause him to withdrawe his present help from vs, wee shall be made a story and a by-word throught the world, wee shall open the mouthes of enemies to speake euill of the wayes of god and all professours for Gods sake; wee shall shame the faces of many of gods worthy seruants, and cause theire prayers to be turned into Cursses vpon vs till wee be consumed out of the good land whether wee are goeing: and to shutt vpp this discourse with that exhortacion of Moses that faithfull seruant of the Lord in his last farewell to Isreell Deut. 30. Beloued there is now sett before vs life, and good, deathe and euill in that wee are Commaunded this day to loue the Lord our God, and to loue one another to walke in his wayes and to keepe his Commaundements and his Ordinance, and his lawes, and the Articles of our Covenant with him that wee may liue and be multiplyed, and that the Lord our God may blesse vs in the land whether wee goe to possesse it: But if our heartes shall turne away soe that wee will not obey, but shall be seduced and worshipp [serue *cancelled*] other Gods our pleasures, and proffitts, and serue them; it is propounded vnto vs this day, wee shall surely perishe out of the good Land whether wee passe over this vast Sea to possess it:

Therefore lett vs choose life,
that wee, and our Seede,
ay liue; by obeying his voyce,
and cleaueing to him,
for hee is our life, and
our prosperity.

Document 2.3 Thomas Hooker, The Importance of Community, 1648

Not all Puritans were pleased with the theocratic commonwealth established in Massachusetts Bay; some led their flocks west to Connecticut. These settlers sought good lands for farming along the region's river valleys. Here, Thomas Hooker and others established the true origins of later New England congregationalism. The first legal code in the area, the Fundamental Orders of Connecticut, did not confine voting to church members, as was the rule in Massachusetts Bay. Free churches in a free land did not mean unlimited freedom and license for individuals, however. What does Hooker see as the relationship between personal freedoms and the success of the community? What freedoms must be surrendered, and why? What is the proper relationship or balance between personal freedoms and the welfare of the community?

For if each man may do what is good in his owne eyes, proceed according to his owne pleasure, so that none may crosse him or controll him by any power; there must of necessity follow the distraction and desolation of the whole, when each man hath liberty to follow his owne imagination and humerous devices, and seek his particular, but oppose one another, and all prejudice the publicke good.

In the building, if the parts be neither mortised nor braced, as there will be so little beauty, so there can be no strength. Its so in setting up the frames of societies among men, when their mindes and hearts are not mortised by mutuall consent of subjection one to another, there is no expectation of any successfull proceeding with the advantage to the publicke. To this appertains that of the Apostle, every one submit unto another.

Mutuall subjection is as it were the sinewes of society, by which it is sustained and supported.

Hence every man is above another, while he walkes according to rule; and when he departs from it, he must be subject to another.

Hence every part is subject to the whole, and must be serviceable to the good thereof, and must be ordered by the power thereof. . . .

It is the highest law in all Policy Civill or Spirituall to preserve the good of the whole; at this all must aime, and unto this all must be subordinate . . .

Hence each man and member of society, in a just way, may be directed, censured, reformed, removed, by the power of the whole: this belongs to all the Members, and therefore to any that shall be in office, if they be Members. They are superiors as Officers, when they keep the rule: but inferior as Members, and in subjection to any when they break the rule. So it is in any corporation; so in the Parliament. The whole can censure any part.

Document 2.4 John Winthrop's Journal Discusses the Importance of Fair Prices for the Community, 1639

Nowadays the Puritans are used to promote unlimited competition and laissez-faire policies, but in reality the Puritan sense of community included fixing prices, profits, and interest rates on lending money. Merchants accused of price-gouging were charged with placing their own welfare above that of the community. Consider the following account from John Winthrop's Journal. He describes the charges and case against Robert Keayne. Keayne would be fined by the General Court, and censured by his own church in Boston. Fourteen years later Keayne felt it necessary to write a 158-page defense of his actions as part of his last will and testament. What are the specific charges against Keayne, and why are they considered wrong, according to this selection? How do the laws, and the charges against Keane, reflect Winthrop's view that the rich and mighty are required by God to nurture qualities of "love, mercy, gentleness, and temperance," and that they are "not to eat up the poor"?

Mo. 9 [Sept. 1639]

At a general court holden at Boston, great complaint was made of the oppression used in the country in sale of foreign commodities; and Mr. Robert Keaine, who kept a shop in Boston, was notoriously above others observed and complained of, and, being convented, he was charged with many particulars; in some, for taking above six-pence in the shilling profit; in some above eight-pence; and, in some small things, above two for one; and being hereof convict, (as appears by the records,) he was fined £200, which came thus to pass: The deputies considered, apart, of his fine, and set it at £200, the magistrates agreed but to £100. So, the court being divided, at length it was agreed, that his fine should be £200, but he should pay but £100, and the other should be respited to the further consideration of the next general court. By this means the magistrates and deputies were, brought to an accord, which otherwise had not been likely, and so much trouble might have grown, and the offender escaped censure. For the cry of the country was so great against oppression, and some of the elders and magistrates had declared such detestation of the corrupt practice of this man (which was the more observable, because he was wealthy and sold dearer than most other tradesmen, and for that he was of ill report for the like covetous practice in England, that incensed the deputies very much against him). And sure the course was very evil, especial circumstances considered: 1. He being an ancient professor of the gospel: 2. A man of eminent parts:

From *A Survey of the Summe of Church-Discipline*, 1648.
From *Winthrop's Journal: The History of New England from 1630–1649*, Boston, 1853.

3. Wealthy, and having but one child: 4. Having come over for conscience' sake, and for the advancement of the gospel here: 5. Having been formerly dealt with and admonished, both by private friends and also by some of the magistrates and elders, and having promised reformation; being a member of a church and commonwealth now in their infancy, and under the curious observation of all churches and civil states in the world. These added much aggravation to his sin in the judgment of all men of understanding. Yet most of the magistrates (though they discerned of the offence clothed with all these circumstances) would have been more moderate in their censure: 1. Because there was no law in force to limit or direct men in point of profit in their trade. 2. Because it is the common practice, in all countries, for men to make use of advantages for raising the prices of their commodities. 3. Because (though he were chiefly aimed at, yet) he was not alone in this fault. 4. Because all men through the country, in sale of cattle, corn, labor, etc., were guilty of the like excess in prices. 5. Because a certain rule could not be found out for an equal rate between buyer and seller, though much labor had been bestowed in it, and divers laws had been made, which, upon experience, were repealed, as being neither safe nor equal. Lastly, and especially, because the law of God appoints no other punishment but double restitution; and, in some cases, as where the offender freely confesseth, and brings his offering, only half added to the principal. After the court had censured him, the church of Boston called him also in question, where (as before he had done in the court) he did, with tears, acknowledge and bewail his covetous and corrupt heart, yet making some excuse for many of the particulars, which were charged upon him, as partly by pretence of ignorance of the true price of some wares, and chiefly by being misled by some false principles, as 1. That, if a man lost in one commodity, he might help himself in the price of another. 2. That if, through want of skill or other occasion, his commodity cost him more than the price of the market in England, he might then sell it for more than the price of the market in New England, etc. These things gave occasion to Mr. Cotton, in his public exercise the next lecture day, to lay open the error of such false principles, and to give some rules of direction in the case.

Some false principles were these:

1. That a man might sell as dear as he can, and buy as cheap as he can.
2. If a man lose by casualty of sea, etc., in some of his commodities, he may raise the price of the rest.
3. That he may sell as he bought, though he paid too dear, etc., and though the commodity be fallen, etc.
4. That, as a man may take the advantage of his own skill or ability, so he may of another's ignorance or necessity.
5. Where one gives time for payment, he is to take like recompense of one as of another.

The rules for trading, were these:

1. A man may not sell above the current price, i.e., such a price as is usual in the time and place, and as another (who knows the worth of the commodity) would give for it, if he had occasion to use it: as that is called current money, which every man will take, etc.
2. When a man loseth in his commodity for want of skill, etc., he must look at it as his own fault or cross, and therefore must not lay it upon another.
3. Where a man loseth by casualty of sea, or, etc., it is a loss cast upon himself by providence, and he may not ease himself of it by casting it upon another; for so a man should seem to provide against all providences, etc., that he should never lose; but where there is a scarcity of the commodity, there men may raise their price; for now it is a hand of God upon the commodity, and not the person.
4. A man may not ask any more for his commodity than his selling price, as Ephron to Abraham, the land is worth thus much.

Document 2.5 Sumptuary Laws of Massachusetts, 1651

Despite all the stereotypes claiming the Puritans only wore drab clothing, many New England settlers wore bright colors, and they accessorized. This was fine, as long as you stayed within your station. Puritans believed different classes of people could dress as befitted their status in society. If someone of a lower class dressed beyond their place, or if someone wore too many accessories, this was not good Christian behavior, but was a sinful pride. How could that harm the Puritan community? What guidelines do you find in these laws regarding what one may or may not wear?

———————————

Although several declarations and orders have been made by this Court against excess in apparell, both of men and women, which have not taken that effect as were to be desired, but on the contrary, we cannot but to our grief take notice that intolerable excess and bravery have crept in upon us, and especially among people of mean condition, to the dishonor of God, the scandal of our profession, the consumption of estates, and altogether unsuitable to our poverty. And, although we acknowledge it to be a matter of much difficulty, in regard of the blindness of men's minds and the stubbornness of their wills, to set down exact rules to confine all sorts of persons, yet we cannot but account it our duty to commend unto all sorts of persons the sober and moderate use of those blessings which, beyond expectation, the Lord has been pleased to afford unto us in this wilderness. And also to declare our utter detestation and dislike that men and women of mean condition should take upon them the garb of gentlemen by wearing gold or silver lace, or buttons, or points at their knees, or to walk in great boots; or women of the same ran to wear silk or tiffany hoods, or scarves which, though allowable to persons of greater estates or more liberal education, we cannot but judge it intolerable. . . .

It is therefore ordered by this Court, and authority thereof, that no person within the jurisdiction, nor any of their relations depending upon them, whose visible estates, real and personal, shall not exceed the true and indifferent value of £200, shall wear any gold or silver lace, or gold and silver buttons, or any bone lace above 2s. per yard, or silk hoods, or scarves, upon the penalty of 10s. for every such offense and every such delinquent to be presented to the grand jury. And forasmuch as distinct and particular rules in this case suitable to the estate or quality of each perrson cannot easily be given: It is further ordered by the authority aforesaid, that the selectmen of every town, or the major part of them, are hereby enabled and required, from time to time to have regard and take notice of the apparel of the inhabitants of their several towns respectively; and whosoever they shall judge to exceed their ranks and abilities in the costliness or fashion of their apparel in any respect, especially in the wearing of ribbons or great boots (leather being so scarce a commodity in this country) lace, points, etc., silk hoods, or scarves, the select men aforesaid shall have power to assess such persons, so offending in any of the particulars above mentioned, in the country rates, at £200 estates, according to that proportion that such men use to pay to whom such apparel is suitable and allowed; provided this law shall not extend to the restraint of any magistrate or public officer of this jurisdiction, their wives and children, who are left to their discretion in wearing of apparel, or any settled militia officer or soldier in the time of military service, or any other whose education and employment have been above the ordinary degree, or whose estate have been considerable, though now decayed.

———————————

From Records of the Governor and Company of the Massachusetts Bay in New England, 1853.

Document 2.6 The Old Deluder Act, 1647

Puritans valued education more than many early colonists. One had to be able to read the Scriptures to find clues about your salvation, to resist temptation, and to bring civilization to the wilderness. Education was another way to preserve civilization, when savagery lurked at the tree line just beyond your settlement. As early as 1642 Massachusetts Bay passed a law requiring parents and masters to teach reading to the children of each household. The government would send officials around to make sure the children were learning, and parents were held responsible if their children were not. How does this 1647 law further demonstrate this concern with education? What does it require communities to do in New England? Who is the "Old Deluder," and why is this law so named?

It being one chief project of that old deluder, Satan, to keep men from the knowledge of the Scriptures, as in former times by keeping them in an unknown tongue, so in these latter times by persuading from the use of tongues, that so that at least the true sense and meaning of the original might be clouded and corrupted with false glosses of saint-seeming deceivers; and to the end that learning may not be buried in the grave of our forefathers, in church and commonwealth, the Lord assisting our endeavors.

It is therefore ordered that every township in this jurisdiction, after the Lord hath increased them to fifty households shall forthwith appoint one within their town to teach all such children as shall resort to him to write and read, whose wages shall be paid either by the parents or masters of such chil-

dren, or by the inhabitants in general, by way of supply, as the major part of those that order the prudentials of the town shall appoint; provided those that send their children be not oppressed by paying much more than they can have them taught for in other towns.

And it is further ordered, that when any town shall increase to the number of one hundred families or householders, they shall set up a grammar school, the master thereof being able to instruct youth so far as they may be fitted for the university, provided that if any town neglect the performance hereof above one year that every such town shall pay 5 pounds to the next school till they shall perform this order.

Document 2.7 Crime, Punishment, and Preserving Social Order in a Puritan Community, Suffolk County Court Records, 1671–1673

Considering the importance of community in New England, and the belief that they were on a godly mission here in the New World, you should not be surprised that the courts dealt with issues of personal behavior and piety as well as the usual cases of theft and assault. Wives were considered essential to the preservation of social order of the community and the moral uplift of her own family. Single males were considered potential troublemakers. As you read through this selection of cases, consider what behaviors the court expected on each occasion. What types of disorder are considered here, and why are they a threat to the Puritan sense of community and mission? Which laws do you think were more seriously enforced, and which were allowed to slide by in the reality of colonial/frontier living?

From Records of the Governor and Company of the Massachusetts Bay in New England, 1853.
From Records of the Suffolk County Court, 1671–1680.

Peter Egerton & Clemence his wife presented for comitting Fornicacion before Marriage they appeared & acknowledged their Evill in a humble peticion. The Court Sentencd them to pay five pounds in Money fine to the County & fees of Court standing comitted till the Sentence be performd.

Upon complaint made against John Tuder of severall incoradgeing speeches he gave to ye persons in Charlestowne Ferry boat by wch he indeavored to forward ye Escape of one Wheeler who violently (with sword Drawne & pistoll cockt) ran from ye Constable the Court sentancd him ye sd Tuder to be comitted to prizon till he finde bonds for his good behavior.

Christopher Webb beeing convicted that he hath beene a disturber of the peace of the Church of Brantry severall years Last past & by his acting an abettor of the Inhabitants in Invading the rights & priviledges of the Church contrary to Law the Court sentances him to pay five pounds fine to the County & to stand henceforward disfranchised during the pleasure of this Court & to be bound to his good behavior. . . .

The Court haveing taken into consideracion the many means yt have beene used with the Church of Brantry & hitherto nothing done to efect as to the obtayning the Ordinances of Christ amongst them, The Court Orders & desires Mr Moses Fiske to improve his Labours in preaching the word at Brantry untill the Church there agree & obtayne suply for the worke of the Ministry or this Court take further Order.

Alice Thomas being accused of severall shamefull notorious crimes & high misdemeanors, she put herselfe upon Tryall of a Jury who brought in theire verdict.

1. That if breaking open warehouses & Vessells in the night & stealing goods thence bee by Law Burglary then ye sd Alice Thomas is guilty of abetting & accessary in Burglary. however that she is guilty of abetting & accessary in Fellonious Theft in receiving buying & concealing severall goods stol"n out of Thomas Beards barque & Mr Hulls & Mr Pincheons warehouses.
2. That she is guilty of giving frequent secret and unseasonable Entertainment in her house to Lewd Lascivious & notorious persons of both Sexes, giving them oppertunity to commit carnall wickedness, & that by common fame she is a common Baud.
3. That She is guilty of Selling Wine & Strong Waters Wthout Licence.

4. That She is guilty of Entertaining Servants and Children from theire Master's and Parent's Families.
5. That She is guilty of the profanation of ye Lord's day, by Selling drinke & entertaining Idle persons & paiing money in a way of Trade upon that day.

The Court upon due consideration of this Verdict Sentenced her to restore to Jon Pinchon Junr forty one pounds fifteen shillings and three pence to Thomas Beard thirteene pounds seaven shillings and eight pence to Capt Jon Hull twelve pounds, all in money being ye proportion of that 3.fold restitution ye Law requireth also to pay fivety pounds fine in money to ye County and fees of Court and prison. Alsoe to bee carried from the prison to ye Gallows, and there stand one hour wth a rope about her necke, one end fastened to ye sd Gallowes, and thence to bee returned to prison. & alsoe to bee carried from the prison to her one house and brought out of the gate or fore-doore strip't to the waste, & there tyed to a Cart's Taile, and soe to be whip't through ye Streete to the prison wth not undr thirty nine Stripes, & there in prison to remaine during the pleasure of this Court.

Robert Marshall being accused by Walter Barefoote for being an Atheist ye Court ordered him ye sd Marshall to bee committed to prison except hee put in bond of two hundred pounds to Appeare at the next Court of Assistance to bee holden at Boston. Accordingly ye sd Robert Marshall in one hundred pounds as principle . . . to ye Treasuror of ye County of Suffolk on condicion that ye sd Marshall shall appear at ye next Court of Assistants to answer what shall bee alledged against him as to his being an Atheist & that . . . in ye meane time bee of good Behavior.

William Carpenter, bound over to this Court to answere for beating his wife, ye Court Sentences him to bee whipt wth fifteen Stripes, & to give in bond for his good behavior paying fees of Court & prison Standing committed till ye Sentence bee performed. . . . Carpenter acknowledged himselfe bound to the Treasuror of ye County of Suffolke in ye Summe of ten pounds upon condicion that he shalbee of good behavior unto all men espetially towards his wife. . . .

Brian Murphey, presented for being a common drunckard, wch hee owned in Court, & also for striking Elinor Shearne that was wth Childe, & other misdemeanors[.] The Court Sentenced him to be whipt wth fifteen Stripes paying fees of Court & prison, Standing committed till the Sentance be performed.

Margarett, the wife of Brian Murphey, presented for common railing & cursing & other misdemeanors, the Court Sentances her to be whipt wth ten Stripes paying fees of Court and prison. Standing committed till the sentence be performed.

William Pollard, presented for taking Eighteen pence for keeping a Horse twenty four hours wth Salt Hey onley, the sd Pollard appeared & alledged hee had take much pains wth the Horse in rubbing him being hot & alsoe that he had other provender, the Court warned him not to exceede in that kinde, & pay fees of Court.

Sarah Carpenter, presented upon strong suspicion of being wth Childe, the Court ordered she should bee Searched by mrs Parker, mrs Williams, & mrs Sands who made return wth Goodwife Tailor a midwife, that she was not wth Childe.

Elizabeth Arnold, convicted of Cursing & Lewd profane Speeches, & other misdemeanors, the Court Sentanced her to pay ten Shillings fine in mony the County & fees of Court & to bee bound to the good behavior. . . .

Ursula the wife of Henry Edwards presented for striking her husband & abusive Carriage & Language the presentment was Owned & she was Sentanced to be whipt wth ten Stripes or pay twenty Shillings fine in money to the County & fees of Court Standing committed till the Sentance bee performed.

Cowesett Indian, convict for his abusive carriage to John Bennett, in comming into his house contrary to his minde & demanding drincke there, throwing Severall Stones at the said John Bennett & pulling him by the haire. The Court Sentanceth him to have his haire cut round close of from his head & to bee whip't wth thirty Stripes, paying fees of Court & prison is discharged, & if hee bee founde in Boston after his discharge hee is to bee taken by the Constable & to bee whipt wth twenty Stripes.

Jonathan Atherton, bound over to this Court for his wounding of an Indian wth his Sword; wch hee owned hee did upon provocacion given him by the Indian. The Court Sentanceth him to defray all the charges about the cure of saide Indian if it bee not already done & disinable him for wearing a Sword during his continuance in this Colony, or till this Court take farther order, & to pay fees of Court.

Jonathan Adams & his wife of Medfielde, presented for absenting themselves from the publique worship of god on the Sabbath dayes, the persons being Summoned & making default in appearance. The Court orders an Attachmt to bee issued forth for them against the next Court.

The Towne of Brantery presented for defect of a Schoolemaster answer was made they were Supplied.

Christopher Mason, convict of getting Mr Rock's Negroe maide Bess with Childe, which hee owned in Court. The Court Sentanceth him to bee whipt with twenty Stripes & to pay fees of Court & prison & to give in bond of twenty pound for the good behaviour till the next Court of this County. . . .

James Robinson presented for rayling in the Streets useing the name of God vainely & a which hee owned in Court, The Court Sentanceth the saide Robinson to bee admonished & to pay fees of Court & to give his owne bond of ten pounds for his good behaviour: accordingly the saide Robinson acknowledged himselfe bound in the Summe of ten pounds to the Treasurer of the County of Suffolke on condicion that hee shalbee of good behaviour especially that hee will not rayle or use the name of god vainly, untill the next Court of this County & that then hee shall appear.

John Veering presented for beeing drunck & abuseing his wife in bad language calling her whore & a reproaching mr Allen & Church members in saying mr Allen was a black hypocriticall Rogue, of all which hee was convict in Court. The Court Sentanceth him to bee whip't with thirty Stripes severely laide on & to stand in the open market place in Boston, exalted upon a Stoole for an houres time on a thursday after Lecture; with a paper fastned to his breast, with this inscription in a lardge character *A Prophane & Wicked Slanderer & Impious Reviler of a minister of the Gosple & Church-members*; & to pay charges of witnesses & Fees of Court standing committed & Upon the peticion of the saide Veering & humble acknowledgment made in open Court The Court reverseth this Sentance & Sentance the saide Veering to pay ten pounds in mony fine to the County & to give in bond for the good behaviour of twenty pounds himselfe & ten pounds apeice two Sureties & to pay the Charge of Witnesses & Fees of Court standing committed.

John Chandler presented for disorder in his house at unseasonable times of night & suffering people to bee singing & fidling at midnight of which hee was convict in Court. The Court Sentanceth him to pay Forty shillings in Mony fine to the County & to pay Charges of Witnesses & Fees of Court & to give bond for his good behaviour of five pounds & fifty shillings apeice two Sureties.

Dr Robert Couch bound over to this Court for making Verses tending to the reproach of the late Govr Richard Bellingham Esqr & of the Ministers: The Court Sentanceth him to give in bond for the good behavior ten pounds himselfe & five pounds apeice two Sureties.

Document 2.8 Proper Behaviors in Puritan Massachusetts, 1675

One of the greatest concerns for Puritans was the upbringing of their children. Children were smaller versions of adults, but with sinful will and readiness to violate the rules. Improper behavior, dress, and deportment among juveniles were considered a sure sign of Satan's activities. What actions are considered improper here by the Massachusetts Bay legislature, known as the General Court? What remedies do they consider appropriate to resolve the offensive behaviors?

Whereas there is manifest pride openly appearing amongst us in that long hair, like women's hair, is worn by some men, either their own or others hair made into periwigs, and by some women wearing borders of hair, and their cutting, curling, and immodest laying out their hair, which practise doth prevail and increase, especially among the younger sort:

This [General] Court doth declare against this ill custom as offensive to them, and divers sober Christians among us, and therefore do hereby exhort and advise all persons to use moderation in this respect; and further, do empower all grand juries to present to the County Court such persons, whether male or female, whom they shall judge to exceed in the premises; and the County Courts are hereby authorized to proceed against such delinquents either by admonition, fine, or correction, according to their good discretion. . . .

Whereas there is much disorder and rudeness in youth in many congregations in time of the worship of God, whereby sin and profaneness is greatly increased, for reformation thereof:

It is ordered by this [General] Court, that the selectmen do appoint such place or places in the meeting house for children or youth to sit in where they may be most together and in public view, and that the officers of the church or selectmen, do appoint some grave and sober person or persons to take a particular care of and inspection over them; who are hereby required to present a list of the names of such who, by their own observance or the information of others, shall be found delinquent, to the next magistrate or Court, who are empowered for the first offense to admonish them, for the second offense to impose a fine of five shillings on their parents or governors, or order the children to be whipped, and if incorrigible, to be whipped with ten stripes or sent to the house of correction for three days.

Aboute some 3. or 4. years before this time, ther came over one Captaine Wolastone, (a man of pretie parts,) and with him 3. or 4. more of some eminencie,

Document 2.9 Coping with Licentiousness and Unlicensed Trade

As you have now observed, the Puritans expected proper behavior as a sign of respect—to God and the community. Improper behavior must be censured by civil authorities, or God would punish the entire community. Thomas Morton (whom you met back in chapter 1) established a trading center near Plymouth long before most of the Puritans arrived in Massachusetts. Before long his trade and lifestyle became an issue for the Puritan leaders. According to William Bradford, what did Morton do that was so objectionable? How did the Plymouth leaders respond to this threat?

From Records of the Governor and Company of the Massachusetts Bay in New England, 1628-1686.

who brought with them a great many servants, with provissions & other implments for to begine a plantation; and pitched them selves in a place within the Massachusets, which they called, after their Captains name, MountWollaston. Amongst whom was one Mr. Morton, who, it should seeme, had some small adventure (of his owne or other mens) amongst them; but had litle respecte amongst them, and was sleghted by the meanest servants. Haveing continued ther some time, and not finding things to answer their expectations, nor profite to arise as they looked for, Captaine Wollaston takes a great part of the sarvants, and transports them to Virginia, wher he puts them of at good rates, selling their time to other men; and writs back to one Mr. Rassdall, one of his cheefe partners, and accounted their marchant, to bring anothcr parte of them to Verginia likewise, intending to put them of ther as he had done the rest. And he, with the consente of the said Rasdall, appoynted one Fitcher to be his Livetenante, and governe the remaines of the plantation, till he or Rasdall returned to take further order theraboute. But this Morton abovesaid, haveing more craft then honestie, (who had been a kind of petiefogger, of Furnefells Inne,) in the others absence, watches an oppertunitie, (commons being but hard amongst them,) and gott some strong drinck & other junkats, & made them a feast; and after they were merie, he begone to tell them, he would give them good counsell. You see (saith he) that many of your fellows are carried to Virginia; and if you stay till this Rasdall returne, you will also be carried away and sould for slaves with the rest. Therfore I would advise you to thruste out this Levetenant Fitcher; and I, having a parte in the plantation, will receive you as my partners and consociats; so may you be free from service, and we will converse, trad, plante, & live togeather as equalls, & supporte & protecte one another, or to like effecte. This counsell was easily received; so, they tooke oppertunitie, and thrust Levetenante Fitcher out a dores, and would suffer him to come no more amongst them, but forct him to seeke bread to eate, and other releefe from his neigbours, till he could gett passages for England. After this they fell to great licenciousnes, and led a dissolute life, powering out them selves into all profanenes. And Morton became lord of misrule, and maintained (as it were) a schoole of Athisme. And after they hadd gott some good into their hands, and gott much by trading with the Indeans, they spent it as vainly, in quaffing & drinking both wine & strong waters in great exsess, &, as some reported, 10. pounds worth in a morning. They also set up a May-polle, drinking and dancing aboute it many days togeather, inviting the Indean women, for their consorts, dancing and frisking togither, (like so many fairies, or furies rather,) and worse practises. As if they had anew revived & celebrated the feasts of the Roman Goddes Flora, or the beasly practiseses of the madd Bacchinalians. Morton likwise (to shew his poetrie) composed sundry rimes & verses, some leading to lasciviousnes, and others to the detraction & scandall of some persons, which he affixed to this idle or idoll May-polle. They chainged allso the name of their place, and in stead of calling it Mounte Wollaston, they call it Merie-mounte, as if this joylity would have lasted ever. But this continued not long, for after Morton was sent for England, (as follows to be declared,) shortly after came over that worthy gentleman, Mr. John Indecott, who brought over a patent under the broad seall, for the govermente of the Massachusets, who visiting those parts caused that May-polle to be cutt downe, and rebuked them for their profanities, and admonished them to looke ther should be better walking; so they now, or others, changed the name of their place againe, and called it Mounte-Dagon.

Now to maintaine this riotous prodigallitie and profuse excess, Morton, thinking him selfe lawless, and hearing what gaine the French & fishermen made by trading of peeces, powder, & shotte to the Indeans, he, as the head of this consortship, begane the practise of the same in these parts; and first he taught them how to use them, to charge, & discharge and what proportion of powder to give the peece, according to the sise or bignes of the same; and what shotte to use for foule, and what for deare. And having this instructed them, he employed some of them to hunte & fowle for him, so as they became farr more active in that imployment then any of the English, by reason of ther swiftnes of foote, & nimblnes of body, being also quick-sighted, and by continual exercise well knowing the hants of all sorts of game. So as when they saw the execution that a peece would doe, and the benefite that might come by the same, they become madd, as it were, after them, and would not stick to give any prise they could attaine too for them; accounting their bowes & arrowes but bables in comparison of them.

From *Of Plymouth Plantation: The Pilgrim in America.*

And here I may take occasion to bewaile the mischefe that this wicked man began in these parts, and which since base covetousnes prevailing in men that should know better, has now at length gott the upper hand, and made this thing commone, notwithstanding any laws to the contrary; so as the Indeans are full of peeces all over, both fouling peeces, muskets, pistols, &c. They have also their moulds to make shotte, of all sorts, as muskett bulletts, pistoll bullets, swane & gose shote, & of smaler sorts; yea, some have seen them have their scruplats to make scrupins them selves, when they wante them, with sundery other implements, wherwith they are ordinarily better fited & furnished then the English them selves. Yea, it is well knowne that they will have powder & shot, when the English want it, nor cannot gett it; and that in a time of warr or danger, as experience hath manifested, that when lead hath been scarce, and men for their owne defence would gladly have given a groat a pound, which is dear enoughe, yet hath it bene bought up & sent to other places, and sould to shuch as trade it with the Indeans, at 12. pence the pound; and it is like they give 3. or 4s. the pound, for they will have it at any rate. And these things have been done in the same times, when some of their neighbors & friends are daly killed by the Indeans, or are in deanger therof, and live but at the Indeans mercies. Yea, some (as they have aquainted them with all other things) have tould them how gunpowder is made, and all the materialls in it, and that they are to be had in their owne land; and I am confidente, could they attaine to make saltpeter, they would teach them to make powder. Oh the horiblnes of this vilanie! how many both Dutch & English have been latly slaine by those Indeans, thus furnished; and no remedie provided, nay, the evill more increased, and the blood of their brethren sould for gaine, as is, to be feared; and in what danger all these colonies are in is too well known. Oh! that princes & parlements would take some timly order to prevent this mischeefe, and at length to suppress it, by some exemplerie punishmente upon some of these gaine thirstie murderers, (for they deserve no better title,) before their collonies in these parts be over throwne by these barbarous savages, thus armed with their owne weapons, by these evill instruments, & traytors to their neighbors & cuntrie. But I have forgott my selfe, and have been to longe in this digression; but now to returne. This Morton having thus taught them the use of peeces, he sould them all he could spare; and he and his consorts detirmined to send for many out of England, and had by some of the ships sente for above a score. The which being knowne, and his neigbours

meeting the Indeans in the woods armed with guns in this sorte, it was a terrour unto them, who lived straglingly, and were of no strength in any place. And other places (though more remote) saw this mischeefe would quietly spread over all, if not prevented. Besides, they saw they should keep no servants, for Morton would entertaine any, how vile soever, and all the scume of the countrie, or any discontents, would flock to him from all places, if this nest was not broken; and they should stand in more fear of their lives & goods (in short time) from this wicked & deboste crue, then from the salvages them selves.

So sundrie of the cheefe of the stragling plantations, meeting together, agreed by mutuall consente to sollissite those of Plimoth (who were then of more strength then them all) to joyne with them, to prevente the further grouth of this mischeefe, and suppress Morton & his consortes before they grewe to further head and strength. Those that joyned in this acction (and after contributed to the charge of sending him for England) were from Pascataway, Namkeake, Winisimett, Weesagascusett, Natasco, and other places wher any English were seated. Those of Plimoth being thus sought too by their messengers & letters, and waying both their reasons, and the commone danger, were willing to afford them their help; though them selves had least cause of fear or hurte. So, to be short, they first resolved joyntly to write to him, and in a freindly and neighborly way to admonish him to forbear these courses, & sent a messenger with their letters to bring his answer. But he was so highe as he scorned all advise, and asked who had to doe with him; he had and would trade peeces with the Indeans in dispite of all, with many other scurillous termes full of disdaine. They sente to him a second time, and bad him be better advised, and more temperate in his termes, for the countrie could not beare the injure he did; it was against their comone saftie, and against the king's proclamation. He answerd in high terms as before, and that the kings proclaimation was no law; demanding what penaltie was upon it. It was answered, more then he could bear, his majesties displeasure. But insolently he persisted, and said the king was dead and his displeasure with him, & many the like things; and threatened withall that if any came to molest him, let them looke to them selves, for he would prepare for them. Upon which they saw ther was no way but to take him by force; and having so farr proceeded, now to give over would make him farr more hautie & insolente. So they mutually resolved to proceed, and obtained of the Governor of Plimoth to send Captaine Standish, & some other aide with him, to take Morton by force. The which accordingly was done; but they found him to stand stifly in his defence, having made fast his dors, armed his consorts, set diverse dishes of powder & bullets ready on the table; and if they had not been over armed with drinke, more hurt might have been done. They sommaned him to yeeld, but he kept his houses and they could gett nothing but scofes & scorns from him; but at length, fearing they would doe some violence to the house, he and some of his crue came out, but not to yeeld, but to shoote; but they were so steeld with drinke as their peeces were to heavie for them; him selfe with a carbine (over charged & almost halfe fild with powder & shote, as was after found) had thought to have shot Captaine Standish; but he stept to him, & put by his peece, & tooke him. Neither was ther any hurte done to any of either side, save that one was so drunke that he rane his owne nose upon the pointe of a sword that one held before him as he entred the house; but he lost but a litle of his hott blood. Morton they brought away to Plimoth, wher he was kepte, till a ship went from the Ile of Shols for England, with which he was sente to the Counsell of New-England; and letters writen to give them information of his course & cariage; and also one was sent at their commone charge to informe their Honors more perticulerly, & to prosecute against him. But he foold of the messenger, after he was gone from hence, and though he wente for England, yet nothing was done to him, not so much as rebukte, for ought was heard; but returned the nexte year. Some of the worst of the company were disperst, and some of the more modest kept the house till he should be heard from. But I have been too long aboute so unworthy a person, and bad a cause.

Document 2.10 The Case Against Anne Hutchinson: A Threat to the Stability of Family, Church, and Community

Knowing your proper role in society was important to the Puritans. Anyone who stepped beyond the proper bounds, or questioned church policies and beliefs, was in trouble. This restriction included the acceptable roles and actions for women in this male-ruled society. Anne Hutchinson, the well-educated daughter of a minister, wife of a prosperous merchant, mother of eleven children, and well-respected midwife, discovered this in 1637. In the following trial transcripts, determine what the charges are against her, and what is considered most serious. What do they claim she has done to attack the Puritan ideals of family, the proper role of women, and their religion? How does she respond to the charges? Do her responses help her case, or make things worse?

Mr. Winthrop, governor. Mrs. Hutchinson, you are called here as one of those that have troubled the peace of the commonwealth and the churches here; you are known to be a woman that hath had a great share in the promoting and divulging of those opinions that are causes of this trouble, and to be nearly joined not only in affinity and affection with some of those the court had taken notice of and passed censure upon. But you have spoken divers things as we have been informed very prejudicial to the honour of the churches and ministers thereof, and you have maintained a meeting and an assembly in your house that hath been condemned by the general assembly as a thing not tolerable nor comely in the sight of God nor fitting for your sex; and notwithstanding that was cried down, you have continued the same. Therefore we have thought good to send for you to understand how things are. . . .

Mrs. Hutchinson. I am called here to answer before you but I hear no things laid to my charge.

Gov. I have told you some already and more I can tell you.

Mrs. H. Name one Sir.

Gov. Have I not named some already?

Mrs. H. What have I said or done?

From *History of the Colony and Province of Massachusetts Bay*, 1767.

Gov. Why for your doings, this you did harbour and countenance those that are parties in this faction that you have heard of.

Mrs. H. That's matter of conscience, Sir.

Gov. Your conscience you must keep, or it must be kept for you. . . .

Gov. Why do you keep such a meeting at your house as you do every week upon a set day?

Mrs. H. It is lawful for me so to do, as it is all your practices; and can you find a warrant for yourself and condemn me for the same thing? The ground of my taking it up was, when I first came to this land, because I did not go to such meetings as those were, it was presently reported that I did not allow of such meetings but held them unlawful, and therefore in that regard they said I was proud and did despise all ordinances. Upon that, a friend came unto me and told me of it and I to prevent such aspersions took it up, but it was in practice before I came; therefore I was not the first.

Gov. For this, that you appeal to our practice you need no confutation. If your meeting had answered to the former it had not been offensive, but I will say that there was no meeting of women alone. But your meeting is of another sort, for there are sometimes men among you.

Mrs. H. There was never any man with us.

Gov. Well, admit there was no man at your meeting and that you was sorry for it, there is no warrant for your doings; and by what warrant do you continue such a course?

Mrs. H. I conceive there is a clear rule in Titus, that the elder women should instruct the younger; and then I must have a time wherein I must do it.

Gov. All this I grant you, I grant you a time for it; but what is this to the purpose that you, Mrs. Hutchinson, must call a company together from their callings to come to be taught of you?

Mrs. H. Will it please you to answer me this and to give me a rule, for then I will willingly submit to any truth? If any come to my House to be instructed in the ways of God, what rule have I to put them away?

Gov. But suppose that a hundred men come unto you to be instructed, will you forbear to instruct them?

Mrs. H. As far as I conceive I cross a rule in it.

Gov. Very well and do you not so here?

Mrs. H. No Sir, for my ground is they are men.

Gov. Men and women all is one for that, but suppose that a man should come and say, "Mrs. Hutchinson, I hear that you are a woman that God hath given his grace unto and you have knowledge in the word of God. I pray instruct me a little." Ought you not to instruct this man?

Mrs. H. I think I may—Do you think it not lawful for me to teach women, and why do you call me to teach the court?

Gov. We do not call you to teach the court but to lay open yourself.

Mr. Dudley, dep. gov. Here hath been much spoken concerning Mrs. Hutchinson's meetings and among other answers she saith that men come not there. I would ask you this one question then, whether never any man was at your meeting?

Gov. There are two meetings kept at their house.

Dep. Gov. How; is there two meetings?

Mrs. H. Ey Sir, I shall not equivocate, there is a meeting of men and women, and there is a meeting only for women.

Dep. Gov, Are they both constant?

Mrs. H. No, but upon occasions they are deferred.

Mr. Endicot. Who teaches in the men's meeting, none but men? Do not women sometimes?

Mrs. H. Never as I heard, not one. . . .

Dep. Gov. Now it appears by this woman's meeting that Mrs. Hutchinson hath so forestalled the minds of many by their resort to her meeting that now she hath a potent party in the country. Now if all these things have endangered us as from that foundation, and if she in particular hath disparaged all our ministers in the land that they have preached a covenant of works, . . . why this is not to be suffered. And therefore being driven to the foundation, and it being found that Mrs. Hutchinson is she that hath depraved all the ministers and hath been the cause of what is fallen out, why we must take away the foundation and the building will fall.

Mrs. H. I pray, Sir, prove it that I said they preached nothing but a covenant of works.

Dep. Gov. Nothing but a covenant of works? Why, a Jesuit may preach truth sometimes.

Mrs. H. Did I ever say they preached a covenant of works, then?

Dep. Gov. If they do not preach a covenant of grace clearly, then they preach a covenant of works.

Mrs. H. No Sir, one may preach a covenant of grace more clearly than another, so I said.

Dep. Gov. We are not upon that now, but upon position.

Mrs. H. Prove this then, Sir, that you say I said.

Dep. Gov. When they do preach a covenant of works, do they preach truth?

Mrs. H. Yes Sir, but when they preach a covenant of works for salvation, that is not truth.

Dep. Gov. I do but ask you this: when the ministers do preach a covenant of works, do they preach a way of salvation?

Mrs. H. I did not come hither to answer to questions of that sort.

Dep. Gov, Because you will deny the thing.

Mrs. H. Ey, but that is to be proved first.

Dep. Gov. I will make it plain that you did say that the ministers did preach a covenant of works.

Mrs. H. I deny that.

Dep. Gov. And that you said they were not able ministers of the new testament. . . .

Mrs. H. If ever I spake that, I proved it by God's word.

Court. Very well, very well. . . .

Mrs. H. If you please to give me leave, I shall give you the ground of what I know to be true. Being much troubled to see the falseness of the constitution of the church of England, I had like to have turned separatist; whereupon I kept a day of solemn humiliation and pondering of the thing; this scripture was brought unto me—he that denies Jesus Christ to be come in the flesh is antichrist—This I considered of, and in considering found that the papists did not deny him to be come in the flesh, nor we did not deny him—who then was antichrist? Was the Turk antichrist only? The Lord knows that I could not open scripture; he must by his prophetical office open it unto me. So after that, being unsatisfied in the thing, the Lord was pleased to bring this scripture out of the Hebrews. He that denies the testament denies the testator, and in this did open unto me and give me to see that those which did not teach the new covenant had the spirit of antichrist, and upon this he did discover the ministry unto me and ever since. I bless the Lord, he hath let me see which was the clear ministry and which the wrong. Since that time I confess I have been more choice, and he hath let me to distinguish between the voice of my beloved and the voice of Moses, the voice of John Baptist and the voice of antichrist, for all those voices are spoken of in scripture. Now if you do condemn me for speaking what in my conscience I know to be truth, I must commit myself unto the Lord.

Mr. Nowell. How do you know that that was the spirit?

Mrs. H. How did Abraham know that it was God that bid him offer his son, being a breach of the sixth commandment?

Dep. Gov. By an immediate voice.

Mrs. H. So to me by an immediate revelation.

Dep. Gov. How! an immediate revelation.

Mrs. H. By the voice of his own spirit to my soul. I will give you another scripture, Jer. 46.27,28—out of which the Lord shewed me what he would do for me and the test of his servants.—But after he was pleased to reveal himself to me, I did presently like Abraham run to Hager. And after that, he did let me see the atheism of my own heart, for which I begged of the Lord that it might not remain in my heart; and being thus, he did shew me this (a twelvemonth after) which I told you of before. Ever since that time I have been confident of what he hath revealed unto me. . . . You see this scripture fulfilled this day, and therefore I desire you that as you tender the Lord and the church and commonwealth to consider and look what you do. You have power over my body, but the Lord Jesus hath power over my body and soul; and assure yourselves thus much, you do as much as in you lies to put the Lord Jesus Christ from you; and if you go on in this course you begin, you will bring a curse upon you and your posterity, and the mouth of the Lord hath spoken it.

Dep. Gov. What is the scripture she brings?

Mr. Stoughton. Behold I turn away from you.

Mrs. H. But now having seen him which is invisible, I fear not what man can do unto me.

Gov. Daniel was delivered by miracle. Do you think to be deliver'd so too?

Mrs. H. I do here speak it before the court. I look that the Lord should deliver me by his providence.

Mr. Harlakenden. I may read scripture and the most glorious hypocrite may read them and yet go down to hell.

Mrs. H. It may be so. . . .

Mr. Endicot. I would have a word or two with leave of that which hath thus far been revealed to the court. I have heard of many revelations of Mr. Hutchinson's, but they were reports, but Mrs. Hutchinson I see doth maintain some by this discourse; and I think it is a special providence of God to hear what she hath said. Now there is a revelation you see which she doth expect as a miracle. She saith she now suffers, and let us do what we will she shall be delivered by a miracle. I hope the court takes notice of the vanity of it and heat of her spirit.

Chapter 2 Worksheet and Questions

1. How do the Puritans describe themselves and their role in the New World? Use the documents to explain the words and concepts Puritans use to describe themselves and why they are in America.

   _____

   _____

   _____

   _____

   _____

   _____

   _____

   _____

2. Summarize the law codes and regulations from this chapter, as well as the various charges brought and punishments imposed by the courts and officials. Why are these issues important? Justify them in terms of the well-being of the community, and people's proper roles in life, as any Puritan would at the time.

   _____

   _____

   _____

   _____

   _____

   _____

   _____

   _____

   _____

   _____

3. You are part of a Puritan congregation crossing the Atlantic in the 1630s, coming to America to establish a new community. What roles and behavior do you expect from people when you arrive? Be sure to use the documents, and especially the ideas of John Winthrop and Thomas Hooker, to guide you in your answer.

_____

_____

_____

_____

_____

_____

_____

_____

_____

4. Puritan Massachusetts Bay Colony demanded that both "order" and "godliness" be maintained at all times. Thomas Morton and Anne Hutchinson are presented as two great threats to Puritan society. Why are they considered such great threats? What do they challenge? How do the Puritans respond to these threats?

_____

_____

_____

_____

_____

_____

_____

_____

_____

Opportunity for All? Rich and Poor in Colonial America

In the early 1770s J. Hector St. John de Crevecoeur, a naturalized Frenchman farming in New York, wrote his famous *Letters of an American Farmer*. In these letters he attempted to explain what transformed European settlers into that unique new being called Americans. One of the keys was prosperity, which he claimed was inevitable for anyone who worked hard. You would start poor, but by acquiring the knowledge to farm the lands, gaining friends, and purchasing land you would eventually own hundreds of acres and be respected throughout your chosen community. This attitude was widely accepted and promoted by those who were successful, but was not always true for the rest of the population. Many did not become large property owners, and even those who did often had to struggle for more than a few years.

Land meant wealth, but only if you could put it into production. That required lots of labor, and labor was is short supply. The ready access to land meant it was harder to get others to willingly work for you. After all, if you can make enough to survive and provide for your family, there is no reason to take orders from someone else. This need to control sufficient labor was a serious issue for the wealthy large land owners in the New World.

Several solutions were failures. English settlers planned to have American Indians work their fields, but the natives were not seduced enough by trade goods to become field hands. Those employed could always escape into the wilderness, and most large Indian groups were too well armed to be enslaved. A second plan saw hundreds of orphans forcibly removed from London from 1617 to 1624 to work in Virginia until they reached the age of 21. Wealthy planters and the government praised this idea, because it transformed financial burdens into wealth producers. Unfortunately (from the planters view), most of the orphans died prematurely from overwork and malnutrition.

Indentured servants and eventually slaves became the solution to the labor problem across the British North American colonies. Recruits were usually single men between the ages of 15 and 24 who, faced with an unbreakable cycle of poverty and unemployment in England, chose to come to America for a chance to gain land and independence. They signed an indenture (contract) pledging to work for four to seven years in return for passage to America. At the end of their employment they would receive a new set of clothes, tools, 50 acres of land, and freedom. Most worked as field hands, planting, caring for, and harvesting the owner's cash crop, but also growing the food for survival. Once this traditional British custom was adapted to Virginia's needs, laborers began arriving. During the 1620s, 75 percent of immigrants were white males, and 15 percent were children. The government of London continued to send over orphans, and after 1720 the British government shipped over 50, 000 convicts to the New World as indentured servants.

Women made up only 10 percent of the early indentured servants. Their work depended on the wealth of their owner. Wealthier planters employed women in a range of domestic tasks such as child rearing, cooking, cleaning the home, and washing clothes. Most owners put the women to work in the fields beside their male indentures, because profits would only come from clearing fields and planting crops.

Life was not easy for indentured servants. Although the law stated they were to be cared for, properly clothed, and fed, this did not always happen. Sometimes conditions were bad for everyone, but masters could work them to exhaustion. Servants slept on dirt floors in crowded quarters, with few blankets to share. When they ate at all, they ate and drank out of common containers passed hand to hand. They relieved themselves just outside the doors of their quarters. Suffering from malnutrition, exhaustion, exposure, and malaria, many succumbed to illness. The property owners felt contempt for anyone so poor they had to work for them. Although the law said servants could take owners to court for maltreatment or breach of contract, this brought little relief in the South because the owners were the local magistrates. Thus, owners could safely physically abuse and beat their servants. Owners brought servants before their fellow magistrates to have them whipped, fined, or branded, or have the length of service extended. Indentured servants could also be bought and sold like slaves, their indentures sold to new masters without any say on their part. Indentures could be lost in games of chance or as payment for debts. Before 1650 as a result of disease, malnutrition, and maltreatment, seven out of ten indentured servants died before their contracts ended; or they reached the age of 50, thus freeing the planters from any obligation to give them land. (By comparison, most settlers in New England lived into their 60s.) After 1650 the elite passed new laws to lengthen service requirements while denying many freed men their 50 acres. Women servants also faced unwanted sexual advances from fellow servants and owners. Twenty percent became pregnant and were punished by additional years of service for bearing bastard children. This provided an incentive for owners to impregnate their own servants, until the law was modified in 1662. In addition, their children could be taken from them and sold to another master.

In the Middle and Northern colonies, labor problems existed also. At first, conditions were good for indentured servants here, with large amounts of good land, better weather, and favorable working conditions available to them. But as the eighteenth century progressed, and as the gap grew between rich and poor, tenancy increased, until almost half of the free inhabitants from the Hudson River Valley to the northern Chesapeake were tenants rather than landowners. Across New York, wealthy landowners established semi-feudal estates, working the land with tenant farmers. Tenants rented land from the owner, and could only sell their lease with his approval; they were required to turn over part of the crop to the owner, and they were obligated to provide gifts when the owner's daughter married. Poor conditions and treatment of tenants led to revolts in the eighteenth century. Indentured servants in the Middle colonies at first were mostly single young males from Southern England. Many were skilled artisans and craftsmen who came to colonial cities like Philadelphia, finished their indentures, and stayed to prosper. By the mid-eighteenth century, however, a majority of indentured servants were young families from Scotland, Ireland, and northern Europe. They tended to work as agricultural workers to pay for their passage to America. Facing harsh treatment by owners, monotonous work, and disputes over compensation, many attempted to run away. When finished, they left the settled areas and their former owners behind and moved to the frontier.

As bad as life could be, indentured servants knew that freedom awaited them. The more skills they had, the better their lives and options would be. For the involuntary African-American immigrants, life was harsh, although they began in the New World as indentured servants because there was no legal basis for chattel slavery in the laws of England. As the labor shortages increased (as well as class troubles with former indentured servants), owners devised a series of justifications and legal tricks to perpetuate African servitude. Owners could claim they were not Christians, and therefore that being enslaved provided the benefit of introducing them to a true religion. (However, many masters chose not to do this seriously.) John Locke argued that slaves were prisoners of war from Africa (as well as criminals and plainly kidnapped civilians). As prisoners of war they could be enslaved until ransomed or exchanged, following legal traditions dating back to Roman days. Black indentured servants caught running away faced enslavement, not just a few additional years of service like whites. Children of slaves would always be slaves. After 1660, laws banned interracial marriages, and banned slaves from carrying weapons or owning land. A slave with special skills and training had no options to improve his life; he was just worth more when sold.

As the decades passed, signs of one's status or place were clear. Magnificent mansions arose on plantations and along the banks of the Connecticut River, often favoring the Georgian style so popular in England. Improved housing and accumulating possessions signaled your rank in society. Clothing distinguished you as well, with the wealthy wearing finer clothes and accesories-including wigs-while the poor farmer wore rough fabrics. Without the British tradition of nobility, rank in the British North American colonies became based on wealth. This new elite aspired to **gentility**, and expected deference from their inferiors in the world. When meeting on the road, the gentleman rode by while the independent yeoman farmer tipped his cap as a sign of respect. Indentured servants stepped aside as their "betters" passed, and slaves moved off the road entirely when a free person walked by. While artisans might still advance in society based on their physical abilities, the expanding number of dependents was obvious to all. Widows and orphans, slaves, and both the urban and rural poor increased every decade.

Considering the Evidence in the Readings

The documents in this module are divided into two larger groups. The first six come from poor immigrants, indentured servants, and slaves, clearly the "have-nots" of colonial society. Their letters and diaries report what life and opportunity meant to the lower classes in the New World. What similarities do you see in their lives, despite the fact they are in different colonies separated by over a hundred years? Are their evils inherent in the indentured servant system? How does their fate compare with slavery? The last four documents originate from men of different circumstances: the wealthy and successful in the colonies. They have a different view of life and the promise of prosperity in America. Be sure to note the differences between their accounts and those of the indentured servants. These differences include how they view the land, the weather, and any hope for success. What accounts for their different points of view? Could it be that America held more promise for those already wealthy, who arrived here free rather than bound? What does each group want (or expect) out of life in this New World?

Document 3.1 Richard Frethorne Describes Life as an Indentured Servant in Virginia

The following is a pathetic appeal from a young man indentured in Virginia shortly before the first great war with the Powhatan Indians in 1622. He lived about ten miles from Jamestown in the small settlement known as Martin's Hundred. As an indentured servant, Frethorne volunteered to come to America as a chance to get ahead. What has gone wrong with his plans? What are his greatest problems and concerns? Do you think his life is so bad because he is lazy, because of conditions in Virginia, or because his owners do not care for him? We do not know if his parents responded, or what happened to Frethorne. When Opecancanough attacked the scattered settlements in Virginia, Martin's Hundred was among those that disappeared. What do you think happened to Frethorne?

Loving and Kind Father and Mother:

My most humble duty remembered to you, hoping in god of your good health, as I myself am at the making hereof. This is to let you understand that I your child am in a most heavy case by reason of the country, [which] is such that it causeth much sic kness, [such] as the scurvy and the bloody flux and diverse other diseases, which maketh the body very poor and weak. And when we are sick there is nothing to comfort us; for since I came out of the ship I never ate anything but peas, and loblollie (that is, water gruel). As for deer or venison I never saw any since I came into this land. There is indeed some fowl, but we are not allowed to go and get it, but must work hard both early and late for a mess of water gruel and a mouthful of bread and beef. A mouthful of bread for a

---

Letter to his Father and Mother, 1623.

penny loaf must serve for four men which is most pitiful. [You would be grieved] if you did know as much as I [do], when people cry out day and night—Oh! That they were in England without their limbs—and would not care to lose any limb to be in England again, yea, though they beg from door to door. For we live in fear of the enemy every hour, yet we have had a combat with them . . . and we took two alive and made slaves of them. But it was by policy, for we are in great danger; for our plantation is very weak by reason of the death and sickness of our company. For we came but twenty for the merchants, and they are half dead just; and we look every hour when two more should go. Yet there came some four other men yet to live with us, of which there is but one alive; and our Lieutenant is dead, and [also] his father and his brother. And there was some five or six of the last year's twenty, of which there is but three left, so that we are fain to get other men to plant with us; and yet we are but 32 to fight against 3000 if they should come. And the nighest help that we have is ten mile of us, and when the rogues overcome this place [the] last [time] they slew 80 persons. How then shall we do, for we lie even in their teeth? They may easily take us, but [for the fact] that God is merciful and can save with few as well as with many, as he showed to Gilead. And like Gilead's soldiers, if they lapped water, we drink water which is but weak.

And I have nothing to comfort me, nor is there nothing to be gotten here but sickness and death, except [in the event] that one had money to lay out in some things for profit. But I have nothing at all—no, not a shirt to my back but two rags (2), not clothes but one poor suit, nor but one pair of shoes, but one pair of stockings, but one cap, [and] but two bands [collars]. My cloak is stolen by one of my fellows, and to his dying hour [he] would not tell me what he did with it; but some of my fellows saw him have butter and beef out of a ship, which my cloak, I doubt [not], paid for. So that I have not a penny, nor a penny worth, to help me too either spice or sugar or strong waters, without the which one cannot live here. For as strong beer in England doth fatten and strengthen them, so water here doth wash and weaken these here [and] only keeps [their] life and soul together. But I am not half [of] a quarter so strong as I was in England, and all is for want of victuals; for I do protest unto you that I have eaten more in [one] day at home than I have allowed me here for a week. You have given more than my day's allowance to a beggar at the door; and if Mr. Jackson had not relieved me, I should be in a poor case. But he like a father and she like a loving mother doth still help me.

For when we go to Jamestown (that is 10 miles of us) there lie all the ships that come to land, and there they must deliver their goods. And when we went up to town [we would go], as it may be, on Monday at noon, and come there by night, [and] then load the next day by noon, and go home in the afternoon, and unload, and then away again in the night, and [we would] be up about midnight. Then if it rained or blowed never so hard, we must lie in the boat on the water and have nothing but a little bread. For when we go into the boat we [would] have a loaf allowed to two men, and it is all [we would get] if we stayed there two days, which is hard; and [we] must lie all that while in the boat. But that Goodman Jackson pitied me and made me a cabin to lie in always when I [would] come up, and he would give me some poor jacks [fish] [to take] home with me, which comforted me more than peas or water gruel. Oh, they be very godly folks, and love me very well, and will do anything for me. And he much marvelled that would send me a servant to the Company; he saith I had been better knocked on the head. And indeed so I find it now, to my great grief and misery; and [I] saith that if you love me you will redeem me suddenly, for which I do entreat and beg. And if you cannot get the merchants to redeem me for some little money, then for God's sake get a gathering or entreat some good folks to lay out some little sum of money in meal and cheese and butter and beef. Any eating meat will yield great profit. Oil and vinegar is very good; but, father, there is great loss in leaking. But for God's sake send beef and cheese and butter, or the more of one sort and none of another. But if you send cheese, it must be very old cheese; and at the cheesemonger's you may buy very food cheese for twopence farthing or halfpenny, that will be liked very well. But if you send cheese, you must have a care how you pack it in barrels; and you must put cooper's chips between every cheese, or else the heat of the hold will rot them. And look whatsoever you send me—be in never so much—look, what[ever] I make of it, I will deal truly with you. I will send it over and beg the profit to redeem me; and if I die before it come, I have entreated Goodman Jackson to send you the worth of it, who hath promised he will. If you send, you must direct your letters to Goodman Jackson, at Jamestown, a gunsmith. (You must set down his freight, because there be more of his name there.) Good father, do not forget me, but have mercy and pity my miserable case. I know if you did but see me, you would weep to see me; for I have but one suit. (But [though] it is a strange one, it is very well guarded.) Wherefore, for God's sake, pity me. I pray you to remember my love to all my friends and kindred. I hope all my brothers and sisters are in good health, and as for my part I have set down my resolution that certainly will be; that is, that the answer of this letter will be life or death to me. Therefore, good father, send as soon as you can; and if you send me any thing let this be the mark.

Richard Frethorne,
Martin's Hundred

Document 3.2 Legal Rulings Against Indentured Servants in Virginia, 1640

Indentured servants were promised certain rights under English and Virginia laws. As British citizens, they had the right to take their owners to court, and testify about their horrendous working conditions and the obvious breach of contract by their master. However, the very group of men who owned their contracts were usually the magistrates operating the courts across the South. After the workers appeals were rejected, their owners used these same courts to ask for punishments (usually in the form of additional service) against their servants. The courts were to sustain the natural order of society, and keep everyone in their place. Look at the hearings listed below. What problems and issues came before this court? What sort of justice do the indentured servants receive?

11th of Dec., 1640

Whereas William Huddleston servant unto Mr. Canhow [or Cantrow?] hath complained to the board against his master for want of all manner of apparel, *the court hath therefore ordered that the said Mr Canhow* [or *Cantrow?*] shall before *christmas* next provide and allow unto the said Huddleston such sufficient apparel of linen and woollen as shall be thought fit by Captain *John West* Esqr or otherwise that the said Captain *West* shall have power to dispose of the said servant until the said Mr. *Canhow* [or *Cantrow?*] do perform this order.

7th of Oct., 1640.

Whereas Thos Pursell servant unto *Robt Brassure* for the term of four years hath petitioned to the board for his freedom, it being denied unto him by the said *Brassure* in regard the said *Pursell* has absented himself from his said service for the space of three months or thereabout the Court *hath therefore ordered* that the said *Pursell* shall be discharged from his said master but shall loose his right in apparel and corn due unto him at the Expiration of his time in respect of his absence from his service as aforesaid & that the said *Brassure* shall Deliver unto the said *Pursell* such apparel beding and what other goods do already belong unto him and are remaining in the custody of the said *Brassure*.

7th of Oct., 1640.

Whereas it appeareth to the Court that *Roger Parke* being bound to serve Capt *Corell* for the space of three Quarters of a year and Thos Loving Being agent for the said Cpt Corell the said Parke was assigned to the said *Loving* to serve the said time which the said *Parke* having not performed the *Court hath ordered* that the said *Parke* shall forthwith put in security for the payment of five pounds *sterling* within twenty days after this order unto the said *Loving* in consideration of his said service being not performed as aforesaid otherwise Execution &c.

June 4, 1640.

Whereas upon information to this Board of two servants that are run away from *Maryland*, and now at the House of *George Minesye* Esqr one of which said

---

From Minutes of the Council and General Court of Colonial Virginia, 1622–1642, 1670–1676.

servants doth belong unto Mr *Snow* as he pretendeth, and the other to the governour of the aforesaid *Maryland* as is informed *the court hath therefore ordered* that the said servant belonging to the said *Snow* be delivered unto him if upon due prooff he make his right appear and the other servant to be returned with all speed unto the said Governour.

June 4, 1640.

Upon the petition of *Hugh Gwyn* gent wherein he complained to this board of three of his servants that are run away to *Maryland* to his much loss and prejudice and wherein he hath humbly requested the board that he may have liberty to make the sale or benifit of the said servants in the said *Mayland* which the Court taking into Consideration and weighing the dangerous consequences of such pernicious precident *do order* that a letter be written unto the said Governour to the intent the said servants may be returned hither to receive such exemplary and condign punishment as the nature of their offence shall justly deserve and then to be returned to their said master.

9th of July, 1640.

Whereas Hugh Gwyn hath by order from this Board Brought back from *Maryland* three servants formerly run away from the said *Gwyn, the court doth therefore order* that the said three servants shall receive the punishment whipping and to have thirty stripes apiece one called *Victor*, a *dutchman*, the other a *Scotchman* called *James Gregory*, shall first serve out their times with their master according to their Indentures, and one whole year apiece after the time of their service is Expired. By their said Indentures in recompense of his Loss sustained by their absence and after that service to their said master is Expired to serve the colony for three whole years apiece, and that the third being a negro named *John Punch* shall serve said master or his assigns for the time of his natural Life here or elsewhere.

July 22, 1640.

Whereas complaint has been made to this Board by Capt *Wm Pierce* Esqr that six of his servants and a negro of Mr *Reginolds* has plotted to run away unto the *Dutch* plantation from their said masters and did assay to put the same in Execution upon *Saturday* night being the 18th day *July* 1640 as appeared to the Board by the Examinations of *Andrew Noxe, Richd Hill, Richd Cookeson* and *John Williams* and likewise

by the confession of *Christopher Miller, Peter Wilcocke,* and *Emanuel* the foresaid Negro who had at the foresaid time, taken the skiff of the said Capt *Wm Pierce* their master, and corn powder and shot and guns, to accomplish their said purposes, which said persons sailed down in the said skiff to *Elizabeth* river where they were taken and brought back again, the Court taking the same into consideration, as a dangerous precident for the future time (if unpunished) did order that *Christopher Miller* a *Dutchman* (a prince agent in the business) should receive the punishment of whipping and to have thirty stripes, and to be burnt in the cheek with the letter R and to work with a shakle on his legg for one whole year, and longer if said master shall see cause and after his full time of service is Expired with his said master to serve the colony for seven whole years, and the said *Peter Wilcocke* to receive thirty stripes and to be Burnt in the cheek with the letter R and, after his term of service is Expired with his said master to serve the colony for three years and the said *Richard Cookson* after his full time expired with his master to serve the colony for two years and a half, and the said *Richd Hill* to remain upon his good behaviour until the next offence and the said *Andrew Noxe* to receive thirty stripes, and the said *John Williams* a *dutchman* and a Chirugeon after his full time of service is Expired with his master to serve the colony for seven years, and *Emanuel* the Negro to receive thirty stripes and to be burnt in the check with the letter R. and to work in shakle one year or more as his master shall see cause, and all those who are condemned to serve the colony after their times are expired with their masters, then their said masters are required hereby to present to this board their said servants so condemned to the colony.

13th of Oct., 1640.

The Court hath ordered that *Wm Wooton* and *John Bradye* as principall actors and contrivers in a most dangerous conspiracy by attempting to run out of the country and Inticing divers others to be actors in the said conspiracy to be whipt from the gallows to the Court door and that the said *Bradye* shall be Branded with an Iron in the shoulder, and *Wotton* in the forehead each of them to serve the Colony seven years, the service due from the said *Wotton* to the said Mr *Sanderson* being first performed, each of them to work in Irons during the time of the said censure for the rest of these that are freemen (*viz John Tomkinson* and *Richr West* for consenting and concealing the said plott that they shall be whipt and serve the colony two years and those that are servants (viz) *John Winchester, Wm Drummer Robt Rouse* and *Robt Mosely* to be whipt only as also *Margarett Beard*, and that the masters of the said servants shall pay the fees due from the servants to the sheriffs and the servants shall make good the same, at the Expiration of their time by a years service apiece to their said masters and that none of them shall be released from their Irons without order from this Board.

Oct. 17, 1640.

Whereas we are daily given to understand of divers servants that run away from their masters whereby much loss and prejudice doth ensue to the masters of such servants, the court therefore conceiving it to be the most necessary and speedy course to apprehend the said servants *doth order* that upon complaint thereof made unto the sheriffs of the counties where any such servant or servants doth run away that the sheriff thereof or his deputies shall hereby have power to hire boat and hands to pursue the said runaways and that the charge thereof shall be borne and defrayed by the said county.

Document 3.3 Former Indentured Servant George Alsop Praises the System, Maryland, 1666

Not all indentured servants denounced their years in bondage. Enough indentured servants prospered, and wrote home describing their situation, to encourage more relatives and countryment to come over to American as workers. George Alsop found his years to be "rewarding." What does he say made it so, and how did his experience differ from other accounts?

They whose abilities cannot extend to purchase their own transportation (from England) over into Mary-Land, (and surely he that cannot command so small a sum for so great a matter, his life must needs be mighty low and dejected) I say they may for the debarment of a four years sordid liberty, go over into this Province and there live plentiously well. And what's a four years Servitude to advantage a man all the remainder of his dayes, making his predecessors happy in his sufficient abilities, which he attained to partly by the restrainment of so small a time?

Now those that commit themselves unto the care of the Merchant to carry them over, they need not trouble themselves with any inquisitive search touching their Voyage; for there is such an honest care and provision made for them all the time they remain aboard the Ship, and are sailing over, that they want for nothing that is necessary and convenient.

The Merchant commonly before they go aboard the Ship, or set themselves in any forwardness for their Voyage, has Conditions of Agreements drawn between him and those that by a voluntary consent become his Servants, to serve him, his Heirs or Assigns, according as they in their primitive acquaintance have made their bargain, some two, some three, some four years; and whatever the Master or Servant tyes himself up to here in England by Condition, the Laws of the Province will force a performance of when they come there: Yet here is this Priviledge in it when they arrive, If they dwell not with the Merchant they made their first agreement withall, they may choose whom they will serve their prefixed time with; and after their curiosity has pitcht on one whom they think fit for their turn, and that they may live well withall, the Merchant makes an Assignment of the Indenture over to him whom they of their free will have chosen to be their Master, in the same nature as we here in England (and no otherwise) turn over Covenant Servants or Apprentices from one Master to another. Then let those whose chaps are always

From *Narratives of Early Maryland 1633–1684*, published 1910.

breathing forth those filthy dregs of abusive exclamations, which are Lymbeckt from their sottish and preposterous brains, against this Country of Mary-Land, saying, That those which are transported over thither, are sold in open Market for Slaves, and draw in Carts like Horses; which is so damnable an untruth, that if they should search to the very Center of Hell, and enquire for a Lye of the most antient and damned stamp, I confidently believe they could not find one to parallel this: For know, That the Servants here in Mary-Land of all Colonies, distant or remote Plantations, have the least cause to complain, either for strictness of Servitude, want of Provisions, or need of Apparel: Five dayes and a half in the Summer weeks is the alotted time that they work in; and for two months, when the Sun predominates in the highest pitch of his heat, they claim an antient and customary Priviledge, to repose themselves three hours in the day within the house, and this is undeniably granted to them that work in the Fields.

In the Winter time, which lasteth three months (*viz.*) December, January, and February, they do little or no work or employment, save cutting of wood to make good fires to sit by, unless their Ingenuity will prompt them to hunt the Deer, or Bear, or recreate themselves in Fowling, to slaughter the Swans, Geese, and Turkeys (which this Country affords in a most plentiful manner:) For every Servant has a Gun, Powder and Shot allowed him, to sport him withall on all Holidayes and leasurable times, if he be capable of using it, or be willing to learn.

Now those Servants which come over into this Province, being Artificers, they never (during their Servitude) work in the Fields, or do any other imployment save that which their Handicraft and Mechanick endeavours are capable of putting them upon, and are esteem'd as well by their Masters, as those that imploy them, above measure. He that's a Tradesman here in Mary-Land (though a Servant), lives as well as most common Handicrafts do in London, though they may want something of that Liberty which Freemen have, to go and come at their pleasure; yet if it were rightly understood and considered, what most of the Liberties of the several poor Tradesmen are taken up about, and what a care and trouble attends that thing they call Liberty, which according to the common translation is but Idleness, and (if weighed in the Ballance of a just Reason) will be found to be much heavier and cloggy then the four years restrainment of a Mary-Land Servitude. He that lives in the nature of a Servant in this Province, must serve but four years by the Custom of the Country; and when the expiration of his time speaks him a Freeman, there's a Law in the Province, that enjoyns his Master whom he hath served to give him Fifty Acres of Land, Corn to serve him a whole year, three Sutes of Apparel, with things necessary to them, and Tools to work withall; so that they are no sooner free, but they are ready to set up for themselves, and when once entred, they live passingly well.

The Women that go over into this Province as Servants, have the best luck here as in any place of the world besides; for they are no sooner on shoar, but they are courted into a Copulative Matrimony, which some of them (for aught I know) had they not come to such a Market with their Virginity, might have kept it by them untill it had been mouldy, unless they had let it out by a yearly rent to some of the Inhabitants of Lewknors-lane, or made a Deed of Gift of it to Mother Coney, having only a poor stipent out of it, untill the Gallows or Hospital called them away. Men have not altogether so good luck as Women in this kind, or natural preferment, without they be good Rhetoricians, and well vers'd in the Art of perswasion, then (probably) they may ryvet themselves in the time of their Servitude into the private and reserved favour of their Mistress, if Age speak their Master deficient.

In short, touching the Servants of this Province, they live well in the time of their Service, and by their restrainment in that time, they are made capable of living much better when they come to be free; which in several other parts of the world I have observed, That after some servants have brought their indented and limited time to a just and legal period by Servitude, they have been much more incapable of supporting themselves from sinking into the Gulf of a slavish, poor, fettered, and intangled life, then all the fastnest of their prefixed time did involve them in before.

Document 3.4 The *Maryland Gazette*, Sales Notices for Skilled Slaves, 1748–1763

The ultimate difference between indentured servants and slaves was that indentured servants were free, their contracts would end, and they could use their skills for their own profit. How different was the situation for slaves, according to the following advertisements? Did having special skills help them in any way? Note how the people being sold are described. Are there any limits to the jobs they are doing, or the skills they have learned? What does the wording of the advertisements suggest about how the wealthy owners viewed their inferiors?

[April 27, 1748]

TO BE SOLD BY THE SUBSCRIBER, IN ANNAPOLIS

A brisk likely Country-born Negro Wench about 18 or 19 years of Age, who is a good Spinner; with a Child, about 18 months Old.

William Reynolds

Very good Nutmegs, by the Pound, or Ounce, to be sold by the same Reynolds.

[December 21, 1748]

A Young Negro Wench, almost sixteen Years of Age, of a Strong, Healthy Constitution, and can do all sorts of Household Work. Enquire of the Printer hereof.

[May 29,1751]

TO BE SOLD

A likely, strong Negro Girl, about 16 Years of Age, fit for Plantation Work, or very capable of making a Good House Wench, having for some Months served as such in a small Family. For further Particulars, Enquire of the Printer Hereof.

[May 28,1752]

TO BE SOLD BY PUBLIC VENDOR

At the House of Mr. Samuel Middleton, in Annapolis, on Wednesday the 10th Day of June next at 4 o'clock in the afternoon:

The Hull of a New Vessel lying now at the Town Dock, together with her Masts, and some of her Yards.
. . .

Also at the same time will be sold a Blacksmith and a Wheelright, with their Tools; both being excellent workmen. Also a Collier and a Sawyer, who have each about 5 Yeares to Serve. . . .

Likewise a Country-born Negro Wench, About 27 Years of Age, very sober and healthy, and understands Household Business very well, with a Mulatto Boy about a year and a half old, who is the said Negro's Child.

Whoever is inclinable to purchase, on giving security (if required), may have two Months time for Payment.

[December 17, 1761]

TO BE SOLD BY THE SUBSCRIBER

being near Upper Marlborough, in Prince George's County, on the Second Day of January next. for good Bills of Exchange:

A Choice Parcel of Country-born Slaves, consisting of Men, Women, Boys, and Girls, all Young and healthy, chief between 10 and 20 years of Age: among these Slaves there are two Wenches about 16 or 17 Years of Age, who Understand Spinning and Knitting, and a young Fellow of 20 Years of Age, a good Plowman and Cartman.

The Sale to be on a Plantation near Mr. William Beall's.

William Parker

[October 20, 1763]

TO BE SOLD

A lusty likely healthy Mulatto Woman, aged about 23 Years, who has been brought up to Household Work, such as Washing, Ironing, Cooking. & C. For terms, enquire at the Printing Office.

Excerpts from *The Maryland Gazette*, 4/27/1748; 12/21/1748; 5/29/1751; 5/28/1752; 12/17/1761; 10/20/1763.

Document 3.5 Letters Home from Indentured Servant Elizabeth Sprigs, 1756

As mentioned earlier, women indentured servants faced many additional horrors. The assumptions about the proper roles for women were left in England, because the labor shortage in the New World required that they work as field labor. Forced to live and work in close quarters with total strangers, women faced sexual abuse in addition to the sufferings men went through. What examples does Sprigs give of her pitiful existence? How did she arrive in this precarious shape? Is life better for indentured servants in eighteenth-century Pennsylvania than in seventeenth-century Virginia?

Maryland, Sept'r 22'd 1756

Honred Father

My being for ever banished from your sight will I hope pardon the Boldness I now take of troubling you with these, my long silence has been purely owning to my undutifullness to you, and well knowing I had offended in the highest Degree, put a tie to my tongue and pen, for fear I should be extinct from your good Graces and add a further Trouble to you, but too well knowing your care and tenderness for me so long as I retain'd my Duty to you, induced me once again to endeavor if possible, to kindle up that flame again. O Dear Father, believe what I am going to relate the words of truth and sincerity, and Balance my former bad Conduct my sufferings here, and then I am sure you'll pity your Destress Daughter, What we unfortunate English People suffer here is beyond the probability of you in England to Conceive, let it suffice that I one of the unhappy Number, am toiling almost Day and Night, and very often in the Horses drudgery, with only this comfort that you Bitch you do not halfe enough, and then tied up and whipp'd to that Degree that you'd not serve an Animal, scarce any thing but Indian Corn and Salt to eat and that even begrudged nay many Negroes are better used, almost naked no shoes nor stockings to wear, and the comfort after slaving during Masters pleasure, what rest we can get is to rap ourselves up in a Blanket and I upon the Ground, this is the deplorable Condition your poor Betty endures, and now I beg if you have any Bowels of Compassion left show it by sending me some Relief, Clothing is the principal thing wanting, which if you should condiscend to, may easily send them to me by any of the ships bound to Baltimore Town Patapsco River Maryland, and give me leave to conclude in Duty to you and Uncles and Aunts, and Respect to all Friends

Honored Father
Your undutifull and Disobedient Child
Elizabeth Sprigs

Document 3.6 Job Johnson Praises Immigration to America, 1767

Before the English colonized North America, they conquered and colonized Ireland. Scottish citizens were recruited in the seventeenth century to settle Northern Ireland to increase the Protestant, pro-British minority in the country. By the eighteenth century their descendants, the Scotch-Irish, left the rising taxes and declining economy of Ireland behind and migrated to the New World. Job Johnson was one of these free immigrants, not an indentured servant. How is his situation different from the earlier accounts by indentured servants? What are his greatest concerns, as addressed in this letter back home?

From Letter to Mr. John Sprigs in White Cross Street near Cripple Gate, London, September 22, 1756.

Oxford Township, November 27th 1767.

My Very dear Brethern,

Not being willing to neglect any opportunity that I have in my power to writ unto you, I have thought proper to address myself to you all in a few lines hopeing that they may find you all in good Health, as thanks be to God they Leave Me. . . . I wrote seven letters home last year . . . but I do not know whether or not you have Got them, and I have Got No answer therefore I have nothing further to writ; only knowing that it is common [ ] at home to expect something Concerning this Country its property and Quality, therefore this is Really my judgement of it, that it is as Good as Country as any Man needs to Dwell in; and it is Much better than I expected it to be in every way I assure you, and I really likes it so well and it is so pleasant to me that it would be a good Estate in Ireland that would Make Me Stay there, and indeed many times when I have been by myself and think of the Lord's Good Dealings unto Me, I cannot but admire him for his Mercies that ever he turned My face hitherward; and Give Me strength and Confidence in himself and boldness by faith, to oppose all Gainsayers, though never so strong, although I cannot say that then, it seemed so Clear for Me to leave the land of My Nativity. Yet Now to Me it is a Certainty that My Removal was right and in what I Did I had peace, and in all My exercises by sea and Land, I never felt the Least in Me, as to Desire I had not come forward, but rather rejoiced (Turn over) in the Midst of them all. My Brother was not so clear in these things untill he had Been a year in the Country, Which indeed is Mostly the Case with all the first year after they Come here: but Blessed be God all is well to our content. And if one heard every objection that lay in the way of Coming here, it would be work enough. But My resolutions were, and my sayings to several opposers, that I would come, if God hindered me not no Man should. And I do not know one that has come here that Desires to be in Ireland again, for to Live there and I have often wondered at our Countryfolk that was hard of belief in regard of what was said of their Country, and would rather live in Slavery, and work all the year round, and not be three-pence the better at the years end than stir out of the Chimney Corner and transport themselves to a place where with the like pains, in two or three years, they might know better things. The only encouragement that I had to Come away was because many Go to America worth nothing yet some of them servants and to hear or see them Come back again, in two or three years worth more than they would have been by staying at home while they lived and yet they would Not Content themselves at home, but went back again which was sufficient to Convince any one that the Country was Good. But there are Many in Ireland that Desire to hear ill of this place, because they would keep their friends there with them, in Bondage and Slavery, rather than let them come here, and they think we never writ enough of the Bad properties of this Country and the Vermin in it. Now this I must say in report that there are Bears, Wolves & Foxes, Rattle snakes, and several other such creatures, but Not in this part as ever I seen, as I have travelled Many Miles to & fro. But I suppose the fear of those Creatures in Ireland is far worse to Some there, than the hurt of them is here. But I believe that this Province of Pennsylvania by all I have seen and heard of it, is a Good a one as any in America. I have seen in all places I have travelled, Orchards Laden with fruit to admiration, their very Limbs torn to pieces with the weight, and Most Delicious to the Taste I have seen a Barrel of Curious Cyder from an apple tree, and peaches in Great plenty. I could Not but at first smile at the Conceit of them, they are a very Delicate fruite, and hang almost like our onions that are tied on a rope. . . . And indeed this is a Brave Country, although no place will please all. And some may be ready to say I writ of Conveniences; but not of Inconveniences; My answer to those I honesly Declare there is some barren Land; as, I suppose there is in Most places of the World; and Land in this part is very high, selling Commonly at six and seven pounds per acre. Neither will such land Produce Corn without something to buy them. Not Bread will not be got with idleness else it would be a Brave Country indeed, and I Question not, but all them would give it a Good work. For my part I never would had the Least thought of returning home only through regard of seeing you all again. . . .

_____

Letters from Scotch-Irish Immigrant in Pennsylvania, 1766–1767 and 1784.

Document 3.7 Gabriel Thomas Describes Conditions in Pennsylvania, 1698

William Penn established Pennsylvania as both a religious haven for English Quakers and a land of economic opportunity for immigrants from all nations. He recruited settlers from across Europe to settle in his colony. Gabriel Thomas, a Quaker, was an early settler whose 1698 book *An Historical and Geographical Account of the Province and Country of Pennsylvania and West New Jersey* praised conditions in this New World. What does he suggest are the greatest attractions in Pennsylvania? How do his account and experiences differ from the indentured servants and others who came to the same area?

And now for their Lots and Lands in City and Country, in their great Advancement since they were first laid out, which was within the compass of about Twelve Years, that which might have been bought for Fifteen or Eighteen Shillings, is now sold for Fourscore Pounds in ready Silver; and some other Lots, that might have been then Purchased for Three Pounds, within the space of Two Years, were sold for a Hundred Pounds a piece. . . .

Now the true Reason why this Fruitful Country and Flourishing City advance so considerably in the Purchase of Lands both in the one and the other, is their great and extended Traffic and Commerce both by Sea and Land, viz. to New-York, New-England, Virginia, Maryland, Carolina, Jamaica, Barbadoes, Nevis, Monsserat, Antigua, St. Christophers, Bermuda, New-Foundland, Madeiras, Saltetudeous, and Old-England; besides several other places. Their Merchandize chiefly consists in Horses, Pipe-Staves, Pork and Beef Salted and Barreled . . . Bread, and Flower, all sorts of Grain, Peas, Beans, Skins, Furs, Tobacco, or Pot-Ashes, Wax &c, which are Barter'd for Rum, Sugar, Molasses, Silver, Negroes, Wine, Linen, Household-Goods, &c. . . .

. . . The Countrey at the first, laying out, was void of inhabitants (except the Heathens, or very few Christians not worth naming) and not many People caring to abandon a quiet and easy (at least tolerable) Life in their Native Country (usually the most agreeable to all Mankind) to seek out a new hazardous, and careful one in a Foreign Wilderness or Desert Country, wholly destitute of Christian inhabitants, and even to arrive at which, they must pass over a vast Ocean, expos'd to some Dangers, and not a few Inconveniences: But now all those Cares, Fears and Hazards are vanished, for the Country is pretty well Peopled, and very much improv'd, and will be more every Day, now the Dove is return'd with the Olive-branch of Peace in her Mouth.

I must needs say, even the Present Encouragements are very great and inviting, for Poor People (both Men and Women) of all kinds, can here get three times the Wages for their Labor they can in England or Wales. . . .

Corn and Flesh, and what else serves Man for Drink, Food and Rayment, is much cheaper here than in England, or elsewhere; but the chief reason why Wages of Servants of all sorts is much higher here than there, arises from the great Fertility and Produce of the Place; besides, if these large Stipends were refused them, they would quickly set up for themselves, for they can have Provision very cheap, and Land for a very small matter, or next to nothing in comparison of the Purchase of Lands in England; and the Farmers there, can better afford to give that great Wages than the Farmers in England can, for several Reasons very obvious.

As first, their land costs them (as I said but just now) little or nothing in comparison, of which the Farmers commonly will get twice the increase of Corn for every Bushel they sow, that the Farmers in England can from the richest Land they have.

In the Second place, they have constantly good price for their Corn, by reason of the great and quick vent into Barbadoes and other Islands; through which means Silver is become more plentiful than here in England, considering the Number of People, and that causes a quick Trade for both Corn and Cattle; and that is the reason that Corn differs now from the Price formerly, else it would be at half the Price it was at then; for a Brother of mine (to my own particular knowledge) sold within the compass of one Week,

---

From *A Historical and Geographical Account of the Province and Country of Pennsylvania and West Jersey*, 1698.

about One Hundred and Twenty fat Beasts, most of them good handsome large Oxen.

Thirdly, They pay no Tithes, and their Taxes are inconsiderable; the Place is free for all Persuasions, in a Sober and Civil way; for the Church of England and the Quakers bear equal Share in the Government. They live Friendly and Well together, there is no Persecution for Religion, nor ever like to be; 'tis this that knocks all Commerce on the Head, together with high Imposts, strict Laws, and cramping Orders. Before I end this paragraph, I shall add another Reason why Womens Wages are so exorbitant; they are not yet very numerous, which makes them stand upon high Terms for their several Services, in Sempstering, Washing, Spinning, Knitting, Sewing, and in all the other parts of their Employments; for they have for Spinning either Worsted or Linen, Two shillings a Pound, and commonly for Knitting a very Coarse pair of Yarn Stockings, they have half a Crown a pair; moreover they are usually Marry'd before they are Twenty Years of Age, and when once in that Noose, are for the most part a little uneasy, and make their Husbonds so too, till they procure them a Maid Servant to bear the burden of the Work, as also in some measure to wait on them too. . . .

Document 3.8 Life Among the Wealthy: William Byrd of Virginia, 1710–1711

William Byrd was one of the leading members of the Virginia aristocracy and one of the wealthiest persons in America. Westover, his mansion of the James River, was known across the colonies for its magnificent gardens, library, and wine cellar. As a member of the aristocracy, he was a member of the House of Burgesses (the Council of State that advised the governor), colonel of the militia, and assorted other positions. Members of the aristocracy, concerned about their manners and public appearance, collected courtesy books to polish their behavior. As you read these pages from his daily logbooks, consider what Byrd's life was like. How does it compare with those examined so far in this section? Do the wealthy and the poor have similar concerns?

November 1711

1. I rose about 8 o'clock and read nothing because I had a great deal to say to my wife. We sent some ducks and pigeons to the Governor and my wife sent to Mrs. Dunn to come to her. I drank chocolate for breakfast and about 10 o'clock went to court but the Governor was not there. I sat till about 3 o'clock and then went to my lodgings where I wrote in my journal till 4 o'clock, and then went to the Governor's to dinner and found my wife there. I ate venison pasty for dinner. In the evening we played at cards and I won. We put a trick [on] the Doctor who left 10 shillings on the table and we took it when he turned his back and left it for the cards when we had done. About 10 o'clock we went home in the Governor's coach. I neglected to say my prayers and had good health, good thoughts, and good humor, thank God Almighty.

2. I rose about 7 o'clock and read nothing because my wife was there, nor did I say my prayers, but ate boiled milk for breakfast. About 10 o'clock I went to the capitol and sat all day in court without once going away and by night we made an end. Then I waited on the Governor home to dinner where we found Mrs. Churchill and several other ladies and my wife among them. The table was so full that the doctor and Mrs. Graeme and I had a little table to ourselves and were more merry than the rest of the company. I ate roast beef for supper. In the meantime the Doctor secured two Fiddlers and candles were sent to the capitol and then the company followed and we

From *The Great American Gentleman: William Byrd of Westover in Virginia, His Secret Diary for the Years 1709–1712*, Capricorn Books, 1763.

had a ball and danced till about 12 o'clock at night and then everybody went to their lodgings, but I neglected to say my prayers but had good health, good thoughts, and good humor, thank God Almighty. Mrs. Russell was my partner.

3. I rogered my wife this morning and rose about 7 o'clock. I neglected to say my prayers but had boiled milk for breakfast. Mr. Beverley came to see my wife and breakfasted with us. About 10 o'clock I went to the capitol to write letters because I would not be disturbed, and my wife went to see her sister. The weather was grown warmer. I wrote three letters to England. About 1 o'clock I ate some gingerbread and drank sage and snakeroot, and then wrote more letters. About 5 o'clock I returned to my lodgings and put up my letters and because Mrs. Churchill and Mrs. Beverley were at Colonel Carter's lodgings I went there and found the Colonel with the President and Mr. Clayton almost drunk. They would fain persuade me to drink with them but I refused and persuaded the Colonel not to suffer the ladies to wait on him so long. Then I went to the coffeehouse and had the misfortune to affront the President without saying anything to provoke a reasonable man. After that we went to [p-l-y] and I won 18 pounds and got home before 11 o'clock. I neglected to say my prayers but had good health, good thoughts, and good humor, thank God Almighty. I let Mrs. Churchill know that I owed her £40 of which her husband had kept no account.

4. I rose about 7 o'clock and read a chapter in Hebrew and some Greek in Homer. I neglected to say my prayers but ate boiled milk for breakfast. About 10 o'clock came my sister Custis to dress here who told me the Major was better. About 11 the coach was sent by the Governor to carry the women to church and I walked. Mr. Commissary gave us an indifferent sermon. When church was done we went to the Governor's to dinner and I ate some boiled venison, though my stomach was not so good as usual. About 4 o'clock we went to see the new house and there we found Mrs. Blair and Mrs. Harrison. When we had tired ourselves there the coach set the women home and the Governor and I went to the coffeehouse where we stayed about half an hour and then I went home to my lodgings and read some of the public news till about 11 o'clock. I neglected to say my prayers but had good health, good thoughts, and good humor, thank God Almighty.

5. I rose about 7 o'clock and read a chapter in Hebrew and some Greek in Lucian. I said my prayers and ate boiled milk for breakfast. About 9 o'clock came Mrs. Bland and invited my wife and Mrs. Dunn to dinner and the Governor sent and invited me by Mr. Robinson, together with all the governors of the College that were in town. The College presented their verses to the Governor by the hands of the Commissary and the master. About 11 o'clock I went to the capitol and wrote a letter to England and set G-r-l to copying letters for me. About 2 o'clock I went to the Governor's to dinner and found there Mr. Commissary and the master of the College and Johnny Randolph as being the first scholar, who at dinner sat on the Governor's right hand. I ate roast mutton for dinner. The Governor was taken sick before we rose from table but it soon went over. In the evening Mr. Bland took a walk to the College, and the Governor, Mrs. Russell, and several ladies came to see the bonfire made by the boys. At night we went to the Governor's to spend the rest of the evening till 10 o'clock and then we went home. I neglected to say my prayers but had good health, good thoughts, and indifferent humor, thank God

7. I rose about 7 o'clock and read two chapters in Hebrew and some Greek in Homer. I said my prayers and ate boiled milk for breakfast. I paid £500 to Mr. Tullitt for the College. About 10 I caused my secretary to be brought to my lodgings from the capitol. The wind blew very hard at northwest so that my wife and her company could not come from Gloucester. Some of the burgesses began to come and the House met and adjourned. I dined upon gingerbread because I could find no company to dine with. About 3 o'clock I went to the capitol and wrote letters to England and danced my dance. About 5 o'clock Mr. Clayton came to me and told me my wife and the other gentlewoman were returned from Gloucester and were at my lodgings. I went to them and gave them some victuals and a bottle of wine from Marot's. My sister Custis and Mrs. Dunn went to Queen's Creek and my wife went to bed and I went to the coffeehouse where I won 5 shillings and stayed till 9 o'clock. I neglected to say my prayers and had good health, good thoughts, and good humor, thank God Almighty.

8. I rose about 7 o'clock and read nothing because my wife was preparing to go away home. I neglected to say my prayers and ate boiled milk for breakfast. About 9 we went to the Governor's

who showed me his speech. I entreated for Gilbert but could not prevail. I drank some tea till about 11 and then went in the Governor's coach to the capitol where he made his speech to the Council and Burgesses. Then I started a project of paying the ministers in money and laying 3 shillings more on tobacco and everybody was pleased with the reason of it. About 2 o'clock I dined with the Council at Marot's and ate mutton for dinner. Harry W-l-s walked from hence to Jimmy Burwell's and back again in less than three hours for a wager of two guineas, but was almost spent. I took a walk to see the College and Governor's house and in the evening returned to the coffeehouse where we played at cards and I won 20 shillings. I returned home about 10 o'clock where I said my prayers and had good health, good humor, and good thoughts, thank God Almighty.

10. I rose about 7 o'clock and read nothing because of writing a letter to Mr. D-k to endeavor to dissuade him from marrying Mrs. Young. I had several people come to see me this afternoon; however I got ready about 9 and went to the Governor's and found him [t-s] with the Commissary. I mentioned to him Mr. D-k's marriage with which he was surprised because he had not heard of it before. I asked the Governor if he had any service at Westover, and took my leave and went to the capitol where I danced my dance and wrote several things and stayed there till 4 o'clock, and then took a walk. About 5 I went to Mr. Bland's and were [sic] there about half an hour. My man Tom brought my horse and a letter from home by which I learned that all was well there, thank God. At night I went to the coffeehouse where came some other gentlemen. I played at cards and won 5 shillings. Then I went to my lodgings where I said my prayers and had good health good thoughts, and good humor, thank God Almighty. At the coffeehouse I ate some chicken pie and drank a bottle of the President's wine.

11. I rose about 7 o'clock and read nothing because I prepared to go home. However I said my prayers and ate some cranberry tart for breakfast. Mr. Graeme came to go home with me and I gave him some Virginia wine. About 10 o'clock we got on our horses and called at Green Springs where we drank tea and then took our leave and proceeded to Frank Lightfoot's and were conducted there by a dog which we found at the ferry. We designed to take Frank with us home but he was obliged to go to court the next day but promised to dine with us on Tuesday. I ate boiled beef for dinner. In the afternoon we sent to Major Harrison to come to us and then took a walk and met a pretty girl and kissed her and so returned. About 6 o'clock Major Harrison came to us but we could not persuade him to go with us to Westover. We sat up and were merry till 11 o'clock and then we went to bed. I neglected to say my prayers but had good health, good thoughts, and good humor, thank God Almighty.

12. I rose about 7 o'clock and said my prayers. Then we ate our breakfast of milk and took our leave and proceeded to Westover, where we found all well, thank God Almighty. Mr. Graeme was pleased with the place exceedingly. I showed him the library and then we walked in the garden till dinner and I ate some wild duck. In the afternoon I paid money to several men on accounts of Captain H-n-t and then we took a walk about the plantation and I was displeased with John about the boat which he was building. In the evening we played at piquet and I won a little. About 8 o'clock my wife was taken with the colic violently but it was soon over. Then Mr. Graeme and I drank a bottle of pressed wine which he liked very well, as he had done the white madeira. About 10 o'clock I went to bed and rogered my wife. I neglected to say my prayers but had good health, good thoughts, and good humor, thank God Almighty.

13. I rose about 7 o'clock and read nothing because of my company. However I said a short prayer and drank chocolate for breakfast and ate some cake. Then Mr. Graeme and I went out with bows and arrows and shot at partridge and squirrel which gave us abundance of diversion but we lost some of our arrows. We returned about one o'clock but found that Frank Lightfoot had broken his word by not coming to us. About 2 o'clock we went to dinner and I ate some venison pasty and were very merry: In the afternoon we played at billiards and I by accident had almost lost some of my fore teeth by putting the stick in my mouth. Then we went and took a walk with the women and Mr. Graeme diverted himself with Mrs. Dunn. In the evening came Mr. Mumford who told me all was well again at Appomattox. We played at cards and drank some pressed wine and were merry till 10 o'clock. I neglected to say my prayers but rogered my wife, and had good health, good thoughts, and good humor, thank God Almighty.

14. I rose about 7 o'clock and gave all the necessary orders to my people. I recommended myself and family to God and then ate some cold venison pasty for breakfast. I settled my business with Captain H-n-t and delivered my letters to him. Then we took our leave and were set over the creek and then proceeded on our journey and about 3 o'clock we got to Green Springs but neither the Colonel nor his lady were at home and therefore we stayed but half an hour and then went on to Williamsburg where we got about 5. I dressed myself and went to Colonel Bray's where the wedding had been kept and found abundance of company there. I dined and ate some chicken pie and then we went to dancing and the bride was my partner but because Colonel Bray was sick we went away before 10 o'clock to the coffeehouse where I won 5 shillings of the President, I said my prayers and had good thoughts, good health, and good humor, thank God Almighty.

16. I rose about 7 o'clock and read two chapters in Hebrew and some Greek in Homer. I said my prayers and ate boiled milk for breakfast. About 9 o'clock I went to the Governor's where I stayed about an hour and then went to the capitol where we read a bill concerning rolling houses the first time. About 11 the Governor came and the President read our address to him with an indifferent grace. About 2 o'clock we dined at Marot's and I ate some fish for dinner. My mouth was sore with the blow I had with the billiard stick. About 4 o'clock Jimmy Burwell and I resolved to go to the wedding at Mr. Ingles' and went away in his coach and found all the company ready to go to supper but we ate nothing with them but some custard. After supper we began to dance, first French dances and after country dances till about 11 o'clock and then most of the company went to Williamsburg but I stayed with Jimmy Burwell and Jimmy Roscow and James Bray, got drunk and went home by myself about 12 o'clock. I neglected to say my prayers but had good health, good thoughts, and good humor, thank God Almighty.

19. I rose about 7 o'clock and read a chapter in Hebrew and some Greek in Homer. I said my prayers and ate boiled milk for breakfast. It rained a little in the morning I went to the Governor's but he was gone to the new house and I went there to him and found him putting up the arms. Captain H-n-t came over and could hardly prevail with the Governor to let him go; however I interceded for him and got leave. About 2

o'clock my sister Custis sent horses for me and about 3 I rode to make her a visit and found them pretty well and their whole family. About 6 o'clock we went to supper and I ate some roast beef. Then we talked about dividing the land of old Colonel Parke between them and me. Some words were spoken concerning selling some of Colonel Parke's land to pay his debts but my sister would not hear of it. I said my prayers and had good health good thoughts, and good humor, thank God Almighty.

20. I rose about 7 o'clock and my brother and I appointed Mr. Bland and Mr. [Keeling.] to divide the land of old Colonel Parke and agreed my sister should have the choice. I said my prayers and ate boiled milk for breakfast. About 9 o'clock I took leave and rode to Williamsburg where I found my man Tom with a letter from home, that told me all were well except my daughter, who had fallen down and cut her forehead. I wrote a letter to my wife and sent Tom home. Then I went to the capitol and read some bills. The Governor was there. We sat till two o'clock and I went to dinner at the Governor's and ate roast beef. About 4 we went away and I went and wrote in my journal and afterwards went and recommended the business of the College to some of the burgesses and then went to the coffeehouse where I won of Dr. Cocke 45 shillings at piquet. About 12 o'clock I went home and said a short prayer and had good thoughts, good humor, and good health, thank God Almighty.

22. I rose about 7 o'clock and read a chapter in Hebrew and some Greek in Homer. I said my prayers and ate boiled milk for breakfast. Mr. Bland came to see me and told me he would go about the dividing of old Colonel Parke's land as we desired. About 11 I went to the capitol where I found the Governor, who had letters from the Governor of North Carolina which gave a terrible account of the state of Carolina. He had also a letter from the Baron by which he had a relation of his being taken with Mr. Lawson by the Indians and of Mr. Lawson's murder. The House of Burgesses brought their address of thanks to which the Governor answered them that he would thank them when he saw them act with as little self interest as he had done. About 3 o'clock we went to dinner and I ate some roast goose. Then I took a walk to the Governor's new house with Frank W-l-s and then returned to the coffeehouse where I lost 12 pounds 10 shillings and about 10 o'clock returned home very much out of

humor to think myself such a fool. I said my prayers and had good health, good thoughts, and good humor, thank God Almighty. It was very hot till about 9 o'clock in the evening and then it grew cold.

23. I rose about 7 o'clock and read a chapter in Hebrew and some Greek in Homer. I said my prayers and ate boiled milk for breakfast. Several gentlemen came to my lodgings. About 10 o'clock I went to the capitol where I danced my dance and then wrote in my journal. It was very cold this morning. About 11 o'clock I went to the coffeehouse where the Governor also came and from thence we went to the capitol and read the bill concerning ports the first time. We stayed till 3 o'clock and then went to dinner to Marot's but could get none there and therefore Colonel Lewis and I dined with Colonel Duke and I ate broiled chicken for dinner. After dinner we went to Colonel Carter's room where we had a bowl of punch of French brandy and oranges. We talked very lewdly and were almost drunk and in that condition we went to the coffeehouse and played at dice and I lost 12 pounds. We stayed at the coffeehouse till almost 4 o'clock in the morning talking with Major Harrison. Then I went to my lodging, where I committed uncleanness, for which I humbly beg God Almighty's pardon.

27. I rose about 7 o'clock and read a chapter in Hebrew and some Greek in Homer. I said my prayers and ate boiled milk for breakfast. The weather was very cold and threatened snow. James Bray invited me to the wedding of his daughter this day but the weather was so bad I made my excuses by the Commissary. We sat at the President's house where we had a good fire. I received a letter from home by my sloop that brought some coal on her way to Kiquotan with palisades. We read several bills and the Governor came to us and made his exceptions to some clauses in the bill concerning probate and administration, which we resolved to amend. We sat till about 4 o'clock and then went to dinner and I ate some roast mutton. In the evening we went to the coffeehouse where I played at cards and won 25 shillings. About 9 I returned to my lodgings where I said my prayers and had good health, good thoughts, and good humor, thank God Almighty.

28. I rose about 7 o'clock and found the weather extremely cold. I read a chapter in Hebrew and some Greek in Homer. I said my prayers and ate boiled milk for breakfast. I had a gentleman that came to buy the quitrents of Nansemond County but we could not agree. About 10 o'clock I went to the capitol where I wrote in my journal and danced my dance, and then went to the coffeehouse where I found several of the council but not ready to go to council, and so some of us took a walk to the Governor's house where we found the Governor looking over the workmen. It was exceedingly cold. Then we returned to the President's lodgings where we read some bills and afterwards adjourned to the capitol where the House of Burgesses brought an address to the Governor in which they desired him to make war on the Indians and the council afterwards advised him if no other method would procure satisfaction from the Indians then to make war on them. About 4 o'clock we went to dinner and I ate some roast beef. In the evening we played at cards till 7 o'clock and then I went home and read some Greek and looked over several papers relating to the estate of old Colonel Parke. I said my prayers and had good health, good thoughts, and good humor, thank God Almighty.

30. I rose about 7 o'clock and read nothing because I prepared for my journey home. However I said my prayers and ate boiled milk for breakfast. I sold the quitrents to Mr. Bland and then took my leave of him and got on horseback about 9 o'clock when it was fair weather, but it was overcast before I got to the ferry. Sometimes I walked to get myself warm, and sometimes I rode, and got there about 3 o'clock in the afternoon, and found all my family well, thank God Almighty. My wife and Mrs. Dunn had worked very hard to put the house in order. In the evening I ate two partridges for my supper and spent the rest of the evening in talking about all the affairs of the neighborhood. My wife told me that Llewellyn Eppes his wife was like not to be very happy because he was cross already to her. I told them all the news of the town and about 8 o'clock we went to bed. I neglected to say my prayers but had good health, good thoughts, and good humor, thank God Almighty. I rogered my wife vigorously.

Document 3.9 Robert Parke Explains Why America Is Good for Free Men with Money, 1725

Robert Parke was also a Scotch-Irish immigrant. Coming to the New World as a free man with enough money to purchase a large piece of property, he and his family were able to live comfortably after the first year. Could this be the reason for his positive letters to family members back in Ireland? Do you think that his arriving in an established and prosperous colony, rather than a new and struggling one, made a difference?

Thee writes in thy letter that there was a talk went back to Ireland that we were not satisfied in coming here, which was utterly false. Now, let this suffice to convince you. In the first place he that carried back this story was an idle fellow, and one of our shipmates, but not thinking this country suitable to his idleness, went back with [Captain] Cowman again. He is sort of a lawyer, or rather a liar, as I may term him; therefore, I would not have you give credit to such false reports for the future, for there is not one of the family but what likes the country very well and would, if we were in Ireland again, come here directly, it being the best country for working folk and tradesmen of any in the world. But for drunkards and idlers, they cannot live well anywhere. . . . Land is of all prices, even from ten pounds to one hundred pounds a hundred [acres] according to the goodness or else the situation thereof, and grows dearer every year by reason of vast quantities of people that come here yearly from several parts of the world. Therefore, thee and thy family or any that I wish well, I would desire to make what speed you can to come here, the sooner the better.

We have traveled over a pretty deal of this country to seek land and though we met with many fine tracts of land here and there in the country, yet my father being curious and somewhat hard to please did not buy any land until the second day of tenth month last, and then he bought a tract of land consisting of five hundred acres for which he gave 350 pounds. It is excellent good land but none cleared, except about twenty acres, with a small log house and orchard planted. We are going to clear some of it directly, for our next summer's fallow. We might have bought land much cheaper but not so much to our satisfaction. We stayed in Chester three months and then we rented a place one mile from Chester with a good brick house and 200 acres of land for ____ pounds a year, where we continue till next May. We have sowed about 200 acres of wheat and seven acres of rye this season. We sowed but a bushel on an acre. . . .

I am grown an experienced plowman and my brother Abell is learning. Jonathan and thy son John drives for us. He is grown a lusty fellow since thou saw him. We have the finest plows here that can be. We plowed up our summer's fallows in May and June with a yoke of oxen and two horses and they go with as much ease as double the number in Ireland. We sow our wheat with two horses. A boy of twelve or fourteen years old can hold plow here; a man commonly holds and drives himself. They plow an acre, nay, some plows two acres a day.

They sow wheat and rye in August and September. We have had a crop of oats, barley, and very good flax and hemp, Indian corn and buckwheat all of our own sowing and planting this last summer. We also planted a bushel of white potatoes which cost us five shillings and we had ten or twelve bushels' increase. This country yields extraordinary increase of all sorts of grain likewise. . . .

This country abounds in fruit, scarce an house but has an apple, peach, and cherry orchard. As for chestnuts, walnuts, and hazelnuts, strawberries, billberries, and mulberries, they grow wild in the woods and fields in vast quantities.

They also make great preparations against harvest. Both roast and boiled [meats], and cakes and tarts and rum, stand at the land's end, so that they may eat and drink at pleasure. A reaper has two shillings and threepence a day, a mower has two

From *The Scotch-Irish in North Britain, North Ireland and North America*, Putnam & Sons, 1902.

shillings and sixpence and a pint of rum, besides meat and drink of the best, for no workman works without their victuals in the bargain throughout the country.

As to what thee writ about the governor's opening letters, it is utterly false and nothing but a lie, and anyone except bound servants may go out of the country when they will and servants when they serve their time may come away if they please. But it is rare any are such fools to leave the country except men's business require it. They pay nine pounds for their passage (of this money) to go to Ireland.

There is two fairs yearly and two markets weekly in Philadelphia; also two fairs yearly in Chester and likewise in Newcastle, but they sell no cattle nor horses, no living creatures, but altogether merchants' goods, as hats, linen and woolen cloth, handerchiefs, knives, scissors, tapes and threads, buckles, ribbons, and all sorts of necessaries fit for our wooden country, and here all young men and women that wants wives or husbands may be supplied. Let this suffice for our fairs. As to [religious] meetings, they are so plenty one may ride to their choice. . . .

Dear sister, I desire thee may tell my old friend Samuel Thornton that he could give so much credit to my words and find no "ifs" nor "ands" in my letter, that in plain terms he could not do better than to come here, for both his and his wife's trade are very good here. The best way for him to do is to pay what money he can conveniently spare at that side and engage himself to pay the rest at this side, and when he comes here, if he can get no friend to lay down the money for him, when it comes to the worst, he may hire out two or three children.

Document 3.10 Dr. Alexander Hamilton Observations on His Travels in North America, 1744

Dr. Alexander Hamilton was born in Edinburgh, Scotland in 1712, graduated from medical school in 1737, and moved to Annapolis, Maryland to join his brother. He became a popular and successful physician. Suffering from tuberculosis, he traveled throughout the summer of 1744 to escape Maryland's heat and humidity. He titled the daily account of his trip through the northern colonies *The Itinerarium*. Hamilton describes the people he meets, their customs and behaviors, the food he eats, and the political and religious issues of the day. What does this member of upper society like during his travels? How do his comments change when he encounters people or ideas he finds distasteful or beneath him? How does his life, concerns, likes, and dislikes compare with the others in this module?

Susquehanna Ferry

When I came near Susquehanna, I looked narrowly in the bottoms for the gensing but could not discover it. The lower ferry of Susquehanna, which I crossed, is above a mile broad. It is kept by a little old man whom I found att vittles with his wife and family upon a homely dish of fish without any kind of sauce. They desired me to eat, but I told them I had no stomach. They had no cloth upon the table, and their mess was in a dirty, deep, wooden dish which they evacuated with their hands, cramming down skins, scales, and all. They used neither knife, fork, spoon, plate, or napkin because, I suppose, they had none to use. I looked upon this as a picture of that primitive simplicity practiced by our forefathers long before the mechanic arts had supplyed them with instruments for the luxury and elegance of life. I drank some of their syder, which was very good, and crossed the ferry in company with a certain Scots-Irishman by name Thomas Quiet. The land about Susquehanna is pritty high and woody, and the channell of the river rockey.

Mr. Quiet rid a little scrub bay mare which he said was sick and ailing and could not carry him, and therefor he 'lighted every half mile and ran a couple

From *Colonial American Travel Narratives*.

of miles att a footman's pace to spell the poor beast (as he termed it). He informed me he lived att Monocosy and had been out three weeks in quest of his creatures (horses), four of which had strayed from his plantation. I condoled his loss and asked him what his mare's distemper was, resolving to prescribe for her, but all that I could gett out of him was that the poor silly beast had choaked herself in eating her oats; so I told him that if she was choaked, she was past my art to recover.

This fellow, I observed, had a particular down hanging look which made me suspect he was one of our New Light biggots. I guessed right, for he introduced a discourse concerning Whitfield and inlarged pritty much and with some warmth upon the doctrines of that apostle, speaking much in his praise. I took upon me, in a ludicrous manner, to impugn some of his doctrines, which, by degrees, put Mr. Quiet in a passion. He told me flatly that I was damnd without redemption. I replyed that I thought his name and behaviour were very incongruous and desired him to change it with all speed, for it was very impropper that such an angry, turbulent mortall as he should be called by the name of Thomas Quiet.

Principio Iron Works—North East

In the height of this fool's passion, I overtook one Mr. B[axte]r, a proprietor in the iron works there, and, after mutual salutation, the topic of discourse turned from religious controversy to politicks; so putting on a little faster, we left this inflammed bigot and his sick mare behind. This gentleman accompanied me to North East and gave me directions as to the road.

Philadelphia

The country round the city of Philadelphia is level and pleasant, having a prospect of the large river of Delaware and the province of East Jersey upon the other side. You have an agreeable view of this river for most of the way betwixt Philadelphia and Newcastle. The plan or platform of the city lyes betwixt the two rivers of Delaware and Skuylkill, the streets being laid out in rectangular squares which makes a regular, uniform plan, but upon that account, altogether destitute of variety.

Att my entering the city, I observed the regularity of the streets, but att the same time the majority of the houses mean and low and much decayed, the streets in generall not paved, very dirty, and obstructed with rubbish and lumber, but their frequent building excuses that. The State House, Assembly House, the great church in Second Street, and Whitefield's church are good buildings.

I observed severall comicall, grotesque phizzes in the inn wher[e] I put up which would have afforded variety of hints for a painter of Hogarth's turn. They talked there upon all subjects—politicks, religion, and trade—some tolerably well, but most of them ignorantly. I discovered two or three chaps very inquisitive, asking my boy who I was, whence come, and whether bound.

I was shaved by a little, finical, hump backed old barber who kept dancing round me and talking all the time of the operation and yet did his job lightly and to a hair. He abounded in compliments and was a very civil fellow in his way. He told me he had been a journeyman to the business for 40 odd years, notwithstanding which, he understood how to trim gentlemen as well (thank God) as the best masters and despaired not of preferment before he dyed.

I delivered my letters, went to dine with Collector Alexander, and visited severall people in town. In the afternoon I went to the coffee house where I was introduced by Dr. Thomas Bond to severall gentlemen of the place, where the ceremony of shaking of hands, an old custom peculiar to the English, was performed with great gravity and the usual compliments. I took private lodgings att Mrs. Cue's in Chestnut Street.

Thursday, June 7th. I remarked one instance of industry as soon as I got up and looked out att my chamber window, and that was the shops open att 5 in the morning. I breakfasted with Mrs. Come and dined by invitation with Dr. Thomas Bond where, after some talk upon physical matters, he showed me some pritty good anatomical preparations of the muscles and blood vessels injected with wax.

After dinner Mr. V[era]bless, a Barbadian gentleman, came in who, when we casually had mentioned the free masons, began to rail bitterly against that society as an impudent, assuming, and vain cabal pretending to be wiser than all mankind besides, an *imperium in imperio*, and therefor justly to be discouraged and suppressed as they had lately been in some foreign countrys. Tho I am no free mason myself, I could not agree with this gentleman, for I abhorr all tyrannicall and arbitrary notions. I believe the free masons to be an innocent and harmless society that have in their constitution nothing mysterious or beyond the verge of common human understanding, and their secret, which has made such a noise, I imagine is just no secret att all.

In the evening att the coffee house, I met Mr. H[asel]l, and enquiring how he did and how he had fared on his way, he replied as to health he was pritty well, but he had almost been devoured with buggs and other vermin and had met with mean, low company which had made him very uneasy. He added that he had heard good news from Barbadoes concerning his friends there—from one, who he imagined called himself Captain Scrotum, a strange name indeed, but this gentleman had always some comicall turn in his discourse. I parted with him and went to the taveren with Mr. Currie and some Scots gentlemen where we spent the night agreeably and went home sober att eleven a'clock.

Friday, June 8. I read Montaign's Essays in the forenoon which is a strange medley of subjects and particularly entertaining.

I dined att a taveren with a very mixed company of different nations and religions. There were Scots, English, Dutch, Germans, and Irish; there were Roman Catholicks, Church men, Presbyterians, Quakers, Newlightmen, Methodists, Seventh day men, Moravians, Anabaptists, and one Jew. The whole company consisted of 25 planted round an oblong table in a great hall well stoked with flys. The company divided into comittees in conversation; the prevailing topick was politicks and conjectures of a French war. A knott of Quakers there talked only about selling of flower and the low price it bore. The[y] touched a little upon religion, and high words arose among some of the sectaries, but their blood was not hot enough to quarrell, or, to speak in the canting phraze, their zeal wanted fervency. A gentleman that sat next me proposed a number of questions concerning Maryland, understanding I had come from thence. In my replys I was reserved, pretending to know little of the matter as being a person whose business did not lye in the way of history and politicks.

In the afternoon I went to see some ships that lay in the river. Among the rest were three vessels a fitting out for privateers—a ship, a sloop, and a schooner. The ship was a large vessel, very high and full rigged; one Capt. Mackey intended to command her upon the cruise. Att 6 a'clock I went to the coffee house and drank a dish of coffee with Mr. H[asel]l.

After staying there an hour or two, I was introduced by Dr. Phitieas Bond into the Governour's Club, a society of gentlemen that met at a taveren every night and converse on various subjects. The Governour gives them his presence once a week, which is generally upon Wednesday, so that I did not see him there. Our conversation was entertaining; the subject was the English poets and some of the foreign writers, particularly Cervantes, author of Don Quixot, whom we loaded with elogiums due to his character. Att eleven a'clock I left this club and went to my lodging.

Saturday, June 9th. This morning there fell a light rain which proved very refreshing, the weather having been very hot and dry for severall days. The heat in this city is excessive, the sun's rays being reflected with such power from the brick houses and from the street pavement which is brick. The people commonly use awnings of painted cloth or duck over their shop doors and windows and, att sun set, throw buckets full of water upon the pavement which gives a sensible cool. They are stocked with plenty of excellent water in this city, there being a pump att almost every 50 paces distance. There are a great number of balconies to their houses where sometimes the men sit in a cool habit and smoke.

The market in this city is perhaps the largest in North-America. It is kept twice a week upon Wednesdays and Saturdays. The street where it stands, called Market Street, is large and spacious, composed of the best houses in the city.

They have but one publick clock here which strikes the hour but has neither index nor dial plate. It is strange they should want such an ornament and conveniency in so large a place, but the chief part of the community consisting of Quakers, they would seem to shun ornament in their publick edifices as well as in their aparrell or dress.

The Quakers here have two large meetings, the Church of England one great church in Second Street, and another built for Whitfield in which one Tennent, a fanatick, now preaches, the Romans one chapell, the Anabaptists one or two meetings, and the Presbyterians two.

The Quakers are the richest and the people of greatest interest in this government; of them their House of Assembly is chiefly composed. They have the character of an obstinate, stiff necked generation and a perpetuall plague to their governors. The present governour, Mr. Thomas, has fallen upon a way to manage them better than any of his predecessors did and, att the same time, keep pritty much in their good graces and share some of their favours. However, the standing or failing of the Quakers in the House of Assembly depends upon their making sure the interest of the Palatines in this province, who of late have turned so numerous that they can sway the votes which way they please.

Here is no publick magazine of arms nor any method of defence, either for city or province, in case of the invasion of an enimy. This is owing to the obstinacy of the Quakers in maintaining their principle of non-resistance. It were a pity but they were put to a sharp triall to see whether they would act as they profess.

I never was in a place so populous where the gout for publick gay diversions prevailed so little. There is no such thing as assemblys of the gentry among them, either for dancing or musick; these they have had an utter aversion to ever since Whitefield preached among them. Their chief employ, indeed, is traffick and mercantile business which turns their thoughts from these levitys. Some Virginia gentlemen that came here with the Commissioners of the Indian Treaty were desirous of having a ball but could find none of the feemale sex in a humour for it. Strange influence of religious enthusiasm upon human nature to excite an aversion at these innocent amusements, for the most part so agreeable and entertaining to the young and gay, and indeed, in the opinion of moderate people, so conducive to the improvement of politeness, good manners, and humanity.

I was visited this morning by an acquaintance from Annapolis of whom, inquiring the news, I could not learn any thing material.

I dined att the taveren, and returning home after dinner I read part of a book lately writ by Fielding entituled The Adventures of Joseph Andrews, a masterly performance of its kind and entertaining; the characters of low life here are naturally delineated, and the whole performance is so good that I have not seen any thing of that kind equal or excell it.

This proved a rainy afternoon which, because it abated the sultry heat, was agreeable. I drank tea with Collector Alexander, where I saw Mr. H[asel]l. Their conversation turned upon the people in Barbadoes, and as I knew nothing of the private history of that island, I only sat and heard, for they went upon nothing but private characters and persons. This is a trespass on good manners which many well bred people fall into thro' inadvertency, two engrossing all the conversation upon a subject which is strange and unknown to a third person there.

At six in the evening I went to my lodging, and looking out att the window, having been led there by a noise in the street, I was entertained by a boxing match between a master and his servant. The master was an unweildy, pott-gutted fellow, the servant muscular, rawbon'd, and tall; therefor tho he was his servant in station of life, yet he would have been his master in single combat had not the bystanders assisted the master and holp him up as often as the fellow threw him down. The servant, by his dialect, was a Scotsman; the names he gave his master were no better than little bastard, and shitten elf, terms ill apply'd to such a pursy load of flesh. This night proved very rainy.

Chapter 3 Worksheet and Questions

1. The writers in this module discussed many common issues or topics. These included food, clothing, labor relations, prosperity, and what the future held. Compare the views of the rich and poor on these issues, and explain both how and why their views differed.

   _____

   _____

   _____

   _____

   _____

   _____

   _____

   _____

   _____

2. The two groups did not always discuss the same issues. Discuss the topics of importance to the poor that were not an issue to the wealthy, and explain why these are important to the have-nots of colonial society. Why are these issues so important to the poor?

   _____

   _____

   _____

   _____

   _____

   _____

   _____

   _____

   _____

   _____

3. Now discuss the topics that the wealthier members of colonial society wrote about that were not important for the poor. Why do the wealthy mention these issues, and what does it indicate about their views on people who have not achieved their wealth and status?

_____

_____

_____

_____

_____

_____

_____

_____

4. Some historians have argued that opportunity in a New World depends on how much wealth you bring with you. Others argue it depends on where or when you arrive. What was true in North America? Show examples from the documents that having money and freedom when arriving made a difference. Was anything else a key to success, according to the writers in this chapter?

_____

_____

_____

_____

_____

_____

_____

_____

The American Revolution: Traitors in an Evil Rebellion or Simple Citizens Defending Their Rights?

As the guns fell silent marking the end of the French and Indian War in 1763, British North American colonists considered themselves a truly blessed people. They were part of the greatest empire in the world. With the French threat gone they were poised to expand westward, through the Cumberland Gap into Kentucky, down the Ohio River to the Old Northwest, and West along the Mohawk Valley of New York. They took great pride in the political, cultural, and economic ties to their Mother Country. North Americans declared their loyalty to the British crown for everyone to hear. But in a little more than a decade, these same colonies declared their independence and actively fought that same government.

To understand the thinking behind such a drastic change of course, you must look at the dominant political thinking of the times. Future Patriot leaders embraced the Whig interpretation of government, which originated in the British civil wars and succession crises of the seventeenth century. Whigs believed there were two major threats to British political freedoms and personal liberties. The first was a general moral decay of the people, which allows evil rulers and their supporters to take over. The second is an encroachment of executive power (i.e., a strong central government) upon the powers of the representative legislature. The colonists believed that England suffered from moral decay in the eighteenth century, both in and out of government. The frequency of bribery in the British Parliament in exchange for votes, and the purchasing of government positions, served as proof that the British government no longer served the interests of the British people. This moral decay led American Congregationalist ministers like Jonathan Mayhew to protest British actions. Whigs also believed that the British constitution embodied certain principles, limiting what Parliament could or could not do, and thus protecting liberty against arbitrary government power. The government existed not only to exercise power or maintain social order, but also to promote the public good by preserving the rights and liberties of British citizens. Property holding was considered an essential liberty. If you owned property you were independent of someone else's will; thus, you could practice the virtue necessary to be a good citizen. Since property ownership was linked to the right to vote, and because land ownership was widespread in America, a larger percentage of British North American citizens were concerned about this issue. Colonists believed that their legislatures, elected by and directly representing them, were the perfect embodiment of these ideas. For this reason they feared that tax collectors and standing armies would be used by a corrupt government to enforce unfair legislation that assaulted their liberties. Standing armies also meant higher taxes to support them, and higher taxes took away your property, and hence your liberty. North American colonists in 1763 professed their loyalty to the Crown, meaning the King, because they believed in his virtue.

The British and the future Loyalists had a different view from the colonists on the workings of government. They accepted the traditional view that all government was the King's, that it existed to maintain the king's peace and provide the king's justice to all citizens. The King shared power with Parliament, especially the House of Commons. Power flowed from the top down in this government. The colonies were dependent children of the "mother country" and subjects of the crown. As British citizens, they owed the Crown allegiance. As subjects they should obey the authority of the Crown whether in the person of the King, the royal governors, the acts of Parliament, or Privy Council vetoes of colonial legislation. To refute this authority would threaten the social order of society and American prosperity. That would lead to a loss of property, and hence American liberties.

The well documented events of the 1750s, 1760s, and 1770s brought these conflicting views out into the open. In the late 1750s the Virginia assembly limited the pay of state-paid Anglican ministers, and the royal government officially rebuked them for doing so. In 1765 the Stamp Act ordered that all legal documents, newspapers, almanacs, printed sermons, and the like must bear a stamp to prove a tax had been paid. Since Parliament directly imposed this internal tax on the colonies without the approval of their local legislatures, many colonists saw the Act as an assault on their liberties. Colonists resisted British policies through written protests, a boycott of British goods, and the use of mob violence against supporters of British policy. These became the standard responses to British actions, which Whig ideology advocates saw as a threat to colonial liberties. In 1767 John Dickinson of Pennsylvania argued in his *Letters From a Pennsylvania Farmer* that any money raised in the colonies through government policies was a tax, and the only legitimate taxes came from local representative assemblies. By 1774 the First Continental Congress declared that anyone importing British goods were "enemies of American liberty." By 1776 Thomas Paine argued that King George III was no more than a "royal Brute," who, with his government, trampled basic American liberties, and thus gave the colonies ample reasons to separate from England.

But not all Americans were prepared to sever their ties with the mother country. Some 500,000 Americans remained loyal to Great Britain during the war (they were called Loyalists), and they represented a true socio-economic and educational cross-section of American society. Loyalists were also concerned with tyranny and threats to their rights, but saw this threat arising from sources other than the royal government. To the Loyalists, the lower ranks of society, the people who made up and directed the mobs, were a greater threat than royal government. Loyalists believed that American colonists needed to respect all forms of authority, and to demonstrate a proper deference to the social elite. Support of tradition and long-established institutions like Parliament were the only real protections of liberty. If such order and obedience to authority disappear, the result is chaos, anarchy, and the tyranny of the popular mob. To Loyalists the actions of the Patriot leaders and the mob was a conspiracy against their rights and liberties. The actions of the First Continental Congress were an "utter subversion of the law, and the total destruction of all liberty." The Patriot leaders would "swear and drink, and lie and whore and cheat, and rob, and pull down houses, and tar and feather, and play the devil in every shape..." according to Loyalist Jonathan Sewell. Their actions would lead to a civil war and would expose the colonies to the greed and attacks of every British enemy in Europe. Loyalists believed they had right and the law on their side. To them the "Revolutionaries" were disloyal rebels, violators of sacred oaths who took up arms against their rightful ruler King George III.

Many Loyalists disagreed with the actions of the British government during the decades before the American Revolution, but their loyalty to the British crown ran deeper than their allegiance to colonial interests. Thomas Hutchinson argued that Parliament could not properly tax the American colonies because they were not represented in that body, but could not accept the conclusion that Parliament had become the enemy of liberty. British authority was necessary to maintain order and to protect property. Joseph Galloway hoped for a return to the days of the 1750s, when the policy of salutary neglect left the colonies largely on their own.

Rebels/patriots outnumbered the Loyalists in every colony. The "revolutionaries" used a variety of methods to keep the Loyalists in check (or to seek revenge for past disagreements). Committees of safety and inspection sought out traitors, tax evaders, and supporters of British policies in 1774. By 1776 the new state governments either created special bodies to investigate charges of treason, or wrote treason acts that allowed the court system to target Loyalists. These laws defined disloyalty to the American nation as writing seditious speeches and letters, supplying arms to the enemy, discouraging enlistments in the Continental Army or local militia, or even actually spying. Penalties included imprisonment, fines, and forfeiture of lands and other property. These laws were frequently used by greedy neighbors to take the property and lands away from their lawful Loyalist owners. The concept of liberty that the revolutionaries held so dear did not mean their neighbors had the individual freedom to disagree with those in power.

Considering the Evidence in the Readings

In this module the documents are paired, with a supporter of the colonial cause matched with a supporter of the King and Parliament. You have the opportunity to make direct comparisons in each case, and decide whose arguments are more believable. The goal is for you to understand the fears, beliefs, and interests that motivated the actions of both Patriots and Loyalists. While most students are exposed to the Patriot arguments from their earliest schooling, they are not often called upon to examine the views of the large number of Americans who remained loyal to the British crown. Be sure to not just assume these people are disloyal traitors to America when you read. They had genuine fears and concerns, and reading these documents will help you understand their positions. Why do the Loyalists oppose American independence, and what do they think about those who support this movement?

Document 4.1 Reverend Jonathan Mayhew on Liberty in America

Religious leaders played a major role shaping public opinion (or reflecting this opinion) during the decade before the War for Independence. The struggle for political liberties was often viewed as an extension of the struggle for religious liberties dating back to sixteenth- and seventeenth-century England and transferred to North America with the colonists. Religious leaders in America divided during the 1760s along the lines of earlier struggles. Congregational leaders in New England, often seen as the most radical region of the 13 colonies, reflected the views of their neighbors and parishioners, and were among the leading proponents of opposition to the British government and the Anglican Church. In Boston, Harvard educator Reverend Jonathan Mayhew spoke out against what he believed was a massive conspiracy. He assumed that the Stamp Act was intended to give the British government control over all printed materials and means of communication, and believed the proposed appointment of an Anglican Bishop for North America was intended to give the Anglican Church control over all the churches in America. The following is from a sermon he gave after the June 1766 repeal of the Stamp Act. What does Mayhew see as the true sources of liberty? What are the greatest threats to liberty?

Having been initiated, in youth, in the doctrines of civil liberty, as they were taught by such men as Plato, Demosthenes, Cicero and other renowned persons among the ancients; and such as Sidney and Milton, Locke and Hoadley, among the moderns; I liked them; they seemed rational. Having, earlier still learnt from the holy scriptures, that wise, brave and vertuous men were always friends to liberty; that God gave the Israelites a King (or absolute Monarch) in his anger, because they had not sense and virtue enough to like a free common-wealth, and to have himself for their King; that the Son of God came down from heaven, to make us "free indeed"; and that "where the Spirit of the Lord is, there is liberty"; this made me conclude, that freedom was a great blessing. Having, also, from my childhood up, by the kind providence of my God, and the tender care of a good parent now at rest with Him, been educated to the love of liberty, tho' not of licentiousness; which chaste and virtuous passion was still increased in me, as I advanced towards, and into, manhood; I would not, I cannot now, tho' past middle age, relinquish the fair object of my youthful affections, LIBERTY; whose charms, instead of decaying with time in my eyes, have daily captivated me more and more. I was, accordingly, penetrated with the most sensible grief, when, about the *first of November last*, that day of darkness, a day hardly to be numbered with the other days of the year, SHE seemed about to take her final departure from America, and to leave that ugly Hag

---

The Snare is Broken, A Thanksgiving Discourse Occasioned by the Repeal of the Stamp Act, Boston, 1766.

Slavery, the deformed child of Satan, in her room. I am now filled with a proportionable degree of joy in God, on occasion of HER speedy return, with new smiles on her face, with augmented beauty and splendor.—Once more then, Hail! celestial Maid, the daughter of God, and, excepting his Son, the first-born of heaven! Welcome to these shores again; welcome to every expanding heart! Long mayest thou reside among us, the delight of the wise, good and brave; the protectress of innocence from wrongs and oppression, the patroness of learning, arts, eloquence, virtue, rational loyalty, religion! And if any miserable people on the continent or isles of Europe, after being weakened by luxury, debauchery, venality, intestine quarrels, or other vices, should, in the rude collisions, or now-uncertain revolutions of kingdoms, be driven, in their extremity, to seek a safe retreat from slavery in some far-distant climate; let them find, O let them find one in America under thy brooding, sacred wings; where our oppressed fathers once found it, and we now enjoy it, by the favor of Him, whose service is the most glorious freedom! Never, O never may He permit thee to forsake us, for our unworthiness to enjoy thy enlivening presence! By His high permission, attend us thro' life AND DEATH to the regions of the blessed, thy original abode, there to enjoy forever the "glorious liberty of the sons of God!"

Document 4.2   Samuel Seabury: An Anglican Minister's Perspective

Anglican ministers (representing the Church of England) also viewed developments with alarm. They were dismayed by the growing defiance of their fellow Americans towards King George III and Parliament. While Patriot ministers called for action and resistance to British laws, Anglicans called for moderation and restraint, reminding their parishioners and legislators of the benefits of British citizenship. According to Tory ministers, liberty comes only from submission to a good and legitimate government. Reverend Samuel Seabury of New York sent the following message to the New York legislature in 1775. How does he view the actions of the colonists? If the colonists persist, what does Seabury believe the ultimate result will be for the citizens in America? What actions does he consider traitorous?

Honourable Gentlemen,

When you reflect upon the present confused and distressed state of this, and the other colonies, I am persuaded, that you will think no apology necessary for the liberty I have taken, of addressing you on that subject. The unhappy contention we have entered into with our parent state, would inevitably be attended with many disagreeable circumstances, with many and great inconveniences to us, even were it conducted on our part, with *propriety* and *moderation.* What then must be the case, when all proper and moderate measures are *rejected*? When not even the *appearance* of decency is regarded? When nothing seems to be consulted, but how to perplex, irritate, and affront, the *British Ministry, Parliament,* *Nation and King*? When every scheme that tends to *peace*, is branded with *ignominy;* as being the machination of slavery! When nothing is called FREEDOM but SEDITION! Nothing LIBERTY but REBELLION! . . .

When the Delegates had met at Philadelphia, instead of settling a reasonable plan of accommodation with the parent country, they employed themselves in censuring acts of the British parliament, which were principally intended to prevent *smuggling*, and all *illicit trade*;—in writing addresses to the people of *Great-Britain*, to the inhabitants of the *colonies* in *general*, and to those of the *province of Quebec*, in *particular*; with the *evident design* of making them *dissatisfied with their present government;* and of *exciting clamours*, and raising *seditions*

Reverend Samuel Seabury to New York Legislature, 1775.

and *rebellions* against the *state*;—and in exercising a *legislative authority over all the colonies.* They had the insolence to proclaim themselves "A FULL AND FREE REPRESENTATION OF HIS MAJESTY'S FAITHFUL SUBJECTS IN ALL THE COLONIES FROM NOVA-SCOTIA TO GEORGIA;" and, as such, have laid a *tax* on all those colonies, viz. the *profits* arising from the *sales of all goods* imported from Great-Britain, Ireland, &c. during the months of December and January: Which *tax* is to be employed for the *relief* of the *Boston poor.* . . .

I must beg leave to enumerate a few of the *effects* of the measures of the Congress.—The government of *Rhode-Island* have dismantled the fort in their harbour, and carried off the cannon, in order to employ them *against his Majesty's forces.* The inhabitants of *New-Hampshire* have, under the command of Major SULLIVAN, one of the *Delegates, attacked,* and by *force of arms taken a* FORT *at Portsmouth,* belonging to his Majesty, and carried off all the powder and small arms found in it. The people of *Maryland* have had a *provincial Congress* who have assessed that colony in the sum of £10,000, to be expended in arming and disciplining the inhabitants, to *fight against the King.* The people in *New-England* are raising, arming and disciplining men, for the same *loyal* and *christian* purpose. . . .

The state to which the GRAND CONGRESS, and the *subordinate Committees,* have reduced the colonies, is *really deplorable.* They have introduced a *system* of the most *oppressive tyranny* that can possibly be imagined;—a *tyranny,* not only over the *actions,* but over the *words, thoughts,* and *wills,* of the *good people of this province.* People have been threatened with the *vengeance of a mob,* for speaking in support of *order* and *good government.* Every method has been used to intimidate the *printers* from publishing any thing, which tended to *peace,* or seem'd in favour of government; while the most *detestable libels* against the *King,* the *British parliament,* and *Ministry,* have been *eagerly read,* and *extravagantly commended.* . . .

Behold, Gentlemen, behold the wretched state to which we are reduced! A *foreign power* is brought in to *govern this province.* Laws made at *Philadelphia,* by factious men from *New-England, New-Jersey, Pennsylvania, Maryland, Virginia,* and the *Carolinas,* are imposed upon us by the most *imperious menaces.* Money is levied upon us without the *consent* of our *representatives:* which very *money,* under colour of relieving *the poor* people of Boston, it is too *probable* will be employed to *raise an army against the King. Mobs* and *riots* are encouraged, in order to *force* submission to the *tyranny of the Congress.* . . .

Act now, I beseech you, as you ever have done, as the faithful representatives of the people; as the real guardians of their Rights and Liberties. Give them deliverance from the tyranny of the *Congress* and *Committees:* Secure them against the horrid carnage of a *civil war:* And endeavour to obtain for them a FREE AND PERMANENT CONSTITUTION. . . .

Be assured, Gentlemen, that a very great majority of your constituents disapprove of the late violent proceedings, and will support you in the pursuit of more *moderate measures,* as soon as You have *delivered* Them from the *tyranny of Committees,* from the *fear of violence,* and the *dread of mobs.* Recur boldly to your good, old, legal and successful way of proceeding, by *petition* and *remonstrance.*

Address yourselves to the *King* and the *two Houses of Parliament.* Let your representations be *decent* and *firm,* and principally directed to obtain a *Solid American Constitution;* such as we can *accept* with *safety,* and *Great-Britain* can *grant* with *dignity.* Try the experiment, and you will assuredly find that our most gracious Sovereign and both Houses of Parliament will readily *meet* you in the *paths of peace.* Only shew your *willingness* towards an accommodation, by *acknowledging the supreme legislative authority of Great-Britain,* and I dare confidently pronounce the attainment of whatever YOU with *propriety,* can *ask,* and the LEGISLATURE OF GREAT-BRITAIN with *honour concede.*

Document 4.3 "An Anonymous Account of the Boston Massacre"

Early in 1770 violence broke out between British troops and crowds incited by the Sons of Liberty. In New York, colonists carrying clubs and swords clashed with British troops. On the evening of March 5, 1770, British soldiers fired into a crowd of 60 people, killing five and wounding eight more. News of this outrage, of British soldiers shooting and killing unarmed British citizens, spread quickly through the colonies, courtesy of inflammatory newspaper accounts and Paul Revere's famous engraving. Revere's work subtly altered facts to suggest unprovoked British brutality to the rest of the colonies. Public opinion in Boston was so inflamed that Governor Bernard ordered all British soldiers out of the city, and the troops responsible were tried for murder. In the ensuing trial, Patriot leader John Adams defended the soldiers, and all but two were acquitted. A Royalist sheriff who stacked the jury in the soldiers' favor helped Adams. In this anonymous Patriot's account of the evening's events, how does he or she connect the massacre to larger issues of colonial liberties? What are given as the causes of the massacre? How would you describe the behavior of the troops in this account? What about the behavior of Boston's citizens? Were the shootings justifiable?

THE HORRID MASSACRE IN BOSTON, PERPETRATED IN THE EVENING OF THE FIFTH DAY OF MARCH, 1770, BY SOLDIERS OF THE TWENTY-NINTH REGIMENT WHICH WITH THE FOURTEENTH REGIMENT WERE THEN QUARTERED THERE; WITH SOME OBSERVATIONS ON THE STATE OF THINGS PRIOR TO THAT CATASTROPHE

It may be a proper introduction to this narrative, briefly to represent the state of things for some time previous to the said Massacre; and this seems necessary in order to the forming a just idea of the causes of it.

At the end of the late [*French and Indian*] war, in which this province bore so distinguished a part, a happy union subsisted between Great Britain and the colonies. This was unfortunately interrupted by the *Stamp Act*; but it was in some measure restored by the repeal of it. It was again interrupted by other acts of parliament for taxing America; and by the appointment of a Board of Commissioners, in pursuance of an act, which by the face of it was made for the relief and encouragement of commerce, but which in its operation, it was apprehended, would have, and it has in fact had, a contrary effect. By the said act the said Commissioners were "*to be resident in some conven-*

ient part of his Majesty's dominions in America." This must be understood to be in some part convenient for the whole. But it does not appear that, in fixing the place of their residence, the convenience of the whole was at all consulted, for Boston, being very far from the centre of the colonies, could not be the place most convenient for the whole. Judging by the act, it may seem this town was intended to be favored, by the Commissioners being appointed to reside here; and that the consequence of that residence would be the relief and encouragement of commerce; but the reverse has been the constant and uniform effect of it; so that the commerce of the town, from the embarrassments in which it has been lately involved, is greatly reduced.

The residence of the Commissioners here has been detrimental, not only to the commerce, but to the political interests of the town and province; and not only so, but we can trace from it the causes of the late horrid massacre. Soon after their arrival here in November, 1767, instead of confining themselves to the proper business of their office, they became partizans of Governor Bernard in his political schemes; and had the weakness and temerity to infringe upon one of the most essential rights of the house of commons of this province—that of giving their votes with freedom, and not being accountable therefor but to their constituents. One of the members of that house, Capt. Timothy Folgier, having voted in some affair contrary to the mind of the said Commissioners, was for so doing dismissed from the office he held under them.

These proceedings of theirs, the difficulty of access to them on office-business, and a supercilious behavior, rendered them disgustful to people in general, who in consequence thereof treated them with neglect. This probably stimulated them to resent it; and to make their resentment felt, they and their

---

From *Boston Gazette and Country Journal,* March 12, 1770.

coadjutor, Governor Bernard, made such representations to his Majesty's ministers as they thought best calculated to bring the displeasure of the nation upon the town and province; and in order that those representations might have the more weight, they are said to have contrived and executed plans for exciting disturbances and tumults, which otherwise would probably never have existed; and, when excited, to have transmitted to the ministry the most exaggerated accounts of them.

Unfortunately for us, they have been too successful in their said representations, which, in conjunction with Governor Bernard's, have occasioned his Majesty's faithful subjects of this town and province to be treated as enemies and rebels, by an invasion of the town by sea and land; to which the approaches were made with all the circumspection usual where a vigorous opposition is expected. While the town was surrounded by a considerable number of his Majesty's ships of war, two regiments landed and took possession of it; and to support these, two other regiments arrived some time after from Ireland; one of which landed at Castle Island, and the other in the town.

Thus were we, in aggravation of our other embarrassments, embarrassed with troops, forced upon us contrary to our inclination—contrary to the spirit of *Magna Charta*—contrary to the very letter of the Bill of Rights, in which it is declared, that the raising or keeping a standing army within the kingdom in time of peace, unless it be with the consent of parliament, is against law, and without the desire of the civil magistrates, to aid whom was the pretence for sending the troops hither; who were quartered in the town in direct violation of an act of parliament for quartering troops in America; and all this in consequence of the representations of the said Commissioners and the said Governor, as appears by their memorials and letters lately published.

As they were the procuring cause of troops being sent hither, they must therefore be the remote and a blameable cause of all the disturbances and bloodshed that have taken place in consequence of that measure.

. . . the challenging the inhabitants by sentinels posted in all parts of the town before the lodgings of officers, which (for about six months, while it lasted), occasioned many quarrels and uneasiness.

Capt. Wilson, of the 59th, exciting the negroes of the town to take away their masters' lives and property, and repair to the army for protection, which was fully proved against him. The attack of a party of soldiers on some of the magistrates of the town—the repeated rescues of soldiers from peace officers—the firing of a loaded musket in a public street, to the endangering a great number of peaceable inhabitants—the frequent wounding of persons by their bayonets and cutlasses, and the numerous instances of bad behavior in the soldiery, made us early sensible that the troops were not sent here for any benefit to the town or province, and that we had no good to expect from such conservators of the peace.

It was not expected, however, that such an outrage and massacre, as happened here on the evening of the fifth instant, would have been perpetrated. There were then killed and wounded, by a discharge of musketry, eleven of his Majesty's subjects, viz.:

- Mr. Samuel Gray, killed on the spot by a ball entering his head.
- Crispus Attucks, a mulatto, killed on the spot, two balls entering his breast.
- Mr. James Caldwell, killed on the spot, by two balls entering his back.
- Mr. Samuel Maverick, a youth of seventeen years of age, mortally wounded; he died the next morning.
- Mr. Patrick Carr mortally wounded; he died the 14th instant.
- Christopher Monk and John Clark, youths about seventeen years of age, dangerously wounded. It is apprehended they will die.
- Mr. Edward Payne, merchant, standing at his door; wounded.
- Messrs. John Green, Robert Patterson, and David Parker; all dangerously wounded.

The actors in this dreadful tragedy were a party of soldiers commanded by *Capt. Preston* of the 29th regiment. This party, including the Captain, consisted of eight, who are all committed to jail.

There are depositions in this affair which mention, that several guns were fired at the same time from the Custom-house; before which this shocking scene was exhibited. Into this matter inquisition is now making. In the meantime it may be proper to insert here the substance of some of those depositions.

Benjamin Frizell, on the evening of the 5th of March, having taken his station near the west corner of the Custom-house in King street, before and at the time of the soldiers firing their guns, declares (among other things) that the first discharge was only of one gun, the next of two guns, upon which he the deponent thinks he saw a man stumble; the third discharge was of three guns, upon which he thinks he saw two men fall; and immediately after were discharged five guns, two of which were by soldiers on his right hand; the other three, as appeared to the deponent, were discharged from the balcony, or the chamber window of the Custom-house, the flashes appearing on the left hand, and higher than the right hand flashes appeared to be, and of which the deponent was very sensible, although his eyes were much turned to the soldiers, who were all on his right hand.

What gave occasion to the melancholy event of that evening seems to have been this. A difference having happened near Mr. Grays ropewalk, between a soldier and a man belonging to it, the soldier challenged the ropemakers to a boxing match. The challenge was accepted by one of them, and the soldier worsted. He ran to the barrack in the neighborhood, and returned with several of his companions. The fray was renewed, and the soldiers were driven off. They soon returned with recruits and were again worsted. This happened several times, till at length a considerable body of soldiers was collected, and they also were driven off, the ropemakers having been joined by their brethren of the contiguous ropewalks. By this time Mr. Gray being alarmed interposed, and with the assistance of some gentlemen prevented any further disturbance. To satisfy the soldiers and punish the man who had been the occasion of the first difference, and as an example to the rest, he turned him out of his service; and waited on Col. Dalrymple, the commanding officer of the troops, and with him concerted measures for preventing further mischief. Though this affair ended thus, it made a strong impression on the minds of the soldiers in general, who thought the honor of the regiment concerned to revenge those repeated repulses. For this purpose they seem to have formed a combination to commit some outrage upon the inhabitants of the town indiscriminately; and this was to be done on the evening of the 5th instant or soon after; as appears by the depositions of the following persons, viz.:

William Newhall declares, that on Thursday night the 1st of March instant, he met four soldiers of the 29th regiment, and that he heard them say, "there were a great many that would eat their dinners on Monday next, that should not eat any on Tuesday."

Daniel Calfe declares, that on Saturday evening the 3d of March, a camp-woman, wife to James McDeed, a grenadier of the 29th, came into his father's shop, and the people talking about the affrays at the ropewalks, and blaming the soldiers for the part they had acted in it, the woman said, "the soldiers were in the right;" adding, "that before Tuesday or Wednesday night they would wet their swords or bayonets in New England people's blood."

Samuel Drowne declares that, about nine o'clock of the evening of the fifth of March current, standing at his own door in Cornhill, he saw about fourteen or fifteen soldiers of the 29th regiment, who came from Murray's barracks, armed with naked cutlasses, swords, &c., and came upon the inhabitants of the town, then standing or walking in Cornhill, and abused some, and violently assaulted others as they met them; most of whom were without so much as a stick in their hand to defend themselves, as he very clearly could discern, it being moonlight, and himself being one of the assaulted persons. All or most of the said soldiers he saw go into King street (some of them through Royal Exchange lane), and there followed them, and soon discovered them to be quarrelling and fighting with the people whom they saw there, which he thinks were not more than a dozen, when the soldiers came first, armed as aforesaid. Of those dozen people, the most of them were gentlemen, standing together a little below the Town House, upon the Exchange. At the appearance of those soldiers so armed, the most of the twelve persons went off, some of them being first assaulted.

The violent proceedings of this party, and their going into King street, "quarrelling and fighting with the people whom they saw there" (mentioned in Mr. Drowne's deposition), was immediately introductory to the grand catastrophe.

These assailants, who issued from Murray's barracks (so called), after attacking and wounding divers persons in Cornhill, as above mentioned, being armed, proceeded (most of them) up the Royal Exchange lane into King street; where, making a short stop, and after assaulting and driving away the few they met there, they brandished their arms and cried out, "where are the boogers! where are the cowards!" At this time there were very few persons in the street beside themselves. This party in proceeding from Exchange lane into King street, must pass the sentry posted at the westerly corner of the Custom House, which butts on that lane and fronts on that street. This is needful to be mentioned, as near that spot and in that street the bloody tragedy was acted, and the street actors in it were stationed: their station being but a few feet from the front side of the said Custom House. The outrageous behavior and the threats of the said party occasioned the ringing of the meeting-house bell near the head of King street, which bell ringing quick, as for fire, it presently brought out a number of inhabitants, who being soon sensible of the occasion of it, were naturally led to King street, where the said party had made a stop but a little while before, and where their stopping had drawn together a number of boys, round the sentry at the Custom House. Whether the boys mistook the sentry for one of the said party, and thence took occasion to differ with him, or whether he first affronted them, which is affirmed in several depositions,—however that may be, there was much foul language between them, and some of them, in consequence of his pushing at them with his bayonet, threw snowballs at him, which occasioned him to knock hastily at the door of the Custom House. From hence two persons thereupon proceeded immediately to the main-guard, which was posted opposite to the State House, at a small distance, near the head of the said street. The officer on guard was Capt. Preston, who with seven or eight soldiers, with fire-arms and charged bayonets, issued from the guardhouse, and in great haste posted himself and his soldiers in front of the Custom House, near the corner aforesaid. In passing to this station the soldiers pushed several persons with their bayonets, driving through the people in so rough a manner

that it appeared they intended to create a disturbance. This occasioned some snowballs to be thrown at them which seems to have been the only provocation that was given. Mr. Knox (between whom and Capt. Preston there was some conversation on the spot) declares, that while he was talking with Capt. Preston, the soldiers of his detachment had attacked the people with their bayonets and that there was not the least provocation given to Capt. Preston or his party; the backs of the people being toward them when the people were attacked. He also declares, that Capt. Preston seemed to be in great haste and much agitated, and that, according to his opinion, there were not then present in King street above seventy or eighty persons at the extent.

The said party was formed into a half circle; and within a short time after they had been posted at the Custom House, began to fire upon the people.

Captain Preston is said to have ordered them to fire, and to have repeated that order. One gun was fired first; then others in succession and with deliberation, till ten or a dozen guns were fired; or till that number of discharges were made from the guns that were fired. By which means eleven persons were killed and wounded, as above represented.

Document 4.4 Captain Thomas Preston's Official Account of the Massacre

A few pertinent facts were missing from the previous account. The year before, 3,000 British troops were summoned to Boston by Governor Bernard in 1769 to help suppress mob resistance to the Townsend Acts and to restore law and order. Captain Thomas Preston, tried with his troops for the massacre, admitted the people in Boston were not pleased that British soldiers were in town. The mere presence of British troops was seen as a threat to colonial liberties. To make matters worse, off-duty British soldiers competed with Boston's lower classes for scarce jobs that were essential to their survival. The week before the Boston Massacre, fistfights between off-duty soldiers and young townsmen were common. Private Hugh White, the sentry on duty at the customhouse, was one of the brawlers. According to Preston's official account, who or what actually caused the shootings? How would you describe or compare the actions of the soldiers with those of the civilians, both before and after the shootings? Having read both accounts, do you think the outcome of the trial was fair? Were the soldiers justified in using their weapons?

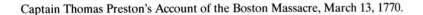

Captain Thomas Preston's Account of the Boston Massacre, March 13, 1770.

It is [a] matter of too great notoriety to need any proofs that the arrival of his Majesty's troops in Boston was extremely obnoxious to its inhabitants. They have ever used all means in their power to weaken the regiments, and to bring them into contempt by promoting and aiding desertions, and with impunity, even where there has been the clearest evidence of the fact, and by grossly and falsely propagating untruths concerning them. On the arrival of the 64th and 65th their ardour seemingly began to abate; it being too expensive to buy off so many, and attempts of that kind rendered too dangerous from the numbers.

And has ever since their departure been breaking out with greater violence after their embarkation. One of their justices, most thoroughly acquainted with the people and their intentions, on the trial of a man of the 14th Regiment, openly and publicly in the hearing of great numbers of people and from the seat of justice, declared *"that the soldiers must now take care of themselves, nor trust too much to their arms, for they were but a handful, that the inhabitants carried weapons concealed under their clothes, and would destroy them in a moment, if they pleased."* This, considering the malicious temper of the people, was an alarming circumstance to the soldiery. Since which several disputes have happened between the townspeople and the soldiers of both regiments, the former being encouraged thereto by the countenance of even some of the magistrates, and by the protection of all the party against government. In general such disputes have been kept too secret from the officers. On the 2d instant two of the 29th going through one Gray's ropewalk, the rope-makers insultingly asked them if they would empty a vault. This unfortunately had the desired effect by provoking the soldiers, and from words they went to blows. Both parties suffered in this affray, and finally the soldiers retired to their quarters. The officers, on the first knowledge of this transaction, took every precaution in their power to prevent any ill consequence. Notwithstanding which, single quarrels could not be prevented, the inhabitants constantly provoking and abusing the soldiery. The insolence as well as utter hatred of the inhabitants to the troops increased daily, insomuch that Monday and Tuesday, the 5th and 6th instant, were privately agreed on for a general engagement, in consequence of which several of the militia came from the country armed to join their friends, menacing to destroy any who should oppose them. This plan has since been discovered.

On Monday night about 8 o'clock two soldiers were attacked and beat. But the party of the townspeople in order to carry matters to the utmost length, broke into two meeting houses and rang the alarm bells, which I supposed was for fire as usual, but was soon undeceived. About 9 some of the guard came to and informed me the town inhabitants were assembling to attack the troops, and that the bells were ringing as the signal for that purpose and not for fire, and the beacon intended to be fired to bring in the distant people of the country. This, as I was captain of the day, occasioned my repairing immediately to the main guard. In my way there I saw the people in great commotion, and heard them use the most cruel and horrid threats against the troops. In a few minutes after I reached the guard, about 100 people passed it and went towards the custom house where the king's money is lodged. They immediately surrounded the sentry posted there, and with clubs and other weapons threatened to execute their vengeance on him. I was soon informed by a townsman their intention was to carry off the soldier from his post and probably murder him. On which I desired him to return for further intelligence, and he soon came back and assured me he heard the mobb declare they would murder him. This I feared might be a prelude to their plundering the king's chest. I immediately sent a non-commissioned officer and 12 men to protect both the sentry and the king's money, and very soon followed myself to prevent, if possible, all disorder, fearing lest the officer and soldiers, by the insults and provocations of the rioters, should be thrown off their guard and commit some rash act. They soon rushed through the people, and by charging their bayonets in half-circles, kept them at a little distance. Nay, so far was I from intending the death of any person that I suffered the troops to go to the spot where the unhappy affair took place without any loading in their pieces; nor did I ever give orders for loading them. This remiss conduct in me perhaps merits censure; yet it is evidence, resulting from the nature of things, which is the best and surest that can be offered, that my intention was not to act offensively, but the contrary part, and that not without compulsion. The mob still increased and were more outrageous, striking their clubs or bludgeons one against another, and calling out, come on you rascals, you bloody backs, you lobster scoundrels, fire if you dare, G-d damn you, fire and be damned, we know you dare not, and much more such language was used. At this time I was between the soldiers and the mob, parleying with, and endeavouring all in my power to persuade them to retire peaceably, but to no purpose. They advanced to the points of the bayonets, struck some of them and even the muzzles of the pieces, and seemed to be endeavouring to close with the soldiers.

On which some well behaved persons asked me if the guns were charged. I replied yes. They then asked me if I intended to order the men to fire. I answered no, by no means, observing to them that I was advanced before the muzzles of the men's pieces, and must fall a sacrifice if they fired; that the soldiers were upon the half cock and charged bayonets, and my giving the word fire under those circumstances would prove me to be no officer. While I was thus speaking, one of the soldiers having received a severe blow with a stick, stepped a little on one side and instantly fired, on which turning to and asking him why he fired without orders, I was struck with a club on my arm, which for some time deprived me of the use of it, which blow had it been placed on my head, most probably would have destroyed me.

On this a general attack was made on the men by a great number of heavy clubs and snowballs being thrown at them, by which all our lives were in imminent danger, some persons at the same time from behind calling out, damn your bloods—why don't you fire. Instantly three or four of the soldiers fired, one after another, and directly after three more in the same confusion and hurry. The mob then ran away, except three unhappy men who instantly expired, in which number was Mr. Gray at whose rope-walk the prior quarrels took place; one more is since dead, three others are dangerously, and four slightly wounded. The whole of this melancholy affair was transacted in almost 20 minutes. On my asking the soldiers why they fired without orders, they said they heard the word fire and supposed it came from me. This might be the case as many of the mob called out fire, fire, but I assured the men that I gave no such order; that my words were, don't fire, stop your firing. In short, it was scarcely possible for the soldiers to know who said fire, or don't fire, or stop your firing. On the people's assembling again to take away the dead bodies, the soldiers supposing them coming to attack them, were making ready to fire again, which I prevented by striking up their firelocks with my hand. Immediately after a townsman came and told me that 4 or 5000 people were assembled in the next street, and had sworn to take my life with every man's with me. On which I judged it unsafe to remain there any longer, and therefore sent the party and sentry to the main guard, where the street is narrow and short, there telling them off into street firings, divided and planted them at each end of the street to secure their rear, momently expecting an attack, as there was a constant cry of the inhabitants to arms, to arms, turn out with your guns; and the town drums beating to arms, I ordered my drums to beat to arms, and being soon after joined by the different companies of the 29th regiment, I formed them as the guard into street firings. The 14th regiment also got under arms but remained at their barracks. I immediately sent a sergeant with a party to Colonel Dalrymple, the commanding officer, to acquaint him with every particular. Several officers going to join their regiment were knocked down by the mob, one very much wounded and his sword taken from him. The lieutenant-governor and Colonel Carr soon after met at the head of the 29th regiment and agreed that the regiment should retire to their barracks, and the people to their houses, but I kept the picket to strengthen the guard. It was with great difficulty that the lieutenant-governor prevailed on the people to be quiet and retire. At last they all went off, excepting about a hundred.

A Council was immediately called, on the breaking up of which three justices met and issued a warrant to apprehend me and eight soldiers. On hearing of this procedure I instantly went to the sheriff and surrendered myself, though for the space of 4 hours I had it in my power to have made my escape, which I most undoubtedly should have attempted and could easily executed, had I been the least conscious of any guilt. On the examination before the justices, two witnesses swore that I gave the men orders to fire. The one testified he was within two feet of me; the other that I swore at the men for not firing at the first word. Others swore they heard me use the word "*fire*," but whether do or do not fire, they could not say; others that they heard the word fire, but could not say if it came from me. The next day they got 5 or 6 more to swear I gave the word to fire. So bitter and inveterate are many of the malcontents here that they are industriously using every method to fish out evidence to prove it was a concerted scheme to murder the inhabitants. Others are infusing the utmost malice and revenge into the minds of the people who are to be my jurors by false publications, votes of towns, and all other artifices. That so from a settled rancour against the officers and troops in general, the suddenness of my trial after the affair while the people's minds are all greatly inflamed, I am, though perfectly innocent, under most unhappy circumstances, having nothing in reason to expect but the loss of life in a very ignominous manner, without the interposition of his Majesty's royal goodness.

Document 4.5 Daniel Leonard "Massachusettensis" Denounces the Desire for Independence

In 1774, delegates to the First Continental Congress voted to assist Massachusetts in resisting British power after the passage of the Coercive Acts. The delegates prohibited imports from England, banned certain social gatherings, voted money and other relief aid to Massachusetts, and declared the Coercive Acts to be unconstitutional. Many members of Congress believed that Parliament would once again back down in the face of united colonial opposition. But many loyal colonists criticized the Congress for its actions, and suspected that radical, treasonous individuals planned more than protecting American liberties. New Jersey Governor William Franklin (Ben's son) believed that the Continental Congress' resolves left Great Britain with two bad choices, to be humiliated "in the eyes of all Europe, or to compel obedience to her laws by a military force." He preferred the latter. Daniel Leonard, a lawyer from Bristol County, Massachusetts, attacked Congress, claiming it was advocating independence from the British Empire, a course filled with indescribable horrors. He charges that members of Congress, by resisting Parliament, are advocating disloyalty to the Crown. According to Leonard, to whom do the colonists owe allegiance? What is the Crown, according to Leonard, king, Parliament, royal ministers, or all three? What will be the evil results if the colonists do not remain subordinate to the authority of the British government?

January 9, 1775

The security of the people from internal rapacity and violence, and from foreign invasion, is the end and design of government. The simple forms of government are monarchy, aristocracy and democracy, that is, where the authority of the state is vested in one, a few, or the many. Each of these species of government has advantages peculiar to itself, and would answer the ends of government, where the persons intrusted with the authority of the state, always guided themselves by unerring wisdom and public virtue; but rulers are not always exempt from the weakness and depravity which make government necessary to society. Thus monarchy is apt to rush headlong into tyranny, aristocracy to beget faction and multiplied usurpations, and democracy to degenerate into tumult, violence and anarchy. A government formed upon these three principles in due proportion, is the best calculated to answer the ends of government, and to endure. Such a government is the British constitution, consisting of King, Lords and Commons, which at once includes the principal excellencies, and excludes the principal defects of the other kinds of government. It is allowed, both by Englishmen and foreigners to be the most perfect system that the wisdom of ages has produced. The distributions of power are so just, and the proportions so exact, as at once to support and controul each other. An Englishman glories in being subject to, and protected by, such a government. The colonies are a part of the British empire. The best writers upon the law of nations, tell us, that when a nation takes possession of a distant country, and settles there, that country though separated from the principal establishment, or mother country, naturally becomes a part of the state, equal with its ancient possessions. Two supreme or independent authorities cannot exist in the same state. It would be what is called *imperium in imperio*, the height of political absurdity. The analogy between the political and human bodies is great. Two independent authorities in a state would be like two distinct principles of volition and action in the human body, dissenting, opposing and destroying each other. *If then we are a part of the British empire, we must be subject to the supreme power of the state which is vested in the estates of parliament*, notwithstanding each of the colonies have legislative and executive powers of their own, delegated or granted to them, for the purposes of regulating their own internal police, which are subordinate to, and must necessarily be subject to

---

From *Massachusetts Gazette*, January 9, 1995.

the checks, controul and regulation of the supreme authority of the state.

This doctrine is not new, but the denial of it is. It is beyond a doubt that it was the sense both of the parent country, and our ancestors, that they were to remain subject to parliament. It is evident from the charter itself, and this authority has been exercised by parliament, from time to time, almost ever since the first settlement of the country, and has been expressly acknowledged by our provincial legislatures. It is not less our interest, than our duty, to continue subject to the authority of parliament, which will be more fully considered hereafter. The principal argument against the authority of parliament, is this, the Americans are entitled to all the privileges of an Englishman, it is the privilege of an Englishman to be exempt from all laws that he does not consent to in person, or by representative; the Americans are not represented in parliament, and therefore are exempt from acts of parliament, or in other words, not subject to its authority. This appears specious; but leads to such absurdities as demonstrate its fallacy. *If the colonies are not subject to the authority of parliament, Great-Britain and the colonies must be distinct states, as completely so as England and Scotland were before the union, or as Great-Britain and Hanover are now;* The colonies in that case will owe no allegiance to the imperial crown, and perhaps not to the person of the King, as the title of the crown is derived from an act of parliament, made since the settlement of this province, which act respects the imperial crown only. Let us waive this difficulty, and suppose allegiance due from the colonies to the person of the King of Great-Britain, he then appears in a new capacity, of King of America, or rather in several new capacities, of King of Massachusetts, King of Rhode Island, King of Connecticut, &c., &c. For if our connexion with Great-Britain by the parliament be dissolved, we shall have none among ourselves, but each colony become as distinct from the others, as England was from Scotland, before the union. . . . But let us suppose the same prerogatives inherent in the several American crowns, as are in the imperial crown of Great-Britain, where shall we find the British constitution that we all agree we are entitled to? We shall seek for it in vain in our provincial assemblies. They are but faint sketches of the estates of parliament. The houses of representatives or Burgesses, have not all the powers of the House of Commons, in the charter governments they have no more than what is expressly granted by their several charters. The first charters granted to this province did not impower the assembly to tax the people at all. Our Council Boards are as

destitute of the constitutional authority of the House of Lords, as their several members are of the noble independence and splendid appendages of Peerage. The House of Peers is the bulwark of the British constitution, and through successive ages, has withstood the shocks of monarchy, and the sappings of Democracy, and the constitution gained strength by the conflict. Thus the supposition of our being independent states, or exempt from the authority of parliament, destroys the very idea of our having a British constitution. The provincial constitutions, considered a subordinate, are generally well adapted to those purpose of government, for which they were intended, that is, to regulate the internal police of the several colonies; but have no principle of stability within themselves, they may support themselves in moderate times, but would be merged by the violence of turbulent ones, and the several colonies become wholly monarchial, or wholly republican, were it not for the checks, controuls, regulations, and support of the supreme authority of the empire. Thus the argument that is drawn from their first principle of our being entitled to English liberties, destroys the principle itself, it deprives us of the Bill of Rights, and all the benefits resulting from the revolution of English laws, and of the British constitution.

Our patriots have been so intent upon building up American rights, that they have overlooked the rights of Great-Britain, and our own interest. Instead of proving that we are entitled to privileges that our fathers knew our situation would not admit us to enjoy, they have been arguing away our most essential rights. If there be any grievance, it does not consist in our being subject to the authority of parliament, but in our not having an actual representation in it. Were it possible for the colonies to have an equal representation in Parliament, and were refused it upon proper application, I confess I should think it a grievance; but at present it seems to be allowed by all parties, to be impracticable, considering the colonies are distant from Great-Britain a thousand transmarine leagues. If that be the case, the right or privilege, that we complain of being deprived of, is not withheld by Britain, but the first principles of government, and the immutable laws of nature, render it impossible for us to enjoy it. . . .

Allegiance and protection are reciprocal. *It is our highest interest to continue a part of the British empire; and equally our duty to remain subject to the authority of parliament.* Our own internal police may generally be regulated by our provincial legislatures, but in national concerns, or where our own assemblies do not answer the ends of government with respect to ourselves, the ordinance or interposition of the great council of the nation is necessary. In this case, the major must rule the minor. After many more centuries shall have rolled away, long after we, who are now bustling upon the stage of life, shall have been received to the bosom of mother earth, and our names are forgotten, the colonies may be so far increased as to have the balance of wealth, numbers and power, in their favour, the good of the empire make it necessary to fix the seat of government here; and some future George, equally the friend of mankind with him that now sways the British sceptre, may cross the Atlantic, and rule Great-Britain, by an American parliament.

Document 4.6 John Adams "Novanglus" Responds to "Massachusettensis"

John Adams, lawyer, Patriot leader, and member of the First Continental Congress, using the persona "Novanglus," exchanged a series of public letters with Leonard. By the late 1760s Adams was convinced that the colonies' traditional relationship with the British Crown was that of allies, not subjects. He also believed the British government was undermining the colonist's loyalty through a series of blunders and legislation attacking colonial rights. Adams ridiculed the notion that the American colonists owed special allegiance to a mystical British Crown or British Empire. According to Adams, to whom do the colonists owe allegiance, and on what basis must they continue to obey the authority of the British government? When does the need for obedience, for an unquestioning acceptance of the total authority of the government, come to an end? What does Adams see as the relationship between representative government and internal rule?

"If then, we are a part of the British empire, we must be subject to the supreme power of the state, which is vested in the estates in parliament."

Here, again, we are to be conjured out of our senses by the magic in the words "British empire," and "supreme power of the state." But, however it may sound, I say we are not a part of the British empire; because the British government is not an empire. The governments of France, Spain, &c. are not empires, but monarchies, supposed to be governed by fixed fundamental laws, though not really. The British government is still less entitled to the style of *an empire*. It is a limited monarchy. If Aristotle, Livy, and Harrington knew what a republic was, the British constitution is much more like a republic than an empire. They define a republic to be a government of laws, and not of men. If this definition is just, the British constitution is nothing more nor less than a republic, in which the king is first magistrate. This office being hereditary, and being possessed of such ample and splendid prerogatives, is no objection to the government's being a republic, as long as it is bound by fixed laws, which the people have a voice in making, and a right to defend. An empire is a despotism, and an emperor a despot, bound by no law or limitation but his own will; it is a stretch of tyranny beyond absolute monarchy. For, although the will of an absolute monarch is law, yet his edicts must be registered by parliaments. Even this formality is not necessary in an empire.

"If the colonies are not subject to the authority of parliament, Great Britain and the colonies must be distinct states, as completely so as England and Scotland were before the union, or as Great Britain and Hanover are now." There is no need of being startled at this consequence. It is very harmless. There is no absurdity at all in it. Distinct states may be united under one king. And those states may be further cemented and united together by a treaty of commerce. This is the case. We have, by our own express consent, contracted to observe the Navigation Act, and by our implied consent, by long usage and uninterrupted acquiescence, have submitted to the other acts of trade, however grievous some of them may be.

Novanglus, February 6, 1775.

This may be compared to a treaty of commerce, by which those distinct states are cemented together, in perpetual league and amity. . . .

The only proposition in all *this writer's* long string of pretended absurdities, which he says follows from the position that we are distinct states, is this: That, "as the king must govern each state by its parliament, those several parliaments would pursue the particular interest of its own state; and however well disposed the king might be to pursue a line of interest that was common to all, the checks and control that he would meet with would render it impossible." Every argument ought to be allowed its full weight; and therefore candor obliges me to acknowledge, that here lies all the difficulty that there is in this whole controversy. There has been, from first to last, on both sides of the Atlantic, an idea, an apprehension that it was necessary there should be some superintending power, to draw together all the wills, and unite all the strength of the subjects in all the dominions, in case of war, and in the case of trade. The necessity of this, in case of trade, has been so apparent, that, as has often been said, we have consented that parliament should exercise such a power. In case of war, it has by some been thought necessary. But, in fact and experience, it has not been found so. . . . The inconveniences of this were small, in comparison of the absolute ruin to the liberties of all which must follow the submission to parliament, in all cases, which would be giving up all the popular limitations upon the government.

But, admitting the proposition in its full force, that it is absolutely necessary there should be a supreme power, coextensive with all the dominions, will it follow that parliament, as now constituted, has a right to assume this supreme jurisdiction? By no means.

A union of the colonies might be projected, and an American legislature; for, if America has 3,000,000 people, and the whole dominions 12,000,000, she ought to send a quarter part of all the members to the house of commons; and instead of holding parliaments always at Westminister, the haughty members for Great Britain must humble themselves, one session in four, to cross the Atlantic, and hold the parliament in America.

There is no avoiding all inconveniences in human affairs. The greatest possible, or conceivable, would arise from ceding to parliament power over us without a representation in it. . . . The least of all would arise from going on as we began, and fared well for 150 years, by letting parliament regulate trade, and our own assemblies all other matters.

But perhaps it will be said, that we are to enjoy the British constitution in our supreme legislature, the parliament, not in our provincial legislatures. To this I answer, if parliament is to be our supreme legislature, we shall be under a complete oligarchy or aristocracy, not the British constitution, which this writer himself defines a mixture of monarchy, aristocracy, and democracy. For king, lords, and commons, will constitute one great oligarchy, as they will stand related to America, as much as the decemvirs did in Rome; with this difference for the worse, that our rulers are to be three thousand miles off . . . If our provincial constitutions are in any respect imperfect, and want alteration, they have capacity enough to discern it, and power enough to effect it, without interposition of parliament. . . . America will never allow that parliament has any authority to alter their constitution at all. She is wholly penetrated with a sense of the necessity of resisting it at all hazards. . . . The question we insist on most is, not whether the alteration is for the better or not, but whether parliament has any right to make any alteration at all. And it is the universal sense of America, that it has none.

That a representation in parliament is impracticable, we all agree; but the consequence is, that we must have a representation in our supreme legislatures here. This was the consequence that was drawn by kings, ministers, our ancestors, and the whole nation, more than a century ago, when the colonies were first settled, and continued to be the general sense until the last peace; and it must be the general sense again soon, or Great Britain will lose her colonies.

"It is our highest interest to continue a part of the British empire; and equally our duty to remain subject to the authority of parliament," says *Massachusettensis.*

We are a part of the British dominions, that is, of the King of Great Britain, and it is our interest and duty to continue so. It is equally our interest and duty to continue subject to the authority of parliament, in the regulation of our trade, as long as she shall leave us to govern our internal policy, and to give and grant our own money, and no longer.

Document 4.7 Thomas Paine attacks the Sanctity of Royal Government, in *Common Sense*, 1776

Thomas Paine arrived in North America only 13 months before the publication of Common Sense. He previously failed at everything he tried, including corset-making, teaching, tax collecting, and shop-keeping. Upon arriving in Philadelphia, he began writing for several newspapers, always promoting the idea of personal liberty. A few months before writing Common Sense, he published an essay denouncing the immorality of the Atlantic slave trade, and the inhumanity of mandating slavery to each generation of African Americans. In Common Sense, he challenged convictions that American rights and liberties were rooted in (and protected by) the British constitution. He also attacked the idea of a sacred bond between colonists and King George III. Paine argued that the British constitution was based on "two ancient tyrannies"—the monarchy and aristocracy. On what basis does Paine attack the monarchy? Why is our connection to England severed, or why should it be? Why is declaring independence just "common sense"? What conspiracy does Paine claim is at work against us, and how is this connected to the monarchy and Parliament? How many of his ideas do you see later in the Declaration of Independence?

Society in every state is a blessing, but government even in its best state is but a necessary evil in its worst state an intolerable one; for when we suffer, or are exposed to the same miseries by a government, which we might expect in a country without government, our calamities is heightened by reflecting that we furnish the means by which we suffer! Government, like dress, is the badge of lost innocence; the palaces of kings are built on the ruins of the bowers of paradise. For were the impulses of conscience clear, uniform, and irresistibly obeyed, man would need no other lawgiver; but that not being the case, he finds it necessary to surrender up a part of his property to furnish means for the protection of the rest; and this he is induced to do by the same prudence which in every other case advises him out of two evils to choose the least. Wherefore, security being the true design and end of government, it unanswerably follows that whatever form thereof appears most likely to ensure it to us, with the least expense and greatest benefit, is preferable to all others.

I draw my idea of the form of government from a principle in nature, which no art can overturn, viz. that the more simple any thing is, the less liable it is to be disordered; and the easier repaired when disordered; and with this maxim in view, I offer a few remarks on the so much boasted constitution of England. That it was noble for the dark and slavish times in which it was erected is granted. When the world was overrun with tyranny the least therefrom was a glorious rescue. But that it is imperfect, subject to convulsions, and incapable of producing what it seems to promise, is easily demonstrated.

Absolute governments (tho' the disgrace of human nature) have this advantage with them, that they are simple; if the people suffer, they know the head from which their suffering springs, know likewise the remedy, and are not bewildered by a variety of causes and cures. But the constitution of England is so exceedingly complex, that the nation may suffer for years together without being able to discover in which part the fault lies, some will say in one and some in another, and every political physician will advise a different medicine.

I know it is difficult to get over local or long standing prejudices, yet if we will suffer ourselves to examine the component parts of the English constitution, we shall find them to be the base remains of two ancient tyrannies, compounded with some new republican materials.

First. The remains of monarchical tyranny in the person of the king.

Secondly. The remains of aristocratical tyranny in the persons of the peers.

Excerpts from *Common Sense* by Thomas Paine.

Thirdly. The new republican materials, in the persons of the commons, on whose virtue depends the freedom of England.

The two first, by being hereditary, are independent of the people; wherefore in a constitutional sense they contribute nothing towards the freedom of the state.

To say that the constitution of England is a union of three powers reciprocally checking each other, is farcical, either the words have no meaning, or they are flat contradictions.

To say that the commons is a check upon the king, presupposes two things.

First. That the king is not to be trusted without being looked after, or in other words, that a thirst for absolute power is the natural disease of monarchy.

Secondly. That the commons, by being appointed for that purpose, are either wiser or more worthy of confidence than the crown.

But as the same constitution which gives the commons a power to check the king by withholding the supplies, gives afterwards the king a power to check the commons, by empowering him to reject their other bills; it again supposes that the king is wiser than those whom it has already supposed to be wiser than him. A mere absurdity!

There is something exceedingly ridiculous in the composition of monarchy; it first excludes a man from the means of information, yet empowers him to act in cases where the highest judgment is required. The state of a king shuts him from the world, yet the business of a king requires him to know it thoroughly; wherefore the different parts, unnaturally opposing and destroying each other, prove the whole character to be absurd and useless.

Some writers have explained the English constitution thus; the king, say they, is one the people another; the peers are an house in behalf of the king; the commons in behalf of the people; but this hath all the distinctions of an house divided against itself; and though the expressions be pleasantly arranged, yet when examined they appear idle and ambiguous; and it will always happen, that the nicest construction that words are capable of, when applied to the description of something which either cannot exist, or is too incomprehensible to be within the compass of description, will be words of sound only, and though they may amuse the ear, they cannot inform the mind, for this explanation includes a previous question, viz. how came the king by a Power which the people are afraid to trust, and always obliged to check? Such a power could not be the gift of a wise people, neither can any power, which needs checking, be from God;

yet the provision, which the constitution makes, supposes such a power to exist.

An inquiry into the constitutional errors in the English form of government is at this time highly necessary; for as we are never in a proper condition of doing justice to others, while we continue under the influence of some leading partiality, so neither are we capable of doing it to ourselves while we remain fettered by any obstinate prejudice. And as a man, who is attached to a prostitute, is unfitted to choose or judge of a wife, so any prepossession in favor of a rotten constitution of government will disable us from discerning a good one.

In the following pages I offer nothing more than simple facts, plain arguments, and common sense; and have no other preliminaries to settle with the reader, than that he will divest himself of prejudice and prepossession, and suffer his reason and his feelings to determine for themselves; that he will put on, or rather that he will not put off, the true character of a man, and generously enlarge his views beyond the present day.

Volumes have been written on the subject of the struggle between England and America. Men of all ranks have embarked in the controversy, from different motives, and with various designs; but all have been ineffectual, and the period of debate is closed. Arms, as the last resource, decide the contest; the appeal was the choice of the king, and the continent hath accepted the challenge.

The sun never shined on a cause of greater worth. 'Tis not the affair of a city, a country, a province, or a kingdom, but of a continent of at least one eighth part of the habitable globe. 'Tis not the concern of a day, a year, or an age; posterity are virtually involved in the contest, and will be more or less affected, even to the end of time, by the proceedings now. Now is the seed time of continental union, faith and honor. The least fracture now will be like a name engraved with the point of a pin on the tender rind of a young oak; The wound will enlarge with the tree, and posterity read it in full grown characters.

I have heard it asserted by some, that as America hath flourished under her former connection with Great Britain, that the same connection is necessary towards her future happiness, and will always have the same effect. Nothing can be more fallacious than this kind of argument. We may as well assert, that because a child has thrived upon milk, that it is never to have meat; or that the first twenty years of our lives is to become a precedent for the next twenty. But even this is admitting more than is true, for I answer roundly, that America would have flourished as much, and probably much more, had no European power had any thing to do with her. The commerce by which she hath enriched herself are the necessaries of life, and will always have a market while eating is the custom of Europe.

But she has protected us, say some. That she hath engrossed us is true, and defended the continent at our expense as well as her own is admitted, and she would have defended Turkey from the same motive, viz. the sake of trade and dominion.

Alas, we have been long led away by ancient prejudices and made large sacrifices to superstition. We have boasted the protection of Great Britain,— Without considering, that her motive was interest not attachment; that she did not protect us from our enemies on our account, but from her enemies on her own account, from those who had no quarrel with us on any other account, and who will always be our enemies on the same account. Let Britain wave her pretensions to the continent, or the continent throw off the dependance, and we should be at peace with France and Spain were they at war with Britain. The miseries of Hanover last war Ought to warn us against connections.

It hath lately been asserted in parliament, that the colonies have no relation to each other but through the parent country, i.e. that Pennsylvania and the Jerseys, and so on for the rest, are sister colonies by the way of England; this is certainly a very roundabout way of proving relationship, but it is the nearest and only true way of proving enemyship, if I may so call it. France and Spain never were, nor perhaps ever will be our enemies as Americans, but as our being the subjects of Great Britain.

But Britain is the parent country, say some. Then the more shame upon her conduct. Even brutes do not devour their young; nor savages make war upon their families; wherefore the assertion, if true, turns to her reproach, but it happens not to be true, or only partly so, and the phrase Parent or mother country hath been jesuitically adopted by the king and his parasites, with a low papistical design of gaining an unfair bias on the credulous weakness of our minds. Europe, and not England, is the parent country of America. This new world hath been the asylum for the persecuted lovers of civil and religious liberty from every Part of Europe. Hither have they fled, not from the tender embraces of the mother, but from the cruelty of the monster; and it is so far true of England, that the same tyranny which drove the first emigrants from home pursues their descendants still.

I challenge the warmest advocate for reconciliation, to show, a single advantage that this continent can reap, by being connected with Great Britain. I repeat the challenge, not a single advantage is derived. Our corn will fetch its price in any market in Europe, and our imported goods must be paid for buy them where we will.

But the injuries and disadvantages we sustain by that connection, are without number; and our duty to mankind at large, as well as to ourselves, instruct us to renounce the alliance: Because, any submission to, or dependance on Great Britain, tends directly to involve this continent in European wars and quarrels; and sets us at variance with nations, who would otherwise seek our friendship, and against whom, we have neither anger nor complaint. As Europe is our market for trade, we ought to form no partial connection with any part of it. It is the true interest of America to steer clear of European contentions, which she never can do, while by her dependance on Britain, she is made the make-weight in the scale of British politics.

Europe is too thickly planted with kingdoms to be long at peace, and whenever a war breaks out between England and any foreign power, the trade of America goes to ruin, because of her connection with Britain. The next war may not turn out like the Past, and should it not, the advocates for reconciliation now will be wishing for separation then, because, neutrality in that case, would be a safer convoy than a man of war. Every thing that is right or natural pleads for separation. The blood of the slain, the weeping voice of nature cries, 'TIS TIME TO PART. Even the distance at which the Almighty hath placed England and America, is a strong and natural proof, that the authority of the one, over the other, was never the design of Heaven. The time likewise at which the continent was discovered, adds weight to the argument, and the manner in which it was peopled increases the force of it. The reformation was preceded by the discovery of America, as if the Almighty graciously meant to open a sanctuary to the persecuted in future years, when home should afford neither friendship nor safety.

The authority of Great Britain over this continent, is a form of government, which sooner or later must have an end: And a serious mind can draw no true pleasure by looking forward, under the painful and positive conviction, that what he calls the present constitution is merely temporary. As parents, we can have no joy, knowing that this government is not sufficiently lasting to ensure any thing which we may bequeath to posterity: And by a plain method of argument, as we are running the next generation into debt, we ought to do the work of it, otherwise we use them meanly and pitifully. In order to discover the line of our duty rightly, we should take our children in our hand, and fix our station a few years farther into life; that eminence will present a prospect, which a few present fears and prejudices conceal from our sight.

Though I would carefully avoid giving unnecessary offence, yet I am inclined to believe, that all those who espouse the doctrine of reconciliation, may be included within the following descriptions. Interested men, who are not to be trusted; weak men who cannot see; prejudiced men who will not see; and a certain set of moderate men, who think better of the European world than it deserves; and this last class by an ill-judged deliberation, will be the cause of more calamities to this continent than all the other three.

It is the good fortune of many to live distant from the scene of sorrow; the evil is not sufficiently brought to their doors to make them feel the precariousness with which all American property is possessed. But let our imaginations transport us for a few moments to Boston, that seat of wretchedness will teach us wisdom, and instruct us for ever to renounce a power in whom we can have no trust. The inhabitants of that unfortunate city, who but a few months ago were in ease and affluence, have now no other alternative than to stay and starve, or turn out to beg. Endangered by the fire of their friends if they continue within the city, and plundered by the soldiery if they leave it. In their present condition they are prisoners without the hope of redemption, and in a general attack for their relief, they would be exposed to the fury of both armies.

Men of passive tempers look somewhat lightly over the offenses of Britain, and, still hoping for the best, are apt to call out, "Come we shall be friends again for all this." But examine the passions and feelings of mankind. Bring the doctrine of reconciliation to the touchstone of nature, and then tell me, whether you can hereafter love, honor, and faithfully serve the power that hath carried fire and sword into your land? If you cannot do all these, then are you only deceiving yourselves, and by your delay bringing ruin upon posterity. Your future connection with Britain, whom you can neither love nor honor, will be forced and unnatural, and being formed only on the plan of present convenience, will in a little time fall into a relapse more wretched than the first. But if you say, you can still pass the violations over, then I ask, Hath your house been burnt? Hath you property been destroyed before your face? Are your wife and children destitute of a bed to lie on, or bread to live on? Have you lost a parent or a child by their hands, and

yourself the ruined and wretched survivor? If you have not, then are you not a judge of those who have. But if you have, and can still shake hands with the murderers, then are you unworthy the name of husband, father, friend, or lover, and whatever may be your rank or title in life, you have the heart of a coward, and the spirit of a sycophant.

A government of our own is our natural right: And when a man seriously reflects on the precariousness of human affairs, he will become convinced, that it is infinitely wiser and safer, to form a constitution of our own in a cool deliberate manner, while we have it in our power, than to trust such an interesting event to time and chance. If we omit it now, some Massenello (note-CmnSns-1) may hereafter arise, who laying hold of popular disquietudes, may collect together the desperate and the discontented, and by assuming to themselves the powers of government, may sweep away the liberties of the continent like a deluge. Should the government of America return again into the hands of Britain, the tottering situation of things, will be a temptation for some desperate adventurer to try his fortune; and in such a case, what relief can Britain give? Ere she could hear the news the fatal business might be done, and ourselves suffering like the wretched Britons under the oppression of the Conqueror. Ye that oppose independence now, ye know not what ye do; ye are opening a door to eternal tyranny, by keeping vacant the seat of government. There are thousands and tens of thousands; who would think it glorious to expel from the continent, that barbarous and hellish power, which hath stirred up the Indians and Negroes to destroy us; the cruelty hath a double guilt, it is dealing brutally by us, and treacherously by them.

To talk of friendship with those in whom our reason forbids us to have faith, and our affections wounded through a thousand pores instruct us to detest, is madness and folly. Every day wears out the little remains of kindred between us and them, and can there be any reason to hope, that as the relationship expires, the affection will increase, or that we shall agree better, when we have ten times more and greater concerns to quarrel over than ever?

Ye that tell us of harmony and reconciliation, can ye restore to us the time that is past? Can ye give to prostitution its former innocence? Neither can ye reconcile Britain and America. The last cord now is broken, the people of England are presenting addresses against us. There are injuries which nature cannot forgive; she would cease to be nature if she did. As well can the lover forgive the ravisher of his mistress, as the continent forgive the murders of Britain. The

Almighty hath implanted in us these inextinguishable feelings for good and wise purposes. They are the guardians of his image in our hearts. They distinguish us from the herd of common animals. The social compact would dissolve, and justice be extirpated the earth, or have only a casual existence were we callous to the touches of affection. The robber and the murderer, would often escape unpunished, did not the injuries which our tempers sustain, provoke us into justice.

O ye that love mankind! Ye that dare oppose, not only the tyranny, but the tyrant, stand forth! Every spot of the old world is overrun with oppression. Freedom hath been hunted round the globe. Asia, and Africa, have long expelled her. Europe regards her like a stranger, and England hath given her warning to depart. O! receive the fugitive, and prepare in time an asylum for mind.

Document 4.8 James Chalmers "Candidus": A Loyalist's Response to Paine

Supporters of the King and Parliament were furious about the attacks in Common Sense. Some attacked the pamphlet as "utopian," or as promoting anarchy and disorder, perhaps even democracy. A structured society was essential to preserving order, property, and liberty. Others argued American liberties could never be secure except under the British constitution. Even some Patriots such as Colonel Langdon Carter of Virginia attacked it for providing a "false notion" of government, by throwing out all "men of principles" and replacing them with egalitarian rabble. James Chalmers' pamphlet Plain Truth espoused common Loyalist sentiments. Chalmers was a Loyalist from the eastern shore of Maryland. According to him, what benefits do the colonists gain from allegiance to Great Britain? How does Chalmers dismiss or explain Paine's attacks on King George III? How would the colonies suffer from independence?

PLAIN TRUTH; CONTAINING, REMARKS ON A LATE PAMPHLET, ENTITLED COMMON SENSE.

I have now before me the Pamphlet, entitled COMMON SENSE; on which I Shall remark with freedom and candour.

His [Paine's] first indecent attack is against the English constitution; which with all its imperfections, is, and ever will be the pride and envy of mankind. To this panegyric involuntarily our author subscribes, by granting individuals to be safer in England, than in any other part of Europe. He indeed insidiously attributes this pre-eminent excellency, to the constitution of the people, rather than to our excellent constitution. To such contemptible subterfuge is our Author reduced. I would ask him, why did not the

constitution of the people afford them superior safety, in the reign of Richard the Third, Henry the Eighth, and other tyrannic princes? Many pages might indeed be filled with encomiums bestowed on our excellent constitution, by illustrious authors of different nations.

This beautiful system (according to MONTESQUIEU) our constitution is a compound of Monarchy, Aristocracy, and Democracy. But it is often said, that the Sovereign, by honours and appointments, influences the Commons. The profound and elegant HUME agitating this question, thinks, to this circumstance, we are in part indebted for our supreme felicity; since without such controul in the Crown, our Constitution would immediately degenerate into Democracy; a Government, which in the sequel, I hope to prove ineligible. Were I asked marks of the best government, and the purpose of political society, I would reply, the encrease, preservation, and prosperity of its members, in no quarter

---

From *Plain Truth* by James Chalmers, 1776.

of the Globe, are those marks so certainly to be found, as in Great Britain, and her dependencies. After our Author has employed several pages, to break the mounds of society by debasing Monarchs: He says, "The plain truth is, that the antiquity of English Monarchy will not bear looking into."

HUME treating of the original contract, has the following melancholy, but sensible observation, "Yet reason tells us, that there is no property in durable objects, such as lands, and houses, when carefully examined, in passing from hand to hand, but must in some period, have been founded in fraud and injustice. The necessities of human society, neither in private or public life, will allow of such an accurate enquiry; and there is no virtue or moral duty, but what may, with facility, be refined away, if we indulge a false philosophy, in sifting and scrutinizing, by every captious rule of logic, in every light or position in which it may be placed."

I will humbly attempt to describe good Kings by the following unerring rule. The best Princes are constantly calumniated by the envenomed tongues and pens of the most worthless of their subjects. For this melancholy truth, do I appeal to the testimony of impartial historians, and long experience. The many unmerited insults offered to our gracious Sovereign; by the unprincipled [John] Wilkes, and others down to this late Author; will forever disgrace humanity. For he says, "that monarchy was the most prosperous invention the Devil ever set on foot for the promotion of idolatry. It is the pride of Kings which throws mankind into confusion: In short, continues this Author, monarchy and succession, have laid not this or that kingdom only, but the world in blood and ashes." How deplorably wretched the condition of mankind, could they believe such execrable flagitious jargon. Unhappily indeed, mankind in every age are susceptible of delusion; but surely our Author's poison carries its antidote with it. Attentive to the spirit of his publication, we fancy ourselves in the barbarous fifteenth century: in which period our Author would have figured with his "Common Sense"—and blood will attend it."

After his terrible anathema against our venerable constitution, and monarchy; let us briefly examine a democratical state; and see whether of not it is a government less sanguinary. This government is extremely plausible, and indeed flattering to the pride of mankind. The demagogues therefore, to seduce the people into their criminal designs ever hold up democracy to them: although conscious it never did, nor ever will answer in practice. If we believe a great Author, "There never existed, nor ever will exist a real democracy in the World." If we examine the republics of Greece and Rome, we ever find them in a state of war domestic or foreign. Our Author therefore makes no mention of these ancient States.

The excellent Montesquieu declares, "that a democracy supposes the concurrence of a number of circumstances rarely united. In the first place, it is requisite that the state itself should be of small extent; so that the people might be easily assembled and personally known to each other. Secondly, the simplicity of their manners, should be such as to prevent a multiplicity of affairs, and perplexity in discussing them: And thirdly, there should subsist a great degree of equality between them, in point of right and authority: Lastly, there should be little or no luxury, for luxury must either be the effect of wealth, or it must make it necessary. It corrupts at once, both rich and poor: The one, by the possession, and the other, by the want of it." To this may be added continues the same Author, "that no government is so subject to CIVIL WARS, and INTESTINE COMMOTIONS, as that of the democratical or popular form; because, no other tends so strongly and so constantly to alter, nor requires so much vigilance, and fortitude to preserve it from alteration. It is indeed, in such a constitution, particularly, that a Citizen should always be armed with fortitude, constancy; and should every day, in the sincerity of his heart, guard against corruption, arising either from selfishness in himself, or in his compatriots; for if it once enters into public transactions, to root it out afterwards would be miraculous.

After impotently attacking our Sovereign; and the constitution: He contradicts the voice of all mankind, by declaring, that America "would have flourished as much, and probably much more, had no European power taken any notice of her."

If he means, that had this Continent been unexplored, the original inhabitants would have been happier: For once, I agree with him. Previous to the settlement of these Provinces by our Ancestors, the kingdom of France was convulsed by religious phrenzy. This, and Sebastian Cabot's prior discovery, perhaps, happily afforded the people of England, an opportunity of locating these Provinces. At length, peace being restored to France, by her Hero, Henry the Fourth: His nation in turn, were seized with the rage of colonizing. Finding the English claimed the Provinces on the Atlantic; they appropriated the snow banks of Canada, which we dare not suppose, they would have preferred to these fertile provinces, had not the prior occupancy, and power of England interfered. I hope it will not be denied, that the notice taken of us, at this time by an European Power, was rather favourable for us.—Certain it is, had not England then taken notice of us, these delectable Provinces would now appertain to France; and the people of New England, horrid to think, would now be counting their beads. Some years after the Æra in question, the civil wars intervening in England, afforded to the Swedes and Dutch, a footing on this Continent. Charles the Second being restored; England reviving her claim, rendered abortive the Swedish pretensions; and by conquest, and granting Surinam to the Dutch, procured the cession of their usurpation, now New York. I do indeed confess, my incapacity to discern the injury sustained by this second "notice taken of us, by an European Power;" in default of which intervention, the Swedes, to this hour, would have retained their settlement, now the famed Pennsylvania; and the Dutch, consequently, had retained theirs. Some time after this period, the people of New England were employed, in framing and executing laws, so intolerant and sanguinary, that to us, they seem adapted for devils, not men.

I shall humbly endeavour to shew, that our author shamefully misrepresents facts, is ignorant of the true state of Great Britain and her Colonies, utterly unqualified for the arduous task, he has presumptuously assumed; and ardently intent on seducing us to that precipice on which himself stands trembling. To elucidate my strictures, I must with fidelity expose the circumstances of Great Britain and her colonies. If therefore, in the energy of description, I unfold certain bold and honest truths with simplicity, the judicious reader will remember, that true knowledge of our situation, is as essential to our safety, as ignorance thereof may endanger it. In the English provinces, exclusive of negroe and other slaves, we have one hundred and sixty thousand; or one hundred and seventy thousand men capable of bearing arms. If we deduct the people called Quakers, Anabaptists, and other religionists averse to arms; a considerable part of the emigrants, and those having a grateful predilection for the ancient constitution and parent state, we shall certainly reduce the first number to sixty or seventy thousand men. Now admitting those equal to the Roman legions, can we suppose them capable of defending against the power of Britain, a country nearly twelve hundred miles extending on the ocean. Suppose our troops assembled in New England, if the Britons see not fit to assail them, they haste to and desolate our other provinces, which eventually would reduce New England. If by dividing our forces, we pretend to defend our provinces, we also are infallibly undone. Our most fertile provinces, filled with unnumbered domestic enemies, slaves, intersected by navigable rivers, every where accessible to the fleets and armies of Britain, can make no defence. If without the medium of passion and prejudice, we view our other provinces, half armed, destitute of money and a navy: We must confess, that no power ever engaged such POTENT ANTAGONISTS, under such peculiar circumstances of infelicity. In the better days of Rome, she permitted no regular troops to defend her. Men destitute of property she admitted not into her militia, (her only army). I have been extremely concerned at the separation of the Connecticut men from our army. It augur'd not an ardent enthusiasm for liberty and glory. We still have an army before Boston, and I should be extremely happy to hear substantial proofs of their glory. I am still hopeful of great things from our army before Boston, when joined by the regiments now forming, which WANT OF BREAD will probably soon fill. Notwithstanding the predilection I have for my countrymen, I remark with grief, that hitherto our troops have displayed but few marks of Spartan or Roman enthusiasm. In the sincerity of my heart, I adjure the reader to believe, that no person is more sensibly afflicted by hearing the enemies of America remark, that no General ever fell singly and so ingloriously unrevenged before the inauspicious affair of Quebec. I am under no doubt, however, that we shall become as famed for martial courage, as any nation ever the sun beheld.

Let us now briefly view the pre-eminently envied state of Great Britain. If we regard the power of Britain, unembarrassed with Continental connections, and the political balance, we may justly pronounce her what our author does, AMERICA; "A match for all Europe." Amazing were the efforts of England, in the war of Queen Ann, when little benefitted by colony commerce, and e'er she had availed herself of the courage, good sense, and numbers of the people of Scotland and Ireland.

That England then prescribed laws to Europe, will be long remembered. Last war, her glory was, if possible, more eminently exalted; in every quarter of the globe did victory hover round her armies and navies, and her fame re-echoed from pole to pole. At present Great Britain is the umpire of Europe.

Can a reasonable being for a moment believe that Great Britain, whose political existence depends on our constitutional obedience, who but yesterday made such prodigious efforts to save us from France, will not exert herself as powerfully to preserve us from our frantic schemes of independency. Can we a moment doubt, that the Sovereign of Great Britain and his ministers, whose glory as well as personal safety depends on our obedience, will not exert every nerve of the British power, to save themselves and us from ruin.

I am perfectly satisfied, that we are in no condition to set the world at defiance, that commerce and the protection of Great Britain will secure us peace, and the friendship of all Europe; but I deny it is the interest of all Europe to have America a free port, unless they are desirous of depopulating their dominions. His assertions, that barrenness of gold and silver will secure us from invaders, is indeed highly pleasant. Have we not a much better security from invasions, viz. the most numerous and best disciplined army under heaven; or has our author already disbanded it. Pray how much gold and silver do the mine of Flanders produce? And what country so often has seen its unhappy fields drenched with blood, and fertilized with human gore. The princes of Europe have long dreaded the migration of their subjects to America; and we are sensible, that the king of Prussia is said more than once to have hanged Newlanders, or those who seduced his subjects to emigrate. I also humbly apprehend, that Britain is a part of Europe. Now, *old gentleman*, as you have clearly shewn, that we have a check upon her West India trade, is it her interest to give us a greater check upon it, by permitting America (as you express it,) to become a free port. Can we suppose it to be her interest to lose her valuable commerce to the Colonies, which effectually she would do, by giving up America to become your free port. If therefore it is the interest of all Europe, to have America a free port: The people of Britain are extremely simple to expend so many millions sterling to prevent it. "It is repugnant to the nature of things, to all examples from former ages, to suppose that this Continent can long remain subject to any external power."

Until the present unhappy period, Great Britain has afforded to all mankind, the most perfect proof of her wise, lenient, and magnanimous government of the Colonies—The proofs to which we already have alluded, viz. Our supreme felicity, and amazing increase. Than the affair of the Connecticut invaders; Omnipotence only could grant us stronger reasons for praying a continuance of our former beneficent government. Most certainly, every dispassionate person, as well as the plundered Pennsylvanians, must confess, that the Arm of Great Britain alone detained those Free-booters aforesaid, from seising the city of Philadelphia, to which without all doubt, they have as just a claim, as to those fertile regions in Pennsylva-

nia, which they surrreptitiously have possessed themselves of. In wrath to mankind, should Heaven permit our Author's new fangled government to exist; I, as a friend to Pennsylvanians, advise them to explore new settlements, and avoid the cruel mortification of being expelled by the *Saints* from their delicious abodes and pleasing field.— "But (says the Author) the most powerful argument is, that nothing but independence, (that is a Continental form of government) can keep the peace of the Continent, and preserve it inviolate from civil wars. I dread the event of a reconciliation now with Britain as it is more than probable, that it will be followed by revolt somewhere; the consequences of which may be far more fatal than all the malice of Britain. Thousands are already ruined by British barbarity, thousands more will probably share the same fate. These men have other feelings, than those who have nothing suffered: All they now possess is liberty, what they before enjoyed is sacrificed to its service, and having nothing more to lose, they disdain all submission."

Our author surely forgets, that when independent, we cannot trade with Europe, without political connections, and that all treaties made by England or other commercial states are, or ought to be, ultimately subservient to their commerce. "But (says our author,) admitting that matters were made up, what would be the event? I answer the ruin of the Continent, and that for several reasons." Reconciliation would conduct us to our former happy state. The happiness of the governed is without doubt the true interest of the governors, and if we aim not at independence, there cannot be a doubt, of receiving every advantage relative to laws and commerce that we can desire.

This Continent fifty years hence, infallibly will be richer, and much better peopled than at present; consequent abler to effect a revolution. But alas! e'er that period, our author will forever be forgotten; impelled therefore by his villainous ambition, he would rashly precipitate his country into every species of horror, misery, and desolation, rather than forego his fancied protectorship. "But if you have, (says our author) and still can shake hands with the murderers, then are ye unworthy the name of husband, father, friend, or lover, and whatever may be your rank or title in life, you have the heart of a coward, and the spirit of a sycophant, &c. To talk of friendship with those in whom our reason forbids us to have faith, and our affections wounded through a thousand pores, instructs us to detest is madness and folly."

Ye that are not drunk with fanaticism answer me? Are these words dictated by peace, or base foul revenge, the constant attendant on cowards and syco-phants? Does our author so perfectly versed in scrip-ture, mean to conduct us to peace or desolation? or is he fit to legislate for men or devils? Nations after des-olating each other, (happily for mankind,) forgive, forget, and reconcile; like individuals who quarrel, reconcile, and become friends. Following the laud-able example of the CONGRESS; we lately have most readily shaken hands with our inveterate ene-mies the Canadians, who have scalped nearly as many of our people as the British troops have done: Why therefore may we not forgive and reconcile—By no means, it blasts our author's ambitious purposes. The English and Scotch, since the first Edward's time, have alternately slaughtered each other, (in the field of Bannockburn, more men fell, than are now in the New-England provinces) to the amount of several hundred thousand: And now view each other as sub-jects, despising the efforts of certain turbulent spirits, tending to rekindle the ancient animosity.

Notwithstanding our Author's fine words about toleration: "Ye sons of peace and true christainity; believe me, it were folly supreme, madness, to expect angelic toleration from New-England, where she has constantly been detested, persecuted and execrated. Even in vain would our Author: or our CROMWELL cherish toleration; for the people of New-England, not yet arrived in the seventeenth or eighteenth cen-tury, would reprobate her." It is more than probable to suppose, that the New-England governments would have no objection to an Agrarian law; nor is it unreasonable to suppose, that such division of prop-erty would be very agreeable to the soldiers. Indeed their General could not perhaps with safety to his existence as a General, refute them so reasonable a gratification, particularly, as he will have more than one occasion for their services. Let us however admit that our General and troops, contradicting the expe-rience of ages; do not assume the sovereignty. Released from foreign war; we would probably be plunged into all the misery of anarchy and intestine war. Can we suppose that the people of the south, would submit to have the seat of Empire at Philadel-phia, or in New England; or that the people oppressed by a change of government, contrasting their misery with their former happy state, would not invite Britain to reassume the sovereignty.

Volumes were insufficient to describe the horror, misery and desolation, awaiting the people at large in the Syren form of American independence. In short, I affirm that it would be most excellent policy in those who wish for TRUE LIBERTY to submit by an advantageous reconciliation to the authority of Great Britain; "to accomplish in the long run, what they cannot do by hypocrisy, fraud and force in the short one."

INDEPENDENCE AND SLAVERY ARE SYNONYMOUS TERMS.

FINIS

Document 4.9   Grace Barclay: Wartime Sufferings of a Patriot Wife

The British army occupied New York City in September 1776, and remained there until the war ended in 1783. For Patriots, this meant years of hardships and insults at the hands of British troops, their Hessian allies, and Loyalist neighbors. Some lost their homes and property; others were forced to open their homes to British and Hessian offices during the occupation. Grace Barclay lived on Long Island with her son and father. She could not communicate safely with her husband, who was an officer in the Continental Army. Her daily journal entries served as unwritten letters to him, and now inform us about life in the occupied city. She details the challenges that Long Island residents faced during these years, including robberies, looting, and harassment. What specific examples of hardships does Grace describe? What are her attitudes toward the Hessian soldiers? Toward her Loyalist neighbors? How does the British occupation affect her support of the Patriot cause?

Tuesday, 1776 The Hessians have been ordered to cut down all the saplings they can find. They pile them along the road about twelve feet high, then by pressing teams and wagons, they cart it away to forts and barracks at a distance.

It is a serious loss; in a few years our farms will be without wood for use. They (the Hessians) burn an immense quantity—even the rail-fences, unless we take care to cut and cart wood for their constant use.
. . .

***

Wednesday, 1776 Charles accompanied John Harris home from school, with my permission, last night. He returned this morning, with a story of the night, which he related to me in breathless excitement.

A family living a mile from us were quietly sitting together in the evening, when a noise was heard at the door like that of a sharp instrument thrust into it. On opening the door, there stood a redcoat with his sabre in his hand, which he had stuck into the wood an inch or two. He was backed by a dozen men. They pushed their way in, and were very unruly, rummaging and ransacking every drawer and closet; but the family had long before taken the precaution to place all their valuables and money in a small room, which opened out of the common sitting-room, putting a large cupboard before the door, which covered it entirely, so that the Hessians quartered there last winter never discovered the existence of the room. A cunning device.

The red-coats, highly enraged at finding nothing, began to threaten terrible things if they did not divulge the hiding place. Mr. W. told them, that if they dared do any violence he would report them to the commanding officer; wereupon they actually went into the kitchen, kindled some light wood, came out, and set a burning brand at each corner of the house. The family were exceedingly alarmed. . . .

A new source of trouble has appeared on the south side—kidnapping negroes.

The ruffians come in sloops from the Delaware and Maryland country, and landing on the island in the night, they steal the poor creatures while asleep, after the labor of cutting the salt meadow grass for their masters. When they get them away, they sell them at the South.

A week since, while the men were at work, four persons, in broad day, their faces blackened, and dressed like negroes, appeared suddenly, each armed with a gun, and before the others could come to the rescue, a man and a boy were forcibly taken, put in a boat, and rowed off to a cutter out at sea. On the deck the villains could be seen putting chains on the poor creatures. I tremble at the thought of the future.

Saturday, Nov. 27, 1776 Received a few hasty lines from White Plains. They mention an engagement on the 28th October; "retreated with loss." The aspect of affairs is gloomy indeed. . . . The army is greatly reduced by killed, wounded, and taken and those whose enlistments have expired daily leaving; the poor creatures remaining, many without shoes or comfortable clothing, are sadly disheartened. The enemy have possession of the city of New York, of Staten Island, and of Long Island. Who can look without trembling at the failure of this struggle to throw off our yoke? . . .

December, 1776 The depredations, robberies, and not seldom murders, committed by the Cow-Boys and Runners, are alarming, and exasperating the people in the extreme. The farmers suffer dreadfully from the levying, taxing, and quartering upon them of the Hessians and British soldiers. They are very insolent, making most unreasonable demands, and the meek-spirited, unresisting Quakers are martyrs to their lawlessness and rapacity. . . .

Monday, 1776 Henry Pattison, the nearest neighbor, has eight sturdy sons, and one little timid daughter. He belongs to the Society of Friends, is a fine specimen of humanity, owns a valuable farm, yet has a pretty hard struggle to bring up his large family. He was beginning to prosper a little, when the war began. . . . He is called hereabouts The Peace-Maker.

Friend Pattison appears to have neither "part nor lot" in the struggle in which the country is engaged. How strange! *To be a man, and remain neutral!* His soul abhors War. This principle of their sect is enrooted in his breast. Yet he is a severe sufferer from it. Six Hessians are quartered upon him. They took possession of the kitchen: swung up their hammocks: cook his (the farmer's) food, and hang about, smoking and drinking the live-long day. Dear, how annoying! When shall we be rid of them?

***

From *Grace Barclay's Diary, or Personal Recollections of the American Revulution*, 2nd edition, 1866.

Thursday, 1776 . . . It is said that many wealthy and influential persons have deserted the American cause. It is indeed a gloomy hour! But we *must* triumph. The descendants of those who sought here a peaceful asylum from oppression,—Huguenots, Puritans, Covenanters, will not submit to oppression here. They will defend it with their lives. . . .

Dec. 30th, 1776 The year has closed disastrous, gloomy; panic and despair reign in many a breast. All the future is uncertain: none can foretell what another year may bring forth. . . . If Congress would appropriate more money, and men could be enlisted on longer terms, say, during the war, and properly equipped, greater things could be done. Now, no sooner are they organized, and become a little drilled, than the term of enlistment expires, and raw recruits take their place.

Jan. 15th, 1777 News of the Battle of Princeton. My husband safe, thank Heaven! General Washington victorious; General Mercer mortally wounded! . . . The Commander-in-Chief, by his judgement, skill, and cool intrepidity, has struck the enemy with surprise. They have looked with contempt on our raw men, many of whom never saw a battle. They expected to crush us: to quell with ease, by their giant power, the rebels, as the lord of the forest crushes the insects beneath his feet. . . .

***

Monday, 1777 On every Monday exercising is practiced opposite our house. Today, when the manoeuvering was over, a man who had been found intoxicated the night before, was stripped and whipped severely, with a rattan, till the blood streamed down his back. Oh, it is dreadful to witness such horrors!

Friday, 1777 Days of agony and nights of tears are my experience; the agony of suspense, the tears of widowhood! In imagination I have no longer a husband! He is slain on the field of battle, of which no tidings have come; or the victim of neglected wounds and disease, he is in the hands of the enemy. If alive and at liberty, we surely should long ago have heard from him. How *can* I endure it? Oh, God, endue me with patience, or I sink! . . .

***

Sunday Evening, 1778 A tale of horror has just come to our ears: we have not heard the details nor do I wish to they are so horrible. It seems the Runners entered the house of John Wilson, and threatened,

until the wife, to save the life of her husband, revealed the hiding-place. But it was too late; he died the next morning from a sabre-cut which he then received, cleaving the skull and occasioning so great loss of blood. The villains took a large sum of money, which was in silver coin, in bags under the hearthstone. Mr. Wilson was much beloved in the neighborhood: his death produced the greatest excitement and indignation.

***

Wednesday, 1778 Last night the Runners appeared round a house near West-Town. and were about forcing a door in front when they were discovered. John Rawlins, the owner, sent a negro up stairs to fire when the word was given. It was a bright moonlight night, and he saw the creatures step up to the door from a window near it with a pane of glass out. In alarm, he looked out for something wherewith to defend himself: seeing the broom, he took it for want of something better, and ran it through the broken window. It touched the shoulder, and grazed the cheek of one of the villains, who, supposing it to be a loaded gun, cried out piteously, "Oh, heavens, don't kill me!" as though he had never an evil intention towards any one.

The signal was now given, and the man above fired; they soon scattered, leaving John Rawlins aiming his broomstick through the broken window-pane!

***

Monday, 1780 This neighborhood is still infested with the odious Hessians. They are so filthy and lazy, lounging about all day long, smoking and sleeping. The patience of the good Friends is inexhaustible. After filling up their parlors, kitchens, and bedrooms, the whole winter with chests, liquor-casks, hammocks, bird-cages, guns, boots, and powder-flasks, they were last week ordered to Jamaica. Oh the rejoicing! It *would* flash out of the eye, though their discreet tongues spake it not.

The moment the Hessians took their leave Friend Pattison caused the broken places in the wall to be repaired, for the Colonel's lady had the room ornamented all around with stuffed parrots, perched on sticks driven in the wall. . . .

Well, all were putting their houses in order, when the appalling news spread like wildfire—*The Hessians are coming back!* . . . They had indeed been ordered back. How many tears of vexation I shed!

Document 4.10 Ann Hulton: Wartime Sufferings of a Loyalist Lady

Patriots were not the only civilians affected by the conflict. Loyalists were often singled out for special treatment by their Patriot neighbors, to intimidate them into cooperation or just force them into silence. By the end of the war, most Loyalists women and families would be driven out of the colonies, or would be allowed to stay and keep their property only if they rejected their spouse's allegiance to the King. Ann Hulton was the sister of Henry Hulton, Commissioner of Customs in Boston from 1767 to 1776. Her letters show a growing pattern of physical intimidation against Loyalists, and clearly express her views of what she believes are the Patriots' "real" motives. Who does Hulton see as the real criminals and enemies of liberty in the colonies? Who is guilty of tyranny—the Patriots or the Tories? How would Hulton explain the causes of the Revolution?

The most shocking cruelty was exercised a few nights ago, upon a poor old man, a tidesman, one Malcolm. . . . A quarrel was picked with him. He was afterward taken, and tarred and feathered. There's no law that knows a punishment for the greatest crimes beyond what this is, of cruel torture. And this instance exceeds any other before it. He was stripped stark naked, one of the severest cold nights this winter, his body covered all over with tar, then with feathers, his arm dislocated in tearing off his clothes. He was dragged in a cart, with thousands attending, some beating him with clubs and knocking him out of the cart, then in again. They gave him several severe whippings, at different parts of the town. This spectacle of horror and sportive cruelty was exhibited for about five hours.

The unhappy wretch they say behaved with the greatest intrepidity and fortitude. All the while before he was taken, he defended himself a long time against numbers; and afterwards, when under torture they demanded of him to curse his masters, the king, governors, etc. which they could not make him do, but still he cried, Curse all Traitors. They brought him to the gallows and put a rope about his neck saying that they would hang him; he said he wished they would, but that they could not for God was above the Devil. The doctors say his flesh comes off his back in stakes.

It is the second time he has been tarred and feathered and this is looked upon more to intimidate the judges and others than a spite to the unhappy victim, though they owe him a grudge for some things, particularly, he was with Governor Tryon in the Battle with the Regulators. . . . The Governor has declared that he was of great service to him in that affair, by his undaunted spirit encountering the greatest dangers.

Governor Tryon had sent him a gift of ten guineas just before this inhuman treatment. He has a wife and family and an aged father and mother who, they say, saw the spectacle which no indifferent person can mention without horror.

These few instances among many serve to show the abject state of government and the licentiousness and barbarism of the times. There's no magistrate that dare or will act to suppress the outrages. No person is secure. There are many objects pointed at, at this time, and when once marked out for vengeance, their ruin is certain.

I imagine you will be desirous to Know how the New Acts of Parliamt operate here, & how y' friends are affected by the Commotions, & disturbances of the Publick. I am sorry to say there appears no disposition yet in the People towards complying with the Port Bill,— They carry thier Melasses & other Goods easily by Land from Salem, & find little inconvenience at present from its operation, The distress it will bring on the Town will not be felt very sever'ly before Winter, when the Roads will be impassible. There's little prospect of Boston Port being Opend this Year. The Leaders of the Faction are only more unwearied, & are pursuing every measure to draw the People onto resistance, & to irritate Governmt more, & more and which probably will end in the total ruin of the Town & the Indivdials.

From *Letters of a Loyalist Lady*, Harvard University Press, 1927.

It is now a very gloomy place, the Streets almost empty, many families have removed from it, & the Inhabitants are divided into several parties, at variance, & quarreling with each other, some appear desponding, others full of rage. The People of Property of best sense & Characters feel the Tyranny of the Leaders, & foresee the Consequences of their proceedings, woud gladly extricate themselves from the difficulties, & distress they are involved in by making their peace with G: Britain, & speedily submiting to the Conditions & penalties required.

These who are well disposed towards Governm^t (more from interest than principle it's to be feard, as there are few will^s to acknowledge the Authority of Parliam^t) are termd Tories. They daily increase, & have made some efforts to take the power out of the hands of the Patriots, but they are intimidated & overpowerd by Numbers, & the Arts, & Machinations of the Leader, who Governs absolutly, the Minds & the Passions of the People—by publishing numberless falshoods to impose on their credulity, & various artifices to influence or terrify. The Ministers from the Pulpit & the Committee of Correspond^{ce} by writing inflame the Minds of the ignorant Country People. Their endeavors to engage the Other Colonies to shut up their Ports, & the Merch^{ts} here to joyn in a Non-importation Agrement, proving without effect. The next plan is in opposition to the Merch^{ts} & which if it spreads must be attended wth the ruin of most of 'em here 'tis a Solemn League & Covenant, not to use any British Manufactures, till the Port is opend, & the New Acts repeald. This is a deep & diabolical scheme, & some people are taken into the Snare, but it's to be hoped the progress of it will be stopd, Genl Gage who conducts himself with great good sense & spirit, issues a Proclaimation Against it to warn 'em of its Consequences, They are startled in general, however, the little Town of Marlborough has had the Audacity to burn the Genl in effigy wth the Proclaimation.

Document 4.11 Legislating an Attack on the Loyalists

In 1774 the First Continental Congress authorized each county or town to establish "committees of safety and inspection" to insure that everyone supported the non-importation agreements and resistance to the Coercive Acts. Those supporting British policy would see their businesses boycotted and would be socially ostracized. Once the Revolutionary War began, the new state legislatures created special agencies to control the "disaffected" population. Loyalists would now face more than just physical harassment. Later these legislatures relied on courts and new laws to punish people for misprision of treason-which could be anything from speaking or writing in opposition to the war to spying for the British. Penalties included imprisonment and confiscation of one's properties. The following are examples of the laws. What do they have in common?

Laws against Freedom of Speech and Action.

New Hamphshire.

January 17, 1777.

An act for preventing and punishing such offences against the State as do not amount to treason or misprision of treason.

Massachusetts.

August (?), 1777.

An act for preventing or punishing crimes that may be committed against the public safety below the degree of treason and misprision of treason.

Rhode Island.

August (third Monday in), 1775.

From *The Loyalists in the American Revolution*, Macmillan, 1902.

An act to punish persons, who shall pilot any armed vessels in or out of any of the harbors . . . in this colony, excepting vessels belonging to some one of the British colonies in America. . . .

October—November, 1775.

An act for the punishment of persons who shall be found guilty of holding a traitorous correspondence with the ministry of Great Britain or any of their officers or agents, or of supplying the ministerial army or navy that now is, or may be, employed in America against the United Colonies, with provisions, cannon, arms, ammunition, warlike or naval stores, or of acting as pilots on board any of their ships and vessels.

New Jersey.

February 11, 1777.

An act for more effectually preventing disaffected and evil minded persons destroying the credit and circulation of the Continental bills of credit. . . .

February 13, 1777.

An act to prevent the counterfeiting or forging the tickets of the United States lottery.

October 8, 1778.

An act to prevent the subjects of this State from going into, or coming out of, the enemy's lines without permissions or passports. . . .

June 13, 1780.

An act more effectually to prevent the passing of counterfeit bills of credit.

June 17, 1780.

An act more effectually to prevent desertion and for the punishment of persons harboring prisoners of war or purchasing the clothing and accoutrements of the soldiers of the army and for the repeal of a certain act therein mentioned.

December 22, 1780.

An act more effectually to prevent the inhabitants of this state from trading with the enemy, or going within their lines, and for other purposes therein mentioned.

June 24, 1782.

An act for preventing illicit trade and intercourse between the subjects of this State and the enemy.

December 24, 1782.

(Amends above.)

Delaware.

May 20, 1778.

To prevent the inhabitants of this State from dealing and furnishing the enemy thereof with supplies . . . .

Virginia.

May, 1780.

An act affixing penalties to certain crimes injurious to the independence of America, but less than treason, and repealing the act for the punishment of certain offences.

South Carolina.

April 11, 1776.

An act to prevent sedition and punish insurgents and disturbers of the public peace. (Estates of offenders confiscated.)

Laws Suppressing, Quarantining, Banishing and Exiling the Loyalists.

New Hampshire.

June 19, 1777.

An act for taking up, imprisoning, or otherwise restraining persons dangerous to this State.

November 19, 1778.

An act to prevent the return to the State of certain persons therein named, and of others who have left or shall leave this State or either of the United States of America and have joined or shall join the enemies thereof.

Massachusetts.

May 10 (?), 1777.

An act for securing this, and the other United States, against the dangers, to which they are exposed by the internal enemies thereof.

May 27—September 16, 1778.

Act to prevent the return of certain persons therein named and others who have left this State or either of the United States and joined the enemies thereof. (See also Laws of Massachusetts 1775–80, pp. 103, 186, 187, 210, 220, 231.)

Rhode Island.

July, 1780.

An act to prevent certain persons therein named . . . from being admitted within this State.

Connecticut.

October 10, (?), 1776.

An act for apprehending and securing such inimical persons as shall be deemed and adjudged dangerous to the State. (Amended May 8, 1777.)

New York.

February 5, 1778.

An act appointing commissioners for detecting and defeating conspiracies and declaring their powers. (Amended April 3, 1778, October 29, 1778, June 14, 1780.)

April 1, 1778.

An act to enable the persons administering the government of this State . . . to remove certain disaffected and dangerous persons and families.

March 22, 1781.

An act to accommodate the inhabitants of the frontiers with habitations.

March 20, 1783.

An act to protect the persons and property of the inhabitants of the county of Westchester from injury and abuse.

North Carolina.

May 13, 1776.

Resolve of Provincial Congress to disarm and imprison all who aid Great Britain.

South Carolina.

October 17, 1778.

An ordinance to empower the President or Commander-in-Chief. . . . with the advice of the privy council to take up and confine all persons whose going at large may endanger the safety of this State.

August 31, 1779.

(Same as above.)

Georgia.

September 16, 1777.

An act for the expulsion of the internal enemies of this State.

March 1, 1778.

An act to prevent the dangerous consequences that may arise from the practices of disaffected . . . persons within this State.

August 21, 1781.

An act for prevention of internal conspiracies and for the empowering certain committees therein named, to examine into the conduct of certain suspicious persons.

January 9, 1782.

An act to repeal an act entitled "An act to draw a line between the good citizens of this State and the enemies thereof and to prevent plundering and detect spies within the same." (Original act January 29, 1780.)

August 5, 1782.

An act for preventing improper or disaffected persons immigrating from other places, and becoming citizens of this State, and for other purposes therein mentioned.

Laws Providing for the Crime of Adhering to Great Britain.

New Hampshire.

January 17, 1777.

An act against treason and misprision of treason and for regulating trials in such cases, and for directing the mode of executing judgments against persons convicted of those crimes.

Massachusetts.

_____, 1777.

An act against treason and misprision of treason. . . . (A general law for treason in general.)

Connecticut.

May 8 (?), 1777.

An act to prevent traitorous conspiracies against this and the United States of America.

New York.

March 30, 1781.

An act more effectually to punish adherence to the king of Great Britain, within this State.

New Jersey.

October 4, 1776.

An act to punish traitors and disaffected persons. (Supplemented October 3, 1782.)

October 2, 1778.

An act for apprehending and delivering up to justice all persons residing or taking refuge in this State, charged with crimes committed in any other of the United States, and for other purposes.

Pennsylvania.

February 11, 1777.

An act declaring what shall be treason and what other crimes . . . shall be misprision of treason.

March 6, 1778.

An act for the attainder of divers traitors, if they render not themselves by a certain day, and for vesting their estates in this commonwealth. . . . (Amended November 26, 1778.)

March 8, 1780.

An act for the amendment of the law relative to the punishment of treasons, robberies, misprisions of treason. . . . (See also November 27, 1778, and March 31, 1781).

Maryland.

July 4, 1776.

Resolve of the Provincial Convention. Adherents to Great Britain to suffer death.

February, 1777.

An act to punish certain crimes and misdemeanors and to prevent the growth of Toryism.

North Carolina.

April 8 (?), 1777.

An act declaring what crimes and practices against the State shall be treason and what shall be misprision of treason . . . and for preventing the dangers which may arise from persons disaffected to the State. (Amended later in 1777.)

September 15, 1777.

(Heading is same as above.)

South Carolina.

February 20, 1779.

An ordinance to prevent persons withdrawing from the defense of this State to join the enemies thereof.

Laws Amercing, Taxing or Confiscating the Estates of Loyalists or Anticipating Such Action.

New Hampshire.

November 29, 1777.

An act to prevent the transfer or conveyance of the estates and property of all such persons who have been or shall be apprehended upon suspicion of being guilty of treason, misprision of treason, or other inimical practices respecting this State, the United States, any or either of them, and also for securing all lands within this State as well of such persons as have traitorously deserted, or may hereafter desert the common cause of America, and have gone over to, or in any way or manner joined our enemies, as of those who belong to, or reside in Great Britain.

December 26, 1778.

An act to make void all attachments which have been or hereafter shall be laid or made on the estates of persons who have left this State or any of the United States, and have gone over to the enemies of the said States since the commencement of hostilities by Great Britain; or on the estates of any inhabitant or subjects of Great Britain.
Preamble.—Whereas such attachments may be made by the collusion of the parties in order to defeat this State of the benefit which may arise from the confiscation of such estates, and to defraud just creditors of their honest demands against such persons.

Massachusetts.

April 10 (?), 1777.

An act to prevent the waste . . . of goods or estates of such persons who have left . . . fled to our enemies for protection. . . . (Amended May—June, 1778.)

April 3O, 1779.

An act for confiscating the estates of certain persons commonly called absentees.

April 3O, 1779.

Act to confiscate the estates of certain notorious conspirators against the government. . . .

Connecticut.

June 14, 1776.

An act in addition to an act. . . . entitled an act for restraining and punishing persons inimical.

May 14 (?), 1778.

An act for confiscating the estates of Persons inimical to the independence and liberties of the United States. . . .

Maryland.

April 25—June 15, 1782.

An act for the liquidation and payment of debts against persons convicted of treason.

October—December, 1780.

(Relates to treble tax on non-jurors.)

Virginia.

December, 1775.

An ordinance for establishing a mode of punishment for the enemies to America in this colony. (Amended, May, 1776.)

May, 1779.

An act to secure the movable property of those who have joined or hereafter may join the enemy.

North Carolina.

May 13, 1776.

Resolve of Provincial Congress—estates of refugees to be seized.

November, 1777.

An act for confiscating the property of all such persons as are inimical to the United States, and of such persons as shall not within a certain time therein mentioned, appear and submit to the State whether they shall be received as citizens thereof and of such persons as shall so appear and shall not be admitted as citizens.

October, 1779.

(Act to carry above into effect; suspended, September, 1780.)

September 5, 1780.

An act for securing the quiet and inoffensive inhabitants of this State from being injured, and for preventing such property as hath or may be confiscated from being wasted or destroyed. . . .

April 13 (?), 1782.

An act directing the sale of confiscated property.

Georgia.

March 1, 1778.

An act for attainting such persons as are herein mentioned, of high treason and for confiscating their estates . . . for establishing boards of commissioners for the sales of such estates. . . . (Amended October 30, 1778.)

November 15, 1778.

An act to compel non-residents to return within a certain time, or in default . . . their estates to be confiscated. . . .

January 11, 1782.

An act for the confiscating of the estates of certain persons . . . and for providing funds for defraying the contingent expenses of this state.

Document 4.12 "The American Times" by Jonathan Odell, 1780

Loyalists were very angry about the way their former neighbors treated them. They believed they were loyal to both the King and America, while the Patriot leaders used inflammatory rhetoric as an excuse to steal, plunder, and deprive good people of their liberty and their property. Jonathan Odell was a physician turned Anglican minister, who later became a writer. During the American Revolution he served as chaplain for the 1st Battalion of Pennsylvania Loyalists, but is best known for his connection to Benedict Arnold's treason. He frequently contributed to the Royal Gazette in British-occupied New York City. In this verse, what are the many sins and crimes committed by Patriots? According to Odell, how have the Patriots' action affected British North America, and what will their punishment be for these injuries?

When Faction, pois'nous as the scorpion's
    sting,
Infects the people and Insults the King;
When foul Sedition skulks no more concealed,
But grasps the sword and rushes to the field;
When Justice, Law, and Truth are in disgrace,
And Treason, Fraud, and Murder fill their place;
Smarting beneath accumulated woes,
Shall we not dare the tyrants to expose?

Bad are the Times, almost too bad to paint;
The whole head sickens, the whole heart is faint;
The State is rotten, rotten to the core,
'Tis all one bruize, one putrefying sore.

Hear thy indictment, Washington, at large;
Attend and listen to the solemn charge;
Thou hast supported an atrocious cause

Against thy King, thy Country, and the laws;
Committed perjury, encourag'd lies,
Forced conscience, broken the most sacred ties;
Myriads of wives and fathers at thy hand
Their slaughter'd husbands, slaughteed sons
    demand;
That pastures hear no more the lowing kine,—
That towns are desolate, all—all is thine.

I swear by Him, who rules the earth and sky,
The dread event shall equally apply;
That Clinton's warfare is the war of God,
And Washington shall feel the vengeful rod.

O! may that hour be soon! for pity's sake,
Genius of Britain, from thy slumber wake,
Too long has mercy spoke, but spoke in vain;
Let justice now in awful terror reign.

From *The American Times*, W. Richardson: London 1780.

Document 4.13 The Declaration of Independence

The Declaration of Independence is one of the greatest documents in United States history. It defines not only the past, but what we hope to stand for as a nation in the future as well. The call that "all men are created equal," at a time when many people were denied rights in their own colonies, would monumentally affect the new United States in the years to come. For the first time, the ideas of equality and liberty are linked together, even though the document does not make it clear what this means. The Declaration contains a huge list of grievances against King George III and his government. This document now charges the King to be the real cause of problems, not the Parliament. Instead of needing the monarchy, the whole people of the new United States have the power to control their own destiny. Consider the preface and the main body carefully, since they summarize the years of struggle before the War for Independence. How do we justify breaking away from the British Empire, and severing all ties of loyalty to the British crown?

The Declaration of Independence of the Thirteen Colonies In CONGRESS, July 4,1776

The unanimous Declaration of the thirteen United States of America,

When in the Course of human events, it becomes necessary for one people to dissolve the political bands which have connected them with another, and to assume among the powers of the earth, the separate and equal station to which the Laws of Nature and of Nature's God entitle them, a decent respect to the opinions of mankind requires that they should declare the causes which impel them to the separation.

We hold these truths to be self-evident, that all men are created equal, that they are endowed by their Creator with certain unalienable Rights, that among these are Life, Liberty, and the pursuit of Happiness. That to secure these rights, Governments are instituted among Men, deriving their just powers from the consent of the governed. That whenever any Form of Government becomes destructive of these ends, it is the Right of the People to alter or to abolish it, and to institute new Government, laying its foundation on such principles and organizing its powers in such form, as to them shall seem most likely to effect their Safety and Happiness.

Prudence, indeed, will dictate that Governments long established should not be changed for light and transient causes; and accordingly all experience hath shewn, that mankind are more disposed to suffer, while evils are sufferable, than to right themselves by abolishing the forms to which they are accustomed.

But when a long train of abuses and usurpations, pursuing invariably the same object evinces a design to reduce them under absolute Despotism, it is their right, it is their duty, to throw off such Government, and to provide new Guards for their future security.

Such has been the patient sufferance of these Colonies; and such is now the necessity which constrains them to alter their former Systems of Government. The history of the present King of Great Britain [George III] is a history of repeated injuries and usurpations, all having in direct object the establishment of an absolute Tyranny over these States. To prove this, let Facts be submitted to a candid world.

He has refused his Assent to Laws, the most wholesome and necessary for the public good.

He has forbidden his Governors to pass Laws of immediate and pressing importance, unless suspended in their operation till his Assent should be obtained, and when so suspended, he has utterly neglected to attend to them.

He has refused to pass other Laws for the accommodation of large districts of people, unless those people would relinquish the right of Representation in the Legislature, a right inestimable to them and formidable to tyrants only.

The Declaration of Independence.

He has called together legislative bodies at places unusual, uncomfortable, and distant from the depository of their public Records, for the sole purpose of fatiguing them into compliance with his measures.

He has dissolved Representative Houses repeatedly, for opposing with manly firmness his invasions on the rights of the people.

He has refused for a long time, after such dissolutions, to cause others to be elected; whereby the Legislative powers, incapable of Annihilation, have returned to the People at large for their exercise; the State remaining in the meantime exposed to all the dangers of invasion from without, and convulsions within.

He has endeavoured to prevent the population of these States; for that purpose obstructing the Laws for Naturalization of Foreigners; refusing to pass others to encourage their migrations hither, and raising the conditions of new Appropriations of Lands.

He has obstructed the Administration of Justice, by refusing his Assent to Laws for establishing Judiciary powers.

He has made Judges dependent on his Will alone, for the tenure of their offices, and the amount and payment of their salaries.

He has erected a multitude of New Offices, and sent hither swarms of Officers to harass our people, and eat out their substance.

He has kept among us, in times of peace, Standing Armies, without the consent of our legislatures.

He has affected to render the Military independent of and superior to the Civil power.

He has combined with others to subject us to a jurisdiction foreign to our constitution and unacknowledged by our laws; giving his Assent to their Acts of pretended Legislation:

- For quartering large bodies of armed troops among us:
- For protecting them by a mock Trial from punishment for any Murders which they should commit on the Inhabitants of these States:
- For cutting off our Trade with all parts of the world:
- For imposing Taxes on us without our Consent:
- For depriving us in many cases of the benefits of Trial by Jury:
- For transporting us beyond Seas to be tried for pretended offences:

- For abolishing the free System of English Laws in a neighbouring Province, establishing therein an Arbitrary government, and enlarging its Boundaries so as to render it at once an example and fit instrument for introducing the same absolute rule into these Colonies:
- For taking away our Charters, abolishing our most valuable Laws and altering fundamentally the Forms of our Governments:
- For suspending our own Legislatures, and declaring themselves invested with power to legislate for us in all cases whatsoever.

He has abdicated Government here by declaring us out of his Protection and waging War against us.

He has plundered our seas, ravaged our Coasts, burnt our towns, and destroyed the lives of our people.

He is at this time transporting large Armies of foreign Mercenaries to complete the works of death, desolation and tyranny, already begun with circumstances of cruelty and perfidy scarcely paralleled in the most barbarous ages, and totally unworthy the Head of a civilized nation.

He has constrained our fellow Citizens taken Captive on the high Seas to bear Arms against their Country, to become the executioners of their friends and Brethren, or to fall themselves by their Hands.

He has excited domestic insurrections amongst us, and has endeavoured to bring on the inhabitants of our frontiers, the merciless Indian Savages, whose known rule of warfare is an undistinguished destruction of all ages, sexes and conditions.

In every stage of these Oppressions We have Petitioned for Redress in the most humble terms. Our repeated Petitions have been answered only by repeated injury. A Prince, whose character is thus marked by every act which may define a Tyrant, is unfit to be the ruler of a free people.

Nor have We been wanting in attentions to our British brethren.

- We have warned them from time to time of attempts by their legislature to extend an unwarrantable jurisdiction over us.
- We have reminded them of the circumstances of our emigration and settlement here.
- We have appealed to their native justice and magnanimity, and we have conjured them by the ties of our common kindred to disavow these usurpations, which would inevitably interrupt our connections and correspondence.

They too have been deaf to the voice of justice and of consanguinity. We must, therefore, acquiesce in the necessity, which denounces our Separation, and hold them, as we hold the rest of mankind, Enemies in War, in Peace Friends.

We, therefore, the Representatives of the United States of America, in General Congress, Assembled, appealing to the Supreme Judge of the world for the rectitude of our intentions, do, in the Name, and by the authority of the good People of these Colonies, solemnly publish and declare.

That these United Colonies are, and of Right ought to be Free and Independent States; that they are Absolved from all Allegiance to the British Crown,

and that all political connection between them and the State of Great Britain is and ought to be totally dissolved;

and that as Free and Independent States, they have full Power to levy War, conclude Peace, contract Alliances, establish Commerce,

and to do all other Acts and Things which Independent States may of right do.

And for the support of this Declaration, with a firm reliance on the protection of Divine Providence, we mutually pledge to each other our Lives, our Fortunes, and our sacred Honor.

Chapter 4 Worksheet and Questions

1. You are part of the legal team either prosecuting or defending the British soldiers after the Boston Massacre. They are charged with numerous crimes against the British citizens of Boston, the most important being intentional (premeditated) murder. How are you going to prove or refute this charge? How do you interpret the series of events that led to the shootings on March 5th? What was the role of the mob, according to your sources? Were they a spontaneous gathering of aggrieved citizens or part of a planned conspiracy?

_____

_____

_____

_____

_____

_____

_____

_____

2. Loyalists and Patriots both claim that they are resisting tyranny, and that they are only defending liberty and their rights as Englishmen. How are their concerns similar, i.e., what rights is each concerned about? How do their definitions of tyranny and the source of the threats to their rights differ? From the documents, use specific examples that demonstrate their views.

_____

_____

_____

_____

_____

_____

_____

3. Loyalists claimed that all Americans owed allegiance to the British Crown. What does this mean, and are there different definitions of what one must be loyal to? Why is such allegiance important, and what evil happenings do they predict if this allegiance is broken?

_____

_____

_____

_____

_____

_____

_____

_____

_____

4. A sharp conflict over the extent and basis of government power developed between Britain and the North American colonies. Why do many colonists question the authority of Parliament, and even that of the King? Using the documents, trace the changes in colonial attitudes from the start of the chapter through the Declaration of Independence.

_____

_____

_____

_____

_____

_____

_____

_____

_____

5. Most trained historians today record that the Patriots grossly mistreated the Loyalists. Earlier historians supported the idea that the Loyalists were all traitors and got just what they deserved. But during a Revolution, it is often difficult to separate who the real traitors and patriots are. American patriots loyal to the Continental Congress labeled supporters of King George as traitors to the cause, while the King's supporters believed the revolutionaries were all traitors to the British Crown. To whom do the ideas of liberty and individual freedoms apply during these years? How did the Patriots treat the Loyalists and their families, and were their actions proper?

_____

_____

_____

_____

_____

_____

_____

_____

_____

_____

Chapter 5

Protecting Our Rights or Stealing Our Liberties?: Debates on the Ratifying of the Constitution

We live in a nation governed by the guidelines and rules set down in the United States Constitution more than 200 years ago. There is a tendency to take the Constitution for granted: It is there, it has always been there, and it will always be there to protect us. But the existence of the United States Constitution was not a sure thing. There were serious doubts in the last part of the eighteenth century whether the Constitution as we know it would even be drafted, or ratified into law, or whether it would survive the century. This chapter looks at the constitutional process, focusing on the struggle over ratification.

The greatest legacy of the struggle in the years before and during the War for Independence was the ideal of a republic. Revolutionary leaders deliberately chose this form of government, even though it had never survived successfully anywhere in history. People of all social classes in the new United States embraced the basis of a **republic**, the idea that the powers of a government come directly from the people. The Declaration of Independence and the 13 new state governments all reflected this belief, that people are born with natural rights and that these basic rights are to be protected by every level of government. Every state created a government dominated by the legislature, with the judiciary and executive branches noticeably less powerful. This arrangement was justified by the fact that the legislature was elected by the people, and therefore was closer to their views, and received the people's grant of power through the elections. Legislatures were trusted by a majority of Americans because they defended the rights of the colonists before the war against the perceived tyranny of the British central government.

Even more radical was the creation of written constitutions, guaranteeing governments that are republican in nature. Most state constitutions included declarations of individual rights, limiting government interference with personal liberties and property (i.e., a bill of rights). Supporters of republics also believed in the necessity of virtuous citizens and government. Educated, virtuous citizens would elect virtuous representatives. These representatives of the people would be willing to put the good of the community before their own personal interests, and the good of the nation before the interests of their community. Virtue was the key to liberty and republicanism. Without virtuous government officials, governments would favor special interests and become tyrannical, eventually costing the people all of their liberties. During the 1770s, most republicans believed that states were the homes and guardians of virtue, because state governments were closer to the people.

Our first national government, under the Articles of Confederation, reflected the concerns of a nation fighting for its rights and liberties. The central government was not too strong; it had no authority to tax its citizens or regulate commerce, it had no courts, and it had no powers to threaten individual civil liberties. In other words, it could not directly impact the lives of its citizens. To do that, it had to go through the state governments.

If so many Americans were happy with their state governments' having most of the power, and content with their relationship with the national government, why was the Constitutional Convention held? Thomas Jefferson observed during the war that once American victory was achieved the greatest reason for national unity would be removed. He believed that public virtue would go "down hill," and that Americans would only be concerned with making money. These concerns arose during the War for Independence, as state governments failed to provide the Confederation Congress with enough money to meet its obligations, or even pay the Continental Army. If the people were not willing to sacrifice through taxes to defend the nation during wartime, what chance did virtue have over self-interest in peacetime? Some observers believed that the Confederation government was unable to function as a central government, to pay its own bills, to handle foreign relations, or to maintain the national economy. To these people, the system of government seemed to be breaking down, and they feared the United States would then cease to exist. A faction of citizens claimed that creating a stronger central government was actually in the people's best interest. Shay's (so-called) Rebellion in 1786 convinced people of property that total collapse of the social order was imminent. This meant their personal possessions and standing in the community were at the mercy of "the people."

Historians have studied and debated the personal motives of the Founding Fathers for years. Most of the men at the Philadelphia Convention were men of substantial property and social standing. They were used to deference from the common people; preserving (or stabilizing) the existing social order was clearly a goal. The growing sense of democracy among some of the "lower sorts" in society made them nervous. The claim by farm laborers, artisans, and street people—that their willingness to risk their lives during the war (a willingness to sacrifice everything) made them equal citizens—shook the elites' sense of place in society. With states issuing their own paper money, creditors and those who made money by lending feared for their livelihoods. Some Convention members feared for the existence of the republic and everything fought for in the American Revolution. They believed a republic without a strong central government would degenerate into "democracy," which to them meant mob rule. This degeneration would lead to disorder, disrespect for the law, and disregard of property rights; it would require a dictator to restore order, but that would mean the end of republican liberty. Others feared the scenario that forecast the nation's splintering into small European-style nations, each eventually ruled by monarchs and aristocrats, as in Europe.

To prevent these disasters and protect their own wealth, the Founding Fathers created the Constitution. The story behind its creation, the famous compromises that brought the document into being, and the Constitution itself are in your textbook. Some of the steps taken at the Convention would be challenged later. The Founding Fathers voted to keep the proceedings secret from the public, nailing windows shut, posting guards at the doors, and forbidding publication of any minutes or proceedings. Officially, this was done to allow members to speak freely and change their minds without fear of criticism, but it was also done to prevent the public from knowing what went on. Convention members knew that the public would not approve a plan for a stronger central government, and would drive them out of Philadelphia if word got out. Officially the convention was only authorized to amend or fix the Articles of Confederation, not create a new government. Critics later commented that this forced secrecy put the drafters of the new Constitution out of touch with the people and their interests. Other Convention measures suggest a distrust of the common people—an argument historians still debate today.

The Constitution abandons the idea that individuals have natural rights, which the Declaration of Independence relies on as the basis of all individual liberties. Distrusting human nature, and believing most citizens from the "lower orders" lacked sufficient education or virtue to be part of the government, the Founding Fathers cut them off from parts of the new national government. While proclaiming that the powers of government rest on the will of the people, the people are not allowed to directly elect Senators; that right is reserved for state legislatures, where it was hoped the "better sorts" would make the right decisions. The common people are not allowed to elect directly the most powerful official in the government: the president. That right is given to a special creation called the Electoral College, which in the beginning was not required to vote for the same person as the people did. Finally, the Founding Fathers claimed to support majority rule at all times, but the multiple Constitutional concessions made to preserve slavery and Southern political power refute this claim. There would be a new central government that directly touched the citizens of the entire nation, without relying on other governments to serve as intermediaries.

Even the ratification process was not turned over to the people, because they might object to a more powerful central government. Unwilling to rely on the people, the state governments, or the Confederation Congress to ratify/approve the new Constitution, the Founders called for special state ratifying conventions. Getting a unanimous vote in the Confederation Congress would be impossible. State legislatures would object to giving up their powers. Finally, the people could not be trusted, and would not likely approve anyway.

This chapter concentrates on the struggle for ratification. James Madison, often called the Father of the Constitution, claimed later that the true meaning of the document was found not in Philadelphia but in the debates at the state ratifying conventions. Here, tough questions were asked, concepts were clarified and defined, problems were identified, and amendments were proposed. Pamphleteers and propagandists produced a steady stream of newspaper editorials and materials supporting, explaining, or denouncing the new Constitution. *The Federalist* is the best known of these materials, aimed at defusing Antifederalist arguments and increasing support for the document. More than 1,700 delegates met in different locations in the 13 states, argued in the press and taverns, and carried the struggle onto the streets and back into the meeting halls. From the time the Constitutional Convention adjourned on September 17, 1787 until Massachusetts, Virginia, and New York ratified the document, the issue was in doubt.

Federalists (supporters of the document) wanted the Constitution accepted as is, without any changes. George Washington and others warned of dire times if not accepted without revision. Washington claimed that there would have to be another convention, and that the document would never be approved, the nation would fall apart, and European powers would come back and take over. Other Federalists wanted no changes because they were sure the document was perfect, and any changes threatened their own protected interests. They were prepared to do anything to get it passed—even use force to get their way. In Pennsylvania they rushed the call for a convention through the legislature, physically dragging opponents from their boardinghouses, carrying them bodily back to the assembly, and forcing them to be counted as present to insure a quorum for voting. Pennsylvania Federalists and others totally disdained popular concerns about the lack of a bill of rights, claiming that the government was either so perfect that a guarantee of rights would be superfluous, or that people asking for such guarantees were actually asking for special favors. They claimed that a standing army was not a threat, because under the Constitution it could only protect the public good, not take away personal liberties; they also claimed that, because this was a good government, opponents need not fear its power to tax.

In Massachusetts, opposition was greater to the new Constitution, largely because a bill of rights was missing. Federalists almost lost the struggle here because they refused to compromise or change the document. They refused to recognize that many patriots from Revolutionary days feared this new government as a return to the old British rule. Power, they believed, was corrupting, and any government given this much power would seek to take even more away from the people. Massachusetts approved the new Constitution only after old Revolutionaries Sam Adams and John Hancock linked approval to a call for amendments after the new government formed. In Virginia, George Mason and Edmund Randolph, two members of the Constitutional Convention, opposed the Constitution as is. Mason was the much-respected architect of the Virginia Constitution, and author of the Declaration of Rights. They feared a government dominated by northern interests, and decried the failure to include a bill of rights in the document, an omission that made its entire structure flawed. To gain approval here, Madison and others promised that the new Congress would amend the Constitution. The Constitution passed some states unanimously (Delaware 30-0), others by large margins (Connecticut 128-40), but very narrowly in key states (Massachusetts 187-186, Virginia 89-79, and New York 30-27).

Most Antifederalists agreed that the Articles of Confederation needed revision and the government needed strengthening, but they were not prepared for a strong national government such as the one proposed. Would the new government be all-powerful? Article I, Section 8 gave the Congress the authority to "make all laws which shall be necessary and proper for carrying into execution" its powers. What would stop the new government from ruling at the point of a bayonet? In some of the state ratifying conventions, local interests dominated the debate. In South Carolina the existence of slavery, and the potential threat of the new government to abolish the institution, dominated the proceedings. Some states, such as Delaware and New Jersey, focused on the potential economic benefits or injuries their state would receive under the new government. Other states dismissed the abstract reasoning of the Constitution's supporters, wanting the new document explained in practical terms. In Massachusetts, most of the Convention delegates were experienced local politicians, veterans of the struggle before independence, the war itself, and several rounds of creating government. They wanted supporters to demonstrate how the new government matched up with lessons learned from their years of political experience.

Other Antifederalists feared that this new document was just a tool of political power for the aggrandizement of wealthy merchants, large landowners, moneylenders, and their attorneys. They would monopolize the centralized powers of the government to create a new elite, an American version of the corrupt *British aristocracy*. Since most of the Antifederalists had fought to liberate the United States from the British monarchy and aristocracy, the potential for creating a new tyranny was alarming. Along the same lines, many Antifederalists feared the loss of state sovereignty, that too much power was leaving the states. State governments were closer to the virtuous people, while a national government was more distant. How could national representatives remain true to their constituents? Wouldn't they be corrupted by special interests? Many of the proposed amendments coming from the state conventions involved clear delineations of state powers versus those of the national government. Across the nation many state delegates found the Federalists' high-handed tactics objectionable. Physical threats, forcing people to vote, refusals to listen to legitimate concerns or consider amendments to the document all reminded Antifederalists of the way the British government acted toward the colonists before the American Revolution. More than anything else, Antifederalists demanded a bill of rights. They were not impressed by Federalist claims that this new "splendid" government would never take away citizens' rights, or that including a bill of rights would actually weaken the new government too much. Federalists' abuses and high-handed tactics used to gain passage in some states suggested evil ulterior motives. A promise of amendments guaranteeing basic rights was necessary to gain ratification in many conventions, and North Carolina did not join the Union until the Bill of Rights became law. Finally, many Antifederalists expressed concerns that this new constitution promoted individual interests instead of rights, and promoted unlicensed individualism at the expense of the community, an attitude that broke with traditional American thinking. Individualism weakens the idea that you owe the public duty, that bonds of community, family, and friendship are more important than the accumulation of personal wealth. The new Constitution promotes a commercial republic, where the public spirit would be endangered by the quest for money. What would happen to public virtue, so necessary for a republic's survival?

Considering the Evidence in the Readings

In the following documents, you will be reading impassioned pleas and reasoned pleas, as well as personal denunciations from Federalists and Antifederalists, supporters and opponents of the Constitution. Would the arguments presented in these documents convince people to ratify a similar constitution today? These materials come from the ratification struggles in several states. Look for similarities in the arguments made for each state. Are there common themes, or do decisions and objections appear dictated by local concerns? How would you use these documents to explain ratification of the Constitution? Finally, look for issues and concerns raised by opponents of the new government and Constitution that might be applicable today.

Document 5.1 David Redick: Worries about the Loss of American Liberty

The loss of liberty is a common concern among Antifederalist writers. It could be the lack of personal liberties because there is no bill of rights, or the loss of state powers to a grasping central government. After all, the new document declared in Article V that the Constitution, and all laws passed by the national government "in pursuance of" it, would be "the supreme law of the land," thus trumping state powers. As you examine this document, what specific liberties is the writer concerned about losing? What does he fear will happen to the nation as a result of losing these liberties?

The new plan of government proposed by the convention has made a bustle in the city & its vicinity, all people, almost, are for Swallowing it down at once without examining its tendencies.—

I have thought it unsafe within the wind of hurricane to utter a Sylable about it: but to you Sir I may venture to Say that in my oppinion the day on which we adopt the present proposed plan of government, from that moment we may Justly date the loss of American liberty, perhaps my fears hath contributed principely to this oppinion. I will change the moment that I See better. My dear Sir why is not the liberty of the press provided for? why will the Congress have power to alter the plan or mode of chusing Representatives? why will they have power to lay direct Taxes? why will they have power to keep Standing Armies in time of peace? why will they have power to make laws in direct contradiction to the forms of government established in the Several States? why will they have power to collect by law ten Dollars for ever German or Irishman which may come to Settle in America? why is the Trial by Jury destroyd in Civil causes before Congress? and above all I cannot imagine why the people in this city are So verry anxious to have it adopted instantly before it can be digested or deliberatly considered. If you were only here to See and hear those people, to observe the means they are useing to effect this purpose, to hear the tories declare they will draw their Sword in its defence, to See the quaquers runing about Signing declarations and Petitions in favor of it before they have time to examine it, to See Gentlemen runing into the Country and neibouring towns haranguing the Rabble. I Say were you to See and hear these things as I do you would Say, with me that: the verry Soul of confidence itself ought to change into distrust. If this government be a good one or even a tollorable one the Necessities and the good Sense of America will lead us to adopt it, if otherwise give us time and it will be amended and then adopted, but I think the measures pursued here is a Strong evidence that these people know it will not bear an examination and therefor wishes to adopt it first and consider it afterward. I hope Congress will be verry deliberate and digest it thoroughly before they Send it recommended to the States. I Sincerely hope that Such Gentlemen as were Members of Convention, and who have Seats in Congress may not be considered as verry proper Judges of their own Works.?

I pray a spirit of Wisdom and a Spirit of integrity prevade Congress, more especially at this time.

Document 5.2 William Findley: Concerns of an Officer of the Late Continental Army

William Findley was born in Ireland in 1741 and immigrated to Pennsylvania in 1763. He served eight years in the Pennsylvania General Assembly, and later served over 20 years in the United States Congress. Representing an area that was lukewarm at best about the new Constitution, his letter to the editor raised

David Redick to William Irvine, September 24, 1787.

several warnings. Knowing the reputations of Washington and Franklin, he urged citizens to not be dazzled by the glorious names and personages at the Constitutional Convention, but to examine the document closely. Should the national government be able to reach into the everyday lives of citizens? Should the states be stripped of powers, and the rights of the people not be openly declared and protected? These are just a few of the issues he raises. Consider the long list of threats to state, local, and individual liberties that he sees from this new central government. What warnings does he issue to the people of Pennsylvania? As part of a generation that fought to gain independence from a tyrannical central government, what does he warn is coming? How does he justify such a claim?

MR. OSWALD,

By inserting the following in your impartial paper, you will oblige yours, &c.

To the Citizens of Philadelphia.

Friends, Countrymen, Brethren and Fellow Citizens,

The important day is drawing near when you are to elect delegates to represent you in a Convention, on the result of whose deliberations will depend, in a great measure, your future happiness.

This convention is to determine whether or not the commonwealth of Pennsylvania shall adopt the plan of government proposed by the late convention of delegates from the different states, which sat in this city.

With a heart full of anxiety for the preservation of your dearest rights, I presume to address you on this important occasion—In the name of sacred liberty, dearer to us than our property and our lives. I request your most earnest attention.

The proposed plan of continental government is now fully known to you. You have read it I trust with the attention it deserves? You have heard the objections that have been made to it? You have heard the answers to these objections.

If you have attended to the whole with candor and unbiassed minds, as becomes men that are possessed and deserving of freedom, you must have been alarmed at the result of your observations. Notwith-standing the splendor of names which has attended the publication of the new constitution, notwithstanding the sophistry and vain reasonings that have been urged to support its principles; alas! you must at least have concluded that great men are not always infallible, and that patriotism itself may be led into essential errors.

The objections that have been made to the new constitution, are these:

1. It is not merely (as it ought to be) a CONFEDERATION of STATES, but a GOVERNMENT of INDIVIDUALS.

2. The powers of Congress extend to the *lives*, the *liberties* and the *property* of every citizen.

3. The *sovereignty* of the different states is *ipso facto* destroyed in its most essential parts.

4. What remains of it will only tend to create violent dissentions between the state governments and the Congress, and terminate in the ruin of the one or the other.

5. The consequence must therefore be, either that the *union* of the states will be destroyed by a violent struggle, or that their sovereignty will be swallowed up by silent encroachments into a universal aristocracy because it is clear, that if two different *sovereign powers* have a co-equal command over the *purses* of the citizens, they will struggle for the spoils, and the weakest will be in the end obliged to yield to the efforts of the strongest.

From *Independent Gazetteer*, November 6, 1787.

6. Congress being possessed of these immense powers, the liberties of the states and of the people are not secured by a bill or DECLARATION OF RIGHTS.

7. The *sovereignty* of the states is not expressly reserved, the *form* only, and not the SUBSTANCE of their government, is guaranteed to them by express words.

8. TRIAL BY JURY, that sacred bulwark of liberty, is ABOLISHED IN CIVIL CASES, and Mr. W—, one of the convention, has told you, that not being able to agree as to the FORM of establishing this point, they have left you deprived of the SUBSTANCE. Here are his own words—*The subject was involved in difficulties. The convention found the task* TOO DIFFICULT *for them, and left the business as it stands.*

9. THE LIBERTY OF THE PRESS is not secured, and the powers of congress are fully adequate to its destruction, as they are to have the trial of *libels*, or *pretended libels* against the United States, and may be a cursed abominable STAMP ACT (as the *Bowdoin administration* has done in Massachusetts) preclude you effectually from all means of information. *Mr. W— has given you no answer to these arguments.*

10. Congress have the power of keeping up a STANDING ARMY in time of peace, and Mr. W— has told you THAT IT WAS NECESSARY.

11. The LEGISLATIVE and EXECUTIVE powers are not kept separate as every one of the American constitutions declares they ought to be; but they are mixed in a manner entirely novel and unknown, even to the constitution of Great Britain; because,

12. In England the king only, has a *nominal negative* over the proceedings of the legislature, which he has NEVER DARED TO EXERCISE since the days of *King William*, whereas by the new constitution, both the president general and the senate TWO EXECUTIVE BRANCHES OF GOVERNMENT, have that negative and are intended to *support each other in the exercise of it.*

13. The representation of the lower house is too small, consisting only of 65 members.

14. That of the senate is so small that it renders its extensive powers extremely dangerous: it is to consist only of 26 members, two-thirds of whom must concur to conclude any *treaty or alliance* with foreign powers: Now we will suppose that five of them are absent, sick, dead, or unable to attend, *twenty-one* will remain, and eight of these (*one-third*, and *one* over) may prevent the conclusion of any treaty, even the most favorable to America. Here will be a fine field for the intrigues and even the *bribery* and *corruption* of European powers.

15. The most important branches of the EXECUTIVE DEPARTMENT are to be put into the hands of a *single magistrate*, who will be in fact an ELECTIVE KING. The MILITARY, the land and naval forces are to be entirely at his disposal, and therefore:

16. Should the *senate*, by the intrigues of foreign powers, become devoted to foreign influence, as was the case of late in *Sweden*, the people will be obliged, as the *Swedes* have been, to seek their refuge in the arms of the *monarch* or PRESIDENT GENERAL.

17. ROTATION, that noble prerogative of liberty, is entirely excluded from the new system of government, and great men may and probably will be continued in office during their lives.

18. ANNUAL ELECTIONS are abolished, and the people are not to reassume their rights until the expiration of *two, four* and *six* years.

19. Congress are to have the power of fixing the *time, place* and *manner* of holding elections, so as to keep them forever subjected to their influence.

20. The importation of slaves is not to be prohibited until the year 1808, and SLAVERY will probably resume its empire in Pennsylvania.

21. The MILITIA is to be under the immediate command of congress, and men *conscientiously scrupulous of bearing arms*, may be compelled to perform military duty.

22. The new government will be EXPENSIVE beyond any we have ever experienced, the *judicial* department alone, with its concomitant train of *judges, justices, chancellors, clerks, sheriffs, coroners, escheators, state attornies and solicitors, constables, &c.* in every state and in every county in each state, will be a burden beyond the utmost abilities of the people to bear, and upon the whole.

23. A government partaking OF MONARCHY and aristocracy will be fully and firmly established, and liberty will be but a name to adorn the short historic page of the halcyon days of America.

These, my countrymen, are the objections that have been made to the new proposed system of government; and if you read the system itself with attention, you will find them all to be founded in truth. But what have you been told in answer?

I pass over the sophistry of Mr. W—, in his equivocal speech at the state house. His pretended arguments have been echoed and reechoed by every retailer of politics, and *victoriously* refuted by several patriotic pens. Indeed if you read this famous speech in a cool dispassionate moment, you will find it to contain no more than a train of pitiful sophistry and evasions, unworthy of the man who spoke them. I have taken notice of some of them in stating the objections, and then must, I am sure, have excited your *pity* and *indignation.* Mr. W— is a man of sense, learning and extensive information, unfortunately for him he has never sought the more solid fame of patriotism. During the late war he narrowly escaped the effects of popular rage, and the people seldom arm themselves against a citizen in vain. The whole tenor of his political conduct has always been strongly tainted with the spirit of *high aristocracy*, he has never been known to join in a truly popular measure, and his talents have ever been devoted to the patrician interest. His lofty carriage indicates the lofty mind that animates him, a mind able to conceive and perform great things, but which unfortunately can see nothing great out of the pale of power and worldly grandeur; despising what he calls the inferior order of the people, popular liberty and popular assemblies offer to his exalted imagination an idea of meanness and contemptribility which he hardly seeks to conceal—He sees at a distance the pomp and pageantry of courts, he sighs after those stately palaces and that apparatus of human greatness which his vivid fancy has taught him to consider as the supreme good. Men of sublime minds, he conceives, were born a different race from the rest of the sons of men, to them, and them only, he imagines, high heaven intended to commit the reins of earthly government, the remaining part of mankind he sees below at an immense distance, they, he thinks were born to serve, to administer food to the ambition of their superiors, and become the footstool of their power—Such is Mr. W—, and fraught with these high ideas, it is no wonder that he should exert all his talents to support a form of govern-

ment so admirably contrived to carry them into execution—But when the people, who possess collectively a mass knowledge superior to his own, inquire into the principles of that government on the establishment or rejection of which depend their dearest concerns, when he is called upon by the voice of thousands to come and explain that favorite system which he holds forth as an object of their admiration, he comes—he attempts to support by reasoning what reason never dictated, and finding the attempt vain, his great mind, made for nobler purposes, is obliged to stoop to mean evasions and pitiful sophistry; himself not deceived, he strives to deceive the people, and the treasonable attempt delineates his true character, beyond the reach of the pencil of a *West* or *Peale,* or the pen of a *Valerius.*

And yet that speech, weak and insidious as it is, is the only attempt that has been made to support by argument that Political monster THE PROPOSED CONSTITUTION. I have sought in vain amidst the immense heap of trash that has been published on the subject, an argument worthy of refutation, and I have not been able to find it. If you can bear the disgust which the reading of those pieces must naturally occasion, and which I have felt in the highest degree, read them, my fellow citizens, and say whether they contain the least shadow of logical reasoning, say (laying your hands upon your hearts) whether there is any thing in them that can impress unfeigned conviction upon your unprejudiced minds.

One of them only I shall take notice of, in which I find that argument is weakly attempted. This piece is signed "AN AMERICAN CITIZEN" and has appeared with great pomp in four succeeding numbers in several of our newspapers. But if you read it attentively, you will find that it does not tell us what the new constitution is, but what it IS NOT, and extolls it on the sole ground that it does not contain ALL the principles of tyranny with which the European Governments are disgraced.

But where argument entirely failed, nothing remained for the supporters of the new constitution but to endeavor to inflame your passions—The attempt has been made and I am sorry to find not entirely without effect. The great names of WASHINGTON and FRANKLIN, have been taken in vain and shockingly prostituted to effect the most infamous purposes. What! because our august chieftain has subscribed his name in his capacity of president of the convention to the plan offered by them to the states, and because the venerable sage of Pennsylvania, has *testified* by his signature that *the majority of the delegates of this state* assented to the same plan, will any one infer from this that it has met with their entire approbation, and that they consider it as the master piece of human wisdom? I am apt to think the contrary, and I have good reasons to ground my opinion on.

In the first place we have found by the publication of *Charles Cotesworth Pinckney*, Esquire, one of the signing members of the convention, who has expressed the most pointed disapprobation of many important parts of the new plan of government, that all the members whose names appear at the bottom of this instrument of tyranny have not concurred in its adoption. Many of them might conceive themselves bound by the opinion of the majority of their state, and leaving the people to their own judgment upon the form of government offered to them, might have conceived it impolitic by refusing to sign their names, to offer to the world the lamentable spectacle of the disunion of a body on the decisions of whom the people had rested all their hopes. We KNOW, and the long sitting of the convention tells us, that, (as it is endeavoured to persuade us) concord and unanimity did not reign exclusively among them. The thick veil of secrecy with which their proceedings have been covered, has left us entirely in the dark, as to the *debates* that took place, and the unaccountable SUPPRESSION OF THEIR JOURNALS, the highest insult that could be offered to the majesty of the people, shews clearly that the whole of the new plan was entirely the work of an *aristrocratic majority*.

But let us suppose for a moment that the proposed government was the unanimous result of the deliberations of the convention—must it on that account preclude an investigation of its merits? Are the people to be dictated to without appeal by any set of men, however great, however dignified? Freedom spurns at the idea and rejects it with disdain—We appeal to the collective wisdom of a great nation, we appeal to the general sense which is easily to be obtained through the channel of a multitude of free presses, from the opinions of *thirty-nine* men, who secluded from the rest of the world, without the possibility of conferring with the rest of their fellow-citizens, have had no opportunity of rectifying the errors into which they may have been led by the *most designing* among them. We have seen names not less illustrious than those of the members of the late convention, subscribed to the present *reprobated* articles of confederation, and if those patriots have erred, there is no reason to suppose that a succeeding set should be more free from error. Nay the very men, who advocate so strongly the new plan of government, and support it with the infallibility of Doctor Franklin, affect to despise the present constitution of Pennsylvania, which was dictated and avowed by that venerable patriot—They are conscious that he does not entirely approve of the new plan, whose principles are so different from those he has established in our ever-glorious constitution, and there is no doubt that it is the reason that has induced them to leave his respected name out of the *ticket* for the approaching election.

Now then my fellow-citizens, my brethren, my friends; if the sacred flame of liberty be not extinguished in your breasts, if you have any regard for the happiness of yourselves, and your posterity, let me entreat you, earnestly entreat you by all that is dear and sacred to freemen, to consider well before you take an awful step which may involve in its consequences the ruin of millions yet unborn—You are on the brink of a dreadful precipice;—in the name therefore of holy liberty, for which I have fought and for which we have all suffered, I call upon you to make a solemn pause before you proceed. One step more, and perhaps the scene of freedom is closed forever in America. Let not a set of aspiring despots, *who make us* SLAVES and *tell us 'tis our* CHARTER, wrest from you those invaluable blessings, for which the most illustrious sons of America have bled and died—but exert yourselves, like men, like freemen and like Americans, to transmit unimpaired to your latest posterity those rights, those liberties, which have ever been so dear to you, and which it is yet in your power to preserve.

Philadelphia, November 3, 1787.
An Officer of the late Continental Army.

Document 5.3 Pennsylvania's Ratifying Convention Debates the Need for a Bill of Rights

Pennsylvania was the first large state to ratify the new Constitution. With the convention meeting literally downstairs from where the legislature was in session, the call for a ratifying convention came almost as soon as the Founding Fathers finished their work. This was the first state where Federalists used strong-arm tactics to force people to be present, rushed through an election for the convention before country opposition to the new Constitution could organize, and haughtily refused to consider any changes in the document. James Wilson was the only member of the Constitutional Convention to also be a member of the Pennsylvania ratifying convention; thus, fellow Federalists treated his views as holy writ. Wilson became the first leading proponent of the view that this was a good government, and good governments never do bad things to their own people. John Smilie, one of the leading proponents of Pennsylvania's own constitution, debated the need for a national bill of rights in the new document. Why does Wilson claim that the national constitution does not need a bill of rights? What arguments does Smilie make for including one?

Mr. Wilson. Mr. President, we are repeatedly called upon to give some reason why a bill of rights has not been annexed to the proposed plan. I not only think that enquiry is at this time unnecessary and out of order, but I expect, at least, that those who desire us to shew why it was omitted, will furnish some arguments to shew that it ought to have been inserted; for the proof of the affirmative naturally falls upon them. But the truth is, Sir, that this circumstance, which has since occasioned so much clamour and debate, never struck the mind of any member in the late convention 'till, I believe, within three days of the dissolution of that body, and even then, of so little account was the idea, that it passed off in a short conversation, without introducing a formal debate, or assuming the shape of a motion. For, Sir, the attempt to have thrown into the national scale an instrument in order to evince that any power not mentioned in the constitution was reserved, would have been spurned at as an insult to the common understanding of mankind. In civil government it is certain, that bills of rights are unnecessary and useless, nor can I conceive whence the contrary notion has arisen. Virginia has no bill of rights, and will it be said that her constitution was the less free?

Mr. Smilie. I beg leave to observe, Mr. President, that although it has not been inserted in the printed volume of state constitutions, yet I have been assured by Mr. Mason, that Virginia has a bill of rights.

Mr. Wilson. I do not rely upon the information of Mr. Mason, or of any other gentleman on a question of this kind, but I refer to the authenticity of the volume which contains the state constitutions, and in that Virginia has no bill of rights. But, Sir, has South Carolina no security for her liberties? that state has no bill of rights. Are the citizens of the Eastern shore of the Delaware more secured in their freedom, or more enlightened on the subject of government than the citizens of the western shore? New Jersey has no bill of rights; New-York has none; Connecticut has none, and Rhode-Island has none. Thus, Sir, it appears from the example of other states, as well as from principle, that a bill of rights is neither an essential nor a necessary instrument in framing a system of government, since liberty may exist and be as well secured without it. But it was not only unnecessary, but on this occasion, it was found impracticable; for who will be bold enough to undertake to enumerate all the rights of the people? and when the attempt to enumerate them is made, it must be remembered that if the enumeration is not complete, every thing not expressly mentioned will be presumed to be purposely omitted. So it must be with a bill of rights, and an omission in stating the powers granted to the government, is not so dangerous as an omission in recapitulating the rights reserved by the people. We have already seen the origin of magna charta, and tracing the subject still further, we find the petition of rights

---

James Wilson and John Smilie Debate, November 28, 1787.

claiming the liberties of the people, according to the laws and statutes of the realm, of which the great charter was the most material; so that here again recourse is had to the old source from which their liberties are derived, the grant of the king. It was not 'till the revolution that the subject was placed upon a different footing, and even then the people did not claim their liberties as an inherent right, but as the result of an original contract between them and the sovereign. Thus, Mr. President, an attention to the situation of England, will shew that the conduct of that country in respect to bills of rights, cannot furnish an example to the inhabitants of the United States, who by the revolution have regained all their natural rights, and possess their liberty neither by grant nor contract. In short, Sir, I have said that a bill of rights would have been improperly annexed to the federal plan, and for this plain reason, that it would imply that whatever is not expressed was given, which is not the principle of the proposed constitution.

Mr. Smilie. The arguments which have been urged, Mr. President, have not in my opinion, satisfactorily shewn that a bill of rights would have been an improper, nay, that it is not a necessary appendage to the proposed system. As it has been denied that Virginia possesses a bill of rights, I shall on that subject only observe, that Mr. Mason, a gentleman certainly of great information and integrity, has assured me that such a thing does exist, and I am persuaded, I shall be able at a future period to lay it before the convention. But, Sir, the state of Delaware has a bill of rights, and I believe one of the honourable members (Mr. M'Kean) who now contests the necessity and propriety of that instrument, took a very conspicuous part in the formation of the Delaware government. It seems however that the members of the federal convention were themselves convinced, in some degree, of the expediency and propriety of a bill of rights, for we find them expressly declaring that the writ of Habeas Corpus and the trial by jury in criminal cases shall not be suspended or infringed. How does this indeed agree with the maxim that whatever is not given is reserved? Does it not rather appear from the reservation of these two articles that every thing else, which is not specified, is included in the powers delegated to the government? This, sir, must prove the necessity of a full and explicit declaration of rights; and when we further consider the extensive, the undefined powers vested in the administrators of this system, when we consider the system itself as a great political compact between the governors and the governed, a plain, strong, and accurate, criterion by which the people might at once determine when, and in what instance, their rights were violated, is a preliminary, without which this plan ought not to be adopted. So loosely, so inaccurately are the powers which are enumerated in this constitution defined, that it will be impossible, without a test of that kind, to ascertain the limits of authority, and to declare when government has degenerated into oppression. In that event the contest will arise between the people and the rulers: "You have exceeded the powers of your office, you have oppressed us," will be the language of the suffering citizens. The answer of the government will be short"—We have not exceeded our power: you have no test by which you can prove it." Hence, Sir, it will be impracticable to stop the progress of tyranny, for there will be no check but the people, and their exertions must be futile and uncertain; since it will be difficult indeed, to communicate to them, the violation that has been committed, and their proceedings will be neither systematical nor unanimous. It is said, however, that the difficulty of framing a bill of rights was insurmountable: but, Mr. President, I can not agree in this opinion. Our experience, and the numerous precedents before us, would have furnished a very sufficient guide. At present there is no security, even for the rights of conscience, and under the sweeping force of the sixth article, every principle of a bill of rights, every stipulation for the most sacred and invaluable privileges of man, are left at the mercy of government.

Document 5.4 "Giles Hickory" Attacks the Opponents of the Constitution

Many writers involved in the pamphlet struggle over the Constitution used pseudonyms to protect themselves from public anger, or from being targeted by their enemies. Some chose the names of famous fighters against tyranny, while supporters chose names to sound as though typical Americans supported the document. So it was with "Giles Hickory," better known as Noah Webster. Noah was born in Hartford, Connecticut in 1758. In 1783 he wrote a three-volume textbook titled *A Grammatical Institute of the English Language*, which most people called the "Blue Backed Speller" because of its cover. Webster had problems copyrighting his books because of the weak national government and conflicting state laws, and for this reason became an outspoken supporter of the new Constitution. Here he attacks Antifederalists who want a bill of rights to protect American liberties. What difference does he make between the need for protections from a monarchy and an elected legislature? Does he ever admit that elected officials can be corrupted by special interests while in office, or be evil to begin with? Could the fact that the new Constitution explicitly protects property rights (e.g., copyrights) influence his arguments?

One of the principal objections to the new Federal Constitution is, that it contains no *Bill of Rights*. This objection, I presume to assert, is founded on ideas of government that are totally false. Men seem determined to adhere to old prejudices, and reason *wrong*, because our ancestors reasoned *right*. A Bill of Rights against the encroachments of Kings and Barons, or against any power independent of the people, is perfectly intelligible; but a Bill of Rights against the encroachments of an elective Legislature, that is, against our *own* encroachments on *ourselves*, is a curiosity in government.

One half the people who read books, have so little ability to apply what they read to their own practice, that they had better not read at all. The English nation, from which we descended, have been gaining their liberties, inch by inch, by forcing concessions from the crown and the Barons, during the course of six centuries. *Magna Charta*, which is called the palladium of English liberty, was dated in 1215, and the people of England were not represented in Parliament till the year 1265. Magna Charta established the rights of the Barons and the clergy against the encroachments of royal prerogative; but the commons or people were hardly noticed in that deed. There was but one clause in their favor, which stipulated that, "no villain or rustic should, by any fine, be bereaved of his carts, plows and instruments of husbandry." As for the rest, they were considered as a part of the property belonging to an estate, and were transferred, as other moveables, at the will of their owners. In the succeeding reign, they were permitted to send Representatives to Parliament; and from that time have been gradually assuming their proper degree of consequence in the British Legislature. In such a nation, every law or statute that defines the powers of the crown, and circumscribes them within determinate limits, must be considered as a barrier to guard popular liberty. Every acquisition of freedom must be established as a *right*, and solemnly recognized by the supreme power of the nation; lest it should be again resumed by the crown under pretence of ancient prerogative; For this reason, the habeas corpus act passed in the reign of Charles 2d, the statute of the 2d of William and Mary, and many others which are declaratory of certain privileges, are justly considered as the pillars of English freedom.

These statutes are however not esteemed because they are unalterable; for the same power that enacted them, can at any moment repeal them; but they are esteemed, because they are barriers erected by the Representatives of the nation, against a power that exists independent of their own choice.

But the same reasons for such declaratory constitutions do not exist in America, where the supreme power is *the people in their Representatives*. The *Bills of Rights*, prefixed to several of the constitutions of the United States, if considered as assigning the reasons of our separation from a foreign government, or as solemn declarations of right against the encroachments of a foreign jurisdiction, are perfectly rational, and were doubtless necessary. But if they are considered as barriers against the encroachments of our own Legislatures, or as constitutions unalterable by posterity, I venture to pronounce them nugatory, and to the last degree, absurd.

In our governments, there is no power of legislation, independent of the people; no power that has an interest detached from that of the public; consequently there is no power existing against which it is necessary to guard. While our Legislatures therefore remain elective, and the rulers have the same interest in the laws, as the subjects have, the rights of the people will be perfectly secure without any declaration in their favor.

But this is not the principal point. I undertake to prove that a standing *Bill of Rights* is *absurd*, because no constitutions, in a free government, can

---

From *American Magazine*, December 1787.

be unalterable. The present generation have indeed a right to declare what they deem a *privilege*; but they have no right to say what the next generation shall deem a privilege. A State is a supreme corporation that never dies. Its powers, when it acts for itself, are at all times, equally extensive; and it has the same right to *repeal* a law this year, as it had to *make* it the last. If therefore our posterity are bound by our constitutions, and can neither amend nor annul them, they are to all intents and purposes our slaves.

But it will be enquired, have we then no right to say, that trial by jury, the liberty of the press, the habeas corpus writ and other invaluable privileges, shall never be infringed nor destroyed? By no means. We have the same right to say that lands shall descend in a particular mode to the heirs of the deceased proprietor, and that such a mode shall never be altered by future generations, as we have to pass a law that the trial by jury shall never be abridged. The right of jury-trial, which we deem invaluable, may in future cease to be a privilege; or other modes of trial more satisfactory to the people, may be devised. Such an event is neither impossible nor improbable. Have we then a right to say that our posterity shall not be judges of their own circumstances? The very attempt to make *perpetual* constitutions, is the assumption of a right to control the opinions of future generations; and to legislate for those over whom we have as little authority as we have over a nation in Asia. Nay we have as little right to say that trial by jury shall be perpetual, as the English, in the reign of Edward the Confessor, had, to bind their posterity forever to decide causes by fiery Ordeal, or single combat. There are perhaps many laws and regulations, which from their consonance to the eternal rules of justice, will always be good and conformable to the sense of a nation. But most institutions in society, by reason of an unceasing change of circumstances, either become altogether improper or require amendment; and

every nation has at all times, the right of judging of its circumstances and determining on the propriety of changing its laws.

The English writers talk much of the omnipotence of Parliament; and yet they seem to entertain some scruples about their right to change particular parts of their constitution. I question much whether Parliament would not hesitate to change, on any occasion, an article of Magna Charta. Mr. Pitt, a few years ago, attempted to reform the mode of representation in Parliament. Immediately an uproar was raised against the measure, as *unconstitutional*. The representation of the kingdom, when first established, was doubtless equal and wise; but by the increase of some cities and boroughs and the depopulation of others, it has become extremely unequal. In some boroughs there is scarcely an elector left to enjoy its privileges. If the nation feels no great inconvenience from this change of circumstances, under the old mode of representation, a reform is unnecessary. But if such a change has produced any national evils of magnitude enough to be felt, the present form of electing the Representatives of the nation, *however constitutional*, and venerable for its antiquity, may at any time be amended, if it should be the sense of Parliament. The *expediency* of the alteration must always be a matter of opinion; but all scruples as to the *right* of making. it are totally groundless.

Magna Charta may be considered as a contract between two parties, the King and the Barons, and no contract can be altered but by the consent of both parties. But whenever any article of that deed or contract shall become inconvenient or oppressive, the King, Lords and Commons may either amend or annul it at pleasure.

The same reasoning applies to each of the United States, and to the Federal Republic in general. But an important question will arise from the foregoing remarks, which must be the subject of another paper.

Document 5.5 Dissent of the Minority of the Pennsylvania Convention

Favored by the actions of the Pennsylvania legislature, supporters of the new Constitution dominated the elections to the ratifying convention and the convention itself. They refused to consider amendments to the Constitution, insulted the sincere opponents of the document, and sometimes utilized physical violence against anyone who opposed them. The Federalists high-handed actions and haughty attitudes raised questions about their motives and tactics outside of Pennsylvania, and some constitutional historians suggest they almost caused the defeat of the new government. Is this the behavior to be expected from the "good government" toward its own citizens? Where is the virtue in their actions? Twenty-one members of the Pennsylvania convention published the "Dissent of the Minority of the Pennsylvania Convention" and distributed it nationally. This lengthy document raised the issues of representation in the new Congress, uses of coercion by the Federalists, and the Founding Fathers' deliberate elimination of many commonly accepted rights and protections. Most of the objections raised in later conventions are first presented in this document. The Pennsylvania Minority raised the threat of the nation's prosperity being determined by a 25-man quorum in Congress, which would have no knowledge of the needs of most of the people in the United States. They warned that the system of election called for in the Constitution would be out of the people's control, and could be rigged so only the wealthy and idle rich could afford to run for office. This would allow a new aristocracy to run the nation. What other charges does the Pennsylvania Minority bring against the Federalists and the new government? What threats to liberty are most obvious?

The Address and Reasons of Dissent of the Minority of the Convention of the State of Pennsylvania to their Constituents.

It was not until after the termination of the late glorious contest, which made the people of the United States an independent nation, that any defect was discovered in the present confederation. It was formed by some of the ablest patriots in America. It carried us successfully through the war; and the virtue and patriotism of the people, with their disposition to promote the common cause, supplied the want of power in Congress.

The requisition of Congress for the five *per cent.* impost was made before the peace, so early as the first of February, 1781, but was prevented taking effect by the refusal of one state; yet it is probable every state in the union would have agreed to this measure at that period, had it not been for the extravagant terms in which it was demanded. The requisition was new moulded in the year 1783, and accompanied with an additional demand of certain supplementary funds for 25 years. Peace had now taken place, and the United States found themselves labouring under a considerable foreign and domestic debt, incurred during the war. The requisition of 1783 was commensurate with the interest of the debt, as it was then calculated; but it has been more accurately ascertained since that time. The domestic debt has been found to fall several millions of dollars short of the calculation, and it has lately been considerably diminished by large sales of the western lands. The

states have been called on by Congress annually for supplies until the general system of finance porposed in 1783 should take place.

It was at this time that the want of an efficient federal government was first complained of, and that the powers vested in Congress were found to be inadequate to the procuring of the benefits that should result from the union. The impost was granted by most of the states, but many refused the supplementary funds; the annual requisitions were set at nought by some of the states, while others complied with them by legislative acts, but were tardy in their payments, and Congress found themselves incapable of complying with their engagements, and supporting the federal government. It was found that our national character was sinking in the opinion of foreign nations. The Congress could make treaties of commerce, but could not enforce the observance of them. We were suffering from the restrictions of foreign nations, who had shackled our commerce, while we were unable to retaliate: and all now agreed that it would be advantageous to the union to enlarge the powers of Congress; that they should be enabled in the amplest manner to regulate commerce, and to lay and collect duties on the imports throughout the United States. With this view a convention was first proposed by Virginia, and finally recommended by Congress for the different states to appoint deputies to meet in convention, "for the purposes of revising and amending the present articles of confederation, so as to make them adequate to the exigencies of the union." This recommendation the legislatures of twelve states complied with so hastily as not to consult their constituents on the subject; and though the different legislatures had no authority from their constituents for the purpose, they probably apprehended

---

From *Pennsylvania Packet*, December 1787.

the necessity would justify the measure; and none of them extended their ideas at that time further than "revising and amending the present articles of confederation." Pennsylvania by the act appointing deputies expressly confined their powers to this object; and though it is probable that some of the members of the assembly of this state had at that time in contemplation to annihilate the present confederation, as well as the constitution of Pennsylvania, yet the plan was not sufficiently matured to communicate it to the public.

The majority of the legislature of this commonwealth, were at that time under the influence of the members from the city of Philadelphia. They agreed that the deputies sent by them to convention should have no compensation for their services, which determination was calculated to prevent the election of any member who resided at a distance from the city. It was in vain for the minority to attempt electing delegates to the convention, who understood the circumstances, and the feelings of the people, and had a common interest with them. They found a disposition in the leaders of the majority of the house to chuse themselves and some of their dependents. The minority attempted to prevent this by agreeing to vote for some of the leading members, who they knew had influence enough to be appointed at any rate, in hopes of carrying with them some respectable citizens of Philadelphia, in whose principles and integrity they could have more confidence; but even in this they were disappointed, except in one member: the eighth member was added at a subsequent session of the assembly.

The Continental convention met in the city of Philadelphia at the time appointed. It was composed of some men of excellent characters; of others who were more remarkable for their ambition and cunning, than their patriotism; and of some who had been opponents to the independence of the United States. The delegates from Pennsylvania were, six of them, uniform and decided opponents to the constitution of this commonwealth. The convention sat upwards of four months. The doors were kept shut, and the members brought under the most solemn engagements of secrecy. Some of those who opposed their going so far beyond their powers, retired, hopeless, from the convention, others had the firmness to refuse signing the plan altogether; and many who did sign it, did it not as a system they wholly approved, but as the best that could be then obtained, and notwithstanding the time spent on this subject, it is agreed on all hands to be a work of haste and accommodation.

Whilst the gilded chains were forging in the secret conclave, the meaner instruments of despotism without, were busily employed in alarming the fears of the people with dangers which did not exist, and exciting their hopes of greater advantages from the expected plan than even the best government on earth could produce.

The proposed plan had not many hours issued forth from the womb of suspicious secrecy, until such as were prepared for the purpose, were carrying about petitions for people to sign, signifying their approbation of the system, and requesting the legislature to call a convention. While every measure was taken to intimidate the people against opposing it, the public papers teemed with the most violent threats against those who should dare to think for themselves, and *tar and feathers* were liberally promised to all those who not immediately join in supporting the proposed government be it what it would. Under such circumstances petitions in favour of calling a convention were signed by great numbers in and about the city, before they had leisure to read and examine the system, many of whom, now they are better acquainted with it, and have had time to investigate its principles, are heartily opposed to it. The petitions were speedily handed into the legislature.

Affairs were in this situation when on the 28th of September last a resolution was proposed to the assembly by a member of the house who had been also a member of the federal convention, for calling a state convention, to be elected within ten days for the purpose of examining and adopting the proposed constitution of the United States, though at this time the house had not received it from Congress. This attempt was opposed by a minority, who after offering every argument in their power to prevent the precipitate measure, without effect, absented themselves from the house as the only alternative left them, to prevent the measure taking place previous to their constituents being acquainted with the business— That violence and outrage which had been so often threatened was now practised; some of the members were seized the next day by a mob collected for the purpose, and forcibly dragged to the house, and there detained by force whilst the quorum of the legislature, *so formed*, compleated their resolution. We shall dwell no longer on this subject, the people of Pennsylvania have been already acquainted therewith. We would only further observe that every member of the legislature, previously to taking his seat, by solemn oath of affirmation, declares, "that he will not do or consent to any act or thing whatever that shall have a tendency to lessen or abridge their rights and priveleges, as declared in the constitution of this state." And that constitution which they are so solemnly sworn to support cannot legally be altered but by a recommendation of the council of censors, who alone are authorised to propose alterations and ammendments, and even these must be published at least *six months*, for the consideration of the people.—The proposed system of government for the United States, if adopted, will alter and may annihilate the constitution of Pennsylvania; and therefore the legislature had no authority whatever to recommend the calling a convention for that purpose. This proceeding could not be considered as binding on the people of this commonwealth. The house was formed by violence, some of the members composing it were detained there by force, which alone would have vitiated any proceedings, to which they were otherwise competent; but had the legislature been legally formed, this business was absolutely without their power.

In this situation of affairs were the subscribers elected members of the convention of Pennsylvania. A convention called by a legislature in direct violation of their duty, and composed in part of members, who were compelled to attend for that purpose, to consider of a constitution proposed by a convention of the United States, who were not appointed for the purpose of framing a new form of government, but whose powers were expressly confined to altering and amending the present articles of confederation. Therefore the members of the continental convention in proposing the plan acted as individuals, and not as deputies from Pennsylvania. The assembly who called the state convention acted as individuals, and not as the legislature of Pennsylvania; nor could they or the convention chosen on their recommendation have authority to do any act or thing, that can alter or annihilate the constitution of Pennsylcania (both of which will be done by the new constitution) nor are their proceedings in our opinion, at all binding on the people.

The election for members of the convention was held at so early a period and the want of information was so great, that some of us did not know of it until after it was over, and we have reason to believe that great numbers of the people of Pennsylvania have not yet had an opportunity of sufficiently examining the proposed constitution. We apprehend that no change can take place that will affect the internal government or constitution of this commonwealth, unless a majority of the people should evidence a wish for such a change; but on examining the number of votes given for members of the present state convention, we find that of upwards of *seventy thousand* freemen who are entitled to vote in Pennsylvania, the whole convention has been elected by about *thirteen thousand* voters, and though *two thirds* of the members of the convention have thought proper to ratify the proposed constitution, yet those *two thirds* were elected by the votes of only *six thousand and eight hundred* freemen.

In the city of Philadelphia and some of the eastern counties, the junto that took the lead in the business agreed to vote for none but such as would solemnly promise to adopt the system in toto, without exercising their judgment. In many of the counties the people did not attend the elections as they had not an opportunity of judging of the plan. Others did not consider themselves bound by the call of a set of men who assembled at the statehouse in Philadelphia, and assumed the name of the legislature of Pennsylvania; and some were prevented from voting, by the violence of the party who were determined at all events to force down the measure. To such lengths did the tools of despotism carry their outrage, that in the night of the election for members of convention, in the city of Philadelphia, several of the subscribers (being then in the city to transact your business) were grossly abused, ill-treated and insulted while they were quiet in their lodgings, though they did not interfere, nor had any thing to do with the said election, but, as they apprehend, because they were supposed to be adverse to the proposed constitution, and would not tamely surrender those sacred rights, which you had committed to their charge.

The convention met, and the same disposition was soon manifested in considering the proposed constitution, that had been exhibited in every other stage of the business. We were prohibited by an express vote of the convention, from taking any question on the separate articles of the plan, and reduced to the necessity of adopting or rejecting in toto.—'Tis true the majority permitted us to debate on each article, but restrained us from proposing amendments." They also determined not to permit us to enter on the minutes our reasons of dissent against any of the articles, nor even on the final question our reasons of dissent against the whole. Thus situated we entered on the examination of the proposed system of government, and found it to be such as we could not adopt, without, as we conceived, surrendering up your dearest rights. We offered our objections to the convention, and opposed those parts of the plan, which, in our opinion, would be injurious to you, in the best manner we were able; and closed our arguments by offering the following propositions to the convention.

1. The right of conscience shall be held inviolable; and neither the legislative, executive nor judical powers of the United States shall have authority to alter, abrogate, or infringe any part of the constitution of the several states, which provide for the preservation of liberty in matters of religion.

2. That in controvesies respecting property, and in suits between man and man, trial by jury shall remain as heretofore, as well in the federal courts, as in those of the several states.

3. That in all capital and criminal prosecutions, a man has a right to demand the cause and nature of his accusation, as well in the federal courts, as in those of the several states; to be heard by himself and his counsel; to be confronted with the accusers and witnesses; to call for evidence in his favor, and a speedy trial by an impartial jury of his vicinage, without whose unanimous consent, he cannot be found guilty, nor can he be compelled to give evidence against himself; and that no man be deprived of his liberty, except by the law of the land or the judgment of his peers.

4. That excessive bail ought not to be required, nor excessive fines imposed, nor cruel nor unusual punishments inflicted.

5. That warrants unsupported by evidence, whereby any officer or messenger may be commanded or required to search suspected places, or to seize any person or persons, his or their property, not particularly described, are grievous and oppressive, and shall not be granted either by the magistrates of the federal government or others.

6. That the people have a right to the freedom of speech, of writing and publishing their sentiments, therefore, the freedom of the press shall not be restrained by any law of the United States.

7. That the people have a right to bear arms for the defence of themselves and their own state, or the United States, or for the purpose of killing game; and no law shall be passed for disarming the people of any of them, unless for crimes committed, or real danger of public injury from individuals; and as standing armies in the time of peace are dangerous to liberty, they ought not to be kept up; and that the military shall be kept under strict subordination to and be governed by the civil power.

8. The inhabitants of the several states shall have liberty to fowl and hunt in seasonable times, on the lands they hold, and on all other lands in the United States not inclosed, and in like manner to fish in all navigable waters, and others not private property, without being restained therein by any laws to be passed by the legislature of the United States.

9. That no law shall be passed to restrain the legislatures of the several states from enacting laws for imposing taxes, except imposts and duties on goods imported or exported, and that no taxes, except imposts and duties upon goods imported and exported, and postage on letters shall be levied by the authority of Congress.

10. That the house of representatives be properly increased in number; that elections shall remain free; that the several states shall have power to regulate the elections for senators and representatives, without being controuled either directly or indirectly by any interference on the part of the Congress; and that elections of representatives be annual.

11. That the power of organizing, arming and disciplining the militia (the manner of disciplining the militia to be prescribed by Congress) remain with the individual states, and that Congress shall not have authority to call or march any of the militia out of their own state, without the consent of such state, and for such length of time only as such state shall agree.

That the sovereignty, freedom and independency of the several states shall be retained, and every power, jurisdication and right which is not by this constitution expressly delegated to the United States in Congress assembled.

12. That the legislative, executive, and judicial powers be kept separate; and to this end that a constitutional council be appointed, to advise and assist the president, who shall be responsible for the advice they give, hereby the senators would be relieved from almost constant attendance; and also that the judges be made completely independent.

13. That no treaty which shall be directly opposed to the existing laws of the United States in Congress assembled, shall be valid until such laws shall be repealed, or made conformable to such treaty; neither shall any treaties be valid which are in contradiction to the constitution of the United States, or the constitutions of the several states.

14. That the judiciary power of the United States shall be confined to cases affecting ambassadors,

other public ministers and consuls; to cases of admiralty and maritime jurisdiction; to controversies to which the United States shall be a party; to controversies between two or more states—between a state and citizens of different states—between citizens claiming lands under grants of different states; and between a state or the citizens thereof and foreign states, and in criminal cases, to such only as are expressly enumerated in the constitution, & that the United States in Congress assembled, shall not have power to enact laws, which shall alter the laws of descents and distribution of the effects of deceased persons, the titles of lands or goods, or the regulation of contracts in the individual states.

After reading these propositions, we declared our willingness to agree to the plan, provided it was so amended as to meet those propositions, or something similar to them: and finally moved the convention to adjourn, to give the people of Pennsylvania time to consider the subject, and determine for themselves; but these were all rejected, and the final vote was taken, when our duty to you induced us to vote against the proposed plan, and to decline signing the ratification of the same.

During the discussion we met with many insults, and some personal abuse; we were not even treated with decency, during the sitting of the convention, by the persons in the gallery of the house; however, we flatter ourselves that in contending for the preservation of those invaluable rights you have thought proper to commit to our charge, we acted with a spirit becoming freemen, and being desirous that you might know the principles which actuated our conduct, and being prohibited from inserting our reasons of dissent on the minutes of the convention, we have subjoined them for your consideration, as to you alone we are accountable. It remains with you whether you will think those inestimable privileges, which you have so ably contended for, should be sacrificed at the shrine of despotism, or whether you mean to contend for them with the same spirit that has so often baffled the attempts of an aristocratic faction, to rivet the shackles of slavery on you and your unborn posterity.

Our objections are comprised under three general heads of dissent, viz.

We Dissent, first, because it is the opinion of the most celebrated writers on government, and confirmed by uniform experience, that a very extensive territory cannot be governed on the principles of freedom, otherwise than by a confederation of republics,

possessing all the powers of internal government; but united in the management of their general, and foreign concerns.

If any doubt could have been entertained of the truth of the foregoing principle, it has been fully removed by the concession of *Mr. Wilson*, one of the majority on this question; and who was one of the deputies in the late general convention. In justice to him, we will give his own words; they are as follows, viz. "The extent of country for which the new constitution was required, produced another difficulty in the business of the federal convention. It is the opinion of some celebrated writers, that to a small territory, the democratical; to a middling territory (as Montesquieu has termed it) the monarchial; and to an extensive territory, the despotic form of government is best adapted. Regarding then the wide and almost unbounded jurisdiction of the United States, at first view, the hand of despotism seemed necessary to controul, connect, and protect it; and hence the chief embarrassment rose. For, we know that, altho' our consitutents would chearfully submit to the legislative restraints of a free government, they would spurn at every attempt to shackle them with despotic power."—And again in another part of his speech he continues.—"It is probable that the dissolution of the state governments, and the establishment of one *consolidated empire* would be eligible in its nature, and satisfactory to the people in its administration? I think not, as I have given reasons to shew that so extensive a territory could not be governed, connected, and preserved, but by the *supremacy of despotic power*. All the exertions of the most potent emperors of Rome were not capable of keeping that empire together, which in extent was far inferior to the dominion of America."

We dissent, secondly, because the powers vested in Congress by this constitution, must necessarily annihilate and absorb the legislative, executive, and judicial powers of the several states, and produce from their ruins one consolidated government, which from the nature of things will be *an iron handed despotism*, as nothing short of the supremacy of despotic sway could connect and govern these United States under one government.

As the truth of this position is of such decisive importance, it ought to be fully investigated, and if it is founded to be clearly ascertained; for, should it be demonstrated, that the powers vested by this constitution in Congress, will have such an effect as necessarily to produce one consolidated government, the question then will be reduced to this short issue, viz. whether satiated with the blessings of liberty; whether repenting of the folly or so recently asserting their unalienable rights, against foreign despots at the expence of so much blood and treasure, and such painful and arduous struggles, the people of America are now willing to resign every privilege of freemen, and submit to the dominion of an absolute government, that will embrace all America in one chain of despotism; or whether they will with virtuous indignation, spurn at the shackles prepared for them, and confirm their liberties by a conduct becoming freemen.

That the new government will not be a confederacy of states, as it ought, but one consolidated government, founded upon the destruction of the several governments of the states, we shall now shew.

The powers of Congress under the new constitution, are complete and unlimited over the *purse* and the *sword*, and are perfectly independent of, and supreme over, the state governments; whose intervention in these great points is entirely destroyed. By virtue of their power of taxation, Congress may command the whole, or any part of the property of the people. They may impose what imposts upon commerce; they may impose what land taxes, poll taxes, excises, duties on all written instruments, and duties on every other article that they may judge proper; in short, every species of taxation, whether of an external or internal nature is comprised in section the 8th, of article the 1st, viz. "The Congress shall have power to lay and collect taxes, duties, imposts, and excises, to pay the debts, and provide for the common defence and general welfare of the United States."

As there is no one article of taxation reserved to the state governments, the Congress may monopolise every source of revenue, and thus indirectly demolish the state governments, for without funds they could not exist, the taxes, duties and excises imposed by Congress may be so high as to render it impracticable to levy further sums on the same articles; but whether this should be the case or not, if the state governments should presume to impose taxes, duties or excises, on the same articles with Congress, the latter may abrogate and repeal the laws whereby they are imposed, upon the allegation that they interfere with the due collection of their taxes, duties or excises, by virtue of the following clause, part of Section 8th, article 1st, viz. "To make all laws which shall be necessary and proper for carrying into execution the foregoing powers, and all other powers vested by this constitution in the government of the United States, or in any department or officer thereof."

The Congress might gloss over this conduct by construing every purpose for which the state legislatures now lay taxes, to be for the "*general welfare,*" and therefore as of their jurisdiction.

And the supremacy of the laws of the United States is established by article 6th, viz. "That this constitution and the laws of the United States, which shall be made in pursuance thereof, and *all treaties* made, or which shall be made, under the authority of the United States, shall be the *supreme law* of the *land;* and *the judges in every state shall be bound thereby; any thing in the constitution or laws of any state to the contrary notwithstanding.*" It has been alledged that the words "pursuant to the constitution," are a restriction upon the authority of Congress; but when it is considered that by other sections they are invested with every efficient power of government, and which may be exercised to the absolute destruction of the state governments, without any violation of even the forms of the constitution, this seeming restriction as well as every other restriction in it, appears to us to be nugatory and delusive; and only introduced as a blind upon the real nature of the government. In our opinion, "pursuant to the constitution," will be co-extensive with the *will* and *pleasure* of Congress, which, indeed, will be the only limitation of their powers.

We apprehend that two co-ordinate sovereignties would be a solecism in politics. That therefore as there is no line of distinction drawn between the general, and state governments; as the sphere of their jurisdiction is undefined, it would be contrary to the nature of things, that both should exist together, one or the other would necessarily triumph in the fullness of dominion. However the contest could not be of long continuance, as the state governments are divested of every means of defence, and will be obliged by "the supreme law of the land" *to yield at discretion.*

It has been objected to this total destruction of the state governments, that the existence of their legislatures is made essential to the organization of Congress; that they must assemble for the appointment of the senators and president general of the United States. True, the state legislatures may be continued for some years, as boards of appointment, merely, after they are divested of every other function, but the framers of the constitution foreseeing that the people will soon be disgusted with this solemn mockery of a government without power and usefulness, have made a provision for relieving them from the imposition, in section 4th, of article 1st, viz. "The times, places, and manner of holding elections for senators and representatives, shall be prescribed in each state by the legislature thereof; *but the Congress may at any time, by law make or alter such regulations; except as to the place of chusing senators."*

As Congress have the controul over the time of the appointment of the president general, of the senators and of the representatives of the United States, they may prolong their existence in office, for life, by postponing the time of their election and appointment, from period to period, under various pretences, such as an apprehansion of invasion, the factious disposition of the people, or any other plausible pretence that the occasion may suggest; and having thus obtained life-estates in the government, they may fill up the vacancies themsleves, by their controul over the mode of appointment; with this exception in regard to the senators, that as the place of appointment for them, must, by the constitution, be in the particular state, they may depute some body in the respective states, to fill up the vacancies in the senate, occasioned by death, until they can venture to assume it themselves. In this manner, may the only restriction in this clause be evaded. By virtue of the foregoing section, when the spirit of the people shall be gradually broken; when the general government shall be firmly established, and when a numerous standing army shall render opposition vain, the Congress may compleat the system of despotism, in renouncing all dependance on the people, by continuing themselves, and children in the government.

The celebrated *Montequieu*, in his Spirit of Laws, vol. I, page 12th, says, "That in a democracy there can be no exercise of sovereignty, but by the suffrages of the people, which are their will; now the sovereigns will is the sovereign himself; the laws therefore, which establish the right of suffrage, are fundamental to this government. In fact, it is as important to regulate in a republic in what manner, by whom, and concerning what suffrages are to be given, as it is in a monarchy to know who is the prince, and after what manner he ought to govern." The *time, mode* and *place* of the election of representatives, senators and president general of the United States, ought not to be under the controul of Congress, but fundamentally ascertained and established.

The new constitution, consistently with the plan of consolidation, contains no reservation of the rights and privileges of the state governments, which was made in the confederation of the year 1778, by article the 2d, viz. "That each state retains its sovereignty, freedom and independence, and every power, jurisdiction and right, which is not by this confederation expressly delegated to the United States in Congress assembled."

The legislative power vested in Congress by the foregoing recited sections, is so unlimited in its nature; may be so comprehensive and boundless in its exercise, that this alone would be amply sufficient to annihilate the state governments, and swallow them up in the grand vortex of general empire.

The judicial powers vested in Congress are also so various and extensive, that by legal ingenuity they may be extended to every case, and thus absorb the state judiciaries, and when we consider the decisive influence that a general judiciary would have over the civil polity of the several states, we do not hesitate to pronounce that this power, unaided by the legislative, would effect a consolidation of the states under one government.

The powers of a court of equity, vested by this constitution, in the tribunals of Congress; powers which do not exist in Pennsylvania, unless so far as they can be incorporated with jury trial, would, in this state, greatly contribute to this event. The rich and wealthy suitors would eagerly lay hold of the infinite mazes, perplexities and delays, which a court of chancery, with the appellate powers of the supreme court in fact as well as law would furnish him with, and thus the poor man being plunged in the bottomless pit of legal discussion, would drop his demand in despair.

In short, consolidation pervades the whole constitution. It begins with an annunciation that such was the intention. The main pillars of the fabric correspond with it, and the concluding paragraph is a confirmation of it. The preamble begins with the words, "We the people of the United States," which is the style of a compact between individuals entering into a state of society, and not that of a confederation of states. The other features of consolidation, we leave before noticed.

Thus we have fully established the position, that the powers vested by this constitution in Congress, will effect a consolidation of the states under one government, which even the advocates of this constitution admit, could not be done without the sacrifice of all liberty.

3. We dissent, Thirdly, Because if it were practicable to govern so extensive a territory as these United States includes, on the plan of a consolidated government, consistent with the principles of liberty and the happiness of the people, yet the construction of this constitution is not calculated to attain the object, for independent of the nature of the case, it would of itself, necessarily produce a despotism, and that not by the usual gradations, but with the celerity

that has hitherto only attended revolutions effected by the sword.

To establish the truth of this position, a cursory investigation of the principles and form of this constitution will suffice.

The first consideration that this review suggests, is the omission of a BILL OF RIGHTS ascertaining and fundamentally establishing those unalienable and personal rights of men, without the full, free and secure enjoyment of which there can be no liberty, and over which it is not necessary for a good government to have the controul. The principal of which are the rights of conscience, personal liberty by the clear and unequivocal establishment of the writ of *habeas corpus*, jury trial in criminal and civil cases, by an impartial jury of the vicinage or county; with the common law proceedings, for the safety of the accused in criminal prosecutions and the liberty of the press, that scourge of tyrants; and the grand bulwark of every other liberty and, privilege; the stipulations heretofore made in favor of them in the state constitutions, are entirely superceded by this constitution.

The legislature of a free country should be so formed as to have a competent knowledge of its constitutents, and enjoy their confidence. To produce these essential requisites, the representation ought to be fair, equal, and sufficiently numerous, to possess the same interests, feelings, opinions, and views, which the people themselves would possess, were they all assembled; and so numerous as to prevent bribery and undue influence, and so responsible to the people, by frequent and fair elections, as to prevent their neglecting or sacrificing the views and interests of their constitutents, to their own pursuits.

We will now bring the legislature under this constitution to the test of the foregoing principles, which will demonstrate, that it is deficient in every essential quality of a just and safe representation.

The house of representatives is to consist of 65 members; that is one for about every 50,000 inhabitants, to be chosen every two years. Thirty-three members will form a quorum for doing business; and 17 of these, being the majority, determine the sense of the house.

The senate, the other constituent branch of the legislature, consists of 26 members, being *two* from each state, appointed by their legislatures every six years—fourteen senators make a quorum; the majority of whom, eight, determines the sense of that body: except in judging on impeachments, or in making treaties, or in expelling a member, when two thirds of the senators present, must concur.

The president is to have the control over the enacting of laws, so far as to make the concurrence of *two* thirds of the representatives and senators present necessary, if he should object to the laws.

Thus it appears that the liberties, happiness, interests, and great concerns of the whole United States, may be dependent upon the integrity, virtue, wisdom, and knowledge of 25 or 26 men.—How unadequate and unsafe a representation! Inadequate, because the sense and views of 3 or 4 millions of people diffused over so extensive a territory comprising such various climates, products, habits, interests, and opinions, cannot be collected in so small a body; and besides, it is not a fair and equal representation of the people even in proportion to its number, for the smallest state has as much weight in the senate as the largest, and from the smallness of the number to be chosen for both branches of the legislature; and from the mode of election and appointment, which is under the controul of Congress; and from the nature of the thing, men of the most elevated rank in life, will alone be chosen. The other orders in the society, such as farmers, traders, and mechanics, who all ought to have a competent number of their best informed men in the legislature, will be totally unrepresented.

The representation is unsafe, because in the exercise of such great powers and trusts, it is so exposed to corruption and undue influence, by the gift of the numerous places of honor and emolument, at the disposal of the executive; by the arts and address of the great and designing; and by direct bribery.

The representation is moreover inadequate and unsafe, because of the long terms for which it is appointed, and the mode of its appointment, by which Congress may not only controul the choice of the people, but may so manage as to divest the people of this fundamental right, and become self-elected.

The number of members in the house of representatives *may* be increased to one for every 30,000 inhabitants. But when we consider, that this cannot be done without the consent of the senate, who from their share in the legislative, in the executive, and judicial departments, and permanency of appointment, will be the great efficient body in this government, and whose weight and predominancy would be abridged by an increase of the representatives, we are persuaded that this is a circumstance that cannot be expected. On the contrary, the number of representatives will probably be continued at 65, although the population of the country may swell to treble what it now is; unless a revolution should effect a change.

We have before noticed the judicial power as it would effect a consolidation of the states into one government; we will now examine it, as it would affect the liberties and welfare of the people, supposing such a government were practicable and proper.

The judicial power, under the proposed constitution, is founded on the well-known principles of the *civil law*, by which the judge determines both on law and fact, and appeals are allowed from the interior tribunals to the superior, upon the whole question; so that *facts* as well as *law*, would be reexamined, and even new facts brought forward in the court of appeals; and to use the words of a very eminent Civilian—"The cause is many times another thing before the court of appeals, than what it was at the time of the first sentence."

That this mode of proceeding is the one which must be adopted under this constitution, is evident from the following circumstances:—1st. That the trial by jury, which is the grand characteristic of the common law, is secured by the constitution, only in criminal cases.—2d. That the appeal from both law and fact is expressly established, which is utterly inconsistent with the principles of the common law, and trials by jury. The only mode in which an appeal from law and fact can be established, is, by adopting the principles and practice of the civil law; unless the United States should be drawn into the absurdity of calling and swearing juries, merely for the purpose of contradicting their verdicts, which would render juries contemptible and worse than useless.—3d. That the courts to be established would decide on all cases *of law and equity*, which is a well known characteristic of the civil law, and these courts would have conusance not only of the laws of the United States and of treaties, and of cases affecting ambassadors, but of all cases of *admiralty and maritime jurisdiction*, which last are matters belonging exclusively to the civil law, in every nation in Christendom.

Not to enlarge upon the loss of the invaluable right of trial by an unbiassed jury, so dear to every friend of liberty, the monstrous expence and inconveniences of the mode of proceeding to be adopted, are such as will prove intolerable to the people of this country. The lengthy proceedings of the civil law courts in the chancery of England, and in the courts of Scotland and France, are such that few men of moderate fortune can endure the expence of; the poor man must therefore submit to the wealthy. Length of purse will too often prevail against right and justice. For instance, we are told by the learned judge *Blackstone*, that a question only on the property of an ox, of the value of *three* guineas, originating under the civil law proceedings in Scotland, after many interlocutory orders and sentences below, was carried at length from the court of sessions, the highest court in that part of Great Britain, by way of *appeal* to the house of lords, where the question of law and fact was finally determined. He adds, that no pique or spirit could in the court of king's bench or common pleas at Westmenster, have given continuance to such a cause for a tenth part of the time, nor have cost a twentieth part of the expence. Yet the costs in the courts of king's bench and common pleas in England, are infinitely greater than those which the people of this country have ever experience. We abhor the idea of losing the transcendant privilege of trial by jury, with the loss of which, it is remarked by the same learned author, that in Sweden, the liberties of the commons were extinguised by an aristocratic senate: and that *trial by jury* and the liberty of the people went out together. At the same time we regret the intolerable delay, the enormous expences and infinite vexation to which the people of this country will be exposed from the voluminous proceedings of the courts of civil law, and especially, from the appellate jurisdiction, by means of which a man may be drawn from the utmost boundaries of this extensive country to the seat of the supreme court of the nation to contend, perhaps with a wealthy and powerful adversary. The consequence of this establishment will be an absolute confirmation of the power of aristocratical influence in the courts of justice; for the common people will not be able to contend or struggle against it.

Trial by jury in criminal cases may also be excluded by declaring that the libeller for instance shall be liable to an action of debt for a specified sum; thus evading the common law prosecution by indictment and trial by jury. And the common course of proceeding against a ship for breach of revenue laws by information (which will be classed among civil causes) will at the civil law be within the resort of a court, where no jury intervenes. Besides, the benefit of jury trial, in cases of a criminal nature, which cannot be evaded, will be rendered of little value, by calling the accused to answer far from home; there being no provision that the trial be by a jury of the neighbourhood or country. Thus an inhabitant of Pittsburgh, on a charge of crime committed on the banks of the Ohio, may be obliged to defend himself at the side of the Delaware, and so *vice versa*. To conclude this head: we observe that the judges of the courts of Congress would not be independent, as they are not debarred from holding other offices, during the pleasure of the president and senate, and as they may derive their support in part from fees, alterable by the legislature.

The next consideration that the constitution presents, is the undue and dangerous mixture of the powers of government: the same body possessing legislative, executive, and judicial powers. The senate is a constituent branch of the legislature, it has judicial power in judging on impeachments, and in this case unites in some measure the characters of judge and party, as all the principal officers are appointed by the president-general, with the concurrence of the senate and therefore they derive their offices in part from the senate. This may biass the judgments of the senators, and tend to screen great delinquents from punishment. And the senate has, moreover, various and great executive powers, viz. in concurrence with the president-general, they form treaties with foreign nations, that may controul and abrogate the constitutions and laws of the several states. Indeed, there is no power, privilege or liberty of the state governments, or of the people, but what may be affected by virtue of this power. For all treaties, made by them, are to be the "supreme law of the land; any thing in the constitution or laws of any state, to the contrary notwithstanding."

And this great power may be exercised by the president and 10 senators (being two-thirds of 14, which is a quorum of that body). What an inducement would this offer to the ministers of foreign powers to compass by bribery *such concessions* as could not otherwise be obtained. It is the unvaried usage of all free states, whenever treaties interfere with the positive laws of the land, to make the intervention of the legislature necessary to give them operation. This became necessary, and was afforded by the parliament of Great-Britain, in consequence of the late commercial treaty between that kingdom and France.—As the senate judges on impeachments, who is to try the members of the senate for the abuse of this power! And none of the great appointments to office can be made without the consent of the senate.

Such various, extensive, and important powers combined in one body of men, are inconsistent with all freedom; the celebrated Montesquieu tells us, that "when the legislative and executive powers are united in the same person, or in the same body of magistrates, there can be no liberty, because apprehensions may arise, lest the same monarch or *senate* should enact tyrannical laws, to execute them in a tyrannical manner."

"Again, there is no liberty, if the power of judging be not separated from the legislative and executive powers. Were it joined with the legislative, the life and liberty of the subject would be exposed to arbitrary controul; for the judge would then be legislator.

Were it joined to the executive power, the judge might behave with all the violence of an oppressor. There would be an end of every thing, were the same man, or the same body of the nobles, or of the people, to exercise those three powers; that of enacting laws; that of executing the public resolutions; and that of judging the crimes or differences of individuals."

The president general is dangerously connected with the senate; his coincidence with the views of the ruling junto in that body, is made essential to his weight and importance in the government, which will destroy all independency and purity in the executive department, and having the power of pardoning without the concurrence of a council, he may skreen from punishment the most treasonable attempts that may be made on the liberties of the people, when instigated by his coadjutors in the senate. Instead of this dangerous and improper mixture of the executive with the legislative and judicial, the supreme executive powers ought to have been placed in the president, with a small independent council, made personally responsible for every appointment to office or other act, by having their opinions recorded; and that without the concurrence of the majority of the quorum of this council, the president should not be capable of taking any step.

We have before considered internal taxation, as it would effect the destruction of the state governments, and produce one consolidated government. We will now consider that subject as it affects the personal concerns of the people.

The power of direct taxation applies to every individual, as congress, under this government, is expressly vested with the authority of laying a capitation or poll tax upon every person to any amount. This is a tax that, however oppressive in its nature, and unequal in its operation, is certain as to its produce and simple in its collection; it cannot be evaded like the objects of imposts or excise, and will be paid, because all that a man hath will he give for his head. This tax is so congenial to the nature of despotism, that it has ever been a favorite under such governments. Some of those who were in the late general convention from this state, have long laboured to introduce a poll-tax among us.

The power of direct taxation will further apply to every individual as congress may tax land, cattle, trades, occupations, &c. to any amount, and every object of internal taxation is of that nature, that however oppressive, the people will have but this alternative, either to pay the tax, or let their property be taken, for all resistance will be vain. The standing army and select militia would enforce the collection.

For the moderate exercise of this power, there is no controul left in the state governments, whose intervention is destroyed. No relief, or redress of grievances can be extended, as heretofore, by them. There is not even a declaration of RIGHTS to which the people may appeal for the vindication of their wrongs in the court of justice. They must therefore, implicitly, obey the most arbitrary laws, as the worst of them will be pursuant to the prinicples and form of the constitution, and that strongest of all checks upon the conduct of adminstration, *responsibility to the people*, will not exist in this government. The permanancy of the appointments of senators and representatives, and the controul the congress have over their election, will place them independent of the sentiments and resentment of the people, and the administration having a greater interest in the government than in the community, there will be no consideration to restrain them from oppression and tyranny. In the government of this state, under the old confederation, the members of the legislature are taken from among the people, and their interests and welfare are so inseparably connected with those of their consituents, that they can derive no advantage from oppressive laws and taxes, for they would suffer in common with their fellow citizens; would participate in the burthens they impose on the community, as they must return to the common level, after a short period; and notwithstanding every exertion of influence, every means of corruption, a necessary rotation excludes them from permanency in the legislature.

This large state is to have but ten members in that Congress which is to have the liberty, property and dearest concerns of every individual in this vast country at absolute command and even these ten persons, who are to be our only guardians; who are to supercede the legislature of Pennsylvania, will not be of the choice of the people, nor amenable to them. From the mode of their election and appointment they will consist of the lordly and high-minded; of men who will have no congenial feelings with the people, but a perfect indifference for, and contempt of them; they will consist of those harpies of power, that prey upon the very vitals; that riot on the miseries of the community. But we will suppose, although in all probability it may never be realized in fact, that our deputies in Congress have the welfare of their constituents at heart, and will exert themselves in their behalf, what security could even this afford; what relief could they extend to their oppressed consituents? To attain this, the majority of the deputies of the twelve other states in Congress must be alike well disposed; must alike forego the sweets of power, and

reliquish the pursuits of ambition, which from the nature of things is not to be expected. If the people part with a responsible representation in the legislature, founded upon fair, certain and frequent elections, they have nothing left they can call their own. Miserable is the lot of that people whose every concern depends on the WILL and PLEASURE of their rulers. Our soldiers will become Janissaries, and our officers of government Bashaws; in short, the system of despotism will soon be compleated.

From the foregoing investigation, it appears that the Congress under this constitution will not possess the confidence of the people, which is an essential requisite in a good government; for unless the laws command the confidence and respect of the great body of the people, so as to induce them to support them, when called on by the civil magistrate, they must be executed by the aid of a numerous standing army, which would be inconsistent with every idea of liberty; for the same force that may be employed to compel obedience to good laws, might and probably would be used to wrest from the people their constitutional liberties. The framers of this constitution appear to have been aware of this great deficiency; to have been sensible that no dependence could be placed on the people for their support: but on the contrary, that the government must be executed by force. They have therefore made a provision for this purpose in a permanent STANDING ARMY, and a MILITIA that may be subjected to as strict discipline and government.

A standing army in the hands of a government placed so independent of the people, may be made a fatal instrument to overturn the public liberties; it may be employed to enforce the collection of the most oppressive taxes, and to carry into execution the most arbitrary measures. An ambitious man who may have the army at his devotion, may step up into the throne, and seize upon absolute power.

The absolute unqualified command that Congress have over the militia may be made instrumental to the destruction of all liberty, both public and private; whether of a personal, civil or religious nature.

First, the personal liberty of every man probably from sixteen to sixty years of age, may be destroyed by the power Congress have in organizing and governing of the militia. As militia they may be subjected to fines to any amount, levied in a military manner; they may be subjected to corporal punishments of the most disgraceful and humiliating kind, and to death itself, by the sentence of a court martial: To this our young men will be more immediately subjected, as a select militia, composed of them, will best answer the purposes of government.

Secondly, The rights of conscience may be violated, as there is no exemption of those persons who are conscientiously scrupulous of bearing arms. These compose a respectable proportion of the community in the state. This is the more remarkable, because even when the distresses of the late war, and the evident disaffection of many citizens of that description, inflamed our passions, and when every person who was obliged to risque his own life, must have been exasperated against such as on any account kept back from the common danger, yet even then, when outrage and violence might have been expected, the rights of conscience were held sacred.

At this momentous crisis, the framers of our state constitution made the most express and decided declaration and stipulations in favour of the rights of conscience: but now when no necessity exists, those dearest rights of men are left insecure.

Thirdly, The absolute command of Congress over the militia may be destructive of public liberty; for under the guidance of an arbitrary government, they may be made the unwilling instruments of tyranny. The militia of Pennsylvania may be marched to New England or Virginia to quell an insurrection occasioned by the most galling oppression, and aided by the standing army, they will no doubt be successful in subduing their liberty and independency; but in so doing, although the magnanimity of their minds will be extinguished, yet the meaner passions of resentment and revenge will be increased, and these in turn will be the ready and obedient instruments of despotism to enslave the others; and that with an irritated vengeance. Thus may the militia be made the instruments of crushing the last efforts of expiring liberty, of riveting the chains of despotism on their fellow citizens, and on one another. This power can be exercised not only without violating the constitution, but in strict conformity with it; it is calculated for this express purpose, and will doubtless be executed accordingly.

As this government will not enjoy the confidence of the people, but be executed by force, it will be a very expensive and burthensome government. The standing army must be numerous, and as a further support, it will be the policy of this government to multiply officers in every department: judges, collectors, tax-gatherers, excisemen and the whole host of revenue officers will swarm over the land, devouring the hard earnings of the industrious. Like the locusts of old, impoverishing and desolating all before them.

We have not noticed the smaller, nor many of the considerable blemishes, but have confined our objections to the great and essential defects; the main pillars of the constitution: which we have shewn to be inconsistent with the liberty and happiness of the people, as its establishment will annihilate the state governments, and produce one consolidated government, that will eventually and speedily issue in the supremacy of despotism.

In this investigation, we have not confined our views to the interests or welfare of this state, in preference to the others. We have overlooked all local circumstances—we have considered this subject on the broad scale of the general good: we have asserted the cause of the present and future ages: the cause of liberty and mankind.

Nathaniel Breading	John Ludwig
John Smilie	Abraham Lincoln
Richard Baird	John Bishop
Adam Orth	Joseph Heister
John A. Hanna	Joseph Powel
John Whitehill	James Martin
John Harris	William Findley
Robert Whitehill	John Baird
John Reynolds	James Edgar
Jonathan Hoge	William Todd.
Nicholas Lutz	

Document 5.6 Noah Webster Ridicules the Pennsylvania Minority

Noah Webster was even less restrained in his attack on the Minority report than in his earlier missives against Antifederalists. He continually hammers home the claim that anyone elected to the new national Congress represents the people, and would never turn on them. Do those claims sound similar to claims that the British government made about Parliament in the 1760s? He also claims that no legislature in North America ever tried to take away the people's rights. What other claims does he make to disparage the Minority report? Does he answer all of their concerns? Are Webster's arguments convincing? Do you see in his responses some of the Federalist belief that "the people's" representatives in the new government should continue to come only from the "better sorts" in society-planters, merchants, lawyers, and the wealthy?

To the DISSENTING MEMBERS of the late CONVENTION of PENNSYLVANIA

Gentlemen, Your long and elaborate publication, assigning the reasons for your refusing to subscribe the ratification of the NEW FEDERAL CONSTITUTION, has made its appearance in the public papers, and, I flatter myself, will be read throughout the United States. It will feed the flame of opposition among the weak, the wicked, the designing, and the factious; but it will make many new converts to the proposed Government, and furnish the old friends of it with new weapons of defence. The very attempt to excite uneasiness and disturbance in a State, about a measure legally and constitutionally adopted, after a long and ample discussion in a Convention of the people's Delegates, marks a disposition, beyond all conception, obstinate, base, and politically wicked. But *obstinacy* is the leading trait in your public characters, and, as it serves to give *consistency* to your actions, even in error, it cannot fail to procure you that share of respect which is paid to the *firmness* of Satan and his fellow apostates, who, after their expulsion from Heaven, had too much pride to *repent* and *ask for a re-admission*. My address to you will not be so lengthy as your publication; your arguments are *few*, altho' your harangue is *long* and *insidious*.

You begin with telling the world, that *no defect was discovered in the present Confederation, till after the war*. Why did you not publish the truth? You know, Gentlemen, that during six years of the war, we had *no Confederation at all*. You know that the war commenced in April, 1775, and that we had *no Confederation* till March, 1781. You know (for some of you are men of abilities and reading) or ought to know, a principle of *fear* in time of war, operates more powerfully in binding together the States which have a common interest, than all the parchment compacts on earth. Could we, then, discover the defects of

our present Confederation, with *two years'* experience only, and an enemy in our country? You know we could not.

I will not undertake to detect the falshood of every assertion, or the fallacy of all your reasoning on each article. In the most of them the public will anticipate any thing I could say, and confute your arguments as fast as they read them. But I must tell you, Gentlemen, that your reasoning against the *New Constitution* resembles that of Mr. Hume on miracles. You begin with some *gratis dicta*, which are denied; you assume *premises* which are *totally false*, and then reason on them with great address. Your whole reasoning, and that of all the opposers of the Federal Government, is built on this *false principle*, that the *Federal Legislature* will be a body *distinct from* and *independent* of the people. Unless your opposition is grounded on *that principle*, it stands on *nothing*; and on any *other* supposition, your arguments are but *declamatory nonsense*.

But the principle is false. The Congress, under the proposed Constitution, will have the *same interest* as the people—they are a *part* of the people—their interest is *inseparable* from that of the people; and this union of interest will eternally remain, while the right of election shall continue in the people. Over this right Congress will have no control: the time and manner of exercising that right are very wisely vested in Congress, otherwise a delinquent State might embarrass the measures of the Union. The safety of the public requires that the Federal body should prevent any particular deliquency; but the *right of election* is above their control: it *must* remain in the people, and be exercised one in two, four or six years. A body thus organized, with thirteen Legislatures watching their measure, and several millions of jealous eyes inspecting their conduct, would not be apt to betray their constituents. Yet this is not the best ground of safety. The first and almost only principle that governs men, is *interest*. *Love of our country* is a powerful auxiliary motive to patriotic actions, but rarely or

---

From *Daily Advertiser*, December 31, 1787.

never operates against *interest*. The only requisite to secure liberty, is to connect the *interest* of the Governors with that of the *governed*. Blend these interests—make them inseparable—and both are safe from voluntary invasion. How shall this union be formed? This question is answered. The union is formed by the equal principles on which the people of these States hold their property and their rights. But how shall this union of interests be perpetuated? The answer is easy—bar all perpetuities of estates—prevent any exclusive rights—preserve all preferment dependent on the choice of the people—suffer no power to exist independent of the people or their Representatives. While there exists no power in a State, which is independent on the will of the electors, the rights of the people are secure. The only barrier against tyranny, that is necessary in any State, is the *election of Legislators* by the yeomanry of that State. Preserve *that*, and every privilege is safe. The Legislators thus chosen to represent the people, should have all the power that the people would have were they assembled in one body to deliberate upon public measures. The distinction between the *powers* of the *people* and of their *Representatives* in the Legislature, is as absurd in *theory*, as it proves pernicious in *practice*. A distinction, which has already countenanced and supported *one rebellion* in America; has prevented many *good* measures; has produced many *bad*; has created animosities in many States, and embarrassments in all. It has taught the people a lesson, which, if they continue to practise, will bring laws into contempt, and frequently mark our country with blood.

You object, Gentlemen, to the powers vested in Congress. Permit me, to ask you, where will you limit their powers? What bounds will you prescribe? You will reply, *we will reserve certain rights, which we deem invaluable, and restrain our rulers from abridging them.* But, Gentlemen, let me ask you, how will you define these rights—would you say, *the liberty of the Press shall not be restrained*? Well, what is this liberty of the Press? Is it an unlimited licence to publish *any thing and every thing* with impunity? If so, the Author, and Printer of any treatise, however obscene and blasphemous, will be screened from punishment. You know, Gentlemen, that there are books extant, so shockingly and infamously obscene and so daringly blasphemous, that no society on earth, would be vindicable in suffering the publishers to pass unpunished. You certainly know that such cases *have* happened, and *may* happen again—nay, you know that they are *probable*. Would not that indefinite expression, *the liberty of the Press*, extend to the justification of every *possible publication*? Yes, Gentlemen, you know, that under such a general licence, a man who should publish a treatise to *prove his maker a knave*, must be screened from legal punishment. I shudder at the thought!—But the truth must not be concealed. The Constitutions of several States *guarantee that very licence.*

But if you attempt to define the *liberty of the Press*, and ascertain what cases shall fall within that privilege, during the course of centuries, where will you *begin*? Or rather, where will you *end*? Here, Gentlemen, you will be puzzled. Some publications certainly may be a breach of civil law: You will not have the effrontery to deny a truth so obvious and intuitively evident. Admit that principle; and unless you can define precisely the cases, which are, and are not a breach of law, you have no right to say, the liberty of the Press shall not be restrained; for such a license would warrant *any breach of law*. Rather than hazard such an abuse of privilege, is it not better to leave the right altogether with your rulers and your posterity? No attempts have ever been made by a Legislative body in America, to abridge that privilege; and in this free enlightened country, no attempts could succeed, unless the public should be convinced that an abuse of it would warrant the restriction. Should this ever be the case, you have no right to say, that a future Legislature, or that posterity shall not abridge the privilege, or punish its abuses. The very attempt to establish a permanent, unalterable Constitution, is an act of consummate arrogance. It is a presumption that we have all possible wisdom—that we can foresee all possible circumstances—and judge for future generations, better than they can for themselves.

But you will say, that trial by jury, is an unalienable right, that ought not to be trusted with our rulers. Why not? If it is such a darling privilege, will not Congress be as fond of it, as their constituents? An elevation into that Council, does not render a man insensible to his privileges, nor place him beyond the necessity of securing them. A member of Congress is liable to all the operations of law, except during his attendance on public business; and should he consent to a law, annihilating any right whatever, he deprives himself, his family and estate, of the benefit resulting from that right, as well as his constituents. This circumstance alone, is a sufficient security.

But, why this outcry about juries? If the people esteem them so highly, why do they ever neglect them, and suffer the trial by them to go into disuse? In some States, *Courts of Admiralty* have no juries—nor Courts of Chancery at all. In the City-Courts of some States, juries are rarely or never called, altho' the parties may demand them; and one State, at least, has lately passed an act, empowering the parties to submit both *law* and *fact* to the Court. It is found, that the judgment of a Court, gives as much satisfaction, as the verdict of a jury, as the Court are as good judges of fact, as juries, and much better judges of law. I have no desire to abolish trials by jury, although the original design and excellence of them, is in many cases superseded.—While the people remain attached to this mode of deciding causes, I am confident, that no Congress can wrest the privilege from them.

But, Gentlemen, our legal proceedings want a reform. Involved in all the mazes of perplexity, which the chicanery of lawyers could invent in the course of 500 years, our road to justice and redress is tedious, fatiguing and expensive. Our judicial proceedings are capable of being simplified, and improved in almost every particular. For God's sake, Gentlemen, do not shut the door against improvement. If the people of America, should ever spurn the shackles of opinion, and venture to leave the road, which is so overgrown with briers and thorns, as to strip a man's cloaths from his back as he passes, I am certain they can devise a more easy, safe, and expeditious mode of administering the laws, than that which harrasses every poor mortal, that is wretched enough to want *legal* justice. In Pennsylvania, where very respectable merchants, have repeatedly told me, they had rather lose a debt of fifty pounds, than attempt to recover it by a legal process, one would think that men, who value liberty and property, would not restrain any Government from suggesting a remedy for such disorders.

Another right, which you would place beyond the reach of Congress, is the writ of *habeas corpus.* Will you say that this right may not be suspended in *any* case? You dare not. If it may be suspended in any case, and the Congress are to judge of the necessity, what security have you in a declaration in its favor? You had much better say nothing upon the subject.

But you are frightened at a standing army. I beg you, Gentlemen, to define a *standing army.* If you would refuse to give Congress power to raise troops, to guard our frontiers, and garrison forts, or in short, to enlist men for any purpose, then we understand you—you tie the hands of our rulers so that they cannot defend you against any invasion. This is protection indeed! But if Congress can raise a body of troops for a year, they can raise them for a *hundred years* and your declaration against *standing*

armies can have no other effect, than to prevent Congress from denominating their troops, a *standing army.* You would only introduce into this country, the English farce of mechanically passing an annual bill for the support of troops which are never disbanded.

You object to the indefinite power of taxation in Congress. You must then limit the exercise of that power by the sums of money to be raised; or leaving the sums indefinite, must prescribe the *particular mode* in which, and the *articles* on which the money is to be raised. But the sums cannot be ascertained, because the necessities of the States cannot be foreseen nor defined. It is beyond even *your* wisdom and profound knowledge, Gentlemen, to ascertain the public exigencies, and reduce them to the provisions of a Constitution. And if you would prescribe the mode of raising money, you will meet with equal difficulty. The different States have different modes of taxation, and I question much whether even your skill, Gentlemen, could invent a uniform system that should sit easy upon every State. It must therefore be left to experiment, with a power that can correct the errors of a system, and suit it to the habits of the people. And if no uniform mode will answer this purpose, it will be in the power of Congress to lay taxes in each State, according to its particular practice. But you know, Gentlemen, that an efficient Federal Government will tender taxes unnecessary—*that it will ease the people of their burdens, and remove their complaints*, and therefore when you raise a clamor about the right of taxation, you must be guilty of the *basest design*—your hearts must be as *malignant* as your actions have been *insidious.* You know that requisitions on the States are ineffectual—That they cannot be rendered effectual, but by a compulsory power in Congress—You know that without an efficient power to raise money, Government cannot secure person, property or justice—Nay, you know further, that such power is as safely lodged in your *Representatives in Congress*, as it is in your *Representatives* in your distinct Legislatures.

You would likewise restrain Congress from requiring *excessive bail*, or imposing *excessive fines* and *unusual punishment.* But unless you can, in every possible instance, previously define the words excessive and *unusual*—if you leave the discretion of Congress to define them on occasion, any restriction of their power by a general indefinite expression, is a nullity—mere *formal nonsense.* What consummate arrogance must you possess, to presume you can *now* make *better* provision for the Government of these States, during the course of ages and centuries, than the future

Legislatures can, on the spur of the occasion! Yet your whole reasoning on the subject implies this arrogance, and a presumption that you have a right to legislate for posterity!

But to complete the list of unalienable rights, you would insert a clause in your declaration, *that every body shall, in good weather, hunt on his own land, and catch fish in rivers that are public property.* Here, Gentlemen, you must have exerted the whole force of your genius! Not even the *all-important* subject of *legislating for a world* can restrain my laughter at this clause! As a supplement to that article of your bill of rights, I would suggest the following restriction:— "That Congress shall never restrain any inhabitant of America from eating and drinking, *at seasonable times,* or prevent his lying on his *left side,* in a long winter's night, or even on his back, when he is fatigued by lying on his *right*."—This article is of just as much consequence as the 8th clause of your proposed bill of rights.

But to be more serious, Gentlemen, you must have had in idea the forest-laws in Europe, when you inserted that article; for no circumstance that ever took place in America, could have suggested the thought of a declaration in favor of hunting and fishing. Will you forever persist in error? Do you not reflect that the state of property in America, is directly the reverse of what it is in Europe? Do you not consider, that the forest-laws in Europe originated in *feudal tyranny,* of which not a trace is to be found in America? Do you not know that in this country almost every farmer is Lord of his own soil? That instead of suffering under the oppression of a Monarch and Nobles, a class of haughty masters, totally independent of the people, almost every man in America is a *Lord himself*—enjoying his property in fee? Where then the necessity of laws to secure hunting and fishing? You may just as well ask for a clause, giving licence for every man to till *his own land,* or milk *his own cows.* The Barons in Europe procured forest-laws to secure the right of hunting on *their own land,* from the intrusion of those who had no property in lands. But the distribution of land in America, not only supersedes the necessity of any laws upon this subject, but renders them absolutely trifling. The same laws which secure the property in land, secure to the owner the right of using it as he pleases.

But you are frightened at the prospect of a *consolidation of the States.* I differ from you widely. I am afraid, after all our attempts to unite the States, that contending interests, and the pride of State-Sovereignties, will either prevent our union, or render our Federal Government weak, slow and inefficient. The danger is all on this side. If any thing under Heaven now endangers our liberties and independence, it is that single circumstance.

You harp upon that clause of the New Constitution, which declares, that the laws of the United States, &c. shall be the supreme law of the land; when you know that the powers of the Congress are defined, to extend only to those matters which are in their nature and effects, *general.* You know, the Congress cannot meddle with the internal police of any State, or abridge its Sovereignty. And you know, at the same time, that all general concerns, the laws of Congress must be *supreme,* or they must be *nothing.*

But the public will ask, who are these men that so violently oppose the New Constitution? I will tell them. You are the heads of that party, Gentlemen, which, on the celebration of a very glorious event in Philadelphia, at the close of the war, collected in a mob, and broke the windows of the Quakers, and committed the most detestable outrages, because their religion would not suffer them to illuminate their windows, and join in the rejoicings. You are the men, Gentlemen, that wanted the Charter from the Bank, without the least justifiable pretence; sporting with a grant which *you* had made, and which had never been forfeited. You are the men, that, without a show of right, took away the Charter of the University, and vested it in the hands of your own tools. Yes, Gentlemen, you are the men, who prescribed a test law and oath of abjuration in Pennsylvania, which excluded more than half the Citizens of the state from all Civil Offices. A law, which, had it not been altered by the efforts of more reasonable men, would have established you, and your adherents, as an Aristocratic junto, in all the offices and emoluments of the State. Could your base designs have been accomplished, *you* would have rioted in all the benefits of Government, and Pennsylvania would now, have been subject to as tyrannical an Aristocracy, as ever cursed Society. Such has been the uniformly infamous conduct of the men, who now oppose the best Constitution of Government, ever devised by human wisdom.

But the most bare-faced act of tyranny and wickedness, which has distinguished your political characters, remains to be mentioned. You are the men, Gentlemen, who have abandoned your parts of duty, and betrayed the constitutional rights of the State of Pennsylvania, by *seceding from the Legislature,* with the design of defeating the measures of a constitutional quorum of the House. Yes, Gentlemen, and to add to the infamy of your conduct, you have the audacity to *avow the intention*. Will you then attempt to palliate the crime, by saying it was *necessary*? Good Heavens! *necessary* that a State should be *ruled by a minority! necessary* that the sense of a legislature should be defeated by a junto, which had labored incessantly, for four years, to establish an *Aristocracy* in the State! The same principle which will vindicate you, will justify any *one* man in defeating the sense of the *whole* State. If a minority may prevent a law, one man may do it; but is this liberty? Is this your concern for the rights of the State? Dare you talk of rights, which you have so flagrantly invaded? Will the world expect you to be the guardians of privileges? No, Gentlemen, they will sooner expect lessons of morality from the wheel-barrowed criminals, that clank their chains along your streets.

Do you know, Gentlemen, that you are treading in the steps of the Governors before the revolution? Do you know that from the first settlement of Pennsylvania, there was a contest between the people and the deputies of the proprietaries? And that when a Governor could not bring the Assembly to resign their rights, he would *prevail on certain members to leave the House*, and prevent their measures. Yes, Gentlemen, you are but following the precedents of your tyrannical Governors. You have begun, and pursued, with unwearied perseverance, the same plan of Despotism which wrought the late revolution; and, with a calm, hypocritical phiz, pretend to be *anxious for the liberties of the people.*

These facts stare you in the face! They are felt in Pennsylvania—and *known* to the world! There is not a spot in the United States, where the solemnity of contracts and grants, has been so sacrilegiously violated—and the rights of men so wantonly and perseveringly abused, as by you and your junto in Pennsylvania—except only, in the little detestable corner of the Continent, called *Rhode-Island*. Thanks be to the Sovereign Ruler of events, you are checked in your career of tyranny—your power is dwindling into impotence—and your abuse of the respectable Convention, and of the friends of our Federal Union, will shroud you in oblivion, or accelerate your progress to merited contempt.

Document 5.7 Letters from "Brutus" Oppose the Constitution as Written

Robert Yates was born in Schenectady, New York in 1738. He received a classical education, read law with William Livingston, and became an attorney in 1760. During the pre-Revolution years he actively warned against English corruption and the need to protect American liberties from a tyrannical central government. During the War for Independence he served on the committee that wrote New York's first constitution. During the 1780s Yates served on the New York Supreme Court. Politically, he opposed any concessions to the Confederation Congress that would reduce state sovereignty and its ability to protect the rights of its citizens. Chosen as a state delegate to the Constitutional Convention, he accepted, because of the convention's mandate to revise the existing articles. Seeing what he believed to be a conspiracy to centralize power in a new national government, he left the convention early and led opposition against ratification in New York. Yates and other New York Antifederalists were alarmed by the lack of a bill of rights in the new Constitution, apparently abandoning the ideas behind the Declaration of Independence and the Revolutionary War. They did not accept Federalist promises that the good and ethical men elected to the new government would never attack individual liberties, or that the separation of powers made government abuse impossible. In the two "Brutus" letters reprinted below, what are Yates' major concerns? What threats, so painfully fought against just years before, does he see returning with the new Constitution? Why does he fear these things so much?

"Brutus" VIII
New York Journal, January 10, 1788

The next powers vested by this constitution in the general government, which we shall consider, are those, which authorise them to "borrow money on the credit of the United States, and to raise and support armies." I take these two together and connect them with the power to lay and collect taxes, duties, imposts and excises, because their extent, and the danger that will arise from the exercise of these powers, cannot be fully understood, unless they are viewed in relation to each other.

The power to borrow money is general and unlimited, and the clause so often before referred to, authorises the passing any laws proper and necessary to carry this into execution. Under this authority, the Congress may mortgage any or all the revenues of the union, as a fund to loan money upon, and it is probable, in this way, they may borrow of foreign nations, a principal sum, the interest of which will be equal to the annual revenues of the country.—By this means, they may create a national debt, so large, as to exceed the ability of the country ever to sink. I can scarcely contemplate a greater calamity that could befal this country, than to be loaded with a debt exceeding their ability ever to discharge. If this be a just remark, it is unwise and improvident to vest in the general government, a power to borrow at discretion, without any limitation or restriction.

It may possibly happen that the safety and welfare of the country may require, that money be borrowed, and it is proper when such a necessity arises that the power should be exercised by the general government.—But it certainly ought never to be exercised, but on the most urgent occasions, and then we should not borrow of foreigners if we could possibly avoid it.

The constitution should therefore have so restricted, the exercise of this power as to have tendered it very difficult for the government to practise it. The present confederation requires the assent of nine states to exercise this, and a number of the other important powers of the confederacy—and it would certainly have been a wise provision in this constitution, to have made it necessary that two thirds of the members should assent to borrowing money—when the necessity was indispensible, this assent would always be given, and in no other cause ought it to be.

The power to raise armies, is indefinite and unlimitted, and authorises the raising forces, as well in peace as in war. Whether the clause which impowers the Congress to pass all laws which are proper and necessary, to carry this into execution, will not authorise them to impress men for the army, is a question well worthy consideration? If the general legislature deem it for the general welfare to raise a body of troops, and they cannot be procured by voluntary enlistments, it seems evident, that it will be proper and necessary to effect it, that men be impressed from the militia to make up the deficiency.

These powers taken in connection, amount to this: that the general government have unlimitted. authority and controul over all the wealth and all the force of the union. The advocates for this scheme, would favor the world with a new discovery, if they would shew, what kind of freedom or independency is left to the state governments, when they cannot command any part of the property or of the force of the country, but at the will of the Congress. It seems to me as absurd, as it would be to say, that I was free and independent, when I had conveyed all my property to another, and was tenant to will to him, and had beside, given an indenture of myself to serve him during life.—The power to keep up standing armies in time of peace, has been justly objected, to this system, as dangerous and improvident. The advocates who have wrote in its favor, have some of them ridiculed the objection, as though it originated in the distempered brain of its opponents, and others have taken pains to shew, that it is a power that was proper to be granted to the rulers in this constitution. That you may be enabled to form a just opinion on this subject, I shall first make some remarks, tending to prove, that this power ought to be restricted, and then animadvert on the arguments which have been adduced to justify it.

I take it for granted, as an axiom in politic, that the people should never authorise their rulers to do any thing, which if done, would operate to their injury.

It seems equally clear, that in a case where a power, if given and exercised, will generally produce evil to the community, and seldom good—and which, experience has proved, has most frequently been exercised to the great injury, and very often to the

From *New York Journal,* January 10, 1788 and January 17, 1788.

total destruction of the government; in such a case, I say, this power, if given at all, should if possible be so restricted, as to prevent the ill effect of its operation.

Let us then enquire, whether standing armies in time of peace, would be ever beneficial to our country—or if in some extraordinary cases, they might be necessary; whether it is not true, that they have generally proved a scourge to a country, and destructive of their liberty.

I shall not take up much of your time in proving a point, in which the friends of liberty, in all countries, have so universally agreed. The following extract from Mr. Pultney's speech, delivered in the house of commons of Great-Britain, on a motion for reducing the army, is so full to the point, and so much better than any thing I can say, that I shall be excused for inserting it. He says, "I have always been, and always shall be against a standing army of any kind; to me it is a terrible thing, whether under that of a parliamentary, or any other designation; a standing army is still a standing army by whatever name it is called; they are a body of men distinct from the body of the people; they are governed by different laws, and blind obedience, and an entire submission to the orders of their commanding officer, is their only principle; the nations around us, sir, are already enslaved, and have been enslaved by those very means; by means of their standing armies they have every one lost their liberties; it is indeed impossible that the liberties of the people in any country can be preserved where a numerous standing army is kept up. Shall we then take our measures from the example of our neighbours" No, sir, on the contrary, from their misfortunes we ought to learn to avoid those rocks upon which they have split.

"It signifies nothing to tell me that our army is commanded by such gentlemen as cannot be supposed to join in any measures for enslaving their country; it may be so; I have a very good opinion of many gentlemen now in the army; I believe they would not join in any such measures; but their lives are uncertain, nor can we be sure how long they will be kept in command, they may all be dismissed in a moment, and proper tools of power put in their room. Besides, sir, we know the passions of men, we know how dangerous it is to trust the best of men with too much power. Where was a braver army than that under Jul. Caesar" Where was there ever an army that had served their country more faithfully? That army was commanded generally by the best citizens of Rome, by men of great fortune and figure in their country, yet that army enslaved their country. The affections of the soldiers towards their country, the honor and integrity of the under officers, are not to be depended on. By the military law the administration of justice is so quick, and the punishment so severe, that neither the officer nor soldier dare dispute the orders of his supreme commander; he must not consult his own inclination. If an officer were commanded to pull his own father out of his house, he must do it; he dares not disobey; immediate death would be the sure consequence of the least grumbling: and if an officer were sent into the court of request, accompanied by a body of musketeers with screwed bayonets, and with orders to tell us what we ought to do, and how we were to vote: I know what would be the duty of this house; I know it would be our duty to order the officer to be hanged at the door of the lobby: but I doubt, sir, I doubt much, if such a spirit could be found in the house, or in any house of commons that will ever be in England.

"Sir, I talk not of imaginary things. I talk of what has happened to an English house of commons, from an English army; not only from an English army, but an army that was raised by that very house of commons, an army that was paid by them, and an army that was commanded by generals appointed by them; therefore do not let us vainly imagine, that an army, raised and maintained by authority of parliament, will always be submissive to them. If an army be so numerous as to have it in their power to overawe the parliament, they wil be submissive as long as the parliament does nothing to disoblige their favourite general; but when that case happens I am afraid, that in place of the parliament's dismissing the army, the army will dismiss the parliament.— "If this great man's reasoning be just, it follows, that keeping up a standing army, would be the highest degree dangerous to the liberty and happiness of the community— and if so, the general government ought not to have authority to do it; for no government should be empowered to do that which if done, would tend to destroy public liberty.

"Brutus" IX
New York Journal, January 17, 1788

The design of civil government is to protect the rights and promote the happiness of the people.

For this end, rulers are invested with powers. But we cannot from hence justly infer that these powers should be unlimited. There are certain rights which mankind possess, over which government ought not to have any controul, because it is not necessary they should, in order to attain the end of its institution. There are certain things which rulers should be absolutely prohibited from doing, because, if they should do them, they would work an injury, not a benefit to the people. Upon the same principles of reasoning, if the exercise of a power, is found generally or in most cases to operate to the injury of the community, the legislature should be restricted in the exercise of that power, so as to guard, as much as possible, against the danger. These principles seem to be the evident dictates of common sense, and what ought to give sanction to them in the minds of every American, they are the great principles of the late revolution, and those which governed the framers of all our state constitutions. Hence we find, that all the state constitutions, contain either formal bills of rights, which set bounds to the powers of the legislature, or have restrictions for the same purpose in the body of the constitutions. Some of our new political Doctors, indeed, reject the idea of the necessity, or propriety of such restrictions in any elective government, but especially in the general one.

But it is evident, that the framers of this new system were of a contrary opinion, because they have prohibited the general government, the exercise of some powers, and restricted them in that of others.

I shall adduce two instances, which will serve to illustrate my meaning, as well as to confirm the truth of the preceding remark.

In the 9th section, it is declared, "no bill of attainder shall be passed." This clause takes from the legislature all power to declare a particular person guilty of a crime by law. It is proper the legislature should be deprived of the exercise of this power, because it seldom is exercised to the benefit of the community, but generally to its injury.

In the same section it is provided, that "the privilege of the writ of habeas corpus shall not be suspended, unless when in cases of rebellion and invasion, the public safety may require it." This clause limits the power of the legislature to deprive a citizen of the right of habeas corpus, to particular cases viz. those of rebellion and invasion; the reason is plain, because in no other cases can this power be exercised for the general good.

Let us apply these remarks to the case of standing armies in times of peace. If they generally prove the destruction of the happiness and liberty of the people, the legislature ought not to have power to keep them up, or if they had, this power should be so restricted, as to secure the people against the danger arising from the exercise of it.

That standing armies are dangerous to the liberties of a people was proved in my last number—If it was necessary, the truth of the position might be confirmed by the history of almost every nation in the world. A cloud of the most illustrious patriots of every age and country, where freedom has been enjoyed, might be adduced as witnesses in support of the sentiment. But I presume it would be useless, to enter into a laboured argument, to prove to the people of America, a position, which has so long and so generally been received by them as a kind of axiom.

Some of the advocates for this new system controvert this sentiment, as they do almost every other that has been maintained by the best writers on free government.—Others, though they will not expressly deny, that standing armies in times of peace are dangerous, yet join with these in maintaining, that it is proper the general government should be vested with the power to do it. I shall now proceed to examine the arguments they adduce in support of their opinions.

A writer, in favor of this system, treats this objection as a ridiculous one. He supposes it would be as proper to provide against the introduction of Turkish janizaries, or against making the Alcoran a rule of faith.

From the positive, and dogmatic manner, in which this author delivers his opinions, and answers objections made to his sentiments—one would conclude, that he was some pedantic pedagogue who had been accustomed to deliver his dogmas to pupils, who always placed implicit faith in what he delivered.

But, why is this provision so ridiculous? because, says this author, it is unnecessary. But, why is it unnecessary? "because, the principles and habits, as well as the power of the Americans are directly opposed to standing armies; and there is as little necessity to guard against them by positive constitutions, as to prohibit the establishment of the Mahometan religion." It is admitted then, that a standing army in time of peace, is an evil. I ask then, why should this government be authorised to do evil? If the principles and habits of the people of this country are opposed to standing armies in time of peace, if they do not contribute to the public good, but would endanger the public liberty and happiness, why should the government be vested with the power? No reason can be given, why rulers should be authorised to do, what, if done, would oppose the principles and habits of the people, and endanger the public safety, but there is every reason in the world, that they should be prohibited from the exercise of such a power. But this author supposes, that no danger is to be apprehended from the exercise of this power, because, if armies are kept up, it will be by the people themselves, and therefore, to provide against it, would be as absurd as for a man to "pass a law in his family, that no troops should be quartered in his family by his consent." This reasoning supposes, that the general government is to be exercised by the people of America themselves—But such an idea is groundless and absurd. There is surely a distinction between the people and their rulers, even when the latter are representatives of the former. They certainly are not identically the same, and it cannot be disputed, but it may and often does happen, that they do not possess the same sentiments or pursue the same interests. I think I have shewn, that as this government is constituted, there is little reason to expect, that the interest of the people and their rulers will be the same.

Besides, if the habits and sentiments of the people of America are to be relied upon, as the sole security against the encroachment of their rulers, all restrictions in constitutions are unnecessary; nothing more is requisite, than to declare who shall be authorized to exercise the powers of government, and about this we need not be very careful—for the habits and principles of the people will oppose every abuse of power. This I suppose to be the sentiments of this author, as it seems to be of many of the advocates of this new system. An opinion like this, is as directly opposed to the principles and habits of the people of America, as it is to the sentiments of every writer of reputation on the science of government, and repugnant to the principles of reason and common sense.

The idea that there is no danger of the establishment of a standing army, under the new constitution, is without foundation.

It is a well known fact, that a number of those who had an agency in producing this system, and many of those who it is probable will have a principal share in the administration of the government under it, if it is adopted, are avowedly in favour of standing armies. It is a language common among them, "That no people can be kept in order, unless the government have an army to awe them into obedience; it is necessary to support the dignity of government, to have a military establishment." And there will not be wanting a variety of plausible reason to justify the raising one, drawn from the danger we are in from the Indians on our frontiers, or from the European provinces in our neighbourhood. If to this we add, that an army will afford a decent support, and agreeable employment to the young men of many families, who are too indolent to follow occupations that will require care and industry, and too poor to live without doing any business we can have little reason to

doubt, but that we shall have a large standing army, as soon as this government can find money to pay them, and perhaps sooner.

A writer, who is the boast of the advocates of this new constitution, has taken great pains to shew, that this power was proper and necessary to be vested in the general government.

He sets out with calling in question the candour and integrity of those who advance the objection, and with insinuating, that it is their intention to mislead the people, by alarming their passions, rather than to convince them by arguments addressed to their understandings.

The man who reproves another for a fault, should be careful that he himself be not guilty of it. How far this writer has manifested a spirit of candour, and has pursued fair reasoning on this subject, the impartial public will judge, when his arguments pass before them in review.

He first attempts to shew, that this objection is futile and disingenuous, because the power to keep up standing armies, in time of peace, is vested, under the present government, in the legislature of every state in the union, except two. Now this is so far from being true, that it is expressly declared, by the present articles of confederation, that no body of forces "shall be kept up by any state, in time of peace, except such number only, as in the judgment of the United States in Congress assembled, shall be deemed requisite to garrison the forts necessary for the defence of such state." Now, was it candid and ingenuous to endeavour to persuade the public, that the general government had no other power than your own legislature have on this head; when the truth is, your legislature have no authority to raise and keep up any forces?

He next tells us, that the power given by this constitution, on this head, is similar to that which Congress possess under the present confederation. As little ingenuity is manifested in this representation as in that of the former.

I shall not undertake to enquire whether or not Congress are vested with a power to keep up a standing army in time of peace; it has been a subject warmly debated in Congress, more than once, since the peace; and one of the most respectable states in the union, were so fully convinced that they had no such power, that they expressly instructed their delegates to enter a solemn protest against it on the journals of Congress, should they attempt to exercise it.

But should it be admitted that they have the power, there is such a striking dissimilarity between the restrictions under which the present Congress can exercise it, and that of the proposed government, that the comparison will serve rather to shew the impropriety of vesting the proposed government with the power, than of justifying it.

It is acknowledged by this writer, that the powers of Congress, under the present confederation, amount to little more than that of recommending. If they determine to raise troops, they are obliged to effect it through the authority of the state legislatures. This will, in the first instance, be a most powerful restraint upon them, against ordering troops to be raised. But if they should vote an army, contrary to the opinion and wishes of the people, the legislatures of the respective states would not raise them. Besides, the present Congress hold their places at the will and pleasure of the legislatures of the states who send them, and no troops can be raised, but by the assent of nine states out of the thirteen. Compare the power proposed to be lodged in the legislature on this head, under this constitution, with that vested in the present Congress, and every person of the least discernment, whose understanding is not totally blinded by prejudice, will perceive, that they bear no analogy to each other. Under the present confederation, the representatives of nine states, out of thirteen, must assent to the raising of troops, or they cannot be levied: under the proposed constitution, a less number than the representatives of two states, in the house of representatives, and the representatives of three states and an half in the senate, with the assent of the pres-ident, may raise any number of troops they please. The present Congress are restrained from an undue exercise of this power, from this consideration, they know the state legislatures, through whose authority it must be carried into effect, would not comply with the requisition for the purpose, if it was evidently opposed to the public good: the proposed constitution authorizes the legislature to carry their determinations into execution, without the intervention of any other body between them and the people. The Congress under the present form are amenable to, and removable by, the legislatures of the respective states, and are chosen for one year only; the proposed constitution does not make the members of the legislature accountable to, or removeable by the state legislatures at all; and they are chosen, the one house for six, and the other for two years; and cannot be removed until their time of service is expired, let them conduct ever so badly.—The public will judge, from the above comparison, how just a claim this writer has to that candour he affects to possess. In the mean time, to convince him, and the advocates for this system, that I possess some share of candor, I pledge myself to give up all opposition to it, on the head of standing armies, if the power to raise them be restricted as it is in the present confederation; and I believe I may safely answer, not only for myself, but for all who make the objection, that they will be satisfied with less.

Document 5.8 Patrick Henry Fears the New Constitution

Patrick Henry of Virginia was one of the great orators of the Revolutionary generation. He was a radical before the American Revolution, opposing British tariffs, taxes, and any actions they took to enforce existing laws. He spoke loudly and often about the threats to American liberty, culminating in his "Give me liberty or give me death" speech in 1775. During the war and afterwards he was elected governor five times. He was an outspoken opponent of strong central government, believing it threatened state powers and individual liberties. Although elected as a delegate, he refused to attend the Constitutional Convention, and took the lead attacking the new Constitution. Ever concerned about individual liberties, he was especially offended by the document's preamble "We the people," denying that the people authorized the Founding Fathers to speak for them in Philadelphia. Henry believed that in times of peace, there was no greater threat to Virginia's interests and liberties than the national government created in the new Constitution. James Madison and other Federalists feared Henry the most, concerned that the magical effect of his oratory would sway the convention against them. For three weeks he spoke against the document at the Virginia ratifying convention. In the following speech from the Virginia Ratifying convention, why does Henry fear for the people? What threats does he see from the new government and the creators of the document?

Mr. Henry—Mr. Chairman.—The public mind, as well as my own, is extremely uneasy at the proposed change of Government. Give me leave to form one of the number of those who wish to be thoroughly acquainted with the reasons of this perilous and uneasy situation—and why we are brought hither to decide on this great national question. I consider myself as the servant of the people of this Commonwealth, as a centinel over their rights, liberty, and happiness. I represent their feelings when I say, that they are exceedingly uneasy, being brought from that state of full security, which they enjoyed, to the present delusive appearance of things. A year ago the minds of our citizens were at perfect repose. Before the meeting of the late Federal Convention at Philadelphia, a general peace, and an universal tranquillity prevailed in this country;— but since that period they are exceedingly uneasy and disquieted. When I wished for an appointment to this Convention, my mind was extremely agitated for the situation of public affairs. I conceive the republic to be in extreme danger. If our situation be thus uneasy, whence has arisen this fearful jeopardy? It arises from this fatal system—it arises from a proposal to change our government:—A proposal that goes to the utter annihilation of the most solemn engagements of the States. A proposal of establishing 9 States into a confederacy, to the eventual exclusion of 4 States. It goes to the annihilation of those solemn treaties we have formed with foreign nations. The present circumstances of France—the good offices rendered us by that kingdom, require our most faithful and most punctual adherence to our treaty with her.

We are in alliance with the Spaniards, the Dutch, the Prussians: Those treaties bound us as thirteen States, confederated together—Yet, here is a proposal to sever that confederacy. Is it possible that we shall abandon all our treaties and national engagements?—And for what? I expected to have heard the reasons of an event so unexpected to my mind, and many others. Was our civil polity, or public justice, endangered or sapped? Was the real existence of the country threatened—or was this preceded by a mournful progression of events? This proposal of altering our Federal Government is of a most alarming nature: Make the best of this new Government— say it is composed by any thing but inspiration—you ought to be extremely cautious, watchful, jealous of your liberty; for instead of securing your rights you may lose them forever. If a wrong step be now made, the republic may be lost forever. If this new Government will not come up to the expectation of the people, and they should be disappointed—their liberty will be lost, and tyranny must and will arise. I repeat it again, and I beg Gentlemen to consider, that a wrong step made now will plunge us into misery, and our Republic will be lost. It will be necessary for this Convention to have a faithful historical detail of the facts, that preceded the session of the Federal Convention, and the reasons that actuated its members in proposing an entire alteration of Government—and to demonstrate the dangers that awaited us: If they were of such awful magnitude, as to warrant a proposal so extremely perilous as this, I must assert, that this Convention has an absolute right to a thorough discovery of every circumstance relative to this great event. And here I would make this enquiry of those worthy characters who composed a part of the late Federal Convention. I am sure they were fully impressed with the necessity of forming a great consolidated Government, instead of a confederation. That this is a consolidated Government is demonstrably clear, and the danger of such a Government, is, to my mind, very striking. I have the highest veneration for those Gentlemen, but, Sir, give me leave to demand, what right had they to say, *We, the People*. My political curiosity, exclusive of my anxious solicitude for the public welfare, leads me to ask, who authorised them to speak the language of, *We, the People*, instead of *We, the States*? States are the characteristics, and the soul of a confederation. If the States be not the agents of this compact, it must be one great consolidated National Government of the people of all the States. I have the highest respect for those Gentlemen who formed the Convention, and were some of them not here, I would express some testimonial of my esteem for them. America had on a former occasion put the utmost confidence in them: A confidence which was well placed: And I am sure, Sir, I would give up any thing to them; I would chearfully confide in them as my Representatives. But, Sir, on this great occasion, I would demand the cause of their conduct.—Even from that illustrious man, who saved us by his valor, I would have a reason for his conduct—that liberty which he has given us by his valor, tells me to ask this reason,—and sure I am, were he here, he would give us that reason: But there are other Gentlemen here, who can give

Patrick Henry, June 4, 1788.

us this information. The people gave them no power to use their name. That they exceeded their power is perfectly clear. It is not mere curiosity that actuates me—I wish to hear the real actual existing danger, which should lead us to take those steps so dangerous in my conception. Disorders have arisen in other parts of America, but here, Sir, no dangers, no insurrection or tumult, has happened—every thing has been calm and tranquil. But notwithstanding this, we are wandering on the great ocean of human affairs. I see no landmark to guide us. We are running we know not whither. Difference in opinion has gone to a degree of inflammatory resentment in different parts of the country—which has been occasioned by this perilous innovation. The Federal Convention ought to have amended the old system—for this purpose they were solely delegated: The object of their mission extended to no other consideration. You must therefore forgive the solicitation of one unworthy member, to know what danger could have arisen under the present confederation, and what are the causes of this proposal to change our Government.

Document 5.9 Another Founding Father Objects to the Constitution

George Mason of Virginia was closely allied with Patrick Henry, George Washington, and other leading Virginians in the resistance movement prior to the American Revolution. Thomas Jefferson credited Mason with helping develop his own ideas about rights and liberties, as well as American Independence. Mason was the architect of the Virginia constitution in 1776, and his Declaration of Rights declared that every free man had the right to "life and liberty...and pursuing and obtaining happiness and safety." Many other states copied his declaration verbatim. At the Constitutional Convention, Mason continually argued for including specific safeguards to preserve state power, restrict presidential power, provide real representative government based solely on population, guarantee real majority rule, and provide for a bill of rights, but his proposals were regularly voted down. As a result, Mason refused to sign the finished document, and wrote a pamphlet explaining his objections to the new Constitution. His first objection was "There is no Declaration of Rights." What concerns does he raise in this speech at the Virginia ratifying convention? How does the new government threaten the people? How does he dismiss some of the Federalists' bland assurances that the government has sufficient safeguards to protect individual and sectional rights?

Mr. George Mason.—Mr. Chairman—Whether the Constitution be good or bad, the present clause clearly discovers, that it is a National Government, and no longer a confederation. I mean that clause which gives the first hint of the General Government laying direct taxes. The assumption of this power of laying direct taxes, does of itself, entirely change the confederation of the States into one consolidated Government. This power being at discretion, unconfined, and without any kind of controul, must carry every thing before it. The very idea of converting what was formerly a confederation, to a consolidated Government, is totally subversive of every principle which has hitherto governed us. This power is calculated to annihilate totally the State Governments.

Will the people of this great community submit to be individually taxed by two different and distinct powers? Will they suffer themselves to be doubly harrassed? These two concurrent powers cannot exist long together; the one will destroy the other: The General Government being paramount to, and in every respect more powerful than, the State governments, the latter must give way to the former. Is it to be supposed that one National Government will suit so extensive a country, embracing so many climates, and containing inhabitants so very different in manners, habits, and customs? It is ascertained by history, that there never was a Government, over a very extensive country, without destroying the liberties of the people: History also, supported by the opinions of

---

Objections to the new Constitution, June 4, 1788.

the best writers, shew us, that monarchy may suit a large territory, and despotic Governments ever so extensive a country; but that popular Governments can only exist in small territories. Is there a single example, on the face of the earth, to support a contrary opinion? Where is there one exception to this general rule? Was there ever an instance of a general National Government extending over so extensive a country, abounding in such a variety of climates, &c. where the people retained their liberty? I solemnly declare, that no man is a greater friend to a firm Union of the American States than I am: But, Sir, if this great end can be obtained without hazarding the rights of the people, why should we recur to such dangerous principles? Requisitions have been often refused, sometimes from an impossibility of complying with them; often from that great variety of circumstances which retard the collection of monies, and, perhaps, sometimes from a wilful design of procrastinating. But why shall we give up to the National Government this power, so dangerous in its nature, and for which its members will not have sufficient information? Is it not well known, that what would be a proper tax in one State would be grievous in another? The Gentleman who hath favored us with an eulogium in favor of this system, must, after all the encomiums he has been pleased to bestow upon it, acknowledge, that our Federal Representatives must be unacquainted with the situation of their constituents: Sixty-five members cannot possibly know the situation and circumstances of all the inhabitants of this immense continent: When a certain sum comes to be taxed, and the mode of levying to be fixed, they will lay the tax on that article which will be most productive, and easiest in the collection, without consulting the real circumstances or convenience of a country, with which, in fact, they cannot be sufficiently acquainted. The mode of levying taxes is of the utmost consequence, and yet here it is to be determined by those who have neither knowledge of our situation, nor a common interest with us, nor a fellow feeling for us:—The subjects of taxation differ in three-fourths; nay, I might say with truth, in four-fifths of the States:—If we trust the National Government with an effectual way of raising the necessary sums, 'tis sufficient; every thing we do further is trusting the happiness and rights of the people: Why then should we give up this dangerous power of individual taxation? Why leave the manner of laying taxes to those, who in the nature of things, cannot be acquainted with the situation of those on whom they are to impose them, when it can be done by those who are well acquainted with it? If instead of giving this

oppressive power, we give them such an effectual alternative as will answer the purpose, without encountering the evil and danger that might arise from it, then I would chearfully acquiesce: And would it not be far more eligible? I candidly acknowledge the inefficacy of the confederation; but requisitions have been made, which were impossible to be complied with: Requisitions for more gold and silver than were in the United States: If we give the General Government the power of demanding their quotas of the States, with an alternative of laying direct taxes, in case of non compliance, then the mischief would be avoided; and the certainty of this conditional power would, in all human probability, prevent the application, and the sums necessary for the Union would be then laid by the States; by those who know how it can best be raised; by those who have a fellow-feeling for us. Give me leave to say, that the same sum raised one way with convenience and ease, would be very oppressive another way: Why then not leave this power to be exercised by those who know the mode most convenient for the inhabitants, and not by those who must necessarily apportion it in such manner as shall be oppressive? With respect to the representation so much applauded, I cannot think it such a full and free one as it is represented; but I must candidly acknowledge, that this defect results from the very nature of the Government. It would be impossible to have a full and adequate representation in the General Government; it would be too expensive and too unweildy: We are then under the necessity of having this a very inadequate representation: Is this general representation to be compared with the real, actual, substantial representation of the State Legislatures? It cannot bear a comparison. To make representation real and actual, the number of Representatives ought to be adequate; they ought to mix with the people, think as they think, feel as they feel, ought to be perfectly amenable to them, and thoroughly acquainted with their interest and condition: Now these great ingredients are, either not at all, or in so small a degree, to be found in our Federal Representatives, that we have no real, actual, substantial representation; but I acknowledge it results from the nature of the Government: The necessity of this inconvenience may appear a sufficient reason not to argue against it: But, Sir, it clearly shews, that we ought to give power with a sparing hand to a Government thus imperfectly constructed. To a Government, which, in the nature of things, cannot but be defective, no powers ought to be given, but such as are absolutely necessary: There is one thing in it which I conceive to be extremely dangerous. Gentlemen may talk of public virtue and confidence; we shall be told that the House of Representatives will consist of the most virtuous men on the Continent, and that in their hands we may trust our dearest rights. This, like all other assemblies, will be composed of some bad and some good men; and considering the natural lust of power so inherent in man, I fear the thirst of power will prevail to oppress the people:—What I conceive to be so dangerous, is the provision with respect to the number of Representatives: It does not expressly provide, that we shall have one for every 30,000, but that the number shall not exceed that proportion: The utmost that we can expect (and perhaps that is too much) is, that the present number shall be continued to us:— "The number of Representatives shall not exceed one for every 30,000." Now will not this be complied with, although the present number should never be increased, nay, although it should be decreased? Suppose Congress should say, that we should have one for every 200,000, will not the Constitution be complied with? For one for every 200,000 does not exceed one for every 30,000. There is a want of proportion that ought to be strictly guarded against: The worthy Gentleman tells us, we have no reason to fear; but I always fear for the rights of the people: I do not pretend to inspiration, but I think, it is apparent as the day, that the members will attend to local partial interests to prevent an augmentation of their number: I know not how they will be chosen, but whatever be the mode of choosing, our present number is but ten: And suppose our State is laid off in ten districts; those Gentlemen who shall be sent from those districts will lessen their own power and influence, in their respective districts, if they increase their number; for the greater the number of men among whom any given quantum of power is divided, the less the power of each individual. Thus they will have a local interest to prevent the increase of, and perhaps they will lessen their own number: This is evident on the face of the Constitution—so loose an expression ought to be guarded against; for Congress will be clearly within the requisition of the Constitution, although the number of Representatives should always continue what it is now, and the population of the country should increase to an immense number. Nay, they may reduce the number from 65, to one from each State, without violating the Constitution; and thus the number which is now too small, would then be infinitely too much so: But my principal objection is, that the confederation is converted to one general consolidated Government, which, from my best judgment of it (and which perhaps will be shewn in the course of this discussion) to be really well founded is one of the worst curses that can possibly befal a nation. Does any man suppose, that one general National Government can exist in so extensive a country as this? I hope that a Government may be framed which may suit us, by drawing the line between the general and State Governments, and prevent that dangerous clashing of interest and power, which must, as it now stands, terminate in the destruction of one or the other. When we come to the Judiciary, we shall be more convinced, that this Government will terminate in the annihilation of the State Governments: The question then will be, whether a consolidated Government can preserve the freedom, and secure the great rights of the people.

If such amendments be introduced as shall exclude danger, I shall most gladly put my hand to it. When such amendments, as shall, from the best information, secure the great essential rights of the people, shall be agreed to by Gentlemen, I shall most heartily make the greatest concessions, and concur in any reasonable measure to obtain the desirable end of conciliation and unanimity. An indispensible amendment in this case, is, that Congress shall not exercise the power of raising direct taxes till the States shall have refused to comply with the requisitions of Congress. On this condition it may be granted, but I see no reason to grant it unconditionally; as the States can raise the taxes with more ease, and lay them on the inhabitants with more propriety, than it is possible for the General Government to do. If Congress hath this power without controul, the taxes will be laid by those who have no fellow-feeling or acquaintance with the people. This is my objection to the article now under consideration. It is a very great and important one. I therefore beg Gentlemen seriously to consider it. Should this power be restrained, I shall withdraw my objections to this part of the Constitution: But as it stands, it is an objection so strong in my mind, that its amendment is with me, a *sine qua non*, of its adoption. I wish for such amendments, and such only, as are necessary to secure the dearest rights of the people.

Document 5.10 James Madison and Alexander Hamilton Support the New Government: *The Federalist #10, #51, #55, #70, #78*

Antifederalist forces were very strong in New York. To win this critical state, Alexander Hamilton, James Madison, and John Jay wrote a series of essays known as *The Federalist*. These essays were works of propaganda, not high political theory. They were intended to address concerns raised by Antifederalists and gain people's confidence in the motives of the new government. Nevertheless, they discuss the key issues surrounding the powers of the new government and preserving the heritage of the American Revolution, with greater clarity than the convention debates. *Federalist #10* addresses the role of factions and special interests in the government. Madison claims that the best way to resist the evils of factions and special interests is to have more of them, and let them balance each other out. Madison also suggests that territorial growth will preserve liberty and representative government. Some scholars think Madison is appealing to landed classes for support here, by giving the rest of society hope for land elsewhere. In *Federalist #51* Madison addresses the lack of guarantees for natural rights of citizens, by arguing that the designed separation of powers will prevent an abusive government, as will competing interests in the government itself. *Federalist #55* addresses concerns that the new Congress is too small to truly represent the people, and as a result they will only represent some of the people. Hamilton addressed other concerns in *# 70 & # 78*. Americans, who fought to get rid of a king and corrupt judges, feared creating a new powerful executive, and having to rid themselves again of judges serving only the government. Together they (an executive and judges) could abuse those who disagreed with them, eliminating their rights and liberties. Hamilton argues that a strong, "energetic" national executive is necessary for the survival of the government and the United States itself. He promised only the "best people" would become federal judges, and they would never become petty tyrants. Do you think that Madison and Hamilton truly address the fears of the Antifederalists? Can you identify areas of concern not touched? Do their answers, and the guarantees they provide, give the same protections as the bill of rights the Antifederalists are calling for? Do you agree with their analysis of how the new government—Congress, President, and Judiciary—will work?

The Federalist No. 10 (1787)

November 22, 1787

To the People of the State of New York:

Among the numerous advantages promised by a well constructed Union, none deserves to be more accurately developed than its tendency to break and control the violence of faction. The friend of popular governments, never finds himself so much alarmed for their character and fate, as when he contemplates their propensity to this dangerous vice. He will not fail therefore to set a due value on any plan which, without violating the principles to which he is attached, provides a proper cure for it. The instabil-

ity, injustice and confusion introduced into the public councils, have in truth been the mortal diseases under which popular governments have every where perished; as they continue to be the favorite and fruitful topics from which the adversaries to liberty derive their most specious declamations. The valuable improvements made by the American constitutions on the popular models, both ancient and modern, cannot certainly be too much admired; but it would be an unwarrantable partiality, to contend that they have as effectually obviated the danger on this side as was wished and expected. Complaints are every where heard from our most considerate and virtuous citizens, equally the friends of public and private faith, and of public and personal liberty; that our governments are too unstable; that the public good is

---

The Federalist Papers, Nos. 10, 51, 55, 70 and 78.

disregarded in the conflicts of rival parties; and that measures are too often decided, not according to the rules of justice, and the rights of the minor party; but by the superior force of an interested and overbearing majority. However anxiously we may wish that these complaints had no foundation, the evidence of known facts will not permit us to deny that they are in some degree true. It will be found indeed, on a candid review of our situation, that some of the distresses under which we labor, have been erroneously charged on the operation of our governments; but it will be found, at the same time, that other causes will not alone account for many of our heaviest misfortunes; and particularly, for that prevailing and increasing distrust of public engagements, and alarm for private rights, which are echoed from one end of the continent to the other. These must be chiefly, if not wholly, effects of the unsteadiness and injustice, with which a factious spirit has tainted our public administrations.

By a faction I understand a number of citizens, whether amounting to a majority or minority of the whole, who are united and actuated by some common impulse of passion, or of interest, adverse to the rights of other citizens, or to the permanent and aggregate interests of the community.

There are two methods of curing the mischiefs of faction: the one, by removing its causes; the other, by controlling its effects.

There are again two methods of removing the causes of faction: the one by destroying the liberty which is essential to its existence; the other, by giving to every citizen the same opinions, the same passions, and the same interests.

It could never be more truly said than of the first remedy, that it is worse than the disease. Liberty is to faction, what air is to fire, an ailment without which it instantly expires. But it could not be a less folly to abolish liberty, which is essential to political life, because it nourishes faction, than it would be to wish the annihilation of air, which is essential to animal life, because it imparts to fire its destructive agency.

The second expedient is as impracticable, as the first would be unwise. As long as the reason of man continues fallible, and he is at liberty to exercise it, different opinions will be formed. As long as the connection subsists between his reason and his self-love, his opinions and his passions will have a reciprocal influence on each other; and the former will be objects to which the latter will attach themselves. The diversity in the faculties of men from which the rights of property originate, is not less an insuperable obstacle to a uniformity of interests. The protection of these faculties is the first object of Government.

From the protection of different and unequal faculties of acquiring property, the possession of different degrees and kinds of property immediately results: and from the influence of these on the sentiments and views of the respective proprietors, ensues a division of the society into different interests and parties.

The latent causes of faction are thus sown in the nature of man; and we see them every where brought into different degrees of activity, according to the different circumstances of civil society. A zeal for different opinions concerning religion, concerning Government and many other points, as well of speculation as of practice; an attachment to different leaders ambitiously contending for preeminence and power; or to persons of other descriptions whose fortunes have been interesting to the human passions, have in turn divided mankind into parties, inflamed them with mutual animosity, and rendered them much more disposed to vex and oppress each other, than to cooperate for their common good. So strong is this propensity of mankind to fall into mutual animosities, that where no substantial occasion presents itself, the most frivolous and fanciful distinctions have been sufficient to kindle their unfriendly passions, and excite their most violent conflicts. But the most common and durable source of factions, has been the various and unequal distribution of property. Those who hold, and those who are without property, have ever formed distinct interests in society. Those who are creditors, and those who are debtors, fall under a like discrimination. A landed interest, a manufacturing interest, a mercantile interest, a monied interest, with many lesser interests, grow up of necessity in civilized nations, and divide them into different classes, actuated by different sentiments and views. The regulation of these various and interfering interests forms the principal task of modern Legislation, and involves the spirit of party and faction in the necessary and ordinary operations of Government.

No man is allowed to be a judge in his own cause; because his interest would certainly bias his judgment, and, not improbably, corrupt his integrity. With equal, nay with greater reason, a body of men, are unfit to be both judges and parties, at the same time; yet, what are many of the most important acts of legislation, but so many judicial determinations, not indeed concerning the rights of single persons, but concerning the rights of large bodies of citizens; and what are the different classes of legislators, but advocates and parties to the causes which they determine? Is a law proposed concerning private debts? It is a question to which the creditors are parties on one side, and the debtors on the other. Justice ought to hold the balance between them. Yet the parties are and must be themselves the judges; and the most numerous party, or, in other words the most powerful faction must be expected to prevail. Shall domestic manufactures be encouraged, and in what degree, by restrictions on foreign manufactures? are questions which would be differently decided by the landed and the manufacturing classes; and probably by neither, with a sole regard to justice and the public good. The apportionment of taxes on the various descriptions of property, is an act which seems to require the most exact impartiality; yet, there is perhaps no legislative act in which greater opportunity and temptation are given to a predominant party, to trample on the rules of justice. Every shilling with which they overburden the inferior number, is a shilling saved to their own pockets.

It is in vain to say, that enlightened statesmen will be able to adjust these clashing interests, and render them all subservient to the public good. Enlightened statesmen will not always be at the helm. Nor, in many cases, can such an adjustment be made at all, without taking into view indirect and remote considerations, which will rarely prevail over the immediate interest which one party may find in disregarding the rights of another, or the good of the whole.

The inference to which we are brought, is, that the causes of faction cannot be removed; and that relief is only to be sought in the means of controlling its *effects*.

If a faction consists of less than a majority, relief is supplied by the republican principle, which enables the majority to defeat its sinister views by regular vote: It may clog the administration, it may convulse the society; but it will be unable to execute and mask its violence under the forms of the Constitution. When a majority is included in a faction, the form of popular government on the other hand enables it to sacrifice to its ruling passion or interest, both the public good and the rights of other citizens. To secure the public good, and private rights, against the danger of such a faction, and at the same time to preserve the spirit and the form of popular government, is then the great object to which our enquiries are directed: Let me add that it is the great desideratum, by which alone this form of government can be rescued from the opprobrium under which it has so long labored, and be recommended to the esteem and adoption of mankind.

By what means is this object attainable? Evidently by one of two only. Either the existence of the same passion or interest in a majority at the same time, must be prevented; or the majority, having such

coexistent passion or interest, must be tendered, by their number and local situation, unable to concert and carry into effect schemes of oppression. If the impulse and the opportunity be suffered to coincide, we well know that neither moral nor religious motives can be relied on as an adequate control. They are not found to be such on the injustice and violence of individuals, and lose their efficacy in proportion to the number combined together; that is, in proportion as their efficacy becomes needful.

From this view of the subject, it may be concluded that a pure Democracy, by which I mean, a Society, consisting of a small number of citizens, who assemble and administer the Government in person, can admit of no cure for the mischiefs of faction. A common passion or interest will, in almost every case, be felt by a majority of the whole; a communication and concert results from the form of Government itself; and there is nothing to check the inducements to sacrifice the weaker party, or an obnoxious individual. Hence it is, that such Democracies have ever been spectacles of turbulence and contention; have ever been found incompatible with personal security, or the rights of property; and have in general been as short in their lives, as they have been violent in their deaths. Theoretic politicians, who have patronized this species of Government, have erroneously supposed, that by reducing mankind to a perfect equality in their political rights, they would, at the same time, be perfectly equalized and assimilated in their possessions, their opinions, and their passions.

A Republic, by which I mean a Government in which the scheme of representation takes place, opens a different prospect, and promises the cure for which we are seeking. Let us examine the points in which it varies from pure Democracy, and we shall comprehend both the nature of the cure, and the efficacy which it must derive from the Union.

The two great points of difference between a Democracy and a Republic are, first, the delegation of the Government, in the latter, to a small number of citizens elected by the rest: secondly, the greater number of citizens, and greater sphere of country, over which the latter may be extended.

The effect of the first difference is, on the one hand to refine and enlarge the public views, by passing them through the medium of a chosen body of citizens, whose wisdom may best discern the true interest of their country, and whose patriotism and love of justice, will be least likely to sacrifice it to temporary or partial considerations. Under such a regulation, it may well happen that the public voice pronounced by the representatives of the people, will be more consonant to the public good, than if pronounced by the people themselves convened for the purpose. On the other hand, the effect may be inverted. Men of factious tempers, of local prejudices, or of sinister designs, may by intrigue, by corruption or by other means, first obtain the suffrages, and then betray the interests of the people. The question resulting is, whether small or extensive Republics are most favorable to the election of proper guardians of the public weal: and it is clearly decided in favor of the latter by two obvious considerations.

In the first place it is to be remarked that however small the Republic may be, the Representatives must be raised to a certain number, in order to guard against the cabals of a few; and that however large it may be, they must be limited to a certain number, in order to guard against the confusion of a multitude. Hence the number of Representatives in the two cases, not being in proportion to that of the Constituents, and being proportionally greatest in the small Republic, it follows, that if the proportion of fit characters, be not less, in the large than in the small Republic, the former will present a greater option, and consequently a greater probability of a fit choice.

In the next place, as each Representative will be chosen by a greater number of citizens in the large than in the small Republic, it will be more difficult for unworthy candidates to practice with success the vicious arts, by which elections are too often carried; and the suffrages of the people being more free, will be more likely to center on men who possess the most attractive merit, and the most diffusive and established characters.

It must be confessed, that in this, as in most other cases, there is a mean, on both sides of which inconveniences will be found to lie. By enlarging too much the number of electors, you render the representative too little acquainted with all their local circumstances and lesser interests; as by reducing it too much, you render him unduly attached to these, and too little fit to comprehend and pursue great and national objects. The Federal Constitution forms a happy combination in this respect; the great and aggregate interests being referred to the national, the local and particular, to the state legislatures.

The other point of difference is, the greater number of citizens and extent of territory which may be brought within the compass of Republican, than of Democratic Government; and it is this circumstance principally which renders factious combinations less to be dreaded in the former, than in the latter. The smaller the society, the fewer probably will be the distinct parties and interests composing it; the fewer the distinct parties and interests, the more frequently will a majority be found of the same party; and the smaller the number of individuals composing a majority, and the smaller the compass within which they are placed, the more easily will they concert and execute their Plans of oppression. Extend the sphere, and you take in a greater variety of parties and interests; you make it less probable that a majority of the whole will have a common motive to invade the rights of other citizens; or if such a common motive exists, it will be more difficult for all who feel it to discover their own strength, and to act in unison with each other. Besides other impediments, it may be remarked, that where there is a consciousness of unjust or dishonorable purposes, communication is always checked by distrust, in proportion to the number whose concurrence is necessary.

Hence it clearly appears, that the same advantage, which a Republic has over a Democracy, in controlling the effects of faction, is enjoyed by a large over a small Republic—is enjoyed by the Union over the States composing it. Does this advantage consist in the substitution of Representatives, whose enlightened views and virtuous sentiments render them superior to local prejudices, and to schemes of injustice? It will not be denied, that the Representation of the Union will be most likely to possess these requisite endowments. Does it consist in the greater security afforded by a greater variety of parties, against the event of any one part being able to outnumber and oppress the rest? In an equal degree does the increased variety of parties, comprised within the Union, increase this security. Does it, in fine, consist in the greater obstacles opposed to the concert and accomplishment of the secret wishes of an unjust and interested majority? Here, again, the extent of the Union gives it the most palpable advantage.

The influence of factious leaders may kindle a flame within their particular States, but will be unable to spread a general conflagration through the other States: a religious sect, may degenerate into a political faction in a part of the Confederacy; but the variety of sects dispersed over the entire fact of it, must secure the national Councils against any danger from that source: a rage for paper money, for an abolition of debts, for an equal division of property, or for any other improper or wicked project, will be less apt to pervade the whole body of the Union, than a particular member of it; in the same proportion as such a malady is more likely to taint a particular county or district, than an entire State.

In the extent and proper structure of the Union, therefore, we behold a Republican remedy for the diseases most incident to Republican Government. And according to the degree of pleasure and pride, we feel in being Republicans, ought to be our zeal in cherishing the spirit, and supporting the character of Federalists.

PUBLIUS.

The Federalist No. 51 (1788)

February 6, 1788

To the People of the State of New York:

To what expedient, then, shall we finally resort, for maintaining in practice the necessary partition of power among the several departments as laid down in the Constitution? The only answer that can be given is that as all these exterior provisions are found to be inadequate, the defect must be supplied, by so contriving the interior structure of the government as that its several constituent parts may, by their mutual relations, be the means of keeping each other in their proper places. Without presuming to undertake a full development of this important idea I will hazard a few general observations which may perhaps place it in a clearer light, and enable us to form a more correct judgment of the principles and structure of the government planned by the convention.

In order to lay a due foundation for that separate and distinct exercise of the different powers of government, which to a certain extent is admitted on all hands to be essential to the preservation of liberty, it is evident that each department should have a will of its own: and consequently should be so constituted that the members of each should have as little agency as possible in the appointment of the members of the others. Were this principle rigorously adhered to, it would require that all the appointments for the supreme executive, legislative, and judiciary magistracies should be drawn from the same fountain of authority, the people, through channels having no communication whatever with one another. Perhaps such a plan of constructing the several departments would be less difficult in practice than it may in contemplation appear. Some difficulties, however, and some additional expense would attend the execution of it. Some deviations, therefore, from the principle must be admitted. In the constitution of the judiciary department in particular, it might be inexpedient to insist rigorously on the principle: first, because peculiar qualifications being essential in the members, the primary consideration ought to be to select that mode of choice which best secures these qualifications; second, because the permanent tenure by which the appointments are held in that department must soon destroy all sense of dependence on the authority conferring them.

It is equally evident, that the members of each department should be as little dependent as possible on those of the others for the emoluments annexed to their offices. Were the executive magistrate, or the judges, not independent of the legislature in this particular, their independence in every other would be merely nominal.

But the great security against a gradual concentration of the several powers in the same department consists in giving to those who administer each department the necessary constitutional means and personal motives to resist encroachments of the other. The provision for defense must in this, as in all other cases, be made to counteract ambition. The interest of the man must be connected with the constitutional rights of the place. It may be a reflection on human nature that such devices should be necessary to control the abuses of government. But what is government itself but the greatest of all reflections on human nature? If men were angels, no government would be necessary. If angels were to govern men, neither external nor internal controls on government would be necessary. In framing a government which is to be administered by men over men, the great difficulty lies in this: you must first enable the government to control the governed: and in the next place oblige it to control itself. A dependence on the people is, no doubt, the primary control on the government; but experience has taught mankind the necessity of auxiliary precautions.

This policy of supplying, by opposite and rival interests, the defect of better motives, might be traced through the whole system of human affairs, private as well as public. We see it particularly displayed in all the subordinate distributions of power, where the constant aim is to divide and arrange the several offices in such a manner as that each may be a check on the other—that the private interest of every individual may be a sentinel over the public rights. These inventions of prudence cannot be less requisite in the distribution of the supreme powers of the State.

But it is not possible to give to each department an equal power of self-defense. In republican government, the legislative authority necessarily predominates. The remedy for this inconveniency is to divide the legislature into different branches: and to render them, by different modes of election and different principles of action, as little connected with each other as the nature of their common functions and their common dependence on the society will admit. It may even be necessary to guard against dangerous encroachments by still further precautions. As the weight of the legislative authority requires that it should be thus divided, the weakness of the executive may require, on the other hand, that it should be fortified. An absolute negative on the legislature appears, at first view, to be the natural defense with which the executive magistrate should be armed. But perhaps it would be neither altogether safe nor alone sufficient. On ordinary occasions it might not be exerted with the requisite firmness, and on extraordinary occasions it might be perfidiously abused. May not this defect of an absolute negative be supplied by some qualified connection between this weaker department and the weaker branch of the stronger department, by which the latter may be led to support the constitutional rights of the former, without being too much detached from the rights of its own departments?

If the principles on which these observations are founded be just, as I persuade myself they are, and they be applied as a criterion to the several State constitutions, and to the federal Constitution, it will be found that if the latter does not perfectly correspond with them, the former are infinitely less able to bear such a test.

There are, moreover, two considerations particularly applicable to the federal system of America, which place that system in a very interesting point of view.

First. In a single republic, all the power surrendered by the people is submitted to the administration of a single government; and the usurpations are guarded against by a division of the government into distinct and separate departments. In the compound republic of America, the power surrendered by the people is first divided between two distinct governments, and then the portion allotted to each subdivided among distinct and separate departments. Hence a double security arises to the rights of the people. The different governments will control each other, at the same time that each will be controlled by itself.

Second. It is of great importance in a republic not only to guard the society against the oppression of its rulers, but to guard one part of the society against the injustice of the other part. Different interests necessarily exist in different classes of citizens. If a majority be united by a common interest, the rights of the minority will be insecure. There are but two methods of providing against this evil: the one by creating a will in the community independent of the majority—that is, of the society itself; the other, by comprehending in the society so many separate descriptions of citizens as will render an unjust combination of a majority of the whole very improbable if not impracticable. The first method prevails in all governments possessing an hereditary or self-appointed authority. This, at best, is but a precarious security; because a power independent of the society may as well espouse the unjust views of the major as the rightful interests of the minor party, and may possibly be turned against both parties. The second method will be exemplified in the federal republic of the United States. Whilst all authority in it will be derived from and dependent on the society, the society itself will be broken into so many parts, interests and classes of citizens, that the rights of individuals, or of the minority, will be in little danger from interested combinations of the majority. In a free government the security for civil rights must be the same as that for religious rights. It consists in the one case in the multiplicity of interests, and in the other in the multiplicity of sects. The degree of security in both cases will depend on the number of interests and sects; and this may be presumed to depend on the extent of country and number of people comprehended under the same government. This view of the subject must particularly recommend a proper federal system to all the sincere and considerate friends of republican government, since it shows that in exact proportion as the territory of the Union may be formed into more circumscribed Confederacies, or States, oppressive combinations of a majority will be facilitated; the best security, under the republican forms, for the rights of every class of citizen, will be diminished; and consequently the stability and independence of some member of the government the only other security, must be proportionally increased. Justice is the end of government. It is the end of civil society. It ever has been and ever will be pursued until it be obtained, or until liberty be lost in the pursuit. In a society under the forms of which the stronger faction can readily unite and oppress the weaker, anarchy may as truly be said to reign as in a state of nature, where the weaker individual is not secured against the violence of the stronger; and as, in the latter state, even the stronger individuals are prompted, by the uncertainty of their condition, to submit to a government which may protect the weak as well as themselves; so, in the former state, will the more powerful factions or parties be gradually induced, by a like motive, to wish for a government which will protect all parties, the weaker as well as the more powerful. It can be little doubted that if the State of Rhode Island was separated from the Confederacy and left to itself, the insecurity of rights under the popular form of government within such narrow limits would be displayed by such reiterated oppressions of factious majorities that some power altogether independent of the people would soon be called for by the voice of the very factions whose misrule had proved the necessity of it. In the extended republic of the United States, and among the great variety of interests, parties, and sects which it embraces, a coalition of a majority of the whole society could seldom take place on any other principles than those of justice and the general good; whilst there being thus less danger to a minor from the will of a major party, there must be less pretext, also, to provide for the security of the former, by introducing into the government a will not dependent on the latter or, in other words, a will independent of the society itself. It is no less certain than it is important, notwithstanding the contrary opinions which have been entertained, that the larger the society, provided it lie within a practicable sphere, the more duly capable it will be of self-government. And happily for the *republican cause*, the practicable sphere may be carried to a very great extent by a judicious modification and mixture of the *federal principle*.

PUBLIUS.

The Federalist Papers: No. 55

No. 55: Madison

The number of which the House of Representatives is to consist forms another and a very interesting point of view under which this branch of the federal legislature may be contemplated. Scarce any article, indeed, in the whole Constitution seems to be tendered more worthy of attention by the weight of character and the apparent force of argument with which it has been assailed. The charges exhibited against it are, first, that so small a number of representatives will be an unsafe depositary of the public interests; second, that they will not possess a proper knowledge of the local circumstances of their numerous constituents; third, that they will be taken from that class of citizens which will sympathize least with the feelings of the mass of the people and be most likely to aim at a permanent elevation of the few on the depression of the many; fourth, that defective as the number will be in the first instance, it will be more and more disproportionate, by the increase of the

people and the obstacles which will prevent a correspondent increase of the representatives.

In general it may be remarked on this subject that no political problem is less susceptible of a precise solution than that which relates to the number most convenient for a representative legislature; nor is there any point on which the policy of the several States is more at variance, whether we compare their legislative assemblies directly with each other, or consider the proportions which they respectively bear to the number of their constituents. Passing over the difference between the smallest and largest States, as Delaware, whose most numerous branch consists of twenty-one representatives, and Massachusetts, where it amounts to between three and four hundred, a very considerable difference is observable among States nearly equal in population. The number of representatives in Pennsylvania is not more than one fifth of that in the State last mentioned. New York, whose population is to that of South Carolina as six to five, has little more than one third of the number of representatives. As great a disparity prevails between the States of Georgia and Delaware or Rhode Island. In Pennsylvania, the representatives do not bear a greater proportion to their constituents than of one for every four or five thousand. In Rhode Island, they bear a proportion of at least one for every thousand. And according to the constitution of Georgia, the proposition may be carried to one to every ten electors; and must unavoidably far exceed the proportion in any of the other States.

Another general remark to be made is that the ratio between the representatives and the people ought not to be the same where the latter are very numerous as where they are very few. Were the representatives in Virginia to be regulated by the standard in Rhode Island, they would, at this time, amount to between four and five hundred; and twenty or thirty years hence, to a thousand. On the other hand, the ratio of Pennsylvania, if applied to the State of Delaware, would reduce the representative assembly of the latter to seven or eight members. Nothing can be more fallacious than to found our political calculations on arithmetical principles. Sixty or seventy men may be more properly trusted with a given degree of power than six or seven. But it does not follow that six or seven hundred would be proportionably a better depositary. And if we carry on the supposition to six or seven thousand, the whole reasoning ought to be reversed. The truth is that in all cases a certain number at least seems to be necessary to secure the benefits of free consultation and discussion, and to guard against too easy a combination for improper purposes; as, on the other hand, the number ought at most to be kept within a certain limit, in order to avoid the confusion and intemperance of a multitude. In all very numerous assemblies, of whatever characters composed, passion never fails to wrest the scepter from reason. Had every Athenian citizen been a Socrates, every Athenian assembly would still have been a mob.

It is necessary also to recollect here the observations which were applied to the case of biennial elections. For the same reason that the limited powers of the Congress, and the control of the State legislatures, justify less frequent election than the public safety might otherwise require, the members of the Congress need be less numerous than if they possessed the whole power of legislation, and were under no other than the ordinary restraints of other legislative bodies.

With these general ideas in our minds, let us weigh the objections which have been stated against the number of members proposed for the House of Representatives. It is said, in the first place, that so small a number cannot be safety trusted with so much power.

The number of which this branch of the legislature is to consist, at the outset of the government, will be sixty-five. Within three years a census is to be taken, when the number may be augmented to one for every thirty thousand inhabitants; and within every successive period of ten years the census is to be renewed, and augmentations may continue to be made under the above limitation. It will not be thought an extravagant conjecture that the first census will, at the rate of one for every thirty thousand, raise the number of representatives to at least one hundred. Estimating the Negroes in the proportion of three fifths, it can scarcely be doubted that the population of the United States will by that time, if it does not already, amount to three millions. At the expiration of twenty-five years, according to the computed rate of increase, the number of representatives will amount to two hundred; and of fifty years, to four hundred. This is a number which, I presume, will put an end to all fears arising from the smallness of the body. I take for granted here what I shall, in answering the fourth objection, hereafter show, that the number of representatives will be augmented from time to time in the manner provided by the Constitution. On a contrary supposition, I should admit the objection to have very great weight indeed.

The true question to be decided, then, is whether the smallness of the number, as a temporary regulation, be dangerous to the public liberty? Whether sixty-five members for a few years, and a hundred or two hundred for a few more, be a safe depositary for a limited and well-guarded power of legislating for the United States? I must own that I could not give a negative answer to this question, without first obliterating every impression which I have received with regard to the present genius of the people of America, the spirit which actuates the State legislatures, and the principles which are incorporated with the political character of every class of citizens. I am unable to conceive that the people of America, in their present temper, or under any circumstances which can speedily happen, will choose, and every second year repeat the choice of, sixty-five or a hundred men who would be disposed to form and pursue a scheme of tyranny or treachery. I am unable to conceive that the State legislatures, which must feel so many motives to watch and which possess so many means of counteracting the federal legislature, would fail either to detect or to defeat a conspiracy of the latter against the liberties of their common constituents. I am equally unable to conceive that there are at this time, or can be in any short time, in the United States, any sixty-five or a hundred men capable of recommending themselves to the choice of the people at large, who would either desire or dare, within the short space of two years, to betray the solemn trust committed to them. What change of circumstances time, and a fuller population of our country may produce requires a prophetic spirit to declare, which makes no part of my pretensions. But judging from the circumstances now before us, and from the probable state of them within a moderate period of time, I must pronounce that the liberties of America cannot be unsafe in the number of hands proposed by the federal Constitution.

From what quarter can the danger proceed? Are we afraid of foreign gold? If foreign gold could so easily corrupt our federal rulers and enable them to ensnare and betray their constituents, how has it happened that we are at this time a free and independent nation? The Congress which conducted us through the Revolution was a less numerous body than their successors will be; they were not chosen by, nor responsible to, their fellow-citizens at large; though appointed from year to year, and recallable at pleasure, they were generally continued for three years, and, prior to the ratification of the federal articles, for a still longer term. They held their consultations always under the veil of secrecy; they had the sole transaction of our affairs with foreign nations; through the whole course of the war they had the fate of their country more in their hands than it is to be hoped will ever be the case with our future representatives; and from the greatness of the prize at stake, and the eagerness of the party which lost it, it may well be supposed that the use of other means than force would not have been scrupled. Yet we know by happy experience that the public trust was not betrayed, nor has the purity of our public councils in this particular ever suffered, even from the whispers of calumny.

Is the danger apprehended from the other branches of the federal government? But where are the means to be found by the President, or the Senate, or both? Their emoluments of office, it is to be presumed, will not, and without a previous corruption of the House of Representatives cannot, more than suffice for very different purposes; their private fortunes, as they must all be American citizens, cannot possibly be sources of danger. The only means, then, which they can possess, will be in the dispensation of appointments. Is it here that suspicion rests her charge? Sometimes we are told that this fund of corruption is to be exhausted by the President in subduing the virtue of the Senate. Now, the fidelity of the other House is to be the victim. The improbability of such a mercenary and perfidious combination of the several members of government, standing on as different foundations as republican principles will well admit, and at the same time accountable to the society over which they are placed, ought alone to quiet this apprehension. But, fortunately, the Constitution has provided a still further safeguard. The members of the Congress are rendered ineligible to any civil offices that may be created, or of which the emoluments may be increased, during the term of their election. No offices therefore can be dealt out to the existing members but such as may become vacant by ordinary casualties: and to suppose that these would be sufficient to purchase the guardians of the people, selected by the people themselves, is to renounce every rule by which events ought to be calculated, and to substitute an indiscriminate and unbounded jealousy, with which all reasoning must be vain. The sincere friends of liberty who give themselves up to the extravagancies of this passion are not aware of the injury they do their own cause. As there is a degree of depravity in mankind which requires a certain degree of circumspection and distrust, so there are other qualitics in human nature which justify a certain portion of esteem and confidence. Republican government presupposes the existence of these qualities in a higher degree than any other form. Were the pictures which have been drawn by the political jealousy of some among us faithful likenesses of the human char-

acter, the inference would be that there is not sufficient virtue among men for self-government; and that nothing less than the chains of despotism can restrain them from destroying and devouring one another.

PUBLIUS.

The Federalist Papers: No. 70

To the People of the State of New York:

There is an idea, which is not without its advocates, that a vigorous executive is inconsistent with the genius of republican government. The enlightened well wishers to this species of government must at least hope that the supposition is destitute of foundation; since they can never admit its truth, without at the same time admitting the condemnation of their own principles. Energy in the executive is a leading character in the definition of good government. It is essential to the protection of the community against foreign attacks: It is not less essential to the steady administration of the laws, to the protection of property against those irregular and high handed combinations, which sometimes interrupt the ordinary course of justice, to the security of liberty against the enterprises and assaults of ambition, of faction and of anarchy. Every man the least conversant in Roman history knows how often that republic was obliged to take refuge in the absolute power of a single man, under the formidable title of dictator, as well against the intrigues of ambitious individuals, who aspired to the tyranny, and the seditions of whole classes of the community, whose conduct threatened the existence of all government, as against the invasions of external enemies, who menaced the conquest and destruction of Rome.

There can be no need however to multiply arguments or examples on this head. A feeble executive implies a feeble execution of the government. A feeble execution is but another phrase for a bad execution: And a government ill executed, whatever it may be in theory, must be in practice a bad government.

Taking it for granted, therefore, that all men of sense will agree in the necessity of an energetic executive; it will only remain to inquire, what are the ingredients which constitute this energy—how far can they be combined with those other ingredients which constitute safety in the republican sense? And how far does this combination characterise the plan, which has been reported by the convention?

The ingredients, which constitute energy in the executive, are first unity, secondly duration, thirdly an adequate provision for its support, fourthly competent powers.

The circumstances which constitute safety in the republican sense are, 1st. a due dependence on the people, secondly a due responsibility.

Those politicians and statesmen, who have been the most celebrated for the soundness of their principles, and for the justness of their views, have declared in favor of a single executive and a numerous legislature. They have with great propriety considered energy as the most necessary qualification of the former, and have regarded this as most applicable to power in a single hand; while they have with equal propriety considered the latter as best adapted to deliberation and wisdom, and best calculated to conciliate the confidence of the people and to secure their privileges and interests.

That unity is conducive to energy will not be disputed. Decision, activity, secrecy, and dispatch will generally characterise the proceedings of one man, in a much more eminent degree, than the proceedings of any greater number; and in proportion as the number is increased, these qualities will be diminished.

This unity may be destroyed in two ways; either by vesting the power in two or more magistrates of equal dignity and authority; or by vesting it ostensibly in one man, subject in whole or in part to the controul and co-operation of others, in the capacity of counsellors to him. Of the first the two consuls of Rome may serve as an example; of the last we shall find examples in the constitutions of several of the states. New-York and New-Jersey, if I recollect right, are the only states, which have entrusted the executive authority wholly to single men. Both these methods of destroying the unity of the executive have their partisans; but the votaries of an executive council are the most numerous. They are both liable, if not to equal, to similar objections; and may in most lights be examined in conjunction. . . .

The Federalist Papers: No. 78

To the People of the State of New York:

We proceed now to an examination of the judiciary department of the proposed government.

In unfolding the defects of the existing Confederation, the utility and necessity of a federal judicature have been clearly pointed out. It is the less necessary to recapitulate the considerations there urged, as the propriety of the institution in the abstract is not disputed; the only questions which have been raised being relative to the manner of constituting it, and to its extent. To these points, therefore, our observations shall be confined.

The manner of constituting it seems to embrace these several objects: 1st. The mode of appointing the judges. 2d. The tenure by which they are to hold their places. 3d. The partition of the judiciary authority between different courts, and their relations to each other.

First. As to the mode of appointing the judges; this is the same with that of appointing the officers of the Union in general, and has been so *fully* discussed in the two last numbers, that nothing can be said here which would not be useless repetition.

Second. As to the tenure by which the judges are to hold their places: this chiefly concerns their duration in office; the provisions for their support; the precautions for their responsibility.

According to the plan of the convention, all judges who may be appointed by the United States are to hold their offices *during good behavior*; which is conformable to the most approved of the State constitutions, and among the rest, to that of this State. Its propriety having been drawn into question by the adversaries of that plan, is no light symptom of the rage for objection, which disorders their imaginations and judgments. The standard of good behavior for the continuance in office of the judicial magistracy, is certainly one of the most valuable of the modern improvements in the practice of government. In a monarchy it is an excellent barrier to the despotism of the prince; in a republic it is a no less excellent barrier to the encroachments and oppressions of the representative body. And it is the best expedient which can be devised in any government, to secure a steady, upright, and impartial administration of the laws.

Whoever attentively considers the different departments of power must perceive, that, in a government in which they are separated from each other, the judiciary, from the nature of its functions, will always be the least dangerous to the political rights of the Constitution; because it will be least in a capacity to annoy or injure them. The Executive not only dispenses the honors, but holds the sword of the community. The legislature not only commands the purse, but prescribes the rules by which the duties and rights of every citizen are to be regulated. The judiciary, on the contrary, has no influence over either the sword or the purse; no direction either of the strength or of the wealth of the society; and can take no active resolution whatever. It may truly be said to have neither FORCE NOR WILL, but merely judgment; and must ultimately depend upon the aid of the executive arm even for the efficacy of its judgments.

This simple view of the matter suggests several important consequences. It proves incontestably, that the judiciary is beyond comparison the weakest of the three departments of power; that it can never attack with success either of the other two; and that all possible care is requisite to enable it to defend itself against their attacks. It equally proves, that though individual oppression may now and then proceed from the courts of justice, the general liberty of the people can never be endangered from that quarter; I mean so long as the judiciary remains truly distinct from both the legislature and the Executive. For I agree, that—there is no liberty, if the power of judging be not separated from the legislative and executive powers.—And it proves, in the last place, that as liberty can have nothing to fear from the judiciary alone, but would have every thing to fear from its union with either of the other departments; that as all the effects of such a union must ensue from a dependence of the former on the latter, notwithstanding a nominal and apparent separation; that as, from the natural feebleness of the judiciary, it is in continual jeopardy of being overpowered, awed, or influenced by its coordinate branches; and that as nothing can contribute so much to its firmness and independence as permanency in office, this quality may therefore be justly regarded as an indispensable ingredient in its constitution, and, in a great measure, as the citadel of the public justice and the public security.

The complete independence of the courts of justice is peculiarly essential in a limited Constitution. By a limited Constitution, I understand one which contains certain specified exceptions to the legislative authority; such, for instance, as that it shall pass no bills of attainder, no *ex-post-facto laws*, and the like. Limitations of this kind can be preserved in practice no other way than through the medium of courts of justice, whose duty it must be to declare all acts contrary to the manifest tenor of the Constitution void. Without this, all the reservations of particular rights or privileges would amount to nothing.

Some perplexity respecting the rights of the courts to pronounce legislative acts void, because contrary to the constitution, has arisen from an imagination that the doctrine would imply a superiority of the judiciary to the legislative power. It is urged that the authority which can declare the acts of another void, must necessarily be superior to the one whose acts may be declared void. As this doctrine is of great importance in all the American constitutions, a brief discussion of the ground on which it rests cannot be unacceptable.

There is no position which depends on clearer principles, than that every act of a delegated authority, contrary to the tenor of the commission under which it is exercised, is void. No legislative act, therefore, contrary to the Constitution, can be valid. To deny this, would be to affirm, that the deputy is greater than his principal; that the servant is above his master; that the representatives of the people are superior to the people themselves; that men acting by virtue of powers, may do not only what their powers do not authorize, but what they forbid.

If it be said that the legislative body are themselves the constitutional judges of their own powers, and that the construction they put upon them is conclusive upon the other departments, it may be answered, that this cannot be the natural presumption, where it is not to be collected from any particular provisions in the Constitution. It is not otherwise to be supposed, that the Constitution could intend to enable the representatives of the people to substitute their *will* to that of their constituents. It is far more rational to suppose, that the courts were designed to be an intermediate body between the people and the legislature, in order, among other things, to keep the latter within the limits assigned to their authority. The interpretation of the laws is the proper and peculiar province of the courts. A constitution is, in fact, and must be regarded by the judges, as a fundamental law. It therefore belongs to them to ascertain its meaning, as well as the meaning of any particular act proceeding from the legislative body. If there should happen to be an irreconcilable variance between the two, that which has the superior obligation and validity ought, of course, to be preferred; or, in other words, the Constitution ought to be preferred to the statute, the intention of the people to the intention of their agents.

Nor does this conclusion by any means suppose a superiority of the judicial to the legislative power. It only supposes that the power of the people is superior to both; and that where the will of the legislature, declared in its statutes, stands in opposition to that of the people, declared in the Constitution, the judges ought to be governed by the latter rather than the former. They ought to regulate their decisions by the fundamental laws, rather than by those which are not fundamental.

This exercise of judicial discretion, in determining between two contradictory laws, is exemplified in a familiar instance. It not uncommonly happens, that there are two statutes existing at one time, clashing in whole or in part with each other, and neither of them containing any repealing clause or expression. In such a case, it is the province of the courts to liquidate and fix their meaning and operation. So far as they can, by any fair construction, be reconciled to each other, reason and law conspire to dictate that this should be done; where this is impracticable, it becomes a matter of necessity to give effect to one, in exclusion of the other. The rule which has obtained in the courts for determining their relative validity is, that the last in order of time shall be preferred to the first. But this is a mere rule of construction, not derived from any positive law, but from the nature and reason of the thing. It is a rule not enjoined upon the courts by legislative provision, but adopted by themselves, as consonant to truth and propriety, for the direction of their conduct as interpreters of the law. They thought it reasonable, that between the interfering acts of an *equal* authority, that which was the last indication of its will should have the preference.

But in regard to the interfering acts of a superior and subordinate authority, of an original and derivative power, the nature and reason of the thing indicate the converse of that rule as proper to be followed. They teach us that the prior act of a superior ought to be preferred to the subsequent act of an inferior and subordinate authority; and that accordingly, whenever a particular statute contravenes the Constitution, it will be the duty of the judicial tribunals to adhere to the latter and disregard the former.

It can be of no weight to say that the courts, on the pretence of a repugnancy, may substitute their own pleasure to the constitutional intentions of the legislature. This might as well happen in the case of two contradictory statutes; or it might as well happen in every adjudication upon any single statute. The courts must declare the sense of the law; and if they should be disposed to exercise WILL instead of JUDGMENT, the consequence would equally be the substitution of their pleasure to that of the legislative body. The observation, if it prove any thing, would prove that there ought to be no judges distinct from that body.

If, then, the courts of justice are to be considered as the bulwarks of a limited Constitution against legislative encroachments, this consideration will afford a strong argument for the permanent tenure of judicial offices, since nothing will contribute so much as this to that independent spirit in the judges which must be essential to the faithful performance of so arduous a duty.

This independence of the judges is equally requisite to guard the Constitution and the rights of individuals from the effects of those ill humors, which the arts of designing men, or the influence of particular conjunctures, sometimes disseminate among the people themselves, and which, though they speedily give place to better information, and more deliberate reflection, have a tendency, in the meantime, to occasion dangerous innovations in the government, and serious oppressions of the minor party in the community. Though I trust the friends of the proposed Constitution will never concur with its enemies, in questioning that fundamental principle of republican government, which admits the right of the people to alter or abolish the established Constitution, whenever they find it inconsistent with their happiness, yet it is not to be inferred from this principle, that the representatives of the people, whenever a momentary inclination happens to lay hold of a majority of their constituents, incompatible with the provisions in the existing Constitution, would, on that account, be justifiable in a violation of those provisions; or that the courts would be under a greater obligation to connive at infractions in this shape, than when they had proceeded wholly from the cabals of the representative body. Until the people have, by some solemn and authoritative act, annulled or changed the established form, it is binding upon themselves collectively, as well as individually; and no presumption, or even knowledge, of their sentiments, can warrant their representatives in a departure from it, prior to such an act. But it is easy to see, that it would require an uncommon portion of fortitude in the judges to do their duty as faithful guardians of the Constitution, where legislative invasions of it had been instigated by the major voice of the community.

But it is not with a view to infractions of the Constitution only, that the independence of the judges may be an essential safeguard against the effects of occasional ill humors in the society. These sometimes extend no farther than to the injury of the private rights of particular classes of citizens, by unjust and partial laws. Here also the firmness of the judicial magistracy is of vast importance in mitigating the severity and confining the operation of such laws. It not only serves to moderate the immediate mischiefs of those which may have been passed but it operates as a check upon the legislative body in passing them; who, perceiving that obstacles to the success of iniquitous intention are to be expected from the scruples of the courts, are in a manner compelled, by the very motives of the injustice they meditate, to qualify their attempts. This is a circumstance calculated to have more influence upon the character of our governments, than but few may be aware of. The benefits of the integrity and moderation of the judiciary have already been felt in more States than one; and though they may have displeased those whose sinister expectations they may have disappointed, they must have commanded the esteem and applause of all the virtuous and disinterested. Considerate men, of every description, ought to prize whatever will tend to beget or fortify that temper in the courts; as no man can be sure that he may not be to-morrow the victim of a spirit of injustice, by which he may be a gainer to-day. And every man must now feel, that the inevitable tendency of such a spirit is to sap the foundations of public and private confidence, and to introduce in its stead universal distrust and distress.

That inflexible and uniform adherence to the rights of the Constitution, and of individuals, which we perceive to be indispensable in the courts of justice, can certainly not be expected from judges who hold their offices by a temporary commission. Periodical appointments, however regulated, or by whomsoever made, would, in some way or other, be fatal to their necessary independence. If the power of making them was committed either to the Executive or legislature, there would be danger of an improper complaisance to the branch which possessed it; if to both, there would be an unwillingness to hazard the displeasure of either; if to the people, or to persons chosen by them for the special purpose, there would be too great a disposition to consult popularity, to justify a reliance that nothing would be consulted but the Constitution and the laws.

There is yet a further and a weightier reason for the permanency of the judicial offices, which is deducible from the nature of the qualifications they require. It has been frequently remarked, with great propriety, that a voluminous code of laws is one of the inconveniences necessarily connected with the advantages of a free government. To avoid an arbitrary discretion in the courts, it is indispensable that they should be bound down by strict rules and precedents, which serve to define and point out their duty in every particular case that comes before them; and it will readily be conceived from the variety of controversies which grow out of the folly and wickedness of mankind, that the records of those precedents must unavoidably swell to a very considerable bulk, and must demand long and laborious study to acquire a competent knowledge of them. Hence it is, that there can be but few men in the society who will have sufficient skill in the laws to qualify them for the stations of judges. And making the proper deductions for the ordinary depravity of human nature, the number must be still smaller of those who unite the requisite integrity with the requisite knowledge. These considerations apprise us, that the government can have no great option between fit character; and that a temporary duration in office, which would naturally discourage such characters from quitting a lucrative line of practice to accept a seat on the bench, would have a tendency to throw the administration of justice into hands less able, and less well qualified, to conduct it with utility and dignity. In the present circumstances of this country, and in those in which it is likely to be for a long time to come, the disadvantages on this score would be greater than they may at first sight appear; but it must be confessed, that they are far inferior to those which present themselves under the other aspects of the subject.

Upon the whole, there can be no room to doubt that the convention acted wisely in copying from the models of those constitutions which have established *good behavior* as the tenure of their judicial offices, in point of duration; and that so far from being blamable on this account, their plan would have been inexcusably defective, if it had wanted this important feature of good government. The experience of Great Britain affords an illustrious comment on the excellence of the institution.

Document 5.11 Congress Debates Proposed Amendments to the United States Constitution, June 8, 1789

To win ratification, the Federalists promised a series of amendments to the Constitution. But after the first elections in 1788, many Federalists balked at revising the document. Madison took this promise more seriously than some Federalists, recognizing the serious concerns and genuine patriotism of those opposing the document. Personally he still believed that the greatest danger to citizens' rights came from state governments, where popular majorities could easily deprive minorities of their rights. Thousands of proposed amendments came to his committee, some minor in nature, others clear attempts to gut the new national government. Some Federalists wanted the whole process ignored; Antifederalists hoped to make structural changes in the government or force a new national convention. Madison sifted through the proposals and presented 17 to Congress for their debate and approval. Twelve amendments went out to the states for ratification. Ten were approved, and they became the Bill of Rights in the United States Constitution. Look closely at Madison's presentation. He is suggesting not just amendments, but integrating actual changes into the existing document. What proposals does he make, and why? What are the justifications for amending the Constitution? Do his arguments sound more like a Federalist or an Antifederalist? What do the amendments restrict the federal government from doing?

I am sorry to be accessary to the loss of a single moment of time by the house. If I had been indulged in my motion, and we had gone into a committee of the whole, I think we might have rose, and resumed the consideration of other business before this time; that is, so far as it depended on what I proposed to bring forward. As that mode seems not to give satisfaction, I will withdraw the motion, and move you, sir, that a select committee be appointed to consider and report such amendments as are proper for Congress to propose to the legislatures of the several States, conformably to the *5th article* of the constitution.

I will state my reasons why I think it proper to propose amendments; and state the amendments themselves, so far as I think they ought to be proposed. If I thought I could fulfil the duty which I owe to myself and my constituents, to let the subject pass over in silence, I most certainly should not trespass upon the indulgence of this house. But I cannot do this; and am therefore compelled to beg a patient hearing to what I have to lay before you. And I do most sincerely believe that if congress will devote but one day to this subject, so far as to satisfy the public that we do not disregard their wishes, it will have a salutary influence on the public councils, and prepare the way for a favorable reception of our future measures.

It appears to me that this house is bound by every motive of prudence, not to let the first session pass over without proposing to the state legislatures some things to be incorporated into the constitution, as will render it as acceptable to the whole people of the United States, as it has been found acceptable to a majority of them. I wish, among other reasons why something should be done, that those who have been friendly to the adoption of this constitution, may have the opportunity of proving to those who were opposed to it, that they were as sincerely devoted to liberty and a republican government, as those who charged them with wishing the adoption of this constitution in order to lay the foundation of an aristocracy or depotism. It will be a desirable thing to extinguish from the bosom of every member of the community any apprehensions, that there are those among his countrymen who wish to deprive them of the liberty for which they valiantly fought and honorably bled. And if there are amendments desired, of such a nature as will not injure the constitution, and they can be ingrafted so as to give satisfaction to the doubting part of our fellow citizens; the friends of the federal government will evince that spirit of deference and concession for which they have hitherto been distinguished.

It cannot be a secret to the gentlemen in this house, that, notwithstanding the ratification of this system of government by eleven of the thirteen United States, in some cases unanimously, in others by large majorities; yet still there is a great number of our constituents who are dissatisfied with it; among whom are many respectable for their talents, their patriotism, and respectable for the jealousy they have for their liberty, which, though mistaken in its object, is laudable in its motive. There is a great body of the people falling under this description, who as present feel much inclined to join their support to the cause of federalism, if they were satisfied in this one point: We ought not to disregard their inclination, but, on principles of amity and moderation, conform to their wishes, and expressly declare the great rights of mankind secured under this constitution. The acquiescence which our fellow citizens shew under the government, calls upon us for a like return of moderation. But perhaps there is a stronger motive than this for our going into a consideration of the subject; it is to provide those securities for liberty which are required by a part of the community. I allude in a

From *Congressional Register*, June 8, 1789.

particular manner to those two states who have not thought fit to throw themselves into the bosom of the confederacy: it is a desirable thing, on our part as well as theirs, that a re-union should take place as soon as possible. I have no doubt, if we proceed to take those steps which would be prudent and requisite at this juncture, that in a short time we should see that disposition prevailing in those states that are not come in, that we have seen prevailing [in] those states which are.

But I will candidly acknowledge, that, over and above all these considerations, I do conceive that the constitution may be amended; that is to say, if all power is subject to abuse, that then it is possible the abuse of the powers of the general government may be guarded against in a more secure manner than is now done, while no one advantage, arising from the exercise of that power, shall be damaged or endangered by it. We have in this way something to gain, and, if we proceed with caution, nothing to lose; and in this case it is necessary to proceed with caution; for while we feel all these inducements to go into a revisal of the constitution, we must feel for the constitution itself, and make that revisal a moderate one. I should be unwilling to see a door opened for a re-consideration of the whole structure of the government, for a re-consideration of the principles and the substance of the powers given; because I doubt, if such a door was opened, if we should be very likely to stop at that point which would be safe to the government itself. But I do wish to see a door opened to consider, so far as to incorporate those provisions for the security of rights, against which I believe no serious objection has been made by any class of our constituents, such as would be likely to meet with the concurrence of two-thirds of both houses, and the approbation of three-fourths of the state legislatures. I will not propose a single alteration which I do not wish to see take place, as intrinsically proper in itself, or proper because it is wished for by a respectable number of my fellow citizens; and therefore I shall not propose a single alteration but is likely to meet the concurrence required by the constitution.

There have been objections of various kinds made against the constitution:

Some were levelled gainst its structure, because the president was without a council; because the senate, which is a legislative body, had judicial powers in trials on impeachments; and because the powers of that body were compounded in other respects, in a manner that did not correspond with a particular theory; because it grants more power than is supposed to be necessary for every good purpose; and controuls

the ordinary powers of the state governments. I know some respectable characters who opposed this government on these grounds; but I believe that the great mass of the people who opposed it, disliked it because it did not contain effectual provison against encroachments on particular rights, and those safeguards which they have been long accustomed to have interposed between them and the magistrate who exercised the sovereign power: nor ought we to consider them safe, while a great number of our fellow citizens think these securities necessary.

It has been a fortunate thing that the objection to the government has been made on the gound I stated; because it will be practicable on that ground to obviate the objection, so far as to satisfy the public mind that their liberties will be perpetual, and this without endangering any part of the constitution, which is considered as essential to the existence of the government by those who promoted its adoption.

The amendments which have occurred to me, proper to be recommended by congress to the state legislatures are these:

First.

That there be prefixed to the constitution a declaration—That all power is orginally vested in, and consequently derived from the people.

That government is instituted, and ought to be exercised for the benefit of the people; which consists in the enjoyment of life and liberty, with the right of acquiring and using property, and generally of pursuing and obtaining happiness and safety.

That the people have an indubitable, unalienable, and indefeasible right to reform or change their government, whenever it be found adverse or inadequate to the purposes of its institution.

Secondly.

That in article 1st. section 2, clause 3, these words be struck out, to wit, "The number of representatives shall not exceed one for every thirty thousand, but each state shall have at least one representative, and until such enumeration shall be made." And that in place thereof be inserted these words, to wit, "After the first actual enumeration, there shall be one representative for every thirty thousand, until the number amount to after which the proportion shall be so regulated by congress, that the number shall never be less than nor more than but each state shall after the first enumeration, have at least two representatives; and prior thereto."

Thirdly.

That in *article 1st, section 6, clause 1*, there be added to the end of the first sentence, these words, to wit, "But no law varying the compensation last ascertained shall operate before the next ensuing election of representatives."

Fourthly.

That in *article 1st, section 9, between clauses 3 and 4*, be inserted these clauses, to wit, The civil rights of none shall be abridged on account of religious belief or worship, nor shall any national religion be established, nor shall the full and equal rights of conscience be in any manner, or on any pretext infringed.

The people shall not be deprived or abridged of their right to speak, to write, or to publish their sentiments; and the freedom of the press, as one of the great bulwarks of liberty, shall be inviolable.

The people shall not be restrained from peaceably assembling and consulting for their common good, nor from applying to the legislature by petitions, or remonstrances for redress of their grievances.

The right of the people to keep and bear arms shall not be infringed; a well armed, and well regulated militia being the best security of a free country: but no person religiously scrupulous of bearing arms, shall be compelled to render military service in person.

No soldier shall in time of peace be quartered in any house without the consent of the owner; nor at any time, but in a manner warranted by law.

No person shall be subject, except in cases of impeachment, to more than one punishment, or one trial for the same office; nor shall be compelled to be a witness against himself; nor be deprived of life, liberty, or property without due process of law; nor be obliged to relinquish his property, where it may be necessary for public use, without a just compensation.

Excessive bail shall not be required, nor excessive fines imposed, nor cruel and unusual punishments inflicted.

The rights of the people to be secured in their persons, their houses, their papers, and their other property from all unreasonable searches and seizures, shall not be violated by warrants issued without probable cause, supported by oath or affirmation, or not particularly describing the places to be searched, or the persons or things to be seized.

In all criminal prosecutions, the accused shall enjoy the right to a speedy and public trial, to be informed of the cause and nature of the accusation, to be confronted with his accusers, and the witnesses against him; to have a compulsory process for obtaining witnesses in his favor; and to have the assistance of counsel for his defense.

The exceptions here or elsewhere in the constitution, made in favor of particular rights, shall not be so construed as to diminish the just importance of other rights retained by the people; or as to enlarge the powers delegated by the constitution; but either as actual limitations of such powers, or as inserted merely for greater caution.

Fifthly.

That in *article 1st, section 10, between clauses 1 and 2,* be inserted this clause, to wit:

No state shall violate the equal rights of conscience, or the freedom of the press, or the trial by jury in criminal cases.

Sixthly.

That article *3d, section 2*, be annexed to the end of clause 2d, these words to wit: but no appeal to such court shall be allowed where the value in controversy shall not amount to _____ dollars: nor shall any fact triable by jury, according to the course of common law, be otherwise re-examinable than may consist with the principles of common law.

Seventhly.

That in *article 3d, section 2*, the third clause be struck out, and in its place be inserted the classes following, to wit:

The trial of all crimes (except in cases of impeachments, and cases arising in the land or naval forces, or the militia when on actual service in time of war or public danger) shall be by an impartial jury of freeholders of the vicinage, with the requisite of unanimity for conviction, of the right of challenge, and other accustomed requisites; and in all crimes punishable with loss of life or member, presentment or indictment by a grand jury, shall be an essential preliminary, provided that in cases of crimes committed within any county which may be in possession of an enemy, or in which a general insurrection may prevail, the trial may by law be authorised in some other county of the same state, as near as may be to the seat of the offence.

In cases of crimes committed not within any county, the trial may by law be in such county as the laws shall have prescribed. In suits at common law, between man and man, the trial by jury, as one of the best securities to the rights of the people, ought to remain inviolate.

Eighthly.

That immediately after *article 6th*, be inserted, as *article 7th*, the clauses following, to wit:

The powers delegated by this constitution, are appropriated to the departments to which they are respectively distributed: so that the legislative department shall never exercise the powers vested in the executive or judicial; nor the executive exercise the powers vested in the legislative or judicial; nor the judicial exercise the powers vested in the legislative or executive departments. The powers not delegated by this constitution, nor prohibited by it to the states, are reserved to the States respectively.

Ninthly.

That *article 7th*, be numbered as *article 8th*.

The first of these amendments, relates to what may be called a bill of rights; I will own that I never considered this provision so essential to the federal constitution, as to make it improper to ratify it, until such an amendment was added; at the same time, I always conceived, that in a certain form and to a certain extent, such a provision was neither improper nor altogether useless. I am aware, that a great number of the most respectable friends to the government and champions for republican liberty, have thought such a provision, not only unnecessary, but even improper, nay, I believe some have gone so far as to think it even dangerous. Some policy has been made use of perhaps by gentlemen on both sides of the question: I acknowledge the ingenuity of those arguments which were drawn against the constitution, by a comparison with the policy of Great-Britain, in establishing a declaration of rights; but there is too great a difference in the case to warrant the comparison: therefore the arguments drawn from that source, were in a great measure inapplicable. In the declaration of rights which that country has established, the truth is, they have gone no farther, than to raise a barrier against the power of the crown; the power of the legislature is left altogether indefinite. Altho' I know whenever the great rights, the trial by jury, freedom of the press, or liberty of conscience, came in question in that body, the invasion of them is resisted by able advocates, yet their Magna Charta does not contain any one provision for the security of those rights, respecting which, the people of America are most alarmed. The freedom of the press and rights of conscience, those choicest privileges of the people, are unguarded in the British constitution.

But altho' the case may be widely different, and it may not be thought necessary to provide limits for the legislative power in that country, yet a different opinion prevails in the United States. The people of many states, have thought it necessary to raise barriers against power in all forms and departments of government, and I am inclined to believe, if once bills of rights are established in all the states as well as the federal constitution, we shall find that altho' some of them are rather unimportant, yet, upon the whole, they will have a salutary tendency.

It may be said, in some instances they do no more than state the perfect equality of mankind; this to be sure is an absolute truth, yet it is not absolutely necessary to be inserted at the head of a constitution.

In some instances they assert those rights which are exercised by the people in forming and establishing a plan of government. In other instances, they specify those rights which are retained when particular powers are given up to be exercised by the legislature. In other instances, they specify positive rights, which may seem to result from the nature of the compact. Trial by jury cannot be considered as a natural right, but a right resulting from the social compact which regulates the action of the community, but is as essential to secure the liberty of the people as any one of the pre-existent rights of nature. In other instances they lay down dogmatic maxims with respect to the construction of the government; declaring, that the legislative, executive, and judicial branches shall be kept separate and distinct: Perhaps the best way of securing this in practice is to provide such checks, as will prevent the encroachment of the one upon the other.

But whatever may be [the] form which the several states have adopted in making declarations in favor of particular rights, the great object in view is to limit and qualify the powers of government, by excepting out of the grant of power those cases in which the government ought not to act, or to act only in a particular mode. They point these exceptions sometimes against the abuse of the executive power, sometimes against the legislative, and, in some cases, against the community itself; or, in other words, against the majority in favor of the minority.

In our government it is, perhaps, less necessary to guard against the abuse in the executive department than any other; because it is not the stronger branch of the system, but the weaker: It therefore must be levelled against the legislative, for it is the most powerful, and most likely to be abused, because it is under the least controul; hence, so far as a declaration of rights can tend to prevent the exercise of undue power, it cannot be doubted but such declaration is proper. But I confess that I do conceive, that in a government modified like this of the United States, the great danger lies rather in the abuse of the community than in the legislative body. The prescriptions in favor of liberty, ought to be levelled against that quarter where the greatest danger lies, namely, that which possesses the highest prerogative of power: But this [is] not found in either the executive or legislative departments of government, but in the body of the people, operating by the majority against the minority.

It may be thought all paper barriers against the power of the community are too weak to be worthy of attention. I am sensible they are not so strong as to satisfy gentlemen of every description who have seen and examined thoroughly the texture of such a defence; yet, as they have a tendency to impress some degree of respect for them, to establish the public opinion in their favor, and rouse the attention of the whole community, it may be one mean to controul the majority from those acts to which they might be otherwise inclined.

It has been said by way of objection to a bill of rights, by many respectable gentlemen out of doors, and I find opposition on the same principles likely to be made by gentlemen on this floor, that they are unnecessary articles of a republican government, upon the presumption that the people have those rights in their own hands, and that is the proper place for them to rest. It would be a sufficient answer to say that this objection lies against such provisions under the state governments as well as under the general government; and there are, I believe, but few gentlemen who are inclined to push their theory so far as to say that a declaration of rights in those cases is either ineffectual or improper.

It has been said that in the federal government they are unnecessary, because the powers are enumerated, and it follows that all that are not granted by the constitution are retained: that the constitution is a bill of powers, the great residuum being the rights of the people; and therefore a bill of rights cannot be so necessary as if the residuum was thrown into the hands of the government. I admit that these arguments are not entirely without foundation; but they are not conclusive to the extent which has been supposed. It is true the powers of the general government are circumscribed; they are directed to particular objects; but even if government keeps within those limits, it has certain discretionary powers with respect to the means, which may admit of abuse to a certain extent, in the same manner as the powers of the state governments under their constitutions may to an indefinite extent; because in the constitution of the United States there is a clause granting to Congress the power to make all laws which shall be necessary and proper for carrying into execution all the powers vested in the government of the United States, or in any department or officer thereof; this enables them to fulfil every purpose for which the government was established. Now, may not laws be considered necessary and proper by Congress, for it is them who are to judge of the necessity and propriety to accomplish those special purposes which they may have in contemplation, which laws in themselves are neither necessary or proper; as well as improper laws could be enacted by the state legislatures, for fulfilling the more extended objects of those governments. I will state an instance which I think in point, and proves that this might be the case. The general government has a right to pass all laws which shall be necessary to collect its revenue; the means for enforcing the collection are within the direction of the legislature: may not general warrants be considered necessary for this purpose, as well as for some purposes which it was supposed at the framing of their constitutions the state governments had in view. If there was reason for restraining the state governments from exercising this power, there is like reason for restraining the federal government.

It may be said, because it has been said, that a bill of rights is not necessary, because the establishment of this government has not repealed those declarations of rights which are added to the several state constitutions: that those rights of the people, which had been established by the most solemn act, could not be annihilated by a subsequent act of the people, who meant, and declared at the head of the instrument, that they ordained and established a new system, for the express purpose of securing to themselves and posterity the liberties they had gained by an arduous conflict.

I admit the force of this observation, but I do not look upon it to be conclusive. In the first place, it is too uncertain ground to leave this provision upon, if a provision is at all necessary to secure rights so important as many of those I have mentioned are conceived to be, by the public in general, as well as those in particular who opposed the adoption of this constitution. Beside some states have no bills of rights, there are others provided with very defective ones, and there are others whose bills of rights are not only defective, but absolutely improper; instead of securing some in the full extent which republican principles would require, they limit them too much to agree with the common ideas of liberty.

It has been objected also against a bill of rights, that, by enumerating particular exceptions to the grant of power, it would disparage those rights which were not placed in that enumeration, and it might follow, by implication, that those rights which were not singled out, were intended to be assigned into the hands of the general government, and were consequently insecure. This is one of the most plausible arguments I have ever heard urged against the admission of a bill of rights into this system; but, I conceive, that may be guarded against. I have attempted it, as gentlemen may see by turning to the last clause of the 4th resolution.

It has been said, that it is necessary to load the constitution with this provision, because it was not found effectual in the constitution of the particular states. It is true, there are a few particular states in which some of the most valuable articles have not, at one time or other, been violated; but does it not follow but they may have, to a certain degree, a salutary effect against the abuse of power. If they are incorporated into the constitution, independent tribunals of justice will consider themselves in a peculiar manner the guardians of those rights; they will be an impenetrable bulwark against every assumption of power in the legislative or executive; they will be naturally led to resist every encroachment upon rights expressly stipulated for in the constitution by the declaration of rights. Beside this security, there is a great probability that such a declaration in the federal system would be enforced; because the state legislatures will jealously and closely watch the operation of this government, and be able to resist with more effect every assumption of power than any other power on earth can do; and the greatest opponents to a federal government admit the state legislatures to be sure guardians of the people's liberty. I conclude from this view of the subject, that it will be proper in itself, and highly politic, for the tranquility of the public mind, and the stability of the government, that we should offer something, in the form I have proposed, to be incorporated in the system of government, as a declaration of the rights of the people.

In the next place I wish to see that part of the constitution revised which declares, that the number of representatives shall not exceed the proportion of one for every thirty thousand persons, and allows one representative to every state which rates below that proportion. If we attend to the discussion of this subject, which has taken place in the state conventions, and even in the opinion of the friends to the constitution, an alteration here is proper. It is the sense of the people of America, that the number of representatives ought to be increased, but particularly that it should not be left in the discretion of the government to diminish them, below that proportion which certainly is in the power of the legislature as the constitution now stands; and they may, as the population of the country increases, increase the house of representatives to a very unwieldy degree. I confess I always thought this part of the constitution defective, though not dangerous; and that it ought to be particularly attended to whenever congress should go into the consideration of amendments.

There are several lesser cases enumerated in my proposition, in which I wish also to see some alteration take place. That article which leaves it in the power of the legislature to ascertain its own emolument is one to which I allude. I do not believe this is a power which, in the ordinary course of government, is likely to be abused, perhaps of all the powers granted, it is least likely to abuse; but there is a seeming impropriety in leaving any set of men without controul to put their hand into the public coffers, to take out money to put in their pockets; there is a seeming indecorum in such power, which leads me to propose a change. We have a guide to this alteration in several of the amendments which the different conventions have proposed. I have gone therefore so far as to fix it, that no law, varying the compensation, shall operate until there is a change in the legislature; in which case it cannot be for the particular benefit of those who are concerned in determining the value of the service.

I wish also, in revising the constitution, we may throw into that section, which interdicts the abuse of certain powers in the state legislatures, some other provisions of equal if not greater importance than those already made. The words, "No state shall pass any bill of attainder, ex post facto law, &c." were wise and proper restrictions in the constitution. I think there is more danger of those powers being abused by the state governments than by the government of the United States. The same may be said of other powers which they possess, if not controuled by the general principle, that laws are unconstitutional which infringe the rights of the community. I should therefore wish to extend this interdiction, and add, as I have stated in the 5th resolution, that no state shall violate the equal right of conscience, freedom of the press, or trial by jury in criminal cases; because it is proper that every government should be disarmed of powers which trench upon those particular rights. I know in some of the state constitutions the power of the government is controuled by such a declaration, but others are not. I cannot see any reason against obtaining even a double security on those points; and nothing can give a more sincere proof of the attachment of those who opposed this constitution to these great and important rights, than to see them join in

obtaining the security I have now proposed; because it must be admitted, on all hands, that the state governments are as liable to attack these invaluable privileges as the general government is, and therefore ought to be as cautiously guarded against.

I think it will be proper, with respect to the judiciary powers, to satisfy the public mind on those points which I have mentioned. Great inconvenience has been apprehended to suitors from the distance they would be dragged to obtain justice in the supreme court of the United States, upon an appeal on an action for a small debt. To remedy this, declare, that no appeal shall be made unless the matter in controversy amounts to a particular sum: This, with the regulations respecting jury trials in criminal cases, and suits at common law, it is to be hoped will quiet and reconcile the minds of the people to that part of the constitution.

I find, from looking into the amendments proposed by the state conventions, that several are particularly anxious that it should be declared in the constitution, that the powers not therein delegated, should be reserved to the several states. Perhaps words which may define this more precisely, than the whole of the instrument now does, may be considered as superfluous. I admit they may be deemed unnecessary; but there can be no harm in making such a declaration, if gentlemen will allow that the fact is as stated. I am sure I understand it so, and do therefore propose it.

These are the points on which I wish to see a revision of the constitution take place. How far they will accord with the sense of this body, I cannot take upon me absolutely to determine; but I believe every gentlemen will readily admit that nothing is in contemplation, so far as I have mentioned, that can endanger the beauty of the government in any one important feature, even in the eyes of its most sanguine admirers. I have proposed nothing that does not appear to me as proper in itself, or eligible as patronised by a respectable number of our fellow citizens; and if we can make the constitution better in the opinion of those who are opposed to it, without weakening its frame, or abridging its usefulness, in the judgment of those who are attached to it, we act the part of wise and liberal men to make such alterations as shall produce that effect.

Having done what I conceived was my duty, in bringing before this house the subject of amendments, and also stated such as wish for and approve, and offered the reasons which occurred to me in their support; I shall content myself for the present with moving, that a committee be appointed to consider of and report such amendments as ought to be proposed by congress to the legislatures of the states, to become, if ratified by three-fourths thereof, part of the constitution of the United States. By agreeing to this motion, the subject may be going on in the committee, while other important business is proceeding to a conclusion in the house. I should advocate greater dispatch in the business of amendments, if I was not convinced of the absolute necessity there is of pursuing the organization of the government; because I think we should obtain the confidence of our fellow citizens, in proportion as we fortify the rights of the people against the encroachments of the government.

Chapter 5 Worksheet and Questions

1. You are an Antifederalist preparing to attend your state's ratification convention. List the major objections you have to the new constitution and government, and why you consider these objections to be important. How are your rights and liberties threatened by this new government?

_____

_____

_____

_____

_____

_____

_____

_____

2. To members of the revolutionary generation the concepts of "liberty," the "will of the people," and "representation" were more than just words. Using the documents in this chapter, how do the Federalists and Antifederalists explain them differently. What is important about each concept? How do their interpretations differ, and why is this important in the debate over the Constitution?

_____

_____

_____

_____

_____

_____

_____

_____

3. Compare the concerns voiced so eloquently by Antifederalists about the new government with the replies to those concerns provided by the Federalists. Do you think the Federalists have sufficiently defused the perceived threats to American liberties? Are there sufficient protections without a bill of rights? What proof is there that no threat to public liberties exists? Judging from what happens today, do you think Madison's and Hamilton's faith in the new government was justified? Is the national government as safe from corruption and abuse as they claim?

_____

_____

_____

_____

_____

_____

_____

_____

_____

4. Comparing both the Federalist and Antifederalist visions of the future, and their concerns for what the future holds, whose arguments do you believe were more accurate? Why? *Be sure to provide examples* to support your answer.

_____

_____

_____

_____

_____

_____

_____

_____

_____

Chapter 6

Beyond the Far Blue Mountains:
Conflict and Cultural Exchange on the American Frontier

Today when people speak of "the West" they usually mean the Trans-Mississippi United States, complete with images of John Wayne, cowboys, Native Americans hunting buffalo, the California Gold Rush, and whatever else Hollywood puts on film. But from the end of the American Revolution to 1850, "the West" meant Trans-Appalachian United States, which had its own stories of survival, struggles between Native Americans and whites, and amazing stories of economic development. The area between the Appalachians and the Mississippi River, but north of the Ohio River, was called the Northwest Territory; the area to the South of the Ohio River was the Southwest Territory. In all, 230 million acres beckoned the adventurous, almost half the landmass of the new nation.

Only one out of every ten Americans lived west of the Appalachians in 1800, but as citizens of the nation swarmed into the region, by 1850 half of the nation's population did. Land was the key to wealth and social status. The independent yeoman farmer was seen as the backbone of the Republic. Because they were economically independent of others, tied to the earth and doing honest labor, they were believed to be the most virtuous of all citizens, and thus the key to the Republic's survival. In 1782 De Crevecoeur declared that Americans were building "the most perfect society now existing in the world," because they were spreading out over immense territories and tilling the soil. Some people heading to the nation's interior did so to escape debts, find excitement, or make scientific discoveries, but most Americans heading west wanted land—somewhere they could have space enough to raise the six to eight children in a normal rural American family.

Land was scarce in the Northeast. After generations of dividing family holdings, there was not enough arable land remaining for new farmers. Southerners felt pressure to head west also. Down South, landholding was not only concentrated in fewer families, but the soil was reaching exhaustion, suffering from repeated plantings of cotton and tobacco. Independent family farmers who did not want to compete with slave labor felt the urge to move, as did the younger sons of planters seeking independence and their own family fortune. Speculators and swindlers were also interested in the west, calling themselves developers and promoters (as they still do today). Groups like the Ohio Company bribed congressmen to give them special land grants in the Old Northwest and, when bribes did not work, threatened to confuse land titles by buying sections directly from state governments instead. Speculators swindled innocent farmers and bribed willing Georgia legislators alike in the Yazoo case, gaining title to millions of dollars worth of land in the future Alabama and Mississippi. But for whatever the reason, citizens of the new United States came west. In three generations, four million people crossed the Appalachians and settled on new lands, creating 12 new states between 1792 and 1848.

The national government promoted and regulated settlement of these areas. The Land Ordinance of 1785 established formal policies on how national lands could be acquired, subdivided, and sold, and created the common measurement of townships: six square miles. Modeled after the Northeastern tradition of surveying to promote orderly development, and the Southern tradition of granting land to individuals, this law also established the procedure for territories to become states. By clearly establishing land boundaries and titles, the Confederation Congress hoped to limit chaos, violence, and conflicting claims along the frontier. The Northwest Ordinance of 1787 guaranteed basic rights to all American citizens moving into these lands, and banned slavery in the territory northwest of the Ohio River. The Southwest Ordinance of 1790 guaranteed the same rights, but specifically opened the lands south of the Ohio River to slavery.

The French and the Spanish arrived in this area before the English, and long before the United States claimed this land. The earlier European visitors did a better job cooperating with the owner/inhabitants of the land. As long as whites were in a minority, they sought what historian Richard White refers to as "mutual accommodation" with the Native Americans. Both groups would use the land; both groups would prosper. This mutuality changed after the American Revolution. The Native Americans in the Trans-Appalachian regions assumed they still owned their lands, but the United States government claimed to own them through the **right of conquest**. This theory suggests that, by defeating the British, the United States also defeated all British allies as well, and thus have the right to all their lands and property. In 1784 the government seized hostages and forced the Iroquois nation to sign the Treaty of Fort Stanwix, ceding most of their land to the United States. The next year, similar tactics were used on the Ohio Indians.

In 1787 the government changed its official policy toward the American Indians. The Northwest Ordinance says that "The utmost good faith shall always be observed toward the Indians, their lands and property shall never be taken from them without their consent…they shall never be invaded or disturbed, *unless in just and lawful wars authorized by Congress.*" The Indian Intercourse Act of 1790 declared that it was official federal policy to "promote civilization among the friendly Indian tribes." All of these changes were to promote peace for the surveyor crews, so that Indian lands could be platted and sold to more white settlers. Such actions did not promote peaceful interaction between whites and Native Americans. Government officials frequently bribed corrupt Indian leaders to sell territory to the national government, even when these leaders did not have the authority to dispose of tribal lands. Then the officials and their speculator allies became rich. William Henry Harrison, governor of the Indian Territory and future president, was one of the most notorious government swindlers.

When diplomacy and treachery did not work, the government relied on force. Open conflict between whites and natives was common, and the national government was eventually forced to step in. Victory was not always certain, however. In the fall of 1790 Little Turtle, a Miami chief, defeated an American Army led by General Harmar; the following year he delivered a crushing defeat to another army under General Arthur St. Clair. Over 900 regulars and militia were casualties in the greatest defeat ever given the American army by Indian warriors. But in 1794 General "Mad" Anthony Wayne defeated Little Turtle, and forced 12 tribes to cede most of present-day Ohio to the United States. The army built forts and connecting roads across the region west of the Appalachians, encouraging the settlement of the region.

Travelers to the Old Northwest constantly commented on the large numbers of Americans heading west; to some it seemed like the entire nation was in motion. Single males, entire families, or clusters of kin followed routes to similar destinations, to create communities. White settlers in the Old Northwest tried to recreate the same farming, family, and community life they had back east. This meant subsistence farming to provide for their family's needs. Since food was the priority, you cleared land to plant corn, let the livestock forage for themselves, and lived in primitive conditions the first year. Settlers lived in their wagon, in lean-tos, dugouts, or cabins with three walls and a roof, with a blazing fire on the open side. You coped with punishing winter winds, swarms of biting, green-eyed flies in the summer, and wind-driven prairie fires in the fall. By the second year, your family cleared more land and you finished a log cabin. It often took ten years to clear 80 acres of farmland out of the forested lands, and it required the assistance of your family and friends. Women seldom were consulted before the family moved out west, and sometimes they stayed at home while their husbands prepared the land for the first year. But wives and daughters helped with the field crops, and the butter and homemade cloth they produced contributed to the family economy even more. These goods went to the nearest town and were sold or bartered for the items that couldn't be produced or manufactured on the farm: salt, sugar, gunpowder and shot, guns, nails, horseshoes, and the like. After ten years, if transportation in the area improved, farmers planted more commercial cash crops to take advantage of the market economy.

The Old Northwest also attracted settlers to boom towns. Some farmers joined speculators to promote towns and urban centers, hoping to increase land values and business opportunities. These communities thrived on the agricultural production of the region, processing and shipping what the farmers brought them. Towns were established along natural travel routes, near river crossings, or near waterfalls where travelers had to stop. Other settlers were drawn to mineral wealth in the territories. Lead deposits attracted people to the region around Galena, Illinois, while coal deposits drew people to west central Illinois.

Political leaders in the Southeast feared it: "Alabama Fever." They believed the desire to leave home and move to more productive lands in Alabama was a sickness, one that would depopulate the slave states along the Atlantic Seaboard. Travelers reported thousands of people on the roads west, with caravans of wagons and livestock stretching as far as the eye could see. The Old Southwest attracted both slaveholding planters and independent yeoman farmers. Planters brought the capital to purchase large amounts of the best land, and used the slaves to make this land profitable. Slaves, fertile land, and a long growing season for cotton made the elite planters even wealthier. This was the story of the South. Their wives were often bitter about the move, being uprooted from their supporting kin networks and nice houses, and moving to what they believed were crude houses and backwoods. The majority of settlers here, as in the Old Northwest, were family farmers. They valued self-sufficiency, just like their northern counterparts, and wanted leisure time to hunt and fish. Plant corn, beans, and squash, and let pigs raise themselves; the family would be fed. Plant a few acres of cotton for clothing and the market, whenever the extra land is cleared.

Considering the Evidence in the Readings

The documents in this chapter all examine life in the Trans-Appalachian west, and how settling there affected lives. You will encounter Native Americans and the effect white settlement has on their lives. You will read many different observations by white settlers about life in this area. Consider who the different sources are, where they come from, and what biases they might have in the observations. What standards do they use to judge the people and towns of the west? Are they fair? Are there some things or places they uniformly like or dislike? The travelers here come west at different times, using different forms of transportation. Do these things make a difference in their observations?

Document 6.1 Tecumseh Speaks Out Against White Aggression and Wrong-Doing

Americans surged into the lands of the Trans-Appalachian west after the American Revolution, into areas known at the time as the Old Northwest and Old Southwest. Believing Providence was on their side, and greedy for more land, they arbitrarily dismissed the rights and land ownership of large groups of Native Americans already living there, and forced them off of their ancestral lands. Shawnee leader Tecumseh and his brother Tenskwatawa attempted to create an Indian confederation to resist white encroachment, because they believed this expansion threatened the lands and cultures of all American Indians. In their lifetimes, the Shawnee were driven from their homes in Kentucky and Southern Ohio to parts of Michigan, Indiana, and Illinois. Tenskwatawa called for a cultural revival, urging the Shawnee and other natives to give up white tools, dress, and liquor, and return to traditional native values and lifestyles. Earlier Indian leaders such as Joseph Brant attempted alliances, but Tecumseh came closer than anyone else to creating a continental political and military alliance, before his death at the Battle of the Thames in the War of 1812. A brilliant speaker, he reminded tribes what happened to other native groups after facing whites on their own: "Where are the Pequot? Where are the Mohican? Where are the Narragansett?" Why does Tecumseh oppose land cessions in his speech? How does he say the United States treats natives unfairly?

. . . It is true I am a Shawnee. My forefathers were warriors. Their son is a warrior. From them I only take my existence; from my tribe I take nothing. I am the maker of my own fortune; and oh! that I could make that of my red people, and of my country, as great as the conceptions of my mind, when I think of the Spirit that rules the universe. I would not then come to Governor Harrison, to ask him to tear the treaty, and to obliterate the landmark; but I would say to him, Sir, you have liberty to return to your own country. The being within, communing with the past ages, tells me, that once, nor until lately, there was no white man on this continent. That it then all belonged to red men, children of the same parents, placed on it by the Great Spirit that made them, to keep it, to traverse it, to enjoy its production, and to fill it with the same race. Once a happy race. Since made miserable by the white people, who are never contented, but always encroaching. The way, and the only way to check and stop this evil, is, for all the red men to unite in claiming a common and equal right in the land, as it was at first, and should be yet; for it never was divided, but belongs to all, for the use of each. That no part has a right to sell, even to each other, much less to strangers; those who want all, and will not do with less. The white people have no right to take the land from the Indians, because they had it first; it is theirs. They may sell, but all must join. Any sale not made by all is not valid. The late sale is bad. It was made by a part only. Part do not know how to sell. It requires all to make a bargain for all. All red men have equal rights to the unoccupied land. The right of occupancy is as good in one place as in another. There cannot be two occupations in the same place. The first excludes all others. It is not so in hunting or travelling; for there the same ground will serve many, as they may follow each other all day; but the camp is stationary, and that is occupancy. It belongs to the first who sits down on his blanket or skins, which he has thrown upon the ground, and till he leaves it no other has a right.

Document 6.2 White Reports of Recent Indian Hostilities

Violence on the western frontier between Native Americans resisting encroachment on their lands (lands guaranteed to them by treaties with the United States government) and white settlers increased steadily before the War of 1812. Native warriors harassed or ambushed supply and trading caravans, postal riders, and others, to discourage illegal settlement on their lands. The United States government acquired millions of acres of land through fraudulent treaties, but even this was not enough, and many settlers deliberately invaded Indian lands. When the Native Americans resisted this trespassing, the settlers claimed the British government was causing Indian hostilities, and called on the United States government and military to force the Indians to give up more land. Settlers rarely accepted any blame for causing hostilities. What is this writer's view of "Indian hostilities"? Who is to blame for these actions, according to the letter?

The following is an extract of a letter from a gentleman at St. Charles, Louisiana Territory, dated Jan. 10, 1812.

"In answer to your enquiry, respecting Indian hostilities in this quarter, I have to inform you, that some of the reports that have found their way into the public prints are much exaggerated, but are generally true. The depredations committed by them have been principally in Indiana and Illinois territories; some horses have been taken in this territory, but I believe no murders have been committed by them for the last ten or twelve months. I had flattered myself that the drubbing given them by the troops under the command of Gov. Harrison would have disposed them to return to order. In this it appears I was mistaken, for this day, by an express from Fort Madison, we are informed of cruel murders committed on some traders, about 100 miles above that Fort, by a party of the Pecant nation

From *Biography and History of the Indians of North America*, Boston: Antiquarian Institute, 1837.

From *The Pennsylvania Gazette*, March 4, 1812.

A Mr. Hunt, son of the late Col. Hunt, of the United States' army, and a Mr. Prior, were trading in that quarter—their houses about 3 miles distance from each other. The party of Indians came to Hunt's house, and appeared friendly until they obtained admittance into the house—they then shot down two men that Mr. Hunt had with him, seized him and a boy, who was his interpreter, tied them, and packed up the goods that were in the house, and carried them off. Mr. Hunt discovered that they believed him to be an Englishman, and on that account saved his life. They told him that they had sent another party to kill Prior, and carry off his goods, and that they intended in a short time to take the Fort—after which they would come on and kill every American they could find. They took Mr. Hunt and his boy with them some distance, but night came on, and proved extremely dark, which fortunately gave them an opportunity of escaping, and they arrived safe at Fort Madison on the sixth day.

"The hostilities that have taken place, together with the mysterious conduct of the few Indians that are passing amongst us, lead me to believe they are determined for war, and that they are set on by British agents. If we go to war with England, I calculate on some very warm work in this quarter."

Document 6.3 Black Hawk's Memory of Sauk Life and White Invasion

The Sauk Indian leader Black Hawk and his tribe were also victims of a fraudulent treaty. In 1804 the United States government got four members of the tribe to sign away all the Sauk land east of the Mississippi River. These four had no authority to surrender these lands, and Black Hawk refused to give up the tribal lands in Illinois. He fought for the British during the War of 1812 and then returned to his land in Illinois. In 1832 the United States army and various militias concentrated to drive Black Hawk and his people out, justifying their actions with the 1804 treaty. The 100-day "Black Hawk War" ended with the so-called battle of Bad Axe, with militia units slaughtering off Sauk men, women, and children in the Mississippi River as the natives tried to surrender. The captive Black Hawk was taken on a tour of the United States, while his tribe was removed to Kansas and Oklahoma. His autobiography, told to an interpreter in the finest oral history tradition, was written down and later published. How does Sauk treatment at the hands of the Spanish and Americans compare? What about his tribe's treatment angers Black Hawk? How important is spiritual life to the Sauk? What injustices against his people does Black Hawk list?

Our enemies having now been driven from our hunting grounds, with so great a loss as they sustained, we returned, in peace, to our villages: and after the seasons of mourning and burying our dead relations, and of feast-dancing had passed, we commenced preparations for our winter's hunt, in which we were very successful.

We generally paid a visit to St. Louis every summer: but, in consequence of the protracted war in which we had been engaged, I had not been there for some years. Our difficulties having all been settled, I concluded to take a small party, that summer, and go down to see our Spanish father. We went—and on our arrival, put up our lodges where the market-house now stands. After painting and dressing, we called to see our Spanish father, and were well received. He gave us a variety of presents, and plenty of provisions. We danced through the town as usual, and its inhabitants all seemed to be well pleased. They appeared to us like brothers—and always gave us good advice.

On my next, and *last*, visit to my Spanish father, I discovered, on landing, that all was not right: every countenance seemed sad and gloomy! I inquired the cause, and was informed that the Americans were coming to take possession of the town and country!—and that we should then lose our Spanish father! This news made myself and band sad—because we had always heard bad accounts of the Americans from Indians who had lived near them!—and we were sorry to lose our Spanish father, who had always treated us with great friendship.

Black Hawk's Own Story.

A few days afterwards, the Americans arrived. I took my band, and went to take leave, for the last time, of our father. The Americans came to see him also. Seeing them approach, we passed out at one door, as they entered another—and immediately started, in canoes, for our village on Rock river—not liking the change any more than our friends appeared to, at St. Louis.

On arriving at our village, we gave the news, that strange people had taken St. Louis—and that we should never see our Spanish father again! This information made all our people sorry!

Some time afterwards, a boat came up the river, with a young American chief, [Lieutenant (afterwards General) Pike] and a small party of soldiers. We heard of him, (by runners,) soon after he had passed Salt river. Some of our young braves watched him every day, to see what sort of people he had on board! The boat, at length, arrived at Rock river, and the young chief came on shore with his interpreter— made a speech, and gave us some presents! We, in return, presented him with meat, and such provisions as we could spare. . . .

Some moons after this young chief descended the Mississippi, one of our people killed an American— and was confined, in the prison at St. Louis, for the offence. We held a council at our village to see what could be done for him—which determined that Quàsh-quà-me, Pà-she-pa-ho, Oú-che-quà-ka, and Hàshe-quar-hi-qua, should go down to St. Louis, see our American father, and do all they could to have our friend released: by paying for the person killed- thus covering the blood, and satisfying the relations of the man murdered! This being the only means with us of saving a person who had killed another-and we *then* thought it was the same way with the whites!

The party started with the good wishes of the whole nation—hoping they would accomplish the object of their mission. The relatives of the prisoner blacked their faces, and fasted—hoping the Great Spirit would take pity on them, and return the husband and father to his wife and children.

Quàsh-quà-me and party remained a long time absent. They at length returned, and encamped a short distance below the village—but did not come up that day—nor did any person approach their camp! They appeared to be dressed in *fine coats,* and had *medals!* From these circumstances, we were in hopes that they had brought good news. Early the next morning, the Council Lodge was Quàsh-quà-me and party came up, and gave us the following account of their mission:

"On their arrival at St. Louis, they met their American father, and explained to him their business, and urged the release of their friend. The American chief told them he wanted land—and they had agreed to give him some on the west side of the Mississippi, and some on the Illinois side opposite the Jeffreon. When the business was all arranged, they expected to have their friend released to come home with them. But about the time they were ready to start, their friend was let out of prison, who ran a short distance, and was *shot dead!* This is all they could recollect of what was said and done. They had been drunk the greater part of the time they were in St. Louis."

This is all myself or nation knew of the treaty of 1804. It has been explained to me since. I find, by that treaty, all our country, east of the Mississippi, and south of the Jeffreon, was ceded to the United States for *one thousand dollars* a year! I will leave it to the people of the United States to say, whether our nation was properly represented in this treaty? or whether we received a fair compensation for the extent of country ceded by those four individuals? I could say much about this treaty, but I will not, at this time. It has been the origin of all our difficulties.

Some time after this treaty was made, a war chief, with a party of soldiers, came up in keel boats, and encamped a short distance above the head of the Des Moines rapids, and commenced cutting timber and building houses. The news of their arrival was soon carried to all the villages—when council after council was held. We could not understand the intention, or reason, why the Americans wanted to build houses at that place—but were told that they were a party of soldiers, who had brought *great guns* with them—and looked like a *war party* of whites!

A number of our people immediately went down to see what was doing—myself among them. On our arrival, we found they were building a *fort!* The soldiers were busily engaged in cutting timber: and I observed that they took their arms with them, when they went to the woods—and the whole party acted as they would do in an enemy's country! . . .

Soon after our return home, news reached us that a war was going to take place between the British and the Americans. Runners continued to arrive from different tribes, all confirming the report of the expected war. The British agent, Col. Dixon, was holding *talks* with, and making presents to, the different tribes. I had not made up my mind whether to join the British, or remain neutral. *I had not discovered one good trait in the character of the Americans that had come to the country!* They made *fair promises but never fulfilled them!* Whilst the *British* made but few—but we could always *rely upon their word!* . . .

The great chief at St. Louis having sent word for us to go down and confirm the treaty of peace, we did not hesitate, but started immediately, that we might smoke the *peace-pipe* with him. On our arrival, we met the great chiefs in council. They explained to us the words of our Great Father at Washington, accusing us of heinous crimes and divers misdemeanors, particularly in not coming down when first invited. We knew very well that *our Great Father had deceived us,* and thereby *forced* us to join the British, and could not believe that he had put this speech into the mouths of these chiefs to deliver to us. I was not a civil chief, and consequently made no reply: but our chiefs told the commissioners that "what they had said was a *lie!*—that our Great Father had sent no such speech, he knowing the situation in which we had been placed had been *caused by him!*" The white chiefs appeared very angry at this reply, and said they "would break off the treaty with us, and *go to war,* as they would not be insulted."

Our chiefs had no intention of insulting them, and told them so—that they merely wished to explain to them that *they had told a lie,* without making them angry; in the same manner that the whites do, when they do not believe what is told them!" The council then proceeded, and the pipe of peace was smoked.

Here, for the first time, I touched the goose quill to the treaty—not knowing, however, that, by that act, I consented to give away my village. Had that been explained to me, I should have opposed it, and never would have signed their treaty, as my recent conduct will clearly prove.

What do we know of the manner of the laws and customs of the white people? They might buy our bodies for dissection, and we would touch the goose quill to confirm it, without knowing what we are doing. This was the case with myself and people in touching the goose quill the first time.

We can only judge of what is proper and right by our standard of right and wrong, which differs widely from the whites, if I have been correctly informed. The whites *may do bad* all their lives, and then, if they are *sorry for it* when about to die, *all is well!* But with us it is different: we must continue throughout our lives to do what we conceive to be good. If we have corn and meat, and know of a family that have none, we divide with them. If we have more blankets than sufficient, and others have not enough, we must give to them that want. But I will presently explain our customs, and the manner we live.

We were friendly treated by the white chiefs, and started back to our village on Rock river. Here we found that troops had arrived to build a fort at Rock Island. This, in our opinion, was a contradiction to what we had done—"to prepare for war in time of peace." We did not, however, object to their building the fort on the island, but we were very sorry, as this was the best island on the Mississippi, and had long been the resort of our young people during the summer. It was our garden (like the white people have near to their big villages) which supplied us with strawberries, blackberries, gooseberries, plums, apples, nuts of different kinds: and its waters supplied us with fine fish, being situated in the rapids of the river. In my early life, I spent many happy days on this island. A good spirit had care of it who lived in a cave in the rocks immediately under the place where the fort now stands, and has often been seen by our people. He was white, with large wings like a *swan's,* but ten times larger. We were particular not to make much noise in that part of the island which he inhabited, for fear of disturbing him. But the noise of the fort has since driven him away, and no doubt a *bad spirit* has taken his place!

Our village was situate on the north side of Rock river, at the foot of its rapids, and on the point of land between Rock river and the Mississippi. In its front, a prairie extended to the bank of the Mississippi: and in our rear, a continued bluff, gently ascending from the prairie. On the side of this bluff we had our cornfields, extending about two miles up, running parallel with the Mississippi: where we joined those of the Foxes whose village was on the bank of the Mississippi, opposite the lower end of Rock island, and three miles distant from ours. We had about eight hundred acres in cultivation, including what we had on the islands of Rock river. The land around our village, uncultivated, was covered with bluegrass, which made excellent pasture for our horses. Several fine springs broke out of the bluff, near by, from which we were supplied with good water. The rapids of Rock river furnished us with an abundance of excellent fish, and the land, being good, never failed to produce good crops of corn, beans, pumpkins, and squashes. We always had plenty—our children never cried with hunger, nor our people were never in want. Here our village had stood for more than a hundred years, during all which time we were the undisputed possessors of the valley of the Mississippi, from the Ouisconsin to the Portage des Sioux, near the mouth of the Missouri, being about seven hundred miles in length.

At this time we had very little intercourse with the whites, except our traders. Our village was healthy, and there was no place in the country possessing such advantages, nor no hunting grounds better than those we had in possession, if another prophet had come to our village in those days, and told us what has since taken place, none of our people would have believed him. What! to be driven from our village and hunting grounds, and not even permitted to visit the graves of our forefathers, our relations, and friends?

This hardship is not known to the whites. With us it is a custom to visit the graves of our friends, and keep them in repair for many years. The mother will go alone to weep over the grave of her child! The brave, with pleasure, visits the grave of his father, after he has been successful in war, and re-paints the post that shows where he lies! There is no place like that where the bones of our forefathers lie, to go to when in grief. Here the Great Spirit will take pity on us!

But, how different is our situation now, from what it was in those days! Then we were as happy as the buffalo on the plains—but now, we are as miserable as the hungry, howling wolf in the prairie! But I am digressing from my story. Bitter reflection crowds upon my mind, and must find utterance.

When we returned to our village in the spring, from our wintering grounds, we would finish trading with our traders, who always followed us to our village. We purposely kept some of our fine furs for this trade; and, as there was great opposition among them, who should get these skins, we always got our goods cheap. After this trade was over, the traders would give us a few kegs of rum, which was generally promised in the fall, to encourage us to make a good hunt, and not go to war. They would then start with their furs and peltries for their homes. Our old men would take a frolic, (at this time our young men never drank.) When this was ended the next thing to be done was to bury our dead, (such as had died during the year.) This is a great *medicine feast*. The relations of those who have died, give all the goods they have purchased, as presents to their friends—thereby reducing themselves to poverty, to show the Great Spirit that they are humble, so that he will take pity on them. We would next open the cashes, and take out corn and other provisions, which had been put up in the fall,—and then commence repairing our lodges. As soon as this is accomplished, we repair the fences around our fields, and clean them off, ready for planting corn. This work is done by our women. The men, during this time, are feasting on dried venison, bear's meat, wild fowl, and corn, prepared in different ways: and recounting to each other what took place during the winter.

Our women plant the corn, and as soon as they get done, we make a feast, and dance the *crane* dance, in which they join us, dressed in their best, and decorated with feathers. At this feast our young braves select the young woman they wish to have for a wife. He then informs his mother, who calls on the mother of the girl, when the arrangement is made, and the time appointed for him to come. He goes to the lodge when all are asleep, (or pretend to be,) lights his matches, which have been provided for the purpose, and soon finds where his intended sleeps. He then awakens her, and holds the light to his face that she may know him—after which he places the light close to her. If she blows it out, the ceremony is ended, and he appears in the lodge the next morning, as one of the family. If she does not blow out the light, but leaves it to burn out, he retires from the lodge. The next day he places himself in full view of it, and plays his flute. The young women go out, one by one, to see who he is playing for. The tune changes, to let them know that he is not playing for them. When his intended makes her appearance at the door, he continues his *courting* tune, until she returns to the lodge. He then gives over playing, and makes another trial at night, which generally turns out favorable. During the first year they ascertain whether they can agree with each other, and can be happy—if not, they part, and each looks out again. If we were to live together and disagree, we should be as foolish as the whites. No indiscretion can banish a woman from her parental lodge—no difference how many children she may bring home, she is always welcome—the kettle is over the fire to feed them.

The crane dance often lasts two or three days. When this is over, we feast again, and have our *national* dance. The large square in the village is swept and prepared for the purpose. The chiefs and old warriors, take seats on mats which have been spread at the upper end of the square—the drummers and singers come next, and the braves and women form the sides, leaving a large space in the middle. The drums beat, and the singers commence. A warrior enters the square, keeping time with the music. He shows the manner he started on a war party—how he approached the enemy—he strikes, and describes the way he killed him. All join in applause. He then leaves the square, and another enters and takes his place. Such of our young men as have not been out in war parties, and killed an enemy, stand back ashamed—not being able to enter the square. I remember that I was ashamed to look where our young women stood, before I could take my stand in the square as a warrior.

What pleasure it is to an old warrior, to see his son come forward and relate his exploits—it makes him feel young, and induces him to enter the square, and "fight his battles o'er again."

This national dance makes our warriors. When I was travelling last summer, on a steam boat, on a large river, going from New York to Albany, I was shown the place where the Americans dance their national dance [West Point]; where the old warriors recount to their young men, what they have done, to stimulate them to go and do likewise. This surprised me, as I did not think the whites understood our way of making braves.

When our national dance is over—our cornfields hoed, and every weed dug up, and our corn about knee-high, all our young men would start in a direction towards sun-down, to hunt deer and buffalo—being prepared, also, to kill Sioux, if any are found on our hunting grounds—a part of our old men and women to the lead mines to make lead—and the remainder of our people start to fish, and get mat stuff. Every one leaves the village, and remains about forty days. They then return: the hunting party bringing in dried buffalo and deer meat, and sometimes *Sioux scalps,* when they are found trespassing on our hunting grounds. At other times they are met by a party of Sioux too strong for them, and are driven in. If the Sioux have killed the Sacs last, they expect to be retaliated upon, and will fly before them, and vice versa. Each party knows that the other has a right to retaliate, which induces those who have killed last, to give way before their enemy—as neither wish to strike, except to avenge the death of their relatives. All our wars are predicated by the relatives of those killed, or by aggressions upon our hunting grounds.

The party from the lead mines bring lead, and the others dried fish, and mats for our winter lodges. Presents are now made by each party; the first, giving to the others dried buffalo and deer, and they, in exchange, presenting them with lead, dried fish and mats.

This is a happy season of the year—having plenty of provisions, such as beans, squashes, and other produce, with our dried meat and fish, we continue to make feasts and visit each other, until our corn is ripe. Some lodge in the village makes a feast daily, to the Great Spirit. I cannot explain this so that the white people would comprehend me, as we have no regular standard among us. Every one makes his feast as he thinks best, to please the Great Spirit, who has the care of all beings created. Others believe in two Spir-its: one good and one bad, and make feasts for the Bad Spirit, *to keep him quiet!* If they can make peace with him, the Good Spirit will not hurt them! For my part, I am of opinion, that so far as we have *reason,* we have a right to use it, in determining what is right or wrong; and should pursue that path which we believe to be right—believing, that "whatever is, is right." If the Great and Good Spirit wished us to believe and do as the whites, he could easily change our opinions, so that we would see, and think, and act as they do. We are *nothing* compared to His power, and we feel and know it. We have men among us, like the whites, who pretend to know the right path, but will not consent to show it without pay! I have no faith in their paths—but believe that every man must make his own path!

When our corn is getting ripe, our young people watch with anxiety for the signal to pull roasting-ears—as none dare touch them—until the proper time. When the corn is fit to use, another great ceremony takes place, with feasting, and returning thanks to the Great Spirit for giving us corn.

I will here relate the manner in which corn first came. According to tradition, handed down to our people, a beautiful woman was seen to descend from the clouds, and alight upon the earth, by two of our ancestors, who had killed a deer, and were sitting by a fire, roasting a part of it to eat. They were astonished at seeing her, and concluded that she must be hungry, and had smelt the meat—and immediately went to her, taking with them a piece of the roasted venison. They presented it to her, and she eat—and told them to return to the spot where she was sitting, at the end of one year, and they would find a reward for their kindness and generosity. She then ascended to the clouds, and disappeared. The two men returned to their village, and explained to the nation what they had seen, done, and heard—but were laughed at by their people. When the period arrived, for them to visit this consecrated ground, where they were to find a reward for their attention to the beautiful woman of the clouds, they went with a large party, and found, where her right hand had rested on the ground, *corn* growing—and where the left hand had rested, *beans*—and immediately where she had been seated, *tobacco.*

The two first have, ever since, been cultivated by our people, as our principal provisions—and the last used for smoking. The white people have since found out the latter, and seem to relish it as much as we do—as they use it in different ways, viz. smoking, snuffing and eating!

We thank the Great Spirit for all the benefits he has conferred upon us. For myself, I never take a drink of water from a spring, without being mindful of his goodness.

Nothing was now talked of but leaving our village. Ke-o-kuck had been persuaded to consent to go; and was using all his influence, backed by the war chief at Fort Armstrong, and our agent and trader at Rock Island, to induce others to go with him. He sent the crier through the village to inform our people that it was the wish of our Great Father that we should remove to the west side of the Mississippi—and recommended the Ioway river as a good place for the new village—and wished his party to make such arrangements, before they started out on their winter's hunt, as to preclude the necessity of their returning to the village in the spring.

The party opposed to removing, called upon me for my opinion. I gave it freely—and after questioning Quàsh-quà-me about the sale of the lands, he assured me that he "never had consented to the sale of our village." I now promised this party to be their leader, and raised the standard of opposition to Ke-o-kuck, with a full determination not to leave my village. I had an interview with Ke-o-kuck, to see if this difficulty could not be settled with our Great Father—and told him to propose to give other land, (any that our Great Father might choose, even our *lead mines,)* to be peaceably permitted to keep the small point of land on which our village and fields were situate. I was of opinion that the white people had plenty of land, and would never take our village from us. Ke-o-kuck promised to make an exchange if possible, and applied to our agent, and the great chief at St. Louis, (who has charge of all the agents,) for permission to go to Washington to see our Great Father for that purpose. This satisfied us for some time. We started to our hunting grounds, in good hopes that something would be done for us. During the winter, I received information that three families of whites had arrived at our village, and destroyed some of our lodges, and were making fences and dividing our corn-fields for their own use—and *were quarreling among themselves about their lines, in the division!* I immediately started for Rock river, a distance of ten day's travel, and on my arrival, found the report to be true. I went to my lodge, and saw a family occupying it. I wished to talk with them, but they could not understand me. I then went to Rock Island, and (the agent being absent,) told the interpreter what I wanted to say to those people, viz: "Not to settle on our lands—nor trouble our lodges or fences—that there was plenty of land in the country for them to settle upon—and they must leave

our village, as we were coming back to it in the spring." The interpreter wrote me a paper, and I went back to the village, and showed it to the intruders, but could not understand their reply. I expected, however, that they would remove, as I requested them. I returned to Rock Island, passed the night there, and had a long conversation with the trader. He again advised me to give up, and make my village with Ke-o-kuck, on the Ioway river. I told him that I would not. The next morning I crossed the Mississippi, on very bad ice—but the Great Spirit made it strong, that I might pass over safe. I travelled three days farther to see the Winnebago subagent, and converse with him on the subject of our difficulties. He gave me no better news than the trader had done. I started then, by way of Rock river, to see the prophet, believing that he was a man of great knowledge. When we met. I explained to him every thing as it was. He at once agreed that I was right, and advised me never to give up our village, for the whites to plough up the bones of our people. He said, that if we remained at our village, the whites would not trouble us—and advised me to get Ke-o-kuck, and the party that had consented to go with him to the Ioway in the spring, to return, and remain at our village.

I returned to my hunting ground, after an absence of one moon, and related what I had done. In a short time we came up to our village, and found that the whites had not left it—but that others had come, and that the greater part of our corn-fields had been enclosed. When we landed, the whites appeared displeased because we had come back. We repaired the lodges that had been left standing, and built others. Ke-o-kuck came to the village; but his object was to persuade others to follow him to the Ioway. He had accomplished nothing towards making arrangements for us to remain, or to exchange other lands for our village. There was no more friendship existing between us. I looked upon him as a coward, and no brave, to abandon his village to be occupied by strangers. What *right* had these people to our village, and our fields, which the Great Spirit had given us to live upon?

My reason teaches me that *land cannot be sold.* The Great Spirit gave it to his children to live upon, and cultivate, as far as is necessary for their subsistence: and so long as they occupy and cultivate it, they have the right to the soil—but if they voluntarily leave it, then any other people have a right to settle upon it. Nothing can be sold, but such things as can be carried away.

In consequence of the improvements of the intruders on our fields, we found considerable difficulty to get ground to plant a little corn. Some of the whites permitted us to plant small patches in the fields they had fenced, keeping all the best ground for themselves. Our women had great difficulty in climbing their fences, (being unaccustomed to the kind,) and were ill-treated if they left a rail down.

One of my old friends thought he was safe. His corn-field was on a small island of Rock river. He planted his corn: it came up well—but the white man saw it!—he wanted the island, and took his team over, ploughed up the corn, and replanted it for himself! The old man shed tears; not for himself, but the distress his family would be in if they raised no corn.

The white people brought whisky into our village, made our people drunk, and cheated them out of their horses, guns, and traps! This fraudulent system was carried to such an extent that I apprehended serious difficulties might take place, unless a stop was put to it. Consequently, I visited all the whites and begged them not to sell whisky to my people. One of them continued the practice openly. I took a party of my young men, went to his house, and took out his barrel and broke in the head and turned out the whisky. I did this for fear some of the whites might be killed by my people when drunk.

Our people were treated badly by the whites on many occasions. At one time, a white man beat one of our women cruelly, for pulling a few suckers of corn out of his field, to suck, when hungry! At another time, one of our young men was beat with clubs by two white men for opening a fence which crossed our road, to take his horse through. His shoulder blade was broken, and his body badly bruised, from which he soon after *died!*

Bad, and cruel, as our people were treated by the whites, not one of them was hurt or molested by any of my band. I hope this will prove that we are a peaceable people—having permitted ten men to take possession of our corn-fields; prevent us from planting corn: burn and destroy our lodges: ill-treat our women, and *beat to death* our men, without offering resistance to their barbarous cruelties. This is a lesson worthy for the white man to learn: to use forbearance when injured.

We acquainted our agent daily with our situation, and through him, the great chief at St. Louis—and hoped that something would be done for us. The whites were *complaining* at the same time that we *were intruding upon their rights!* THEY made themselves out the *injured* party, and *we* the *intruders!* and called loudly to the great war chief to protect their property!

How smooth must be the language of the whites, when they can make right look like wrong, and wrong like right. . . .

We now resumed some of our games and pastimes—having been assured by the prophet that we would not be removed. But in a little while it was ascertained, that a great war chief, with a large number of soldiers, was on his way to Rock river. I again called upon the prophet, who requested a little time to see into the matter. Early next morning he came to me, and said he had been *dreaming!* "That he saw nothing bad in this great war chief. [Gen. Gaines.] who was now near Rock river. That the *object* of his mission was to *frighten* us from our village, that the white people might get our land for *nothing!*" He assured us that this "great war chief dare not, and would not, hurt any of us. That the Americans were at peace with the British, and when they made peace, the British required, (which the Americans agreed to,) that they should never interrupt any nation of Indians that was at peace—and that all we had to do to retain our village, was to *refuse* any, and every offer that might be made by this war chief." . . .

Early in the morning a party of whites, being in advance of the army, came upon our people, who were attempting to cross the Mississippi. They tried to give themselves up—the whites paid no attention to their entreaties—but commenced *slaughtering* them! In a little while the whole army arrived. Our braves, but few in number, finding that the enemy paid no regard to age or sex, and seeing that they were murdering helpless women and little children, determined to *fight until they were killed!* As many women as could, commenced swimming the Mississippi, with their children on their backs. A number of them were drowned, and some shot, before they could reach the opposite shore.

One of my braves, who gave me this information, piled up some saddles before him, (when the fight commenced,) to shield himself from the enemy's fire, and killed three white men! But seeing that the whites were coming too close to him, he crawled to the bank of the river, without being perceived, and hid himself under it, until the enemy retired. He then came to me and told me what had been done. After hearing this sorrowful news. I started, with my little party, to the Winnebago village at Prairie La Cross. On my arrival there, I entered the lodge of one of the chiefs, and told him that I wished him to go with me to his father—that I intended to give myself up to the American war chief, and *die,* if the Great Spirit saw proper! He said he would go with me. I then took my *medicine bag,* and addressed the chief. I told him that it was "the soul of the Sac nation—that it never had been dishonored in any battle—take it, it is my life—dearer than life—and give it to the American chief!" He said he would keep it, and take care of it, and if I was suffered to live, he would send it to me.

During my stay at the village, the squaws made me a white dress of deer skin. I then started, with several Winnebagoes, and went to their agent, at Prairie du Chien, and gave myself up.

Document 6.4 A Trip Down the Ohio River by Flatboat in 1803

Thomas Rodney was born in Dover, Delaware on June 4, 1744. His famous older brother Caesar was a member of the Continental Congress, a signer of the Declaration of Independence, and leader of the Delaware militia, as well as Thomas' political mentor. In many ways, Thomas' life is a reflection of the economic uncertainties in the developing nation. He served as an admiralty court judge and was colonel of the state militia regiment, but was also accused of theft and thrown in debtor's prison for 14 months. Nevertheless, in July 1803 President Jefferson appointed Rodney as one of the Mississippi territorial judges and as federal land commissioner for the district west of the Pearl River. At age 59, Rodney traveled across half the continent to assume his post. His travel journal of August to December 1803 describes the hardships of western travel, as well as his observations on the Northwest Territory and its settlers. Rodney rode overland coaches to Wheeling, West Virginia, and then took flatboats down the Ohio and Mississippi rivers to Natchez. From there he traveled the last six miles on horseback. Most travelers down the Ohio River were enchanted by the trip the first few days, and then boredom set in. Most observers found more to complain about than to praise in their comments. What types of things does Rodney consider important enough to comment on? What problems do they encounter on the Ohio River? What food do they eat? What does Thomas Rodney think about Cincinnati?

Ohio River, October 1st 1803. The morning became after sun up very thick and foggy, yet we put off and so did Wood. 2 miles on we passed Little Sciota and a rocky bar just below it. We passed the bar at the upper end and then run along the side of it across oblikely to the Ohio State shore, this reach of the river runing west SW. We proceed a mile and came to a long sand bar on the Kentucky shore and kept the channel which is close to the Ohio State shore (the Ohio Pilot says it is next to the Kaintuky shore but is mistaken or the bar has altered).

We met with no further impediment to Great Siota which we arrived at about half after eleven: and I went on shore to git some whisky and to see the town of Alexandria, which stands on a hill of high land on the uper side of the Sciota but facing the Ohio. In a street parrallel with the river there is about 20 ordinary logged houses and cabbins in it and one

framed and one stone house, but few of the buildings finished and the inhabitants miserably poor. Chillecothe the seat of government of the Ohio State stands on this river 60 miles up it. The Great Sciota is some thing larger than Little Sciota but is but small at the mouth tho it is said to be a hansome river. The reach of the Ohio by Alexandria is SSW. Wood left us while we stopped.

It was just 12 o'clock at noon when we left Alexandria. 5 miles below passed Turkey Creek and a large sand bar on the NW shore. Just after we had left Alexandria some person hailed the boat away behind on the shore near the lower and of the town. We thought it was a man who had disputed a dollar Brown had paid him and we would not stop again. They put off in a canoe and persued us trailing from time to time. At length he got out on the bar and seemed in great distress. The Major went to him in

---

From *A Journal through the West: Thomas Rodney's 1803 Journal from Delaware to the Mississippi Territory*.

the skiff while the batteau persued her way. It was Shields who had persued us by land and got to Alexandra just time enough to see the boat. The Major brot him on board fatragued [sic] half to death for when we saw them coming the boy slacked rowing for them to come up.

At 3 o'clock we passed Canoconneque Creek on the Kentucky shore. This is a fine creek and the only one we have seen that was not dry. There was a flow of water out of this, but there is two ugly bars here, one runing of[f] from the mouth of the creek and one from an island on the NW shore; but we found a good channel between and round them by passing between them and then runing over to and along the Kentucky shore a little way and then gliding off into the middle of the river between the island and Kentucky shore. After passing said island the river assumed its natural form again.

Here I recollect that I omitted to mention the appearance of a cuerious rock on the mountain on the Kentucky shore just before we saw Alexandria round the point. It was an oblong laying like a table on one edge and the upper corners ovalled off a little. It stood on the top of a nob of the mountain and perhaps was 60 ft. long and 15 ft. high. The face was green as if covered with moss and the top edge was crowned with a row of ceadars.

While passing the last island we came in sight of Woods boat again but the wind slacked and he has got out of sight again. At 1/4 before 5 o'clock P.M. passed a creek on the NW shore and a stone bar just below it. Good channel close under the Kentucky shore. We overtook Woods boat at Vance Ville where he had encamped for the night and we come to ankor just above him. There is a very hansom settlement and little town here on the Kentuky shore and a salt works 1/4 mile out of town on Salt Lick Creek. The Major and Brown lodged on shore. This 17 miles below Sciota and 28 miles above Lime Stone. 20 ft. water by the shore.

Sunday, October the 2d 1803. We weighed ankor at day light tho the fog was very thick. In earnest to reach Limestone today to git our boat repaired as she leaks too much, esspecially every night. Wood over took us about 3 miles on the way again. Just time enough to pass over a dangerous riffle before us. The best channel was on the Kentucky shore but we followed Wood and crossed short over the middle of the riffle in the middle of the river. They rubed hard and we just touched as we passed over. Just below this riffle we passed Pond Run on the Kentuky shore and Stouts Run on the NW shore, and 4 Miles below there past Prestonville a little town of ten or twelve poor

logged houses on the Kentucky shore, and passed a riffle just below the village. Channel good on NW shore.

2 miles below we passed a small island surrounded by a large sand barr. Channel on NW shore but next to the barr at the uper end and at the lower end over the riffle at the mouth of a creek on the NW shore. Keep nearest to that shore and then the middle of the river by the floating mill, and thence toward the Kentucky shore by the mouth of a run or small creek on that shore. Thence the channel inclines over towards the NW shore but is good from the middle of the river to that shore and no danger any where but by timber near the shore: but low as the water is both Woods boat and ours passed the island without touching. This is the uppermost of what is called The Three Islands.

At 2 miles below the island we passed Cycamore Creek on the Kentucky shore, at 11 o'clock A.M. No riffle here. The Major and Shields went on shore in the skiff for wood and fire where Woods boat had landed on Kentucky shore and are now persuing us. At 40 minutes after 11 o'clock A.M. passed Donelsons Creek on the NW shore 2 miles below the last creek. At 12 o'clock we passed a long sand bar and creek on the Kentucky shore a mile below the last creek. We go now between 3 and 4 miles an hour there being no wind ahead on stern. (The last mentioned creek and bar are not mentioned by the Pilot.)

At one o'clock we entered it into the channel on the Kentuck shore at the upper end of what the Pilot calls the Two Islands. The upper one we call Tinn Pan Island because the Major here droped one of our tinn basons overboard and then persued it in the skiff and took it up again. The lower island we called Manchester Island from the little village of Manchester on the NW shore opposite the lower end of it. This villiage has a very hansome situation and contains about 20 wooden houses, some of them pretty decent looking ones.

Wood gave us an Ohio sucker which we had for diner boiled and butter with it and found it a good fish. It was remarkably fat. Before cooking we took near at [a] pint tin cup of leaf fat out of it which lay all along its back interior. It would have weighed as we suppose about six pounds. It was in shape or form like a fatback and in color like a yellow perch. It lives by suction on muscles, etc.

Below the last island the river resumed its natural size again. There is a ridge of mountain on the Caintucky shore opposite these island[s]. Indeed the mountains have appeared on both shores for two days past, and thereby spoiled our wind so that we have had but little sailing.

At 1/4 after 3 o'clock past a small creek or run on the NW shore and a fine extensive settlement along the river below it. At half after 3 o'clock we passed a small creek on the Kentucky shore. A pretty neat logged house and small settlement below. A person passing by told us this is Cabbin Creek 6 miles above Lime Stone. We passed Crooked Creek while I was laying down two miles back or higher up. At half past 5 o'clock we passed another small creek or run, and 10 minutes after passed another just above Brooks's settlement and a sand barr on the NW shore opposite said settlement, which is on the point on the Kentucky shore. As soon as we turn said poi[n]t we saw Lime Stone about 2 miles off and arrived there at 7 o'clock, that is just before dark and came to ankor.

Limestone on the Ohio. October 3d 1803. This morning after some trouble got the batteau up and got her overhalled and new corked by Brown and another carpenter and got off again at 4 o'clock P.M. Wood waited for us till 2 o'clock and then went off. While there I wrote a letter to Caesar my son and one to J. Fisher and put them in the Post Office: and the Major and I took a walk to see the town and ship yard.

There is about 50 houses in the town and a few large good houses but I observed but one of brick. Mr. Gallahar has a very fine ship of about 240 tuns on the stocks and will be done by the swell of the river. We viewed her and she appears to be well built and of excellent stuff such as mulbery, locust, white oak, etc. Crispin is the master workman and he told me people and mechanecks at that place are the idlest he ever met with. Indeed this appeared to be the case. I saw no body at work and no body about the town took notice of us or offered to afford us the least assistance except one poor man; and we had to pay extravagantly for every thing we bought or had done only [except for] the assistance of Mr. Woods men, our fellow travellers. Indeed, the present disposition of the people on this beautiful river is very unfavorable to its improvement. They mostly seem as if they were only waylayers to take advantage of travellers in[s]tead of aiding and incurraging the navigation of the river. Every thing raised in the country even, is as high here as in the market towns near the Atlantic.

We saw a very few genteel people in Lime Stone. We were introduced by Mr. Wood last evening to a Major Brown tavern keeper and we invited him to drink a glass of wine with us in our cabin and we were back and forward at his house today but he paid very little attention to us. Mr. Gallahar indeed was obliging enough to let us have what we paid for.

We left Limestone at a little before 5 o'clock P.M. and at a 1/4 before six passed a creek on the NW shore. P. Stout had passed Limestone 10 days ago. Here Brown and his companion ship carpenter left us and we had only Buckhanan our pilot beside our selves, 4 in all; but expect to git another hand. Coud not meet with one at Limestone: but our batteau goes better with one hand now she is dry than with two before. We travel about three miles an hour, without wind. The town at Limestone is called Maysville. I know not why. As to the Limestone Creek it is but a small stream and is now quite dry. This place is a great thorofare and more might be expected of it than is seen. The situation is pleasant and gives a good prospect of the river. I here discovered that I had omitted to leave letters brought to J. Rumford at Washington and a Mister Taylor at this place as well as all J. Lees letters to Connels Ville, such has been my haste and attention to my journey.

We dropt ankor at 7 o'clock in the evening near the Kentucky shore opposite a little town called Charles Town the Cou[n]ty Town of Mason County. The Major and Shields went on shore to see the place tho [it was] after dark. It contains only about 20 or 30 houses. The river below Limestone is said to be navigable for loaded boats at all seasons of the year and but little danger any where but at the falls; nevertheless I shall continue my observations on whatever may seem worth notice as we go.

The Major and Shields returned with a nice line [loin] of veal and half a bushel of sweet potatoes as a present from a Mr. Mitchel of Charleston aforesaid whose wife is sister to Mr. Ignatious Smith of Natchez. This is an instance of the greatest hospitality we have met with on the Ohio, not evin excepting Mr. Blany Hazard. He lives in a decent loged house and every thing decent round them, etc. Such men do honor to this wild uncultivated country. It is only to be lamented there is but few of them in it.

Our boat has been quite dry since her dressing at Limestone and floats much lighter by that, and by gitting clear of the young carpenters and their baggage and tools so that she goes faster now with Buckhanan alone than 2 rowers before.

Cincinnati on the N bank of Ohio opposite the mouth of Lycking River, Fryday, October 7th 1803. A very thick fog this morning and cleared up. Summer warm. Early in the morning Mr. Thomas H. Williams came on board the Iris and delivered me a letter of introduction from Captain Lewes, etc. His business was to git a passage with us down to the Natches. He said he had no baggage except what he had brought on horseback and wood take such fare on board as we had to spare and shift as well as he could: whereupon I consented to his going if he would lodge with the Major, as our spare berth was allotted to P. Stout at Louisville if he should meet us there.

After breakfast Shields and I took a walk through the town to vew it, and visited the Court House and old Fort Washington, etc.: and returned by the tavern where we met with the Major and old General St. Clair, and stoped and sat awhile with the General. He pressed us to take a family diner with him, but I excused myself as I had ordered diner on board, but wou'd wait on him in the afternoon. Shields and I returnd and the Major went with the General.

The Court House is a large stone building with a cupala and belfry on it and will make a neat appearance when finished. For the large room now intended for the Court has an arched raling for the advantage of sound in speaking, and there is a gallery on one side and the sealing is 18 or 20 ft. high. The whole building appears in good proportion and contains room for the publick officers, etc. There are 4 niches in front, of size for a statue to stand in each, but for what purpose intended do not know. As I went to the Court House I passed through the burying ground which exhibited a vast number of graves indeed for so young a place. From the Court House we went to view Fort Washington. This appears to have been origionally nothing more than a kind of block house fort calculated only to frighten or repell Indians. It covers about half an acre but is now partly in ruins and the whole will be so soon as it is of no longer [any] use.

This town, when we consider the recentness of it[s] date, the ground being all in woods only 14 years ago, is astonishingly large. It now contains about 400 houses and a great many new ones building and many of them large good houses. It has nearly a south front on the Ohio. The lower town is evidently built on what was once an island, as the vally between that and the hill back (where the Court House and uper town is) shews evidently that it has been once one bed of the river, but having got choaked up has risen in the course of time and united the island to the main land. Several other islands are now in this progress, the smaller channel round them being dry and no doubt yearly filling up as the larger channel becomes more roomy: and this effect is also apparent at many other places along this, river. Indeed, all the bottom land on this river appears to have been united to the highland in this manner.

In the afternoon Mr. Shields and I walked up to Genl. St. Clairs and the Major soon after came to us there w[h]ere we stayed and drank wine while with the Genl. and then returnd. The Genl. came with me and we called again to see the Court House. Then the Genl. came with me to the bank, and we took leave of each other, but as we came along he spoke of the antient fortifications just beyond the town which upon reflection I determined to see in the morning before we go.

Soon after I got on board the Major came down and brought Mrs. Finley['s] complements for us to drink tea there, and the Major and I went. Mr. Williams, Doctor Sulman and his wife, and a Mr. Vaughn and his wife, and a Mr. and Mrs. [blank] were there. Mr. Finley introduced us to them all and we drank tea with them. Then whist was proposed and Mrs. Finley and myself played against Mr. Vaughn and Mrs. Sulman and the Major and Mrs. Vaughn played against Mr. Finley and Mrs. [blank]. We ended at 11 o'clock and we returned on board: but while we were playing, the Majors partner sang "Drink to me only with thine eyes and I will pledge with mine." I expected to hear the Major reply in the next verse, "Or leave a kiss within the cup and I'll not look for wine:" but he hung his head and was beat. So he lost a paper of pins. Thus politely treated we spent a pleasant evening at Cincinnati. Mr. Finley is receiver for this district. At our table we left off even games. The ladies were all genteel and agreeable.

Cincinnati on the Ohio. Saturday, October 8th 1803. Foggy morning as usual. As soon as I got up I went alone to examine the old supposed fortifications a little to the westward of the Court House. They are in the form of a regular uniform circle with an opening of about a hundred yards on the eas[t]. The surrounding wall is about 6 feet high and uniform in hight and size all round. The area within contains about ten acres. The trees that grew on it are cut down. The larges[t] stump remaining counted 150 years groth. This grew on the highest part of the ridge. There is no appearance of mote or ditch round it, nor could there be after such a length of time: and therefore it must be supposed there was a ditch without and a parrapet within, and that the wall was origionally ten or twelve feet high, and that the wall has gradually sunk till the ditch and parrapet being filled up are lost to appearance, and the wall of course sunk into its present form. This is the natural operation, for I have seen this effect in respect to banks and ditches in a much shorter time.

Genl. St. Clair says that there is one at Musk-ingum that contains 40 acres; and it is said there is another up that river that includes 600 acres: but the accounts I heard of them differed as to their size and also as to their form. They appear indeed similar in age and workmanship to those mounds in this coun-try called Indian mounds, but are supposed by some to be the work of nations anticeedent to the present Indian tribes.

Genl. St. Clair says he has seen one of these mounds 40 feet high and another 70 feet: but all I have seen are near about the same hight and none of them exceeding ten feet in hight: and all these are known to be burying places from the human bones found in them and frequently Indian trinkets which shews that these are the works of the Indians only but perhaps of nations more advanced in the arts than the present tribes: but I can find no traces of those ori-gional white inhabitants which I have no doubt once inhabited this country unless these works are the only remains of the extent of their knowledge and that they were buried in that distrucktion which put an end to the mamoth tribe of beasts.

Apropus, Finley told us last evening that a tusk had been lately found at Big Bonelick that measured in a straight line from the root to the point ten feet and from the root to the point tracing the middle of its circular limb 15 feet, that it is 19 inches round at the root and 23 inches round in the thickest part.

We left Cincinnati at 11 o'clock. Just as we set off Williams came down with his baggage and the Major brot him on board but he returned again to Meet us at Louisville.

Just below the town we passed a stoney bar on Kentucky shore and rapid. A mile below this we passed another stoney bar in the river nearest to the Kentucky shore, yet the best channel tho small is next the Kentucky shore; however we passed in the middle of the river over the rapid, but the shoal is very full of wood. Just below this is Mill Creek on NW shore, a very large creek and not dry like others. On the Ken-tucky shore just below this seat is Col. Sandfords seat who is said to be the richest man in Kentucky. We saw not any thing to denote this but a large plantation. About 6 miles below C.Cinati we passed a very large sand bar in the middle of the river, a narrow channel by it close along each shore. We passed it on the NW shore. This bar will no doubt soon be an island.

About sun down we passed Bushes Ferry and a little below it a small riffle and rapid along the old French settlement on the most northerly bend of the Ohio; and little below said settlement came to ankor at dusk in the north point of said bend 3 miles above the Great Miama, having come about [17?] miles only today.

A little while after diner today we saw a large flock of wild turkies on the bank of the river. The Major and Shield went on shore with the gun; and the Major shot at two of them at 30 yds. distance but did not kill either. Our shot is too small. It require swan shot to kill them. By the information we had received set down the above distance but found in the morning that the extreme part of the N bend at the old French settlement is 3 miles above the mouth of the Miama.

Document 6.5 An English Immigrant Describes the Northwestern Territories

Morris Birkbeck emigrated from England to the United States in 1817 with a large family. He was deter-mined to establish a farming settlement for English Quakers in the Northwest Territory. In a series of let-ters published in England, he announced the creation of 1,500-acre English-style estates in Edwards County, Illinois. He encouraged prospective settlers to apply to him for sections of land, and guaranteed "a cabin, an enclosed garden, a cow, and a hog" for all settlers. As a farmer and developer, he wanted to see the land's potential for crops, so instead of traveling easily by boat down the Ohio River, he chose to go west overland to Cincinnati, then on to Vincennes, Indiana, finally entering the Illinois territory. Birkbeck observed the land, the morals, and the work habits of frontiersmen, and the prospects of the cities. What does he praise about the frontier and the people he finds there? What does he condemn, and why? What does he mean when he says "America was bred in a cabin"? If you were a farmer reading this account in England, what is most likely going to make you want to join his community in Illinois?

June 11. In my stroll among the lovely inclosures of this neighbourhood, I called to enquire my way at a small farm-house, belonging to an old Hibernian, who was glad to invite me in for the sake of a little conversation. He had brought his wife with him from his native island, and two children. The wife was at a neighbour's on a "wool-picking frolic," which is a merry-meeting of gossips at each other's houses, to pick the year's wool and prepare it for carding. The son and daughter were married, and well settled; each having eight children. He came to this place fourteen years ago, before an axe had been lifted, except to make a blaze road, a track across the wilderness, marked by the hatchet on the trees, which passed over the spot where the town now stands. A free and independent American, and a warm politician, he now discusses the interests of the state as one concerned in its prosperity:—and so he is, for he owns one hundred and eighteen acres of excellent land, and has twenty descendants. He has also a right to scrutinize the acts of the government, for he has a share in its appointment, and pays eight dollars a year in taxes:—five to the general treasury, and three to his own country:—in all about four-pence per acre. He still inhabits a *cabin,* but it is not an *Irish* cabin.

As particular histories lead to correct general notions, I shall give another little tale of early difficulties, related to us by a cheerful intelligent farmer, from the neighbourhood of Chillicothe, who made one of our party at the inn this evening: Fourteen years ago, he also came into this new settlement, and "unloaded his family under a tree," on his present estate; where he has now two hundred acres of excellent land, cleared and in good cultivation, capable of producing from eighty to one hundred bushels of Indian corn per acre.

The settlers in a country entirely new, are generally of the poorer class, and are exposed to difficulties, independent of unhealthy situations, which may account for the mortality that sometimes prevails among them. The land, when intended for sale, is laid out in the government surveys in quarter sections of 160 acres, being one fourth of a square mile. The whole is then offered to the public by auction, and that which remains unsold, which is generally a very large proportion, may be purchased at the land office of the district, at two dollars per acre, one fourth to

be paid down, and the remaining three-fourths at several instalments, to be completed in five years.

The poor emigrant, having collected the eighty dollars, repairs to the land office, and enters his quarter section, then works his way, without another "cent" in his pocket, to the solitary spot, which is to be his future abode, in a two horse waggon, containing his family and his little all, consisting of a few blankets, a skillet, his rifle, and his axe. Suppose him arrived in the spring: after putting up a little log cabin, he proceeds to clear, with intense labour, a plot of ground for Indian corn, which is to be their next year's support; but, for the present, being without means of obtaining a supply of flour, he depends on his gun for subsistence. In pursuit of the game, he is compelled, after his day's work, to wade through the evening dews, up to the waist, in long grass or bushes, and returning, finds nothing to lie on but a bear's skin on the cold ground, exposed to every blast through the sides, and every shower through the open roof of his wretched dwelling, which he does not even attempt to close, till the approach of winter, and often not then. Under these distresses of extreme toil and exposure, debarred from every comfort, many valuable lives have sunk, which have been charged to the climate.

The individual whose case is included in this seeming digression, escaped the ague, but he lay three weeks delirious in a nervous fever, of which he yet feels the remains, owing, no doubt, to excessive fatigue. Casualties, doubly calamitous in their forlorn estate, would sometimes assail them. He, for instance, had the misfortune to break his leg at a time when his wife was confined by sickness, and for three days they were only supplied with water, by a child of two years old, having no means of communicating with their neighbours (neighbours of ten miles off perhaps) until the fourth day. He had to carry the little grain he could procure twelve miles to be ground, and remembers once seeing at the mill, a man who had brought his, sixty miles, and was compelled to wait three days for his turn.

Such are the difficulties which these pioneers have to encounter; but they diminish as settlements approach each other, and are only heard of by their successors. The number of emigrants who passed this way was greater last year than in any preceding; and the present spring they are still more numerous than

From Notes on a Journey in America, from the Coast of Virginia to the Territory of Illinois, With Proposals for the Establishment of a Colony of English, London: 1818.

the last. Fourteen waggons yesterday, and thirteen to-day, have gone through this town. Myriads take their course down the Ohio. The waggons swarm with children. I heard to-day of three together, which contain forty-two of these young citizens. The wildest solitudes are to the taste of some people. General Boon, who was chiefly instrumental in the first settlement of Kentucky, is of this turn. It is said, that he is now, at the age of seventy, pursuing the daily chase, two hundred miles to the westward of the last abode of civilized man. He had retired to a chosen spot, beyond the Missouri, which, after him is named Boon's Lick, out of the reach, as he flattered himself, of intrusion; but white men even there, incroached upon him, and two years ago, he went back two hundred miles further.

June 22. As we approach the little Miami river, the country becomes more broken and much more fertile, and better settled. After crossing this rapid and clear stream, we had a pleasant ride to Lebanon, which is not a mountain of cedars, but a valley, so beautiful and fertile, that it seemed, on its first opening on our view, enriched as it was by the tints of evening, rather a region of fancy than a real back-wood scene.

Lebanon is itself, one of those wonders which are the natural growth of these backwoods. In fourteen years, from two or three cabins of half-savage hunters, it has grown to be the residence of a thousand persons, with habits and looks no way differing from their brethren of the east. Before we entered the town, we beard the supper bells of the taverns, and arrived just in time to take our seats at the table, among just such a set as I should have expected to meet at the ordinary in Richmond;—travellers like ourselves, with a number of store-keepers; lawyers and doctors; men who board at the taverns, and make up a standing company for the daily public table.

This morning we made our escape from this busy scene, in defiance of the threatening rain. A crowded tavern in an American town, though managed as is that we have just quitted, with great attention and civility is a place from which you are always willing to depart. After all, the wonder is, that so many comforts are provided for you, at so early a period.

Cincinnati, like most American towns, stands too low; it is built on the banks of the Ohio, and the lower part is not out of the reach of spring-floods.

As if "life was not more than meat, and the body than rainment," every consideration of health and enjoyment yields to views of mercantile convenience. Short-sighted and narrow economy, by which the lives of thousands are shortened, and the comfort of all sacrificed to mistaken notions of private interest!

Cincinnati is, however, a most thriving place, and backed as it is already by a great population and a most fruitful country, bids fair to be one of the first cities of the west. We are told, and we cannot doubt the fact, that the chief of what we see is the work of four years. The hundreds of commodious, well-finished brick houses, the spacious and busy markets, the substantial public buildings, the thousands of prosperous well-dressed, industrious inhabitants, the numerous waggons and drays, the gay carriages and elegant females;—the shoals of craft on the river, the busy stir prevailing every where, houses building, boat building, paving and levelling streets; the numbers of country people, constantly coming and going, with the spacious taverns, crowded with travellers from a distance.

All this is so much more than I could comprehend, from a description of a new town, just risen from the woods, that I despair of conveying an adequate idea of it to my English friends. It is enchantment, and Liberty is the fair enchantress.

I was assured by a respectable gentleman, one of the first settlers, and now a man of wealth and influence, that he remembers when there was only one poor cabin where this noble town now stands. The county of Hamilton is something under the regular dimensions of twenty miles square, and it already contains 30,000 inhabitants. Twenty years ago, the vast region comprising the states of Ohio and Indiana, and the territory of Illinois and Michigan, only counted 30,000 inhabitants; the number that are now living, and living happily, in the little county of Hamilton, in which stands Cincinnati.

Why do not the governments of Europe afford such an asylum, in their vast and gloomy forests, for their increasing myriads of paupers! This would be an object worthy a convention of sovereigns, if sovereigns were really the fathers of their people; but jealous as they are of emigration to America, this simple and sure mode of preventing it will never occur to them.

Land is rising rapidly in price, in all well-settled neighbourhoods. Fifty dollars per acre for improved land is spoken of familiarly: I have been asked thirty for a large tract, without improvements, on the Great Miami, fifty miles from Cincinnati, and similar prices in other quarters. An estate of a thousand acres, partially cleared, is spoken of, on the road to Louisville, at twenty dollars. Many offers occur, all at a very great advance of price. It now becomes a question, whether to fix in this comparatively populous state of

Ohio, or join the vast tide of emigration that is flowing farther west, where we may obtain lands of equal value, at the government price of two dollars per acre, and enjoy the advantage of choice of situation.

Though I feel some temptation to linger here, where society is attaining a maturity truly astonishing, when we consider its early date, I cannot be satisfied without seeing that remoter country, before we fix in this; still enquiring and observing as we proceed. If we leave behind us eligible situations, it is like securing a retreat to which we may return with good prospects, if we think it advisable.

The probability is that, in these more remote regions, the accumulation of settlers will shortly render land as valuable as it is here at present; and in the interim, this accession of inhabitants will create a demand for the produce of the new country, equal to the supply. It is possible too, that we may find ourselves in as good society there as here. Well-educated persons are not rare amongst the emigrants who are moving farther west; for the spirit of emigration has reached a class somewhat higher in the scale of society than formerly. Some too may be aiming at the same point with ourselves; and others, if we prosper, will be likely to follow our example.

We are also less reluctant at extending our views westward, on considering that the time is fast approaching, when the grand intercourse with Europe, will not be, as at present, through eastern America, but through the great rivers which communicate by the Mississippi with the ocean, at New Orleans. In this view, we approximate to Europe, as we proceed to the west.

The upward navigation of these streams is already coming under the control of steam, an invention which promises to be of incalculable importance to this new world.

Such is the reasoning which impels us still forward; and in a few days we propose setting out to explore the state of Indiana, and probably the Illinois. With so long a journey before us, we are not comfortable under the prospect of separation. Our plan had been to lodge our main party at Cincinnati, until we had fixed on our final abode; but this was before our prospects had taken so wide a range. We now talk of Vincennes, as we did before of this place, and I trust we shall shortly be again under weigh.

June 27. Cincinnati.—All is alive here as soon as the day breaks. The stores are open, the markets thronged, and business is in full career by five o'clock in the morning; and nine o'clock is the common hour for retiring to rest.

As yet I have felt nothing oppressive in the heat of this climate. Melting, oppressive, sultry nights, succeeding broiling days, and forbidding rest, which are said to wear out the frames of the languid inhabitants of the eastern cities, are unknown here. A cool breeze always renders the night refreshing, and generally moderates the heat of the day.

June 28. The numerous creeks in this country, which are apt to be swelled suddenly by heavy rains, render travelling perplexing, and even perilous to strangers, in a showery season like the present. On my way this morning from an excursion of about fifteen miles to view an estate, a man who was mowing at some distance from the road, hailed me with the common, but to us quaint appellation of "stranger:" I stopped to learn his wishes. "Are you going to ride the creek?" "I know of no creek," said I; "but I am going to Cincinnati."— "I guess it will swim your horse." "How must I avoid it?" "Turn to your left, and go up to the mill, and you will find a bridge." Now if this kind man had rested on his scythe, and detained the "stranger" a few minutes, to learn his country, his name, and the object of his journey, as he probably would, had he been nearer to the road, he would but have evinced another trait of the friendly character of these good Americans.

In this land of plenty, young people first marry, and then look out for the means of a livelihood, without fear or cause for it. The ceremony of marriage is performed in a simple family way, in my opinion more delicate, and corresponding to the nature of the contract, than the glaring publicity adopted by some, or the secrecy, not so respectable, affected by others.

The near relations assemble at the house of the bride's parents. The minister or magistrate is in attendance, and when the candidates make their appearance, he asks them severally the usual questions, and having called on the company to declare if there be any objections, he confirms the union by a short religious formula;—the bridegroom salutes the bride, and the ceremony is over. Tea and refreshments follow. Next day the bridegroom holds his levée, his numerous friends, and sympathy makes them numerous on these happy occasions, pour in to offer their congratulations. Abundance of refreshments of the most substantial kind, are placed on side-tables which are taken, not as a formal meal, but as they walk up and down the apartments in cheerful conversation. This running meal continues from noon till the close of the evening, the bride never making her appearance on the occasion; an example of delicacy worthy the imitation of more refined societies.

There are about two thousand people regularly employed as boatmen on the Ohio, and they are proverbially ferocious and abandoned in their habits, though with many exceptions, as I have good grounds for believing. People who settle along the line of this grand navigation, generally possess or acquire similar habits; and thus profligacy of manners seems inseparable from the population on the banks of these great rivers.

It is remarked, indeed, every where that in land navigators are worse than sailors.

This forms a material objection to a residence on the Ohio: outweighing all the beauty and local advantages of such a situation.

August 1. Dagley's, twenty miles north of Shawnee Town. After viewing several beautiful prairies, so beautiful with their surrounding woods as to seem like the creation of fancy, gardens of delight in a dreary wilderness; and after losing our horses and spending two days in recovering them, we took a hunter as our guide, and proceeded across the Little Wabash, to explore the country between that river and the Skillet-fork.

Since we left the Fox settlement, about fifteen miles north of the Big-Prairie, cultivation has been very scanty, many miles intervening between the little "clearings." This may therefore be truly called, a new country.

These lonely settlers are poorly off;—their bread corn must be ground thirty miles off, requiring three days to carry to the mill, and bring back, the small horse-load of three bushels. Articles of family manufacture are very scanty, and what they purchase is of the meanest quality and excessively dear: yet they are friendly and willing to share their simple fare with you. It is surprising how comfortable they seem, wanting every thing. To struggle with privations has now become the habit of their lives, most of them having made several successive plunges into the wilderness; and they begin already to talk of selling their "improvements," and getting farther "back," on finding that emigrants of another description are thickening about them.

Our journey across the Little Wabash was a complete departure from all mark of civilization. We saw no bears as they are now buried in the thickets, and seldom appear by day; but, at every few yards, we saw recent marks of their doings, "wallowing" in the long grass; or turning over the decayed logs in quest of beetles or worms, in which work the strength of this animal is equal to that of four men. Wandering without track; where even the sagacity of out hunter-guide

had nearly failed as, we at length arrived at the cabin of another hunter, where we lodged.

This man and his family are remarkable instances of the effect on the complexion, produced by the perpetual incarceration of a thorough woodland life. Incarceration may seem to be a term less applicable to the condition of a roving backwoods man than to any other, and especially unsuitable to the habits of this individual and his family; for the cabin in which he entertained us, is the third dwelling be has built within the last twelve months; and a very slender motive would place him in a fourth before the ensuing winter. In his general habits, the hunter ranges as freely as the beasts he pursues: labouring under no restraint, his activity is only bounded by his own physical powers: still he is incarcerated—"Shut from the common air." Buried in the depth of a boundless forest, the breeze of health never reaches these poor wanderers; the bright prospect of distant hills fading away into the semblance of clouds, never cheered their sight : they are tall and pale, like vegetables that grow in a vault, pining for light.

The man, his pregnant wife, his eldest son, a tall half-naked youth, just initiated in the hunters' arts, his three daughters, growing up into great rude girls, and a squalling tribe of dirty brats of both sexes, are of one pale yellow, without the slightest hint of healthful bloom.

In passing through a vast expanse of the backwoods, I have been so much struck with this effect, that I fancy I could determine the colour of the inhabitants, if I was apprised of the depth of their immersion; and, *vice versa,* I could judge of the extent of the "clearing" if I saw the people. The blood, I fancy, is not supplied with its proper dose of oxygen from their gloomy atmosphere, crowded with vegetables growing almost in the dark or decomposing; and in either case, abstracting from the air this vital principle.

Our stock of provisions being nearly exhausted we were anxious to provide ourselves with a supper by means of our guns; but we could meet with neither deer nor turkey; however, in our utmost need, we shot three racoons, an old one to be roasted for our dogs; and the two young ones to be stewed up daintily for ourselves. We soon lighted a fire, and cooked the old racoon for the dogs; but, famished as they were, they would not touch it, and their squeamishness so far abated our relish for the promised stew, that we did not press our complaining landlady to prepare it: and thus our supper consisted of the residue of our "corn" bread, and *no* racoon. However, we laid our bearskins on the filthy earth, (floor there was none,) which they assured us was "too damp for fleas," and wrapped in our blankets, slept soundly enough; though the collops of venison, hanging in comely rows in the smoky fire-place, and even the shoulders put by for the dogs, and which were suspended over our heads, would have been an, acceptable prelude to our night's rest, had we been invited to partake of them; but our hunter and our host were too deeply engaged in conversation to think of supper. In the morning the latter kindly invited us to cook some of the collops, which we did by toasting them on a stick; and he also divided some shoulders among the dogs:—so we all fared sumptuously.

The cabin, which may serve as a specimen of these rudiments of houses, was formed of round logs, with apertures of three or four inches between: no chimney, but large intervals between the "clap-boards," for the escape of the smoke. The roof was, however, a more effectual covering than we have generally experienced, as it protected us very tolerably from a drenching night. Two bedsteads of unhewn logs, and cleft boards laid across;—two chairs, one of them without a bottom, and a low stool, were all the furniture required by this numerous family. A string of buffalo hide, stretched across the hovel, was a wardrobe for their rags; and their utensils, consisting of a large iron pot, some baskets, the effective rifle and two that were superannuated, stood about in corners, and the fiddle, which was only silent when we were asleep, hung by them.

Our racoons, though lost to us and our hungry dogs, furnished a new set of strings for this favourite instrument. Early in the morning the youth had made good progress in their preparation, as they were cleaned and stretched on a tree to dry.

Many were the tales of dangerous adventures in their hunting expeditions, which kept us from our pallets till a late hour; and the gloomy morning allowed our hunters to resume their discourse, which no doubt would have been protracted to the evening, had not our impatience to depart caused us to interrupt it, which we effected, with some difficulty, by eleven in the forenoon.

These hunters are as persevering as savages, and as indolent. They cultivate indolence as a privilege:—"You English are very industrious, but we have freedom." And thus they exist in yawning indifference, surrounded with nuisances, and petty wants, the first to be removed, and the latter supplied by a tenth of the time loitered away in their innumerable idle days.

Indolence, under various modifications, seems to be the easily besetting sin of the Americans, where I have travelled. The Indian probably stands highest on the scale, as an example; the backwoods' man the next; the new settler, who declines hunting takes a lower degree, and so on. I have seen interesting exceptions even among the hunting tribe; but the malady is a prevailing one in all classes:—I note it again, and again, not in the spirit of satire, but as a hint for reformation:

"To know ourselves diseas'd is half a cure."

The Little Wabash, which we crossed in search of some prairies, which had been described to us in glowing colours, is a sluggish and scanty stream at this season, but for three months of the latter part of winter and spring, it covers a great space by the overflow of waters collected in its long course. The Skillet-fork is also a river of similar character; and the country lying between them must labour under the inconvenience of absolute seclusion for many months every year, until bridges and ferries are established: this would be a bar to our settling within the Fork, as it is called: we therefore separated this morning, without losing the time that it would require to explore this part thoroughly. I proceed to Shawnee Town land office, to make some entries which we had determined on, between the Little and the Big Wabash. Mr. Flower spends a day or two in looking about, and returns to our families at Princeton. Having made my way through this wildest of wildernesses to the Skillet-fork, I crossed it at a shoal, which affords a notable instance out of a thousand, of the utter worthlessness of reports about remote objects in this country, even from *soi-disant* eye-witnesses.

A grave old hunter, who had the air of much sagacity, declared to me, that he had visited this shoal, that it is a bed of limestone, a substance greatly wanting in this country. The son confirmed the father's account, adding, that he had seen the stone burnt into lime. It is micaceous sandstone slate, without the least affinity to limestone!

It is a dreadful country, on each side of the Skillet-fork; flat and swampy; so that the water in many places, even at this season, renders travelling disagreeable; yet here and there, at ten miles distance perhaps, the very solitude tempts some one of the family of Esau to pitch his tent for a season.

At one of these lone dwellings we found a neat, respectable-looking female, spinning under the little piazza at one side of the cabin, which shaded her from the sun: her husband was absent on business, which would detain him some weeks: she had no family, and no companion but her husband's faithful dog, which usually attended him in his bear hunting in the winter: she was quite overcome with "*lone*" she said, and hoped we would tie our horses in the wood, and sit awhile with her, during the heat of the day. We did so, and she rewarded us with a basin of coffee. Her husband was kind and good to her, and never left her without necessity, but a true lover of bear hunting; which he pursued alone, taking only his dog with him, though it is common for hunters to go in parties to attack this dangerous animal. He had killed a great number last winter; five, I think, in one week. The cabin of this hunter was neatly arranged, and the garden well stocked.

Document 6.6 Anne Royal Promotes Alabama Settlement, 1821

After the American Revolution, pioneer farmers and other settlers began moving into the Old Southwest, into lands later called Alabama and Mississippi. But the greatest exodus to the Old Southwest came after the Indian Land sessions of 1815-1818 opened the way to settlement. As the local Native Americans vacated the land (or were forced out), white settlers moved in, often carrying little more than a few tools and driving a few livestock. At first they lived off the resources of the land, as the Native Americans had; later, they turned to commercial agriculture. Elite migrants drove their slaves into the rich lands of the delta, and helped create the cotton frontier, with its emphasis on the price of cotton and the value of slaves. Other settlers congregated in boom towns and new communities, hoping to benefit from the exertions of the local farmers. Florence, Alabama was one of these boom towns. In 1821, two years after Alabama gained statehood, Anne Royal wrote this letter describing Florence to her sister back east. What accomplishments does she take pride in noting? Is there a community spirit, or simply rampant individualism evident in the town's growth? How does this compare with the descriptions of towns in the Old Northwest?

Florence is one of the new towns of this beautiful and rapid rising state. It is happily situated for commerce at the head of steamboat navigation, on the north side of Tennessee river, in the county of Lauderdale, five miles below the port of the Muscle Shoals, and ten miles from the line of the state of Tennessee.

Florence is to be the great emporium of the northern part of this state. I do not see why it should not; it has a great capital and is patronized by the wealthiest gentlemen in the state. It has a great state at its back; another in front, and a noble river on all sides, the steamboats pouring every necessary and every luxury into its lap. Its citizens, bold, enterprising, and industrious—much more so than any I have seen in the state.

Many large and elegant brick buildings are already built here, (although it was sold out, but two years since,) and frame houses are putting up daily. It is not uncommon to see a framed building begun in the morning and finished by night.

Several respectable mercantile houses are established here, and much business is done on commis-sion also. The site of the town is beautifully situated on an eminence, commanding an extensive view of the surrounding country, and Tennessee River, from which it is three quarters of a mile distant. It has two springs of excellent and never failing water. Florence has communication by water with Mississippi, Missouri, Louisiana, Indiana, Illinois, Ohio, Kentucky, West Pennsylvania, West Virginia, and East Tennessee, and very shortly will communicate with the Eastern States, through the great canal!!! The great Military road that leads from Nashville to New Orleans, by way of Lake Ponchartrain, passes through this town, and the number of people who travel through it, and the numerous droves of horses for the lower country, for market, are incredible. Florence contains one printing press, and publishes a paper weekly called the *Florence Gazette;* it is ably patronized, and edited by one of our first men, and said to be the best paper in the state. Florence is inhabited by people from almost all parts of Europe and the United States; here are English, Irish, Welsh, Scotch, French, Dutch, Germans, and Grecians. The first

From *Letters from Alabama on Various Subjects,* Washington DC: 1830.

Greek I ever saw was in this town. I conversed with him on the subject of his country, but found him grossly ignorant. He butchers for the town, and has taken to his arms a mulatto woman for a wife. He very often takes an airing on horseback of a Sunday afternoon, with his wife riding by his side, and both arrayed in shining costume.

The river at Florence is upwards of five-hundred yards wide; it is ferried in a large boat worked by four horses, and crosses in a few minutes.

There are two large and well kept taverns in Florence, and several Doggeries. A Doggery is a place where spirituous liquors are sold; and where men get drunk, quarrel, and fight, as often as they choose, but where there is nothing to eat for man or beast. Did you ever hear any thing better named. "I sware!" said a Yankee peddlar, one day, with both his eyes bunged up, "that are Doggery, be rightly named. Never seed the like on't. If I get to hum agin it 'il be a nice man 'il catch me in these here parts. Awfullest place one could be at." It appeared the inmates of the Doggery enticed him under pretence of buying his wares, and forced him to drink; and then forced him to fight; but

the poor little Yankee was sadly beaten. Not content with blacking up his eyes, they over-turned his tin-cart, and scattered his tins to the four winds; frightened his horse, and tormented his very soul out about lasses, &c. He was a laughable object—but to hear his dialect in laying off the law, was a complete farce, particularly when Pat came to invite him into the same Doggery to drink friends— "I ben't a dog to go into that are dog house."

The people, you see, know a thing or two, here; they call things by their right names. But to proceed—there may be about one hundred dwelling houses and stores, a court house, and several warehouses in Florence. The latter are however on the river. One of the longest buildings I ever saw, is in Florence. It was built by a company of gentlemen, and is said to have cost $90,000, and is not yet finished. The proprietors, being of this place, are men of immense wealth, and are pushing their capital with great foresight and activity. For industry and activity, Florence outstrips all the northern towns in the state. More people travel this road than all our western roads put together. . . .

Document 6.7 Harriet Noble Describes Her Family Move to Michigan

The end of the War of 1812, the destruction of Tecumseh's confederacy, and the forced removal of natives promoted a surge of migration into the Old Northwest as well. Since the best lands in New England and the East were exhausted from generations of tillage and over-grazing, hundreds of thousands of people emigrated to the newly opened lands of Ohio, Indiana, Illinois, Wisconsin, and Michigan. In many towns across the region, New Englanders recreated the classic village green, surrounded by the public buildings and stores. For many women, the move west was a nightmare. Often forced to leave their homes without any input, wives were expected to recreate all aspects of civilization in their new settlements, as well as maintain some sense of normalcy during their travels. Gone are the amenities of settled communities and the established social networks. Harriet Noble and her family traveled through New York and Lake Erie to reach the Detroit area. How does she describe her travels and new home? What complaints does she have about life on the farming frontier?

My husband was seized with the mania, and accordingly made preparation to start in January with his brother. They took the Ohio route, and were nearly a month in getting through; coming by way of Monroe, and thence to Ypsilanti and Ann Arbor. Mr. John Allen and Walter Rumsey with his wife and two

men had been there some four or five weeks, had built a small house, moved into it the day my husband and his brother arrived, and were just preparing their first meal, which the newcomers had the pleasure of partaking. They spent a few days here, located a farm a little above the town on the river Huron, and

Harriet Noble, account of emigration to Michigan in Elizabeth F. Ellet *Pioneer Women of the West* [New York: Charles Scribner's Sons, 1852], pp. 388–396.

returned through Canada. They had been so much pleased with the country, that they immediately commenced preparing to emigrate; and as near as I can recollect, we started about the 20th of September, 1824, for Michigan. We travelled from our house in Geneva to Buffalo in wagons. The roads were bad, and we were obliged to wait in Buffalo four days for a boat, as the steamboat "Michigan" was the only one on the lake. After waiting so long we found she had put into Erie for repairs, and had no prospect of being able to run again for some time. The next step was to take passage in a schooner, which was considered a terrible undertaking for so dangerous a voyage as it was then thought to be. At length we went on board "the Prudence," of Cleveland, Capt. Johnson. A more inconvenient little hark could not well be imagined. We were seven days on Lake Erie, and so entirely prostrated with seasickness, as scarcely to be able to attend to the wants of our little ones. I had a little girl of three years, and a babe some months old, and Sister Noble had six children, one an infant. It was a tedious voyage; the lake was very rough most of the time, and I thought if we were only on land again, I should be satisfied, it was a wilderness. I could not then realize what it would be to live without a comfortable house through the winter, but sad experience afterwards taught me a lesson not to be forgotten.

We came into the Detroit river; it was beautiful then as now; on the Canada side, in particular, you will scarce perceive any change. As we approached Detroit, the "Cantonment" with the American flag floating on its walls, was decidedly the most interesting of any part of the town; for a city it was certainly the most filthy, irregular place I had ever seen; the streets were filled with Indians and low French, and at that time I could not tell the difference between them. We spent two days in making preparations for going out to Ann Arbor, and during that time I never saw a genteelly-dressed person in the streets. There were carriages; the most wealthy families rode in French carts, sitting on the bottom upon some kind of mat; and the streets were so muddy these were the only vehicles convenient for getting about. I said to myself, "if this be a Western city, give me a home in the woods." I think it was on the 3rd of October we started from Detroit, with a pair of oxen and a wagon, a few articles for cooking, and such necessaries as we could not do without. It was necessary that they should be few as possible, for our families were a full load for this mode of travelling. After travelling all day we found ourselves but ten miles from Detroit (at what is now Dearborn); here we spent the night at a kind of tavern, the only one west of the city. Our lodg-

ing was the floor, and the other entertainment was to match. The next day we set out as early as possible, in hopes to get through the woods before dark, but night found us about half way through, and there remained no other resource but to camp out, and make ourselves contented. The men built a large fire and prepared our supper. My sister and myself could assist but little, so fatigued were we with walking and carrying our infants. There were fifteen in our company. Two gentlemen going to Ypsilanti had travelled with us from Buffalo; the rest were our own families. We were all pretty cheerful, until we began to think of lying down for the night. The men did not seem to dread it, however, and were soon fast asleep, but sleep was not for me in such a wilderness. I could think of nothing but wild beasts, or something as bad; so that I had the pleasure of watching while the others slept. It seemed a long, long night, and never in my life did I feel more grateful for the blessing of returning day. We started again as early as possible, all who could walk moving on a little in advance of the wagon; the small children were the only ones who thought of riding. Every few rods it would take two or three men to pry the wagon out of the mud, while those who waked were obliged to force their way over fallen timber, brush, &c. Thus passed the day; at night we found ourselves on the plains, three miles from Ypsilanti. My feet were so swollen I could walk no further. We got into the wagon and rode as far as Woodruff's grove, a little below Ypsilanti. There were some four or five families at this place. The next day we left for Ann Arbor. We were delighted with the country before us, it was beautiful in its natural state; and I have sometimes thought that cultivation has marred its loveliness. Where Ypsilanti now stands, there was but one building—an old trading-house on the west side of the river; the situation was fine—there were scattering oaks and no brushwood. Here we met a large number of Indians; and one old squaw followed us some distance with her papoose, determined to swap babies. At last she gave it up, and for one I felt relieved.

We passed two log houses between this and Ann Arbor. About the middle of the afternoon we found ourselves at our journey's end—but what a prospect? There were some six or seven log huts occupied by as many inmates as could be crowded into them. It was too much to think of asking strangers to give us a place to stay in even for one night under such circumstances. Mr. John Allen himself made us the offer of sharing with him the comfort of a shelter from storm, if not from cold. His house was large for a log one, but quite unfinished; there was a ground floor and a small piece above. When we got our things stored in this place, we found the number sheltered to be twenty-one women and children, an fourteen men. There were but two bedsteads in the house, and those who could not occupy these, slept on feather beds upon the floor. When the children were put in bed you could not set a foot down without stepping on a foot or hand; the consequence was we had music most of the time.

We cooked our meals in the open air, there being no fire in the house but a small box-stove. The fall winds were not very favorable to such business; we would frequently find our clothes on fire, but fortunately we did not often get burned. When one meal was over, however, we dreaded preparing the next. We lived in this way until our husbands got a log house raised and the roof on; this took them about six weeks, at the end of which time we went into it, without door, floor, chimney, or anything but logs and roof. There were no means of getting boards for a floor, as everything must be brought from Detroit, and we could not think of drawing lumber over such a road. The only alternative was to split slabs of oak with an axe. My husband was not a mechanic, but he managed to make a floor in this way that kept us from the ground. I was most anxious for a door, as the wolves would come about in the evening, and sometimes stay all night and keep up a serenade that would almost chill the blood in my veins. Of all noises I think the howling of wolves and the yell of Indians the most fearful; at least it appeared so to me then, when I was not able to close the door against them. I had the greatest terror of Indians; for I had never seen any before I came to Michigan but Oneidas, and they were very different, being partially civilized.

We had our house comfortable as such a rude building could be, by the first of February. It was a mild winter; there was snow enough to cover the ground only four days, a fortunate circumstance for us. We enjoyed uninterrupted health, but in the spring the ague with its accompaniments gave us a call, and by the middle of August there were but four out of fourteen who could call themselves well. We then fancied we were too near the river for health. We sold out and bought again ten miles west of Ann Arbor, a place which suited us better; and just a year form the day we came to Ann Arbor, moved out of it to Dexter. There was one house here, Judge Dexter's; he was building a sawmill, and had a number of men at work at the time; besides these there was not a white family west of Ann Arbor in Michigan territory. Our log house was just raised, forming only the square log pen. Of course it did not look very inviting,

but it was our home, and we must make the best of it. I helped to raise the rafters and put on the roof, but it was the last of November before our roof was completed. We were obliged to wait for the mill to run in order to get boards for making it. The doorway I had no means of closing except by hanging up a blanket, and frequently when I would raise it to step out, there would be two or three of our dusky neighbors peeping in to see what was there. It would always give me such a start, I could not suppress a scream, to which they would reply with "Ugh!" and a hearty laugh. They knew I was afraid, and liked to torment me. Sometimes they would throng the house and stay two or three hours. If I was alone they would help themselves to what they liked. The only way in which I could restrain them at all, was to threaten that I would tell Cass; he was governor of the territory, and they stood in great fear of him. At last we got a door. The next thing wanted was a chimney; winter was close at hand and the stone was not drawn. I said to my husband, "I think I can drive the oxen and draw the stones, while you dig them from the ground and load them." He thought I could not, but consented to let me try. He loaded them on a kind of sled; I drove to the house, rolled them off, and drove back for another load. I succeeded so well that we got enough in this way to build our chimney. My husband and myself were four days building it. I suppose most of my lady friends would think a woman quite out of "her legitimate sphere" in turning mason, but I was not at all particular what kind of labor I performed, so we were only comfortable and provided with the necessaries of life. Many times I had been obliged to take my children, put on their cloaks, and sit on the south side of the house in the sun to keep them warm; anything was preferable to smoke. When we had a chimney and floor, and a door to close up our little log cabin, I have often thought it the most comfortable little place that could possibly be built in so new a country; and but for the want of provisions of almost every kind, we should have enjoyed it much. The roads had been so bad all the fall that we had waited until this time, and I think it was December when my husband went to Detroit for supplies. Fifteen days were consumed in going and coming. We had been without flour for three weeks or more, and it was hard to manage with young children thus. After being without bread three or four days, my little boy, two years old, looked me in the face and said, "Ma, why don't you make bread; don't you like it? I do." His innocent complaint brought forth the first tears I had shed in Michigan on account of any privations I had to suffer, and they were about the last. I am not of a desponding disposition, nor often low-spirited, and having left New York to make Michigan my home, I had no idea of going back, or being very unhappy. Yet the want of society, of church privileges, and in fact almost every thing that makes life desirable, would often make me sad in spite of all effort to the contrary. I had no ladies' society for one year after coming to Dexter, except that of sister Noble and a Mrs. Taylor, and was more lonely than either of them, my family being so small.

The winter passed rather gloomily, but when spring came, everything looked delightful. We thought our hardships nearly at an end, when early in the summer my husband was taken sick with the ague. He had not been sick at all the first year; of course he must be acclimated. He had never suffered from ague or fever of any kind before, and it was a severe trial for him, with so much to do and no help to be had. He would break the ague and work for a few days, when it would return. In this way he made his garden, planted his corn, and thought he was quite well. About August he harvested his wheat and cut his hay, but could get no help to draw it, and was again taken with ague. I had it myself, and both my children. Sometimes we would all be ill at a time. Mr. Noble and I had it every other day. He was almost discouraged, and said he should have to sell his cattle or let them starve. I said to him, "to-morrow we shall neither of us have the ague, and I believe I can load and stack the hay, if my strength permits." As soon as breakfast was over, I prepared to go into the meadow, where I loaded and stacked seven loads that day. The next day my husband had the ague more severely than common, but not so with me; the exercise broke the chills, and I was able to assist him whenever he was well enough, until our hay was all secured. In the fall we had several added to our circle. We were more healthy then, and began to flatter ourselves that we could live very comfortably through the winter of 1826; but we were not destined to enjoy that blessing,

for in November my husband had his left hand blown to pieces by the accidental discharge of a gun, which confined him to the house until April. The hay I had stacked during the summer I had to feed out to the cattle with my own hands sin the winter, and often cut the wood for three days at a time. The logs which I alone rolled in, would surprise any one who has never been put to the test of necessity, which compels people to do what under other circumstances they would not have thought possible. This third winter in Michigan was decidedly the hardest I had yet encountered. In the spring, Mr. Noble could go out by carrying his hand in a sling. He commenced ploughing to prepare for planting his corn. Being weak from his wound, the ague returned again, but he worked every other day until his corn was planted. He then went to New York, came back in July, and brought a nephew with him, who relived me from helping him at the work out of doors. Although I was obliged to stack the hay this third fall, I believe it was the last labor of the kind I ever performed. At this time we have began to have quite a little society; we were fortunate in having good neighbors, and for some years were almost like one family, our interests being the same, and envy, jealousy, and all bitter feelings unknown among us. We cannot speak so favorably of the present time.

When I look back upon my life, and see the ups and downs, the hardships and privations I have been called upon to endure, I feel no wish to be young again. I was in the prime of life when I came to Michigan—only twenty-one, and my husband was thirty-three. Neither of us knew the reality of hardship. Could we have known what it was to be pioneers in a new country, we should never come, but I am satisfied that with all the disadvantages of raising a family in a new country, there is a consolation in knowing that our children are prepared to brave the ills of life, I believe, far better than they would have been had we never left New York.

Document 6.8 A New Englander's Views of the Mississippi Valley, 1826

Timothy Flint was a Massachusetts-born, Harvard-trained clergyman. After repeated disputes with his congregation over doctrine and salary, he resigned in June 1814. Thirty-four years old, with a wife and three children to support, Flint took employment as a missionary in the Trans-Appalachian west. Most New England missionary societies were more concerned with reclaiming the fallen rather than converting the heathen Indians. Flint's job was to make backwoods communities realize they needed a church, help them form a congregation, and then move on to repeat the process again. Starting with three years in St. Charles, Missouri, Flint lived, worked, and traveled in the Mississippi River Valley for ten years, from 1816 to 1826. His book, *Recollections of the Last Ten Years: Passed in Occasional Residences and Journeyings in the Valley of the*

Mississippi, presented a largely favorable view of the Trans-Appalachian west and the people living there. Flint's writing all stress the triumph of civilization and progress over white and native barbarism. Change and increasing settlement equaled progress, so Flint described change in great detail. Some eastern writers characterized westerners as drunken, lazy good-for-nothings. Does Flint agree with this? If not, how does he describe westerners? How does Flint demonstrate the advance of civilization?

Letter XVII.—St. Charles

The people in the Atlantic states have not yet recovered from the horror, inspired by the term "backwoodsman." This prejudice is particularly strong in New England, and is more or less felt from Maine to Georgia. When I first visited this country, I had my full share, and my family by far too much for their comfort. In approaching the country, I heard a thousand stories of gougings, and robberies, and shooting down with the rifle. I have travelled in these regions thousands of miles under all circumstances of exposure and danger. I have travelled alone, or in company only with such as needed protection, instead of being able to impart it; and this too, in many instances, where I was not known as a minister, or where such knowledge would have had no influence in protecting me. I never have carried the slightest weapon of defence. I scarcely remember to have experienced any thing that resembled insult, or to have felt myself in danger from the people. I have often seen men that had lost an eye. Instances of murder, numerous and horrible in their circumstances, have occurred in my vicinity. But they were such lawless rencounters, as terminate in murder every where, and in which the drunkenness, brutality, and violence were mutual. They were catastrophes, in which quiet and sober men would be in no danger of being involved. When we look round these immense regions, and consider that I have been in settlements three hundred miles from any court of justice, when we look at the position of the men, and the state of things, the wonder is, that so few outrages and murders occur. The gentlemen of the towns, even here, speak often with a certain contempt and horror of the backwoodsmen. I read, and not without feelings of pain, the bitter representations of the learned and virtuous Dr. Dwight, in speaking of them. He represents these vast regions, as a grand reservoir for the scum of the Atlantic states. He characterizes in the mass the emigrants from New England, as discontented coblers, too proud, too much in debt, too unprincipled, too much puffed up with self-conceit, too strongly impressed that their fancied talents could not find scope in their own country, to stay there. It is true there are worthless people here, and the most so, it must be confessed, are from New England. It is true there are gamblers, and gougers, and outlaws; but there are fewer of them, than from the nature of things, and the character of the age and the world, we ought to expect. But it is unworthy of the excellent man in question so to designate this people in the mass. The backwoodsman of the west, as I have seen him, is generally an amiable and virtuous man. His general motive for coming here is to be a freeholder, to have plenty of rich land, and to be able to settle his children about him. It is a most virtuous motive. And notwithstanding all that Dr. Dwight and Talleyrand have said to the contrary, I fully believe, that nine in ten of the emigrants have come here with no other motive. You find, in truth, that he has vices and barbarisms, peculiar to his situation. His manners are rough. He wears, it may be, a long beard. He has a great quantity of bear or deerskins wrought into his household establishment, his furniture, and dress. He carries a knife, or a dirk in his bosom, and when in the woods has a rifle on his back, and a pack of dogs at his heels. An Atlantic stranger, transferred directly from one of our cities to his door, would recoil from a rencounter with him. But remember, that his rifle and his dogs are among his chief means of support and profit. Remember, that all his first days here were passed in dread of the savages. Remember, that he still encounters them, still meets bears and panthers. Enter his door, and tell him you are benighted, and wish the shelter of his cabin for the night. The welcome is

---

From *Recollections of the Last Ten years, Passed in Occasional Residences and Journeyings of the Valley of the Mississippi*, Boston: Cummings, Hilliard and Company, 1826.

indeed seemingly ungracious: "I reckon you can stay," or "I suppose we must let you stay." But this apparent ungraciousness is the harbinger of every kindness that he can bestow, and every comfort that his cabin can afford. Good coffee, corn bread and butter, venison, pork, wild and tame fowls are set before you. His wife, timid, silent, reserved, but constantly attentive to your comfort, does not sit at the table with you, but like the wives of the patriarchs, stands and attends on you. You are shown to the best bed which the house can offer. When this kind of hospitality has been afforded you as long as you choose to stay, and when you depart, and speak about your bill, you are most commonly told with some slight mark of resentment, that they do not keep tavern. Even the flaxen-headed urchins will turn away from your money.

In all my extensive intercourse with these people, I do not recollect but one instance of positive rudeness and inhospitality. It was on the waters of the Cuivre of the upper Mississippi; and from a man to whom I had presented bibles, who had received the hospitalities of my house, who had invited me into his settlement to preach. I turned away indignantly from a cold and reluctant reception here, made my way from the house of this man,—who was a German and comparatively rich,—through deep and dark forests, and amidst the concerts of wolves howling on the neighbouring hills. Providentially, about midnight, I heard the barking of dogs at a distance, made my way to the cabin of a very poor man, who arose at midnight, took me in, provided supper, and gave me a most cordial reception.

With this single exception, I have found the backwoodsmen to be such as I have described; a hardy, adventurous, hospitable, rough, but sincere and upright race of people. I have received so many kindnesses from them, that it becomes me always to preserve a grateful and affectionate remembrance of them. If we were to try them by the standard of New England customs and opinions, that is to say, the customs of a people under entirely different circumstances, there would be many things in the picture, that would strike us offensively. They care little about ministers, and think less about paying them. They are averse to all, even the most necessary restraints. They are destitute of the forms and observances of society and religion; but they are sincere and kind without professions, and have a coarse, but substantial morality, which is often rendered more striking by the immediate contrast of the graceful bows, civility, and professions of their French Catholic neighbours, who have the observances of society and the forms of wor-ship, with often but a scanty modicum of the blunt truth and uprightness of their unpolished neighbours.

In the towns of the upper country on the Mississippi, and especially in St. Louis, there is one species of barbarism, that is but too common; I mean the horrid practice of duelling. But be it remembered, this is the barbarism only of that small class that denominate themselves "the gentlemen." It cannot be matter of astonishment that these are common here, when we recollect, that the fierce and adventurous spirits are naturally attracted to these regions, and that it is a common proverb of the people, that when we cross the Mississippi, "we travel beyond the Sabbath."

It would lead me to such personalities as I mean to avoid, were I to give you details, and my views of the fatal duels, of which there were so many while I was here. I can only say, that I lost, in this dreadful way, two individuals with whom I had personal intercourse, and from whom I had received many kindnesses. One of them was one of the most promising and apparently the most sober and moral young men in the state, the hope of his family, and the prop of the old age of his father. All that fell were men in office, of standing and character. I am not here going to start a dissertation upon the trite subject of duelling, the most horrible and savage relic of a barbarous age. If any thing could disgust reasoning beings with this dreadful practice, it would be to have seen its frequency and its terminations and consequences in this region. The best encomium of regulated society, and of the restraints of order and religion, is found in the fact, that the duels that occur here, compared with those that occur in New England, in proportion to the population, are as a hundred to one. But even here, it would be unjust to infer that the mass of the people favour duelling. A single consideration will go far to explain its frequency of occurrence among the upper classes. As we have said, the ambitious, fiery, and ungovernable spirits emigrate to obtain consequence, and make their fortune. There is a continual chaos of the political elements, occasioned by this continual addition of new and discordant materials. The new adventurers that arrive, have not as yet had their place or their standing assigned them in public opinion. In process of time, this new timber is inwrought into the old political fabric, and thus it becomes continually repaired and new moulded. In other words, people come here and find themselves in a position to start for a new standing in society. No new man can ascend to eminence, without displacing some one who is already there. Where character and estimation are settled by prescription, the occupant of the high station gives place peaceably to him that public opinion has mounted to his place. Not so to the newly arrived emigrant, who makes this way to public favour, before his standing and character have been settled by general estimation. A few partisans find it convenient to cry up their friend, who has recently emigrated here from abroad. This is the very country and region for this kind of crying up and crying down. We know that every circle, however small, has its prodigious great man, like Sancho's beauty, the greatest within three leagues. How often have I heard of these great men on a small circle, the actual monopolists of all the talents and all the virtues, and yet men, of whom on acquaintance I was compelled to form but a very indifferent opinion. To express a doubt in this case is treason. Even "faint praise" is almost a ground of offence. At the mouth of the pistol it must be settled, which is the greater man of the opposing circles. The partisans of the opposing great men meet. Recklessness about justice, and even life, is generated by the blasphemy and abuse that grow out of the idle quarrel. They throw away their lives, and the desperate indifference with which they do it, creates a kind of respect in the minds of them that contemplate it.

Document 6.9 The Promise of the West Judged by a Foreign Observer

Foreign visitors frequently visited the United States during antebellum days. Some, like Alexis De Tocqueville, saw much to praise in our democratic process. But most foreign observers were critical of everything they encountered. Harriet Martineau complained that all Americans talked about while eating was money: making money, the income of the speaker, the price of crops, and so on. Charles Dickens complained about frontier manners, especially chewing and spitting tobacco; he claimed Americans even spat in their sleep! Francis Trollope complained about the lack of gardens, the dirty streets, and the infestations of insects. Michael Chevalier came to the United States in 1834 at the order of the French Minister of the Interior, to inspect our public works. He spent two years studying the country and the people in it. Because his response to the United States was largely positive, American reviewers of his book, *Society, Manners and Politics in the United States*, were overwhelming in their praises. Keeping his original mission in mind, what does Chevalier find worth praising in the United States? According to him, what demonstrates the great promise of the American west?

Letter XVIII

Cincinnati.

Memphis, (Tenn.), Jan. 1, 1835.

Cincinnati has been made famous by Mrs Trollope, whose aristocratic feelings were offended by the pork-trade, which is here carried on on a great scale. From her accounts many persons have thought that every body in Cincinnati was a pork merchant, and the city a mere slaughter-house. The fact is that Cincinnati is a large and beautiful town, charmingly situated in one of those bends which the Ohio makes, as if unwilling to leave the spot. The hills which border the *Belle Riviereè* (Beautiful River, the French name of the Ohio) through its whole course, seem here to have receded from the river bank, in order to form a lofty plain, to which they serve as walls, whenever the Ohio does not serve as a foss, and on which man might build a town above the reach of the terrible floods of the river. Geologists, who have no faith in the favours of the fabled Oreads, will merely attribute this table-land to the washing away of the mountains, in the diluvian period, by the River Licking, now a modest little stream, which, descending from the highlands of Kentucky, empties itself into the Ohio opposite Cincinnati. However this may be, there is not, in the whole course of the river, a single spot which offers such attractions to the founders of a town.

From *Society, Manners and Politics in the United States,* 1835.

The architectural appearance of Cincinnati is very nearly the same with that of the new quarters of the English towns. The houses are generally of brick, most commonly three stories high, with the windows shining with cleanliness, calculated each for a single family, and regularly placed along well paved and spacious streets, sixty feet in width. Here and there the prevailing uniformity is interrupted by some more imposing edifice, and there are some houses of hewn stone in very good taste, real palaces in miniature, with neat porticoes, inhabited by the aristocratical portion of Mrs Trollope's hog-merchants, and several very pretty mansions surrounded with gardens and terraces. Then there are the common schoolhouses, where girls and boys together learn reading, writing, cyphering, and geography, under the simultaneous direction of a master and mistress. In another direction you see a small, plain church, without sculpture or paintings, without coloured glass or gothic arches, but snug, well carpeted, and well-warmed by stoves. In Cincinnati, as everywhere else in the United States, there is a great number of churches; each sect has its own, from Anglican Episcopalianism, which enlists under its banner the wealth of the country, to the Baptist and Methodist sects, the religion of the labourers and negroes. On another side, stands a huge hotel, which from its exterior you would take for a royal residence, but in which, as I can testify, you will not experience a princely hospitality; or a museum, which is merely a private speculation, as all American museums are, and which consists of some few crystals, some mammoth-bones, which are very abundant in the United States, an Egyptian mummy, some Indian weapons, and dresses, and a half-dozen wax-figures, representing, for instance, Washington, General Jackson, and the Indian Chiefs, Black Hawk and Tecumseh, a figure of Napoleon afoot or on horseback, a French cuirass from Watterloo, a collection of portraits of distinguished Americans comprising Lafayette and some of the leading men of the town, another of stuffed birds, snakes preserved in spirits, and particularly a large living snake, a boa constrictor, or an anaconda. One of these museums in Cincinnati is remarkable for its collection of Indian antiquities, derived from the huge caves of Kentucky, or from the numerous mounds on the banks of the Ohio, of which there were several on the site of Cincinnati.

As for the banks they are modestly lodged at Cincinnati, but a plan of a handsome edifice, worthy of their high fortune, and sufficient to accommodate them all, is at present under consideration. The founderies for casting steam-engines, the yards for building steamboats, the noisy, unwholesome, or unpleasant work-shops, are in the adjoining village of Fulton, in Covington or Newport on the Kentucky bank of the river, or in the country. As to the enormous slaughter of hogs, about 150,000 annually, and the preparation of the lard, which follows, the town is not in the least incommoded by it; the whole process takes place on the banks of a little stream called Deer Creek, which has received the nickname of the Bloody Run, from the colour of its waters during the season of the massacre, or near the basins of the great canal, which extends from Cincinnati towards the Maumee of Lake Erie. Cincinnati has, however, no squares planted with trees in the English taste, no parks nor walks, no fountains, although it would be very easy to have them. It is necessary to wait for the ornamental, until the taste for it prevails among the inhabitants: at present the useful occupies all thoughts. Besides, all improvements require an increase of taxes, and in the United States it is not easy to persuade the people to submit to this. Cincinnati also stands in need of some public provision for lighting the streets, which this repugnance to taxes has hitherto prevented.

Cincinnati has had water-works, for supplying the inhabitants with water, for about 20 years; for an annual rate, which amounts to about 8 or 12 dollars for a family, each has a quantity amply sufficient for all its wants. A steam-engine on the banks of the river raises the water to a reservoir on one of the hills near the city, 300 feet high, whence it is conducted in iron pipes in every direction. The height of the reservoir is such that the water rises to the top of every house, and fire-plugs are placed at intervals along the streets to supply the engines in case of fire. Several of the new towns in the United States have water-works, and Philadelphia among the older cities, has an admirable system of works, which, owing to a series of unsuccessful experiments, have cost a large sum. At this moment, a plan for supplying Boston with water is under discussion, which will cost several millions, because the water must be brought from a distance. New York is also engaged in a similar work, the expense of which will be about five millions. The Cincinnati water-works have not cost much above 150,000 dollars, although they have been several times completely reconstructed. It is generally thought in the United States, that the water-works ought to be owned by the towns, but those in Cincinnati belong to a company, and the water-rate is, therefore, higher than in Philadelphia and Pittsburg. The city has three times been in negociation for the purchase of the works, and has always declined buying on advantageous terms; the first time the establishment was offered for 35,000 dollars, and the second time for 80,000; the third time, 125,000 dollars were demanded, and 300,000 or 400,000 will finally be paid for it. In this case, as in regard to lighting the streets, the principal cause of the refusal of the city to buy was the unwillingness to lay new taxes.

The appearance of Cincinnati as it is approached from the water, is imposing, and it is still more so when it is viewed from one of the neighbouring hills. The eye takes in the windings of the Ohio and the course of the Licking, which enters the former at right angles, the steamboats that fill the port, the basin of the Miami canal, with the warehouses that line it and the locks that connect it with the river, the white-washed spinning works of Newport and Covington with their tall chimnies, the Federal arsenal, above which floats the starry banner, and the numerous wooden spires that crown the churches. On all sides the view is terminated by ranges of hills, forming an amphitheatre yet covered with the vigorous growth of the primitive forest. This rich verdure is here and there interrupted by country houses surrounded by colonnades, which are furnished by the forest. The population which occupies this amphitheatre lives in the midst of plenty; it is industrious, sober, frugal, thirsting after knowledge and if, with a very few exceptions, it is entirely a stranger to the delicate pleasures and elegant manners of the refined society of our European capitals, it is equally ignorant of its vices, dissipation and follies.

At the first glance one does not perceive any difference between the right and left bank of the river: from a distance the prosperity of Cincinnati seems to extend to the opposite shore. This is an illusion: on the right bank, that is, in Ohio, there are none but freemen; slavery exists on the other side. You may descend the river hundreds of miles, with slavery on the left and liberty on the right, although it is the same soil, and equally capable of being cultivated by the white man. When you enter the Mississippi you have slavery on both sides of you. A blind carelessness, or rather a fatal weakness in the rulers, and a deplorable selfishness in the people, have allowed this plague to become fixed in a country where there was no need of tolerating its existence. Who can tell when and how, and through what sufferings, it will be possible to eradicate it?

Letter XIX

Cincinnati

NATCHEZ, (MISS.) Jan. 4, 1835.

Cincinnati contains about 40,000 inhabitants, inclusive of the adjoining villages; although founded 40 years ago, its rapid growth dates only about 30 years back. It seems to be the rendezvous of all nations; the Germans and Irish are very numerous, and there are some Alsacians; I have often heard the harsh accents of the Rhenish French in the streets. But the bulk of the population, which gives its tone to all the rest, is of New England origin. What makes the progress of Cincinnati more surprising is, that the city is the daughter of its own works. Other towns, which have sprung up in the United States in the same rapid manner, have been built on shares, so to speak. Lowell, for example, is an enterprise of Boston merchants, who, after having raised the necessary funds, have collected workmen and told them, "Build us a town." Cincinnati has been gradually extended and embellished, almost wholly without foreign aid, by its inhabitants, who have for the most part arrived on the spot poor. The founders of Cincinnati brought with them nothing but sharp-sighted, wakeful, untiring industry, the only patrimony which they inherited from their New England fathers, and the other inhabitants have scrupulously followed their example and adopted their habits. They seem to have chosen Franklin for their patron-saint, and to have adopted Poor Richard's maxims as a fifth gospel.

I have said that Cincinnati was admirably situated; this is true in respect of its geographical position, but, if you follow the courses of the rivers on the map, and consider the natural resources of the district, you will find that there are several points on the long line of the rivers of the West as advantageously placed, both for trade and manufactures, and that there are some which are even more favoured in these respects. Pittsburg, which has within reach both coal and iron, that is to say, the daily bread of industry, which stands at the head of the Ohio, at the starting point of steam-navigation, at the confluence of the Monongahela and the Alleghany, coming the one from the south and the other from the north; Pittsburg, which is near the great chain of lakes, appears as the pivot of a vast system of roads, railroads, and canals, several of which are already completed. Pittsburg was marked out by nature at once for a great manufacturing centre and a great mart of trade. Louisville, built at the falls of the Ohio, at the head of navigation for the largest class of boats, is a natural medium between the commerce of the upper Ohio and that of the Mississippi and its tributaries. In respect to manufacturing resources, Louisville is as well provided as Cincinnati, and the latter, setting aside its enchanting situation, seemed destined merely to become the market of the fertile strip between the Great and Little Miami.

But the power of men, when they agree in willing any thing and in willing it perseveringly, is sufficient to overbear and conquer that of nature. In spite of the superior advantages of Louisville as an *entrepôt*, in spite of the manufacturing resources of Pittsburg, Cincinnati is able to maintain a population twice that of Louisville and half as large again as that of Pittsburg in a state of competence, which equals, if it does not surpass, the average condition of that of each of the others. The inhabitants of Cincinnati have fixed this prosperity among them, by one of those instinctive views with which the sons of New England are inspired by their eminently practical and calculating genius. A half-word, they say, is enough for the wise, but cleverer than the wisest, the Yankees understand each other without speaking, and by a tacit consent direct their common efforts toward the same point. To work Boston fashion means, in the United States, to do anything with perfect precision and without words. The object which the Cincinnatians have had in view, almost from the origin of their city has been nothing less than to make it the capital, or great interior mart of the West. The indirect means which they have employed, have been to secure the manufacture of certain articles, which, though of little value separately considered, form an important aggregate when taken together, and getting the start of their neighbours, with that spirit of diligence that characterises the Yankees, they have accordingly distributed the manufacture of these articles among themselves. This plan has succeeded.

Thus with the exception of the pork trade, one is surprised not to see any branch of industry carried on on the great scale of the manufacturing towns of England and France. The Cincinnatians make a variety of household furniture and utensils, agricultural and mechanical implements and machines, wooden clocks, and a thousand objects of daily use and consumption, soap, candles, paper, leather, &c., for which there is an indefinite demand throughout the flourishing and rapidly growing States of the West, and also in the new States of the Southwest, which are wholly devoted to agriculture, and in which, on account of the existence of slavery, manufactures cannot be carried on. Most of these articles are of ordinary quality; the furniture, for instance, is rarely such as would be approved by Parisian taste, but it is cheap and neat, just what is wanted in a new country, where, with the exception of a part of the South, there is a general ease and but little wealth, and where plenty and comfort are more generally known than the little luxuries of a more refined society. The prosperity of Cincinnati, therefore, rests upon the sure basis of the prosperity of the West, upon the supply of articles of the first necessity to the bulk of the community; a much more solid foundation than the caprice of fashion, upon which, nevertheless, the branches of industry most in favour with us, depend. The intellectual also receives a share of attention; in the first place, there is a large type-foundery in Cincinnati, which supplies the demand of the whole West, and of that army of newspapers that is printed in it. According to the usual English or American mode of proceeding, the place of human labour is supplied as much as possible by machinery, and I have seen several little contrivances here, that are not probably to be found in the establishments of the Royal Press or of the Didots. Then the printing-presses are numerous, and they issue nothing but publications in general demand, such as school-books, and religious books, and newspapers. By means of this variety of manufactures, which, taken separately appear of little consequence, Cincinnati has taken a stand, from which it will be very difficult to remove her, for, in this matter, priority of occupation is no trifling advantage. The country trader, who keeps an assortment of everything vendible, is sure to find almost everything he wants in Cincinnati, and he, therefore, goes thither in preference to any other place in order to lay in his goods. Cincinnati is thus in fact the great central mart of the West; a great quantity and variety of produce and manufactured articles find a vent here, notwithstanding the natural superiority of several other sites, either in regard to the extent of water-communication or mineral resources.

Document 6.10 Traveling in Frontier Illinois

In 1836 John Gates Thurston of South Lancaster, Massachusetts traveled to Illinois with his brother-in-law George Lee. Lee planned to speculate with land investments in Illinois, but we are not sure why Thurston made the trip. He might have had plans for investment; he had brothers living in Vincennes, Indiana and Rockford, Illinois; or he might have made the trip for health reasons. We do know that he made detailed observations about potential prosperity and profits for towns and villages they visited, and also commented on the fertility of farmland. As you read the following selections from his travel diary, determine where he considers great prospects to be, and why he thinks communities are good or bad investment risks.

Cincinnati, May 20th. This may justly be styled the Queen of Cities. I was prepared to see a fine city, but the one half had not been told me. The beautiful site on which it stands, the elegance of the houses, the immense number of buildings for public institutions, the large and elegant churches, the spacious markets, the wide paved streets, the extensive warehouses, and the hive of business which is every where seen—all conspire to render it the most beautiful city in America. It is laid out in a manner similar to Philadelphia: but the streets being much wider gives it a more airy and inviting appearace. To a man who began business here but a few years ago as it were, when the place was a howling wilderness, to view it now in its prosperous and flourishing state which appear to have been the work of ages, it must indeed seem like enchantment.

The wealth of the place will compare with an Eastern city of three times the age of it. And when one considers that it has all been accumulated here within the last fifty years and nearly all within the last twenty years, it is truly astonishing. The suburbs extend several miles on the eastern shore of the river, and the whole region is in a high state of cultivation. Opposite the city are two large towns or villages divided only by a small creek which empties into the Ohio, one of which is called Covington and the other Newport. The landing, as it is called, is a spacious place or square from the river to the top of the bank, a gradual ascent of 20 or 30 rods till you rise 60 or 70 feet. The landing is lined with a row of steamboats which are continually arriving and departing. The city is built mostly of brick. Some spacious houses, or more properly speaking—palaces, are of stone, and will compare with any buildings in Boston or New York in every respect; but Trollope's Bazaar is the worst looking building I have ever seen. It is said however if it had been built in a more central part of the town, it would have been good property. We took a ride over the city and its environs and every part seems to be in the same flourishing state; and upon inquiry, we learnt that the mechanicks were more independent than in any other city in the union.

We walked through the market in the morning, and a greater variety and abundance I never saw in any market, and prices much cheaper than at the East. To sum up every thing in regard to this city, it must be acknowledged to be a magnificent place. We left here at 4 or 5 in the afternoon and arrived at Louisville at 9 A.M. next morning. This place is finely laid out with streets 90 feet wide. The city is not very compact, excepting the business part of it. It is well built but will not compare with Cincinnati, and is far from being as neat. The main part of the city being on a level, it is difficult to drain it which must render it sickly during the warm season. It is a place of great trade and wealth and must eventually be a large city. The public buildings are few and small. There are but few churches in the place compared with Cincinnati. The finest building I have seen in the whole city is "Galts House," a new hotel which has been opened but a few weeks.

After leaving Cincinnati, the valley of the river grows wider and many rich fields are seen and in some places the bottom lands extend to a great distance. About twenty miles below Cincinnati, we passed the mansion house of Gen. Harrison. The grounds appear to be well cultivated, but not much of the ornamental is to be seen. The river for a great distance is skirted with beautiful trees and the forests

---

From *A Journal of a Trip to Illinois*, 1836.

look like parks. No underwood is seen, and the grass looks as fresh as in a cultivated field.

A few miles below Louisville is New Albany on the other side of the river. The boat did not stop at this place, much to our regret. The city is on a fine site, and its appearance is very inviting. It is regulary laid out, well built, neat, and showed many ornamental trees. The river on the city side is skirted by a ledge of rock in regular strata ten or fifteen feet thick for a mile or two below the town. This ledge commences at low water and is graded from about three feet on the river to a distance of forty feet on the bank which affords an excellent landing place like a paved street which will ever remain without change. We passed many other towns of small note; some of them were quite flourishing, especially those on the Indiana side. The next place of importance we touched at was Evansville. We stopped at this place half an hour and walked over the thickest settled part of town. It is a flourishing place of only a few years growth; and the price of building lots centrally situated is from 100 to 150 dollars per foot on front for 75 ft. rear. I noticed several wholesale stores and a large number of smaller ones of different descriptions. Farming lands in the vicinity were from 100 to 150 dollars per acre. This place is to be the termination of a canal and some other internal improvements which are projected, and it is thought it will be a place of great importance in a few years. They have in my opinion, however, fixed prices on their lots which cannot be obtained to any advantage by the purchaser at present unless the place should have a very rapid growth. The boat we are in carries the mail and of course stops at every town where a post office is kept on the river. A few miles further down we stopped at Henderson, a town which has a beautiful site, it being many feet above high water mark, which is a thing seldom found on these shores where there are no mountains near the river. This place has been settled forty years, and though it is said that some years ago the village could not have been purchased by covering it with dollars, yet at this time it seemed to be in a state of complete dilapidation. A corner lot in the center of the village could be bought for 400 or 500 $ and land in the vicinity at very low prices, and the only cause which can be assigned for this state of things is that it is in a slave-holding state. The spirit of enterprise which is making such rapid strides in the West will not fix itself on soil which is polluted by slavery. But whatever may be the opinions of those who have only heard of slavery and who are disposed to believe in all the tales of fiction that are fabricated against it, I can assure them that so far as my observation goes, and I

have examined with all the care that I was capable of whenever, an opportunity presented itself, I can truly say that the slaves are decidedly the happiest beings I have seen in this part of the country. I have seen several of them chained up for running away, but they wore the same happy countenances and cared as little for the consequences of their escapement as any of the bystanders did for them.

A few miles below Henderson, a signal of distress was hoisted from the shore of the river and the boat meandered up along side of a large wood float and made fast to the shore. Here we found a group of not less than fifty persons consisting of men, women, and children of all ages, from the infant in the mothers arms to the grey head of three score years, all mingled together in one common herd, with nothing but a shanty of loose boards open wholly at either end to shelter them from the weather which had now been quite cold and rainy for several days. Around this hut were strewed in admirable confusion tables, beds, chairs, pots, kettles, bureaus, boxes, chests, bags and bedding, together with dogs, guns, and powder horns. The history of these people was that they were run down by a steamboat which struck the one they were in and disabled her so that she could not proceed. She lay a little below where they were, partly capsized which was the cause of their leaving the boat and encamping on the bank of the river. They had been in this situation nearly a fortnight and what added more to their distress they had met with their sad disaster in the dead of night. In fifteen minutes after we had anchored, this whole colony were taken on board and stowed away into comfortable quarters, together with their household furniture and bag and baggage of every description, and in twenty minutes from the anchoring of the boat we were again on our passage down the Ohio. One would naturally suppose that these persons must have suffered from such an exposure to the night and with young infants to take care of and all the inconvenience of sheltering themselves from the rain, and I expected to find them in a sorrowing and dejected state of mind, but it was far otherwise. On inquiry we found they were emigrating from Ohio to Illinois, and in answer to our inquiry of a young woman who had an infant in her arms if she had not suffered from the inclemency of the weather. The reply was that she had "suffered *right smart* last night and the night before but the rest of the time she had been very comfortable" and so far from being down-hearted or repining, not a single complaint was uttered and for aught I could discover after mingling with them some moments, I could not perceive but what they were perfectly happy. I afterwards learnt that part of their number had taken passage in another boat, and that they were obliged to remain in consequence of their *plunder*, as they expressed it, being in the lower hold of the boat and could not be got out. I learnt further that a child belonging to one of the families who had left had fallen overboard during the disaster and was drowned.

During the whole of this days voyage the lands on the banks were low and but few places were seen high enough to place the buildings above high water. This makes the population thin on the shore—but few huts are seen and the only object of the squatters seems to be to sell his wood to the steam boats.

We stopped a half an hour at a place called Shawnee Town—which had been settled many years, and tho price of lots was low, they found no buyers. It had been remarked by a young gent. from Conn. that he had not seen a handsome young lady since he left N. York when much to our astonishment, we took on board about this time, with a gentleman in company with her who was considerably older than herself and we were in doubt whether he was her husband, suitor, or father—one thing however was certain—she was exceedingly beautiful. I suggested to my friend that he had better make the attempt to ogle with her, but he observed that he had already made the attempt and found that the gent. was much more disposed to ogle than the lady. She remained on board several days and my friend altho much disposed to be attentive to her had had little opportunity of gratifying his feelings. He learnt however that she was in the market, and we regretted that so fair a flower should have been left in a place where she must "blush unseen"

for the place where she landed had but two dwellings at the settlement.

Today our visions were greeted with a sight of the "father of waters." We turned our course from the Ohio and began to ascend the mighty river. It did not appear to be larger at the mouth of the Ohio than the Ohio itself; but as soon as we began to ascend, I found a far more powerful stream and much more rapid than I had expected. Our progress was rather slow for some miles but after proceeding about fifty miles, it became rather less rapid.

The shores of the Mississippi are entirely different from those of the Ohio. The river does not assume a regular appearance, but is so full of islands that a stranger could not tell half of the time which was the channel. The banks, are constantly wasting away, and in high water it is not uncommon for many acres to disappear in one season. New banks are constantly forming which as soon as they are left above water are covered with a thick growth of trees which are exactly of a size and shape, and the shores of the river are continually presenting a field of different growths from one year till it, assumes the size of full grown forest. The, verdure of these groves is exceedingly beautiful. The heavy timbered lands on the Mississippi are full of underwood which is so dense in many places that a chicken could not crawl through it. The large trees of elm, cotton wood, ash, and sycamore which often rear their immense trunks eighty or a hundred feet without limbs are covered entirely with ivy or something which exactly resembles it, and gives the forest a rich and verdant appearance.

Document 6.11 Different Frontier Towns in 1842 Illinois

Most writers published their travel accounts in newspapers, for immediate impact. They were frequently intended as booster material, promoting the growth of one region or town at the expense of another. Such travel letters are one of the greatest bodies of information historians have about the antebellum Midwest. Many letters speak in generalities and repeat truisms about frontier life, such as that the land is fertile or the women are all fairer than elsewhere. But several letters by Charles Carter Langdon, published in the Peoria *Register and Northwest Gazetteer*, provide detailed looks at two Illinois River towns: Quincy and Meredosia. Langdon was a Whig politician and editor from Alabama, supposedly scouting out prospective settlements for Alabamans. What does he like or dislike about these two communities? What makes one the better place to be? What standards does the author use to judge the two towns, and do you detect any bias in his comments?

Quincy, (Illinois,) Sept. 3, 1842.

This is without doubt one of the most pleasant and thriving towns in the west. I was prepared by descriptions I had heard, to find a very pretty and comfortable place, but had formed but a very Imperfect conception of the size and business capacities of the city, the elegant refinements of its inhabitants, or the unrivaled beauty of the surrounding country. I found here some Mobile friends, who have spent the two last summers in this delightful place, to whom I am under many obligations for their kind attentions, and the facilities they have extended to me in forming acquaintances, and making me familiar with a section of country so full of interest, so rich in landscape beauty. I know not when I have spent time more pleasantly than the last three days in this city of Quincy, and I leave this evening with sincere regret, yielding to that stern necessity which compels me to prosecute my journey.

The city of Quincy is handsomely situated on a high and commanding bluff on the east bank of the Mississippi, is the county seat of the county of Adams, and contains some 2800 or 3000 inhabitants. In the center of town is a large public square, gently sloping to the west, neatly enclosed, and covered with nature's simplest and most beautiful carpet of green; fronting which on the east side is the large brick court house, on the south side the Quincy house, a splendid hotel which cost $100,000, and the remainder on the four sides filled up with substantial brick buildings, stores, &c. Around the city are many private dwellings of taste and beauty, and under the bluff on the bank of the river are numerous large warehouses, a flour mill, a steam saw mill, a paper mill, a castor oil factory, a lard oil factor, &c, &c. The city also contains no less than nine churches, which speaks well for the cause of religion. The population of the city is mostly from New England, and the society partakes much, of course, of the New England character. The city is remarkable for the good morals and the sobriety of its inhabitants. During my three days visit I have not only not seen a person intoxicated, but I have not seen even a drop of ardent spirits. The town is steadily improving, there being now some thirty or forty brick buildings in the course of erection.

The county of Adams is one of the richest in the state, almost every foot of its land being not only fit for cultivation, but of remarkable fertility. The country directly back of Quincy, for miles in extent, as far as the eye can reach, is a continued prairie, agreeably diversified with gentle undulations of hill and dale, with a soil of unsurpassed fertility, a considerable portion of which is in a state of cultivation. The view is magnificent beyond description, and one which I shall not attempt to describe. But in truth I can say,

"The sun in all his broad career,
Ne'er looked upon a fairer land."

From the fact that there are no trees in view, the country wears the appearance of an old settled region in a high state of cultivation. The rich natural meadows of prairie remind me of the beautiful meadows on the banks of the Connecticut, the Hudson and the Schuylkill. The principal productions are wheat, corn and oats, though there are large fields of hemp, tobacco, buckwheat, castor oil bean, &c., while vegetables, and all the fruits common to the eastern and middle states, are produced with ease in the greatest abundance. The prairies are covered with cattle and sheep roaming at large, and horses are raised in large numbers, at small expense, and sell remarkably low. There never was a country blessed with a greater abundance of the good things of the world than this, but all produce is selling low, and money is hard to get. The land produces astonishingly,—seventy-five bushels of corn, or forty bushels of wheat to the acre, being very common. Wheat is selling in this place at 30 to 31 cents, and extremely dull at that. A man here with a good farm and free from debt, can live like a lord; but if he is in debt, he must stay so for the present. The population of the county is composed mostly of Kentuckians.

The manufacture of lamp oil from lard, I predict, will become immediately a business of great importance throughout this country. Both the oil and the candles are in constant use at the Quincy house, and the proprietor informs me that they are equal for light and durability, and in every other respect, to sperm. There is no loss by the process of manufacturing—100 pounds of lard will produce the hundred pounds in oil and candles. Of course the candles and oil can be furnished very low. The latter is selling here now at 75 cents per gallon, but can be afforded much lower. Instead of paying 50 cents a pound for sperm candles, these, equal to sperm, can be furnished at the price of lard. What an immense saving to the country; and what an important discovery for this "hog killing" region of the west!

Quincy and Meredosia in 1842: Charles Carter Langdon's Travel Letters.

The public houses I have visited, so far, I have found very excellent. The Quincy house in this place is kept in a style that would do credit to any city in the union. The building (to which I have before alluded) is a noble edifice of brick, pleasantly situated on the south side of the public square, affording an agreeable view of the city from the front, while from the back part, on one wing you have the bed of the "Eternal river," with its steamboats, barges, and rafts; and on the other, the beautiful prairie, in full view. It is really a most comfortable house, and the gentlemanly proprietor, Mr. Monroe, spares no pains to make his guests feel "at home."

I shall leave in a few minutes for Peoria, from which place I will write again.

Springfield, Sept. 7, 1842.

I left Quincy Saturday afternoon for Meredosia, on the Illinois river, intending to take a steamboat there for Peoria; but finding no boat after waiting two tedious days, I took the stage for this place, where I arrived last evening.

After leaving Quincy, the route for thirty miles is in the county of Adams, which, from the uniform fertility of its soil, and the density of its population, has already acquired the designation of the "empire county." It contains 3200 votes, and elects a senator and five representatives to the legislature; and what, in my estimation, is still higher recommendation, it is a decided whig county. The county is admirably diversified with prairie and timber land, which renders settlements convenient, and every foot of soil is susceptible of cultivation. It therefore possesses advantages over many other sections of the state, where the immense rich prairies are rendered valueless for the want of timber. The little village of Columbus is located near the center of the county, in the midst of a beautiful prairie, and in the eastern extremity is the town of Clayton. In the latter village I spent the night.

The next morning I passed through the county of Brown, a new county formed from Schuyler, the county seat of which is Mount Sterling, a place presenting no attractions.

As you approach the Illinois river there are tracts of heavy timber, and the prairies are of smaller compass, though extremely fertile. Crossing the river, I arrived at Meredosia, situated on the eastern bank, on a small bluff of deep sand—as uncomfortable and disagreeable a place, I will venture to say, as can be found any where in this wide world. Its only importance is derived from its being the termination of the rail road from Springfield; consequently, all the goods, passengers, &c. for Jacksonville, Springfield, and the surrounding country, and in return all the produce of that rich and fertile region, are compelled to land here. It is therefore a mere landing place, and the only buildings are two or three good warehouses, two sorry looking taverns, and a half dozen dilapidated dwellings stuck in the sand banks.

The public house where I stopped is worthy of a special notice. The exterior, as I approached it, was *not inviting. An* old-fashioned signboard hung to a post proclaimed, "Entertainment by Wm. H. Long"; and a half dozen cross-eyed Dutchmen were standing in the door of the bar-room (which proved to be also the post office), who were not very attractive in their appearance. It was Sabbath morning, and the interesting group were luxuriating over a bottle of whiskey. I was ushered, fortunately, into another apartment, which I had the pleasure of occupying in solitude during the day. A boat, it was said, was immediately expected, which would convey me to Peoria. I waited with tolerable patience till dinner was announced. The dinner!—it was a *great dinner*—though much better than any of the subsequent meals of which I was compelled to partake. As it was *Sunday,* It appears they had killed a *sheep*—"extra doings" for Sunday! The table presented three large dishes of boiled mutton, three large plates of boiled cabbage, and as many of boiled potatoes—this constituted the bill of fare. Chickens were running around the table and under it, to catch a crumb that might fall; and it took one hand constantly employed to *drive the hogs out of the* room—attracted thither, I suppose, by the flavor of the smoking viands.

Dinner being over, I strolled for an hour on the bank of the river in the hope of hearing the welcome sound of a boat; but in vain. I returned to my room, wrote a letter, smoked at least half a dozen cigars, and finally supper was announced; and still no boat. The supper was *cold* mutton, and *cold* cabbage, without the potatoes. This over, I indulged in another stroll on the river bank, with the same result as before. All was as silent there as the grave, not a ripple on the bosom of the river, and the sluggish stream seemed to mock at my anxiety. I went back despondingly, and retired for the night—and such a night as I had! The reader who has traveled much knows what a peculiarly *funky* odor arises from a dirty old bed on which every body sleeps, and which never enjoys the benefit of an airing. But this was not half. No sooner was I stretched than I was beset by musketoes, fleas, bedbugs, and all sorts of vermin, and in such droves too—my stars! what a time! Sleep utterly refused to come to my relief, and the night seemed a week long. Well, still another day and another night passed in which I went through the same routine of misery (except in the way of eating, the *mutton* had given out, and *salt pork* was substituted in its place)—and *still no boat*. As the stage was to leave for Springfield that morning, I was resolved to wait no longer for a boat, and accordingly took my departure.

Now such taverns are a gross imposition, and should be exposed by travelers oftener than they are. Mine host may be a very clever man, in his way, and I have no doubt is, but he is not fit for a tavern keeper, and should be made to "haul down his sign." In a country like this, where there is such superabundance of every thing that is good, there is no excuse for such fare. It is worse than any thing I have ever met with, even in Alabama. Mr. Long should know that in a dining room, *chickens* would appear better on the table than *under* the table, and a separate apartment should be given to the *old sow and her pigs*. Mr. Long is Postmaster of the village, says he was four years acting constable, and is now a justice of the peace. Of course, he is a man of *consequence,* but I still insist *he is not fit for a tavern-keeper.* Aside from this, I have no doubt *Long* is a very good fellow—and *long* may *Long* live—long may *Long* prosper in every thing but *tavern-keeping;* but *long* may it be before I am again caught in *Long's* "house of entertainment!"

The distance from Meredosia to this place is fifty-five miles, through a most delightful country. The settlements on this side of the Illinois river are much older than those upon the other, the country presents a higher degree of cultivation, and the farms are exceedingly beautiful. Here there is constantly presented to the eye of the traveler the neat and comfortable dwelling of the farmer, with his large barn, the flourishing orchards, apple and peach, laden with fruit, and all other conveniences and comforts that the heart of man could desire,—denoting abundance, ease, and independence.

Jacksonville is the county seat of Morgan county, and is a very pretty place, though possessing no other advantages for trade than are derived from the wealthy and densely populated county in which it is situated. This is the residence of ex-governor Duncan, and the county gives from two to three hundred whig majority, yet notwithstanding this, three out of the four members of the legislature are locos!

Document 6.12 The Proper Role of Women on the Frontier: Two Points of View in 1846

Eliza Woodson Burhans was born in Rensselaerville, New York in 1815. She was five when her mother died, and was separated from her siblings for 11 years and sent to live with other relatives. Her sister Mary moved to a homestead in Tazewell County, Illinois in 1831, and Eliza moved out with them four years later. Her experiences over the next four and a half years are the basis for this selection from her book, *Life in Prairie Land.* She married Thomas Jefferson Farnham, a noted western explorer and travel writer, in 1836. Eliza later became involved in prison reform, asylum reform, and women's rights movements, and served as a volunteer nurse at Gettysburg. Her book is a detailed look at antebellum Illinois, with an interest in the role of women in society. Her views on marriage and freedom are challenged in this selection, where she encounters a newly married farmer and his bride on a steamboat headed west. What did the farmer look for in a frontier wife, and what did he expect her contributions to be to his life? What did he expect her limitations to be? How do these ideas compare with Farnham's?

From *Life in Praire Land,* 1846.

The strange character of the feeling manifested by [the] husband, made me very desirous of drawing him into an expression of it in words before he left us, and as their landing-place would probably be reached on the third morning, I availed myself of a chance meeting . . . to engage him in conversation. A few words about the height of the water, the timber, and the prairies, served the purpose.

"You are going to become a prairie farmer?" I said.

"No, I've been one afore, I've got a farm up the river hyur that I've *crapped* twice a'ready; there's a good cabin on it, and it's about as good a place, I reckon, as can be found in these diggins."

"Then you built a cage," I said, "and went back for your bird to put in it?"

He looked at me, and his face underwent a contortion, of which words will convey but a faint idea. It was a mingled expression of pride and contempt, faintly disguised by a smile that was intended to hide them.

"Why, I don't know what you Yankees call a bird," he replied, "but I call her a woman. I shouldn't make much account of havin a bird in my cabin, but a good, stout woman I should calculate was worth somethin. She can a her way, and do a handsome thing besides, helpin me on the farm."

Think of that, ye belles and fair-handed maidens! How was my sentiment rebuked!

"Well, we'll call her a woman, which is, in truth, much the more rational appellation. You intend to make her useful as well as ornamental to your home?"

"Why, yes; I calculate 'taint of much account to have a woman if she ain't of no use. I lived up hyur two year, and had to have another man's woman do all my washin and mendin and so on, and at last I got tired o' totin my plunder back and forth, and thought I might as well get a woman of my own. There's a heap of things beside these, that she'll do better than I can, I reckon; every man ought to have a woman to do his cookin and such like, 'kase it's easier for them than it is for us. They take to it kind o' naturally."

I could scarcely believe that there was no more human vein in the animal, and determined to sound him a little deeper.

"And this bride of yours is the one, I suppose, that you thought of all the while you were making your farm and building your cabin? You have, I dare say, made a little garden, or set out a tree, or done something of the kind to please her alone?"

"No, I never allowed to get a woman till I found my neighbors went ahead of me with 'em, and then I

should a got one right thar, but there wasn't any stout ones in our settlement, and it takes so long to make up to a *stranger,* that I allowed I mought as well go back and see the old folks, and git somebody that I know'd thar to come with me."

"And had you no choice made among your acquaintances? was there no one person of whom you thought more than another?" said I.

"Yas, there was a gal I used to know that was stouter and bigger than this one. I should a got her if I could, but she'd got married and gone off over the *Mississippi,* somewhar."

The cold-hearted fellow! it was a perfectly business matter with him.

"Did you select this one solely on account of her size?" said I.

"Why, pretty much," he replied; "I reckon women are some like horses and oxen, the biggest can do the most work, and that's what I want one for."

"And is that all?" I asked, more disgusted at every word. "Do you care nothing about a pleasant face to meet you when you go home from the field, or a soft voice to speak kind words when you are sick, or a gentle friend to converse with you in your leisure hours?"

"Why, as to that," he said. "I reckon a woman ain't none the worse for talk because she's stout and able to work. I calculate she'll mind her own business pretty much, and if she does she won't talk a great deal to me; that ain't what I got her for."

"But suppose when you get home she should be unhappy, and want to see her parents and other friends?"

"Why I don't allow she will; I didn't get her for that . . . I shall give her enough to eat and wear, and I don't calculate she'll be very *daunsey* if she gets that; if she is she'll git *shet* of it after a while."

My indignation increased at every word.

"But you brought her away from her home to be treated as a human being, not as an animal or machine. Marriage is a moral contract, not a mere bargain of business. The parties promise to study each other's happiness, and endeavor to promote it. You could not marry a woman as you could buy a washing machine, though you might want her for the same purpose. If you take the machine there is no moral obligation incurred, except to pay for it. If you take the woman, there is. Before you entered into this contract I could have shown you a machine that would have answered your purpose admirably. It would have washed and ironed all your clothes, and when done, stood in some out-of-the-way corner till it was wanted again. You would have been under no obligation, not even to feed and clothe it, as you now are. It would have been the better bargain, would it not?"

"Why that would be according to what it cost in the fust place; but it wouldn't be justly the same thing as havin a wife, I reckon, even if it was give to you."

"No, certainly not; it would free you from many obligations that you are under to a wife" (it was the first time, by the way, he had used the word), "and leave you to pursue your own pleasure without seeing any sorrowful or sour faces about you."

"Oh, I calculate sour faces won't be of much account to me. If a woman'll mind her business, she may look as thunderin as a live airthquake, I shan't

mind it. . . . I reckon the Yankees may do as they like about them things, and I shall do jist the same. I don't think a woman's of much account anyhow, if she can't help herself a little and me too. If the Yankee women was *raised up like the women* here *aar,* they'd cost a heap less and be worth more."

I turned away, saying that I trusted his wife would agree with him in these opinions, or they might lead to some unpleasant differences.

"Oh, as to that," said he, "I reckon her pinions won't go fur anyhow; she'll think pretty much as I do, or not at all."

Document 6.13 Life on an 1851 Illinois Farm

In September 1850, a young German named Carl Kohler left Germany to travel to the United States. He would spend eight weeks on an Illinois farm near Belleville owned by Friedrich Karl Hecker. Kohler took notes on the people he met and the sights he saw, including his life and work on the farm, and sent these images home in letters to his parents. By the time you are finished, you should be able to describe what life and labor are like on the farm, and how people ate, dressed, worked, and interacted.

II

June

At the end of April we planted fifty acres of oats that have already grown to a splendid stand. Planting was at five different times—ten acres each, with a few days between—so that all would not ripen simultaneously, for we would not have enough hands if mowing had to be done at once. Help is hard to find and costly at harvest, when every farmer has plenty to do. We pay a day-laborer $1.00 a day now. Later he'll demand $1.50. Having to get other people to help is very inconvenient; but, with our extensive acreage and pressing work, we must do it. Here, unlike Germany, there are no professional farm laborers. Those available here are referred to with the tactful work *hand.* We had a German hand who had to be let go for the rudeness of his drunken behavior. That was at the critical time when the corn had to be planted, 150 acres.

The corn is planted and mostly up and growing now. Thank God, that fiendishly essential task is done and we can be more relaxed at our work. I am abut to start painting the wooden parts of our buildings white, using an oil paint, which from a distance contrasts beautifully with the dark oak trees. I have replaced all broken windows. I got the glass and putty in Lebanon, where glass is sold precut in the *grocery* store. My latest project was a sawbuck. I'm making a pushcart now, something I could very much have used recently, when I carried home a quarter of a hog, butchered at our next-to-nearest neighbor's, too small a load to bother hitching up a horse. The lard melted in the hot sun and ran down my back and legs. But it didn't matter: here a man is not judged by how he dresses.

My entire wardrobe consists of a shirt, some linen trousers, a straw hat, and shoes—very simple and practical. Indeed, the more frugal a farmer is, the better able he is to get ahead. He must be equipped to live independently of the world: and he can—if he has conscientiously prepared himself to do so. Farmers' cash outlay here is very small: farmers build their own

---

Eight Weeks on a St. Clair County Farm in 1851: Letters by a young German.

houses, make their own clothes, produce their own food, and need little else or try to barter for what they need.

To round out for you my picture of farm life, I'll try to describe what happens at our farm on a day in planting time.

In the morning when the glowing horizon proclaims daybreak, Mr. H. wakes us. At every job he is Number One and Mr. Energetic, setting a good example. The buffalo hide, which must serve as a blanket until there is a mistress of the house, is thrown aside and the morning toilet [putting on trousers and shoes] is done in half a minute. Arms and legs are still stiff and sore from yesterday, but the well contains the most delicious potion for refreshing the body and banishing sleep. Then the animals to be used for todays work are driven from the pasture towards the farm and fed corn, and then watered.

Meanwhile the housekeeper, a woman, has made breakfast, and now blows on the horn used on every farm here to call people home from the fields at mealtimes. Breakfast consists usually of warm *corncakes,* fried pork and coffee. [Corncakes are cornmeal mixed with milk, measured out in small round cakes, fried in fat, and served with molasses in the way we eat mustard with beef.] They taste very good. For a change eggs, potatoes, preserves, radishes etc. are served: but pork and corncakes remain the favorite. During breakfast the days jobs are discussed and assigned. Then everyone goes to work. Horses are harnessed and oxen yoked . . .

Let us assume that today we will plant corn in a field that has been plowed and harrowed. Now it is to be checkrowed. With a light, one-horse rig, furrows for planting are dug as two—four feet apart and exactly parallel. As soon as the furrows in one direction are dug and the cross furrow started, the man doing the planting follows the furrow-maker as closely as possible and at every point that the furrows intersect drops four to six kernels, which a third man, using a hoe, covers with soil. The seed must be put as soon as possible into the fresh furrow and covered at once with the moist soil essential to rapid germination. As a way of seeing the whole layout clearer, take a chessboard, let the sides of the squares represent furrows, think of seeds planted where the corners of the square touch, and you have an Illinois cornfield.

Between now and harvest the corn needs even more troublesome care and hard work. Corn's two worst enemies are weeds and the cornworm. Worms chew off the sprouts, often necessitating replanting: and weeds threaten with their luxuriance to choke the young plants. Therefore, when the corn has reached a certain height, it is cultivated several times, to plow weeds under and bank soil around the plants. Corn grown to a height of six to eight feet here, and the entire [immature] plant is used for green feed. The ears grow to a length of a foot to a foot and a half, and as thick as the wrist of a strong man. Some ears are picked before they ripen, cooked in water, and seasoned with butter, salt, and pepper. Ripe corn is sold—to be used to make whiskey or ground and exported to all parts of the world. But back to work!

It continues until noon. At 10:00 the sun is already so fierce that heat waves can be seen dancing over the field. The forests, filled in the morning with the chirping of birds, are now as silent as the grave. The oxen breathe with difficulty and often will not move. A man wipes sweat from his face and has increasing trouble seeing his shrinking shadow.

At noon the horn blows a sound welcome to everyone. The animals recognize it and will no longer be made to work. They are unhitched, brought into the farmyard, unharnessed, and fed. Then they lie down in the shade of the trees. Their masters take a shot of whiskey before slaking their burning thirsts with water, then sit down to their simple meal. It is about the same, morning, noon, and night, though it is varied with game in season. Presently we would have no trouble shooting a dozen of the wild pigeons that frequent our corncrib. Cooked with rice, they make good soup. From the bounty of our garden we enjoy many a tasty dish that Americans miss because they take no pains to grow salad-greens and other vegetables. Sundays the table is crowned with a fresh roast of beef, which one of us has had to ride to Mascoutah to get. Whenever a farmer butchers, he always informs his neighbors of it: and they come for fresh meat against payment. After eating we rest. We lie on the ground, because everywhere else is too hot, and smoke a pipe. Nobody has strength to talk: sleep is preferred.

We go back to work at 2:00 now. Later, when the heat is worse, not until 3:00. The first hours of work after the noon meal are unbearably hot: but the prairie wind, which I mentioned earlier, rises about 4:00 and refreshes body and soul. At first the heat gave us much trouble. We are more used to it now, and even do not sweat so profusely. As soon as the sun sinks behind the treetops, we stop for the day, because darkness soon follows: dusk, nonexistent to the south and in the tropics, is very short here. After the animals have been unharnessed and watered, they are driven to the pasture and six to eight ears of corn thrown out for each. Here the animals stay overnight. One of our mares gets some oats because she has just foaled: for the rest of her nourishment she grazes in the pasture.

After dinner, pipes are lit; and with considerable talent, Mr. H. tells stories, spiced with witty jokes, about his eventful life. Or a neighbor stops by for the evening, and there is chatting about farming or politics. Through the open windows the delightful fragrance of the acacias fills the room. Of the millions of fireflies swarming outside, one occasionally loses it way, zooms inside, and draws a glowing line across the dark ceiling. From the tenebrous forest we hear the sad cry of the whippoorwill. . . . The cry ceases with the rising of the moon, a friend that lights our way to bed. For, with the last puffs on the pipe, intractable sleep approaches: and one after another, with a sleep-choked "Good Night," we slip off to bed.—Good Night!

An Excursion to the Prairie

On this beautiful Pentecost, four of us went out onto the . . . immense Looking-Glass Prairie. It is about two miles away on a road partly through forest, partly past farms.

A morning shower had moistened the soil and invigorated the vegetation, which emerged from its bath clad in bright green. The air was alive with a thousand fragrances, often making me pause involuntarily to search out the source of a particularly delightful one. I usually found it in one of the many varieties of trees and vines that compose American forests. Here—where the lack of wood endemic in most of Europe is unheard of, where profusion of trees is instead often a hindrance to people, and where forestry is therefore unknown—forests grow in the wild tangle of Nature as first created . . .

A long walk in the forest so tires the novice that he grows dizzy and trees seem to dance around him, until his eyes grow accustomed to picking out with a quick glance the best path through the colonnades of trees. How often, in such perplexing situations, when I didn't know whether to go this way or that, I wished for a signpost of the kind in our [German] forests, showing in black and white the right direction to take. Here a stranger can press toward his destination all day in vain, and learn in the end, if lucky enough to meet another person, that he has indeed covered a lot of ground but has not advanced one step. More skilled are Americans who have lived all their lives in the forest and know every tree. They are also crack shots and carry the familiar rifle that is as long as a man is tall and of very small caliber. They hunt only the bigger creatures—deer, raccoon and turkeys—

while the quick little birds evade the small bullets. These marksmen look with a certain contempt on our short [German] shotguns—toys to them, and indeed, unable to reach the tops of some tall trees. It should certainly seem that these vast forests teem with game. Not so. Years ago the deer withdrew to distant places away from people. Hence hunters must travel a day away from settlements to hunt deer. Our neighbor Pyle, the robust son of Kentucky forebears, told me that even ten years ago he saw herds of deer near his farm and on many a day shot three or four. Those Nimrod times are gone: and now, in our immediate area, we go for rabbit, partridge, prairie chicken, turkey, woodcock and grey squirrel. Superabundant because Americans don't hunt them, they are frequent and welcome additions to our simple diet.

The closer we get to the prairie, the more the size and age of the forest diminishes . . . At the edge of the forest, where the trees stop but before grass is in complete control, the Prairie is girdled in sporadic brush, sometimes a mile wide . . .

On the Prairie strawberries have just ripened and flourish in such extraordinary quantities that they color long stretches red. They have such short stalks that the strawberries seem to rest on the ground. They are very juicy, though lacking the aroma of our German varieties. From the countless splendid flowers I saw today I gathered a bouquet . . . I can name none except roses and lilies . . .

Strawberries and especially long-legged birds, nesting now in marshy places and not shy, interested us more than we realized—until the absence of any trace of people told us we had gone into the truly wild Prairie, and fatigue and hunger admonished us to return. All day the sky was covered uniformly in grey, and the unwavering horizon gave us no points of reference, so we headed into the direction we thought we had come. It must have been 5:00 when we found a lone farm: and the owner, a gaunt American ravaged by fever, gave us the in-no-way agreeable assurance that we had strayed for two hours in the opposite direction from home. So can people err in seemingly simple things. After too many strawberries, our palates enjoyed, and our stomachs welcomed, the bread and whiskey given us. We all laughed about losing the way and headed happily home. In the evening we came again to settled parts. Seeing the many herds of livestock and distant log cabins on the horizon, we became nimble again and we greeted with a cheer the dark grove where we had entered the Prairie in the morning.

The day's bag—in all, we had shot thirty-six snipes and some prairie chickens—brought welcome variety to our simple table, replacing pork for at least two days. But worth far more to me was the sense of having experienced a grand phenomenon, whose scenes stamped on me an unforgettable, indescribable impression. What stuff for memories in days to come!

III

[June?]

In the forest, ten minutes from our farm, shaded by giant sycamores, stands the church attended by neighboring farmers. It is Methodist, the faith that prevails locally [amid the many faiths and sects flourishing in America's religious freedom]. . . .

Sundays the church is a joyful sight, when the congregation, partly in wagons, partly on horseback, comes in colorful groups from all directions out of the forest and rests under the trees until services begin. . . .

The life of these prairie farmers is very monotonous and dreary because, in their remoteness from human society and the problematical sale of their products, they miss all the little joys that make life agreeable. Their only relief from humdrum existence is church, where young and old from far and wide attend on Sunday. If the prairie is empty of people on Sunday, great cavalcades of men, women, and children crowd the common house of prayer. . . .

The school is in our vicinity, too, and I pass it often . . . a very modest structure of logs, with one door that also admits the light and therefore stands open during instruction. Inside is one room with a dirt floor. Rude benches and a writing table are the only furnishings. The teacher—supported by the farmers, with whom he boards by turns—is to teach his charges reading, writing, and arithmetic, as well as the country's history. Pupils living farther away come on horseback and bring their lunches in tin buckets.

As soon as these young Americans have learned to spell, they reach fearlessly for their fathers' newspapers and begin at once to form political opinions. I have heard twelve-year-olds express themselves about politics and religion with a maturity that amazed me. At the age of sixteen, the young American male has more independence and greater masculinity than our German twenty-year-olds. Very early he hears the American motto, "Be independent," and tries to acquire the skills and sharpen the capacities necessary for daily life. Free from pedantic pedagoguery, his mind grows uncommonly fast and bespeaks a sagacity common to all Americans, which

must result from the purely practical method of schooling, free of all excessive erudition.

The Americans living around us are thoroughly good neighbors, ready and willing to be of help. But in business they are just as crafty as all their countrymen. When doing business they have no conscience at all, and follow implicitly the advice an Old Yankee once gave his son: "Boy, make money; if you can, make it honestly—but make money." Therefore be on guard in business, for I'm convinced they enjoy getting the better of a good *"Dutchman."*

Sundays, after church, men of the neighborhood often visit our place. Talk is of domestic matters, what's new in St. Louis, the price of corn, and what the congressional representative said in the last session. As long as there is no mistress of the house, no American woman will step across the threshold . . .

Recently we were given an exquisite *hound,* glossy-brown in color. He made the farm his home and became everyone's pet, when he committed a crime that led to his death and that of his accomplice, a powerful bulldog. To elaborate: Every farmer here keeps a dozen or so sheep in the pasture, to supply wool for household needs. We were at work in the fields at midday when we heard a savage barking of dogs at Pyles'. Immediately, our hound, jaws bloody, bounded over the fence in a mighty leap. Hot after him came the whole crew from Pyles', firing rifles at him even as they ran. At first we could not explain this seeming assault on our property, but learned only too soon that our dogs had just mangled seven sheep. Our handsome bulldog had been shot on the spot while his henchman tried to flee to safety. We went with Pyle to his pasture and found the seven sheep scattered about on the ground, their throats bitten apart. Our bulldog, shot through the shoulder, lay in a puddle. Pyle told us that by mutual agreement among local farmers, we did not have to pay for the dead sheep, but that the other dog had to be shot to prevent future calamity, and the dog was shot.

Sheep raising should be very successful in this country, which is so uncommonly suited for it, if hounds—of which every farmer keeps four to six— did not do so much damage. It has happened that they have killed thirty sheep in a night.

We suffered a double loss with the bulldog, for he was an excellent pig-chaser. Pigs, especially young ones, force their way through fences and do great damage to cornfields. When a pig was in our corn, all we had to do was call the dog by shouting "Hey, Morou!" and he went for the intruder vehemently, seized it by the ear, and held on until we arrived and threw it back over the fence. Now we have to chase, often for hours, these destroyers of what we have worked so hard to create—no fun when the weather is hot. It so irritates us that many a little pig, once caught, leaves the encounter on an injured leg.

The life of a farmer, like any other, has its good and bad sides. From a distance it seems very attractive. Scrutinized, its apparent charms diminish to ordinary amenities, while the hardships loom larger than before. Indeed, the farmer, as owner of his own business, can celebrate only one unalloyed good: priceless independence. . . . Many educated people in Germany, enthusiastic about farming in America, think it a paradise. I built such castles in the air myself, before I got to know the farmer's life first-hand. Let me give you some advice: the life is only for those who are already skilled at the plow in Germany, or are young and strong enough to learn the plow by force of will, or have enough capital to hire help and put money out at interest [for supplemental income]. . . .

In my neighborhood there are many German farmers who arrived in this country poor ten years ago and now own one hundred acres and more. The money they brought along they put out at interest—it was not enough to buy a farm—and hired themselves and their children out to strangers until the necessary sum was saved. Then, with the help of the children (now grown), a log cabin was built and a small farm begun with a yoke of oxen and a cow. When the first essential work was done, out for daily wages went members of the family not needed on the farm. The initial harvests were enough to keep the family going, and the supplemental income of daily wages bought the needed additions to equipment and livestock. Thus things went slowly but surely forward. Too small an acreage fully to occupy all the family can be augmented by renting from a neighbor at a cost of part of the harvest or in exchange for labor. Land to rent is seldom lacking. On the contrary: owners of large acreage are often happy to get income from their fallow fields without having to work them themselves.

To give a rough estimate of the cost of a farm here, let me list the chief expenditures: (1) Land, Federal land: $1.25 an acre at auction, if no one else bids it higher. Land already under cultivation: $6.00 to $14, depending on location. (2) Fences. If built by hired labor: $1.00 an acre. If the owner can turn a capable hand to this hard work, the cost is significantly less. (3) A yoke of oxen: $40 to $60. (4) A good milk cow: $10 to $14. (5) A team of horses: $80 to $120. (6) A plow: $9.00. (7) A wagon: $80. (8) A harrow: $8.00. (9) A dozen hens: $0.80 to $1.00. (10) Swine: $3.00 to $4.00 each. (11) Household furnishings and kitchen equipment: $40 in all. (12) Seed and enough food for the first six months: variable according to size of property and family.

Having experienced firsthand the joys and sorrows of farm life here, I'm convinced it does not measure up to what I expected. . . . So a quick but hearty Farewell!

Your faithful son,
C.

Chapter 6 Worksheet and Questions

1. Your job is to recruit settlers for a new speculative boom town out west. The more settlers you convince to move to this area, the more money you and your partners make. Using the accounts in this chapter, what facts/stories will you use to attract settlers to your town? What accounts will you avoid?

    _____

    _____

    _____

    _____

    _____

    _____

    _____

    _____

    _____

2. Many travelers opted to move to new cities in the west rather than to farm. Other travelers provided descriptions of the towns they passed through. Cincinnati is named as a promising community in several of the accounts. Why? What about Cincinnati do the travelers and potential investors like, and why? According to the documents, what makes other communities not as promising?

    _____

    _____

    _____

    _____

    _____

    _____

    _____

    _____

    _____

3. Tecumseh, Black Hawk, and several of the white writers mention the treatment of the local Indian populations, and how the two cultures view each other. Using the documents, clearly explain how the two sides feel about their "interaction" on the frontier. What are the major problems each side claims that the other causes?

_____

_____

_____

_____

_____

_____

_____

_____

_____

4. Assume you are a farmer, now in your fifth year living on the frontier. What advice do you have for newcomers heading west? What real issues should they be prepared for in traveling, and what problems will they face in developing their farms? Use specific examples from the documents in your answer.

_____

_____

_____

_____

_____

_____

_____

_____

_____

At What Price Change?
The Impact of the Free Market Economy
and Industrialization in Antebellum America

When President Thomas Jefferson assumed office at the beginning of the nineteenth century, the United States was a nation of 5.3 million people. We were a rural nation, with only six cities over 10,000, and these six eastern seaports totaled 183,000 people. In cities and towns across America, manufacturing was done by artisans/craftsmen and their assistants, a combination of journeymen and apprentices. In separate buildings and small shops attached to their homes, employers and workers toiled side by side, using their skills as tailors, carpenters, coopers, shoemakers, and the like, to meet the needs of their community. Because of the poor transportation network, most goods they made were consumed in their local market.

Most Americans lived and worked on family farms, a life that provided comfort and security if you earned a competency each year. This meant you remained independent of others' orders, stayed out of debt, and had something left to pass on to your children when your life ended. A competency, not massive profits, was each farmer's goal. Self-sufficient family farms consumed 75 percent of what they produced each year, and bartered the rest in nearby towns for the goods and services they could not make by themselves.

Seldom did they look to market goods beyond their local community, usually because poor transportation limited their options. Unnavigable rivers and bad roads meant isolation for most farming communities. River travel meant dangerous falls, rapids, snags, shifting sand bars, and even beaver dams to obstruct your path. Most roads were sandy or dirt paths, originally Indian trails now widened to take a horse or perhaps a wagon. In summer heat, travelers choked on clouds of dust; in rainy seasons, wagons and carriages could sink almost out of sight. The only ways for commercial-minded farmers to ship goods to distant markets were to convert grains to alcohol and pack it out on a mule train, or else feed grain to livestock, and then drive the pigs to market. Any other attempt was cost-prohibitive: it cost as much to ship a ton of goods 30 miles overland as it did to ship the same goods all the way across the Atlantic. Thus there was little incentive for farmers to grow surplus crops.

But farming was more than just the common lifestyle; agrarianism was the accepted philosophy of life in the new republic. Good citizens lived and worked in the country, *not* in the city. Family farmers possessed honesty and virtue, and thus guaranteed the existence of the republic. Dr. Benjamin Rush claimed that "farmers and tradesmen are the pillars of national happiness and prosperity." President Jefferson stated what generations of Americans believed, when he said "Those who labor on the earth are the chosen people of God, if he ever had a chosen people, whose breasts he has made his peculiar deposit for substantial and genuine virtue." He went on to declare "cultivators of the earth are the most valuable citizens . . . the most independent, the most virtuous, and they are tied to their country and wedded to its liberty and interest by the most lasting bonds."

Coupled with the nation's veneration of the plow and its master was a fear of urban masses and non-farm labor. Benjamin Franklin declared "it is the multitude of poor without land in a country, who must work for others at low wages or starve, that enables undertakers to carry on manufactures." He, James Madison, Jefferson and others believed that republics collapse into despotism when citizens lose their virtue. If the number of property-less urban workers increased, then national virtue and public morality would disappear.

During the first half of the nineteenth century, agriculture expanded west with the United States, even as industry developed. By 1860, three of the five largest industries in the United States were processing agricultural goods (cotton and woolen textiles), milling, and meat-packing. Transportation improvements increased market opportunities for farmers. Many farmers increased specialized production for the expanding marketplace, decreased barter, increased cash transactions in their local stores, and bought more basic goods as well as luxuries. Other changes prompted by the market economy took place, creating what the new middle class referred to as "progress," including government intervention and promotion of economic development, industrialization, and reform movements. Transportation improvements were key to the new market economy, a fact well known to early national leaders such as Secretary of the Treasury Albert Gallatin, when they called for government promotion of internal improvements.

Critical improvements came in water transportation. While the governments assumed responsibility for clearing away snags, sand bars, and other water hazards, private investors sped up travel with the steamboat. In 1807 the *Clermont* first steamed from New York City to Albany and back in five days, cutting the trip time by more than half. In 1811 the steamboat *New Orleans*, built in Pittsburgh, traveled down the Ohio and Mississippi Rivers to its namesake city, opening the western rivers for trade. In 1817 there were 17 steamboats operating on the Great lakes and western rivers; by 1855 the 727 operating steamboats were a common sight. Along the East Coast, steamboats replaced sailing vessels in the coastal trade.

Other than blowing up, the greatest problem with steamboats is they could only go where rivers and lakes did, which meant they could not cross the western mountains or go directly where many Americans wanted to go. To solve this problem, Americans resorted to man-made rivers, better known as canals. The major East Coast cities were competing for western trade, but needed government assistance to build major canals. After the United States government refused, Governor DeWitt Clinton of New York led the way. Justifying the expense because a western canal would benefit the entire state, he and others promoted and built the Erie Canal. This legendary canal became the success story and model for all others. Historian Carol Sheriff explains how the Erie Canal prompted all the changes, and raises the issues repeated throughout the market economy. The canal promoted town growth along its path, converting frontier towns like Cleveland, Rochester, Buffalo, and Columbus into commercial centers. Canals increased the value of farmlands along their paths, cut shipping costs, made travel more efficient, cut the cost of goods purchased, and made New York City the largest city in the nation. Along any canal, you could see goods, people, and materials moving along. Other states built canals to compete with the Erie Canal; some used canals to connect and improve transportation along existing rivers. By 1840, over 3,300 miles of canals stretched across the eastern United States.

But the transportation improvements did not benefit everyone. Rural breweries, small gristmill owners, and other local manufacturers were often forced out of business when forced to compete with distant companies, which were now able to invade their local markets. Some farms specialized by switching from grain production to raising sheep, in order to sell wool to the mills. This practice reduced the need for farm labor and eliminated the need for women to produce woolen cloth at home. With jobs lost, people left the dying rural towns and surrounding farms, and migrated to newer communities.

Newer communities meant textile mills, and the textile industry spearheaded industrialization in the United States, just as it did in England. First, however, the Boston Associates had to overcome the traditional anti-industry attitude of most Americans. Since Americans all "knew" that European industrial workers had weak intelligence and weaker morals, and that large numbers of such workers would corrupt the virtue of everyone around them, the Boston Associates had to guarantee that American industrial centers would not become "crowded, dark, immoral Manchesters." They needed to show how American industry was close to nature, how manufacturing was a part of the agrarian philosophy. Powering mills by natural waterfalls instead of coal-powered steam engines helped a lot. Early manufacturers would claim that machines were good, not evil, and (just like agriculture) would help conquer the continent and make use of the natural resources. When Lafayette toured the nation in 1824 and 1825, and visited the Lowell mills, manufacturers claimed that his link to Washington and other Founding Fathers gave their blessing to industry.

The Boston Associates sold industrialization and the market economy to Americans, actively promoting (and myth-making) the good that industry brings to a virtuous republic. They claimed industry would never destroy the agricultural basis of the nation. With farming in decline, young women would not be regularly occupied. They would be slothful and underemployed, and would develop bad habits and poor morals. Factory labor would take these "not formerly productive" persons and make them honest and industrious. Thus industry and morality go hand in hand. Besides, with these workers assembled in mill towns, the demand for farm products would increase, improving agriculture in the nation. To further prove that they were not creating "American Manchesters," factory owners planned entire moral communities. Churches, schools, clean boardinghouses, parks, strict living rules, and company-owned moral police to monitor workers behavior meant virtue was important.

But it wasn't enough to convince American society of their intentions; the owners had to attract New England farm girls away from home and into the mills. They did this with "high" wages—high compared to what they could make at other jobs or back home on the farm. They used well planned boardinghouses, idealized to be new, extended families. They appealed to a chance for women to gain some independence and control of their lives, to meet new friends, and to have new social opportunities. The rules they established for mills and life outside the mills were intended to both assure the mill operatives of their concern for them, and to enable the owners to control their actions.

No matter what else they said, the Boston Associates created the mills to make money. They built their own railroads to connect the mill towns to larger markets. They assumed farmers daughters were used to hard work, long hours, and low pay, and also assumed women would accept male authority in the mills better than men would. With smaller hands, and better hand-to-eye coordination than men, the female operatives could reach into running machines better to retrieve broken threads. Since they were women, you could justify paying them less.

Not everyone accepted the mythology about industry, even in the early years. Timothy Flint (whom you met in Chapter 6) saw industry leading to luxuries for the rich and to declining morality. As for the special care for mill workers, he observed: "It is only a besieged city that requires martial law, and the constant guard of armed sentinels." The famous French observer of democracy, Alexis de Tocqueville, pointed out how the factory system degrades the workmen and elevates a class of masters. The end of social equality, he feared, would end real democracy in America as well.

By the 1830s and 1840s the mill towns of New England and other industrial centers were becoming typical factory towns. Competition and new owners' greed diminished their concern for the workers' welfare. The new generation of mill owners did not accept as relevant the moral concerns of the original Boston Associates. They saw the New England farm girls as a thorn in their sides. If cutting wages drove out the mill girls, that was fine. By 1847, pauperism among mill operatives was common. Many were forced into prostitution to make ends meet. The owners closed the boardinghouses, and filled in the open spaces with larger, filthier, poorly ventilated factories. The owner's attitude was announced by Ithamar A. Beard, paymaster of the Hamilton Manufacturing Company in Lowell. Stressing the need for order in society, he declared that in manufacturing towns most inhabitants had to be under the control of a master, and that while this may lead to the creation of an aristocracy, that is the only way master and servant could be friends.

Historians still debate the lasting impacts of the market economy and how it transformed the United States. We do know the following positive effects in antebellum society: First, American factory workers received wages 30 percent higher than in England, and enjoyed lower food prices and more to eat. Second, early mill workers enjoyed the independence and incomes that mill work provided. Third, the nation's appearance and cleanliness improved. Instead of people owning few sets of clothes, which they seldom washed (and never wearing underwear), mass-produced clothing became available and affordable. This meant cleaner clothes and healthier people; in fact, clean clothes became an accepted standard for middle-class America.

This new wardrobe opportunity did not mean that the claims of owners and their legion of sycophants and apologists were correct that "anything which benefited owners and industry benefited the workers as well." Many observers from all classes saw the new market economy and industrialization as a threat to the nation, fearful how the marketplace promoted material ambition and greed, undermining the happiness of the nation and destroying the virtue of each succeeding generation. No virtue in the citizens meant an end of the republic.

The mill operatives clearly suffered and saw their lives change. Most were forced to marry later than their peers, which meant fewer children. They also tended to change their family tradition by not marrying a farmer, but someone with urban connections. Slashed wages threatened them with slavery. Protestors at the 1834 Lowell strike complained that "the oppressing hand of avarice would enslave us," a fate not becoming the daughters of freemen whose ancestors fought for independence. Overwork ruined the health of many workers; poverty forced others into prostitution. Conditions worsened enough for Herman Melville to publicize them in his short story "The Tartarus of Maids."

Workers in other industries suffered as well. Most working families, when fully employed in good times, earned no more than $100 to $250 per year, when it was estimated you needed $400 to $600 to live "decently." You had money for food, clothing, and shelter only if other family members worked. That meant mothers/wives not staying home with small children, and older children not attending school. You had no money in savings, no insurance, no money for medical expenses, and little margin for error. If one of the wage earners fell ill or died, you could be homeless and never recover. If you stayed healthy, it meant working 10- to 14-hour days, six days a week in dangerous conditions. In many industries (e.g., printing, carpentry, shoe-making, tailoring), the factory system and new machinery meant lost opportunity for advancement or ownership.

Workers responded by forming labor unions and becoming politically active, sure that their cause was keyed to preserving democracy and opportunity in the United States. Besides better pay and shorter hours, they wanted free common schools, in order to provide educational opportunities to their children. They wanted an end to imprisonment for debt, mandatory militia service, and first claim on employer's assets when they filed for bankruptcy. They embraced a more traditional American labor theory of value: that workers were entitled to sales proceeds from the products of their labors. Like many Founding Fathers, they attacked those who accumulated wealth while not producing it, but merely benefited from the hard work of others. Merchants, bankers, speculators, and factory owners fell into these categories. Supporters repeated these ideas in writing; James Fenimore Cooper declared that "wealth not gained through hard labor is unnatural."

Considering the Evidence in the Readings

The following accounts expose you to the changes in American society caused by the market economy. Some of the writers have fond, nostalgic memories of their early years during the period of change, while others remember the pain and injustices they encountered. You will encounter professional writers, propagandists, and apologists for both sides. As you examine the documents, remember to consider who is writing, why they are writing, and who their audience is supposed to be. When finished, ask yourself how you would feel about all the changes talking place if you had lived through them. Would it matter what your position in society was at the start of the Civil War?

Document 7.1 George Bagby Remembers Life and Activities along the Canals

The first recorded descriptions of building canals come from Roman days. Early in the new America, George Washington and other investors created the Potomac Company in 1785 to improve transportation along that river. Another early canal effort came in 1787 in South Carolina, as the Santee Canal Company attempted to connect the Santee and Cooper rivers, to facilitate upstate planters' shipping crops to Charleston. People tended to romanticize canal days, remembering lazy summer days, American expansion to the west, and songs such as "I got me a mule, her name is Sal, fifteen miles on the Erie Canal"—all part of a supposedly simpler life before newer travel technology like railroads changed the pace of life. What memories of canal days does George Bagby have? Do you see evidence of the canal's commercial value in his account? Are these impressions nostalgia for days gone by or relief that the past is gone?

Fleets of these *batteaux* used to be moored on the river bank near where the depot of the Virginia and Tennessee Railroad now stands; and many years after the "Jeems and Kanawha" was finished, one of them used to haunt the mouth of Blackwater creek above the toll-bridge, a relic of departed glory. For if ever man gloried in his calling,—the negro batteau-man was that man. His was a hardy calling, demanding skill, courage and strength in a high degree. I can see him now striding the plank that ran along the gunwale to afford him footing, his long iron-shod pole trailing in the water behind him. Now he turns, and after one or two ineffectual efforts to get his pole fixed in the rocky bottom of the river, secures his purchase, adjusts the upper part of the pole to the pad at his shoulder, bends to his task, and the long, but not ungraceful bark mounts the rapids like a sea-bird breasting the storm. His companion on the other side plies the pole with equal ardor, and between the two the boat bravely surmounts every obstacle, be it rocks, rapids, quicksands, hammocks, what not. A third negro at the stern held the mighty oar that served as a rudder. A stalwart, jolly, courageous set they were, plying the pole all day, hauling in to shore at night under the friendly shade of a mighty sycamore, to rest, to eat, to play the banjo, and to snatch a few hours of profound, blissful sleep.

The up-cargo, consisting of sacks of salt, bags of coffee, barrels of sugar, molasses and whiskey, afforded good pickings. These sturdy fellows lived well, I promise you, and if they stole a little, why, what was their petty thieving compared to the enormous pillage of the modern sugar refiner and the crooked-whiskey distiller? They lived well. Their cook's galley was a little dirt thrown between the ribs of the boat at the stern, with an awning on occasion to keep off the rain, and what they didn't eat wasn't worth eating. Fish of the very best, both salt and fresh, chickens, eggs, mill: and the invincible, never-satisfying ash-cake and fried bacon. I see the frying-pan, I smell the meat, the fish, the Rio coffee!—I want the *batteau* back again, aye! and the brave, light-hearted slave to boot. What did he know about the State debt? There was no State debt to speak of. Greenbacks? Bless, you! the Farmers Bank of Virginia was living and breathing, and its money was good enough for a king. Re-adjustment, funding bill, tax-receivable coupons—where were all these worries then? I think if we had known they were coming, we would have stuck to the batteaux and never dammed the river. Why, shad used to run to Lynchburg! The world was merry, butter-milk was abundant; Lynchburg a lad, Richmond a mere youth, and the great "Jeems and Kanawha canell" was going to—oh! it was going to do everything. . . .

The perfect cultivation, the abundance, the elegance the ducal splendor, one might almost say, of the great estates that lay along the canal in the old days have passed away in a great measure. Here were gentlemen, not merely refined and educated, fitted to display a royal hospitality and to devote their leisure to the study of the art and practice of government, but they were great and greatly successful farmers as well. The land teemed with all manner of products, cereals, fruits, what not! Negroes by the hundreds and the thousands, under wise direction, gentle but firm control, plied the hoe to good purpose.

There was enough and to spare for all—to spare? aye! to bestow with glad and lavish hospitality. A mighty change has been wrought. What that change is in all of its effects mine eyes have happily been spared the seeing; but well I remember—I can

---

George William Bagby, *Canal Reminiscences: Recollections of Travel in Old Days on the James River and Kanawha Canal*, electronic edition. Found at docssouth.unc.edu/bagby/bagby.html.

never forget—how from time to time the boat would stop at one of these estates, and the planter, his wife, his daughters, and the guests that were going home with him, would be met by those who had remained behind, and how joyous the greetings were! It was a bright and happy scene, and it continually repeated itself as we went onward.

In fine summer weather, the passengers, male and female, stayed most of the time on deck, where there was a great deal to interest, and naught to mar the happiness, except the oft-repeated warning, *"braidge!" "low braidge!"* No well-regulated packet-hand was ever allowed to say plain "bridge;" that was an etymological crime in canal ethics. . . .

There is a point at which the passengers would get off, and taking a near cut across the hills, would stretch their legs with a mile or two of walking. It was unmanly, I held, to miss that. Apropos of scenery, I must not forget the haunted house near Manchester, which was pointed out soon after we left Richmond, and filled me with awe; for though I said I did not believe in ghosts, I did. The ruined mill, a mile or two further on was always an object of melancholy interest to me; and of all the locks from Lynchburg down,

the Three-Mile Locks pleased me most. It is a pretty place, as every one will own on seeing it. It was so clean and green, and white and thrifty-looking. To me it was simply beautiful. I wanted to live there; I ought to have lived there. I was built for a lock-keeper—have that exact moral and mental shape. Ah! to own your own negro, who would do all the drudgery of opening the gates. Occasionally you would go through the form of putting your shoulder to the huge wooden levers, if that is what they call them, by which the gates are opened: to own your own negro and live and die calmly at a lock! What more could the soul ask! I do think that the finest picture extant of peace and contentment—a little abnormal, perhaps, in the position of the animal—is that of a sick mule looking out of the window of a canal freight-boat. And that you could see every day from the porch of your cottage, if you lived at a lock, owned your own negro, and there was no great rush of business on the canal, (and there seldom was) on the "Jeems and Kanawhy," as old Capt. Sam Wyatt always called it, leaving out the word "canal," for that was understood. Yes, one ought to live as a pure and resigned lock-keeper, if one would be blest, really blest.

Document 7.2 Rules of Employment for Those Who Worked in the Mills

English industrial cities, such as Manchester, were known in the United States as "hell above ground." Horror stories about working conditions, abuse by managers, depravity, and vanishing morality of workers, and the consequential decline of the entire region made this a model to avoid. The Boston Associates had to overcome the image of English industry, both to attract young women into the workforce and to convince their New England farming parents that it was safe to allow their daughters to enter the mills. The paternalistic rules were designed to protect the reputations of the female workers and the image of the American companies. Rule violators were fired and blacklisted from future mill work. As you read the following work rules, do you think they accomplish the goals of the company? What here would prompt British visitors to praise American industrial centers as superior to their own?

The overseers are to be punctually in their Rooms at the starting of the Mill, and not to be absent unnecessarily during working hours. They are to see that all those employed in their Rooms are in their places in due season; they may grant leave of absence to those employed under them, when there are spare hands in the Room to supply their places; otherwise they are not to grant leave of absence, except in cases of absolute necessity.

All persons in the employ of the Lowell Manufacturing Company are required to observe the Regulations of the overseer of the Room where they are employed; they are not to be absent from work without his consent, except in cases of sickness, and then they are to send him word of the cause of their absence.

They are to board in one of the Boarding-Houses belonging to the Company, and to conform to the

Edith Abbott, *Women in Industry*, [New York: Appleton Crofts, 1910], pp. 374–377.

regulations of the House where they board; they are to give information at the Counting-Room, of the place where they board, when they begin; and also give notice whenever they change their boarding-place.

The Company will not employ any one who is habitually absent from public worship on the Sabbath.

It is considered a part of the engagement that each person remains twelve months if required; and all persons intending to leave the employment of the Company are to give two weeks' notice of their intention to their Overseer, and their engagement is not considered as fulfilled unless they comply with this Regulation.

The Pay Roll will be made up to the last Saturday of every month, and the payment made to the Carpet Mill the following Saturday, and the Cotton Mill the succeeding Tuesday, when every person will be expected to pay their board.

The Company will not continue to employ any person who shall be wanting in proper respect to the females employed by the Company, or who shall smoke within the Company's premises, or be guilty of inebriety, or other improper conduct.

The Tenants of the Boarding-Houses are not to board or permit any part of their houses to be occupied by any person, except those in the employ of the Company.

They will be considered answerable for any improper conduct in their Houses, and are not to permit their Boarders to have company at unseasonable hours.

The doors must be closed at ten o'clock in the evening, and no person admitted after that time without some reasonable excuse.

The keepers of the Boarding-Houses must give an account of the number, names and employment of the Boarders when required, and report the names of such as are guilty of any improper conduct.

The Buildings, and yards about them, must be kept clean and in good order, and if they are injured otherwise than from ordinary use; all necessary repairs will be made and charged to the occupant.

It is desirable that the families of those who live in the Houses, as well as the Boarders, who have not had the Kine Pox, should be vaccinated; which will be done at the expense of the Company for such as wish it.

Some suitable chamber in the House must be reserved, and appropriated for the use of the sick, so that others may not be under the necessity of sleeping in the same room.

No one will be continued as a Tenant who shall suffer ashes to be put into any place other than the place made to receive them, or shall, by any carelessness in the use of fire, or lights, endanger the Company's property.

These regulations are considered a part of the contract with the persons entering into the employment of the Lowell Manufacturing Company.

Document 7.3 Harriet Hanson Robinson Remembers Early Life in Lowell

Some of the mill girls started under unhappy circumstances, such as the death of their father depriving the family of the bread-winner. Harriet Hanson Robinson entered the mills in 1835 at age 10, and left in 1848 when she married at age 23. During her years at the mills, working conditions slowly deteriorated. After she left, Harriet became an activist in the Abolition and women's suffrage movements. In her book about life in Lowell, she describes the conditions that entice women to enter the mills to take advantage of economic opportunities, what they face, and why they went on strike. What does she remember about Lowell before the mills were built? How does she describe her work? Take note of how she describes the mill girls, the managers, and other people in Lowell. Are there clear class lines? Why does she think the mill operatives went on strike?

Harriet Hanson Robinson, *Loom and Spindle, or Life among the Early Mill Girls* [New York: Crowell, 1898], pp. 1-3, 7-10, 16-20, 37-44, 51-52

The life of a people or of a class is best illustrated by its domestic scenes, or by character sketches of the men and women who form a part of it. The historian is a species of mental photographer of the life and times he attempts to portray; he can no more give the whole history of events than the artist can, in detail, bring a whole city into his picture. And so, in this record of a life that is past, I can give but incomplete views of that long-ago faded landscape, views taken on the spot.

It is hardly possible to do this truthfully without bringing myself into the picture,—a solitary traveler revisiting the scenes of youth, and seeing with young eyes a city and a people living in almost Arcadian simplicity, at a time which, in view of the greatly changed conditions of factory labor, may well be called a lost Eden for that portion of our working-men and working-women.

Before 1836 the era of mechanical industry in New England had hardly begun, the industrial life of its people was yet in its infancy, and nearly every article in domestic use that is now made by the help of machinery was then "done by hand." It was, with few exceptions, a rural population, and the material for clothing was grown on the home-farm, and spun and woven by the women. Even in comparatively wealthy families, the sons were sent to college in suits of homespun, cut and made by the village seamstress, and every household was a self-producing and self-sustaining community. "Homespun was their only wear," homespun their lives.

There was neither railway, steamboat, telegraph, nor telephone, and direct communication was kept up by the lumbering stage-coach, or the slow-toiling canal, which tracked its sinuous way from town to city, and from State to State. The daily newspaper was almost unknown, and the "news of the day" was usually a week or so behind the times. Money was scarce, and most of the retail business was done by "barter"—so many eggs for a certain quantity of sugar, or so much butter or farm produce for tea, coffee, and other luxuries. The people had plenty to eat, for the land, though sterile, was well cultivated; but if the children wanted books, or a better education than the village school could give them, the farmer seldom had the means to gratify their wishes.

These early New Englanders lived in pastoral simplicity. They were moral, religious, and perhaps content. They could say with truth,—

"We are the same things that our fathers have been,
We see the same sights that our fathers have seen,

We drink the same stream, we feel the same sun,
And run the same course that our fathers have run."

Their lives had kept pace for so many years with the stage-coach and the canal that they thought, no doubt, if they thought about it at all, that they should crawl along in this way forever. But into this life there came an element that was to open a new era in the activities of the country.

This was the genius of mechanical industry, which would build the cotton-factory, set in motion the loom and the spinning-frame, call together an army of useful people, open wider fields of industry for men and (which was quite as important at that time) for women also. For hitherto woman had always been a money-*saving*, rather than a money-earning, member of the community, and her labor could command but small return. If she worked out as servant, or "help," her wages were from fifty cents to one dollar a week if she went from house to house by the day to spin and weave, or as tailoress, she could get but seventy-five cents a week and her meals. As teacher her services were not in demand, and nearly all the arts, the professions, and even the trades and industries, were closed to her, there being, as late as 1840, only seven vocations, outside the home, into which the women of New England had entered.

The Middlesex Canal was one of the earliest factors in New England enterprise. It began its course at Charlestown Mill-pond, and ended it at Lowell. It was completed in 1804, at the cost of $700,000, and was the first canal in the United States to transport both passengers and merchandise. Its charter was extinguished in 1859, in spite of all opposition, by a decision of the Supreme Court. And thus, in less than sixty years, this marvel of engineering skill, as it was then considered, which was projected to last for all time, was "switched off the track" by its successful rival, the Boston and Lowell Railroad, and, with the stage-coach and the turnpike road became a thing of the past.

The course of the old Middlesex Canal can still be traced, as a cow-path or a woodland lane, and in one place, which I have always kept in remembrance, very near the Somerville Station on the Western Division of the Boston and Maine Railroad, can still be seen a few decayed willows, nodding sleepily over its grass-grown channel and ridgy paths,—a reminder of those slow times when it took a long summer's day to travel the twenty-eight miles from Boston to Lowell.

. . .

Before 1840, the foreign element in the factory population was almost an unknown quantity. The first immigrants to come to Lowell were from England. The Irishman soon followed; but not for many years did the Frenchman, Italian, and German come to take possession of the cotton mills. The English were of the artisan class, but the Irish came as "hewers of wood and drawers of water." The first Irishwomen to work in the Lowell mills were usually scrubbers and waste-pickers. They were always good-natured, and when excited used their own language; the little mill-children learned many of the words (which all seemed to be joined together like compound words), and these mites would often answer back, in true Hibernian fashion. These women, as a rule, wore peasant cloaks, red or blue, made with hoods and several capes, in summer (as they told the children), to "kape cool," and in winter to "kape warrum." They were not intemperate, nor "bitterly poor." They earned good wages, and they and their children, especially their children, very soon adapted themselves to their changed conditions of life, and became as "good as anybody."

To show the close connection in family descent of the artisan and the artist, at least in the line of color, it may be said here that a grandson of one of the first blue-dyers in this country is one of the finest American marine painters, and exhibited pictures at the World's Columbian Exposition of 1893.

In 1832 the factory population of Lowell was divided into four classes. The agents of the corporations were the aristocrats, not because of their wealth, but on account of the office they held, which was one of great responsibility, requiring, as it did, not only some knowledge of business, but also a certain tact in managing, or utilizing the great number of operatives so as to secure the best return for their labor. The agent was also something of an autocrat, and there was no appeal from his decision in matters affecting the industrial interests of those who were employed on his corporation.

The agents usually lived in large houses, not too near the boarding-houses, surrounded by beautiful gardens which seemed like Paradise to some of the home-sick girls, who, as they came from their work in the noisy mill, could look with longing eyes into the sometimes open gate in the high fence, and be reminded afresh of their pleasant country homes. And a glimpse of one handsome woman, the wife of an agent, reading by an astral lamp in the early evening, has always been remembered by one young girl, who looked forward to the time when she, too,

might have a parlor of her own, lighted by an astral lamp!

The second class were the overseers, a sort of gentry, ambitious mill-hands who had worked up from the lowest grade of factory labor; and they usually lived in the end-tenements of the blocks, the short connected rows of houses in which the operatives were boarded. However, on one corporation, at least, there was a block devoted exclusively to the overseers, and one of the wives, who had been a factory girl, put on so many airs that the wittiest of her former work-mates fastened the name of "Puckersville" to the whole block where the overseers lived. It was related of one of these quondam factory girls, that, with some friends, she once re-visited the room in which she used to work, and, to show her genteel friends her ignorance of her old surroundings, she turned to the overseer, who was with the party, and pointing to some wheels and pulleys over her head, she said, "What's them things up there?"

The third class were the operatives, and were all spoken of as "girls" or "men;" and the "girls," either as a whole, or in part, are the subject of this volume.

The fourth class, lords of the spade and the shovel, by whose constant labor the building of the great factories was made possible, and whose children soon became valuable operatives, lived at first on what was called the "Acre," a locality near the present site of the North Grammar schoolhouse. Here, clustered around a small stone Catholic Church, were hundreds of little shanties, in which they dwelt with their wives and numerous children. Among them were sometimes found disorder and riot, for they had brought with them from the *ould counthrey* their feuds and quarrels, and the "Bloody Far-downers" and the "Corkonians" were torn by intestinal strife. The boys of both these factions agreed in fighting the "damned Yankee boys," who represented to them both sides of the feud on occasion; and I have seen many a pitched battle fought, all the way from the Tremont Corporation (then an open field) to the North Grammar schoolhouse, before we girls could be allowed to pursue our way in peace.

We were obliged to go to school with our champions, the boys, for we did not dare to go alone. These "Acreites" respected one or two of us from our relationship to the "bullies," as some of the fighting leaders of our boys were called; and when caught alone by Acreites coming home from school, we have been in terror of our lives, till we heard some of them say, in a language used by all sides, air-o-there owes-o-gose e-o-the ooly-o-boos' ister-o-see. (There goes the bully's sister.) This language was called Hog Latin by the boys; but it is found in one of George Borrows' books, as a specimen of the Rommany or gypsy language. These fights were not confined to the boys on each side; after mill-hours the men joined in the fray, and evenings that should have been better employed were spent in carrying on this senseless warfare. The authorities interfered, and prevented these raids of the Acreites upon the school-children, and the warfare was kept within their own domain. It lasted after this for more than ten years, and was ended by the "bloody battle" of Suffolk Bridge, in which a young boy was killed.

The agents were paid only fair salaries, the overseers generally two dollars a day, and the help all earned good wages. By this it will be seen that there were no very rich persons in Lowell, nor were there any "suffering poor," since every man, woman, and child, (over ten years of age) could get work, and was paid according to the work each was capable of doing.

Chapter II
Child-Life in the Lowell Cotton-Mills

In attempting to describe the life and times of the early mill-girls, it has seemed best for me to write my story in the first person; not so much because my own experience is of importance, as that it is, in some respects, typical of that of many others who lived and worked with me.

Our home was in Boston, in Leverett Court, now Cotting Street, where I was born the year the corner-stone was laid for the Bunker Hill Monument, as my mother told me always to remember. We lived there until I was nearly seven years of age, and, although so young, I can remember very vividly scenes and incidents which took place at that time. We lived under the shadow of the old jail (near where Wall Street now runs), and we children used to hear conversation, not meant for small ears, between the prisoners and the persons in the court who came there to see them.

All the land on which the North Union Station now stands, with the railway lines connected with it, and also the site of many of the streets, particularly Lowell Street, was then a part of the Mill-pond, or was reclaimed from the Bay. The tide came in at the foot of Leverett Court, and we could look across the water and see the sailing vessels coming and going. There the down-east wood-coasters landed their freight; many a time I have gone "chipping" there, and once a generous young skipper offered me a stick of wood, which I did not dare to take.

In 1831, under the shadow of a great sorrow, which had made her four children fatherless,—the oldest but seven years of age,—my mother was left to struggle alone; and, although she tried hard to earn bread enough to fill our hungry mouths, she could not do it, even with the help of kind friends. And so it happened that one of her more wealthy neighbors, who had looked with longing eyes on the one little daughter of the family, offered to adopt me. But my mother, who had had a hard experience in her youth in living amongst strangers, said, "No; while I have one meal of victuals a day, I will not part with my children." I always remembered this speech because of the word "victuals," and I wondered for a long time what this good old Bible word meant.

My father was a carpenter, and some of his fellow-workmen helped my mother to open a little shop, where she sold small stores, candy, kindling-wood, and so on, but there was no great income from this, and we soon became poorer than ever. Dear me! I can see the small shop now, with its jars of striped candy, its loaves of bread, the room at the back where we all lived, and my oldest brother (now a "D.D.") sawing the kindling-wood which we sold to the neighbors.

That was a hard, cold winter; and for warmth's sake my mother and her four children all slept in one bed, two at the foot and three at the head,—but her richer neighbor could not get the little daughter; and, contrary to all the modern notions about hygiene, we were a healthful and a robust brood. We all, except the baby, went to school every day, and Saturday afternoons I went to a charity school to learn to sew. My mother had never complained of her poverty in our hearing, and I had accepted the conditions of my life with a child's trust, knowing nothing of the relative difference between poverty and riches, And so I went to the sewing-school, like any other little girt who was taking lessons in sewing and not as a "charity child;" until a certain day when something was said by one of the teachers, about me, as a "poor little girl,"—a thoughtless remark, no doubt, such as may be said to-day in "charity schools." When I went home I told my mother that the teacher said I was *poor*, and she replied in her sententious manner, "You need not go there again."

Shortly after this my mother's widowed sister, Mrs. Angeilne Cudworth, who kept a factory boarding-house in Lowell, advised her to come to that city. She secured a house for her, and my mother, with her little brood and her few household belongings, started for the new-factory town.

We went by the canal-boat, The Governor Sullivan, and a long and tiresome day it was to the weary mother and her four active children, though the children often varied the scene by walking on the tow-path under the Lombardy poplars, riding on the gates when the locks were swung open, or buying glasses of water at the stopping-places along the route.

When we reached Lowell, we were carried at once to my aunt's house, whose generous spirit had well provided for her hungry relations; and we children were led into her kitchen, where, on the longest and whitest of tables, lay, oh, so many loaves of bread!

After our feast of loaves we walked with our mother to the Tremont Corporation, where we were to live, and at the old No. 5 (which imprint is still legible over the door), in the first block of tenements then built, I began my life among factory people. My mother kept forty boarders, most of them men, mill-hands, and she did all her housework, with what help her children could give her between schools; for we all, even the baby three years old, were kept at school. My part in the housework was to wash the dishes, and I was obliged to stand on a cricket in order to reach the sink!

My mother's boarders were many of them young men, and usually farmers' sons. They were almost invariably of good character and behavior, and it was a continual pleasure for me and my brothers to associate with them. I was treated like a little sister, never hearing a word or seeing a look to remind me that I was not of the same sex as my brothers. I played checkers with them, sometimes "beating," and took part in their conversation, and it never came into my mind that they were not the same as so many "girls." A good object-lesson for one who was in the future to maintain, by voice and pen, her belief in the equality of the sexes!

I had been to school constantly until I was about ten years of age, when my mother, feeling obliged to have help in her work besides what I could give, and also needing the money which I could earn, allowed me, at my urgent request (for I wanted to earn *money* like the other little girls), to go to work in the mill. I worked first in the spinning-room as a "doffer." The doffers were the very youngest girls, whose work was to doff, or take off, the full bobbins, and replace them with the empty ones.

I can see myself now, racing down the alley, between the spinning-frames, carrying in front of me a bobbin-box bigger than I was. These mites had to be very swift in their movements, so as not to keep the spinning-frames stopped long, and they worked only about fifteen minutes in every hour. The rest of the time was their own, and when the overseer was kind they were allowed to read, knit, or even to go outside the mill-yard to play.

Some of us learned to embroider in crewels, and I still have a lamb worked on cloth, a relic of those early days, when I was first taught to improve my time in the good old New England fashion. When not doffing, we were often allowed to go home, for a time, and thus we were able to help our mothers in their housework. We were paid two dollars a week; and how proud I was when my turn came to stand up on the bobbin-box, and write my name in the paymaster's book, and how indignant I was when he asked me if I could "write." "Of course I can," said I, and he smiled as he looked down on me.

The working-hours of all the girls extended from five o'clock in the morning until seven in the evening, with one-half hour for breakfast and for dinner. Even the doffers were forced to be on duty nearly fourteen hours a day, and this was the greatest hardship in the lives of these children. For it was not until 1842 that the hours of labor for children under twelve years of age were limited to ten per day; but the "ten-hour law" itself was not passed until long after some of these little doffers were old enough to appear before the legislative committee on the subject, and plead, by their presence, for a reduction of the hours of labor.

I do not recall any particular hardship connected with this life, except getting up so early in the morning, and to this habit, I never was, and never shall be, reconciled, for it has taken nearly a lifetime for me to make up the sleep lost at that early age. But in every other respect it was a pleasant life. We were not hurried any more than was for our good, and no more work was required of us than we were able easily to do.

Chapter IV
The Characteristics of the Early Factory Girls

When I look back into the factory life of fifty or sixty years ago, I do not see what is called "a class" of young men and women going to and from their daily work, like so many ants that cannot be distinguished one from another; I see them as individuals, with personalities of their own. This one has about her the atmosphere of her early home. That one is impelled by a strong and noble purpose. The other,—what she is, has been an influence for good to me and to all womankind.

Yet they were a class of factory operatives, and were spoken of (as the same class is spoken of now) as a set of persons who earned their daily bread, whose condition was fixed, and who must continue to spin and to weave to the end of their natural existence. Nothing but this was expected of them, and they were not supposed to be capable of social or mental improvement. That they could be educated and developed into something more than mere work-people, was an idea that had not yet entered the public mind. So little does one class of persons really know about the thoughts and aspirations of another! It was the good fortune of these early mill-girls to teach the people of that time that this sort of labor is not degrading; that the operative is not only "capable of virtue," but also capable of self-cultivation.

At the time the Lowell cotton mills were started, the factory girl was the lowest among women. In England, and in France particularly, great injustice had been done to her real character; she was represented as subjected to influences that could not fail to destroy her purity and self-respect. In the eyes of her overseer she was but a brute, a slave, to be beaten, pinched, and pushed about. It was to overcome this prejudice that such high wages had been offered to women that they might be induced to become mill-girls, in spite of the opprobrium that still clung to this "degrading occupation." At first only a few came; for, though tempted by the high wages to be regularly paid in "cash," there were many who still preferred to go on working at some more *genteel* employment at seventy-five cents a week and their board.

But in a short time the prejudice against factory labor wore away, and the Lowell mills became filled with blooming and energetic New England women. They were naturally intelligent, had mother-wit, and fell easily into the ways of their new life. They soon began to associate with those who formed the community in which they had come to live, and were invited to their houses. They went to the same church, and sometimes married into some of the best families. Or if they returned to their secluded homes again, instead of being looked down upon as "factory girls" by the squire's or the lawyer's family, they were more often welcomed as coming from the metropolis, bringing new fashions, new books, and new ideas with them.

In 1831 Lowell was little more than a factory village. Several corporations were started, and the cotton-mills belonging to them were building. Help was in great demand; and stories were told all over the country of the new factory town, and the high wages that were offered to all classes of work-people,—stories that reached the ears of mechanics' and farmers' sons, and gave new life to lonely and dependent women in distant towns and farmhouses. Into this Yankee El Dorado, these needy people began to pour by the various modes of travel known to those slow old days. The stagecoach and the canal-boat came every day, always filled with new recruits for this army of useful people. The mechanic and machinist came, each with his homemade chest of tools, and often-times his wife and little ones. The widow came with her little flock and her scanty housekeeping goods to open a boarding-house or variety store, and so provided a home for her fatherless children. Many farmers' daughters came to earn money to complete their wedding outfit, or buy the bride's share of housekeeping articles.

Women with past histories came, to hide their griefs and their identity, and to earn an honest living in the "sweat of their brow." Single young men came, full of hope and life, to get money for an education, or to lift the mortgage from the home-farm. Troops of young girls came by stages and baggage-wagons, men often being employed to go to other States and to Canada, to collect them at so much a head, and deliver them at the factories.

A very curious sight these country girls presented to young eyes accustomed to a more modern style of things. When the large covered baggage-wagon arrived in front of a block on the corporation, they would descend from it, dressed in various and outlandish fashions, and with their arms brimful of bandboxes containing all their worldly goods. On each of these was sewed a card, on which one could read the old-fashioned New England name of the owner. And sorrowful enough they looked, even to the fun-loving child who has lived to tell the story; for they had all left their pleasant country homes to try their fortunes in a great manufacturing town, and they were homesick even before they landed at the doors of their boarding-houses. Years after, this scene dwelt in my memory; and whenever anyone said anything about being homesick, there rose before me the picture of a young girl with a sorrowful face and a big tear in each eye, clambering down the steps at the rear of a great covered wagon, holding fast to a cloth-covered bandbox, drawn up at the top with a string, on which was sewed a paper bearing the name of Plumy Clay!

Some of these girls brought diminutive hair trunks covered with the skin of calves, spotted in dun and white, even as when they did skip and play in daisy-blooming meads. And when several of them were set together in front of one of the blocks, they looked like their living counterparts: reposing at noontide in the adjacent field. One of this kind of trunks has been handed down to me as an heirloom. The hair is worn off in patches: it cannot be invigorated, and it is now become a hairless heirloom. Within its hide-bound sides are safely stowed away the love-letters of a past generation,—love-letters that agitated the hearts of the grandparents of to-day; and I wonder that their resistless ardor has not long ago burst its wrinkled sides. It is relegated to distant attics, with its ancient crony, "ye bandbox," to enjoy an honored and well-earned repose.

Ah me! when some of us, its contemporaries, are also past our usefulness, gone clean out of fashion, may we also be as resigned, yea, as willing, to be laid quietly on some attic shelf!

These country girls had queer names, which added to the singularity of their appearance. Samantha, Triphena, Plumy, Kezia, Aseneth, Elgardy, Leafy, Ruhamah, Lovey, Almaretta, Sarepta, and Flotilla were among them.

Their dialect was also very peculiar. On the broken English and Scotch of their ancestors was ingrafted the nasal Yankee twang; so that many of them, when they had just come *daown*, spoke a language almost unintelligible. But the severe discipline and ridicule which met them was as good as a school education, and they were soon taught the "city way of speaking."

Their dress was also peculiar, and was of the plainest of homespun, cut in such an old-fashioned style that each young girl looked as if she had borrowed her grandmother's gown. Their only head-covering was a shawl, which was pinned under the chin; but after the first payday, a "shaker" (or "scooter") sunbonnet usually replaced this primitive head-gear of their rural life.

But the early factory girls were not all country girls. There were others also, who had been taught that "work is no disgrace." There were some who came to Lowell solely on account of the social or literary advantages to be found there. They lived in secluded parts of New England, where books were scarce, and there was no cultivated society. They had comfortable homes, and did not perhaps need the *money* they would earn; but they longed to see this new "City of Spindles," of which they had heard so much from their neighbors and friends, who had gone there to work.

And the fame of the circulating libraries, that were soon opened, drew them and kept them there when no other inducement would have been sufficient.

The laws relating to women were such, that a husband could claim his wife wherever he found her, and also the children she was trying to shield from his influence; and I have seen more than one poor woman skulk behind her loom or her frame when visitors were approaching the end of the aisle where she worked. Some of these were known under assumed names, to prevent their husbands from trusteeing their wages. It was a very common thing for a male person of a certain kind to do this, thus depriving his wife of *all* her wages, perhaps, month after month. The wages of minor children could be trusteed, unless the children (being fourteen years of age) were given their time. Women's wages were also trusteed for the debts of their husbands, and children's for the debts of their parents.

As an instance, my mother had some financial difficulties when I was fifteen years old, and to save herself and me from annoyance, she gave me my time. The document reads as follows:—

"Be it known that I, Harriet Hanson, of Lowell, in consideration that my minor daughter Harriet J. has taken upon herself the whole burden of her own support, and has undertaken and agreed to maintain herself henceforward without expense to me, do hereby release and quitclaim unto her all profits and wages which she may hereafter earn or acquire by her skill or labor in any occupation,—and do hereby disclaim all right to collect or interfere with the same. And I do give and release unto her the absolute control and disposal of her own time according to her own discretion, without interference from me. It being understood that I am not to be chargeable hereafter with any expense on her account.

(Signed) HARRIET HANSON. *July* 2, 1840."

It must be remembered that at this date woman had no property rights. A widow could be left without her share of her husband's (or the family) property, a legal "incumbrance" to his estate. A father could make his will without reference to his daughter's share of the inheritance. He usually left her a home on the farm as long as she remained single. A woman was not supposed to be capable of spending her own or of using other people's money. In Massachusetts, before 1840, a woman could not legally be treasurer of her own sewing-society, unless some man were responsible for her.

The law took no cognizance of woman as a money-spender. She was a ward, an appendage, a relict. Thus it happened, that if a woman did not choose to marry, or, when left a widow, to remarry, she had no choice but to enter one of the few employments open to her, or to become a burden on the charity of some relative.

In almost every New England home could be found one or more of these women, sometimes welcome, more often unwelcome, and leading joyless, and in many instances unsatisfactory, lives. The cotton-factory was a great opening to these lonely and dependent women. From a condition approaching pauperism they were at once placed above want; they could earn money, and spend it as they pleased; and could gratify their tastes and desires without restraint, and without rendering an account to anybody. At last they had found a place in the universe; they were no longer obliged to finish out their faded lives mere burdens to male relatives. Even the time of these women was their own, on Sundays and in the evening after the day's work was done. For the first time in this country woman's labor had a money value. She had become not only an earner and a producer, but also a spender of money, a recognized factor in the political economy of her time. And thus a long upward step in our material civilization was taken; woman had begun to earn and hold her own money, and through its aid had learned to think and to act for herself.

Among the older women who sought this new employment were very many lonely and dependent ones, such as used to be mentioned in old wills as "incumbrances" and "relicts," and to whom a chance of earning money was indeed a new revelation. How well I remember some of these solitary ones! As a child of eleven years, I often made fun of them—for children do not see the pathetic side of human life—and imitated their limp carriage and inelastic gait. I can see them now, even after sixty years, just as they looked,—depressed, modest, mincing, hardly daring to look one in the face, so shy and sylvan had been their lives. But after the first pay-day came, and they felt the jingle of silver in their pockets, and had begun to feel its mercurial influence, their bowed heads were lifted, their necks seemed braced with steel, they looked you in the face, sang blithely among their looms or frames, and walked with elastic step to and from their work. And when Sunday came, homespun was no longer their only wear; and how sedately gay in their new attire they walked to church, and how

proudly they dropped their silver four-pences into the contribution-box! It seemed as if a great hope impelled them,—the harbinger of the new era that was about to dawn for them and for all women-kind.

In passing, let me not forget to pay a tribute, also, to those noble single and widowed women, who are "set solitary in families," but whose presence cements the domestic fabric, and whose influence is unseen and oftentimes unappreciated, until they are taken away and the integral part of the old home-life begins to crumble.

Except in rare instances, the rights of the early mill-girls were secure. They were subject to no extortion, if they did extra work they were always paid in full, and their own account of labor done by the piece was always accepted. They kept the figures, and were paid accordingly. This was notably the case with the weavers and drawing-in girls. Though the hours of labor were long, they were not overworked; they were obliged to tend no more looms and frames than they could easily take care of, and they had plenty of time to sit and rest. I have known a girl to sit idle twenty or thirty minutes at a time. They were not driven, and their work-a-day life was made easy. They were treated with consideration by their employers, and there was a feeling of respectful equality between them. The most favored of the girls were sometimes invited to the houses of the dignitaries of the mills, showing that the line of social division was not rigidly maintained.

Their life in the factory was made pleasant to them. In those days there was no need of advocating the doctrine of the proper relation between employer and employed. *Help was too valuable to be ill-treated.* If these early agents, or overseers, had been disposed to exercise undue authority, or to establish unjust or arbitrary laws, the high character of the operatives, and the fact that women employees were scarce would have prevented it. A certain agent of one of the first corporations in Lowell (an old sea-captain) said to one of his boarding-house keepers, "I should like to rule my help as I used to rule my sailors, but so many of them are women I do not dare to do it."

. . .

One of the first strikes of cotton-factory operatives that ever took place in this country was that in Lowell, in October, 1836. When it was announced that the wages were to be cut down, great indignation was felt, and it was decided to strike, *en masse.* This was done. The mills were shut down, and the girls went in procession from their several corporations to the "grove" on Chapel Hill, and listened to "incendiary" speeches from early labor reformers.

One of the girls stood on a pump, and gave vent to the feelings of her companions in a neat speech, declaring that it was their duty to resist all attempts at cutting down the wages. This was the first time a woman had spoken in public in Lowell, and the event caused surprise and consternation among her audience.

Cutting down the wages was not their only grievance, nor the only cause of this strike. Hitherto the corporations had paid twenty-five cents a week towards the board of each operative, and now it was their purpose to have the girls pay the sum; and this, in addition to the cut in wages, would make a difference of at least one dollar a week. It was estimated that as many as twelve or fifteen hundred girls turned out, and walked in procession through the streets. They had neither flags nor music, but sang songs, a favorite (but rather inappropriate) one being a parody on "I won't be a nun."

"Oh! isn't it a pity, such a pretty girl as I—
Should be sent to the factory to pine away and die?
Oh! I cannot be a slave,
I will not be a slave,
For I'm so fond of liberty
That I cannot be a slave."

My own recollection of this first strike (or "turn out" as it was called) is very vivid. I worked in a lower room, where I had heard the proposed strike fully, if not vehemently, discussed; I had been an ardent listener to what was said against this attempt at "oppression" on the part of the corporation, and naturally I took sides with the strikers. When the day came on which the girls were to turn out, those in the upper rooms started first, and so many of them left

that our mill was at once shut down. Then, when the girls in my room stood irresolute, uncertain what to do, asking each other, "Would you?" or "Shall we turn out?" and not one of them having the courage to lead off, I, who began to think they would not go out, after all their talk, became impatient, and started on ahead, saying, with childish bravado, "I don't care what you do, *I* am going to turn out, whether any one else does or not;" and I marched out, and was followed by the others.

As I looked back at the long line that followed me, I was more proud than I have ever been since at any success may have achieved, and more proud than I shall ever be again until my own beloved State gives to its women citizens the right of suffrage.

The agent of the corporation where I then worked took some small revenges on the supposed ringleaders; on the principle of sending the weaker to the wall, my mother was turned away from her boarding-house, that functionary saying, "Mrs. Hanson, you could not prevent the older girls from turning out, but your daughter is a child, and *her* you could control."

It is hardly necessary to say that so far as results were concerned this strike did no good. The dissatisfaction of the operatives subsided, or burned itself out, and though the authorities did not accede to their demands, the majority returned to their work, and the corporation went on cutting down the wages.

And after a time, as the wages became more and more reduced, the best portion of the girls left and went to their homes, or to the other employments that were fast opening to women, until there were very few of the old guard left; and thus the *status* of the factory population of New England gradually became what we know it to be today.

Document 7.4 Lucy Larcom Describes How Life Changed in New England

Despite the Boston Associates' claims, not all of their operatives were cheerful farm girls, choosing to leave home and enter the mills of their own accord, to direct their own future and gain independence. Often younger girls, tearful and not desiring a mill life, were forced into labor out of economic necessity. Lucy Larcom, like Harriet Robinson, was the daughter of a widow running a company boardinghouse. Her employment was not entirely her choice. After she left the mills, she moved to Illinois, attended college, taught school, and returned to New England and became a prolific author. What steps does she go through to start working? What does she leave behind that she regrets? How well does she like working in the mills?

During my father's life, a few years before my birth, his thoughts had been turned towards the new manufacturing town growing up on the banks of the Merrimack. He had once taken a journey there, with the possibility in his mind of making the place his home, his limited income furnishing no adequate promise of a maintenance for his large family of daughters. From the beginning, Lowell had a high reputation for good order, morality, piety, and all that was dear to the old-fashioned New Englander's heart.

After his death, my mother's thoughts naturally followed the direction his had taken; and seeing no other opening for herself, she sold her small estate, and moved to Lowell, with the intention of taking a corporation-house for mill-girl boarders. Some of the family objected, for the Old World traditions about factory life were anything but attractive; and they were current in New England until the experiment at Lowell had shown that independent and intelligent workers invariably give their own character to their occupation. My mother had visited Lowell, and she was willing and glad, knowing all about the place, to make it our home.

The change involved a great deal of work. "Boarders" signified a large house, many beds, and an indefinite number of people. Such piles of sewing accumulated before us! A sewing-bee, volunteered by the neighbors, reduced the quantity a little, and our child-fingers had to take their part. But the seams of those sheets did look to me as if they were miles long!

My sister Lida and I had our "stint"—so much to do every day. It was warm weather, and that made it the more tedious, for we wanted be running about the fields we were so soon to leave. One day, in sheer desperation, we dragged a sheet up with us into an apple-tree in the yard, and sat and sewed there through the summer afternoon, beguiling the irksomeness of our task by telling stories and guessing riddles.

It did not take long to turn over the new leaf of our home experience. One sunny day three of us children, my youngest sister, my brother John, and I, took with my mother the first stage-coach journey of our lives, across Lynnfield plains and over Andover hills to the banks of the Merrimack. We were set down before an empty house in a yet unfinished brick block, where we watched for the big wagon that was to bring our household goods.

It came at last; and the novelty of seeing our old furniture settled in new rooms kept us from being homesick. One after another they appeared,—bed-steads, chairs, tables, and, to me most welcome of all, the old mahogany secretary with brass-handled drawers, that had always stood in the "front room" at home. With it came the barrel full of books that had filled its shelves, and they took their places as naturally as if they had always lived in this strange town.

Other familiar articles journeyed with us: the brass-headed shovel and tongs, that it had been my especial task to keep bright; the two card-tables (which were as unacquainted as ourselves with ace, face, and trump); the two china mugs, with their eighteenth-century lady and gentleman figures, curiosities brought from over the sea; and reverently laid away by my mother with her choicest relics in the secretary-desk, my father's miniature, painted in Antwerp, a treasure only shown occasionally to us children as a holiday treat; and my mother's easy-chair,—I should have felt as if I had lost *her*, had that been left behind. The earliest unexpressed ambition of my infancy had been to grow up and wear a cap, and sit in an easy-chair knifing, and look comfortable, just as my mother did.

Filled up with these things, the little one-windowed sitting-room easily caught the home feeling and gave it back to us. Inanimate objects do gather into themselves something of the character of those who live among them, through association; and this alone makes heirlooms valuable. They are family treasures, because they are part of the family life, full of memories and inspirations. Bought or sold, they are nothing but old furniture. Nobody can buy the old associations; and nobody who has really felt how everything that has been in a home makes part of it, can willingly bargain away the old things.

My mother never thought of disposing of her best furniture, whatever her need. It traveled with her in every change of her abiding-place, as long as she lived, so that to us children home seemed to accompany her wherever she went. And, remaining yet in the family, it often brings back to me pleasant reminders of my childhood. No other Bible seems quite so sacred to me as the old Family Bible, out of which my father used to read when we were all gathered around him for worship. To turn its leaves and look at its pictures was one of our few Sabbath-day indulgences; and I cannot touch it now except with feelings of profound reverence.

For the first time in our lives, my little sister and I became pupils in a grammar school for both girls and boys, taught by a man. I was put with her into the

Lucy Larcom, *A New England Girlhood Outlined From Memory* [Boston: Houghton Mifflin, 1889], pp. 144–156.

sixth class, but was sent the very next day into the first. I did not belong in either, but somewhere between. And I was very uncomfortable in my promotion, for though the reading and spelling and grammar and geography were perfectly easy, I had never studied anything but mental arithmetic, and did not know how to "do a sum." We had to show, when called up to recite, a slateful of sums, "done" and "proved." No explanations were ever asked of us.

The girl who sat next to me saw my distress, and offered to do my sums for me. I accepted her proposal, feeling, however, that I was a miserable cheat. But I was afraid of the master, who was tall and gaunt, and used to stalk across the school-room, right over the desk-tops, to find out if there was any mischief going on. Once, having caught a boy annoying a seatmate with a pin, he punished the offender by pursuing him around the school-room, sticking a pin into shoulder whenever he could overtake him. And he had a fearful leather strap, which was sometimes used even upon the shrinking palm of a little girl. If he should find out that I was a pretender and deceiver, as I knew that I was, I could not guess what might happen to me. He never did, however. I was left unmolested in the ignorance which I deserved. But I never liked the girl who did my sums, and I fancied she had a decided contempt for me.

There was a friendly looking boy always sitting at the master's desk; they called him "the monitor." It was his place to assist scholars who were in trouble about their lessons, but I was too bashful to speak to him, or to ask assistance of anybody. I think that nobody learned much under that regime, and the whole school system was soon after entirely reorganized.

Our house was quickly filled with a large feminine family. As a child, the gulf between little girlhood and young womanhood had always looked to me very wide. I supposed we should get across it by some sudden jump, by and by. But among these new companions of all ages, from fifteen to thirty years, we slipped into womanhood without knowing when or how.

Most of my mother's boarders were from New Hampshire and Vermont, and there was a fresh, breezy sociability about them which made them seem almost like a different race of beings from any we children had hitherto known.

We helped a little about the housework, before and after school, making beds, trimming lamps, and washing dishes. The heaviest work was done by a strong Irish girl, my mother always attending to the cooking herself. She was, however, a better caterer than the circumstances required or permitted. She liked to make nice things for the table, and, having been accustomed to an abundant supply, could never learn to economize. At a dollar and a quarter a week for board, (the price allowed for mill-girls by the corpora-tions) great care in expenditure was necessary. It was not in my mother's nature closely to calculate costs, and in this way there came to be a continually increasing leak in the family purse. The older members of the family did everything they could, but it was not enough. I heard it said one day, in a distressed tone, "The children will have to leave school and go into the mill."

There were many pros and cons between my mother and sisters before this was positively decided. The mill-agent did not want to take us two little girls, but consented on condition we should be sure to attend school the full number of months prescribed each year. I, the younger one, was then between eleven and twelve years old.

I listened to all that was said about it, very much fearing that I should not be permitted to do the coveted work. For the feeling had already frequently come to me, that I was the one too many in the overcrowded family nest. Once, before we left our old home, I had heard a neighbor condoling with my mother because there were so many of us, and her emphatic reply had been a great relief to my mind:—

"There isn't one more than I want. I could not spare a single one of my children."

But her difficulties were increasing, and I thought it would be a pleasure to feel that I was not a trouble or burden or expense to anybody. So I went to my first day's work in the mill with a light heart. The novelty of it made seem easy, and it really was not hard, just to change the bobbins on the spinning-frames every three quarters of an hour or so, with half a dozen other little girls who were doing the same thing. When I came back at night, the family began to pity me for my long, tiresome day's work, but I laughed and said,—

"Why, it is nothing but fun. It is just like play."

And for a little while it was only a new amusement; I liked it better than going to school and "making believe" I was learning when I was not. And there was a great deal of play mixed with it. We were not occupied more than half the time. The intervals were spent frolicking around among the spinning-frames, teasing and talking to the older girls, or entertaining ourselves with games and stories in a corner, or exploring, with the overseer's permission, the mysteries of the carding-room, the dressing-room, and the weaving-room.

I never cared much for machinery. The buzzing and hissing and whizzing of pulleys and rollers and spindles and flyers around me often grew tiresome. I could not see into their complications, or feel interested in them. But in a room below us we were sometimes allowed to peer in through a sort of blind door at the great waterwheel that carried the works of the whole mill. It was so huge that we could only watch a few of its spokes at a time, and part of its dripping rim, moving with a slow, measured strength through the darkness that shut it in. It impressed me with something of the awe which comes to us in thinking of the great Power which keeps the mechanism of the universe in motion. Even now, the remembrance of its large, mysterious movement, in which every little motion of every noisy little wheel was involved, brings back to me a verse from one of my favorite hymns: —

"Our lives through various scenes are drawn,
And vexed by trifling cares,
While Thine eternal thought moves on
Thy undisturbed affairs."

There were compensations for being shut in to daily toil so early. The mill itself had its lessons for us. But it was not, and could not be, the right sort of life for a child, and we were happy in the knowledge that, at the longest, our employment was only to be temporary.

When I took my next three months at the grammar school, everything there was changed, and I too was changed. The teachers were kind and thorough in their instruction; and my mind seemed to have been ploughed up during that year of work, so that knowledge took root in it easily. It was a great delight to me to study, and at the end of the three months the master told me that I was prepared for the high school.

But alas! I could not go. The little money I could earn—one dollar a week, besides the price of my board—was needed in the family, and I must return to the mill. It was a severe disappointment to me, though I did not say so at home. I did not at all accept the conclusion of a neighbor whom I heard talking about it with my mother. His daughter was going to the high school,—and my mother was telling him how sorry she was that I could not.

"Oh," he said, in a soothing tone, "my girl hasn't got any such head-piece as yours has. Your girl doesn't need to go."

Of course I knew that whatever sort of a "head-piece" I had, I did need and want just that very opportunity to study. I think the resolution was then formed, inwardly, that I *would* go to school again, some time, whatever happened. I went back to my work, but now without enthusiasm. I had looked through an open door that I was not willing to see shut upon me.

Document 7.5 Mary Paul Corresponds about Life in the Mills

New England farm girls were among the most literate group in the early republic. Letter writers often expressed concerns about events outside of the factory, while sharing descriptions of life on the inside. Mary Paul worked as a domestic in Bridgewater, Vermont before entering the mills in 1845, where she worked on and off for the next four years. In her late teens she returned home to care for her ill father, moved to New Jersey, and started a coat-making business with a contact from mill days, and then became a housekeeper in New Hampshire. Eventually she married the son of her factory boardinghouse keeper and became a New England housewife. What concerns does Mary talk about in her letters? What problems occurring at the mill does she describe? How important is her family, based on the topics in the letters?

———

Lowell Dec 21st 1845
Dear Father
I received your letter on Thursday the 14th with much pleasure. I am well which is one comfort. My life and health are spared while others are cut off. Last Thursday one girl fell down and broke her neck which caused instant death. She was going in or coming out of the mill and slipped down it being very icy. The same day a man was killed by the cars. Another had nearly all of his ribs broken. Another was nearly killed by falling down and having a bale of cotton fall on him. Last Tuesday we were paid. In all I had six dollars and sixty cents paid $4.68 for board. With the rest I got me a pair of rubbers and a pair of 50.cts

Mary Paul letters in Thomas Dublin ed. *Farm to Factory: Women's Letters, 1830–1860 2e* [New York: Columbia University Press, 1993], pp. 126–131.

shoes. Next payment I am to have a dollar a week beside my board. We have not had much snow the deepest being not more than 4 inches. It has been very warm for winter. Perhaps you would like something about our regulations about going in and coming out of the mill. At 5 o'clock in the morning the bell rings for the folks to get up and get breakfast. At half past six it rings for the girls to get up and at seven they are called into the mill. At half past 12 we have dinner are called back again at one and stay till half past seven. I get along very well with my work. I can doff as fast as any girl in our room. I think I shall have frames before long. The usual time allowed for learning is six months but I think I shall have frames before I have been in three as I get along so fast. I think that the factory is the best place for me and if any girl wants employment I advise them to come to Lowell. Tell Harriet that though she does not hear from me she is not forgotten. I have little time to devote to writing that I cannot write all I want to. There are half a dozen letters which I ought to write to day but I have not time. Tell Harriet I send my love to her and all of the girls. Give my love to Mrs. Clement. Tell Henry this will answer for him and you too for this time.

This from
Mary S Paul

Bela Paul
Henry S Paul

———————

Lowell April 12th 1846

Dear Father

I received your letter with much pleasure but was sorry to hear that you had been lame. I had waited for a long time to hear from you but no letter came so last Sunday I thought I would write again which I did and was going to send it to the [post] office Monday but at noon I received a letter from William and so I did not send it at all. Last Friday I received a letter from you. You wanted to know what I am doing. I am at work in a spinning room and tending four sides of warp which is one girls work. The overseer tells me that he never had a girl get along better than I do and that he will do the best he can by me. I stand it well, though they tell me that I am growing very poor. I was paid nine shillings a week last payment and am to have more this one though we have been out considerable for backwater which will take off a good deal. The Agent promises to pay us nearly as much as we should have made but I do not think that he will. The payment was up last night and we are to be paid this week. I have a

very good boarding place have enough to eat and that which is good enough. The girls are all kind and obliging. The girls that I room with are all from Vermont and good girls too. Now I will tell you about our rules at the boarding house. We have none in particular except that we have to go to bed about 10 o'clock. At half past 4 in the morning the bell rings for us to get up and at five for us to go into the mill. At seven we are called out to breakfast are allowed half an hour between bells and the same at noon till the first of May when we have three quarters [of an hour] till the first of September. We have dinner at half past 12 and supper at seven. If Julius should go to Boston tell him to come this way and see me. He must come to the Lawrence Counting room and call for me. He can ask some one to show him where the Lawrence is. I hope he will not fail to go. I forgot to tell you that I have not seen a particle of snow for six weeks and it is settled going we have had a very mild winter and but little snow. I saw Ann Hersey last Sunday. I did not know her till she told me who she was. I see the Griffith girls often. I received a letter from a girl in Bridgewater in which she told me that Mrs. Angell had heard some way that I could not get work and that she was much pleased and said that I was so bad that no one would have me. I believe I have written all so I will close for I have a letter to write to William this afternoon.

Yours affectionately
Mary S Paul

Mr. Bela Paul
P.S. Give my love to all that enquire for me and tell them to write me a long long letter. Tell Harriet I shall send her a paper.

———————

Lowell Nov 5th 1848

Dear Father

Doubtless you have been looking for a letter from me all the week past. I would have written but wished to find whether I should be able to stand it— to do the work that I am now doing. I was unable to get my old place in the cloth room on the Suffolk or on any other corporation. I next tried the dressrooms on the Lawrence Cor[poration], but did not succe[e]d in getting a place. I almost concluded to give up and go back to Claremont, but thought I would try once more. So I went to my old overseer on the Tremont Cor. I had no idea that he would want one, but he *did*, and I went to work last Tuesday—warping—the same work I used to do.

It is *very* hard indeed and sometimes I think I shall not be able to endure it. I never worked so hard in my life but perhaps I shall get used to it. I shall try hard to do so for there is no other work that I can do unless I spin and that I shall not undertake on any account. I presume you have heard before this that the wages are to be reduced on the 20th of this month. It is *true* and there seems to be a good deal of excitement on the subject but I can not tell what will be the consequence. The companies pretend they are losing immense sums every *day* and therefore they are obliged to lessen the wages, but this seems perfectly absurd to me for they are constantly making *repairs* and it seems to me that this would not be if there were really any danger of their being obliged to *stop the mills*.

It is very difficult for anyone to get into the mill on any corporation. All seem to be very full of help. I expect to be paid about two dollars a week but it will be dearly earned. I cannot tell how it is but never since I have worked in the mill have I been so very tired as I have for the last week but it may be owing to the long rest I have had for the last six months. I have not told you that I do not board on the Lawrence. The reason of this is because I wish to be nearer the mill and I do not wish to pay the extra \$.12-1/2 per week (I should not be obliged to do it if I boarded at 15) and I know that they are not able to give it me. Beside this I am so near I can go and see them as often as I wish. So considering all things I think I have done the best I could. I do not like here very well and am very sure I never shall as well as at Mother Guilds. I can now realize how very kind the whole family have ever been to me. It seems like going *home* when I go there which is every day. But now I see I have not told you yet where I do board. It is at No. 5 Tremont Corporation. Please enlighten all who wish for information. There is one thing which I forgot to bring with me and which I want very much. That is my *rubbers*. They hang in the back room at uncle Jerrys. If Olive comes down here I presume you can send them by her, but if you should not have the opportunity to send them do not trouble yourself about them. There is another thing I wish to mention—about my fare down here. If you paid it all the way as I understand you did there is something wrong about it. When we stopped at Concord to take the cars, I went to the ticket office to get a ticket which I knew I should be obliged to have. When I called for it I told the man that my fare to Lowell was paid all the way and I wanted a ticket to Lowell. He told me if this was the case the Stagedriver would get the ticket for me and I supposed of course he would. But he did *not*, and when the ticket master called for my ticket in the *cars*, I was obliged to give him a dollar. Sometimes I have thought that the fare might *not* have been paid beside farther than Concord. If this is the case all is right. But if it is not, then I have paid a dollar too much and gained the character of trying to cheat the company out of my fare, for the man thought I was lying to him. I suppose I want to know how it is and wish it could be settled for I do not like that *any* one should think *me* capable of such a thing, even though that person be an utter stranger. But enough of this. The Whigs of Lowell had a great time on the night of the 3rd. They had an immense procession of men on foot bearing *torches* and *banners* got up for the occasion. The houses were illuminated (Whigs houses) and by the way I should think the whole of *Lowell* were Whigs. I went out to see the illuminations and they did truly look splendid. The Merrimack house was illuminated from attic to cellar. Every pane of glass in the house had a half candle to it and there were many others lighted in the same way. One entire block on the Merrimack Cor[poration] with the exception of one tenement which doubtless was occupied by a free soiler who would not illuminate on any account whatever.

(Monday Eve) I have been to work today and think I shall manage to get along with the work. I am not so tired as I was last week. I have not yet found out what wages I shall get but presume they will be about \$2.00 per week exclusive of board. I think of nothing further to write excepting I wish you to prevail on *Henry* to write to me, also tell *Olive* to write and *Eveline* when she comes.

Give my love to uncle Jerry and aunt Betsey and tell little Lois that "Cousin Carra" thanks her very much for the *apple* she sent her. Her health is about the same that it was when she was at Claremont. No one has much hope of her ever being any better.

Write soon. Yours affectionately
Mary S Paul

Document 7.6 "Susan" Defends Life in the Mills and the Mill Girls' Reputations

The *Lowell Offering* was a literary magazine published by supporters of the mills and their owners in Lowell. The letters, essays, and stories, mostly creations of the operatives themselves, were edited by Harriet Farley, a former operative who contributed many articles and then was hired to edit the magazine. Some of the selections were poetry, stories of nature, and fiction, but some described life in the mills. Many letters praised life in the mills, claiming the operatives all took jobs for selfless or charitable reasons, and insisting that mill work was an enlightening experience for women. Most critical descriptions of conditions were rejected by editor Farley, who believed management worked for the good of the employees. The "letters from Susan" are correspondence between a fictional operative and her home. They were actually written by Farley to defend the reputation of the employers. Based on the letters, how happy is "Susan" with her job? How does she describe the other workers? Do they, in her opinion, have any legitimate complaints?

Letters from Susan

LETTER SECOND

Lowell, April ___, ____.

Dear Mary: In my last I told you I would write again, and say more of my life here; and this I will now attempt to do.

I went into the mill to work a few days after I wrote to you. It looked very pleasant at first, the rooms were so light, spacious, and clean, the girls so pretty and neatly dressed, and the machinery so brightly polished or nicely painted. The plants in the windows, or on the overseer's bench or desk, gave a pleasant aspect to things. You will wish to know what work I am doing. I will tell you of the different kinds of work.

There is, first, the carding-room, where the cotton flies most, and the girls get the dirtiest. But this is easy, and the females are allowed time to go out at night before the bell rings—on Saturday night at least, if not on all other nights. Then there is the spinning-room, which is very neat and pretty. In this room are the spinners and doffers. The spinners watch the frames; keep them clean, and the threads mended if they break. The doffers take off the full bobbins, and put on the empty ones. They have nothing to do in the long intervals when the frames are in motion, and can go out to their boardinghouses, or do any thing else that they like. In some of the factories the spinners do

their own doffing, and when this is the ease they work no harder than the weavers. These last have the hardest time of all—or can have, if they choose to take charge of three or four looms, instead of the one pair which is the allotment. And they are the most constantly confined. The spinners and dressers have but the weavers to keep supplied, and then their work can stop. The dressers never work before breakfast, and they stay out a great deal in the afternoons. The drawers-in, or girls who draw the threads through the harnesses, also work in the dressing-room, and they all have very good wages—better than the weavers who have but the usual work. The dressing-rooms are very neat, and the frames move with a gentle undulating motion which is really graceful. But these rooms are kept very warm, and are disagreeably scented with the "sizing," or starch, which stiffens the "beams," or unwoven webs. There are many plants in these rooms, and it is really a good green-house for them. The dressers are generally quite tall girls, and must have pretty tall minds too, as their work requires much care and attention.

I could have had work in the dressing-room, but chose to be a weaver; and I will tell you why. I disliked the closer air of the dressing-room, though I might have become accustomed to that. I could not learn to dress so quickly as I could to weave, nor have work of my own so soon, and should have had to stay with Mrs. C. two or three weeks before I could go in at all, and I did not like to be "lying upon my oars" so long.

"Letters from Susan" in Benita Eisler ed. *The Lowell Offering: Writings by New England Mill Women* [New York: Harper & Row, 1977], pp. 51–60.

And, more than this, when I get well learned I can have extra work, and make double wages, which you know is quite an inducement with some.

Well, I went into the mill, and was put to learn with a very patient girl—a clever old maid. I should be willing to be one myself if I could be as good as she is. You cannot think how odd every thing seemed to me. I wanted to laugh at every thing, but did not know what to make sport of first. They set me to threading shuttles, and tying weaver's knots and such things, and now I have improved so that I can take care of one loom. I could take care of two if I only had eyes in the back part of my head, but I have not got used to "looking two ways of a Sunday" yet.

At first the hours seemed very long, but I was so interested in learning that I endured it very well; and when I went out at night the sound of the mill was in my ears, as of crickets, frogs, and jewsharps, all mingled together in strange discord. After that it seemed as though cotton-wool was in my ears, but now I do not mind at all. You know that people learn to sleep with the thunder of Niagara in "their ears, and a cotton mill is no worse, though you wonder that we do not have to hold our breath in such a noise.

It makes my feet ache and swell to stand so much, but I suppose I shall get accustomed to that too. The girls generally wear old shoes about their work, and you know nothing is easier; but they almost all say that when they have worked here a year or two they have to procure shoes a size or two larger than before they came. The right hand, which is the one used in stopping and starting the loom, becomes larger than the left; but in other respects the factory is not detrimental to a young girl's appearance. Here they look delicate, but not sickly; they laugh at those who are much exposed, and get pretty brown; but I, for one, had rather be brown than pure white. I never saw so many pretty looking girls as there are here. Though the number of men is small in proportion there are many marriages here, and a great deal of courting. I will tell you of this last sometime.

You wish to know minutely of our hours of labor. We go in at five o'clock; at seven we come out to breakfast; at half-past seven we return to our work, and stay until half-past twelve. At one, or quarter-past one four months in the year, we return to our work, and stay until seven at night. Then the evening is all our own, which is more than some laboring girls can say, who think nothing is more tedious than a factory life.

When I first came here, which was the last of February, the girls ate their breakfast before they went to their work. The first of March they came out at the present breakfast hour, and the twentieth of March they ceased to "light up" the rooms, and come out between six and seven o'clock.

You ask if the girls are contented here: I ask you, if you know of *any one* who is perfectly contented. Do you remember the old story of the philosopher, who offered a field to the person who was contented with his lot; and, when one claimed it, he asked him why, if he was so perfectly satisfied, he wanted his field. The girls here are not contented; and there is no disadvantage in their situation which they do not perceive as quickly, and lament as loudly, as the sternest opponents of the factory system do. They would scorn to say they were contented, if asked the question; for it would compromise their Yankee spirit—their pride, penetration, independence, and love of "freedom and equality" to say that they were *contented* with such a life as this. Yet, withal, they are cheerful. I never saw a happier set of beings. They appear blithe in the mill, and out of it. If you see one of them, with a very long face, you may be sure that it is because she has heard bad news from home, or because her beau has vexed her. But, if it is a Lowell trouble, it is because she has failed in getting off as many "sets" or "pieces" as she intended to have done; or because she had a sad "break-out," or "break-down," in her work, or something of that sort.

You ask if the work is not disagreeable. Not when one is accustomed to it. It tried my patience sadly at first, and does now when it does not run well; but, in general, I like it very much. It is easy to do, and does not require very violent exertion, as much of our farm work does.

You also ask how I get along with the girls here. Very well indeed; only we came near having a little flurry once. You know I told you I lodged in the "long attic." Well, a little while ago, there was a place vacated in a pleasant lower chamber. Mrs. C. said that it was my "chum's" turn to go down stairs to lodge, unless she would waive her claim in favor of me. You must know that here they get up in the world by getting down, which is what the boys in our debating society used to call a paradox. Clara, that is the girl's name, was not at all disposed to give up her rights, but maintained them staunchly. I had nothing to do about it—the girls in the lower room liked me, and disliked Clara, and were determined that it should not be at all pleasant weather there if she did come. Mrs. C. was in a dilemma. Clara's turn came first. The other two girls in the chamber were sisters, and would not separate, so they were out of the question. I wanted to go, and knew Clara would not be happy with them. But I thought what was my duty to do. She was not happy now, and would not be if deprived of her privilege. She had looked black at me for several days, and slept with her face to the wall as many nights. I went up to her and said, "Clara, take your things down into the lower chamber, and tell the girls that *I will not come*. It is your turn now, and mine will come in good time."

Clara was mollified in an instant. "No," said she; "I will not go now. They do not wish me to come, and I had rather stay here." After this we had quite a contest—I trying to persuade Clara to go, and she trying to persuade me, and I "*got beat.*" So now I have a pleasanter room, and am quite favorite with all the girls. They have given me some pretty plants, and they go out with me whenever I wish it, so that I feel quite happy.

You think we must live very nice here to have plum-cake, &c. The plum-cake, and crackers, and such things as the bakers bring upon the corporations, are not as nice as we have in the country, and I presume are much cheaper. I seldom eat any thing that is not cooked in the family. I should not like to tell you the stories they circulate here about the bakers, unless I *knew* that they were true. Their brown bread is the best thing that I have tasted of their baking.

You see that I have been quite *minute* in this letter, though I hardly liked your showing the former to old Deacon Gale, and 'Squire Smith, and those old men. It makes me feel afraid to write you all I should like to, when I think so many eyes are to pore over my humble sheet. But if their motives are good, and they can excuse all defects, why I will not forbid.

'Squire Smith wishes to know what sort of men our superintendents are. I know very well what he thinks of them, and what their reputation is up our way. I am not personally acquainted with any of them; but, from what I hear, I have a good opinion of them. I suppose they are not faultless, neither are those whom they superintend; but they are not the overbearing tyrants which, many suppose them to be. The abuse of them, which I hear, is so very low that I think it must be unjust and untrue; and I do frequently hear them spoken of as *men*—whole-hearted full-souled men. Tell 'Squire Smith they are not what he would be in their places—that they treat their operatives better than he does his "hired girls," and associate with them on terms of as much equality. But I will tell you who are almost universally unpopular: the "runners," as they are called, or counting-room boys. I suppose they are little whipper-snappers who will grow better as they grow older.

My paper is filling up, and I must close by begging your pardon for speaking of the Methodists as having lost their simplicity of attire. It was true, nevertheless, for I have not seen one of the old "Simon Pure" Methodist bonnets since I have been here. But they may be as consistent as other denominations. Had few of us follow in the steps of the primitive Christians.

Yours as ever,
Susan

Letters from Susan

LETTER THIRD

Lowell, July ___, ____.

Dear Mary: You complain that I do not keep my promise of being a good correspondent, but if you could know how sultry it is here, and how fatigued I am by my work this warm weather, you would not blame me. It is now that I begin to dislike these hot brick pavements, and glaring buildings. I want to be at home—to go down to the brook over which the wild grapes have made a natural arbor, and to sit by the cool spring around which the fresh soft brakes cluster so lovingly. I think of the time when, with my little bare feet, I used to follow in aunt Nabby's footsteps through the fields of corn—stepping high and long till we came to the bleaching ground; and I remember—but I must stop, for I know you wish me to write of what I am now doing, as you already know of what I have done.

Well; I go to work every day—not earlier than I should at home, nor do I work later, but I mind the confinement more than I should in a more unpleasant season of the year. I have extra work now—I take care of three looms; and when I wrote you before I could not well take care of two. But help is very scarce now, and they let us do as much work as we please; and I am highly complimented upon my "powers of execution." Many of the girls go to their country homes in the summer. The majority of the operatives are country girls. These have always the preference, because, in the fluctuations to which manufactures are liable, there would be much less distress among a population who could resort to other homes, than if their entire interest was in the city. And in the summer these girls go to rest, and recruit themselves for another "yearly campaign"—not a bad idea in them either. I shall come home next summer; I have been here too short a time to make it worth while now. I wish they would have a *vacation* in "dog days"—stop the mills, and *make* all the girls rest; and let their "menfolks" do up their "ditching," or whatever else it is they now do Sundays.

But these mills are not such dreadful places as you imagine them to be. You think them dark damp holes; as close and black as—as the Black Hole at Calcutta. Now, dear M., it is no such thing. They are high spacious well-built edifices, with neat paths around them, and beautiful plots of greensward. These are kept fresh by the "force-pumps" belonging to every corporation. And some of the corporations have beautiful flower gardens connected with the factories. One of the overseers, with whom I am acquainted, gave me a beautiful bouquet the other morning, which was radiant with all the colors of the rainbow, and fragrant with the sweet perfume of many kinds of mints and roses. He has a succession of beautiful blossoms from spring till "cold weather." He told me that he could raise enough to bring him fifty dollars if he chose to sell them; and this from a little bit of sand not larger than our front yard, which you know is small for a country house. But it is so full—here a few dollars have brought on a fresh soil, and "patience has done its perfect work." What might not be accomplished in the country with a little industry and taste.

But I have said enough of the outside of our mills—now for the inside. The rooms are high, very light, kept nicely whitewashed, and extremely neat; with many plants in the window seats, and white cotton curtains to the windows. The machinery is very handsomely made and painted, and is placed in regular rows; thus, in a large mill, presenting a beautiful and uniform appearance. I have sometimes stood at one end of a row of green looms, when the girls were gone from between them, and seen the lathes moving back and forth, the harnesses up and down, the white cloth winding over the rollers, through the long perspective; and I have thought it beautiful.

Then the girls dress so neatly, and are so pretty. The mill girls are the prettiest in the city. You wonder how they can keep neat. Why not? There are no restrictions as to the number of pieces to be washed in the boarding-house. And, as there is plenty of water in the mill, the girls can wash their laces and muslins and other nice things themselves, and no boarding woman ever refuses the conveniences for starching and ironing. You say too that you do not see how we can have so many conveniences and comforts at the price we pay for board. You must remember that the boarding-houses belong to the companies, and are let to the tenants far below the usual city rent—sometimes the rent is remitted. Then there are large families, so that there are the profits of many individuals. The country farmers are quite in the habit of bringing their produce to the boarding-houses for sale, thus reducing the price by the omission of the market-man's profit, So you see there are many ways by which we get along so well.

You ask me how the girls behave in the mill, and what are the punishments. They behave very well while about their work, and I have never heard of punishments, or scoldings, or anything of that sort. Sometimes an overseer finds fault, and sometimes offends a girl by refusing to let her stay out of the mill, or some deprivation like that; and then, perhaps, there are tears and pouts on her part, but, in general, the tone of intercourse between the girls and overseers is very good—pleasant, yet respectful. When the latter are fatherly sort of men the girls frequently resort to them for advice and assistance about other affairs than their work. Very seldom is this confidence abused; but, among the thousands of overseers who have lived in Lowell, and the tens of thousands of girls who have in time been here, there are legends still told of wrong suffered and committed. "To err is human," and when the frailties of humanity are exhibited by a factory girl it is thought of for worse than are the errors of any other persons.

The only punishment among the girls is dismission from their places. They do not, as many think, withhold their wages; and as for corporal punishment—mercy on me! To strike a female would cost any overseer his place. If the superintendents did not take the affair into consideration the girls would turn out, as they did at the Temperance celebration, "Independent day;" and if they didn't look as pretty, I am sure they would produce as deep an impression.

By the way, I almost forgot to tell you that we had a "Fourth of July" in Lowell, and a nice one it was too. The Temperance celebration was the chief dish in the entertainment. The chief, did I say? It was almost the whole. It was the great turkey that Scroggs sent for Bob Cratchet's Christmas dinner. But, perhaps you don't read Dickens, so I will make no more "classical allusions." In the evening we had the Hutchinsons, from our own Granite State, who discoursed sweet music so sweetly. They have become great favorites with the public. It is not on account of their fine voices only, but their pleasant modest manners—the perfect sense of propriety which they exhibit in all their demeanor; and I think they are not less popular *here* because they sing the wrongs of the slave, and the praises of cold water.

But, dear Mary, I fear I have tired you with this long letter, and yet I have not answered half your questions. Do you wish to hear anything more about the Overseers? Once for all, then, there are many very likely intelligent public-spirited men among them. They are interested in the good movements of the day; teachers in the Sabbath schools; and some have represented the city in the State Legislature. They usually marry among the factory girls, and do not connect themselves with their inferiors either. Indeed, in almost all the matches here the female is superior in education and manner, if not in intellect, to her partner.

The overseers have good salaries, and their families live very prettily. I observe that in almost all cases the mill girls make excellent wives. They are good managers, orderly in their households, and "neat as waxwork." It seems as though they were so delighted to have houses of their own to take care of, that they would never weary of the labor and the care.

The boarding women you ask about. They are usually widows or single women from the country; and many questions are always asked, and references required, before a house is given to a new applicant. It is true that mistakes are sometimes made, and *the wrong person gets into the pew, but*

"Things like this you know must be,"
Where'er there is a factory.

I see I have given you rhyme; it is not all quotation, nor *entirely original.*

I think it requires quite a complication of good qualities to make up a good boarding woman. "She looks well to the ways of her household," and must be even more than all that King Solomon describes in the last chapter of Proverbs. She not only in winter "riseth while it is yet night, and giveth meat to her household, a portion to her maidens," but she sitteth up far into the night, and seeth that her maidens are asleep, and that their lamps are gone out. Perhaps she doth not "consider a field to buy it," but she considereth every piece of meat, and bushel of potatoes, and barrel of flour, and load of wood, and box of soap, and every little thing, whether its quantity, quality, and price are what discretion would recommend her to purchase. "She is not afraid of the snow for her household," for she maketh them wear rubber overshoes, and thick cloaks and hoods, and seeth that the paths are broken out. "Her clothing is silk and purple," and she looketh neat and comely. It may be that her husband sitteth not "in the gates," for it is too often the case that he hath abandoned her, or loafeth in the streets. "She openeth her mouth with wisdom, and in her tongue is the law of kindness." Her maidens go to her for counsel and sympathy, if a decayed tooth begins to jump, or a lover proves faithless; and to keep twoscore young maidens in peace with themselves, each other, and her own self, is no slight task. The price of such a woman is, indeed, *above rubies.* "Give her of the fruit of her hands, and let her own works praise her."

I have now told you of mill girls, overseers and their wives, and boarding-housekeepers, and I feel that I have won forgiveness for neglecting you so long. You think that I have too high an opinion of our superintendents. I hope not. I do think that many of them are chosen as combining, in their characters, many excellent qualities. Some of them may be as selfish as you suppose. But we must remember that they owe a duty to their employers, as well as to those they employ. They are agents of the companies, as well as superintendents of us. Where those duties conflict I hope the sympathies of the man will always be with the more dependent party.

Country people are very suspicious. I do not think them perfect. A poet will look at a wood-cutter, and say "there is an honest man;" and as likely as not the middle of his load is rotten punk, and crooked sticks make many interstices, while all looks well without. A rustic butcher slays an animal that is dying of disease, and carries his meat to the market. The butcher and the woodman meet, and say all manner of harsh things against the *"grandees"* of the city, and quote such poetry as,

"God made the country—
Man made the town," &c.

It is true that with the same disposition for villany the man of influence must do the most harm. But, where there is most light, may there not be most true knowledge? And, even if there is no more principle, may there not be, with more cultivation of mind, a feeling of honor and of self-respect which may be of some benefit in its stead.

But I have written till I am fairly wearied. Good by.

Yours always,
Susan
(*Harriet Farley, Vol. IV, 1844 , pp. 237–240*)

Document 7.7 Amelia Sargent Describes "Lowell Slavery"

As related on previous pages, conditions in the mills worsened as years went on. The women in Lowell responded by organizing the Lowell Female Labor Reform Association, conducting work stoppages, and making appeals for freedom and justice. They asserted that corporate actions threatened their status as free daughters of the Revolutionary generation, as well as depriving them of their economic independence. Sarah Bagley edited the *Voice of Industry*, a publication for factory workers that discussed the worsening factory conditions. She also spearheaded a movement to limit the work day to ten hours for health reasons, testifying in front of the Massachusetts legislature. The following is written by Amelia Sargent, a member of the Association. What evidence does she give of worsening work conditions? How does her writing support the charge that management is undermining the well-being of its female employees?

For the purpose of illustration, let us go with that light-hearted, joyous young girl who is about for the first time to leave the home of her childhood; that home around which clusters so many beautiful and holy associations, pleasant memories, and quiet joys; to leave, too, a mother's cheerful smile, a father's care and protection; and wend her way toward this far famed "city of spindles," this promised land of the imagination, in whose praise she has doubtless heard so much.

Let us trace her progress during her first year's residence, and see whether she indeed realizes those golden prospects which have been held out to her. Follow her now as she enters that large gloomy looking building—she is in search of employment, and has been told that she might here obtain an eligible situation. She is sadly wearied with her journey, and withal somewhat annoyed by the noise, confusion, and strange faces all around her. So, after a brief conversation with the overseer, she concludes to accept the first situation which offers; and reserving to herself a sufficient portion of time in which to obtain the necessary rest after her unwanted exertions, and the gratification of a strangers curiosity regarding the place in which she is now to make her future home, she retires to her boarding house, to arrange matters as much to her mind as may be.

The intervening time passes rapidly away, and she soon finds herself once more within the confines of that close noisy apartment, and is forthwith installed in her new situation—first, however, premising that she has been sent to the Counting-room, and receives there from a Regulation paper, containing

the rules by which she must be governed while in their employ; and lo! here is the beginning of mischief; for in addition to the tyrannous and oppressive rules which meet her astonished eyes, she finds herself compelled to remain for the space of twelve months in the very place she then occupies, however reasonable and just cause of complaint might be hers, or however strong the wish for dismission; thus, in fact constituting herself a slave, a very slave to the caprices of him for whom she labors. Several incidents coming to the knowledge of the writer, might be somewhat interesting in this connection, as tending to show the prejudicial influence exerted upon the interests of the operative by this unjust requisition. The first is of a lady who has been engaged as an operative for a number of years, and recently entered a weaving room on the Massachusetts Corporation; the overseer having assured her previous to her entrance, that she should realize the sum of $2.25 per week, exclusive of board; which she finding it impossible to do, appealed to the Counting-room for a line enabling her to engage elsewhere, but it was peremptorily refused.

The next is of a more general bearing, concerning quite a number of individuals employed on the Lawrence Corporation, where the owners have recently erected and put in motion a new mill, at the same time stopping one of the old, in which said persons were employed. Now as they did not voluntarily leave their situations, but were discharged therefrom on account of suspension of operations by the company; they had an undoubted right to choose their own place of labor; and as the work in the new mill is

Amelia Sargent, "Lowell Slavery" in *Factory Life as it Is: Factory Traits No. 1* [Lowell, MA: Female Labor Reform Association, 1845], pp. 4–7.

vastly more laborious, and the wages less than can be obtained in many parts of the city, they signified their wish to go elsewhere, but are insolently told that they shall labor there or not at all; and will not be released until their year has expired, when if they can *possibly* find *no* further excuse for delay, they *may* deign to bestow upon them what is in common parlance termed a "regular discharge;" thus enabling them to pass from one prison house to another. Concerning this precious document, it is only necessary to say, that it very precisely reminds one of that which the dealers in human flesh at the South are wont to give and receive as the transfer of one piece of property from one owner to another.

Now, reader, what think you? is not this the height of the beautiful? and are not we operatives an ungrateful set of creatures that we do not properly appreciate and be highly thankful for such unparalleled generosity on the part of our employers!

But to return to our toiling Maiden,—the next beautiful feature which she discovers in this *glorious* system is, the long number of hours which she is obliged to spend in the above named close, unwholesome apartment. It is not enough, that like the poor peasant of Ireland, or the Russian serf who labors from sun to sun, but during one half of the year, she must still continue to toil on, long after Nature's lamp has ceased to lend its aid—not will even this suffice to satisfy the grasping avarice of her employer; for she is also through the winter months required to rise, partake of her morning meal, and be at her station in the mill, while the sun is yet sleeping behind the eastern hills; thus working on an average, at least twelve hours and three fourths per day, exclusive of the time allotted for her hasty meals, which is in winter simply one half hour at noon,—in the spring is allowed the same at morn, and during the summer is added 15 minutes to the half hour at noon. Then too, when she is at last released from her wearisome day's toil, still may she not depart in peace. No! Her footsteps must be dogged to see that they do not stray beyond the corporation limits, and she *must*, whether she will or no, be subjected to the manifold inconveniences of a large crowded boarding-house, where too, the price, paid for her accommodation is so utterly insignificant, that it will not ensure to her the common comforts of life; she is obliged to sleep in a small comfortless, half ventilated apartment containing some half a dozen occupants each; but no matter, *she is an operative*—it is all well enough for her; there is no "abuse" about it; no, indeed; so think our employers—but do we think so? Time will show. Here, too, comes up a case which strikingly illustrates the petty tyranny of the employer. A little girl, some 12 or 13 years of age, the daughter of a poor widow, dependent on her daily toil for a livelihood, worked on one of the Corporations, boarding with her mother; who dying left her to the care of an aunt, residing but a few steps from the Corporation—but the poor little creature all unqualified as she was, to provide for her own wants, was *compelled* to leave her home and the motherly care bestowed upon her, and enter one of those same large crowded boarding-houses. We do but give the facts in this case and they need no comment for every one *must* see the utter heartlessness which prompted such conduct toward a mere child.

Reader will you pronounce this a mere fancy sketch, written for the sake of effect? It is not so. It is a real picture of "Factory life;" nor is it one half so bad as might truthfully and justly have been drawn. But it has been asked, and doubtless will be again, why, if these evils are so aggravating, have they been so long and so peacefully borne? Ah! and why have they? It is a question well worthy of our consideration, and we would call upon every operative in *our* city, aye, throughout the length and breadth of the land to awake from the lethargy which has fallen upon them, and assert and maintain their rights. We call upon you for action—*united and immediate action*. But, says one, let us wait till we are stronger. In the language of one of old, we ask, when shall we be stronger? Will it be the next week, or the next year? Will it be when we are reduced to the servile condition of the poor operatives of England? for verily we shall be and that right soon, if matters be suffered to remain as they are. Says another, how shall we act? we are but one amongst a thousand, what shall we do that our influence may be felt in this vast multitude? We answer, there is in this city an Association called the Female Labor Reform Association, having for its professed object, the amelioration of the condition of the operative. Enrolled upon its records are the names of five hundred members—come then, and add thereto five hundred or rather five thousand more, and in the strength of our united influence we will soon show these *drivelling* cotton lords, this mushroom aristocracy of New England, who so arrogantly aspire to lord it over God's heritage, that our rights cannot be trampled upon with impunity; that we WILL not longer submit to that arbitrary power which has for the last ten years been so abundantly exercised over us.

One word ere we close, to the hardy independent yeomanry and mechanics, among the Granite Hills of New Hampshire, the woody forests of Maine, the cloud capped mountains of Vermont, and the busy, bustling towns of the old Bay State—ye! who have daughters and sisters toiling in those sickly prison-houses which are scattered far and wide over each of these States, we appeal to *you* for aid in this matter. Do you ask how that aid can be administered? We answer through the Ballot Box: Yes! if you have one spark of sympathy for our condition, carry it *there*, and see to it that you send to preside in the Councils of each Commonwealth, men who have hearts as well as heads, souls as well bodies; men who will watch zealously over the interests of the laborer in every department; who will protect him by the strong arm of the law from the encroachments of arbitrary power; who will see that he is not deprived of those rights and privileges which God and Nature have bestowed upon him—yes,

> From every rolling river,
>   From mountain, vale and plain,
> We call on you to deliver
>   Us, From the tyrant's chain:

And shall we call in vain! We trust not. More anon.

Amelia

Document 7.8 Ely Moore on the Need of Workers to Unionize

Besides changing the lives of family farmers and promoting immigration and the growth of cities, new technology and the factory system fundamentally changes the traditional social relations between workers and employers, and significantly reduced the opportunities for ownership by workers. As workers saw conditions deteriorate and their futures disappear, they equated the new industrial poverty with anti-democracy, considering it nothing more than a new form of slavery. One solution to their problems was labor unions. Leaders of early unions came from threatened communities of craftsmen, such as Thomas Skidmore of New York, Seth Luther of New England, and Ely Moore, a printer by trade, a land speculator by preference, and a labor leader and politician out of necessity. He was the first president of the New York General Trades Union, editor of the *National Trades Union* labor journal, and was elected to Congress as a workingman's candidate in 1836. He moved to Kansas in 1855 and died in Lecompton, Kansas in 1861. According to Moore, what economic and political forces are dividing the nation into separate classes? What is his proposed remedy for the dangerous drift in the nation? Why would his speech upset conservatives and the newly wealthy business class?

We have assembled, on the present occasion, for the purpose of publicly proclaiming the motives which induced us to organize a general union of the various trades and arts in this city and its vicinity, as well as to defend the course and to vindicate the measures we deign to pursue. This is required of us by a due regard to the opinions of our fellow men. . . .

Wherever man exists, under whatever form of government, or whatever be the structure or organization of society, . . . selfishness will appear, operating either for evil or for good. To curb it sufficiently by legislative enactments is impossible. Much can be done, however, towards restraining it within proper limits by unity of purpose and concert of action on the part of the *producing* classes. To contribute toward the achievement of this great end is one of the objects of the "General Trades' Union." Wealth, we all know, constitutes the aristocracy of this country. Happily no distinctions are known among us save what wealth and worth confer. . . . The greatest danger, therefore, which threatens the stability of our Government and the liberty of the people is an undue accumulation and distribution of wealth. And I do conceive that real danger is to be apprehended from this source, notwithstanding that tendency to distribution which naturally grows out of the character of our statutes of conveyance, of inheritance, and descent of property; but by securing to the producing classes a fair, certain, and equitable compensation for their toil and skill, we insure a more just and equal distribution of wealth than can ever be effected by statutory law.

Ely Moore, *Address Before the General Trades' Union of New York City* [New York: 1833], pp. 7–14, 18–20.

... We ask ... what better means can be devised for promoting a more equal distribution of wealth than for the producing classes to claim, and by virtue of union and concert, *secure their claims* to their respective portions? And why should not those who have the toil have the enjoyment also? Or why should the sweat that flows from the brow of the laborer be converted into a source of revenue for the support of the crafty or indolent?

It has been averred, with great truth, that all governments become cruel and aristocratical in their character and bearing in proportion as one part of the community is elevated and the other depressed, and that misery and degradation to the many is the inevitable result of such a state of society. And we regard it to be equally true that, in proportion as the line of distinction between the employer and employed is *widened*, the condition of the latter inevitably verges toward a state of vassalage, while that of the former as certainly approximates toward supremacy; and that whatever system is calculated to make the many dependent upon or subject to the few not only tends to the subversion of the natural rights of man, but is hostile to the best interests of the community, as well as to the spirit and genius of our Government. Fully persuaded that the foregoing positions are incontrovertible, we, in order to guard against the encroachments of aristocracy, to preserve our natural and political rights, to elevate our moral and intellectual condition, to promote our pecuniary interests, to narrow the line of distinction between the journeyman and employer, to establish the honor and safety of our respective vocations upon a more secure and permanent basis, and to alleviate the distresses of those suffering from want of employment have deemed it expedient to form ourselves into a "General Trades' Union."

It may be asked, how these desirable objects are to be achieved by a general union of trades? How the encroachments of aristocracy, for example, are to be arrested by our plan? We answer, by enabling the producer to enjoy the full benefit of his productions, and thus diffuse the streams of wealth more generally and, consequently, more equally throughout all the ramifications of society. . . .

There are, doubtless, many individuals who are resolved, right or wrong, to misrepresent our principles, impeach our measures, and impugn our motives. Be it so. They can harm us not. . . . We have the consolation of knowing that all good men, all who love their country, and rejoice in the improvement of the condition of their fellow men, will acknowledge the policy of our views and the purity of our motives. . . .

And why, let me ask, should the character of our Union be obnoxious to censure? Wherefore is it wrong in principle? Which of its avowed objects reprehensible? What feature of it opposed to the public good? I defy the ingenuity of man to point to a single measure which it recognizes that is wrong in itself or in its tendency. What, is it wrong for men to unite for the purpose of resisting the encroachments of aristocracy? Wrong to restrict the principle of selfishness to its proper and legitimate bounds and objects? Wrong to oppose monopoly and mercenary ambition? Wrong to consult the interests and seek the welfare of the producing classes? Wrong to attempt the elevation of our moral and intellectual standing? Wrong to establish the honor and safety of our respective vocations upon a more secure and permanent basis? I ask—in the name of heaven I ask—can it be wrong for men to attempt the melioration of their condition and the preservation of their natural and political rights?

I am aware that the charge of "illegal combination" is raised against us. The cry is as senseless as 'tis stale and unprofitable. Why, I would inquire, have not journeymen the same right to ask their own price for their own property or services that employers have? or that merchants, physicians, and lawyers have? Is that equal justice which makes it an offense for journeymen to combine for the purpose of maintaining their present prices or raising their wages, while employers may combine with impunity for the purpose of lowering them? I admit that such is the common law. All will agree, however, that it is neither wise, just, nor politic, and that it is directly opposed to the spirit and genius of our free institutions and ought therefore, to be abrogated. . . .

Again, it is alleged that it is setting a dangerous precedent for journeymen to combine for the purpose of coercing a compliance with their terms. It may, indeed, be dangerous to aristocracy, dangerous to monopoly, dangerous to oppression, but not to the general good or the public tranquility. Internal danger to a state is not to be apprehended from a general effort on the part of the people to improve and exalt their condition, but from an alliance of the crafty, designing, and intriguing few. What! tell us, in this enlightened age, that the welfare of the people will be endangered by a voluntary act of the people themselves? That the people will wantonly seek their own destruction? That the safety of the state will be plotted against by three-fourths of the members comprising the state! O how worthless, how poor and pitiful, are all such arguments and objections! . . .

My object in inviting you to a consideration of this subject at the present time is to impress upon your minds the importance of the situation which you, in reality, ought to occupy in society. This you seem to have lost sight of in a very great degree; and, from some cause or other, have relinquished your claims to that consideration to which, as mechanics and as men, you are entitled. You have, most unfortunately for yourselves and for the respectability of your vocations, become apparently unconscious of your own worth, and been led to regard your callings as humble and inferior, and your stations as too subordinate in life. And why? why is it so? Why should the producer consider himself inferior to the consumer? Or why should the mechanic, who builds a house, consider himself less important than the owner or occupant? It is strange, indeed, and to me perfectly unaccountable that the artificer, who prepares the accommodations, the comforts, and embellishments of life, should consider himself of less consequence than those to whose pleasure and convenience he ministers. . . .

Document 7.9 Massachusetts Investigates Conditions in the Mills

As conditions in the mills deteriorated, workers began agitating for reform, especially safeguards for their health. In the 1840s, mill workers and others began calling for state governments to mandate a ten-hour work day. This was a key goal of the Lowell Female Labor Reform Association. The Massachusetts legislature was the first to conduct hearings into labor conditions, in 1845, but did not enact a ten-hour law until 1874. By that time the New England mill girls were all replaced by immigrants. What working conditions are described here as "usual" by the mill workers? How could these conditions harm women and prevent them from fulfilling their roles in society? How did the legislature respond in this document?

. . . The first petition which was referred to your committee, came from the city of Lowell, and was signed by Mr. John Quincy Adams Thayer, and eight hundred and fifty others, "peaceable, industrious, hard working men and women of Lowell." The Petitioners declare that they are confined "from thirteen to fourteen hours per day in unhealthy apartments," and are thereby "hastening through pain, disease and privation, down to a premature grave." They therefore ask the Legislature "to pass a law providing that ten hours shall constitute a day's work," and that no corporation or private citizen "shall be allowed, except in cases of emergency, to employ one set of hands more than ten hours per day.". . .

The first petitioner who testified was Eliza R. Hemmingway. She had worked two years and nine months in the Lowell Factories; two years in the Middlesex, and nine months in the Hamilton Corporations. Her employment is weaving—works by the piece. The Hamilton Mill manufactures cotton fabrics. The Middlesex, woolen fabrics. She is now at work in the Middlesex Mills, and she attends one loom. Her wages average from $16 to $23 a month exclusive of board. She complained of the hours for labor being too many, and the time for meals too limited. in the summer season the work is commenced at 5 o'clock, A.M. and continued till 7 o'clock, P.M., with half an hour for breakfast and three quarters of an hour for dinner. During eight months of the year, but half an hour is allowed for dinner. The air in the room she considered not to be wholesome. There were 293 small lamps and 61 large lamps lighted in the room in which she worked, when evening work is required. These lamps are also lighted sometimes in the morning. About 130 females, 11 men and 12 children (between the ages of 11 and 14) work in the room with her. She thought the children enjoyed about as good health as children usually do. The children work but nine months out of twelve. The other three months they must attend school. Thinks there is no day when there are less than six females out of the mill from sickness. Has known as many as thirty. She, herself, is out quite often, on account of sickness.

"The First Official Investigation into Labor Conditions by the Massachusetts Legislature," Massachusetts House Document 50 [March 1845].

There was more sickness in the summer than in the winter months; though in the summer, lamps were not lighted. She thought there was a general desire among females to work but ten hours, regardless of pay. . . .

Miss Sarah G. Bagley said she had worked in the Lowell Mills eight and a half years, six years and a half on the Hamilton Corporation, and two years on the Middlesex. She is a weaver and works by the piece. She worked in the mills three years before her health began to fail. She is native of New Hampshire and went home six weeks during the summer. Last year she was out of the mill a third of the time. She thinks the health of the operatives is not as good as the health of the females who do house-work or the millinery business. The chief evil, as far as health is concerned, is the shortness of the time allowed for meals. The next evil the length of time employed— not giving them time to cultivate their minds. . . . She thought that girls were generally favorable to the ten hour system. She had presented a petition, same as the one before the Committee, to 132 girls, most of whom said that they would prefer to work but ten hours. In a pecuniary point of view, it would be better as their health would be improved. They would have more time for sewing. Their intellectual, moral and religious habits would be benefited by the change. . . .

Your Committee have not been able to give the petitions from the other towns in this state a hearing. We believe that the whole case was covered by the petition from Lowell, and to the consideration of that petition we have given our undivided attention, and we have come to the conclusion unanimously, that legislation is not necessary at the present time and for the following reasons:

1st. That a law limiting the hours of labor, if enacted at all, should be of a general nature. That it should apply to individuals or copartnerships as well as corporations. Because, if it is wrong to labor more than ten hours in a corporation it is also wrong when applied to individual employers, and your Committee are not aware that more complaint can justly be made against incorporated companies in regard to hours of labor than can be against individuals or co-partnerships. . . .

2d. Your Committee believe that the factory system as it is called, is not more injurious to health than other kinds of indoor labor. That a law which would compel all of the factories in Massachusetts to run their machinery but ten hours out of the 24, while those in Maine, New Hampshire, Rhode Island and other States in the Union, were not restricted at all, the effect would be to close the gate of every mill in the State. . . .

3d. It would be impossible to legislate to restrict the hours of labor, without affecting very materially the question of wages; and that is a matter which experience has taught us can be much better regulated by parties themselves than by the Legislature. Labor in Massachusetts is a very different commodity from what it is in foreign countries. Here labor is on an equality with capital, and indeed controls it, and so it ever will be while free education and free constitutions exist. . . . Labor is intelligent enough to make its own bargains, and look out for its own interest without any interference from us. . . .

4th. The Committee do not wish to be understood as conveying the impression, that there are no abuses in the present system of labor; we think there are abuses; we think that many improvements may be made, and we believe will be made, by which labor will not be so severely tasked as it now is. We think that it would be better if the hours for labor would be less, if more time was allowed for meals, if more attention were paid to ventilation and pure air in our manufactories, and workshops, and many other matters. We acknowledge all this, but we say, the remedy is not with us.

Document 7.10 Reverend Henry Bellows Bemoans Greed and Materialism

While most labor leaders focused on the economic consequences of changes caused by the market economy, other reformers saw even darker forces unleashed upon the land. Young men and women drawn to the industrial centers and away from the controlling influences of family, church, and home meant increases in violence, vice, crime, and immorality. Others feared the loss of virtue and morality in a nation only motivated by greed and the desire to get ahead at all costs. Orestes Brownson believed Lowell and its sister cities were as exploitive as southern slavery, wearing out the mill girls both morally and physically, till they quit the mills to either turn to prostitution or go home to die. Henry W. Bellows, a New York City

Unitarian minister, examined the widespread darker influences of the free market and free labor system in the following article. What does he fear? What evil does he see now, and coming to the nation in the future? What is the cost to both the people and the country of "doing business in America"?

Influence of the Trading Spirit Upon the Social and Moral Life of America

Those influences which affect the characters of a whole people are less observed, although more important, than such as peculiar to classes or individuals. The exertions which one may make to protect himself from error, or demeaning influences, are sometimes rendered ineffectual from his ignorance of the tremendous biases which he receives from a corrupt public opinion; as the most careful observations of the mariner are sometimes vitiated by an unknown current which insensibly drifts him from his supposed position. What everybody does in our own community, we are apt to suppose to be universal with men; and universal custom is, by general consent, not to be disputed. We are not disposed to suspect public opinion, or to question common custom.—Nay, we do not even, for the most part, distinguish between a prevailing sentiment and an innate idea—between a universal or national habit and a law of nature. The customs of the city in which we are brought up seem to most persons of divine appointment. We are apt to account a foreigner who prefers (in accordance with his own national manners and prejudices) a different division of the day, different hours at the table, a different style of dress, as almost immoral. This proves how little aware we may be of the nature of the social habits and sentiments which greatly influence our characters. We propose to offer a few observations upon some of our national habits and tendencies.

There is but one thing to discourage such an inquiry, and that is, that after understanding the direction and force of the current on which we are borne, there is little hope of withstanding it, or guiding ourselves upon it. But to this it must be replied, that public opinion is made up of private opinions, and that the only way of ever changing it is by commencing to correct, be it ever so little, the judgments of one's own mind and of the few others under our

influence. We must not despise humble means of influence, nor hesitate to do a little good, because an almost hopeless amount of evil surrounds us.

All strangers who come among us remark the excessive anxiety written in the American countenance. The wide-spread comfort, the facilities for livelihood, the spontaneous and cheap lands, the high price of labor, are equally observed, and render it difficult to account for these lines of painful thoughtfulness. It is not poverty, nor tyranny, nor over-competition which produces this anxiety; that is clear. It is the concentration of the faculties upon an object, which in its very nature is unattainable—the perpetual improvement of the outward condition. There are no bounds among us to the restless desire to be better off; and this is the ambition of all classes of society. We are not prepared to allow that wealth is more valued in America than elsewhere, but in other countries the successful pursuit of it is necessarily confined to a few, while here it is open to all. No man in America is contented to be poor, or expects to continue so. There are here no established limits within which the hopes of any class of society must be confined, as in other countries. There is consequently no condition of hopes realized, in other words, of contentment. In other lands, if children can maintain the station and enjoy the means, however moderate, of their father, they are happy. Not so with us. This is not the spirit of our institutions. Nor will it long be otherwise in other countries. That equality, that breaking down of artificial barriers which has produced this universal ambition and restless activity in America, is destined to prevail throughout the earth. But because we are in advance of the world in the great political principle, and are now experiencing some of its first effects, let us not mistake these for the desirable fruits of freedom. Commerce is to become the universal pursuit of men. It is to be the first result of freedom, of popular institutions everywhere. Indeed, every land not steeped in tyranny is now feeling this impulse. But while trade is destined to free and employ the masses, it is also destined to destroy for the time much of the

Reverend Henry W. Bellows, "The Influence of the Trading Spirit upon the Social and Moral Life of America," in *The American Whig Review* Volume 1, pp. 94–99.

beauty and happiness of every land. This has been the result in our own country. We are free. It is a glorious thing that we have no serfs, with the large and unfortunate exception of our slaves—no artificial distinctions—no acknowledged superiority of blood—no station which merit may not fill—no rounds in the social ladder to which the humblest may not aspire. But the excitement, the commercial activity, the restlessness, to which this state of things has given birth, is far from being a desirable or a natural condition. It is natural to the circumstances, but not natural to the human soul. It is good and hopeful to the interests of the race, but destructive to the happiness, and dangerous to the virtue of the generation exposed to it.

Those unaccustomed by reading or travel, to other states of society, are probably not aware how very peculiar our manner of life here is. The laboriousness of Americans is beyond all comparison, should we except the starving operatives of English factories. And when we consider that here, to the labor of the body is added the great additional labor of mental responsibility and ambition, it is not to be wondered at that as a race, the commercial population is dwindling in size, and emaciated in health, so that *palor* is the national complexion. If this devotion to business were indispensable to living, it would demand our pity. It is unavoidable, we know, in one sense. That is, it is customary—it is universal. There is no necessity for the custom; but there is a necessity, weakly constituted as men are, that every individual should conform greatly to the prevailing habits of his fellows, and the expectations of the community in and with which he deals. It is thus that those who deeply feel the essentially demoralizing and wretched influences of this system are yet doomed to be victims of it. Nay, we are all, no matter what our occupations, more or less, and all greatly, sufferers from the excessive stimulus under which every thing is done. We are all worn out with thought that does not develop our thinking faculties in a right direction, and with feeling expended upon poor and low objects. There is no profession that does not feel it. The lawyer must confine himself to his office, without vacation, to adjust a business which never sleeps or relaxes. The physician must labor day and night to repair bodies, never well from over-exertion, over-excitement, and over-indulgence. The minister must stimulate himself to supply the cravings of diseased moral appetites, and to arouse the attention of men deafened by the noise, and dizzy with the whirl in which they constantly live.

We call our country a *happy* country; happy, indeed, in being the home of noble political institutions, the abode of freedom; but very far from being happy in possessing a cheerful, light-hearted, and joyous people. Our agricultural regions even are infected with the same anxious spirit of gain. If ever the curse of labor was upon the race, it is upon us; nor is it simply now "by the sweat of thy brow thou shalt earn thy bread." Labor for a livelihood is dignified. But we labor for bread, and labor for pride, and *labor* for pleasure. A man's life with us *does* consist of the abundance of the things which he possesseth. To get, and to have the reputation of possessing, is the ruling passion. To it are bent all the energies of nine-tenths of out population. Is it that our people are so much more miserly and earth-born than any other? No, not by any constitutional baseness; but circumstances have necessarily given this direction to the American mind. In the hard soil of our common mother, New England—the poverty of our ancestors—their early thrift and industry—the want of other distinctions than those of property—the frown of the Puritans upon all pleasures; these circumstances combined, directed our energies from the first into the single channel of trade. And in that they have run till they have gained a tremendous head, and threaten to convert our whole people into mere money-changers and producers. Honor belongs to our fathers, who in times of great necessity met the demand for a most painful industry with such manly and unflinching hearts. But what was their hard necessity we are perpetrating as our willing servitude! what they bore as evil we seek as good. We cannot say that the destiny of this country did not demand that the spirit of trade should rule it for centuries. It may be that we are now carrying out only the decree of Providence. But if so, let us consider ourselves as in the wilderness, and not in the promised land. Let us bear the dispensation of God, but not glory in our bondage. If we are doomed to be tradesmen, and nothing but tradesmen—if money, and its influences and authority, are to reign for a season over our whole land, let us not mistake it for the kingdom of heaven, and build triumphal arches over our avenues of trade, as though the Prince of Peace and the Son of God were now and thus to enter in.

It is said that we are not a happy people. And it is true; for we most unwisely neglect all those free fountains of happiness which Providence has opened for all its children. Blessed beyond any people with the means of living, supplied to an unparalleled extent with the comforts and luxuries of life, our American homes are somber and cheerless abodes. There is even in the air of comfort which their well-furnished apartments wear something uncomfortable. They are the habitations of those who do not live at home.

They are wanting in a social and cheerful aspect. They seem fitted more to be admired than to be enjoyed. The best part of the house is for the occasional use of strangers, and not to be occupied by those who might, day by day, enjoy it, which is but one proof among many that we love to appear comfortable rather than to be so. Thus miserable pride hangs like a mill-stone about our hospitality. "We sacrifice the hospitality of a year to the prodigality of a night." We are ashamed of any thing but affluence, and when we cannot make an appearance, or furnish entertainments as showy as the richest, we will do nothing. Thus does pride close our doors. Hospitality becomes an event of importance. It is not our daily life, one of our chiefest enjoyments, but a debt, a ceremony, a penance. And not only pride, but anxiety of mind, interferes with sociality. Bent upon one aim, the merchant grudges his thoughts. He cannot expend his energies in social enjoyment. Nay, it is not enjoyment to him; society has nothing of the excitement of business. The excessive pursuit of gain begets a secrecy of thought, a contradiction of ideas, a barrenness of interest, which renders its votary any thing but social or companionable. Conversation incessantly takes an anxious and uninteresting turn; and the fireside becomes only a narrower exchange, and the parlor a more private news-room.

It is rare to see a foreigner without some taste for amusement, some power of relaxing his mind, some interest in the arts or in literature. This is true even of the less privileged classes. It is rare, on the contrary, to find a *virtuous* American past middle life, who does not regard amusements of all sorts either as childish or immoral; who possesses any acquaintance with or taste for the arts, except it be a natural and rude taste for music; or who reads any thing except newspapers, and only the political or commercial columns of those. It is the want of tastes for other things than business which gives an anxious and unhappy turn to our minds. It cannot be many years before the madness of devoting the whole day to the toils of the counting-house will be acknowledged; before the claim of body and mind to relaxation and cheerful, exhilarating amusement will be seen. We consider the common suspicion which is felt of amusements among thoughtful people to be one of the most serious evils to which our community is exposed. It outlaws a natural taste, and violates and ruins the consciences of the young, by stamping as sinful what they have not the force to refrain from. It makes our places if amusement low, divides the thoughtful and the careless, the grave and the gay, the old and the young, in their pleasures. Children are without the

protection of their parents in their enjoyments. And thus, too, is originated one of the greatest curses of our social state—the great want of intimacy and confidence between children and their parents, especially between fathers and sons.

The impulses that incline to pleasure, if opposed, tend to vice. Nature finds a vent for her pent-up forces. Alas! for what are called *strict morals* in this view; when, by an unnatural restriction, innocent and open pleasures make way for secret vices or sins of the heart.

While the commercial spirit in this extravagant form gives a certain sobriety and moral aspect to society, it occasions an excessive barrenness of real moral excellencies. This is a very difficult and delicate distinction to render popularly apparent, although of the most vital and substantial reality. There is a very great difference between what are called strict morals, and morals that are really profound in their sources, and pervading in their influence. We are more strict in our morals in these Northern States than anywhere in the world, but it is questionable whether our morality is not of a somewhat inferior quality, and in a too narrow view. It is artificial, conventional. There is no quarter of the earth where the Sabbath is more scrupulously observed—where religious institutions are so well supported, or where more abstinence from pleasure is practiced. The great virtue of industry prevails. Overt sins are more rare here than elsewhere. As far as morality is restrictive in its nature, it has accomplished a great work in America. The vices or sins which are reducible to statute, or known by name, are generally restrained. We have a large class of persons of extraordinary propriety and faultlessness of life. Our view of morals has a tendency to increase this class. Our pursuits are favorable to it. The love of gain is one of the most sober of all desires. The seriousness of a miser surpasses the gravity of a devotee. Did not every commercial city draw a large body of strangers to it, and attract many reckless and vicious persons, it would wear a very solemn aspect. The pleasure-seeking, the gay, the disorderly, are never the trading population. Large commercial cities tend to great orderliness and decency of manners and morals. But they also tend to very low and barren views of moral excellence. And the American spirit of our own day illustrates this. Our moral sense operates only in one direction. Our virtues are the virtues of merchants, and not of men. We run all to honesty, and mercantile honesty. We do not cultivate the graces of humanity. We have more conscience than heart, and more propriety than either. The fear of evil consequences is more influential than the love of goodness. There is nothing hearty, gushing, eloquent, in the national virtue. You do not see goodness leaking out from the full vessel at every motion it feels. Our goodness is formal, deliberate, premeditated. The upright man is not benevolent, and the just man is not generous. The good man is not cheerful. The religious man is not agreeable. In other words, our morals are partial and therefore barren. It is not generally understood how great scrupulousness of character may be united with great selfishness, and how, along with a substantial virtue, there may exist the most melancholy deficiencies. This seems to be very common with us, and to be the natural result of our engrossing pursuits. Every one minds his own business, to the extreme peril of his own soul. The apostolic precept, Mind not thine own things, but also the things of another, is in danger of great neglect. Our social condition makes us wary, suspicious, slow to commit ourselves too far in interest for others. The shyness of the tradesman communicates itself to the manners of the visitor; we learn to live within ourselves; we grow unsocial, unfraternal in feeling; and the sensibility, the affection, the cordiality, the forth-putting graces of a warm and virtuous heart, die of disuse. For our part, we are ready to say, let us have more faults and more virtues; more weaknesses and more graces; less punctilio, and more affluence of heart. Let us be less dignified and more cordial; less sanctimonious and more unselfish; less thriving and more cheerful; less toilsome and more social.

We want, as a people, a rounder character. Our humanity is pinched; our tastes are not generous. The domestic and social virtues languish. The dearest relations of life are stripped of beauty; a wretched utility usurps that proper theatre of beautiful sentiment, our very homes. Children grow up unknown to their parents. The mature despise their own youth, and have no sympathy with the romance, the buoyancy, the gayety of their children. Enterprise is our only enthusiasm. We grow to be ashamed of our best affections. We are afraid to acknowledge that we derive enjoyment from trifles, and make apologies for being amused with any thing. Thus is the beautiful field of life burnt over, and all its spontaneous flowers and fruitage destroyed; a few towering trunks alone redeeming the landscape. Happiness is made up of little things, and he who would be happy at all, must enjoy the little things day by day. So fraternal love, benevolence, virtue, consist in small acts prompted by love, and binding the day with a chain of delicate moral links. Character, too, is the result of right purposes, and pure feelings, and generous emotions,

exercised upon trivial occasions day after day; and heroic and high virtue is the necessary result of this mode of life. We fear that the ruling passion of our community, the habits of business which it has established, the anxious and self-concentrated mind which ensues, the morals which it engenders, are very hostile to any thing like perfected humanity. It is very probable that we may have erred in supposing a greatly better state of things to exist in other communities. But we know that we are right as to the positive state of our own, whatever it may be relatively to others. We know, too, very well the almost insuperable difficulties in the way of any individual who shall attempt to withstand the prevailing current of sentiment, or of business habits. But if *none* are to escape, it is well to be aware of the danger; nor must it be assumed that a firm will cannot do much to emancipate a man from the general bondage of trade. Sooner than slave from morning to night at business, we would counsel any man conscious of inward resources, of the desire to cultivate his better nature, his social feelings, his tastes, his generous and cheerful sentiments, to give it up altogether as soon as the most moderate competency is secured; to seek the country—to occupy some of our rich western lands—to do any thing which will give him time to enjoy domestic pleasures, to rear his children, to acquaint himself with nature, to read, to meditate. The excitement, the bustle, the toil of our life render us dead to the voice of the highest truth. We cannot stop to consider the matter. How few are aware that Christianity is a call to freedom—a call to happiness. Would we but listen, it would break these very chains whose galling wounds we have been opening; it would allay these feverish anxieties; it would restore to us contentment; it would legitimate our pleasures; it would re-establish, or for the first time build, our homes; it would give our children parents, and us parents children; it would teach us that happiness resides ever in the simple and impartial bounties of God—in a domestic love—in social intercourse—in generous sympathy—in a mind pleased with little things—in the gratification of our various innocent tastes—in the love of nature—in thought—in doing good. We meanwhile barter the substance for the shadow—delve for the means instead of quietly enjoying the end—keep up appearances, deceive others with the show of happiness, and fall at length from the top of life's laborious gains into our graves, worn out with anxieties that have benefited no one, and carrying neither the recollection nor the capacity of happiness with us into the spiritual existence.

Document 7.11 Hezikiah Niles Defends the New Economy as the Great National Interest

Hezikiah Niles was born during the American Revolution. He apprenticed as a printer in Philadelphia, and attempted several unsuccessful publishing enterprises before beginning *Niles' Weekly Register* in 1811. Niles was part of a group of publishers and writers, along with Mathew Carey of Philadelphia and Daniel Raymond of Baltimore, who were dedicated to the new economic system. He promoted protective tariffs, industrial growth, massive internal improvements, and a national banking system to promote United States wealth and power. Always positive about economic development, he made *Niles' Weekly Register* the most popular weekly publication in the country. In many ways he was "preaching to the choir"; his subscribers were mostly urban and middle-class citizens benefiting the most from the market economy, possessed by a spirit of ambition and a desire to get ahead. What accomplishments does Niles document in the following editorial? Does he note any negative impacts of the national changes?

Illustrative of the progress and present condition of manufactures in the United States, and concerning internal improvements, aiding and assisting every branch of the national industry.

The making of the New York canals did not really cost the people of the state the value of one cent, except so far as *foreign* materials may have been employed in the construction of them, or for that small portion of the profits on labor which the artists and laborers may have carried *out of the state.* On the contrary, they gave a large and wholesome circulation to money, and enriched many individuals; and the increased value of property, and of profit, resulting from them, must be supposed by counting up hundreds of millions of dollars, if, indeed, the benefits of them be within *supposition* at all! The rise in the value of lands and lots on their borders—at Albany, Troy, Rochester, Utica, Buffalo, and an hundred new and thrifty villages which have started into existence as if created by magic—the *new* employment of tens of thousands of persons—the *new* commodities transported to market, many of which, of great value, were hitherto as quiescent, or useless, because of the want of such market, with the *new* products of a teeming, busy, bustling and happy population—make up an aggregate of benefits that the mind cannot grasp with any degree of confidence in itself; and to all these should be added, the wealth and power caused by the increased inhabitants of the state on account of these things; perhaps directly and already, to the number of

three or four hundred thousand persons! Such are the general effects of canals, roads and bridges. And besides, the revenue arising from tolls will not only pay the interest on the money expended, but speedily extinguish the debt, and then supply the chief part of all the funds required for the support of the government of New York! These canals cost $9,123,000, but the actual debt created was only 7,771,000, the interest payable on which was 419,000—but the tolls of the present year will amount to a million!—and the business of the canals will go *on, on, on,* and increase every year, for years to come, until the utmost shore of lake Superior teems with civilized men, and cities are located where the wolf has his home, and the bear takes up his winter-quarters.

Up to the 18th August last, and for the present season, about 9,000 tons of coal, 4,000 tons of wheat, 2,000 tons of iron ore, 1,500 tons of flour, and 4,000 tons of other articles, arrived at Philadelphia by the improved navigation of the Schuylkill—one hundred vessels laden with Schuylkill coal will have arrived at New York from Philadelphia, during the present season. What is the *new* profit, or value, of the products or employments caused by this comparatively small work, yet in the very infancy of its usefulness? What the amount of *new* capital put into useful operation? *Let it be calculated!*

Some particulars might be given about other canals; but these two cases have been referred to only to shew general results, and they speak a language that cannot be mistaken—to the glory of those who

---

Hezikiah Niles, "Great National Interests, *Niles Weekly Register* [Baltimore, October 21, 1826]

have supported INTERNAL IMPROVEMENTS, to the shame of some who have opposed them, and the [what shall I say?]—the *something* of others who were so much interested in *arguing* while others were employed in *digging!* But such will always be the difference between talking and doing—the talkers will become poorer and poorer, and the doers richer and richer. One spade-full of earth removed in New York or Pennsylvania, has rendered more service, in either state, than a *ten-column essay* in the Richmond "Enquirer" has benefitted Virginia. The policy of the first, is to make even a small state a great one—of the other, to reduce a great state into a small one. Witness, Vermont and New York, and Maryland and Virginia. Population and power and wealth will centre where labor is honored, and business abounds. The little rough and rugged state of Vermont, has had as great an accession of citizens, since 1790, as the mighty state of Virginia—though the capital for increase in the latter was five times greater than the former had in the year just stated; and as to Maryland, Vermont *now* contains more of the people than she does, though the first numbered 208,000, and the last only 85,000, in 1790! These things speak in most intelligible language. Maryland has done nothing, (though we have talked much), in favor of internal improvements, or to encourage domestic industry, except through the public spirit of some private individuals located in Baltimore or Frederick—and, by a strange waywardness of policy, our representatives and delegates have generally, in fact, discouraged those who would have effected them, to increase the population and wealth of the state. A great field is open for improvement in Maryland—the Susquehannah and the Potomac, and the abundance of waterpower adjacent to Baltimore, with our valuable mines and minerals, invite capital and enterprise—and they must be promptly exerted, or the state will retrograde yet further and further.

There are about 100 sail of coasters on the American side of lake Erie—500 will be required after the Ohio canal is finished, and fairly in use. Buffalo, a mere village before the war, has 5,000 inhabitants, and the number is *daily* increasing. One steam boat on the lake had not sufficient business two years since—six are now well employed. We shall soon have *ports* on Huron and Michigan. Green Bay will be an important point, and Michilimackinac the centre of a very extensive trade which will pass either to New York, Philadelphia, or New Orleans, by canals and river navigation, every foot of the way! A thousand miles of space has been reduced as if to fifty. Distance is subdued by science, supported by public spirit.

By means of the canals made, or making, the coal trade will be a mighty business, and the price of fuel be much reduced in those parts where wood is becoming scarce. It abounds in the immediate neighborhood of Pittsburg, and, in 1822, a million of bushels were used by 10,000 inhabitants, including the manufactories—1,500,000 bushels will probably be used in that city during the present year, because of the increased population and business. What then will the great cities require?

* * *

It is probable that the domestic consumption of cotton in the present year, [in 1816, 90,000 bales], will amount to about or more than one hundred and fifty thousand bales—possibly, to 175,000. Next year, unless because of some unlooked-for events, to 200,000! Suppose this were thrown into the European market! The price of cotton, paid to our planters, by our own manufacturers, has been greater, on the average, than they have received of the British purchasers of their staple. About 30,000 bales annually arrive at Providence, R. I. for the mills in the neighborhood. Many single establishments at other places use 1,000—some 1,500, some 2,000! The consumption at Baltimore is 4,000.

* * *

There are between 50 and 60 cotton and woolen factories in New Hampshire, and it is supposed that they make 33,000,000 yards of cloth per annum. In 1810, the quantity made was only 4,274,185 yards. At Dover, 21,000 spindles and 750 power looms were lately at work, or preparing. At Salmon Falls, a village with 1,600 inhabitants has *jumped* up. Many mills are building with brick—one finished is 390 by 40, another 220 by 49, and six stories high! At New Market there is also a new village with 1,000 inhabitants—the capital of this last company is $600,000. This establishment now makes, or speedily will make, 3,600 yards of cloth, daily—though it has only just started, as it were. When the works are completed, a million and a half of yards of cloth will be made in a year, at New Market.

The capital vested in manufactures in Massachusetts, including the new works, may be estimated at between twenty-five and thirty millions of dollars—the factories, in 1824, were 161. At Lowell, 1,700,000 dollars have been recently employed. At Waltham, about the same sum; its stock has been sold at 40 per cent above par. At Merrimack 1,200,000, all paid in; the Hamilton company has 600,000. At Taunton, 250 pieces of calico are made daily—employing 1,000, persons!—The furnaces at Wareham make 4,000 tons of metal annually, and there are two rolling and slitting mills and three forges at the same place, with large cotton mills, fulling mills, &c. Several villages, with from 1,000 to 1,500 inhabitants have been built within a few years, all whose inhabitants were employed or subsisted by the factories. A busy, healthful population teems on spots over which a rabbit, a little while since, could hardly have made his way— . . .

The manufactories of Rhode Island, Connecticut and Vermont make up a large amount of capital—In Rhode Island there are about ninety cotton mills, and new ones are building! We venture to assert that the surplus product of the people of Rhode Island, aided as they are by scientific power, is of greater value than the *surplus* products of the whole state of Virginia, in which that power is not much used. By "surplus" I mean a value beyond what is required for the subsistence of the people. One person, assisted by machinery, is equal to from 100 to 200 without it. One hundred and fifty persons are employed in making lace at Newport, R.I. It is made at several other places, splendid, and as good, and at a less price than the imported. Providence is, perhaps, the richest town of its size in the world—and its population rapidly increases.

* * *

[Mr. Webster, at a late public dinner, gave the following appropriate and veritable sentiment:

"The mechanics and manufacturers of New England—Men who teach us how a little country is to be made a great one."

The females employed in the factories are remarkable for the propriety of their conduct—to be suspected of bad behaviour is to be dismissed.]

The cotton and woollen cloths made in New York are valued at from 15 to 18,000,000 dollars per ann. There are large manufactories of iron, wool, cotton, leather, glass, paper, &c. &c. One brewery at Newburg covers 7,500 square feet of ground. Hudson teems with manufacturing establishments, and the splendid cotton and woollen works at Matteawan are famous—they support a large population. Duchess, Oneida and many other counties, are *filled* with factories.

A grand display of manufactures has just been made at the Franklin Institute, Philadelphia. It was estimated that the rooms were visited by seven thousand persons in one day, and the crowd was great during the whole time of the exhibition. Cloths, cottons, glass-wares, porcelain, silks, works in wood, in metals, and of almost every description of materials, many of the very best and most beautiful kinds, were shewn and in astonishing variety and quantity. . . . All these things were, of course, of American manufacture.

* * *

Four thousand weavers find employment in Philadelphia—and several new villages of manufacturers have been built in the neighborhood. Among them Manyunk, with 2,000 inhabitants. The furnaces of Huntingdon county, only, make 6,000 tons of iron, annually. There are 165 hatters in the small town of Reading.

The city of Pittsburg contains 1,873 buildings and 12,796 inhabitants. One paper mill employs 190 persons—there are seven other paper mills in the city or its immediate neighborhood—seven rolling and slitting mills; eight air foundries, six steam engine factories, one large wire factory, seven glass works, &c. &c. Some of these are mighty establishments—one of them has two steam engines, of 100 and 120 horse power, to drive the machinery! *One* of the factories at Pittsburg makes glass to the value of 160,000 dollars a year—and others do nearly as much business. The whole glass manufacture in the United States is worth not less than three millions annually.

* * *

Delaware has many valuable cotton mills—several important woollen factories, and of paper, &c. The powder works of Mr. Dupont are said to be the largest in the world; and there are few more extensive establishments for making paper than one of those on the Brandywine.

In Maryland, there are various large and respectable factories in Cecil, Baltimore, Frederick and Washington counties—but we cannot give many particulars, just now.

* * *

Many extensive iron works are going into operation in the northern part of *Ohio*, in consequence of the market about to be opened by the canals. There are large establishments of various kinds at Steubenville and Cincinnati, and respectable ones scattered through the country, and the flocks of sheep of Mr. Dickinson and others, are justly famous. . . . In Jefferson county, in which Steubenville is located, there are 25,000 sheep. Mr. Dickinson's flock is 8,000. At Steubenville, besides the great cloth manufactory, there are 2 steam flour mills, 2 do. cotton mills, 1 do. paper mill. 2 breweries, 2 copperas manufactories, 1 air foundry, 1 steam engine factory, 1 machine factory, 2 carding machines, &c. some of them very extensive. There are numerous valuable factories in

Kentucky, Indiana and Tennessee—and some in western Virginia, North Carolina, &c. but we have little or not any particular information concerning them.

* * *

Before the perfect establishment of the cotton manufacture in the United States, those kind of goods which now sell for 12 cents, cost the consumers 25 cents! Cotton, for the last two or three years, has averaged a greater price for American consumption than it sold for in Europe! Let the planter look to this—it is true.

In 1815, in a congressional report, it was estimated that 200,000 persons were employed in the cotton and woollen manufactories of the United States! The present number engaged in *all* sorts of manufactories cannot be less than *two millions*. What a market do they *create*. We shall attempt to *calculate* it hereafter.

The hats, caps and bonnets, of straw or grass, manufactured in the United States, employ about 25,000 persons, chiefly females, and produce $825,000, in Massachusetts, only! The whole value of this manufacture is, probably, about a million and a half yearly.

The quantity of flannel now made in the United States is considerably greater than the whole importation ever amounted to—as reported at the custom houses.

Silk begins to be extensively cultivated in several of the states. The silk raised and manufactured in the town of Mansfield, Con. in 1825, was 3,000 lbs. worth $15,000, and in Windham county, in the same state, silk worth 54,000 dollars a year. We have seen fine specimens from North Carolina and one from Missouri. It is a very profitable cultivation, and nearly the whole business is done by women and children, who would otherwise be idle, and so it is pretty nearly a clear gain. One acre of land planted with mulberry trees, will feed as many worms as will make silk worth $200, in a good season.

* * *

There are probably not less than fifteen millions of sheep in the United States, and their numbers is increasing, though the price of woollen goods is very low—*too low.* But our farmers must raise less grain, and more of other articles than heretofore. Flax is

exceedingly wanted—we import large quantities for our manufactories. It is abundantly proved in the neighborhood of Philadelphia and York, Pa. Georgetown, (Col.) Vevay, Indiana, &c. that the vine will flourish, and that excellent wine may be made in the United States; and 20,000 hands detached from the cultivation of wheat to that of the vine, would make a great difference in the general products of our agriculture. The olive begins to be cultivated as a crop in the south, and the Palma Christi grows bountifully. A moderate degree of attention to a few *new* articles of agriculture, would save us from five to eight millions of dollars a year, *and be so much of a clear gain.* The cultivation of the vine, especially in the neighborhood of cities, wherein the grapes may be sold, is wonderfully profitable. Half an acre of land, Mr. Carr's vineyard, near Philadelphia, produced 260 gallons of wine, the value of which, with that of the grapes sold, is estimated at $670, for the present year: *one* vine yielded 300 lbs. of fine grapes. . . .

* * *

It may generally be observed, that migrations from the eastern and middle Atlantic states to the west are not nearly so common as they were, except to particular sections. Employment and profit is found at home. The facts shewn at the next census will probably surprise even those who may have calculated the probable population of the several states.

* * *

What then would be the state of our country, if our work-shops were in Europe? We should have, as it were, to live in caves and be clothed in skins. But we shall speak of these things hereafter—the whole intent of my present undertaking being to afford some faint idea of the importance of the manufacturing interest, and to show the people what has been done by the encouragement of the national industry, that they may more and more attend to the subject, and resolve that their public agents, whether of the general government or of the states, *shall* rather accelerate than impede the progress of things so indispensable to the general welfare—so inseparably connected with the employment and profit of every citizen of the United States.

* * *

Document 7.12 Henry Carey Defends Laboring Conditions and Pay in the United States

Henry Carey, son of Mathew Carey, is often called the first political economist in United States history. He firmly believed that economic growth and development must be promoted by the government and individuals at all times. Capitalists and industry are keys to national prosperity. He also believed that whatever benefited the owners would benefit the employees; thus, high tariffs were a must. Everyone would prosper, Carey believed, unless the government interfered with the "natural process" of economic growth by regulating wages or working conditions. How does he "prove" these ideas in this essay? What does he see as the only comparison of European and American workers that counts? Does he believe we should consider working conditions between nations, or alter them here? What does he say about government actions to protect workers?

Wages and profits have been represented by many political economists as natural antagonists, the Ormuzd and Ahriman of political economy, one of which could rise only at the expense of the other. Such has been the belief of the great mass of the people who receive wages, which belief has given rise to trades' unions, so numerous in England. and obtaining in the United States; as well as to the cry of the *poor against the rich.* A large portion of those who pay as well as those who receive wages, believe that the rate is altogether arbitrary, and that changes may be made at will. To this belief we are indebted for the numerous "'strikes," or "'turns out" we have seen, the only effect of which has been loss to both employers and workmen. Had the journeymen tailors of London understood the laws by which the distribution of the proceeds between the workman and the capitalist is regulated, they would have saved themselves and their employers the enormous loss that has arisen out of their recent combination, and would have retained their situations instead of seeing themselves pushed from their stools by the influx of Germans, who seized gladly upon the places vacated by their English fellow workmen. Believing as they do that their wages are depressed for the benefit of their employers, they believe also that those employers are bound to give them a portion of their profits in the advance of wages, when, in fact, the employers are also sufferers by the same causes which produce the depression, and are unable to advance them, however willing they may be. If the real causes of the depression were understood, instead of combining against their employers, they would unite with them to free their country from those restrictions and interferences which produce the effect of which they complain, and would thus secure permanent advantage, instead of a temporary advance of wages, which is all that can be hoped for from combination, even if successful, which is rarely the case. Fortunately, in the United States there have been fewer interferences, and there is therefore less to alter, than in any other country; and if the workmen and labourers could be made to understand the subject, they would see that the division between themselves and the capitalist, or the rate of wages, is regulated by a law immutable as are those which govern the motion of the Heavenly bodies; that attempts at legislative interference can produce only disadvantageous effects; and, that the only mode of increasing wages is by rendering labour more productive, which can only be accomplished by allowing every man to employ his capital and talent in the way which he deems most advantageous to himself. They would see that all attempts on the part of the capitalist, to reduce wages below the natural rate, as well as all on their part to raise it above that rate, must fail, as any such reduction must be attended with an unusual rate of profit to the employer, which must, in its turn. beget competition among the possessors of capital, and raise the rate of wages: while such elevation in any employment must reduce the rate of profit so far as to drive capital therefrom, and reduce wages again to the proper standard.

They should see in the fact that the great majority of the master workmen have risen by their own

---

Henry C. Carey, *Essay on Rate of Wages with an Examination of the Causes of the Differences in the Condition of the Labouring Populations Throughout the World* [Philadelphia: Carey, Lea and Blanchard, 1835], pp. 15–18.

exertions to the situations they at present occupy, abundant evidence that nothing is wanting to them but industry and economy. They should desire nothing but freedom of action for themselves, and that security both of person and property which prompts the capitalist to investment; and so far should they be from entertaining feelings of jealousy towards those who, by industry and economy, succeed in making themselves independent, that they should see with pleasure the increase of capital certain that such increase must produce new demands for their labour, accompanied by increased comfort and enjoyment for them. With such a system the population of this country might increase still more rapidly than it has done; the influx of people from abroad might be triple or quadruple what it has been, and each successive year find the comforts of the labouring population in a regular course of increase, as the same causes which drive the labourers of Europe here, to seek that employment and support denied them at home, impel the capitalist to seek here a market for his capital, at the higher rate of interest which our system enables us to pay him with profit to ourselves.

Document 7.13 Reverend Henry A. Miles Defends the Mill Owners and Workers

As described earlier, the Boston Associates took great pains, before building any factories or boarding houses, to dispel the arguments against industrializing, assuring the nation that American factory owners would put the moral and physical well-being of their employees first. As the Lowell mills came under attack for their treatment of workers in the 1830s and 1840s, the Associates assembled apologists to defend the investor/owners. Foremost among these apologists was Henry A. Miles, a Unitarian minister in Lowell. In 1845 Miles wrote the first official history of Lowell and the mills. This was actually another (albeit larger) manufactured myth about Lowell. As you read from his book, determine how Miles "proves" that the Lowell mills beneficially influence the mill workers. How does he claim the owners demonstrate that they truly cared for their workers? Do you find his arguments convincing?

A Lowell Corporation

From this sketch of the growth and extent of the operations of this city, we come now to some branches of our subject, which are of the highest interest and importance; we mean the method upon which business is here conducted, the provisions made for the health, comfort, and moral protection of the operatives, and the actual character which the mass of these operatives sustain. On this last point, all know that conflicting statements have been put forth. Lowell has been highly commended by some, as a model community, for its good order, industry, spirit of intelligence, and general freedom from vice. It has been strongly condemned, by others, as a hotbed of corruption, tainting and polluting the whole land. We all, in New England, have an interest in knowing what are the exact facts of the case. We are destined to be a great manufacturing people. The influences that go forth from Lowell, will go forth from many other manufacturing villages and cities. If these influences are pernicious, we have a great calamity impending over us. Rather than endure it, we should prefer to have every factory destroyed; the character of our sons and daughters being of infinitely more importance than any considerations "wherewithal they shall be clothed." If, on the other hand, a system has been introduced, carefully provided with checks and safeguards, and strong moral and conservative influences, it is our duty to see that this system be faithfully carried out, so as to prevent the disastrous results which have developed themselves in the manufacturing towns of other countries. Hence the topics above named assume the importance of the highest moral questions. They will justify and demand the most careful consideration. The author writes after a nine years' residence in this city, during which he has closely observed the working of the factory system, and has gathered a great amount of statistical facts which have a bearing upon this subject. He believes

Reverend Henry A. Miles, *Lowell, As It Was and As It Is* [Lowell: Powers & Bagley, 1845], pp. 61–63, 67–69, 128–147.

himself to be unaffected by any partisan views, as he stands wholly aside from the sphere of any interested motives. He enters upon this part of his work, feeling, in the outset, that he has no case, one way or the other, to make out, and intending principally to confine himself to the presentation of the facts which he has collected.

A Lowell Boarding-House

Each of the long blocks of boarding-houses is divided into six or eight tenements, and are generally three stories high. These tenements are finished off in a style much above the common farm-houses of the country, and more nearly resemble the abodes of respectable mechanics in rural villages. They are all furnished with an abundant supply of water, and with suitable yards and out-buildings. These are constantly kept clean, the buildings well painted, and the premises thoroughly whitewashed every spring, at the Corporation's expense. The front room is usually the common eating-room of the house, and the kitchen is in the rear. The keeper of the house, (commonly a widow, with her family of children,) has her parlor in some part of the establishment; and in some houses there is a sitting-room for the use of the boarders. The remainder of the apartments are sleeping-rooms. In each of these are lodged two, four, and in some cases six boarders; and the room has an air of neatness and comfort, exceeding what most of the occupants have been accustomed to in their paternal homes. In many cases, these rooms are not sufficiently large for the number who occupy them; and oftentimes that attention is not paid to their ventilation which a due regard to health demands. These are points upon which a reform is called for; and, in the construction of new boarding-houses, this reform should be attempted. At the same time, it should in justice be added, that the evil alluded to is not peculiar to Lowell, and will not probably appear to be a crying one, if the case should be brought into comparison with many of the apartments of milliners and seamstresses in the boarding-houses of our cities.

Moral Police of the Corporations

It has been seen what a large amount of capital is here invested, and what manifold and extensive operations this capital sets in motion. The productiveness of these works depends upon one primary and indispensable condition—the existence of an industrious, sober, orderly, and moral class of operatives. Without this, the mills in Lowell would be worthless. Profits would be absorbed by cases of irregularity, carelessness, and neglect; while the existence of any great moral exposure in Lowell would cut off the supply of help from the virtuous homesteads of the country. Public morals and private interests, identical in all places, are here seen to be linked together in an indissoluble connection. Accordingly, the sagacity of self-interest, as well as more disinterested considerations, has led to the adoption of a strict system of moral police.

Before we proceed to notice the details of this system, there is one consideration bearing upon the character of our operatives, which must all the while be borne in mind. *We have no permanent factory population.* This is the wide gulf which separates the English manufacturing towns from Lowell. Only a very few of our operatives have their homes in this city. The most of them come from the distant interior of the country, as will be proved by statistical facts which will be presented in a subsequent chapter.

To the general fact, here noticed, should be added another, of scarcely less importance to a just comprehension of this subject,—*the female operatives in Lowell do not work, on an average, more than four and a half years in the factories.* They then return to their homes, and their places are taken by their sisters, or by other female friends from their neighborhood. Returns will hereafter be given which will establish the fact of the average above named.

Here, then, we have two important elements of difference between English and American operatives. The former are resident operatives, and are operatives for life, and constitute a permanent, dependent factory caste. The latter come from distant homes, to which in a few years they return, to be the wives of the farmers and mechanics of the country towns and villages. The English visitor to Lowell, when he finds it so hard to understand why American operatives are so superior to those of Leeds and Manchester, will do well to remember what a different class of females we have here to *begin* with—girls well educated in virtuous rural homes; nor must the Lowell manufacturer forget, that we forfeit the distinction, from that moment, when we cease to obtain such girls as the operatives of the city.

To obtain this constant importation of female hands from the country, it is necessary to secure *the moral protection of their characters while they are resident in Lowell.* This, therefore, is the chief object of that moral police referred to, some details of which will now be given.

It should be stated, in the outset, that no persons are employed on the Corporations who are addicted to intemperance, or who are known to be guilty of any immoralities of conduct. As the parent of all other vices, intemperance is most carefully excluded. Absolute freedom from intoxicating liquors is understood, throughout the city, to be a prerequisite to obtaining employment in the mills, and any person known to be addicted to their use is at once dismissed. This point has not received the attention, from writers upon the moral condition of Lowell, which it deserves; and we are surprised that the English traveller and divine, Dr. Scoresby, in his recent book upon Lowell, has given no more notice to this subject. A more strictly and universally temperate class of persons cannot be found, than the nine thousand operatives of this city; and the fact is as well known to all others living here, as it is of some honest pride among themselves. In relation to other immoralities, it may be stated, that the suspicion of criminal conduct, association with suspected persons, and general and habitual light behavior and conversation, are regarded as sufficient reasons for dismissions, and for which delinquent operatives are discharged.

In respect to discharged operatives, there is a system observed, of such an effectual and salutary operation, that it deserves to be minutely described.

Any person wishing to leave a mill, is at liberty to do so, at any time, after giving a fortnight's notice. The operative so leaving, if of good character, and having worked a year, is entitled, as a matter of right, to an honorable discharge, made out after a printed form, with which every counting-room is supplied. That form is as follows:

Mr. or Miss _____ _____, has been employed by the _____ Manufacturing Company, in a _____ Room, _____ years ___ months, and is honorably discharged.

_____ _____, Superintendent.

Lowell, _____ _____

This discharge is a letter of recommendation to any other mill in the city, and not without its influence in procuring employment in any other mill in New England. A record of all such discharges is made in each counting-room, in a book kept for that purpose.

So much for honorable discharges. Those dishonorable have another treatment. The names of all persons dismissed for bad conduct, or who leave the mill irregularly, are also entered in a book kept for that purpose, and these names are sent to all the counting-rooms of the city, and are there entered on *their* books. *Such persons obtain no more employment throughout the city.* The question is put to each applicant, "Have you worked before in the city, and if so, where is your discharge?" If no discharge be presented, an inquiry of the applicant's name will enable the superintendent to know whether that name stands on his book of dishonorable discharges, and he is thus saved from taking in a corrupt or unworthy hand. This system, which has been in operation in Lowell from the beginning, is of great and important effect in driving unworthy persons from our city, and in preserving the high character of our operatives.

A record book, of honorable and dishonorable discharges, kept on one of the Corporations, and running through the years 1836, 1837, 1838, and a part of 1839, is now lying before the author; a few quotations from which will enable the reader to understand still better the operation of the above system. Opening it at random, a few quotations will be given first of honorable discharges, transcribing, for obvious reasons, only the Christian name of the operative; and as these quotations record the length of time in which the operative has worked, the reader will be here furnished with some incidental and exact evidence bearing upon that point.

"1838, *March* 10. Julia _____. From No. 5 weaving room; worked three years; discharged to go home.

March 12. Hannah _____. From No. 3, spinning room; worked five years; discharged to go on the Boott.

March 13. Elizabeth _____. From No. 3, carding room; worked twelve months; to go home; will return probably.

March 13. Acsah _____. From No. 5, weaving room; worked three years; to go home.

March 15. Nancy _____. From No. 2, weaving room; worked twenty-seven months; to go home.

March 16. Eliza _____. From No. 5 lower weaving room; worked fourteen months; to go home.

March 19. Lucy _____. From No. 1, weaving room; worked one week; not wanted; to go on the Boott.

March 19. Lucy _____. From No. 1, dressing room; worked nine months; not wanted.

March 20. Otis _____. From repair shop, blacksmith; worked twelve months.

March 21. Almira _____. From No. 5, lower weaving room; worked three years; to go home.

March 21. Nathaniel _____. From No. 3, spinning room; worked three month; discontented with wages.

March 21. William _____. Worked ten months; cannot stand it.

March 21. Lucy _____. From No. 1, spinning room; worked ten months; not wanted.

March 24. Luretta _____. From No. 4, spinning room; worked one month.

March 24. Catharine _____. No. 4, cloth room; worked twenty-five months; to go home.

March 26. Elizabeth _____. From No. 1, spinning room; worked twelve months; to go on the Tremont."

The above is the unselected and connected record of one page.

From the record of dishonorable discharges, a connected page, opened at random, will be quoted, only with the same omission as before. The reader will notice the kind of offences recorded, and, from the dates, will be able to judge how frequently such cases occur.

"1838, *Dec*. 31. Ann _____. No. 4, weaving room; discharged for altering her looms and thinning her cloth.

1839, *Jan*. 2. Lydia _____. No. 1, spinning room; obtained an honorable discharge by false pretences. Her name has been sent round to the other Corporations as a thief and a liar.

Jan. 3. Harriet _____. and Judith _____. From No. 4, spinning, room, and No. 5, weaving room; discharged as worthless characters.

Jan. 9. Lydia _____. From No. 2, spinning room; left irregularly; name sent round.

Feb. 15. Hadassah _____. From No. 3, lower weaving room; discharged for improper conduct—stealing from Mrs. _____.

March 8. Abby _____. No. 2, spinning room; discharged for improper conduct.

March 14. Ann _____. No. 2, spinning room; discharged for reading in the mill; gave her a line stating the facts.

March 26. Harriet _____, No. 4, carding room; Laura _____, No. 4, spinning room; Ellen _____, No. 1, carding room; George _____, repair shop—all discharged for improper conduct.

March 29. Martha _____, No. 2, spinning room; Apphia _____, No. 2, spinning room; left irregularly, and names sent round.

April 3. Emily _____. No. 5, carding room; discharged for profanity, and sundry other misdemeanors. Name sent round."

It must be unnecessary to accompany the above quotations with any comment. The facts, selected with as much impartiality as is possible, speak for themselves. We have here sixteen honorable discharges given in sixteen days; and fourteen dishonorable discharges given in three months and four days, and of the offences specified, five of them indicate no deep moral delinquency. The care with which these records are kept is creditable to the officers of the Corporation, as the results of the records are honorable to the characters of their operatives.

Any description of the moral care, studied by the Corporations, would be defective if it omitted a reference to the overseers. Every room in every mill has its first and second overseer. The former, or, in his absence, the latter, has the entire care of the room, taking in such operatives as he wants for the work of the room, assigning to them their employment, superintending each process, directing the repairs of disordered machinery, giving answers to questions of advice, and granting permissions of absence. At his small desk, near the door, where he can see all who go out or come in, the overseer may generally be found; and he is held responsible for the good order, propriety of conduct, and attention to business, of the operatives of that room. Hence, this is a post of much importance, and the good management of the mill is almost wholly dependent upon the character of its overseers. It is for this reason that peculiar care is exercised in their appointment. Raw hands, and of unknown characters, are never placed in this office. It is attained only by those who have either served a regular apprenticeship as machinists in the Repair Shop, or have become well known and well tried, as third hands, and assistant overseers. It is a post for which there are always many applicants, the pay being two dollars a day, with a good house, owned by the company, and rented at the reduced charge before noticed. The overseers are almost universally married men, with families; and as a body, numbering about one hundred and eighty, in all, are among the most permanent residents, and most trustworthy and valuable citizens of the place. A large number of them are members of our churches, and are often chosen as council men in the city government, and representatives in the State legislature. The guiding and salutary influence which they exert over the operatives, is one of the most essential parts of the moral machinery of the mills.

As closely connected with the foregoing statements, the following note from a superintendent may be here republished, which was sent in reply to questions proposed to him in the Spring of 1841:—

"DEAR SIR: —

I employ in our mills, and in the various departments connected with them, thirty overseers, and as many second overseers. My overseers are married men, with families, with a single exception, and even he has engaged a tenement, and is to be married soon. Our second overseers are younger men, but upwards of twenty of them are married, and several others are soon to be married. Sixteen of our overseers are members of some regular church, and four of them are deacons. Ten of our second overseers are also members of the church, and one of them is the superintendent of a Sunday School. I have no hesitation in saying that in all the sterling requisites of character, in native intelligence, and practical good sense, in sound morality, and as active, useful, and exemplary citizens, they may as a class, safely challenge comparison with any class in our community. I know not, among them all, an intemperate man, nor, at this time, even what is called a moderate drinker.

Yours truly,
Lowell, May 10, 1841."

* * *

Still another source of trust which a Corporation has, for the good character of its operatives, is the moral control which they have over one another. Of course this control would be nothing among a generally corrupt and degraded class. But among virtuous and high-minded young women, who feel that they have the keeping of their characters, and that any stain upon their associates brings reproach upon themselves, the power of opinion becomes an ever-present, and ever-active restraint. A girl *suspected* of immoralities, or serious improprieties of conduct at once loses caste. Her fellow-boarders will at once leave the house, if the keeper does not dismiss the offender. In self-protection, therefore, the matron is obliged to put the offender away. Nor will her former companions walk with or work with her; till at length, finding herself everywhere talked about and pointed at, and shunned, she is obliged to relieve her fellow-operatives of a presence which they feel brings disgrace. From this power of opinion, there is no appeal; and as long as it is exerted in favor of propriety of behavior and purity of life, it is one of the most active and effectual safeguards of character.

It may not be out of place to present here the regulations, which are observed alike on all the Corporations, which are given to the operatives when they are first employed, and are posted up conspicuously in all the mills.

They are as follows: —

Regulations to be observed by all persons employed by the _____ Manufacturing Company, in the Factories.

Every overseer is required to be punctual himself, and to see that those employed under him are so.

The overseers may, at their discretion, grant leave of absence to those employed under them, when there are sufficient spare hands in the room to supply their place; but when there are not sufficient spare hands, they are not allowed to grant leave of absence unless in cases of absolute necessity.

All persons are required to observe the regulations of the room in which they are employed. They are not allowed to be absent from their work without the consent of their overseer, except in case of sickness, and then they are required to send him word of the cause of their absence.

All persons are required to board in one of the boarding houses belonging to the company, and conform to the regulations of the house in which they board.

All persons are required to be constant in attendance on public worship, at one of the regular places of worship in this place.

Persons who do not comply with the above regulations will not be employed by the company.

Persons entering the employment of the company, are considered as engaging to work one year.

All persons intending to leave the employment of the company, are required to give notice of the same to their overseer, at least two weeks previous to the time of leaving.

Any one who shall take from the mills, or the yard, any yarn, cloth, or other article belonging to the company will be considered guilty of STEALING—and prosecuted accordingly.

The above regulations are considered part of the *contract with* all persons entering the employment of the _____ MANUFACTURING COMPANY. All persons who shall have complied with them, on leaving the employment of the company, shall be entitled to an honorable discharge, which will serve as a recommendation to any of the factories in Lowell. No one who shall not have complied with them will be entitled to such a discharge.

_____ _____, Agent."

Chapter 7 Worksheet and Questions

1. Assume the role of a former mill girl in 1850. Using examples from the documents, explain why you entered the mills, what was positive about your experience, and why you would recommend this life to others.

_____

_____

_____

_____

_____

_____

_____

_____

2. Now take the position of a labor reformer, and denounce the person above as a corporate flunky. Describe what you see as the reality of the mill experience. Why are people forced into the life of an operative? What are the real working conditions like, and how do the owners treat the workers?

_____

_____

_____

_____

_____

_____

_____

_____

3. One of the classic American myths is the idea that we have a classless society, a nation of equals. This was clearly not the case demonstrated in these documents. Provide examples of the thinking and attitudes in these documents about class, and the workers' place in the class structure.

_____

_____

_____

_____

_____

_____

_____

_____

4. Since you first read the preface of this book, the authors have told you that people always have motives for what they write. In this chapter, people tended to be "pro" and "anti the impact of the market economy. Choose four authors and provide examples how their position is clear on one side of this issue or another.

_____

_____

_____

_____

_____

_____

_____

_____

What Kind of Equality? The Debate over Women's Rights and Duties in the Antebellum United States

The traditionally prescribed status of American women began to change with the development of the market economy and industrialization. Prior to this time, most families lived on farms, where everyone in the household was responsible for economic production and prosperity. Women and children created goods and services vital to the family's survival, either by contributing labor in the fields or creating goods for barter in the local town. But with the coming of industrialization and the market economy, homes declined as centers of production, and goods traditionally made by women shifted to factories and workshops. Bulk textiles as well as finished clothes, shoes, various foods, and specialty items became available in standardized forms to most Americans. Transportation improvements hastened this development by expanding the marketplace, making manufactured items available and inexpensive enough to replace home-made goods.

These economic changes and new opportunities meant upward success and social mobility for some, but failure and loss of status for others. Rural inhabitants left behind their homes, churches, and families for the opportunities and excitement of the growing cities. There they joined a burgeoning immigrant population. Middle-class Americans embraced the notion that successful people had ambition and a winner-take-all mentality, and that the wealth they accumulated symbolized status. They also feared loss of status and downward mobility for themselves, and the threat of violence and an end to social order across society as the market economy expanded.

For women this notion supposedly meant they were no longer tied to the spinning wheel and loom, hearth, or kitchen. While the husband left home daily to earn an income in his chosen profession, his wife took over the home to rule as her own—the middle-class ideal of home life. While men remained the family head, his domain was out in the "real world" of business, because the family's status depended on the income he brought home. This wealth, the middle class believed, allowed him to support his non-working wife and children. The new standard became that if your job did not produce an income large enough to support a family, then you were not really working. In fact, society valued housework less now than before, even though washing clothes, caring for children, cooking meals, and cleaning the home remained day-long activities. As historian Jeanne Boydston explained, this arrangement now became a form of "unpaid labor." A woman's responsibilities to produce a competency changed, but housework remained a constant. Her work and world remained largely the same, even as the male sphere was changing.

The household took on new importance as a "home," a refuge from the outside world of the marketplace, competition, and greed. Middle-class families decreased in size, as children became more important as symbols of what the family produced, instead of being part of the production unit. Now time spent with children became important, teaching and educating them, molding them with middle-class values. Motherhood became valued more as the nineteenth century progressed, and the home where "Mother" ruled was a source of stability and order. Of course, women did not escape the labor and drudgery of housework, even if they could afford domestic help. Neatness and cleanliness of the home became symbols of success and the ability to "mother"; thus, time spent on housework increased rather than diminished.

The spiritual ferment of the Second Great Awakening also destabilized traditional gender roles. Reform movements, attempting to free individuals from evils such as alcohol, ignorance, or slavery, attracted many men and women. These movements allowed women to be forceful and nurturing outside of the home. They could also take steps to protect the home from the growing social disorder of modern society, disorder they believed stemmed from people leaving their traditional foundations of moral support: the home, family, church, and community. Although reform movements at first separated all female auxiliaries from the male bodies, women still joined the communities of reformers, and crusaded for and kept in touch with other women on issues important to them. Some women first joined bible and tract societies to spread the gospel and save souls. All of these associations outside of the home allowed women to network with their peers. Many created lifelong friendships and correspondence, and anguished during extended periods of separation. Although their backgrounds varied, most women reformers were part of the emerging middle class, and being involved in such activities helped define that status to others as much as their husband's income.

The focus of the benevolent associations reflected more female concerns as more women joined their ranks. For example, the Daughters of Temperance not only wanted to save the drunkard, but also focused their concern on his victims—the abused wife and children. Convincing men to cut back on alcohol consumption meant preventing job loss; more money came home for the family, raising their stature and assuring the success of the woman's sphere. Prostitutes were seen as fallen sisters seduced by men, who now needed saving from male depravity. The seducers should be prosecuted, not the victims, a stance unpopular with many male reformers.

But the woman's sphere was supposed to be in the home, and her powers were supposed to be subtle and silent. Women authors used pen names because writing for publications was considered a male arena. Women reformers were not often allowed freedom to speak in public, especially to mixed (the nineteenth-century term was "promiscuous") crowds. Speaking on separate platforms to gender-segregated crowds was accepted, but any woman bold enough to speak to men supposedly "unsexed" herself by speaking out of place. Woe be unto the women who dared criticize any male speaker or minister speaking at the same meeting. The first time noted anti-slavery writer and orator Abigail Kelley spoke to a mixed audience, outraged Philadelphians threw rocks and brickbats through the windows, and after she left they torched the building, ironically a new hall dedicated to the right of free discussion. Later she would be attacked for her style of dressing, accused of being a prostitute or unsexed monster, and pelted with rotten eggs by civilized gentlemen.

Middle-class America pictured the ideal wife, mother, and daughter to be at home in her own sphere. The ideal of domesticity emerged from both the economic changes and the post-Revolutionary ideas about "republican motherhood." Women's magazines began paying tribute to the mother of George Washington, and held her up as the model for all modern nineteenth-century women. The middle-class home was the safe retreat from the evils of the outside world, a refuge from the greed and corruption of the commercial world and market economy. More than that, the home was the key to maintaining stability and culture in the nation, to preserving the very existence of the Republic itself. This would be so because the home would be a bastion of feminine values—piety, morality, and self-sacrifice—virtues all missing from the male world on the outside. Women would raise the children to be virtuous, and restore their husbands' virtues and values when they came home from earning the family income. Earlier in the United States, household work and childcare were rarely noticed, but now the home became the most important social institution, and stay-at-home mothers became vital to preserving virtue in the population. The *Seneca Falls Democrat* in 1840 explained "a good wife" should be ". . . like a snail, always keep within her own house . . . second, be like an echo, to speak when she is spoken to; but like an echo she should not always have the last word." Any woman who did not conform to this middle-class model of womanhood was either immoral or a threat to society.

Of course, many women had to work outside the home because they were poor or left without male support (such as the mill workers in Chapter 7), but they were still criticized for being "bad" wives and mothers. Catherine Beecher advocated that women, as nurturers and submissive wives, maintained the democratic social order, which she believed was the existing social order. Women would be the agents of middle-class culture, and thus be the ultimate force for national unity in troubled times. Beecher opposed women's suffrage but advocated women as teachers, believing they could nurture and mold more children in the classroom than they do at home. Since the nation faced a shortage of teachers to staff the growing number of common schools, women could fill this need and provide service to the republic. Besides, they were single women doing what had been men's jobs, and they could be paid less because they had no families to support.

As they promoted other reforms, women recognized the unequal treatment they received from the law and society in general. Decades of activism in other reform movements, and attempts to rescue female victims of poverty, slavery, and prostitution led to calls for women's rights and greater access to life in the public sphere. Elizabeth Cady Stanton came from the anti-slavery movement, Susan B. Anthony from the Temperance movement, and Paulina W. Davis from the property rights struggle. Gender-based legal discrimination was nothing new; wives were legal possessions, not legal persons. They had no control over real or personal property, and no rights to their own earnings—these belonged to either their husband or closest male relative. Few states allowed women to make contracts or even claim rights to their own children in a divorce.

There was a growing movement to equalize these laws. Mississippi first recognized women's rights to property they brought into the marriage, in 1839, and New York followed in 1848. But the general attitude was that women were less accountable under the law than "infants, idiots, and lunatics." In the 1850s, Massachusetts refused to lift restrictions on women's legal standing or grant them the right to vote, claiming that since most women were not actively calling for these rights, a majority of women must not want them. George Fitzhugh wrote that "women, like children, have but one right, and that is the right to protection. The right to protection involves the obligation to obey."

Legal changes were good, but the majority of Americans opposed any movement for greater female participation in the public sphere. Most women's sense of security and identity was rooted in the home. Although men accused female activists of abandoning the home, most proponents of women's rights never really questioned a woman's primary responsibility for the home and children. Some were aware of how the idea of domesticity negatively shaped the lives of working-class and poor women. Utilizing the assumption that all "good women" should be working in their homes caring for their families, employers justified paying women lower wages and denying them access to higher-paying jobs. This argument ignored the obvious fact that many women were the primary income producers for their families. Other women became prostitutes to feed their families, because it paid more. In 1859 a New York survey of prostitutes found 25 percent were married but abandoned by their husbands, while most worked in factories or as domestic servants at the same time but could not survive on the wages. At least 10 percent of urban women were forced to choose prostitution as a survival option before the Civil War. Male-led public charities, however, labeled poor women as "failed women," attributing prostitution to moral collapse rather than economic necessity and sexual exploitation by men. Poor or working mothers were blamed for the large numbers of hungry, dirty children learning to become thieves on New York streets, because of their failure to stay at home and teach them proper values. As one solution, the New York Children's Aid Society regularly swooped up such children and shipped them by train to foster homes in the Midwest.

Outspoken male critics went further. Conservative Protestant ministers claimed that the idea of a woman's public rights was absurd, that female subordination to man is God-given due to the "sin of Eve" and the fact that Jesus was a man. Many opposed women becoming teachers, since schools provided them a public place of authority over young men. In 1837 the Reverend Jonathan Stearns of Massachusetts claimed that denying women the right to speak in public was not a matter of capability, but of *decency*. She should stay at home because "it is her province to adorn social life, to throw a charm over the intercourse of the world, by making it lovely and attractive." The *New York Herald* and other newspapers questioned the femininity of women activists, calling them old maids, unattractive, and "mannish men" unable to get husbands. These papers also attacked the masculinity of the movement's male supporters, suggesting they were all weak-willed, hen-pecked husbands who "ought to wear petticoats." If women were given public rights, the editors warned, wives would start wearing pants, smoking cigars, and staying out all night, while men would be forced to stay home and care for children. Southerners attacked the movement because many women's rights activists were also abolitionists. Sarah and Angelina Grimke formed the first women's abolitionist society, the Anti-Slavery Convention of American Women. The City of Charleston formally exiled the sisters for incendiary talk (abolition and women's rights) and accused them of moral turpitude for appearing in public with men of both races.

Women activists ignored the critics and pushed ahead with their calls for public rights and freedoms. These included freedom of speech without interference, whether expressing themselves in print, aloud, or in parades; freedom to appear in forbidden (public) places without attacks on their character; and an end to exclusion from profitable employment, higher education, the pulpit, and voting. The movement had little formal organization at first, consisting of isolated speaking tours and petition campaigns aimed at state legislatures. Conventions such at the ones at Seneca Falls in 1848 and Worcester in 1850 usually invited men, recognizing that their support would be useful in convincing legislatures to change the laws. Success would be slow in coming, but the push for equal rights had begun.

Considering the Evidence in the Readings

This chapter contains the opinions of men and women on both sides of the women's rights issue. The writers use a variety of methods to make their points. Some talk about tradition, some appeal to emotion, some speak out of anger, and others paint a picture of future disaster if changes occur. Various selections advocate the ideal of domesticity and argue that the only proper place for women is at home. You should take note of the arguments they give for women's staying at home, and what they fear will be the result of women's entering the public sphere. The other selections discuss the reality of life for women in the antebellum United States. Be sure to observe the injustices they describe, as well as the solutions they propose. Who opposes their call for equality and justice, and what is the response to the women's rights conventions during the antebellum years?

Document 8.1 A Pastoral Letter from the Massachusetts Congregational Clergy, 1837

Conservative clergy led the attack on women's rights activists. Unlike English clergy who led the attack on slavery, most Northern clergymen did not actively support abolition until shortly before the Civil War. Instead, they supported maintaining the status quo and the existing social order. They were especially upset by the attempt to link the abolition movement with the new calls for women's rights. Women who spoke in public, they believed, were little more than brazen hussies who by their actions forfeited the protection of all good men and the law. Ministers urged women to remain within their "God ordained" sphere, and to give up public speaking, teachings, or initiating public discussions of private issues like rape and contraception. Conservative clergy vehemently opposed abolitionist women testifying about the sexual exploitation of slave women. The following letter responds to the Grimke sisters speaking at mixed-gender abolition meetings, and represents a desire by the clergy to control the women in their own congregations, as well as forbidding the sisters to speak in any other churches. What "obtrusive and ostentatious" behaviors does the clergy believe are unnatural and a violation of Christian guidelines? What arguments does the clergy give to support female subordination and silence? Do they have anything good to say about women here?

From *The Liberator*, August 11, 1837.

... The appropriate duties and influence of woman are clearly stated in the New Testament. Those duties and that influence are unobtrusive and private, but the source of mighty power. When the mild, dependent, softening influence of woman upon the sternness of man's opinions is fully exercised, society feels the effects of it in a thousand forms. The power of woman is in her dependence, flowing from the consciousness of that weakness which God has given her for her protection, and which keeps her in those departments of life that form the character of individuals and of the nation. There are social influences which females use in promoting piety and the great objects of Christian benevolence which we cannot too highly commend. We appreciate the unostentatious prayers and efforts of woman in advancing the cause of religion at home and abroad; in Sabbath-schools; in leading religious inquirers to the pastors for instruction; and in all such associated effort as becomes the modesty of her sex; and earnestly hope that she may abound more and more in these labors of piety and love.

But when she assumes the place and tone of man as a public reformer, our care and protection of her seem unnecessary; we put ourselves in self-defence against her; she yields the power which God has given her for protection, and her character becomes unnatural. If the vine, whose strength and beauty is to lean upon the trellis-work and half conceal its clusters, thinks to assume the independence and the overshadowing nature of the elm, it will not only cease to bear fruit, but fall in shame and dishonor into the dust. We cannot, therefore, but regret the mistaken conduct of those who encourage females to bear an obtrusive and ostentatious part in measure of reform, and countenance any of that sex who so far forget themselves as to itinerate in the character of public lecturers and teachers.—We especially deplore the intimate acquaintance and promiscuous conversation of females with regard to things "which ought not to be named"; by which that modesty and delicacy which is the charm of domestic life, and which constitutes the true influence of woman in society, is consumed, and the way opened, as we apprehend, for degeneracy and ruin. We say these things, not to discourage proper influences against sin, but to secure such reformation as we believe is Scriptural, and will be permanent.

Document 8.2 Sarah M. Grimke Responds to the Pastoral Letter, 1837

Born and raised in Charleston, South Carolina, Sarah and Angelina Grimke were the daughters of a prominent slaveholding family who converted to the antislavery cause. Beginning in June 1837, they commenced a lecturing tour, speaking before thousands of New England men and women. Their vivid, personal accounts of the horrors of slavery caused the previous pastoral letter. But Sarah also angered the New England clergy by writing letters in Boston newspapers. These letters were later bound and published as the first feminist treatise in the United States, *Letters on the Equality of the Sexes, and the Condition of Women.* Her written response to the Congregationalist clergy was published in the same antislavery newspaper as their letter, William Lloyd Garrison's *Liberator.* In this letter Sarah challenged the clergy's interpretation of the proper sphere for women, and argued against their theological justification. In what ways did the male ministers utilize a "perverted" interpretation of the New Testament? What is the biblical basis for women's activism and involvement in reform movements, according to Ms. Grimke? According to Sarah, is there any biblical justification for inequality of pay or educational opportunity? Is there a biblical requirement that all women marry, or is this just another male-based interpretation?

Haverhill, 7th Mo. 1837.

DEAR FRIEND,—When I last addressed thee, I had not seen the Pastoral Letter of the General Association. It has since fallen into my hands, and I must digress from my intention of exhibiting the condition of women in different parts of the world, in order to make some remarks on this extraordinary document. I am persuaded that when the minds of men and women become emancipated from the thraldom of superstition and "traditions of men," the sentiments contained in the Pastoral Letter will be recurred to

From *The Liberator*, October 6, 1837.

with as much astonishment as the opinions of Cotton Mather and other distinguished men of his day, on the subject of witchcraft; nor will it be deemed less wonderful, that a body of divines should gravely assemble and endeavor to prove that woman has no right to "open her mouth for the dumb," than it now is that judges should have sat on the trials of witches, and solemnly condemned nineteen persons and one dog to death for witchcraft.

But to the letter. It says, "We invite your attention to the dangers which at present seem to threaten the FEMALE CHARACTER with wide-spread and permanent injury." I rejoice that they have called the attention of my sex to this subject, because I believe if woman investigates it, she will soon discover that danger is impending, though from a totally different source from that which the Association apprehends,—danger from those who, having long held the reins of *usurped* authority, are unwilling to permit us to fill that sphere which God created us to move in, and who have entered into league to crush the immortal mind of woman. I rejoice, because I am persuaded that the rights of woman, like the rights of slaves, need only be examined to be understood and asserted, even by some of those, who are now endeavoring to smother the irrepressible desire for menial and spiritual freedom which glows in the breast of many, who hardly dare to speak their sentiments.

"The appropriate duties and influence of women are clearly stated in the New Testament. Those duties are unobtrusive and private, but the sources of *mighty power*. When the mild, *dependent*, softening influence of woman upon the sternness of man's opinions is fully exercised, society feels the effects of it in a thousand ways." No one can desire more earnestly than I do, that woman may move exactly in the sphere which her Creator has assigned her; and I believe her having been displaced from that sphere has introduced confusion into the world. It is, therefore, of vast importance to herself and to all the rational creation, that she should ascertain what are her duties and her privileges as a responsible and immortal being. The New Testament has been referred to, and I am willing to abide by its decisions, but must enter my protest against the false translation of some passages by the MEN who did that work, and against the perverted interpretation by the MEN who undertook to write commentaries thereon. I am inclined to think, when we are admitted to the honor of studying Greek and Hebrew, we shall produce some various readings of the Bible a little different from those we now have.

The Lord Jesus defines the duties of his followers in his Sermon on the Mount. He lays down grand principles by which they should be governed, without any reference to sex or condition.—"Ye are the light of the world. A city that is set on a hill cannot be hid. Neither do men light a candle and put it under a bushel, but on a candlestick, and it giveth light unto all that are in the house. Let your light so shine before men, that they may see your good works, and glorify your Father which is in Heaven." I follow him through all his precepts, and find him giving the same directions to women as to men, never even referring to the distinction now so strenuously insisted upon between masculine and feminine virtues: this is one of the antichristian "traditions of men" which are taught instead of the "commandments of God." Men and women were CREATED EQUAL; they are both moral and accountable beings, and whatever is *right* for man to do, is *right* for woman.

But the influence of woman, says the Association, is to be private and unobtrusive, her light is not to shine before man like that of her brethren; but she is passively to let the lords of the creation, as they call themselves, put the bushel over it, lest peradventure it might appear that the world has been benefitted by the rays of *her* candle. So that her quenched light, according to their judgment, will be of more use than if it were set on the candlestick. "Her influence is the source of mighty power." This has ever been the flattering language of man since he laid aside the whip as a means to keep woman in subjection. He spares her body; but the war he has waged against her mind, her heart, and her soul, has been no less destructive to her as a moral being. How monstrous, how antiChristian, is the doctrine that woman is to be dependent on man! Where, in all the sacred Scriptures, is this taught? Alas! she has too well learned the lesson, which MAN has labored to teach her. She has surrendered her dearest RIGHTS, and been satisfied with the privileges which man has assumed to grant her; she has been amused with the show of power, whilst man has absorbed all the reality into himself. He has adorned the creature whom God gave him as a companion, with baubles and gewgaws, turned her attention to personal attractions, offered incense to her vanity, and made her the instrument of his selfish gratification, a plaything to please his eye and amuse his hours of leisure. "Rule by obedience and by submission sway," or in other words, study to be a hypocrite, pretend to submit, but gain your point, has been the code of household morality which woman has been taught. The poet has sung, in sickly strains, the loveliness of woman's dependence upon man, and now we find it reechoed by those who profess to teach the religion of the Bible. God says, "Cease ye from man whose breath is in his nostrils, for wherein is he to be accounted of?" Man says, depend upon me. God says, "HE will teach us of his ways." Man says, believe it not, I am to be your teacher. This doctrine of dependence upon man is utterly at variance with the doctrine of the Bible. In that book I find nothing like the softness of woman, nor the sternness of man: both are equally commanded to bring forth the fruits of the Spirit, love, meekness, gentleness, &c.

But we are told, "the power of woman is in her dependence, flowing from a consciousness of that weakness which God has given her for her protection." If physical weakness is alluded to, I cheerfully concede the superiority; if brute force is what my brethren are claiming, I am willing to let them have all the honor they desire; but if they mean to intimate, that mental or moral weakness belongs to woman, more than to man, I utterly disclaim the charge. Our powers of mind have been crushed, as far as man could do it, our sense of morality has been impaired by his interpretation of our duties; but no where does God say that he made any distinction between us, as moral and intelligent beings.

"We appreciate," say the Association, "the unostentatious prayers and efforts of woman in advancing the cause of religion at home and abroad, in leading religious inquirers to THE PASTOR for instruction." Several points here demand attention. If public prayers and public efforts are necessarily ostentatious, then "Anna the prophetess, (or preacher,) who departed not from the temple, but served God with fastings and prayers night and day," "and spake of Christ to all them that looked for redemption in Israel," was ostentatious in her efforts. Then, the apostle Paul encourages women to be ostentatious in their efforts to spread the gospel, when he gives them directions how they should appear, when engaged in praying, or preaching in the public assemblies. Then, the whole association of Congregational ministers are ostentatious, in the efforts they are making in preaching and praying to convert souls.

But woman may be permitted to lead religious inquirers to the PASTORS for instruction. Now this is assuming that all pastors are better qualified to give instruction than woman. This I utterly deny. I have suffered too keenly from the teaching of man, to lead any one to him for instruction. The Lord Jesus says,— "Come unto me and learn of me." He points his followers to no man; and when woman is made the favored instrument of rousing a sinner to his lost and helpless condition, she has no right to substitute any teacher for Christ; all she has to do is, to turn the contrite inquirer to the "Lamb of God which taketh away

the sins of the world." More souls have probably been lost by going down to Egypt for help, and by trusting in man in the early stages of religious experience, than by any other error. Instead of the petition being offered to God,—"Lead me in thy truth, and TEACH me, for thou art the God of my salvation,"—instead of relying on the precious promises—"What man is he that feareth the Lord? him shall HE TEACH in the way that he shall choose"—"I will instruct thee and TEACH thee in the way which thou shalt go—I will guide thee with mine eye"—the young convert is directed to go to man, as if he were in the place of God, and his instructions essential to an advancement in the path of righteousness. That woman can have but a poor conception of the privilege of being taught of God, what he alone can teach, who would turn the "religious inquirer aside" from the fountain of living waters, where he might slake his thirst for spiritual instruction, to those broken cisterns which can hold no water, and therefore cannot satisfy the panting spirit. The business of men and women, who are ORDAINED OF GOD to preach the "unsearchable riches of Christ" to a lost and perishing world, is to lead souls to Christ, and not to Pastors for instruction.

The General Association say, that "when woman assumes the place and tone of man as a public reformer, our care and protection of her seem unnecessary; we put ourselves in self-defence against her, and her character becomes unnatural." Here again the unscriptural notion is held up, that there is a distinction between the duties of men and women as moral beings; that what is virtue in man, is vice in woman; and women who dare to obey the command of Jehovah, "Cry aloud, spare not, lift up thy voice like a trumpet, and show my people their transgression," are threatened with having the protection of the brethren withdrawn. If this is all they do, we shall not even know the time when our chastisement is inflicted; our trust is in the Lord Jehovah, and in him is everlasting strength. The motto of woman, when she is engaged in the great work of public reformation should be,—"The Lord is my light and my salvation; whom shall I fear? The Lord is the strength of my life; of whom shall I be afraid?" She must feel, if she feels rightly, that she is fulfilling one of the important duties laid upon her as an accountable being, and that her character, instead of being "unnatural," is in exact accordance with the will of Him to whom, and to no other, she is responsible for the talents and the gifts confided to her. As to the pretty simile, introduced into the "Pastoral Letter," "if the vine whose strength and beauty is to lean upon the trellis work, and half conceal its clusters, thinks to assume the independence and the overshadowing nature of the elm," &c. I shall only remark that it might well suit the poet's fancy, who sings of sparkling eyes and coral lips, and knights in armor clad; but it seems to me utterly inconsistent with the dignity of a Christian body, to endeavor to draw such an antiscriptural distinction between men and women. Ah! how many of my sex feel in the dominion, thus unrighteously exercised over them, under the gentle appellation of *protection*, that what they have leaned upon has proved a broken reed at best, and oft a Spear.

Thine in the bonds of womanhood,

SARAH M. GRIMKE.

Document 8.3 Mrs. A.J. Graves Argues in Favor of the Domestic Sphere

Supporters of what historian Nancy Cott called the "Cult of Domesticity" believed that a woman's place was in the home. She should use all her moral, pious, and emotional skills to shape her children into model citizens, and restore her husband's virtue when he came home corrupted by his efforts in the jungle-like economic world. Any problem arising at home was by definition her fault, and she was responsible for finding solutions to keep the sphere functioning properly. This meant staying home, not venturing out in public. Male supporters of the women's sphere, such as novelist John Neal, argued that women did not need rights outside the home because they were already superior to men inside the home, that "she is as free and independent as the wild winds of heaven." Sarah Hale argued that women's intuition, "an innate, feminine form of intelligence," made women superior, and that "what man shall become depends on the secret, silent influence of women." Mrs. A.J. Graves described this role in her 1841 book *Woman in America*. How would Mrs. Graves describe a woman's "intellectual life"? What is a woman supposed to learn and know, and how should she apply her knowledge? What is Mrs. Graves' solution to communication problems between husband and wife?

To woman it belongs, also, to elevate the intellectual character of her household, to kindle the fires of mental activity in childhood, and to keep them steadily burning with advancing years. "It is in educating the women of your country," says Mademoiselle Montgolfier, in a letter to one of our female writers, "that its future is prepared. It is by this that the land will be purified, where the men are too much absorbed by material interests. The intellectual life of America seems to have passed into the souls of the women." This may appear somewhat extravagant; but whether the fact be so or not, there can be no doubt that "intellectual life" should have an existence in the souls of American women. The men of our country, as things are constituted among us, find but little time for the cultivation of science and general literature—studies so eminently calculated to refine the mind and purify the taste, and which furnish so exhaustless a fund of elevated enjoyment to the heart. And this is the case even with those who have acquired a fondness for intellectual pursuits in early life. The absorbing passion for gain, and the pressing demands of business, engross their whole attention. Thus the merchant becomes a merchant, and nothing more; and the mind of the lawyer is little else than a library of cases and precedents, of legal records and commentaries. The physician loses sight of the scientific studies to which his profession so naturally directs him, contents himself with the same beaten track, and becomes a mere practitioner or operator. And the mechanic and agriculturist too often settle down into mere manual laborers, by suffering practical details wholly to occupy their minds as well as their bodies. The only relief to this absorbing devotion to "material interests" is found in the excitement of party politics.

These two engross the whole moral, intellectual, and physical man; and, to be convinced of this, we need not follow the American to his place of business or to political meetings—we have only to listen to his fireside conversation. It might be supposed that the few waking hours he spends at home in the bosom of his family, he would delight to employ upon such subjects as would interest and improve his wife and children, and that he would avail himself of these

From *Woman in America*, New York, 1858.

opportunities to refresh his wearied mind with new matters of thought. But in place of this, what is the perpetual theme of his conversation? Business and politics, six per cent., bank discounts, stock-jobbing, insolvencies, assets, liabilities—cases at court, legal opinions and decisions—neuralgia, gastric irritation, fevers, &c.—Clay, Webster, the Bank bill, and other political topics of the day: these are the subjects incessantly talked about by the male members of the family when at home, and which the females, of course, are neither expected to take any special interest in nor to understand. Or perhaps the wife may take her turn in relating the history of the daily vexations she experiences in her household arrangements, while the husband's eye is gazing on vacancy, or his mind is occupied by his business cares. Woman should be made to take an intelligent interest in her husband's affairs, and may be benefited by a knowledge of the value of money, its best mode of investment; or by being instructed in the laws of physiology and of hygiene; but she can receive neither pleasure nor profit from hearing the cabalistic terms familiar only to the initiated in the mysteries of financiering, or the occult words and phrases which the professional man employs to communicate his knowledge or the results of his observations. The husband should doubtless sympathize with the wife in her domestic trials; but he cannot, nor ought he to, become interested in every trivial vexation she may meet with. There should, then, be some common ground on which both may meet with equal pleasure and advantage to themselves and to their offspring; and what is there so appropriate to this end as intellectual pursuits? . . .

Document 8.4 A Southern Matron Promotes Deference and Self-Control for a Planter's Bride

The Cult of Domesticity enjoyed great support in the north, where the growing wealth of the middle class allowed women to stay at home and focus their time on family rather than economic survival. In more rural areas to the south and west, women still spent time producing goods to increase or maintain household income. But the idea of the feminine sphere, where women stay at home and demonstrate piety, innocence, and submission were celebrated across the south as well. Here, however, the Cult of Domesticity enforced the dominant patriarchy, suppressed women's activities in reform movements or writing, and became part of the defense of slavery. Native New Englander Caroline Howard Gilman was the wife of a Unitarian minister transferred to Charleston, South Carolina. In addition to having seven children, she wrote articles for Sarah Hale's *Ladies Magazine*, which actively promoted male authority and female domesticity, and published several novels with the New York publisher Harper & Brothers. Her novels promoted the ideal of middle-class domestic bliss. One novel, *Recollections of a Southern Matron*, included a chapter called "The Planter's Bride," which offered advice to Southern wives. What complaints about a Southern woman's life does Gilman make? Why are these problems not as important as domestic harmony? Why is deference so important? According to Gilman, what are the three "golden threads" of domestic happiness?

———

The planter's bride, who leaves a numerous and cheerful family in her paternal home, little imagines the change which awaits her in her own retired residence. She dreams of an independent sway over her household, devoted love and unbroken intercourse with her husband, and indeed longs to be released from the eyes of others, that she may dwell only beneath the sunbeam of his. And so it was with me. After our bustling wedding and protracted journey, I looked forward to the retirement at Bellevue as a quiet port in which I should rest with Arthur, after drifting so long on general society. The romance of our love was still in its glow, as might be inferred by the infallible sign of his springing to pick up my pocket-handkerchief whenever it fell. . . .

For several weeks all kinds of droll associations were conjured up, and we laughed at anything and nothing. What cared we for fashion and pretension?

———

From *Recollections of a Southern Matron*, Harper & Brothers, 1838.

There we were together, asking for nothing but each other's presence and love. At length it was necessary for him to tear himself away to superintend his interests. I remember when his horse was brought to the door for his first absence of two hours; an observer would have thought that he was going a far journey, had he witnessed that parting; and so it continued for some days, and his return at each time was like the sun shooting through a three days' cloud.

But the period of absence was gradually protracted; then a friend sometimes came home with him, and their talk was of crops and politics, draining the fields and draining the revenue. . . . I was not selfish, and even urged Arthur to go to hunt and to dinner-parties, although hoping that he would resist my urging. He went frequently, and a growing discomfort began to work upon my mind. I had undefined forebodings; I mused about past days; my views of life became slowly disorganized; my physical powers enfeebled, a nervous excitement followed; I nursed a moody discontent, and ceased a while to reason clearly. Woe to me had I yielded to this irritable temperament! I began immediately, on principle, to busy myself about my household. The location of Bellevue was picturesque—the dwelling airy and commodious; I had, therefore, only to exercise taste in external and internal arrangement to make it beautiful throughout. I was careful to consult my husband in those points which interested him, without annoying him with mere trifles. If the reign of romance was really waning, I resolved not to chill his noble confidence, but to make a steadier light rise on his affections. If he was absorbed in reading, I sat quietly waiting the pause when I should be rewarded by the communication of ripe ideas; if I saw that he prized a tree which interfered with my flowers, I sacrificed my preference to a more sacred feeling; if any habit of his annoyed me, I spoke of it once or twice calmly, and then bore it quietly if unreformed; I welcomed his friends with cordiality, entered into their family interests, and stopped my yawns, which, to say the truth, was sometimes an almost desperate effort, before they reached eye or ear.

This task of self-government was not easy. To repress a harsh answer, to confess a fault, and to stop (right or wrong) in the midst of self-defence, in gentle submission, sometimes requires a struggle like life and death: but these *three* efforts are the golden threads with which domestic happiness is woven: once begin the fabric with this woof, and trials shall not break or sorrow tarnish it.

Men are not often unreasonable: their difficulties lie in not understanding the moral and physical structure of our sex. They often wound through ignorance, and are surprised at having offended. How clear is it, then, that woman loses by petulance and recrimination! Her first study must be self-control, almost to hypocrisy. A good wife must smile amid a thousand perplexities, and clear her voice to tones of cheerfulness when her frame is drooping with disease, or else languish alone. Man, on the contrary, when trials beset him, expects to find her ear and heart a ready receptacle. . . .

I have not meant to suggest that, in ceasing to be a mere lover, Arthur was not a tender and devoted husband. I have only described the natural progress of a sensible, independent married man, desirous of fulfilling all the relations of society. Nor in these remarks would I chill the romance of some young dreamer, who is reposing her heart on another. Let her dream on. God has given this youthful, luxurious gift of trusting love, as he has given hues to the flower and sunbeams to the sky. It is a superadded charm to his lavish blessings; but let her be careful. . . .

Let him know nothing of the struggle which follows the first chill of the affections; let no scenes of tears and apologies, be acted to agitate him, until he becomes accustomed to agitation; thus shall the star of domestic peace arise in fixedness and beauty above them, and shine down in gentle light on their lives, as it has on ours.

Document 8.5 Catherine Beecher Exalts the Middle-Class Home and a Woman's Role

Catherine Beecher was the daughter of Reverend Lyman Beecher, sister of the equally prominent Reverend Henry Ward Beecher and sister of the novelist Harriet Beecher Stowe. She was the champion of middle-class female domesticity and republican motherhood. In her writings she agreed that housework was hard work, but told her readers it was never as difficult as any field of male labor. Beecher also praised female subordination to men as a vital key to American democracy. Refusing to go on the lecture circuit herself, she declared that a woman's entering masculine public realms was a violation of nature. In 1846 Beecher presented a public address by sitting on the dais and listening while *her brother* read her speech.

Women had all the equality necessary, and should realize men subordinated women only when their concern for the female sex's "best interests demanded it." However, Beecher supported women's dominating the teaching profession, because they could morally shape entire generations of future citizens. She established a female seminary in Hartford, Connecticut, as well as the Western Female Institute in Cincinnati. Her schools rounded up, trained, and sent west young women as common school teachers. In this opening chapter of her *Treatise on Domestic Economy*, how does she demonstrate that democracy is consistent with social hierarchies? How is a woman's concentration on teaching and domesticity the key to American democracy?

Chapter 1
The Peculiar Responsibilities of American Women

There are some reasons, why American women should feel an interest in the support of the democratic institution of their Country, which it is important that they should consider. The great maxim, which is the basis of all our civil and political institutions, is, that "all men are created equal," and that they are equally entitled to "life, liberty, and the pursuit of happiness."

But it can readily be seen, that this is only another mode of expressing the fundamental principle which the Great Ruler of the Universe has established, as the law of His eternal government. "Thou shalt love thy neighbor as thyself;" and "Whatsoever ye would that men should do to you, do ye even so to them," are the Scripture forms, by which the Supreme Lawgiver requires that each individual of our race shall regard the happiness of others, as of the same value as his own; and which forbid any institution, in private or civil life, which secures advantages to one class, by sacrificing the interests of another.

The principles of democracy, then, are identical with the principles of Christianity.

But, in order that each individual may pursue and secure the highest degree of happiness within his reach, unimpeded by the selfish interests of others, a system of laws must be established, which sustain certain relations and dependencies in social and civil life. What these relations and their attending obligations shall be, are to be determined, not with reference to the wishes and interests of a few, but solely with reference to the general good of all; so that each individual shall have his own interest, as well as the public benefit, secured by them.

For this purpose, it is needful that certain relations be sustained, which involve the duties of subordination. There must be the magistrate and the subject, one of whom is the superior, and the other the inferior. There must be the relations of husband and wife, parent and child, teacher and pupil, employer and employed, each involving the relative duties of subordination. The superior, in certain particulars, is to direct, and the inferior is to yield obedience. Society could never go forward, harmoniously, nor could any craft or profession be successfully pursued, unless these superior and subordinate relations be instituted and sustained.

But who shall take the higher, and who the subordinate, stations in social and civil life? This matter, in the case of parents and children, is decided by the Creator. He has given children to the control of parents, as their superiors, and to them they remain subordinate, to a certain age, or so long as they are members of their household. And parents can delegate such a portion of their authority to teachers and employers, as the interests of their children require.

In most other cases, in a truly democratic state, each individual is allowed to choose for himself, who shall take the position of his superior. No woman is forced to obey any husband but the one she chooses for herself; nor is she obliged to take a husband, if she prefers to remain single. So every domestic, and every artisan or laborer, after passing from parental control, can choose the employer to whom he is to accord obedience, or, if he prefers to relinquish certain advantages, he can remain without taking a subordinate place to any employer.

Each subject, also, has equal power with every other, to decide who shall be his superior as a ruler. The weakest, the poorest, the most illiterate, has the same opportunity to determine this question, as the richest, the most learned, and the most exalted.

From A Treatise on Domestic Economy, for the Use of Young Ladies at Home, at School, Harper & Brothers, 1846.

And the various privileges that wealth secures, are equally open to all classes. Every man may aim at riches, unimpeded by any law or institution which secures peculiar privileges to a favored class, at the expense of another. Every law, and every institution, is tested by examining whether it secures equal advantages to all; and, if the people become convinced that any regulation sacrifices the good of the majority to the interests of the smaller number, they have power to abolish it.

The institutions of monarchical and aristocratic nations are based on precisely opposite principles. They secure, to certain small and favored classes, advantages, which can be maintained, only by sacrificing the interests of the great mass of the people. Thus, the throne and aristocracy of England are supported by laws and customs, which burden the lower classes with taxes, so enormous, as to deprive them of all the luxuries, and of most of the comforts, of life. Poor dwellings, scanty food, unhealthy employments, excessive labor, and entire destitution of the means and time for education, are appointed for the lower classes, that a few may live in palaces, and riot in every indulgence.

The tendencies of democratic institutions, in reference to the rights and interests of the female sex, have been fully developed in the United States; and it is in this aspect, that the subject is one of peculiar interest to American women. In this Country, it is established, both by opinion and by practice, that woman has an equal interest in all social and civil concerns; and that no domestic, civil, or political, institution, is right, which sacrifices her interest to promote that of the other sex. But in order to secure her the more firmly in all these privileges, it is decided, that, in the domestic relation, she take a subordinate station, and that, in civil and political concerns, her interests be intrusted to the other sex, without her taking any part in voting, or in making and administering laws. The result of this order of things has been fairly tested, and is thus portrayed by M. De Tocqueville, a writer, who, for intelligence, fidelity, and ability, ranks second to none.

"There are people in Europe, who, confounding together the different characteristics of the sexes, would make of man and woman, beings not only equal, but alike. They would give to both the same functions, impose on both the same duties, and grant to both the same rights. They would mix them in all things—their business, their occupations, their pleasures. It may readily be conceived that, by thus attempting to make one sex equal to the other, both are degraded; and, from so preposterous a medley of

the works of Nature, nothing could ever result, but weak men and disorderly women.

"It is not thus that the Americans understand the species of democratic equality, which may be established between the sexes. They admit, that, as Nature has appointed such wide differences between the physical and moral constitutions of man and woman, her manifest design was, to give a distinct employment to their various faculties; and they hold, that improvement does not consist in making beings so dissimilar do pretty nearly the same things, but in getting each of them to fulfil their respective tasks, in the best possible manner. The Americans have applied to the sexes the great principle of political economy, which governs the manufactories of our age, by carefully dividing the duties of man from those of woman, in order that the great work of society may be the better carried on. . . .

"Thus the Americans do not think that man and woman have either the duty, or the right, to perform the same offices, but they show an equal regard for both their respective parts; and, though their lot is different, they consider both of them, as beings of equal value. They do not give to the courage of woman the same form, or the same direction, as to that of man; but they never doubt her courage: and if they hold that man and his partner ought not always to exercise their intellect and understanding in the same manner, they at least believe the understanding of the one to be as sound as that of the other, and her intellect to be as clear. Thus, then, while they have allowed the social inferiority of woman to subsist, they have done all they could to raise her, morally and intellectually, to the level of man; and, in this respect, they appear to me to have excellently understood the true principle of democratic improvement.

"As for myself, I do not hesitate to avow, that, although the women of the United States are confined within the narrow circle of domestic life, and their situation is, in some respects, one of extreme dependence, I have nowhere seen women occupying a loftier position; and if I were asked, now I am drawing to the close of this work, in which I have spoken of so many important things done by the Americans, to what the singular prosperity and growing strength of that people ought mainly to be attributed, I should reply,—*to the superiority of their women.*"

This testimony of a foreigner, who has had abundant opportunities of making a comparison, is sanctioned by the assent of all candid and intelligent men, who have enjoyed similar opportunities.

It appears, then, that it is in America, alone, that women are raised to an equality with the other sex;

and that, both in theory and practice, their interests are regarded as of equal value. They are made subordinate in station, only where a regard to their best interests demands it, while, as if in compensation for this, by custom and courtesy, they are always treated as superiors. Universally, in this Country, through every class of society, precedence is given to woman, in all the comforts, conveniences, and courtesies, of life.

In civil and political affairs, American women take no interest or concern, except so far as they sympathize with their family and personal friends; but in all cases, in which they do feel a concern, their opinions and feelings have a consideration, equal, or even superior, to that of the other sex.

In matters pertaining to the education of their children, in the selection and support of a clergyman, in all benevolent enterprises, and in all questions relating to morals or manners, they have a superior influence. In such concerns, it would be impossible to carry a point, contrary to their judgment and feelings; while an enterprise, sustained by them, will seldom fail of success.

If those who are bewailing themselves over the fancied wrongs and injuries of women in this Nation, could only see things as they are, they would know, that, whatever remnants of a barbarous or aristocratic age may remain in our civil institutions, in reference to the interests of women, it is only because they are ignorant of them, or do not use their influence to have them rectified; for it is very certain that there is nothing reasonable, which American women would unite in asking, that would not readily be bestowed.

The preceding remarks, then, illustrate the position, that the democratic institutions of this Country are in reality no other than the principles of Christianity carried into operation, and that they tend to place woman in her true position in society, as having equal rights with the other sex; and that, in fact, they have secured to American women a lofty and fortunate position, which, as yet, has been attained by the women of no other nation.

There is another topic, presented in the work of the above author, which demands the profound attention of American women.

The following is taken from that part of the Introduction to the work, illustrating the position, that, for ages, there has been a constant progress, in all civilized nations, towards the democratic equality attained in this Country.

"The various occurrences of national existence have every where turned to the advantage of democracy; all men have aided it by their exertions; those who have intentionally labored in its cause, and those who have served it unwittingly; those who have fought for it, and those who have declared themselves its opponents, have all been driven along in the same track, have all labored to one end;" "all have been blind instruments in the hands of God."

"The gradual development of the equality of conditions, is, therefore, a Providential fact; and it possesses all the characteristics of a Divine decree: it is universal, it is durable, it constantly eludes all human interference, and all events, as well as all men, contribute to its progress." . . .

It thus appears, that the sublime and elevating anticipations which have filled the mind and heart of the religious world, have become so far developed, that philosophers and statesmen are perceiving the signs, and are predicting the approach, of the same grand consummation. There is a day advancing, "by seers predicted, and by poets sung," when the curse of selfishness shall be removed; when "scenes surpassing fable, and yet true," shall be realized; when all nations shall rejoice and be made blessed, under those benevolent influences, which the Messiah came to establish on earth.

And this is the Country, which the Disposer of events designs shall go forth as the cynosure of nations, to guide them to the light and blessedness of that day. To us is committed the grand, the responsible privilege, of exhibiting to the world, the beneficent influences of Christianity, when carried into every social, civil, and political institution, and, though we have, as yet, made such imperfect advances, already the light is streaming into the dark prison-house of despotic lands, while startled kings and sages, philosophers and statesmen, are watching us with that interest, which a career so illustrious, and so involving their own destiny, is calculated to excite. They are studying our institutions, scrutinizing our experience, and watching for our mistakes, that they may learn whether "a social revolution, so irresistible, be advantageous or prejudicial to mankind."

There are persons, who regard these interesting truths merely as food for national vanity; but every reflecting and Christian mind, must consider it as an occasion for solemn and anxious reflection. Are we, then, a spectacle to the world? Has the Eternal Lawgiver appointed us to work out a problem, involving the destiny of the whole earth? Are such momentous interests to be advanced or retarded, just in proportion as we are faithful to our high trust? "What manner of persons, then, ought we to be," in attempting to sustain so solemn, so glorious a responsibility?

But the part to be enacted by American women, in this great moral enterprise, is the point to which special attention should here be directed.

The success of democratic institutions, as is conceded by all, depends upon the intellectual and moral character of the mass of the people. If they are intelligent and virtuous, democracy is a blessing; but if they are ignorant and wicked, it is only a curse, and as much more dreadful than any other form of civil government, as a thousand tyrants are more to be dreaded than one. It is equally conceded, that the formation of the moral and intellectual character of the young is committed mainly to the female hand. The mother forms the character of the future man; the sister bends the fibres that are hereafter to be the forest tree; the wife sways the heart, whose energies may turn for good or for evil the destinies of a nation. Let the women of a country be made virtuous and intelligent, and the men will certainly be the same. The proper education of a man decides the welfare of an individual; but educate a woman, and the interests of a whole family are secured.

If this be so, as none will deny, then to American women, more than to any others on earth, is committed the exalted privilege of extending over the world those blessed influences, which are to renovate degraded man, and "clothe all climes with beauty."

No American woman, then, has any occasion for feeling that hers is an humble or insignificant lot. The value of what an individual accomplishes, is to be estimated by the importance of the enterprise achieved, and not by the particular position of the laborer. The drops of heaven which freshen the earth, are each of equal value, whether they fall in the lowland meadow, or the princely parterre. The builders of a temple are of equal importance, whether they labor on the foundations, or toil upon the dome.

Thus, also, with those labors which are to be made effectual in the regeneration of the Earth. And it is by forming a habit of regarding the apparently insignificant efforts of each isolated laborer, in a comprehensive manner, as indispensible portions of a grand result, that the minds of all, however humble their sphere of service, can be invigorated and cheered. The woman, who is rearing a family of children; the woman, who labors in the schoolroom; the woman, who, in her retired chamber, earns, with her needle, the mite, which contributes to the intellectual and moral elevation of her Country; even the humble domestic, whose example and influence may be moulding and forming young minds, while her faithful services sustain a prosperous domestic state;— each and all may be animated by the consciousness, that they are agents in accomplishing the greatest work that ever was committed to human responsibility. It is the building of a glorious temple, whose base shall be coextensive with the bounds of the earth, whose summit shall pierce the skies, whose splendor shall beam on all lands; and those who hew the lowliest stone, as much as those who carve the highest capital, will be equally honored, when its top-stone shall be laid, with new rejoicings of the morning stars, and shoutings of the sons of God.

Document 8.6 Senator Daniel Webster Praises Women's Activities Outside of Politics

Senator Daniel Webster (1782-1852) was arguably the greatest orator in the history of the United States Congress. Hundreds if not thousands of onlookers traveled great distances to hear Webster speak, each straining to hear his magnificent voice deliver well-crafted arguments. He was an ardent nationalist, an unqualified supporter of capitalism and the market economy, and a firm believer in the need for a strong central government to protect property owners. He served as Secretary of State, and argued cases before the Supreme Court with great success, contributing to our nation's Constitutional development. His greatest ambition was to be president, but in this he was repeatedly frustrated. When he gave the following speech to the ladies of Richmond, Virginia, he was campaigning for the Whig party's 1840 presidential candidate William Henry Harrison. One of the Whig campaign strategies was to accuse the incumbent president, Democrat Martin Van Buren, of being corrupt and immoral. These qualities made him the antithesis of middle-class women, as portrayed in the ideals of domesticity. According to Webster, what role do women play in preserving the right administration in the nation? Why is the moral training of young people so vital to the preservation of free government? Could Webster's support of the market economy influence his arguments, or is this all just politics?

LADIES,—I am very sure I owe the pleasure I now enjoy to your kind disposition, which has given me the opportunity to present my thanks and my respects to you thus collectively, since the shortness of my stay in the city does not allow me the happiness of calling upon those, severally and individually, from members of whose families I have received kindness and notice. And, in the first place, I wish to express to you my deep and hearty thanks, as I have endeavored to do to your fathers, your husbands, and your brothers, for the unbounded hospitality I have received ever since I came among you. This is registered, I assure you, in a grateful heart, in characters of an enduring nature. The rough contests of the political world are not suited to the dignity and the delicacy of your sex; but you possess the intelligence to know how much of that happiness which you are entitled to hope for, both for yourselves and for your children, depends on the right administration of government, and a proper tone of public morals. That is a subject on which the moral perceptions of woman are both quicker and juster than those of the other sex. I do not speak of that administration of government whose object is merely the protection of industry, the preservation of civil liberty, and the securing to enterprise of its due reward. I speak of government in a somewhat higher point of view; I speak of it in regard to its influence on the morals and sentiments of the community. We live in an age distinguished for great benevolent exertion, in which the affluent are consecrating the means they possess to the endowment of colleges and academies, to the building of churches, to the support of religion and religious worship, to the encouragement of schools, lyceums, and athenaeums, and other means of general popular instruction. This is all well; it is admirable; it augurs well for the prospects of ensuing generation. But I have sometimes thought, that, amidst all this activity and zeal of the good and the benevolent, the influence of government on the morals and on the religious feelings of the community is apt to be overlooked or underrated. I speak, of course, of its indirect influence, of the power of its example, and the general tone which it inspires.

A popular government, in all these respects, is a most powerful institution; more powerful, as it has sometimes appeared to me, than the influence of most other human institutions put together, either for good or for evil, according to its character. Its example, its tone, whether of regard or disregard for moral obligation, is most important to human happiness; it is among those things which most affect the political morals of mankind, and their general morals also. I advert to this, because there has been put forth, in modern times, the false maxim, that there is one morality for politics, and another morality for other things; that, in their political conduct to their opponents, men may say and do that which they would never think of saying or doing in the personal relations of private life. There has been openly announced a sentiment, which I consider as the very essence of false morality, which declares that "all is fair in politics." If a man speaks falsely or calumniously of his neighbor, and is reproached for the offence, the ready excuse is this:—"It was in relation to public and political matters; I cherished no personal ill-will whatever against that individual, but quite the contrary; I spoke of my adversary merely as a political man." In my opinion, the day is coming when falsehood will stand for falsehood, and calumny will be treated as a breach of the commandment, whether it be committed politically or in the concerns of private life.

It is by the promulgation of sound morals in the community, and more especially by the training and instruction of the young, that woman performs her part towards the preservation of a free government. It is generally admitted that public liberty, and the perpetuity of a free constitution, rest on the virtue and intelligence of the community which enjoys it. How is that virtue to be inspired, and how is that intelligence to be communicated? Bonaparte once asked Madame de Staël in what manner he could best promote the happiness of France. Her reply is full of political wisdom. She said, "Instruct the mothers of the French people." Mothers are, indeed, the affectionate and effective teachers of the human race. The mother begins her process of training with the infant in her arms. It is she who directs, so to speak, its first mental and spiritual pulsations. She conducts it along the impressible years of childhood and youth, and hopes to deliver it to the stern conflicts and tumultuous scenes of life, armed by those good principles which her child has received from maternal care and love.

If we draw within the circle of our contemplation the mothers of a civilized nation, what do we see? We behold so many artificers working, not on frail and perishable matter, but on the immortal mind, moulding and fashioning beings who are to exist for ever. We applaud the artist whose skill and

From *The Writings and Speeches of Daniel Webster,* Little Brown & Company, 1903.

genius present the mimic man upon the canvas; we admire and celebrate the sculptor who works out that same image in enduring marble; but how insignificant are these achievements, though the highest and the fairest in all the departments of art, in comparison with the great vocation of human mothers! They work, not upon the canvas that shall perish, or the marble that shall crumble into dust, but upon mind, upon spirit, which is to last for ever, and which is to bear, for good or evil, throughout its duration, the impress of a mother's plastic hand.

I have already expressed the opinion, which all allow to be correct, that our security for the duration of the free institutions which bless our country depends upon habits of virtue and the prevalence of knowledge and of education. The attainment of knowledge does not comprise all which is contained in the larger term of education. The feelings are to be disciplined; the passions are to be restrained; true and worthy motives are to be inspired; a profound religious feeling is to be instilled, and pure morality inculcated, under all circumstances. All this is comprised in education. Mothers who are faithful to this great duty will tell their children, that neither in political nor in any other concerns of life can man ever withdraw himself from the perpetual obligations of conscience and of duty; that in every act, whether public or private, he incurs a just responsibility; and that in no condition is he warranted in trifling with

important rights and obligations. They will impress upon their children the truth, that the exercise of the elective franchise is a social duty, of as solemn a nature as man can be called to perform; that a man may not innocently trifle with his vote; that every free elector is a trustee, as well for others as himself; and that every man and every measure he supports has an important bearing on the interests of others, as well as on his own. It is in the inculcation of high and pure morals such as these, that, in a free republic, woman performs her sacred duty, and fulfils her destiny. The French, as you know, are remarkable for their fondness for sententious phrases, in which much meaning is condensed into a small space. I noticed lately, on the title-page of one of the books of popular instruction in France, this motto:—"Pour instruction on the heads of the people! you owe them that baptism." And, certainly, if there be any duty which may be described by a reference to that great institute of religion, a duty approaching it in importance, perhaps next to it in obligation,—it is this.

I know you hardly expect me to address you on the popular political topics of the day. You read enough, you hear quite enough, on those subjects. You expect me only to meet you, and to tender my profound thanks for this marked proof of your regard, and will kindly receive the assurances with which I tender to you, on parting, my affectionate respects and best wishes.

Document 8.7 Nancy Cummings Johnson Speaks Out Against Domestic Abuse, 1854

Traditionalists talked a great deal about a "woman's power" to influence men, but this subtle power was unenforceable in court. Legally, women were subject first to their fathers and then to their husbands, who could do anything they pleased, short of murder. In colonial days, this meant the "rule of thumb," where a husband could beat his wife senseless as long as he did not use a rod or staff wider than his thumb. Domestic abuse was still widespread in the 1850s, when enlightened law codes still authorized husbands to use "moderate force" to discipline wives and children, and to call on public authorities to track down runaway wives. Some observers noted that these were the same rights that Slave Codes gave masters. Nancy Cummings Johnson was one of the first woman writers to boldly speak out against domestic abuse. Women writers often used pseudonyms, to protect themselves, their families, and their publishers from abuse, since many men did not believe women should be writing for public consumption. Writing as Minnie Myrtle, Johnson contributed sketches and poems to the *New York Times* that were later published as *The Myrtle Wreath or Stray Leaves Recalled*. As you read this excerpt, consider why Johnson says the phrase "power is corrupting" applies to domestic abuse, and how this problem can be fixed. What examples of male hypocrisy does Minnie Myrtle point out?

"Power is corrupting," says the politician—"Power is corrupting," says the foe to hierarchies. "Good men, the best men, should not be intrusted with absolute power." "Power is corrupting," says the enemy of slavery, "men should not be permitted the absolute control of human beings; however good the master may be, he will be tempted to indulge in tyranny, if there is nothing external to restrain him."

These are sentiments which I have often heard expressed by one who still exclaims, "I *will* be master in my own house; those who live with me shall *obey* me." And the obedience which is required of a wife is as servile as that which is rendered by any bond slave.

To his daughter he says, "Whilst you are in my house you will do as I say, if you are a hundred years old"; not because she would not obey willingly and happily, but because there is such pleasure in *exacting* obedience. All would gladly do right of their own accord; but that would not be sufficient; they must be compelled; they must feel in every nerve, and bone and muscle, that they are subject to the will of another. To order, thwart and torture, is a peculiar pleasure, and I am fully convinced, is not enjoyed by Princes, and Popes, and slaveowners alone.

I have seen the staunchest advocates of "Woman's rights" and "human freedom," exercise the most brutal tyranny over wives and daughters. I have seen a quiet Christian woman beaten, by a man who was ever railing against oppression. I have seen the marks of an *inch cable* on the shoulders of a grown up daughter, placed there by a man who was ever uttering anathemas against those, who, for any reason applied the lash to those over whom the law gave them power!

I have seen a little girl drop lifeless under the infliction of the rod, which was used not merely as an instrument of punishment, but to prove that he who wielded it had a right to do what he pleased with his own.

If those who rule with such authority lived where human beings are property, they would exult in its peculiar privileges, and triumph in the wrongs they could commit with impunity.

"Power is indeed corrupting." I have seen a young girl dragged from room to room by her hair, beaten and trodden upon, for only slight offence, by one whom she called mother, because *tyranny was sweet*—to inspire fear more pleasant than to inspire love.

I have seen in many families, wives and daughters and sisters, afraid with a fear not less slavish than that which inspires the most abject among those who are bought and sold, and all because those who held it delighted in swaying the iron sceptre and ruling with an iron rod. And those who are ruled are expected meekly to endure; their lips must be even wreathed in smiles and breathless gladness for those who have crushed all gladness from their hearts. "Power is corrupting," but it is not Kings and Politicians alone whom it corrupts.

Document 8.8 *The Lily* Comments on Women's Rights

During the 1840s and 1850s, the number of journals women owned and produced increased. Hannah Barnard's *Dialogues on Domestic and Rural Economy* and Lydia Marie Childs' *The Frugal Housewife* dispensed recipes, household hints on cleaning and childcare, and advice on running a household on a small budget. Journals such as Elizabeth Cady Stanton's *Revolution,* Lucy Stone's *Woman's Journal,* and *Una,* a journal dedicated to elevating women's legal status in the United States, all championed a combination of reform issues along with women's rights. *The Lily,* known best as a temperance publication, was edited by Amelia Bloomer, the assistant postmaster of Seneca Falls, New York. Bloomer was also an advocate of dress reform, proposing a shortened skirt over a pairs of pantaloons, which allowed women freer movement and was less likely to collect dust and mud at the hem. According to this editorial, what are the problems facing women that everyone can see? Why aren't these problems discussed publicly, where something could be done about them? What are the solutions, according to Bloomer?

From *The Myrtle Wreath or Stray Leaves Recalled,* New York: Charles Scribner, 1854.

Some of our gentlemen readers are a little troubled lest we should injure ourself and our paper by saying too much in behalf of the rights and interests of our own sex, and it has even been intimated to us that we are controlled in the matter by some person or persons. Now while we feel very thankful for the disinterested kindness of friends, we wish them to give themselves no uneasiness on our account, as we feel perfectly competent to manage our own affairs, and wish not to hold them responsible for our doings. We would here say distinctly that no one besides ourself has any control over the columns of the Lily and we know not that we are controlled in our actions by any one. We may sometimes publish articles with the sentiments of which we do not fully agree, but we have the right, and shall fearlessly use it should occasion require, of expressing our disapprobation of any such sentiments.—Our readers must bear in mind that the Lily is a woman's paper, and one of its objects as stated in our prospectus is, *to open a medium through which woman's thoughts and aspirations might be developed*. Gentlemen have no reason to complain if women avail themselves of this medium, and here dare utter aloud their thoughts, and protest against the wrongs and grievances which have been so long heaped upon their sex.

When we look around us and see the extreme misery and degradation of many of our sex who were cradled in luxury and reared with care and tenderness—when we behold so many dragging out a wretched existence—mere slaves to men, who in everything save physical strength are far inferior to them—when we see them toiling to earn a bare subsistence and then through fear and brutal force compelled to yield up the pittance they have earned, to idle and dissolute husbands—when we look upon the drunkard's wife and his scantily clothed and half starved children and witness their sufferings, we are more astonished that women have not long ere this arisen *en masse* and demanded their rights, and forcibly obtained them if they could not do so peacefully, than we are that a few should now, when opportunity offers, plead in behalf of their sorrowing sisters, and raise their united voices against the indignities to which they are subjected.

Women are awakening to a sense of their inferior position, and beginning to question the right of man to dictate laws for their observance—laws which they have no voice in making and at which their feelings revolt. They see that the evils which afflict society and which bear so heavily upon them are all the effects of these laws, and the question arises, "who gave man the right to make laws and sanction means calculated to oppress, degrade and render wretched woman's whole life?" They look in vain for an answer. If he has such authority it is only human. Divine law does not sanction it. God never designed man to be a tyrant, or woman to be a slave and bow to his dictates. We rejoice that the barriers to woman's equality are being thrown down, or overleaped; we are glad that she now has the press at her command, and may, if she will, stir up the mighty mass of people to give heed to her behests. We only wish there were more of them willing to devote their talents to the good of their sex, and the moral elevation of their race; and we can only hope that the spirit which has enkindled in the breasts of the few, may pervade the many, and that they may fully consider the part which it is their duty to take in arresting the terrible evils which have spread to such fearful extent over our beloved country.

Document 8.9 The Seneca Falls Declaration of Sentiments, 1848

For most historians, the summer 1848 gathering in Seneca Falls, New York marks the beginning of the formal women's rights movement in the country. More than 300 men and women attended the convention, which discussed the roles and rights of women in the United States. Elizabeth Cady Stanton, at the time a mother of three boys under the age of six, was the primary author of the declaration. This document compiles the complaints about how men treat women, and establishes an agenda for women's rights that is still valid today. Using the Declaration of Independence as a formal model, but inserting gender-neutral language, this document bases its appeal on the idea of basic democratic rights for all United States' citizens. As you read the Declaration, consider why patriarchy is seen as the cause of all female problems and

From *The Lily 2*, Number 4, April 1850.

grievances. What rights have women been denied? What meaning does this document and the convention hold for us today? If you compare this document with the Declaration of Independence (see Chapter 4), are their arguments just as accurate and compelling?

---

1. Declaration of Sentiments

When, in the course of human events, it becomes necessary for one portion of the family of man to assume among the people of the earth a position different from that which they have hitherto occupied, but one to which the laws of nature and of nature's God entitle them, a decent respect to the opinions of mankind requires that they should declare the causes that impel them to such a course.

We hold these truths to be self-evident: that all men and women are created equal; that they are endowed by their Creator with certain inalienable rights; that among these are life, liberty, and the pursuit of happiness; that to secure these rights governments are instituted, deriving their just powers from the consent of the governed. Whenever any form of government becomes destructive of these ends, it is the right of those who suffer from it to refuse allegiance to it, and to insist upon the institution of a new government, laying its foundation on such principles, and organizing its powers in such form, as to them shall seem most likely to effect their safety and happiness. Prudence, indeed, will dictate that governments long established should not be changed for light and transient causes; and accordingly all experience hath shown that mankind are more disposed to suffer, while evils are sufferable, than to right themselves by abolishing the forms to which they are accustomed. But when a long train of abuses and usurpations, pursuing invariably the same object, evinces a design to reduce them under absolute despotism, it is their duty to throw off such government, and to provide new guards for their future security. Such has been the patient sufferance of the women under this government, and such is now the necessity which constrains them to demand the equal station to which they are entitled. The history of mankind is a history of repeated injuries and usurpations on the part of man toward woman, having in direct object the establishment of an absolute tyranny over her. To prove this, let facts be submitted to a candid world.

He has never permitted her to exercise her inalienable right to the elective franchise.

He has compelled her to submit to laws, in the formation of which she had no voice.

He has withheld from her rights which are given to the most ignorant and degraded men—both natives and foreigners.

Having deprived her of this first right of a citizen, the elective franchise, thereby leaving her without representation in the halls of legislation, he has oppressed her on all sides.

He has made her, if married, in the eye of the law, civilly dead. He has taken from her all right in property, even to the wages she earns.

He has made her, morally, an irresponsible being, as she can commit many crimes with impunity, provided they be done in the presence of her husband.

In the covenant of marriage, she is compelled to promise obedience to her husband, he becoming, to all intents and purposes, her master—the law giving him power to deprive her of her liberty, and to administer chastisement.

He has so framed the laws of divorce, as to what shall be the proper causes, and in case of separation, to whom the guardianship of the children shall be given, as to be wholly regardless of the happiness of women—the law, in all cases, going upon a false supposition of the supremacy of man, and giving all power into his hands.

After depriving her of all rights as a married woman, if single, and the owner of property, he has taxed her to support a government which recognizes her only when her property can be made profitable to it.

He has monopolized nearly all the profitable employments, and from those she is permitted to follow, she receives but a scanty remuneration. He closes against her all the avenues to wealth and distinction which he considers most honorable to himself. As a teacher of theology, medicine, or law, she is not known.

The Seneca Falls Declaration of Sentiments, 1848.

He has denied her the facilities for obtaining a thorough education, all colleges being closed against her.

He allows her in Church, as well as State, but a subordinate position, claiming Apostolic authority for her exclusion from the ministry, and, with some exceptions, from any public participation in the affairs of the Church.

He has created a false public sentiment by giving to the world a different code of morals for men and women, by which moral delinquencies which exclude women from society, are not only tolerated, but deemed of little account in man.

He has usurped the prerogative of Jehovah himself, claiming it as his right to assign for her a sphere of action, when that belongs to her conscience and to her God.

He has endeavored, in every way that he could, to destroy her confidence in her own powers, to lessen her self-respect and to make her willing to lead a dependent and abject life.

Now, in view of this entire disfranchisement of one-half the people of this country, their social and religious degradation—in view of the unjust laws above mentioned, and because women do feel themselves aggrieved, oppressed, and fraudulently deprived of their most sacred rights, we insist that they have immediate admission to all the rights and privileges which belong to them as citizens of the United States.

In entering upon the great work before us, we anticipate no small amount of misconception, misrepresentation, and ridicule; but we shall use every instrumentality within our power to effect our object. We shall employ agents, circulate tracts, petition the State and National legislatures, and endeavor to enlist the pulpit and the press in our behalf. We hope this Convention will be followed by a series of Conventions embracing every part of the country.

2. Resolutions

WHEREAS, The great precept of nature is conceded to be, that "man shall pursue his own true and substantial happiness." Blackstone in his Commentaries remarks, that this law of Nature being coeval with mankind, and dictated by God himself, is of course superior in obligation to any other. It is binding over all the globe, in all countries and at all times; no human laws are of any validity if contrary to this, and such of them as are valid, derive all their force, and all their validity, and all their authority, mediately and immediately, from this original; therefore,

Resolved, That such laws as conflict, in any way with the true and substantial happiness of woman, are contrary to the great precept of nature and of no validity, for this is "superior in obligation to any other."

Resolved, That all laws which prevent woman from occupying such a station in society as her conscience shall dictate, or which place her in a position inferior to that of man, are contrary to the great precept of nature, and therefore of no force or authority.

Resolved, That woman is man's equal—was intended to be so by the Creator, and the highest good of the race demands that she should be recognized as such.

Resolved, That the women of this country ought to be enlightened in regard to the laws under which they live, that they may no longer publish their degradation by declaring themselves satisfied with their present position, nor their ignorance, by asserting that they have all the rights they want.

Resolved, That inasmuch as man, while claiming for himself intellectual superiority, does accord to woman moral superiority, it is pre-eminently his duty to encourage her to speak and teach, as she has an opportunity, in all religious assemblies.

Resolved, That the same amount of virtue, delicacy, and refinement of behavior that is required of woman in the social state, should also be required of man, and the same transgressions should be visited with equal severity on both man and woman.

Resolved, That the objection of indelicacy and impropriety, which is so often brought against woman when she addresses a public audience, comes with a very ill-grace from those who encourage, by their attendance, her appearance on the stage, in the concert. Or in feats of the circus.

Resolved, That woman has too long rested satisfied in the circumscribed limits which corrupt customs and a perverted application of the Scriptures have marked out for her, and that it is time she should move in the enlarged sphere which her great Creator has assigned her.

Resolved, That it is the duty of the women of this country to secure to themselves their sacred right to the elective franchise.

Resolved, That the equality of human rights results necessarily from the fact of the identity of the race in capabilities and responsibilities.

Resolved, therefore, That, being invested by the creator with the same capabilities, and the same consciousness of responsibility for their exercise, it is demonstrably the right and duty of woman, equally with man, to promote every righteous cause by every righteous means; and especially in regard to the great subjects of morals and religion, it is self-evidently her right to participate with her brother in teaching them, both in private and in public, by writing and by speaking, by any instrumentalities proper to be used, and in any assemblies proper to be held; and this being a self-evident truth growing out of the divinely implanted principles of human nature, any custom or authority adverse to it, whether modern or wearing the hoary sanction of antiquity, is to be regarded as a self-evident falsehood, and at war with mankind.

Resolved, That the speedy success of our cause depends upon the zealous and untiring efforts of both men and women, for the overthrow of the monopoly of the pulpit, and for the securing to women an equal participation with men in the various trades, professions, and commerce.

Document 8.10 Paula Wright Davis Gives the Presidential Address at the 1850 Worcester Women's Rights Convention

Paulina Wright Davis of Rhode Island chaired the Worcester Women's Rights Convention in 1850 and gave the following address. Davis, a long-time crusader for equal legal rights, was the first American woman speaker to charge lecture fees equal to her male counterparts. Women attending this meeting came from many walks of life, but all were experienced participants of national reform movements. Most were liberal Protestants, with parents who lived through the American Revolution and actively believed most of the ideals of equality. While advocating equality, most participants relied on a well-educated white elite to set the agenda of reform and lead the cause. At this convention, speakers regularly declared that the roots of women's oppression in the United States were unfair laws regulating domestic relations, and male misreading of the Bible. In the following excerpts from Davis' keynote address, from what basic human rights principles does she claim women's right arise? Who or what serves as tyrants preventing women's equality, and why do they take this stance? How will changes in women's status advance the cause of humanity?

Human societies have been long working and fighting their way up from what we scornfully call barbarism, into what we boastfully call modern civilization; but, as yet, the advancement has been chiefly in ordering and methodizing the lower instincts of our nature, and organizing society under their impulses. The intellect of the masses has received development, and the gentler affections have been somewhat relieved from the dominion of force; but the institutions among men are not yet modelled after the highest laws of our nature. The masterdom of the strong hand and bold spirit is not yet over. . . . But the age of war is drawing towards a close, and that of peace (whose methods and end alike are harmony) is dawning, and the uprising of womanhood is its prophecy and foreshadow.

The first principles of human rights have now for a long time been abstractly held and believed, and both in Europe and America whole communities have put them into practical operation in some of their bearings. Equality before the laws, and the right of the governed to choose their governors, are established maxims of reformed political science; but in the countries most advanced, these doctrines and their actual benefits are as yet enjoyed exclusively by the sex that in the battle-field and the public forum has wrenched them from the old time tyrannies. They are yet denied to Woman, because she has not yet so asserted or won them for herself; for political justice pivots itself upon the barbarous principle that "Who would be free, themselves must strike the blow." Its furthest progress toward magnanimity is to give arms to helplessness. It has not yet learned to give justice. For this rule of barbarism there is this much justification, that although every human being is naturally entitled to every right of the race, the enjoyment and administration of all rights require such culture and conditions in their subject as usually lead him to claim and struggle for them; and the contented slave is left in slavery, and the ignorant man in darkness, on the

From the Presidential Address at the 1850 Worcester Women's Rights Convention.

inference that he cannot use what he does not desire. This is indeed true of the animal instincts, but it is false of the nobler soul; and men must learn that the higher faculties must be first awakened, and then gratified, before they have done their duty to their race. The ministry of angels to dependent humanity is the method of Divine Providence, and among men the law of heaven is, that the "elder shall serve the younger." But let us not complain that the hardier sex overvalue the force which heretofore has figured most in the world's affairs. "They know not what they do" is the apology that crucified womanhood must concede in justice and pity to the wrong doers. In the order of things, the material world was to be first subdued. For this coarse conflict, the larger bones and stronger sinews of manhood are especially adapted, and it is a law of muscles and of all matter that might shall overcome right. This is the law of the vegetable world, and it is the law of the animal world, as well as the law of the animal instincts and of the physical organization of men; but it is not the law of spirit and affection.

. . . Besides the feebler frame, which under the dynasty of muscles is degraded, there remains, even after justice has got the upper hand of force in the world's judgments, a mysterious and undefined difference of sex that seriously embarrasses the question of equality; or, if that is granted, in terms of equal fitness for avocations and positions which heretofore have been the monopoly of men. Old ideas and habits of mind survive the facts which produced them, as the shadows of night stretch far into the morning, sheltered in nooks and valleys from the rising light; and it is the work of a whole creation-day to separate the light from the darkness.

The rule of difference between the sexes must be founded on the traits which each estimates most highly in the other; and it is not at all wonderful that some of woman's artificial incapacities and slaveries may seem to be necessary to some of her excellencies; just as the chivalry that makes man a butcher of his kind still glares like a glory in the eyes of admiring womanhood, and all the more because it seems so much above and unlike her own powers and achievements. Nature does not teach that men and women are unequal, but only that they are unlike; an unlikeness so naturally related and dependent that their respective differences by their balance establish, instead of destroying, their equality.

Men are not in fact, and to all intents, equal among themselves, but their theoretical equality for all the purposes of justice is more easily seen and allowed than what we are here to claim for women.

Higher views, nicer distinctions, and a deeper philosophy are required to see and feel the truths of woman's rights; and besides, the maxims upon which men distribute justice to each other have been battlecries for ages, while the doctrine of woman's true relations in life is a new science, the revelation of an advanced age,—perhaps, indeed, the very last grand movement of humanity towards its highest destiny,— too new to be yet fully understood, too grand to grow out of the broad and coarse generalities which the infancy and barbarism of society could comprehend.

The rule of force and fraud must be well nigh overturned, and learning and religion and the fine arts must have cultivated mankind into a state of wisdom and justice tempered by the most beneficent affections, before woman can be fully installed in her highest offices. We must be gentle with the ignorance and patient under the injustice which old evils induce. Long suffering is a quality of the highest wisdom, and clarity beareth all things for it hopeth all things.

. . . The tyrant sex, if such we choose to term it, holds such natural and necessary relations to the victims of injustice, that neither rebellion nor revolution, neither defiance nor resistance, nor any mode of assault or defence incident to party antagonism, is either possible, expedient, or proper. Our claim must rest on its justice, and conquer by its power of truth. We take the ground, that whatever has been achieved for the race belongs to it, and must not be usurped by any class or caste. The rights and liberties of one human being cannot be made the property of another, though they were redeemed for him or her by the life of that other; for rights cannot be forfeited by way of salvage, and they are in their nature unpurchasable and inalienable.

We claim for woman a full and generous investiture of all the blessings which the other sex has solely or by her aid achieved for itself. We appeal from men's injustice and selfishness to their principles and affections.

I will not accept the concession of any equality which means identity or resemblance of faculty and function. I do not base her claims upon any such parallelism of constitution or attainment. I ask only freedom for the natural unfolding of her powers, the conditions most favorable for her possibilities of growth, and the full play of all those incentives which have made man her master, and then, with all her natural impulses and the whole heaven of hope to invite. I ask that she shall fill the place that she can attain to, without settling any unmeaning questions of sex and sphere, which people gossip about for want of principles of truth, or the faculty to reason upon them.

But it is not with the topics of our reform and the discussion of these that I am now concerned. It is of its position in the world's opinion, and the causes of this, that I am thinking; and I seek to derive hints and suggestions as to the method and manner of successful advocacy, from the inquiry. Especially am I solicitous that the good cause may suffer no detriment from the theoretical principles its friends may assume, or the spirit with which they shall maintain them. It is fair to presume that such causes as have obscured these questions in the general judgement of the governing sex, must also more or less darken the counsels of those most anxious for truth and right. If our demand were simply for chartered rights, civil and political, such as get acknowledgement in paper constitutions, there would be no ground of doubt. We could plead our common humanity, and claim an equal justice. We might say that the natural right of self-government is so clearly due to every human being alike, that it needs no argument to prove it; and if some or a majority of women would not exercise this right, this is no ground for taking it from those who would. And the right to the control and enjoyment of her own property and partnership in all that she helps her husband to earn and save, needs only to be stated to command instant assent. Her appropriate avocations might not be so easily settled that a programme could be completed on the theoretical principles merely; but we need discuss no such difficulties while we ask only for liberty of choice, and opportunities of adaptation; and the question of her education is solved by the simple principle, that whatever she can receive is her absolute due.

Yet all these points being so easily disposed of, so far as they are mere matters of controversy, the advocates of the right need none the less the wisest and kindest consideration for all the resistance we must encounter, and the most forbearing patience under the injustice and insolence to which we must expose

ourselves. And we can help ourselves to much of the prudence and some of the knowledge we shall need, by treating the prejudices of the public as considerately as if they were principles, and the customs of society as if they once had some temporary necessity, and so meet them with the greater force for the claim to respect which we concede to them. For a prejudice is just like any other error of judgment, and a custom has sometimes had some fitness to things more or less necessary, and is nor an utter absurdity, even though the reason on which it was based is lost or removed. Who shall say that there is nothing serious, or respectable, or just, in the repugnance with which our propositions are received? The politician who knows his own corruption may be excused for an earnest wish to save his wife and daughter from the taint, and he must be excused, too, for not knowing that the corruption would be cured by the saving virtue which he dreads to expose to risk.

In principle these truths are not doubtful, and it is therefore not impossible to put them in practice, but they need great clearness in system and steadiness of direction to get them allowance and adoption in the actual life of the world. The opposition should be consulted where it can be done without injurious consequences. Truth must not be suppressed, nor principles crippled, yet strong meat should not be given to babes. Nor should the strong use their liberties so as to become a stumbling block to the weak. Above all things, we owe it to the earnest expectation of the age, that stands trembling in mingled hope and fear of the great experiment, to lay its foundations broadly and securely in philosophic truth, and to form and fashion it in practical righteousness. To accomplish this, we cannot be too careful or too brave, too gentle or too firm: and yet with right dispositions and honest efforts, we cannot fail of doing our share of the great work, and thereby advancing the highest interests of humanity.

Document 8.11 Debate over Women's Rights and Duties, the *New York Tribune*, November 2, 1850

As you would expect, there were a variety of responses to the convention. Conservative James Gordon Bennett, editor of the *New York Herald*, compared the gathering of women with "the jubilee of the Devil and his angels." Other male editors praised the proceedings and the "awakening of women's senses." Pioneering woman doctor Elizabeth Blackwell condemned what she saw as the "anti-man" attitude of the convention; but her sister and mother attended the gathering. The following exchange took place in the editorial columns of the *New York Tribune* after the Worcester convention. The first letter writer is obviously male, and just as obviously opposed to changes in women's status outside of the domestic sphere. Replying is Editor Horace Greeley, at times a supporter of almost every reform movement in the nation. What are the arguments against the Worcester convention, and the condemnations of the women who attended? Do the arguments sound familiar; are they still used against women today? What is Horace Greeley's response, and does he give a blanket endorsement of the women's cause? What reservations does he have?

H. Greeley. Esq.

Dear Sir: I notice that in publishing the proceedings of "the Mothers of our Republic," you refrain from all comment or remarks. I enjoy hearing your opinion, and am particularly anxious to know what you really think of this late [i.e., recent] movement in favor of "Woman's Rights."

Now, I am at a loss to what the Women of the Worcester Convention are aiming at. It is clear that, if we are going to live, or have any private comforts, there must be dinners cooked, children's faces must be washed, and there must be a home—a home to which the mind of the weary husband will turn to bear him up and urge him on in his toils for the inmates of that sanctuary—a home where he can for a time forget, in his wife's and children's society, the toils and troubles of this weary world—a home which he can never leave without carrying with him a new grace, a new strength, drawn from Woman's influence, to enable him victoriously and manfully to withstand the trials and temptations of the world. Now, if Women are given the right to vote, to electioneer, to become stateswomen, why it is an incontrovertible fact (that is, if they attend properly to politics) that the dinners must go *un*cooked, the children's faces *un*washed, and home be forgotten unless, indeed, the men exchange duties with them, as was proposed at the Convention [by C. C. Burleigh], and stay at home and help their wives cook and wash the dishes.

So far from thinking Women "slaves," I do not see how it can appear in such a light to any thinking mind, any true-hearted woman. There is something so superior about Woman that would make one shrink as from profanation at the idea of her mingling in public with "the sterner and worser sex"—a spiritualization that raises her far above the intrigues of politicians and the vulgarity of rowdies—a superiority which, if not acknowledged in words. is confessed in actions, even by men who, however degraded they may be, refrain from the slightest word or action that could be commented upon, in the presence of a woman.

The Women of the Worcester Convention seem to have entirely overlooked the immense power given to women in the form of Home Influence. What power can be greater than a mother's holy and elevated example, which has given to the world so many shining lights? than a mother's gentle but impressive remonstrance to a straying son, or a wife's earnest pleadings to a wayward husband? all of which would be of no avail the moment a woman condescended to become a rowdy Senator or intriguing politician. For my part, I look on Women as missionary angels, sent among men to remind them of their high calling and high duties. It is not because men think that women have no intellect, etcetera that they consider it inexpedient for them to vote. No, it is common sense directs them to this judgment. They know that there are two great duties to be performed in the world, *public* and *domestic* duties; and as no one can deny but that men are stronger than women, the former generally choose the more laborious and inferior duties.

We must also remember, that if women gained these absurd "rights," they would be obliged to maintain them; and this they have not the strength to do; for which of the women at the Worcester Convention could knock a man down if he chose to stand up? and what man would come forward to protect a woman as long as she claimed to herself the right of self-protection? It would be well enough for the ladies to endeavor to protect themselves, if it were practicable; but what rowdy, if he met Miss Dr. So & So out on a sick call at 12 o'clock at night, would stand to listen to her explanations of "Woman's Rights"?

I acknowledge there are some gross injustices done to Women in regard to property and their very low wages; and if it were to reform such abuses as these that Women held conventions, it would be laudable; but such injustices seem to take up but a small share of their attention, and, strange as it may appear, their ambition seems to aim principally at gaining the right to be just as uninteresting and bad as men. One of the ladies [Lucretia Mott] outdid even the Nineteenth Century, when she thought the

---

From the *New York Daily Tribune,* November 2, 1850.

inspired Apostles, the companions of our blessed Savior, "might have imbibed some of the ignorance of the age." Truly, we of the Nineteenth Century are wondrous wise, or either, I fear, we are imbibing some of the infidelity and self conceit of this same wonderful age. There can be no fault found with Miss Lucy Stone's desire not to have it placed on her grave-stone that she was "relict of somebody," as she can easily avoid being the "relict" [widow] of anybody.

I am sorry, dear Sir, to have trespassed so long upon your valuable time, but as I know that on any subject you are always willing to give both sides a chance, as we Yankees say, I could not refrain from the above remarks.

Yours sincerely, A.

Remarks. [Greeley's Editorial Response]

That there is great injustice and evil in the present circumscriptions of Woman's sphere, we firmly believe: that the Worcester Convention indicated precisely the right *remedies* therefor, we are not sure. That the full and equal enjoyment of Political Franchises would improve the lot of Woman, may be doubtful; but we are willing to give the Democratic theory a full and fair trial. Whenever so many Women shall petition for the Right of Suffrage as to indicate that a majority of the sex virtually concur in the demand, then we shall insist that the Franchise shall be extended to them. Being a disciple of the faith which holds that "all just government is founded on the *consent* of the *governed*," we could do not less, even though we knew that the Women would make a bad use of the power thus accorded them. Right first; Expediency afterward.

As to our correspondent's fear that buttered toast will run short, and children's faces get crusted over, in case the Political Rights of Women are recognized as equal to and identical with those of Men, we do not share it. We know people who supposed that, when Slavery was abolished, there could be no more boots blacked, no wood chopped, bacon fried, et cetera. But we see that all needful operations go on, though Slavery *is* abolished throughout this region. We see not why it may not be so in case the slavery of Woman should in like manner be abolished. We do not see how an enlargement of her liberties and duties is to make a mother neglect her children or her household. She now performs her maternal duties

because she delights in so doing, and not because man requires it.

Our friend's delightful picture of the home presided over by an exemplary wife and mother we appreciate, but all women are not wives and mothers. Marriage is indeed "honorable in all," when it is marriage; but accepting a husband for the sake of a position, a home and a support, is not marriage. (We must be excused from stating what it *is*.) Now one radical vice of our present system is that it morally *constrains* women to take husbands (not to say, fish for them) without the least impulse of genuine affection. Ninety-nine of every hundred young women are destitute of an independent income adequate to their comfortable support; they must work or marry for a living. But in industry, Woman's sphere is exceedingly circumscribed, and her reward, as compared with the recompense of masculine effort, very inadequate. Except as household drudges, it is very difficult for seven single women out of eight to earn a comfortable, reputable, independent livelihood in this country, and it is generally much worse in others. Hence false marriages and degradations more scandalous if not more intrinsically vicious.

What Woman imminently needs is a far wider sphere of action, larger opportunities for the employment of her faculties, and a juster reward for her labor. It is a shame, for example, that there should be several thousand male Clerks in our City dealing out dry goods mainly to women; these Clerks should have more masculine employments, and their places should be filled by women. The teachers in our schools should nearly all be women; the number should be doubled and the compensation largely increased. Watchmaking, tailoring, and many other branches of manufacturing industry, should in good part be relinquished to women. Women's work should command in the average two-thirds to three-fourths that of men: the present rates range from one-third to one-half.

Political franchises are but means to an end, which end is the securing of social and personal rights. Other classes have found the Elective Franchise serviceable toward the attainment of these rights, and we see not why it would lose its efficacy in the hands of Women. And as to the exposure of Women to insult and outrage in the Town or Ward Meeting, or at the Election, we trust the effect would be just opposite to that anticipated—namely, that men would be constrained by the presence of ladies to keep sober and behave themselves. The presence of Woman has this effect ever in those public assemblages honored by her presence; and we trust its virtue is far from having been exhausted.

As to Woman having to fight and knock down to maintain their Rights if once conceded, we don't believe a word of it. Knock down whom? Certainly not those who cheerfully concede them all they ask; and if there are any of the other sort, such brutes as choose to commence the game of knocking down, (they) would be very sure to get enough of it before coming to the Women. But there would be no knocking down in the premises.

We heartily rejoice that the Women's Rights Convention was held, and trust it will be followed by others. Our correspondent admits that Woman endures great wrongs which cry aloud for redress, but thinks the Worcester Convention misunderstood both the disease and the remedy. Very well; let the discussion go on, until wiser heads shall be interested and safer counsels prevail. For our part, we are well satisfied with the general scope and bearing of the Worcester discussions, and trust they will be followed up. [Ed.]

Chapter 8 Worksheet and Questions

1. Conservative clergy and other male opponents of women's rights predicted that if women left the home or gained any justice under the laws, the world would end. What specific evils and problems do they predict will happen? On what grounds do conservative clergy and other male supporters of domesticity oppose women's basic rights?

_____

_____

_____

_____

_____

_____

_____

_____

2. Catherine Beecher and other women do not support the calls for public equality for or public activism by women. Why not? What is the basis of women's power, and how or where should they use it? Do they ever really address the issues and concerns raised by women's rights activists? Why not?

_____

_____

_____

_____

_____

_____

_____

_____

3. Using the documents and personal testimony in this chapter, describe all of the abuses, discriminations, unmet needs, and lack of rights that nineteenth-century women suffered.

_____

_____

_____

_____

_____

_____

_____

_____

_____

4. How many of the issues and problems that you described in question #3 still exist today? What are the unmet goals of nineteenth-century activists? What arguments are used against these goals today? How are they similar to arguments used by women's rights opponents in the antebellum United States?

_____

_____

_____

_____

_____

_____

_____

_____

_____

_____

Master and Slave: Two Perspectives on the Antebellum South and Its "Peculiar Institution"

The image remains strong in American minds, as vivid as a Currier and Ives print, as romantic and appealing as a Stephen Foster song: One sees magnolias and moonlight, and a large plantation house with white colonnades, where tall handsome gentlemen are dancing with beautiful hoop-skirted ladies. Warm laughter and rich songs are floating up from the slave quarters. This is the myth of the antebellum South and slavery, one repeated after the Civil War to deny the importance of slavery in causing the conflict. In reality, slavery was vitally important to the Southern economy. Production of short-staple cotton soared with the creation of the mechanical "gin" to separate the green seeds from the precious white fibers, and planters spread cotton cultivation across the Appalachians into the Black Belt lands of Alabama, Mississippi, and other areas of the Old Southwest. In 1790 the South produced only 3,000 bales of cotton, an amount that increased to 178,000 bales in 1810 and surged past 4 million bales annually by 1860.

Slaves produced almost all of this cotton. By 1860 the exports of cotton exceeded the dollar value of all other American exports combined. Slaves cleared the land and broke the soil, planted the cotton and kept the plants weed-free as they grew, picked the bolls from the fields, and packed them into bales. Cotton produced an economic boom across the South. In the region known as the Old Southwest, the free residents of the "cotton belt" enjoyed a per capita income twice as high as anywhere else in the nation. As cotton prices raised, so too did the demand for slaves, and non-cotton producing states "produced" and shipped over one million slaves to areas further south and west. Slave families were ripped apart as traders purchased them in the upper tier of Southern states and moved them south and west. By 1860, some 65 percent of Southern slaves lived in the cotton belt region.

Slavery was intertwined with every facet of Southern life. In 1833 one Southerner admitted as much, declaring "So interwoven is it with our interest, our manners, our climate and our very being, that no change can ever possibly be effected without a civil commotion." Slavery supported Southern ideas about paternalism and a patriarchal society, satisfied the need for profit, and increased one's net worth and social standing. For White Southerners, liberty and slavery were intertwined so much that, in their view, the existence of liberty depended on the preservation of slavery. In fact, Southern Whites insisted that true liberty meant the right to own slaves; freedom meant the right to treat their property as they chose and take it with them wherever they went. Freedom meant preserving their society and culture, their way of life and property—and that property meant first and foremost African-American slaves. In 1861 secession would mean a defense of freedom as they defined it.

When historians search through the traditional records, they reveal White Southerners justifying slavery, and praising and glorifying the master-slave relationship in the antebellum South. Sources include public speeches and government documents, plantation records, slave owner diaries, newspapers, traveler's accounts, and Southern sermons. Recognizing their need for slaves, Southerners went to great lengths to justify the existence of an institution considered by the rest of the western world to be foul, loathsome, and anachronistic. Their accounts described Southern paternalism working its best, where slavery was a benign and benevolent institution, caring for child-like slaves in a cruel world. Masters were father figures, who cared for their "people" like an extended family, usually at great cost to themselves. Thomas R. Dew of Virginia, in his 1832 *Review of the Debate in the Virginia Legislature*, explained that slavery was the only "fitting condition" for African Americans; it was the best way to civilize them. They were like children, incapable of higher learning, skilled tasks, or even caring for themselves. He claimed, "Slaves of a good master are his warmest, most constant and most devoted friends." To release the slaves, to require them to fend for themselves, would be a catastrophe. Besides, slavery was good for Whites as well, teaching them to be more benevolent and responsible toward others. Since the South needed slave labor to insure economic success, and African Americans "needed" slavery to survive, slavery could be excused as a "necessary evil."

After the 1831 Nat Turner revolt in Virginia, Southerners aggressively defended slavery as a "positive good." Southern clergy, politicians, and writers furiously defended slavery in a variety of ways. They justified slavery on religious grounds, claiming both New and Old Testament approval of this institution. They repeated and expanded arguments about African-American inferiority, claiming they could only survive in an authority relationship. Southern Whites frequently referred to slaves' "childlike simplicity" or "childlike irresponsibility," suggesting that they were a race of permanent children in need of a permanent father/authority figure. It was the duty of White masters to permanently shelter, feed, and own Black people. It was the duty of African Americans to always serve Whites. James Henry Hammond of South Carolina combined these arguments to deny that slavery was either evil or immoral. It could not be either one, he argued, because "civilized gentlemen" organized the institution rationally and thoughtfully. Any problems for slaves or masters should be blamed on Abolitionist agitators. Besides, argued Hammond, all great societies built themselves on a social "mud sill" of inferiors, whose job was to "perform the drudgery of life" while Whites achieved cultural and economic greatness. George Fitzhugh and other writers argued that the chattel slaves in the South lived better than the "wage slaves" working in Northern factories. Southern paternalism meant African-American slaves were cared for from cradle to grave, whether sick or healthy. Northern employers cared nothing for their workers, abandoning them to starve and die in the elements when they needed help the most. (Be sure to consider what you have read in chapter 7 of this book.) Slavery draws the workers and slaves together into one great, close-knit community.

Luckily we have many accounts from former slaves to balance this slanted view of slavery. Abolitionists and anti-slavery societies collected some stories from fugitive slaves before the Civil War. A larger source comes from the Federal Writers' Project, undertaken as part of the New Deal's Great Depression employment efforts. Thousands of writers traveled across the South, interviewing former slaves now very old. Their stories were collected and stored in the Library of Congress where, starting in the 1960s, they became the basis of increased research on American slavery. From these records we know that slaves had to strike a balance between accepting their fate and open rebellion, to find ways to define and control their own lives while appearing to follow the guidelines their masters set down for them. Slaves' lives varied, depending on the tasks they did, the size of their master's farm/plantation, and the innate human qualities of each master. Far beyond the shadow of the plantation there were industrial slaves, urban slaves, and others hired out as craftsmen. We now know that slaves helped make their own world. They were not merely docile recipients of whatever their owners dished out, but were proactive in creating their own lives. Historians cannot study slaves or masters alone; their lives are so intertwined they must be studied together. To study only one provides a distorted view of Southern life and culture.

How did African-American descriptions of their lives differ from White accounts? Systematic violence anchored slavery, not warm paternalism and caring masters. Owners had a monopoly on force and violence, and used it to keep slaves under control. Whippings were the most frequent form of punishment; slaves were whipped for working too slowly, for being insolent, or for any other reason the master chose. Many slaves wore permanent scars on their backs, pictures of which created great sensations in the North. Frequent Southern responses were that whippings were necessary to keep the slaves under control; it was "for their own good" or they could not "be controlled without the whip." Owners pointed out that school children, soldiers, sailors, and even women were corporally punished, so why not the slaves as well? This is a defense of slavery still used by some Southern historians today.

Besides whippings, owners could brand, burn, or mutilate their slaves, because the African Americans were their private property. These actions could include chopping off the toes of runaways so they "won't run so fast next time," or requiring slaves who do a bad job picking worms off of cotton leaves to eat a handful of worms as a punishment. Owners used religion to sway slaves into submission as well, by teaching them only parts of the gospel. White ministers told slaves that the Bible instructed them to "not lie and steal," that "it is the devil who tells you to try and be free," and that God made slaves/servants to "obey their masters at all times and make crops." Slaves rejected Southern religious leaders' attempts to make Christianity a doctrine of passive submission to slavery. African Americans adapted elements of Christianity to their daily needs and incorporated parts of their traditional religions and rituals from past generations. They accepted the idea of a better future, and took to heart the idea that all should love their brothers and sisters as children of God. Slaves identified with the people of the Old Testament and their escape from bondage, and looked forward to a Judgment day that would bring salvation for them, but damnation for their owners and abusers.

African-American slaves sought to sanction their personal relationships through marriage. Although sometimes forced together by masters for procreation, slaves formed their own bonds and created families. Unlike Southern Whites, they preserved the African tradition of not marrying cousins. Marriage also avoided the traditional shame of unwed motherhood. To preserve family traditions in an institution that frequently broke up family units, newborns were often given African names, or were named after fathers to preserve the family name. Extended kinship relationships throughout the slave community helped families survive, because they were under attack. Women endured repeated rapes by Whites, mothers and fathers were beaten in front of their children, or their children were beaten in front of them, and the slaves were helpless to prevent these acts of violence. Black women were the most vulnerable group in the antebellum United States. As historian Deborah Gray White declared, they were "black in a white society, women in a society ruled by men" and thus had less formal power than any other group in the nation. But African-American women and families survived and grew stronger.

Considering the Evidence in the Readings

In this chapter you will examine slavery from the viewpoint of the owners and defenders of the institution, as well as from the slaves who suffered in its existence. We know that most masters did not purposely starve or beat their slaves to death—slaves were too valuable for that. Minimum housing, clothing, and food were provided, enough so that the slaves could survive and be productive workers. You should determine what life was really like for slaves on antebellum plantations, how much the owners controlled them, and to what extent slaves could shape their own world. Consider how slavery impacted the lives of everyone in the South. Another point to consider is how the experience of slavery differed for men and women.

Document 9.1 Last Will and Testament of James Richey, Deceased

The most basic fact of slavery is that African Americans were chattel; they were human property. They were, however, very valuable property. The expansion of cotton production greatly increased the demand for slaves in the South. This increased demand, combined with the 1808 ban on the external slave trade, saw the going price for slaves increase every antebellum decade. By 1850, prime male field hands sold for more than $800, while women doubling as field hands and breeders of this same age (20-40 years old) sold for $600. It should not be too surprising, then, that slave owners accounted for their most valuable property first when writing a will. In the following document, James Richey reinforces that African Americans were human property, owned by another human being. What ages are the slaves that Richey wills to his own children? What ages do his own children seem to be? Do the slaves' own family ties or forthcoming children affect Richey's plans for dividing his property in any way?

In the Name of God, Amen!

I James Richey of the District and State aforesaid being in sound mind, but frail in body do make this my last will and Testament in manner and form following:

1st. Item viz. I will and bequeath unto my daughter Nancy one Negro boy named Peter about the age of seven years old.

2nd. Item. I will and bequeath unto my daughter Peggy one Negro, (Viz) Jesse about the age of sixteen years old—

3rd. Item. I will and bequeath unto my son Samuel two Negroes (Viz) Esther, about the age of 6 years, and George, about 4 years of age—

4th. Item. I will and bequeath unto my son William two Negroes (Viz) Isabell, about the age of seven years and Will about 3 years of age—

5th. Item. I will and bequeath unto my son John a Negro woman (viz), Hannah.

6th. Item. I will and bequeath unto my daughter Betty two Negroes (viz) Phillis (Whom she is now in possession of) and Charlotte, during her life and at her demise I will and bequeath them to her children, with their increase—

7th. Item. I will and bequeath unto my daughter Sally one Negro (Viz) Jen whom she is now in possession of, together with her children—

8th. Item. I direct and allow Reuben and Ann his wife, together with the child she is now suckling, to be sold and the amount to be equally divided among my children.

9th. Item. I will and bequeath unto my grandson James, (son of my son James) a Negro viz Aaron about the age of four years old—

10th. Item. I will and bequeath unto my gran Polly, (daughter of my son James) one Negro (Viz) Ameu about 18 month old.

11th. Item. I will and bequeath unto my son Samuel the Plantation whereon he now lives.

12th. Item. I will and bequeath unto my son Samuel the Plantation adjoining that on which my son William lives containing about 150 acres.

13th. Item. I will and bequeath unto my son John the Plantation whereon I now live.

14th. Item. I direct and allow Samuel my son to take one cow, and then, the balance of my cattle with all my other stock to be sold and the proceeds to be equally divided among my children. I direct and allow a certain note which I hold on William Lord to be given up to my daughter Mary his wife, and that he shall not be called on to pay it nor the interest on it.

15th. Item. I also direct and allow whatever Notes and money may be remaining at the time of my death to be equally divided among my children.

16th. Item. I also direct and allow, whatever property I may possess at the time of my death which is not herein specified, to be sold and the proceeds to be equally divided among my children.

17th. Item. I will and bequeath unto my daughter Peggy a horse (viz) her choice of those that are remaining at the time of my decease.

18th. Item. I nominate and appoint William Richey (my brother), Robert Dunn and James Wilson to be my Executors of this my last Will and Testament and hereby utterly renounce and nullify all other wills and testaments which I may have heretofore made, subscribing to this as my last will and testament this 8th. day of May in the year of our Lord one thousand eight hundred and thirty two.

James Richey, L. S.

William Hill
Hezekiah Elgin
John McCullough, Jr.

Proven by the oath of John McCullough, Junr. and Jas. Wilson qualified Executors 7th. of June, 1833 before Moses Taggart.

A true copy:

Wilbur J. Blake
SEAL Judge of Probate
March 28th, 1944

_____

From State of South Carolina, Abbeville District.

Document 9.2 John C. Calhoun Pronounces Slavery a Positive Good

Born in the back country of South Carolina in 1782, John C. Calhoun was left fatherless at age 14, and struggled to complete his education. To gain the wealth and social position he wanted in society, he married Floride Bouneau Calhoun in 1811, instantly becoming a wealthy slave owner. An outspoken nationalist before 1816, Calhoun became the foremost defender of states' rights, slavery, and the slave-owning aristocracy of the South. Later slavery apologists adopted his views and deified the man. Calhoun emphasized the defense of slavery as early as 1828 in his writings on nullification theory. The real cause behind his arguments for states' rights was the potential danger to the "peculiar domestic institution of the Southern states." He was one of the earliest proponents of slavery as a positive good, the attitude that dominated pro-slavery arguments from the 1840s onward. Calhoun's ideas are first introduced in his February 6, 1837 Senate speech "On the Reception of Abolitionist Petitions," which is printed below. According to Calhoun, what do all advanced communities throughout history have in common? Why is the South's slave system an advantage in the ongoing conflict between labor and capital? How is the slave treated better than workers and the poor elsewhere?

I do not belong, said Mr. C., to the school which holds that aggression is to be met by concession. Mine is the opposite creed, which teaches that encroachments must be met at the beginning, and that those who act on the opposite principle are prepared to become slaves. In this case, in particular, I hold concession or compromise to be fatal. If we concede an inch, concession would follow concession—compromise would follow compromise, until our ranks would be so broken that effectual resistance would be impossible. We must meet the enemy on the frontier, with a fixed determination of maintaining our position at every hazard. Consent to receive these insulting petitions, and the next demand will be that they be referred to a committee in order that they may be deliberated and acted upon. At the last session we were modestly asked to receive them, simply to lay them on the table, without any view to ulterior action. . . . I then said, that the next step would be to refer the petition to a committee, and I already see indications that such is now the intention. If we yield, that will be followed by another, and we will thus proceed, step by step, to the final consummation of the object of these petitions. We are now told that the most effectual mode of arresting the progress of abolition is, to reason it down; and with this view it is urged that the petitions ought to be referred to a committee. That is the very ground which was taken at the last session in the other House, but instead of arresting its progress it has since advanced more rapidly than ever. The most unquestionable right may be rendered doubtful, if once admitted to be a subject of controversy, and that would be the case in the present instance. The subject is beyond the jurisdiction of Congress—they have no right to touch it in any shape or form, or to make it the subject of deliberation or discussion. . . .

As widely as this incendiary spirit has spread, it has not yet infected this body, or the great mass of the intelligent and business portion of the North; but unless it be speedily stopped, it will spread and work upwards till it brings the two great sections of the Union into deadly conflict. This is not a new impression with me. Several years since, in a discussion with one of the Senators from Massachusetts (Mr. Webster), before this fell spirit had showed itself, I then predicted that the doctrine of the proclamation and the Force Bill—that this Government had a right, in the last resort, to determine the extent of its own powers, and enforce its decision at the point of the bayonet, which was so warmly maintained by that Senator, would at no distant day arouse the dormant spirit of abolitionism. I told him that the doctrine was tantamount to the assumption of unlimited power on the part of the Government, and that such would be the impression on the public mind in a large portion of the Union. The consequence would be inevitable. A large portion of the Northern States

---

Slavery a Positive Good Speech to the United States Senate.

believed slavery to be a sin, and would consider it as an obligation of conscience to abolish it if they should feel themselves in any degree responsible for its continuance, and that this doctrine would necessarily lead to the belief of such responsibility. I then predicted that it would commence as it has with this fanatical portion of society, and that they would begin their operations on the ignorant, the weak, the young, and the thoughtless,—and gradually extend upwards till they would become strong enough to obtain political control, when he and others holding the highest stations in society, would, however reluctant, be compelled to yield to their doctrines, or be driven into obscurity. But four years have since elapsed, and all this is already in a course of regular fulfilment.

Standing at the point of time at which we have now arrived, it will not be more difficult to trace the course of future events now than it was then. They who imagine that the spirit now abroad in the North, will die away of itself without a shock or convulsion, have formed a very inadequate conception of its real character; it will continue to rise and spread, unless prompt and efficient measures to stay its progress be adopted. Already it has taken possession of the pulpit, of the schools, and, to a considerable extent, of the press; those great instruments by which the mind of the rising generation will be formed. However sound the great body of the non-slaveholding States are at present, in the course of a few years they will be succeeded by those who will have been taught to hate the people and institutions of nearly one-half of this Union, with a hatred more deadly than one hostile nation ever entertained towards another. It is easy to see the end. By the necessary course of events, if left to themselves, we must become, finally, two people. It is impossible under the deadly hatred which must spring up between the two great nations, if the present causes are permitted to operate unchecked, that we should continue under the same political system. The conflicting elements would burst the Union asunder, powerful as are the links which hold it together. Abolition and the Union cannot coexist. As the friend of the Union I openly proclaim it,—and the sooner it is known the better. The former may now be controlled, but in a short time it will be beyond the power of man to arrest the course of events. We of the South will not, cannot, surrender our institutions. To maintain the existing relations between the two races, inhabiting that section of the Union, is indispensable to the peace and happiness of both. It cannot be subverted without drenching the country or the other of the races. . . . But let me not be understood as admitting, even by implication, that the existing relations between the two races in the slaveholding States is an evil:—far otherwise; I hold it to be a good, as it has thus far proved itself to be to both, and will continue to prove so if not disturbed by the fell spirit of abolition. I appeal to facts. Never before has the black race of Central Africa, from the dawn of history to the present day, attained a condition so civilized and so improved, not only physically, but morally and intellectually.

In the meantime, the white or European race, has not degenerated. It has kept pace with its brethren in other sections of the Union where slavery does not exist. It is odious to make comparison; but I appeal to all sides whether the South is not equal in virtue, intelligence, patriotism, courage, disinterestedness, and all the high qualities which adorn our nature.

But I take higher ground. I hold that in the present state of civilization, where two races of different origin, and distinguished by color, and other physical differences, as well as intellectual, are brought together, the relation now existing in the slaveholding States between the two, is, instead of an evil, a good— a positive good. I feel myself called upon to speak freely upon the subject where the honor and interests of those I represent are involved. I hold then, that there never has yet existed a wealthy and civilized society in which one portion of the community did not, in point of fact, live on the labor of the other. Broad and general as is this assertion, it is fully borne out by history. This is not the proper occasion, but, if it were, it would not be difficult to trace the various devices by which the wealth of all civilized communities has been so unequally divided, and to show by what means so small a share has been allotted to those by whose labor it was produced, and so large a share given to the non-producing classes.

The devices are almost innumerable, from the brute force and gross superstition of ancient times, to the subtle and artful fiscal contrivances of modern. I might well challenge a comparison between them and the more direct, simple, and patriarchal mode by which the labor of the African race is, among us, commanded by the European. I may say with truth, that in few countries so much is left to the share of the laborer, and so little exacted from him, or where there is more kind attention paid to him in sickness or infirmities of age. Compare his condition with the tenants of the poor houses in the more civilized portions of Europe—look at the sick, and the old and infirm slave, on one hand, in the midst of his family and friends, under the kind superintending care of his master and mistress, and compare it with the forlorn and wretched condition of the pauper in the poorhouse. But I will not dwell on this aspect of the question; I turn to the political; and here I fearlessly assert that the existing relation between the two races in the South, against which these blind fanatics are waging war, forms the most solid and durable foundation on which to rear free and stable political institutions. It is useless to disguise the fact. There is and always has been in an advanced stage of wealth and civilization, a conflict between labor and capital. The condition of society in the South exempts us from the disorders and dangers resulting from this conflict; and which explains why it is that the political condition of the slaveholding States has been so much more stable and quiet than that of the North. . . .

Surrounded as the slaveholding States are with such imminent perils, I rejoice to think that our means of defense are ample, if we shall prove to have the intelligence and spirit to see and apply them before it is too late. All we want is concert, to lay aside all party differences and unite with zeal and energy in repelling approaching dangers. Let there be concert of action, and we shall find ample means of security without resorting to secession or disunion. I speak with full knowledge and a thorough examination of the subject, and for one see my way clearly. . . . I dare not hope that anything I can say will arouse the South to a due sense of danger; I fear it is beyond the power of mortal voice to awaken it in time from the fatal security into which it has fallen.

Document 9.3 George Fitzhugh Compares Free and Slave Society

Although Thomas Dew, Josiah Nott, and other Southern writers actively defended slavery and the Southern way of life, few were as eloquent as George Fitzhugh. Fitzhugh openly endorsed Calhoun's indictment of Northern capitalism. Owner of a small plantation in Port Royal, Virginia, Fitzhugh trained as a lawyer, and clerked in the Attorney General's office during the Buchanan administration. His fame came from his books defending the ideal of Southern paternalism versus the Northern free market economy. According to Fitzhugh, liberty and equality—concepts any free society embraces—turn everyone into cannibals who are selfish and uncaring of anyone else's needs. Liberty in Northern capitalism meant liberty for the few but slavery in other forms for everyone else. It meant you were free to be exploited by the rich and powerful. Liberty and equality meant increased crime in the North, in England, and in France. These ideas meant class warfare and unions, because employers did not care about their workers' needs. The South did things differently, Fitzhugh claimed, and thus rivaled Rome in its greatness. He envisioned a South that would be industrial as well as agricultural, but always a slave-holding society. If White and Black labor were brought under slavery, then the endless greed and self-absorption of Northern capitalism would vanish, and the nation would be saved. In this excerpt from *The Sociology for the South: Or, The Failure of Free Society*, how is Southern society superior to that in the North? What Northern problems is the South avoiding, and how are they escaping these problems?

At the slaveholding South all is peace, quiet, plenty and contentment. We have no mobs, no trades unions, no strikes for higher wages, no armed resistance to the law, but little jealousy of the rich by the poor. We have but few in our jails, and fewer in our poor houses. We produce enough of the comforts and necessaries of life for a population three or four times as numerous as ours. We are wholly exempt from the torrent of pauperism, crime, agrarianism, and infidelity which Europe is pouring from her jails and

alms houses on the already crowded North. Population increases slowly, wealth rapidly. In the tide water region of Eastern Virginia, as far as our experience extends, the crops have doubled in fifteen years, whilst the population has been almost stationary. In the same period in the lands, owing to improvements of the soil and the many fine houses erected in the country, have nearly doubled in value. This ratio of improvement has been approximated or exceeded wherever in the South slaves are numerous. We have

From *The Sociology of the South*, Richmond: J. W. Randolph, 1854.

enough for the present, and no Malthusian spectres frightening us for the future. Wealth is more equally distributed than at the North, where a few millionaires own most of the property of the country. (These millionaires are men of cold hearts and weak minds; they know how to make money, but not how to use it, either for the benefit of themselves or of others.) High intellectual and moral attainments, refinement of head and heart, give standing to a man in the South, however poor he may be. Money is, with few exceptions, the only thing that ennobles at the North. We have poor among us, but none who are over-worked and under-fed. We do not crowd cities because lands are abundant and their owners kind, merciful and hospitable. The poor are as hospitable as the rich, the negro as the white man. Nobody dreams of turning a friend, a relative, or a stranger from his door. The very negro who deems it no crime to steal, would scorn to sell his hospitality. We have no loafers, because the poor relative or friend who borrows our horse, or spends a week under our roof, is a welcome guest. The loose economy, the wasteful mode of living at the South, is a blessing when rightly considered; it keeps want, scarcity and famine at a distance, because it leaves room for retrenchment. The nice, accurate economy of France, England and New England, keeps society always on the verge of famine, because it leaves no room to retrench, that is to live on a part only of what they now consume. Our society exhibits no appearance of precocity, no symptoms of decay. A long course of continuing improvement is in prospect before us, with no limits which human foresight can descry. Actual liberty and equality with our white population has been approached much nearer than in the free States. Few of our whites ever work as day laborers, none as cooks, scullions, hostlers, body servants, or in other menial capacities. One free citizen does not lord it over another; hence that feeling of independence and equality that distinguishes us; hence that pride of character, that self-respect, that give us ascendence when we come in contact with Northerners. It is a distinction to be a Southerner, as it once was to be a Roman citizen. . . .

Document 9.4 Reverend Thorton Stringfellow's Christian Defense of Slavery

From the time of the first Great Awakening in the eighteenth century, through the first decades of the nineteenth century, many Southern religious leaders criticized slavery. Baptists, Methodists, and other evangelical Protestants condemned both slavery and slaveowners as evil. But during the nineteenth century, Southern ministers abandoned their high moral ground and instead allied themselves with wealthy patrons and politicians to defend the institution, causing splits in national churches that continue to the present day. In fact, Southern ministers played a leading role justifying slavery, using the Bible as a tool to appeal to common Whites. The Reverend Thorton Stringfellow was one of slavery's most strident defenders. This Baptist minister from Culpepper County, Virginia used both Old and New Testament scripture to demonstrate what Southerners claimed was a "holy" sanction for human slavery. The following excerpts are from Stringfellow's 1856 pamphlet *Scriptural and Statistical Views in Favor of Slavery.* What are his major religious arguments in favor of slavery? What examples (biblical "facts" to Stringfellow) does he use to support his arguments? Would everyone find his use of the Bible and his arguments convincing?

. . . I PROPOSE . . . To EXAMINE the sacred volume briefly, and if I am not greatly mistaken, I shall be able to make it appear that the institution of slavery has received, in the first place.

1st. The sanction of the Almighty in the Patriarchal age.

2d. That it was incorporated into the only National Constitution which ever emanated from God.

3d. That its legality was recognized, and its relative duties regulated, by Jesus Christ in his kingdom. . . .

From *Scriptural and Statistical Views in Favor of Slavery,* Richmond: J. W. Raldolph, 1856.

The first recorded language which was ever uttered in relation to slavery, is the inspired language of Noah. In God's stead he says, "Cursed be Canaan; a servant of servants shall he be to his brethren." "Blessed be the Lord God of Shem; and Canaan shall be his servant." "God shall enlarge Japheth, and he shall dwell in the tents of Shem; and Canaan shall be his servant."—Gen. ix: 25, 26, 27. Here, language is used, showing the *favor* which God would exercise to the posterity of Shem and Japheth, while they were holding the posterity of Ham in a state of *abject bondage*. May it not be said in truth, that God decreed this institution before it existed; and has he not connected its *existence* with prophetic tokens of special favor, to those who should be slave owners or masters? . . . The sacred records occupy but a short space from this inspired ray on this subject, untill they bring to our notice, a man that is held up as a model, in all that adorns human nature, and as one that God delighted to honor. This man is Abraham, honored in the sacred records, with the appellation, "Father" of the "faithful." Abraham was a native of Ur, of the Chaldees. From thence the Lord called him to go to a country which he would show him; and he obeyed, not knowing whither he went. He stopped for a time at Haran, where his father died. From thence he "took Sarai his wife, and Lot his brother's son, and all their substance that they had gathered, and the souls they had gotten in Haran, and they went forth to go into the land of Canaan."—Gen. xii: 5.

All the ancient Jewish writers of note, and Christian commentators agree, that by the "souls they had gotten in Haran," as our translators render it, are meant their slaves or those persons they had bought with their money in Haran. In a few years after their arrival in Canaan, Lot with all he had was taken captive. So soon as Abraham heard it, he armed three hundred and eighteen slaves that were born in his house, and retook him. How great must have been the entire slave family, to produce at this period of Abraham's life, such a number of young slaves able to bear arms.—Gen. xiv: 14. . . .

God had promised Abraham's seed the land of Canaan, and that in his seed all the nations of the earth should be blessed. He reached the age of eighty-five, and his wife the age of seventy-five, while as yet, they had no child. At this period, Sarah's anxiety for the promised seed, in connection with her age, induced her to propose a female slave of the Egyptian stock, as a secondary wife, from which to obtain the promised seed. This alliance soon puffed the slave with pride, and she became insolent to her mistress— the mistress complained to Abraham, the master.

Abraham ordered Sarah to exercise her authority. Sarah did so, and pushed it to severity, and the slave absconded. The divine oracles inform us, that the angel of God found this run-away bond-woman in the wilderness; and if God had commissioned his angel to improve this opportunity of teaching the world how much he abhorred slavery, he took a bad plan to accomplish it. For, instead of repeating a homily upon doing to others as we "would they should do unto us," and heaping reproach upon Sarah, as a hypocrite, and Abraham as a tyrant, and giving Hagar direction how she might get into Egypt, from whence (according to abolitionism) she had been unrighteously sold into bondage, the angel addressed her as "Hagar, Sarah's maid,"—Gen. xvi: 1, 9; (thereby recognizing the relation of master and slave,) and asks her, "whither wilt thou go?" and she said "I flee from the face of my mistress." . . .

. . . Judge for yourself, reader, by the angel's answer: "And the angel of the Lord said unto her, Return unto thy mistress, and submit thyself under her hands."—Gen. xvi: 9.

But, says the spirit of abolition, with which the Bible has to contend, you are building your house upon the sand, for these were nothing but hired servants; and their servitude designates no such state, condition, or relation, as that, in which one person is made the property of another, to be bought, sold, or transferred forever. To this, we have two answers in reference to the subject, *before giving the law*. In the first place, the term servant, in the schedules of property among the patriarchs, *does designate* the state, condition, or relation in which one person is the legal property of another, as in Gen. xxiv: 35, 36. Here Abraham's servant, who had been sent by his master to get a wife for his son Isaac, in order to prevail with the woman and her family, states, that the man for whom he sought a bride, was the son of a man whom God had greatly blessed with riches; which he goes on to enumerate thus, in the 35th verse: "He hath given him flocks, and herds, and silver, and gold, and menservants, and maid-servants, and camels, and asses;" then in verse 36th, he states the disposition his master had made of his estate: "My master's wife bare a son to my master when she was old, and unto him he hath given all that he hath." Here, servants are enumerated with silver and gold as part of the patrimony. And, reader, bear it in mind; as if to rebuke the doctrine of abolition, servants are not only inventoried as property, but as property which *God had given to Abraham*. After the death of Abraham, we have a view of Isaac at Gerar, when he had come into the possession of this estate; and this is the description given of him: "And the man waxed great, and went forward, and grew until he became very great; for he had possession of flocks, and possession of herds, and *great store of servants.*"—Gen. xxvi: 13, 14. This state in which servants are made chattels, he received as an inheritance from his father, and passed to his son Jacob.

Again, in Genesis xvii, we are informed of a covenant God entered into with Abraham; in which he stipulates to be a God to him and his *seed,* (not his servants,) and to give to his seed the land of Canaan for an everlasting possession. He expressly stipulates, that Abraham shall put the token of this covenant upon every servant born in his house, and upon every servant *bought with his money of any stranger.*—Gen. xvii: 12, 13. Here again servants are property. Again, more than four hundred years afterward, we find the *seed* of Abraham, on leaving Egypt, directed to celebrate the rite, that was ordained as a memorial of their deliverance, viz: the Passover, at which time the same institution which makes *property of men and women*, is recognized, and the *servant bought with money*, is given the privilege of partaking, upon the ground of his being circumcised *by his master*, while the hired servant, over whom the master had no such control, is excluded until he voluntarily submits to circumcision; showing clearly that the institution of involuntary slavery then carried with it a right, on the part of the master, *to choose* a religion *for the* servant who was his money, as Abraham did, by God's direction, when he imposed circumcision on those he had bought with his money,—when he was circumcised himself, with Ishmael his son, who was the only individual beside himself, on whom he had a right to impose it, except the bond-servants bought of the stranger with his money, and their children born in his house. The next notice we have of servants as property, is from God himself, when clothed with all the visible tokens of his presence and glory, on the top of Sinai, when he proclaimed his law to the millions that surrounded its base: "Thou shalt not covet thy neighbor's house, thou shalt not covet thy neighbor's wife, nor his man-servant, nor his maid-servant, nor his ox, nor his ass, nor any thing that is thy neighbor's."—Ex. xx: 17. Here is a patriarchal catalogue of property, having God for its author, the wife among the rest, who was then purchased, as Jacob purchased his two, by fourteen years' service. Here the term servant, as used by the Almighty, under the circumstances of the case could not be understood by these millions, as meaning any thing but property, because the night they left Egypt, a few weeks before, Moses,

by Divine authority, recognized their servants as property, which they had bought with their money. . . .

. . . Job himself was a great slaveholder, and, like Abraham, Isaac, and Jacob, won no small portion of his claims to character with God and men from the manner in which he discharged his duty to his slaves. Once more: the conduct of Joseph in Egypt, as *Pharaoh's counsellor*, under all the circumstances, proves him a friend to absolute slavery, as a form of government better adapted to the state of the world at that time, than the one which existed in Egypt; for certain it is, that he peaceably effected a change in the fundamental law, by which a *state, condition, or relation*, between Pharaoh and the Egyptians was established, which answers to the one now denounced as sinful in the sight of God. Being warned of God, he gathered up all the surplus grain in the years of plenty, and sold it out in the years of famine, until he gathered up all the money; and when money failed, the Egyptians came and said, "Give us bread;" and Joseph said, "Give your cattle, and I will give for your cattle, if money fail." When that year was ended, they came unto him the second year, and said, "There is not aught left in sight of my Lord, but our bodies and our lands. Buy us and our lands for bread." And Joseph bought all the land of Egypt for Pharaoh.

So the land became Pharaoh's, and as for the people, he removed them to cities, from one end of the borders of Egypt, even to the other end thereof. Then Joseph said unto the people, "Behold! I have bought you this day, and your land for Pharaoh;" and they said, "we will be Pharaoh's servants."—See Gen. xlvii: 14, 16, 19, 20, 21, 23, 25. Having thus changed the fundamental law, and created a state of entire *dependence* and *hereditary bondage*, he enacted in his sovereign pleasure, that they should give Pharaoh one part, and take the other four parts of the productions of the earth to themselves. How far the hand of God was in this overthrow of liberty, I will not decide; but from the fact that he has singled out the greatest slaveholders of that age, as the objects of his special favor, it would seem that the institution was one furnishing great opportunities to exercise grace and glorify God, as it still does, where its duties are faithfully discharged.

. . . We will therefore proceed to our second proposition, which is—

Second.—That it was incorporated in the only national constitution emanating from the Almighty. By common consent, that portion of time stretching from Noah, until the law was given to Abraham's posterity, at Mount Sinai, is called the patriarchal age; *this is the period we have reviewed*, in relation to this subject. From the giving of the law until the coming of Christ, is called the Mosaic or legal dispensation. From the coming of Christ to the end of time, is called the Gospel dispensation. The legal dispensation is *the period of time, we propose now to examine,* in reference to the institution of involuntary and hereditary slavery; in order to ascertain, whether, during this period, *it existed at all,* and *if it did exist,* whether with the *divine sanction,* or *in violation of the divine will.* This dispensation is called the legal dispensation, because it was the pleasure of God to take Abraham's posterity by miraculous power, then numbering near three millions of souls, and give them a written constitution of government, a country to dwell in, and a covenant of special protection and favor, for their obedience to his law until the coming of Christ. The laws which he gave them emanated from his sovereign pleasure, and were designed, in the first place, to make himself known in his essential perfections; second, in his moral character; third, in his relation to man; and fourth, to make known those principles of action by the exercise of which man attains his highest moral elevation, viz: supreme love to God, and love to others as to ourselves.

All the law is nothing but a perceptive exemplification of these two principles; consequently, the existence of a precept in the law, utterly irreconcilable with these principles, would destroy all claims upon us for an acknowledgment of its divine original. Jesus Christ himself has put his finger upon these two principles of human conduct, (Deut. vi: 5—Levit. xix: 18,) revealed in the law of Moses, and decided, that on them hang all the law and the prophets. . . .

. . . For the fifteen hundred years, during which these laws were in force, God raised up a succession of prophets to reprove that people for the various sins into which they fell; yet there is not a reproof uttered against the institution of *involuntary slavery,* for any species of abuse that ever grew out of it. A severe judgment is pronounced by Jeremiah, (chapter xxxiv: see from the 8th to the 22d verse,) for an abuse or violation of the law, concerning the *voluntary* servitude of Hebrews; but the prophet pens it with caution, as if to show that it had no reference to any abuse that had taken place under the system of *involuntary slavery,* which existed by law among that people; the sin consisted in making hereditary bond-men and bond-women of Hebrews, which was positively forbidden by the law, and not for buying and holding one of another nation in hereditary bondage, which was as positively allowed by the law. And really, in view of what is passing in our country, and elsewhere, among men who profess to reverence the Bible, it would

seem that these must be dreams of a distempered brain, and not the solemn truths of that sacred book.

Well, I will now proceed to make them good to the letter, see Levit. xxv: 44, 45, 46; "Thy bond-men and thy bond-maids which thou shalt have, shall be of the heathen that are round about you; of them shall ye buy bond-men and bond-maids. Moreover, of the children of the strangers that do sojourn among you, of them shall ye buy, and of their families that are with you, which they begat in your land. And they shall be your possession. And ye shall take them as an inheritance for your children after you, to inherit them for a possession they shall be your bond-men forever." I ask any candid man, if the words of this institution could be more explicit? It is from God himself; it authorizes that people, to whom he had become *king and law-giver*, to purchase men and women as property; to hold them and their posterity in bondage; and to will them to their children as a possession forever; and more, it allows foreign *slave-holders* to *settle* and *live among them*; to *breed slaves* and *sell* them. Now, it is important to a correct understanding of this subject, to connect with the right to *buy* and *possess*, as property, the amount of authority *to govern,* which is granted by the *law-giver;* this amount of authority is implied, in the first place, in the law which prohibits the exercise of rigid authority upon the Hebrews, who are allowed to sell themselves for limited times. "If thy brother be waxen poor, and be sold unto thee, thou shalt not *compel him* to serve as a *bond servant*, but as a *hired servant*, and as a *sojourner* he shall be with thee, and shall serve thee until the year of jubilee—*they shall not be sold as bond-men; thou shalt not rule over them with rigor.*"— Levit. xxv: 39, 40, 41, 42, 43. It will be evident to all, that here are *two states* of servitude; in reference to *one* of which, *rigid* or *compulsory* authority, is *prohibited*, and that its *exercise is authorized in the other.*

Second.—In the criminal code, that conduct is punished with death, when done to a *freeman*, which is not punishable at all, when done *by a master to a slave*, for the express reason, that the slave is the *master's money.* "He that smiteth a man so that he die, shall surely be put to death."—Exod. xxi: 20, 21. "If a man smite his servant or his maid, with a rod, and he die under his hand, he shall be surely punished; notwithstanding, if he continue a day or two, he shall not be punished, for he is his money."—Exod. xxi: 20. Here is precisely the same crime: smiting a man so that he die; if it be a freeman, he shall surely be put to death, whether the man die under his hand, or live a day or two after; but if it be a servant, and the master continued the rod until the servant died under his hand, then it must be evident that such a chastisement could not be necessary for any purpose of wholesome or reasonable authority, and therefore he may be punished,—but not with death. But if the death did not take place for a day or two, then it is to be *presumed*, that the master only aimed to use the rod, so far as was necessary to produce subordination, and for this, the law which allowed him to lay out his money in the slave, would protect him against all punishment. This is the common-sense principle which has been adopted substantially in civilized countries, where involuntary slavery has been instituted, from that day until this. . . .

Again, the divine Law-giver, in guarding the property right in slaves among his chosen people, sanctions principles which may work the separation of man and wife, father and children. . . . "If thou buy a Hebrew servant, six years shall he serve thee, and in the seventh he shall go out free for nothing; if he came in by himself, he shall go out by himself; if he were married, then his wife shall go out with him; if his master have given him a wife (one of his bond-maids) and she have borne him sons and daughters, the wife and her children shall be her master's and he shall go out by himself."—Exod. xxi: 2, 3, 4. Now, the God of Israel gives this man the option of being separated by the master, from his wife and children, or becoming himself a servant forever, with a mark of the fact, like our cattle, in the ear, that can be seen wherever he goes; for it is enacted, "If the servant shall plainly say, I love my master, my wife, and my children, I will not go out free, then his master shall bring him unto the judges, (in open court,) he shall also bring him unto the door, or unto the door post, (so that all in the court-house, and those in the yard may be witnesses, and his master shall bore his ear through with an awl; and he shall serve him forever." It is useless to spend more time in gathering up what is written in the Scriptures on this subject, from the giving of the law until the coming of Christ. . . . We propose—

Third. To show that Jesus Christ recognized this institution as one that was lawful among men, and regulated its relative duties.

. . . I affirm then, first, (and no man denies,) that Jesus Christ has not abolished slavery by a prohibitory command: and second, I affirm, he has introduced no new moral principle which can work its destruction, under the gospel dispensation; and that the principle relied on for this purpose, is a fundamental principle of the Mosaic law, under which slavery was instituted by Jehovah himself: and third, with this absence of positive prohibition, and this absence

of principle, to work its ruin, I affirm, that in all the Roman provinces, where churches were planted by the apostles, hereditary slavery existed, as it did among the Jews, and as it does now among us, (which admits of proof from history that no man will dispute who knows any thing of the matter,) and that in instructing such churches, the Holy Ghost by the apostles, has recognized the institution, as one *legally existing* among them, to be perpetuated in the church, and that its duties are prescribed.

Now for the proof: To the church planted at Ephesus, the capital of the lesser Asia, Paul ordains by letter, subordination in the fear of God,—first between wife and husband; second, child and parent; third, servant and master; *all, as states, or conditions, existing among the members.*

The relative duties of each state are pointed out; those between the servant and master in these words: "Servants be obedient to them who are your masters, according to the flesh, with fear and trembling, in singleness of your heart as unto Christ; not with eye service as men pleasers, but as the servants of Christ, doing the will of God from the heart, with good-will, doing service, as to the Lord, and not to men, knowing that whatsoever good thing any man doeth, the same shall he receive of the Lord, whether he be bond or free. And ye masters do the same things to them, forbearing threatening, knowing that your master is also in heaven, neither is there respect of persons with him." Here, by the Roman law, the servant was property, and the control of the master unlimited, as we shall presently prove.

To the church at Colosse, a city of Phrygia, in the lesser Asia, Paul in his letter to them, recognizes the three relations of wives and husbands, parents and children, servants and masters, as relations existing among the members; (here the Roman law was the same;) and to the servants and masters he thus writes: "Servants obey in all things your masters, according to the flesh: not with eye service, as men pleasers, but in singleness of heart, fearing God: and whatsoever you do, do it heartily, as to the Lord and not unto men; knowing that of the Lord ye shall receive the reward of the inheritance, for ye serve the Lord Christ. But he that doeth wrong shall receive for the wrong he has done; and there is no respect of persons with God. Masters give unto your servants that which is just and equal, knowing that you also have a master in heaven."

The same Apostle writes a letter to the church at Corinth;—very important city, formerly called the eye of Greece, either from its location, or intelligence, or both, and consequently, an important point, for radiating light in all directions, in reference to subjects connected with the cause of Jesus Christ; and particularly, in the bearing of its practical precepts on civil society, and the political structure of nations. Under the direction of the Holy Ghost, he instructs the church, that, on this particular subject, *one general principle* was ordained of God, applicable alike in all countries and at all stages of the church's future history, and that it was this: "*as the Lord has called every one, so let him walk.*" "Let every man abide in the same calling wherein he is called." "Let every man wherein he is called, therein abide with God."—1 Cor. vii: 17, 20, 24. "*And so ordain I in all churches;*" vii: 17. The Apostle thus explains his meaning:

"Is any man called being circumcised? Let him not become uncircumcised."

"Is any man called in uncircumcision? Let him not be circumcised."

"Art thou called, being a servant? Care not for it, but if thou mayest be made free, use it rather;" vii: 18, 21. Here, by the Roman law, slaves were property,— yet Paul ordains, in this, and all other churches, that Christianity gave them no title to freedom, but on the contrary, required them not to care for being slaves, or in other words, to be contented with their *state*, or *relation*, unless they could be *made free*, in a lawful way.

Again, we have a letter by Peter, who is the Apostle of the circumcision—addressed especially to the Jews, who were scattered through various provinces of the Roman empire; comprising those provinces especially, which were the theater of their dispersion, under the Assyrians and Babylonians. . . . He thus instructs them: "Submit yourselves to every ordinance of man for the Lord's sake." "For so is the will of God." "Servants, be subject to your masters with all fear, not only to the good and gentle, but also to the froward."—l Peter ii: 11, 13, 15, 18. What an important document is this! enjoining political subjection to *governments of every form*, and Christian subjection on the part of servants to their masters, whether good or bad; for the purpose of showing forth to advantage, the *glory of the gospel*, and putting to silence the ignorance of foolish men, who might think it seditious.

By "every ordinance of man," as the context will show, is meant governmental regulations or laws, as was that of the Romans for enslaving their prisoners taken in war, instead of destroying their lives.

When such enslaved persons came into the church of Christ let them (says Peter) "be subject to their masters with all fear," whether such masters be good or bad. It is worthy of remark, that he says much

to secure civil subordination to the State, and hearty and cheerful obedience to the masters, on the part of servants; yet he says nothing to masters in the whole letter. It would seem from this, that danger to the cause of Christ was on the side of *insubordination among the servants, and a want of humility with inferiors,* rather than *haughtiness among superiors* in the church. . . .

. . . It is taken for granted, on all hands pretty generally, that Jesus Christ has at least been silent, or that he has not personally spoken on the subject of slavery. Once for all, I deny it. Paul, after stating that a slave was to honor an unbelieving master, in the 1st verse of the 6th chapter, says, in the 2d verse, that to a believing master, he is the rather to do service, because he who partakes of the benefit is his brother. He then says, if any man teach otherwise, (as all abolitionists then did, and now do,) and consent not to wholesome words, "even the words of our Lord Jesus Christ." Now, if our Lord Jesus Christ uttered such words, how dare we say he has been silent? If he has been silent, how dare the Apostle say these are the words of our Lord Jesus Christ, if the Lord Jesus Christ never spoke them? . . .

We will remark, in closing under this head, that we have shown from the text of the sacred volume, that when God entered into covenant with Abraham, it was with him as a slaveholder; that when he took his posterity by the hand in Egypt, five hundred years afterward to confirm the promise made to Abraham, it was done with them as slaveholders; that when he gave them a constitution of government, he gave them the right to perpetuate hereditary slavery; and that he did not for the fifteen hundred years of their national existence, express disapprobation toward the institution.

We have also shown from authentic history that the institution of slavery existed in every family, and in every province of the Roman Empire, at the time the gospel was published to them.

We have also shown from the New Testament, that all the churches are recognized as composed of masters and servants; and that they are instructed by Christ how to discharge their relative duties; and finally that in reference to the question which was then started, whether Christianity did not abolish the institution, or the right of one Christian to hold another Christian in bondage, we have shown, that "the words of our Lord Jesus Christ" are, that so far from this being the case, it adds to the obligation of the servant to render service with good-will to his master, and that gospel fellowship is not to be entertained with persons who will not consent to it! . . .

Document 9.5 Advice from the Editor on "Managing Slaves"

James Dunwoody Brownson DeBow (J.D.B. DeBow) actively promoted slavery, cotton production, and the Southern economy from the pages of *DeBow's Review*. He published this magazine on and off from 1846 until his death in 1867, achieving the greatest circulation of any Southern magazine at the time. DeBow was also a professor of political economy at the University of Louisiana (now Tulane University), and served as the Superintendent of the Census from 1853 to 1855. In his editorials, he routinely defended slavery and Southern nationalism, discussing such topics as the "Destiny of Cotton Culture" and the "Destiny of the Slave States." One of his themes was the benevolent, paternal nature of slavery. Slaves were like children who needed rules and training. A good master should lay down written rules and enforce them, so that he, his family, and their slaves "can take pleasure" in their natural relations. The earlier these rules are laid down, the better for everyone. Strict rules would help the slaves improve themselves, guarantee decent behavior, and help the plantations be more productive. In this editorial from *DeBow's Review*, why does the editor believe masters should impose daily living rules on their slaves? What types of rules does he believe are most important to increase slaves' satisfaction with their role in life?

The negroes should be required to keep their houses and yards clean; and in case of neglect should receive such punishment as will be likely to insure more cleanly habits in future.

In no case should two families be allowed to occupy the same house. The crowding a number into one house is unhealthy. It breeds contention; is destructive of delicacy of feeling, and it promotes immorality between the sexes. . . .

The master should never establish any regulation among his slaves until he is fully convinced of its propriety and equity. Being thus convinced, and having issued his orders, implicit obedience should be required and rigidly enforced. Firmness of manner, and promptness to enforce obedience, will save much trouble, and be the means of avoiding the necessity for much whipping. The negro should feel that his master is his lawgiver and judge; and yet is his protector and friend, but so far above him, as never to be approached save in the most respectful manner. That where he has just cause, he may, with due deference, approach his master and lay before him his troubles and complaints; but not on false pretexts or trivial occasions. If the master be a tyrant, his negroes may be so much embarrassed by his presence as to be incapable of doing their work properly when he is near.

It is expected that servants should rise early enough to be at work by the time it is light. In sections of country that are sickly, it will be found conductive

to health in the fall to make the hands eat their breakfast before going into the dew. In winter, as the days are short and nights long, it will be no encroachment upon their necessary rest to make them eat breakfast before daylight. One properly taken care of, and supplied with good tools, is certainly able to do more work than under other circumstances. While at work they should be brisk. If one is called to you, or sent from you, and he does not move briskly, chastise him at once. If this does not answer, repeat the dose and double the quantity. When at work I have no objection to their whistling or singing some lively tune, but no drawling tunes are allowed in the field, for their motions are almost certain to keep time with the music.

In the intercourse of negroes among themselves, no quarreling nor opprobrious epithets, no swearing nor obscene language, should ever be allowed. Children should be required to be respectful to those who are grown, more especially to the old, and the strong should never be allowed to impose on the weak. Men should be taught that it is disgraceful to abuse or impose on the weaker sex, and if a man should so far forget and disgrace himself as to strike a woman, the women should be made to give him the hickory and ride him on a rail. The wife, however, should never be required to strike her husband, for fear of its unhappy influences over their future respect for and kindness to each other.

From *DeBow's Review,* September 1855.

The negroes should not be allowed to run about over the neighborhood; they should be encouraged to attend church, when it is within convenient distance. Where there are pious negroes on a plantation who are so disposed, they should be allowed and encouraged to hold prayer meetings among themselves; and when the number is too great to be accommodated in one of the negro houses, they should have a separate building for the purpose of worship. Where it can be done, the services of a minister should be procured for their special business. By having the appointments for preaching at noon, during summer, and at night during winter, the preacher could consult his own convenience as to the day of the week, without, in the least, interfering with the duties of the farm.

A word to those who think and care but little about their own soul or the soul of the negro, and yet desire a good reputation for their children. Children are fond of the company of negroes, not only because the deference shown them makes them feel perfectly at ease, but the subjects of conversation are on a level with their capacity; while the simple tales, and the witch and ghost stories so common among negroes, excite the young imagination and enlist the feelings. If in this association the child becomes familiar with indelicate, vulgar, and lascivious manners and conversation, an impression is made upon the mind and heart which lasts for years—perhaps for life. Could we, in all cases, trace effects to their real causes, I doubt not but many young men and women of respectable parentage and bright prospects, who have made shipwreck of all their earthly hopes, have been led to the fatal step by the seeds of corruption which, in the days of childhood and youth, were sown in their hearts by the indelicate and lascivious manners and conversation of their father's negroes.

Document 9.6 Rules for a Louisiana Plantation

Slave states passed laws outlawing the use of extreme physical abuse against slaves, but such laws were rarely enforced. Slave owners could bend the rules as they saw fit on their land, when it applied to their own property. Every master made rules for their own slaves, and set down the law for everyone else living on the farm or plantation as well. Slave owners had many concerns. What are the best ways to keep slaves under control? What are the best ways to keep slaves happy, motivated, and productive? These concerns often clashed, because the most common answers to the first concern were whippings and the sale or breakup of families. Such action usually defeated the second goal. The following rules come from Bennett Barrow, who established these guidelines for the 200 slaves on his Louisiana plantation in 1838. Note how Barrow tries to balance his two concerns. What are his rules regarding slave marriage, and why does he establish these guidelines? How does he plan to motivate his slaves? What does he forbid them to do, and why?

No negro shall leave the place at any time without my permission, or in my absence that of the Driver the driver in that case being responsible, for the cause of such absence which ought never to be omitted to be enquired into—

The Driver should never leave the plantation, unless on business of the plantation.

No negro shall be allowed to marry out of the plantation.

No negro shall be allowed to sell anything without my express permission. I have ever maintained the doctrine that my negroes have no time Whatever, that they are always liable to my call without questioning for a moment the propriety of it, I adhere to this on the grounds of expediency and right. The very security of the plantation requires that a general and uniform control over the people of it should be exercised. Who are to protect the plantation from the intrusions of ill designed persons When every body is a broad—Who can tell the moment When a plantation might be threatened with destruction from Fire—could the flames be arrested if the negroes are scattered throughout the neighborhood, seeking their amusement. Are these not duties of great

Diary of Bennett H. Barrow, May 1, 1838.

importance, and in which every negro himself is deeply interested to render this part of the rule justly applicable, however, it would be necessary that such a settled arrangement should exist on the plantation as to make it unnecessary for a negro to leave it. . . . You must, therefore make him as comfortable at Home as possible, affording him What is essentially necessary for his happiness—you must provide for him Your self and by that means create in him a habit of perfect dependence on you—Allow it once to be understood by a negro that he is to provide for himself, and you that moment give him an undeniable claim on you for a portion of his time to make this provision, and should you from necessity, or any other cause, encroach upon his time—disappointment and discontent are seriously felt—if I employ a labourer to perform a certain quantum of work per day and I agree to pay him, a certain amount for the performance of said work When he had accomplished it I of course have no further claim on him for his time or services—but how different is it with a slave— Who can calculate the exact profit or expence of a slave one year with another, if I furnish my negro with every necessary of life, without the least care on his part—if I support him in sickness, however long it may be, and pay all his expenses, though he does nothing—if I maintain him in his old age, when he is incapable of rendering either himself or myself any service, am I not entitled to an exclusive right to his time good feelings, and a sense of propriety would all ways prevent unnecessary employment on the Sabbath, and policy would check any exaction of excessive labor in common. . . . I never give a negro a Pass to go from home without he first states particularly where he wishes to go, and assigns a cause for his desiring to be absent. If he offers a good reason, I never refuse, but otherwise, I never grant him a Pass, and feel satisfied that no practice is more prejudicial to the community, and to the negroes themselves, than that of giving them general Passes to go Where they please I am so opposed to this plan that I never permit any negro to remain on my plantation, whose Pass does not authorize him expressly to come to it— Some think that after a negro has done his work it is an act of oppression to confine him to the plantation, when he might be strolling about the neighborhood for his amusement and recreation—this is certainly a mistaken humanity. Habit is every thing—The negro who is accustomed to remain constantly at Home, is just as satisfied with the society on the plantation as that which he would find elsewhere, and the very restrictions laid upon him being equally imposed on others, he does not feel them, for society is kept at

Home for them. . . . No rule that I have stated is of more importance than that relating to negroes marrying out of the plantation it seems to me, from What observations I have made it is utterly impossible to have any method, or regularity when the men and women are permitted to take wives and husbands indiscriminately off the plantation, negroes are very much desposed to pursue a course of this kind, and without being able to assign any good reason, though the motive can be readily perceived, and is a strong one with them, but one that tend not in the Least to the benefit of the Master, or their ultimate good. [T]he inconveniences that at once strikes one as arising out of such a practice are these—

First—in allowing the men to marry out of the plantation, you give them an uncontrolable right to be frequently absent

2d—Wherever their wives live, there they consider their homes, consequently they are indifferent to the interest of the plantation to which they actually belong—

3d—it creates a feeling of independence, from being, of right, out of the control of the masters for a time—

4th—They are repeatedly exposed to temptation from meeting and associating with negroes from different directions, and with various habits & vices—

5th—Where there are several women on a plantation, they may have husbands from different plantations belonging to different persons. These men possess different habits are accustomed to different treatment, and have different privileges, so your plantation every day becomes a rendezvous of a medly of characters. Negroes who have the privilege of a monthly Passes to go where they please, and at any hour that they say they have finished their work, to leave their Master's plan'tn come into yours about midday, When your negroes are at work, and the Driver engaged, they either take possession of houses their wives live—and go to sleep or stroll about in perfect idleness—feeling themselves accessible to every thing. What an example to those at work at the time—can any circumstance be more Intrusive of good order and contentment—

Sixthly—When a man and his wife belong to different persons, they are liable to be separated from each other, as well as their children, whether by caprice of either of the parties, or When there is a sale of property this keeps up an unsettled state of things, and gives rise to repeated new connections. . . . I prefer giving them money of Christmas to their making any thing thereby creating an interest with you and yours. . . . I furnish my negroes regularly with their full share of allowance weakly. 4 pound & 5 pound of meat to every thing that goes in the field—pound over 4 years 1 1/2 between 15 months and 4 years old—Clear good meat—I give them cloths twice a year, two suits one pair shoes for winter every third year a blanket. . . . I supply them with tobacco if a negro is suffered to sell any thing he chooses without any inquiry being made, a spirit of trafficing at once is created. to carry this on, both means and time are necessary, neither of which is he of right possessed. A negro would not be content to sell only What he raises or makes either corn (should he be permitted) or poultry, or the like, but he would sell part of his allowance also, and would be tempted to commit robberies to obtain things to sell. Besides, he would never go through his work carefully, particularly when other engagements more interesting and pleasing are constantly passing through his mind, but would be apt to slight his work That the general conduct of master has a very considerable influence on the character and habits of his slave, will be readily admitted. When a master is uniform in his own habits & conduct, his slaves know his wishes, and What they are to expect if they act in opposition to, or conformity with them, therefore, the more order and contentment Exist.

A plantation might be considered as a piece of machinery, to operate successfully, all of its parts should be uniform and exact, and the impelling force regular and steady; and the master, if he pretended at all to attend to his business, should be their impelling force, if a master exhibits no extraordinary interest in the proceedings on his plantation, it is hardly to be expected that any other feelings but apathy, and perfect indifference could exist with his negroes, and it would be unreasonable for him . . . to expect attention and exaction from those, Who have no other interest than to avoid the displeasure of their master. in the different departments on the plantation as much distinction and separation are kept up as possible with a view to create responsibility—The Driver has a directed charge of every thing, but there are subordinate persons, who take the more immediate care of the different departments. For instance, I make one person answerable for my stock. Horses cattle hogs, &c. another the plantation utensils &c. one the sick—one the poultry. [A]nother providing for and taking care of the children whose parents are in the field &c. As good a plan as could be adopted, to establish security and good order on the plantation is that of constituting a watch at night, consisting of two or more men, they are answerable for all trespasses commited during their watch, unless they produce the offender, or give immediate alarm. When the protection of a plantation is left to the negroes generally, you at once perceive the truth of the maxim that what is every one's business, is no one's business. but when a regular watch is Established, Each in turn performs his tour of duty, so that the most careless is at times, made to be observant and watchful—the very act of organizing a watch bespeaks a care and attention on the part of a master, Which has the due influence on the negro—

Most of the above rules "in fact with the exception of the last" I have adopted since 1833. And with success—get your negroes once disciplined and planting is a pleasure—A Hell without it never have an Overseer—Every negro to come up Sunday after their allowance Clean & head well combed—it gives pride to every one, the fact of master feeling proud of them, When clean &c.

Never allow any man to talk to your negroes, nothing more injurious.

Document 9.7 1824 Louisiana Slave Laws

Every Southern state created its own slave code; these laws varied from state to state, but had much in common. They were intended to regulate the behavior of slaves anytime they were not on their masters' home plantation, and make sure they did not compete, interfere with, or threaten White society in any way. The primary feature of these laws was the lack of legal rights for slaves. They could not testify against their masters, use the courts, serve on juries, or press charges against any Whites. Slaves could not own guns or property, and had to have written permission to be off the plantation after dark. Slaves could not compete in skilled jobs against Whites. Any White man could legally kill a slave outlawed for running away. No slave could defend himself against attack. To strike a White man once, even in self-defense, meant mutilation; to do so a second time meant death. As you read through the Louisiana code, determine what rights slaves have. Do the laws talk more about the rights of masters, or slaves? What can you tell about a slave's life from these laws?

ART. 172.—The rules prescribing the police and conduct to be observed with respect to slaves in this State, and the punishment of their crimes and offences, are fixed by special laws of the Legislature.

ART. 173.—The slave is entirely subject to the will of his master, who may correct and chastise him, though not with unusual rigor, nor so as to maim or mutilate him, or to expose him to the danger of loss of life, or to cause his death.

ART. 174.—The slave is incapable of making any kind of contract, except those which relate to his own emancipation.

ART. 175.—All that a slave possesses, belongs to his master; he possesses nothing of his own, except his *peculium*, that is to say, the sum of money, or moveable estate, which his master chooses he should possess.

ART. 176.—They can transmit nothing by succession or otherwise; but the succession of free persons related to them which they would have inherited had they been free, may pass through them to such of their descendants as may have acquired their liberty before the succession is opened.

ART. 177.—The slave is incapable of exercising any public office, or private trust; he cannot be tutor, curator, executor nor attorney; he cannot be a witness in either civil or criminal matters, except in cases provided for by particular laws. He cannot be a party in any civil action, either as plaintiff or defendant, except when he has to claim or prove his freedom.

ART. 178.—When slaves are prosecuted in the name of the State, for offences they have committed, notice must be given to their masters.

ART. 179.—Masters are bound by the acts of their slaves done by their command, as also by their transactions and dealings with respect to the business in which they have entrusted or employed them; but in case they should not have authorised or entrusted them, they shall be answerable only for so much as they have benefitted by the transaction.

ART. 180.—The master shall be answerable for all the damages occasioned by an offence or quasi-offence committed by his slave, independent of the punishment inflicted on the slave.

ART. 181.—The master however may discharge himself from such responsibility by abandoning his slave to the person injured; in which case such person shall sell such slave at public auction in the usual form, to obtain payment of the damages and costs; and the balance, if any, shall be returned to the master of the slave, who shall be completely discharged, although the price of the slave should not be sufficient to pay the whole amount of the damages and costs; provided that the master shall make the abandonment within three days after the judgment awarding such damages, shall have been rendered; provided also that it shall not be proved that the crime or offence was committed by his order; for in case of such proof the master shall be answerable for all damages resulting therefrom, whatever be the amount, without being admitted to the benefit of the abandonment.

ART. 182.—Slaves cannot marry without the consent of their masters, and their marriages do not produce any of the civil effects which result from such contract.

ART. 183.—Children born of a mother then in a state of slavery, whether married or not, follow the condition of their mother; they are consequently slaves and belong to the master of their mother.

ART. 184.—A master may manumit his slave in this State, either by an act *inter vivos* or by a disposition made in prospect of death, provided such manumission be made with the forms and under the conditions prescribed by law; but an enfranchisement, when made by a last will, must be express and formal, and shall not be implied by any other circumstances of the testament, such as a legacy, an institution of heir, testamentary executorship or other dispositions of this nature, which, in such case, shall be considered as if they had not been made.

ART. 185.—No one can emancipate his slave, unless the slave has attained the age of thirty years, and has behaved well at least for four years preceding his emancipation.

ART. 186.—The slave who has saved the life of his master, his master's wife, or one of his children, may be emancipated at any age.

ART. 187.—The master who wishes to emancipate his slave, is bound to make a declaration of his intentions to the judge of the parish where he resides; the judge must order notice of it to be published during forty days by advertisement posted at the door of the court house; and if, at the expiration of this delay, no opposition be made that shall authorise the master to pass an act of emancipation.

ART. 188.—The act of emancipation imports an obligation on the part the person granting it, to provide the subsistence of the slave emancipated, if he should be unable to support himself.

From Civil Code of the State of Louisiana, 1825.

ART. 189.—An emancipation or perfected, is irrevocable, on the part of the master or his heirs.

ART. 190.—Any enfranchisement made in fraud of creditors, or of the portion reserved by law to forced heirs is null and void; and such fraud shall be considered as proved, when it shall appear that at the moment of executing the enfranchisement, the person granting it had not sufficient property to pay his debts or to leave to his heir the portion to them reserved by law the same rule will apply if the slave thus manumitted, was specially mortgaged; but in this case the enfranchisement shall take effect, provided the slave or any one in his behalf shall pay the debt for which the mortgage was given.

ART. 191.—No master of slaves shall be compelled, either directly or indirectly, to enfranchise any of them, except only in cases where the enfranchisement shall be made for services rendered to the State, by virtue of an act of the Legislature of the same, and on the State satisfying to the master the appraised value of the manumitted slave . . .

Document 9.8 Southern Slavery Indicted by Its Own Hand

Prior to the 1830s, Abolitionists and other anti-slavery advocates relied on education and religious arguments to convince Southerners and Northerners alike that slavery was wrong. For their efforts they were physically attacked by Northern opponents and subjected to verbal denunciations by Southerners. The Executive Committee of the American Anti-Slavery Society commissioned Theodore Weld to compile evidence proving the evil effects of slavery. His goal was to overcome the claims that slave owners were incapable of mistreating "their people," that slave owners would never mistreat slaves because they were too valuable, and that the Southern public would never allow slaves to be abused. Weld's book, *American Slavery As It Is: The Testimony of a Thousand Witnesses,* proved to be a devastating attack. Besides using the eyewitness accounts of former slave owners and reliable Northern visitors, he concluded that Southern slave owners could provide the most damning evidence themselves. He gathered clippings from Southern newspaper stories and advertisements to destroy the South's own myths about how well their slaves were treated. The selection below contains advertisements for runaway slaves pulled from Southern newspapers. The ads, written by the owners themselves, detail the inhumanity of slavery. As you read over the advertisements, compile a list of physical abuses slaves endured. Consider whether the slave system, which gives White masters complete power over their fellow human beings, is responsible for this violence. Also, note how widespread the physical abuse is.

III. Brandings, Maimings, Gun-Shot Wounds, &c.

The slaves are often branded with hot irons, pursued with fire arms and *shot,* hunted with dogs and torn by them, shockingly maimed with knives, dirks, &c.; have their ears cut off, their eyes knocked out, their bones dislocated and broken with bludgeons, their fingers and toes cut off, their faces and other parts of their persons disfigured with scars and gashes, *besides* those made with the lash.

We shall adopt, under this head, the same course as that pursued under previous ones,—first give the testimony of the slaveholders themselves, to the mutilations, &c. by copying their own graphic descriptions of them, in advertisements published under their own names, and in newspapers published in the slave states, and generally, in their own immediate vicinity. We shall, as heretofore, insert only so much of each advertisement as will be necessary to make the point intelligible.

From *American Slavery As It Is: Testimony of a Thousand Witnesses*, New York: American Anti-Slavery Society, 1839.

Witnesses.	Testimony.
Mr. Micajah Ricks, Nash County, North Carolina, in the Raleigh "Standard," July 18, 1838.	"Ranaway, a negro woman and two children; a few days before she went off, *I burnt her with a hot iron*, on the left side of her face, *I tried to make the letter M.*"
Mr. Asa B. Metcalf, Kingston, Adams Co. Mi. in the "Natchez Courier," June 15, 1832.	"Ranaway Mary, a black woman, has a scar on her back and right arm near the shoulder, *caused by a rifle ball.*"
Mr. William Overstreet, Benton, Yazoo Co. Mi. in the "Lexington (Kentucky) Observer," July 22, 1838.	"Ranaway a negro man name Henry, *his left eye out*, some scars from a *dirk* on and under his left arm, and *much scarred* with the whip."
Mr. R. P. Carney, Clark Go. Ala. in the Mobile Register, Dec. 22, 1832.	One hundred dollars reward for a negro fellow Pompey, 40 years old, he is *branded* on the *left jaw.*
Mr. J. Guyler, Savannah Georgia, in the "Republican," April 12, 1837.	"Ranaway Laman, an old negro man, grey, *has only one eye.*"
J. A. Brown, jailor, Charleston, South Carolina, in the "Mercury," Jan. 12, 1837.	"Committed to jail a negro man, has *no toes* on his left foot."
Mr. J. Scrivener, Herring Bay, Anne Arundel Co. Maryland, in the "Annapolis Republican," April 18, 1837.	"Ranaway negro man Elijah, has a scar on his left cheek, apparently occasioned by a *shot.*"
Madame Burvant, corner of Chartres and Toulouse streets, New Orleans, in the "Bee," Dec. 21, 1838.	"Ranaway a negro woman named Rachel, *has lost all her toes* except the large one."
Mr. O. W. Lains, in the "Helena, (Ark.) Journal," June 1, 1833.	"Ranaway Sam, he was *shot* a short time since, through the hand, and has *several shots in his left arm and side.*"
Mr. R. W. Sizer, in the "Grand Gulf, [Mi.] Advertiser," July 8, 1837.	"Ranaway my negro man Dennis, said negro has been *shot* in the left arm between the shoulder and elbow, which has paralyzed the left hand."
Mr. Nicholas Edmunds, in the "Petersburgh [Va.] Intelligncer," May 22, 1838.	"Ranaway my negro man named Simon, *he has been shot badly* in his back and right arm."
Mr. J. Bishop, Bishopville, Sumpter District, South Carolina, in the "Camden [S.C.] Journal," March 4, 1837.	"Ranaway a negro named Arthur, has a considerable *scar* across his *breast* and *each arm*, made by a knife; loves to talk much of the goodness of God."
Mrs. S. Neyle, Little Ogeechee, Georgia, in the "Savannah Republican," July 3, 1837.	"Ranaway George, he has a *swordcut* lately received on his left ar."
Mrs. Sarah Walsh, Mobile, Ala. in the "Georgia Journal," March 27, 1837.	"Twenty five dollars reward for my man Isaac, he has a scar on his forehead caused by a *blow*, and one on his back made by *a shot from a pistol.*"
Mr. J. P. Ashford, Adams Co. Mi. in the "Natchez Courier," August 24, 1838.	"Ranaway a negro girl called Mary, has a small scar over her eye, a *good many teeth missing*, the letter A. *is branded on her cheek and forehead.*"

Mr. Ely Townsed, Pike Co. Ala. in the "Pensacola Gazette," Sep. 16, 1837.

S. B. Murphy, jailer, Irvington, Ga. in the "Milledgeville Journal," May 20, 1838.

Mr. A. Luminais, Parish of St. John, Louisiana, in the New Orleans "Bee," March 3, 1838.

Mr. Isaac Johnson, Pulaski Co. Georgia, in the "Milledgeville Journal," June 19, 1838.

Mr. Thomas Hudnall, Madison Co. Mi. in the "Vicksburg Register," September 5, 1838.

Mr. John McMurrain, Columbus, Ga. in the "Southern Sun," August 7, 1838.

Mr. Moses Orme, Annapolis, Maryland, in the "Annapolis Republican," June 20, 1837.

William Strickland, Jailor, Kershaw District, S.C. in the "Camden [S.C.] Courier," July 8, 1837.

The Editor of the "Grand Gulf Advertiser," Dec. 7, 1838.

Mr. William Bateman, in the "Grand Gulf Advertiser," Dec. 7, 1838.

Mr. B.G. Simmons, in the "Southern Argus," May 30, 1837.

Mr. James Artop, in the "Macon [Ga.] Messenger," May 25, 1837.

J.L. Jolley, Sheriff of Clinton, Co. Mi., in the "Clinton Gazette," July 23, 1836.

Mr. Thomas Ledwith, Jacksonville East Florida, in the "Charleston [S.C.] Courier," Sept. 1, 1838.

"Ranaway negro Ben, has a scar on his right hand, his thumb and forefinger being injured by being *shot* last fall, a part of *the bone came out,* he has also one or two *large scars* on his back and hips."

"Committed a negro man, is *very badly shot in the right side* and right hand."

"Detained at the jail, a mulatto named Tom, has a *scar* on the right cheek and appears to have been *burned with powder* on the face."

"Ranaway a negro man named Ned, *three of his fingers* are drawn into the palm of his hand by a *cut,* has a *scar* on the back of his neck nearly half round, done by a *knife.*"

"Ranaway a negro named Hambleton, *limps* on his left foot where he was *shot* a few weeks ago, while runaway."

"Ranaway a negro boy named Mose, he has a *wound* in the right shoulder near the back bone, which was occasioned by a *rifle shot.*"

"Ranaway my negro man Bill, he has *a fresh wound in his head* above his ear."

"Committed to jail a negro, says his name is Cuffee, he is lame in one knee, occasioned *by a shot.*"

"Ranaway Joshua, his thumb is off of his left hand.

"Ranaway William, *scar* over his left eye, one between his eye brows, one on his breast, and his right leg has been *broken.*"

"Ranaway Mark, his left arm has been *broken,* right *leg also.*"

"Ranaway, Caleb, 50 years old, has an awkward gait occasioned by his being *shot* in the thigh."

"Was committed to jail a negro man, says his name is Josiah, his back very much scarred by the whip, and *branded on the thigh and hips in three or four places,* thus (J.M.) *the rim of his right ear has been bit or cut off.*

"Fifty dollars reward, for my fellow Edward, he has a *scar* on the corner of his mouth, two *cuts* on and under his arm, and the *letter E. on his arm.*"

Mr. Joseph James, Sen., Pleasant Ridge, Paulding Co. Ga., in the "Milledgeville Union," Nov. 7, 1837.

Mr. W. Riley, Orangeburg District, South Carolina, in the "Columbia [S.C.] Telescope," Nov. 11, 1837.

Mr. Samuel Mason, Warren Co, Mi., in the "Vicksburg Register," July 18, 1838.

Mr. F. L. C. Edwards, in the "Southern Telegraph," Sept. 25, 1837."

Mr. Stephen M. Jackson, in the "Vicksburg Register," March 10, 1837.

Philip Honerton, deputy sheriff of Halifax Co. Virginia, Jan. 1837.

Stearns & Co. No. 28, New Levee, New Orleans, in the "Bee," March 22, 1837.

Mr. John W. Walton, Greensboro, Ala. in the "Alabama Beacon," Dec. 13, 1838.

Mr. R. Furman, Charleston, S. C., in the "Charleston Mercury," Jan. 12, 1839.

Mr. John Tart, Sen., in the "Fayetteville [N. C.] Observer," Dec. 26, 1838.

Mr. Richard Overstreet, Brook Neal, Campbell Co. Virginia, in the "Danville [Va.] Reporter," Dec 21, 1838.

The editor of the New Orleans "Bee," in that paper, August 27, 1837.

Mr. Bryant Johnson, Fort Valley, Houston county, Georgia, in the Milledgeville "Union," Oct. 2, 1838.

Mr. Lemuel Miles, Steen's Creek, Rankin County, Mi., in the "Southern Sun," Sept. 22, 1838.

Mr. Bezou, New Orleans, in the "Bee," May 23, 1838.

"Ranaway, negro boy Ellic, has a *scar* on one of his arms *from the bite of a dog.*"

"Ranaway a negro man, has a *scar* on the ankle produced by a *burn* and a *mark on his arm* resembling the letter S."

"Ranaway, a negro man named Allen, he has a scar on his breast, also a scar under the left eye, and has *two buck shot in his right arm.*"

"Ranaway from the plantation of James Surgette, the following negroes, Randal, *has one ear cropped*; Bob, *has lost one eye*, Kentucky Tom, *has one jaw broken.*"

"Ranaway, Anthony, one of his *ears cut off*, and his left hand cut with an axe."

"Was committed, a negro man, has a *scar* on his right side by a burn, one on his knee, and one on the calf of his leg *by the bite of a dog.*"

"Absconded, the mulatto boy Tom, his fingers *scarred* on his right hand, and had a *scar* on his right cheek."

"Ranaway my black boy Frazier, with a *scar* below and one above his right ear."

"Ranaway, Dick, about 19, has lost the small toe of one foot."

"Stolen a mulatto boy, *ten* years old, he has a *scar* over his eye which was made by an axe."

"Absconded my negro man Coleman, has a *very large scar* on one of his legs, also one on *each* arm, by a burn, and his heels have been frosted."

"Fifty dollars reward, for the negro Jim Blake–has a *piece cut out of each ear*, and the middle finger of the left hand *cut off* to the second joint."

"Ranaway, a negro woman named Maria—has a scar on one side of her cheek, by a *cut*—some scars on her back."

"Ranaway, Gabriel—has *two* or *three scars across his neck* made with a knife."

"Ranaway, the mulatto wench Mary—*has a cut on the left arm, a scar on the shoulder, and two upper teeth missing.*"

Mr. James Kimborough, Memphis, Tenn., in the "Memphis Enquirer," July 13, 1838.

Mr. Robert Beasley, Macon, Georgia, in the "Georgia Messenger," July 27, 1837.

Mr. B. G. Barrer, St. Louis, Missouri, in the "Republican," Sept. 6, 1837.

Mr. John D. Turner, near Norfolk, Virginia, in the "Norfolk Herald," June 27, 1838.

Mr. William Stansell, Picksville, Ala., in the "Huntsville Democrat," August 29, 1837.

Hon. Ambrose H. Sevier, Senator in Congress, from Arkansas, in the "Vicksburg Register," of Oct. 13.

Mr. R. A. Greene, Milledgeville, Georgia, in the "Macon Messenger," July 27, 1837.

Benjamin Russel, deputy sheriff, Bibb County, Ga., in the "Macon Telegraph," December 25, 1837.

Hon. H. Hitchcock, Mobile, judge of the Supreme Court, in the "Commercial Register," Oct. 27, 1837.

Mrs. Elizabeth L. Carter, near Groveton, Prince William County, Virginia, in the "National Intelligencer," Washington, D. C. June 10, 1837.

Mr. William D. Buckels, Natchez, Mi. in the "Natchez Courier," July 28, 1838.

Mr. Walter R. English, Monroe county, Ala., in the "Mobile Chronicle," Sept. 2, 1837.

Mr. James Saunders, Grany Spring, Hawkins county, Tenn., in the "Knoxville Register," June 6, 1838.

Mr. John Jenkins, St. Joseph's, Florida, captain of the steamboat Ellen, "Apalachicola Gazette," June 7, 1838.

"Ranaway, a negro boy, named Jerry—has a *scar* on his right cheek two inches long, from the cut of a knife."

"Ranaway, my man Fountain—*has holes in his ears, a scar on the right side of his forehead—has been shot in the hind parts of his legs*—is marked on the back with the whip."

"Ranaway, a negro man named Jarrett—*has a scar* on the under part of one of his arms, occasioned by a wound from a knife."

"Ranaway, a negro by the name of Joshua—he has a cut across one of his ears, which he will conceal as much as possible—one of his ankles is *enlarged by an ulcer.*"

"Ranaway, negro boy Harper—*has a scar* on one of his hips in the form of a G."

"Ranaway, Bob, a slave—has a scar *across his breast,* another on the *right side of his head*—his back is *much scarred* with the whip."

"Two hundred and fifty dollars reward, for my negro man Jim—he is much marked with *shot* in his right thigh,—the shot entered on the outside, half way between the hip and knee joints."

"Brought to jail, John—*left ear cropt.*"

"Ranaway, the slave Ellis—he has *lost one of his ears.*"

"Ranaway, a negro man, Moses—he has *lost a part* of one of his ears."

"Taken up, a negro man—is *very much scarred* about the face and body, and has the left *ear bit off.*"

"Ranaway, my slave Lewis—he has lost *a piece of one ear,* and a *part of one of his fingers,* a *part of one of his toes* is also lost."

"Ranaway, a black girl named Mary—has a *scar* on her cheek, and the end of one of her toes *cut off.*"

"Ranaway, the negro boy Caesar—he has *but one eye.*"

Mr. Peter Hanson, Lafayette city, La. in the New Orleans "Bee," July 28, 1838.

Mr. Orren Ellis, Georgeville, Mi., in the "North Alabamian," Sept. 15, 1837.

Mr. Zadock Sawyer, Cuthbert, Randolph County, Georgia, in the "Milledgeville Union," Oct. 9, 1838.

Mr. Abraham Gray, Mount Morino, Pike county, Ga., in the "Milledgeville Union," Oct. 9, 1838.

S. B. Tuston, jailer, Adams County, Mi., in the "Natchez Courier," June 15, 1838."

Mr. Joshua Antrim, Nineveh, Warren County, Virginia, in the "Winchester Virginian," July 11, 1837.

J. B. Randall, jailor, Marietta, Cobb County, Ga., in the "Southern Recorder," Nov. 6, 1838.

Mr. John N. Dillahunty, Woodville, Mi., in the "N. O. Commercial Bulletin," July 21, 1837.

William K. Ratcliffe, sheriff, Frankin County, Mi., in the "Natchez Free Trader," August 23, 1838.

Mr. Preston Halley, Barnwell, South Carolina, in the "Augusta [Ga.] Chronicle," July 27, 1838.

Mr. Welcome H. Robbins, St. Charles County, Mo., in the "St. Louis Republican," June 30, 1838.

G. Gourdon & Co. druggists, corner of Rampart and Hospital streets, New Orleans, in the "Commercial Bulletin," Sept. 18, 1838.

Mr. William Brown, in the "Grand Gulf Advertiser," August 29, 1838.

Mr. James McDonnell, Talbot County, Georgia, in the "Columbus Enquirer," Jan. 18, 1938.

Mr. John W. Cherry, Marengo County, Ala., in the "Mobile Register," June 15, 1838.

"Ranaway, the negress Martha—she has *lost her right eye.*"

"Ranaway, George—has had the lower part of *one of his ears bit off.*"

"Ranaway, my negro Tom—has a piece *bit off the top of his right ear,* and his little finger *is stiff.*"

"Ranaway, my mulatto woman Judy—she has had her *right arm broke.*"

"Was committed to jail, a negro man named Bill—has had the *thumb of his left hand split.*"

"Ranaway, a mulatto man named Joe—his fingers on the left hand are *partly amputated.*"

"Lodged in jail, a negro man named Jupiter—is very *lame in his left hip,* so that he can hardly walk—has lost a joint of the middle finger of his left hand."

"Ranaway, Bill—has a scar over one eye, also one on his leg, from *the bite of a dog—has a burn on his buttock, from a piece of hot iron in shape of a T.*"

"Committed to jail, a negro name Mike—*his left ear off.*"

"Ranaway, my negro man Levi—his left hand has been *burnt,* and I think the end of his fore finger is *off.*"

"Ranaway, a negro named Washington—has *lost a part of his* middle finger and the end of his little finger."

"Ranaway, a negro named David Drier—has *two toes cut.*"

"Ranaway, Edmund—has a *scar* on his right temple, and under his right eye, and *holes in both ears.*"

"Ranaway, a negro boy *twelve or thirteen* years old—has a scar on his left cheek *from the bite of a dog.*"

"Fifty dollars reward, for my negro man John—he has a considerable scar on his *throat,* done with a *knife.*"

Mr. Thos. Brown, Roane co. Tenn., in the "Knoxville Register," Sept. 12, 1838.

Messrs. Taylor, Lawton & Co., Charleston, South Carolina, in the "Mercury," Nov. 1838.

Mr. Louis Schmidt, Taubourg, Sivaudais, La., in the New Orleans "Bee," Sept. 5, 1837.

W. M. Whitehead, Natchez, in the "New Orleans Bulletin," July 21, 1837.

Mr. Conrad Salvo, Charleston, South Carolina, in the "Mercury," August 10, 1837.

William Baker, jailer, Shelby County, Ala., in the "Montgomery (Ala.) Advertiser," Oct. 5, 1838."

Mr. S. N. Hite, Camp Street, New Orleans, in the "Bee," Feb. 19, 1838.

Mr. Stephen M. Richards, Whitesburg, Madison County, Alabama, in the "Huntsville Democrat," Sept. 8, 1838.

"Mr. A. Brove, parish of St. Charles, La. in the "New Orleans Bee," Feb. 19, 1838.

Mr. Needham Whitefield, Aberdeen, Mi., in the "Memphis (Tenn.) Enquirer," June 15, 1838.

Col. M. J. Sheith, Charleston, South Carolina, in the "Mercury," Nov. 27, 1837.

Mr. R. Lancette, Haywood, North Carolina, in the "Raleigh Register," April 30, 1838.

Mr. G. C. Richardson, Owen Station, Mo., in the St. Louis "Republican," May 5, 1838.

Mr. E. Han, La Grange, Fayette County, Tenn., in the Gallatin "Union," June 23, 1837.

D. Herring, warden of Baltimore city jail, in the "Marylander," Oct. 6, 1837.

Mr. James Marks, near Natchitoches, La. in the "Natchitoches Herald," July 21, 1838.

Mr. James Barr, Amelia Court House, Virginia, in the "Norfolk Herald," Sept. 12, 1838.

"Twenty-five dollars reward, for my man John—the *tip* of his nose is *bit off.*"

"Ranaway, a negro fellow called Hover—has a *cut* above the right eye."

"Ranaway, the negro man Hardy—has a *scar* on the upper lip, and another made with a *knife* on his neck."

"Ranaway, Henry—has half of one *ear bit off.*"

"Ranaway, my negro man Jacob—he has but *one eye.*"

"Committed to jail, Ben—his *left thumb off* at the first joint."

"Twenty-five dollars reward for the negro slave Sally—walks as through *crippled* in the back."

"Ranaway, a negro man named Dick—has a *little finger off* the right hand."

"Ranaway, the negro Patrick—has his little finger of the right hand *cut close to the hand.*"

"Ranaway, Joe Dennis—has a small *notch* in one of his ears."

"Ranaway, Dick—has *lost the little toe* of one of his feet."

"Escaped, my negro man Eaton—his *little finger* of the right hand has been *broke.*"

"Ranaway, my negro man named Top—has had one of his *legs broken.*"

"Ranaway, negro boy Jack—has a small *crop out of his left ear.*"

"Was committed to jail, a negro man—has *two scars* on his forehead, and the *top of his left ear cut off.*"

"Stolen, a negro man named Winter—has a *notch* cut out of the left ear, and the mark of *four or five buck shot* on his legs."

"Ranaway, a negro man—*scar back of his left eye* as if from the *cut* of a knife."

Mr. Isaac Michell, Wilkinson County, Georgia, in the "Augusta Chronicle," Sept. 21, 1837.

Mr. P. Bayhi, captain of the police, Suburb Washington, third municipality, New Orleans, in the "Bee," Oct. 13, 1837.

Mr. Willie Paterson, Clinton, Jones County, Ga., in the "Darien Telegraph," Dec. 5, 1837.

Mr. Samuel Ragland, Triana, Madison County, Alabama, in the "Huntsville Advocate," Dec. 23, 1837.

Mr. Moses E. Bush, near Clayton, Ala., in the "Columbus [Ga.] Enquirer," July 5, 1838.

C. W. Wilkins, sheriff Baldwin Co. Ala., in the "Mobile Advertiser," Sept. 22, 1837.

Mr. James H. Taylor, Charleston South Carolina, in the "Courier," August 7, 1837.

N. M. C. Robinson, jailer, Columbus, Georgia, in the "Columbus (Ga.) Enquirer," August 2, 1838.

Mr. Littlejohn Rynes, Hinds Co. Mi., in the "Natchez Courier," August 17, 1838.

The Heirs of J. A. Alston, near Georgetown, South Carolina, in the "Georgetown [S. C.] Union," June 17, 1837.

A. S. Ballinger, Sheriff, Johnston Co., North Carolina, in the "Raleigh Standard," Oct. 18, 1838.

Mr. Thomas Crutchfield, Atkins, Ten., in the "Tennessee Journal" Oct. 17, 1838.

J. A. Brown, jailer, Orangeburg, South Carolina, in the "Charleston Mercury," July 18, 1838.

S. B. Turton, jailer, Adams Co. Miss. in the "Natchez Courier," Sept. 28, 1828,

Mr. John H. King, High street, Georgetown, in the "National Intelligencer," August 1, 1837.

Mr. John B. Fox, Vicksburg, Miss., in the "Register," March 29, 1837.

Messrs. Fernandez and Whiting, auctioneers, New Orleans, in the "Bee," April 8, 1837.

"Ranaway, negro man Buck—has a very *plain mark* under his ear on his jaw, about the size of a dollar, having been *inflicted by a knife.*"

"Detained at the jail, the negro boy Hermon—has a scar below his left ear, from the *wound of a knife.*"

"Ranaway, a negro man by the name of John—he has a *scar* across his cheek, and one on his right arm, apparently done with a *knife.*"

"Ranaway, Isham—has a *scar* upon the breast and upon the under lip, from the *bite of a dog.*"

"Ranaway, a negro man—has a *scar* on his hip and on his breast, and *two front teeth out.*"

"Committed to jail, a negro man, he is *crippled* in the right leg."

"Absconded, a colored boy, named Peter, *lame* in the right leg."

"Brought to jail, a negro man, his left ankle has been *broke.*"

"Ranaway, a negro man named Jerry, has a small peice *cut out of the top of each ear.*"

"Absconded a negro named Cuffee, has *lost one finger; has an *enlarged leg.*"

"Committed to jail, a negro man; has a *very sore leg.*"

"Ranaway, my mulatto boy Cy, has but *one hand*, all the fingers of his right hand were *burnt* off when young."

"Was committed to jail, a negro named Bob, appears to be *crippled* in the right leg."

"Was committed to jail, a negro man, has his *left thigh broke.*"

"Ranaway, my negro man, he has the *end of one* of his fingers *broken.*"

"Ranaway, a yellowish negro boy named Tom, has a *notch* in the back of one of his ears."

"Will be sold Martha, aged nineteen, *has one eye out.*"

Mr. Marshall Jett, Farrowsville, Fauquier Co. Virginia, in the "National Intelligencer," May 30, 1837.

S. B. Turton, jailer Adams Co. Miss. in the "Natches Courier," Oct. 12, 1838.

John Ford, sheriff of Mobile County, in the "Mississipipian," Jackson Mi., Dec. 28, 1838.

E. W. Morris, sheriff of Warren County, in the "Vicksburg [Mi.] Register," March 28, 1838.

Mr. John P. Holcombe, in the "Charleston Mercury," April 17, 1838.

Mr. Willis Patterson, in the "Charleston Mercury," December 11, 1837.

Wm. Magee, sheriff, Mobile Co., in the "Mobile Register," Dec. 27, 1837.

Mr. Henry M. McGregor, Prince George County, Maryland, in the "Alexandria [D. C.] Gazett," Feb. 6, 1838.

Green B. Jourdan, Baldwin County Ga., in the "Georgia Journal," April 18, 1837.

Messrs. Daniel and Goodman, New Orleans, in the "N. O. Bee," Feb. 2, 1838.

Jeremiah Woodward, Goochland, Co., Va., in the "Richmond Va. Whig," Jan. 30, 1838.

Samuel Rawlins, Gwinet Co., Ga., in "Columbus Sentinel," Nov. 29, 1838."

"Ranaway, negro man Ephraim, has a *mark* over one of his eyes, occasioned by a *blow*."

"Was committed a negro, calls himself Jacob, has been *crippled* in his right leg."

"Committed to jail, a negro man Cary, a *large scar on his forehead.*"

"Committed as a runaway, a negro man Jack, has *several scars* on his face."

"Absented himself, his negro man Ben, *has scars* on his throat, occasioned by the *cut of a knife.*"

"Ranaway, a negro man, John, a *scar* across his cheek, and one on his right arm, apparently done *with a knife.*"

"Committed to jail, a runaway slave, Alexander, a *scar* on his left cheek."

"Ranaway, negro Phil, *scar through the right eye brow, part of the middle toe* on the *right foot cut off.*"

"Ranaway, John, has a *scar* on one of his hands extending from the wrist joint to the little finger, also a *scar* on one of his legs."

"Absconded, mulatto slave Alick, has a *large scar over* one of his cheeks."

"200 DOLLARS REWARD for Nelson, has a *scar* on his forehead occasioned by a *burn* and one on his lower lip and one about the knee."

"Ranaway, a negro man and his wife, named Nat and Priscilla, he has a small *scar* on his left cheek, *two stiff fingers* on his right hand with a *running sore* on them; his wife has a *scar* on her left arm, and one *upper tooth out.*"

Document 9.9 A Slave's Testimony: Lewis Clark

Anti-slavery societies also collected first-hand accounts from runaway slaves. These stories were often shocking to hear, so shocking that those opposed to abolition claimed they couldn't possibly be true, that no human could do these things to another human being. This is, of course, the classic defense used by those defending genocide as well. No part of slavery seemed more appalling than the tearing apart of families, when children were loaded into carts and hauled away while their mothers cried. While the accounts could be shocking and titillating, many were actually toned down to not outrage listeners. Northern visitors who went to border states like Kentucky often reported back that slavery was fine there, that the evils must be farther south. Consider the account of Lewis Clark. What horrors and outrages does he report happened? Does this sound like slaves are treated well in Kentucky?

"There was a widower in Kentucky, who took one of his women slaves into the house. She told her master one day that seven of the young girls had poked fun at her for the way she was living. This raised his *ambition*. 'I'll teach 'em to make fun!' said he. So he sent the woman away, and ordered the young girls to come to him, one by one." (An ill-mannered and gross laughter, among the boys of the audience, here seemed to embarrass him.) "Perhaps I had better not try to tell this story," he continued; "for I cannot tell it as it was; though surely it is more shameful to have such things *done*, than it is to *tell* of 'em. He got mad with the girls, because they complained to their mothers; but he didn't like to punish 'em for that, for fear it would make a talk. So he ordered 'em to go out into the field to do work that was too hard for 'em. Six of 'em said they couldn't do it; but the mother of the seventh, guessing what it was for, told her to go, and do the best she could. The other six was every one of 'em tied up naked, and flogged, for disobeying orders. Now, who would like to be a slave, even if there was nothing bad about it but such treatment of his sisters and daughters? But there's a worse thing yet about slavery; the worst thing in the whole lot; though it's all bad, from the butt end to the *pint*. I mean the *patter-rollers* (patrols.) . . . If a slave don't open his door to them at any time of night they break it down. They steal his money if they can find it, and act just as they please with his wives and daughters. If a husband dares to say a word, or even look as if he wasn't quite satisfied, they tie him up and give him thirty-nine lashes. If there's any likely young girls in a slave's hut, they're mighty apt to have business there, especially if they think any colored young man takes a fancy to any of 'em. Maybe he'll get a pass from his master, and go to see the young girl for a few hours. The patter-rollers break in and find him there. They'll abuse the girl as bad as they can, a purpose to provoke him. If he looks cross, they give him a flogging, tear up his pass, turn him out of doors, and then take him up and whip him for being out without a pass. If the slave says they tore it up, they swear he lies; and nine times out of ten the master won't come out agin 'em; for they say it won't *do* to let the niggers suppose they may complain of the patter-rollers; they must be taught that it's their business to obey 'em in everything; and the patter-roller knows that very well. Oh, how often I've seen the poor girls sob and cry, when there's been such goings on! Maybe you think, because they're slaves, they an't got no feeling and no shame? A woman's being a slave, don't stop her having genteel ideas; that is, according to their way, and as far as they can. They know they must submit to their masters; besides, their masters, maybe, dress 'em up, and make 'em little presents, and give 'em more privileges, while the whim lasts; but that an't like having a parcel of low, dirty, swearing, drunk patter-rollers let loose among 'em, like so many hogs. This breaks down their spirits dreadfully, and makes 'em wish they was dead.

"Now who among you would like to have your wives, and daughters, and sisters, in such a situation? This is what every slave in all these States is exposed to.—Yet folks go from these parts down to Kentucky, and come back, and say the slaves have enough to eat and drink, and they are very happy, and they wouldn't mind it much to be slaves themselves. I'd like to have 'em try it; it would teach 'em a little more than they know now."

From *National Anti-Slavery Standard*, October 20, 1842.

Document 9.10 A Slave's Testimony: Solomon Northup

Most slaves worked as field hands. Men and women alike were lined up early and sent out into the fields for long hours of hard work. This meant starting before sunup and ending after sunset, and then having other work to do around the house before quitting for the day. If you slowed down because you were tired, you would be punished. If you made a mistake, damaged the cotton plants, or did not produce as much as your master wanted, you would likely be punished. This usually meant lashes with a whip. With enough "incentive" the slaves could work with the efficiency of a piece of machinery, according to their owners. The following account is by Solomon Northrup, a free Black kidnapped from New York and forced to work as a slave in central Louisiana for 12 years. After being released in 1853, he wrote this account to promote the anti-slavery movement. As you read this material, calculate the amount of work, and the different types of tasks, slaves were required to do. How many people would volunteer to work this way? How many would work this hard even for pay?

The hands are required to be in the cotton field as soon as it is light in the morning, and, with the exception of ten or fifteen minutes, which is given them at noon to swallow their allowance of cold bacon, they are not permitted to be a moment idle until it is too dark to see, and when the moon is full, they oftentimes labor until the middle of the night. They do not dare to stop even at dinner time, nor return to the quarters, however late it be, until the order to halt is given by the driver.

The day's work over in the field, the baskets are "toted," or in other words, carried to the gin-house, where the cotton is weighed. No matter how fatigued and weary he may be—no matter how much he longs for sleep and rest—a slave never approaches the gin-house with his basket of cotton but with fear. If it falls short in weight—if he has not performed the full task appointed him, he knows that he must suffer. And if he has exceeded it by ten or twenty pounds, in all probability his master will measure the next day's task accordingly. So, whether he has too little or too much, his approach to the gin-house is always with fear and trembling. Most frequently they have too little, and therefore it is they who are not anxious to leave the field. After weighing, follow the whippings; and then the baskets are carried to the cotton house, and their contents stored away like hay, all hands being sent in to tramp it down. If the cotton is not dry, instead of taking it to the gin-house at once, it is laid upon plat-forms, two feet high, and some three times as wide, covered with boards or plank, with narrow walks running between them.

This done, the labor of the day is not yet ended, by any means. Each one must then attend to his respective chores. One feeds the mules, another the swine—another cuts the wood, and so forth; besides, the packing is all done by candle light. Finally, at a late hour, they reach the quarters, sleepy and overcome with the long day's toil. Then a fire must be kindled in the cabin, the corn ground in the small hand-mill, and supper, and dinner for the next day in the field, prepared. All that is allowed them is corn and bacon, which is given out at the corncrib and the smoke-house every Sunday morning. Each one receives, as his weekly allowance, three and a half pounds of bacon, and corn enough to make a peck of meal. That is all—no tea, coffee, sugar, and with the exception of a very scanty sprinkling now and then, no salt. . . .

An hour before daylight the horn is blown. Then the slaves arouse, prepare their breakfast, fill a gourd with water, in another deposit their dinner of cold bacon and corn cake, and hurry to the field again. It is an offense invariably followed by a flogging, to be found at the quarters after daybreak. Then the fears and labors of another day begin; and until its close there is no such thing as rest.

From *Twelve Years a Slave: Narrative of Solomon Northrup*, Auburn, New York: 1853.

Document 9.11 A Slave's Testimony: William Brown

All slaves were "disciplined" at some time. If not lashed yourself, you were forced to witness the whipping of your peers, hear the sound of the whip cutting into the flesh, and then see the bleeding cuts and visible pain. Owners wanted slaves to witness this "discipline" so they could imagine the same thing happening to themselves if they disobeyed. William Brown escaped from slavery in 1835, after living in the border states of Kentucky and Missouri. His account of slave life, *Narrative of William Brown, A Fugitive Slave*, appeared 13 years later. This account details both the physical and mental abuses of slavery. According to this testimony, how does slavery affect Whites and Blacks? What evils come to both races? Are some Southerners better than others, according to Brown? What makes some masters better than others, and what is the basis for making this judgment?

I was born in Lexington, Ky. The man who stole me as soon as I was born, recorded the births of all the infants which he claimed to be born [on] his property, in a book which he kept for that purpose. My mother's name was Elizabeth. She had seven children, viz.: Solomon, Leander, Benjamin, Joseph, Millford, Elizabeth, and myself. No two of us were children of the same father. My father's name, as I learned from my mother, was George Higgins. He was a white man, a relative of my master, and connected with some of the first families in Kentucky.

My master owned about forty slaves, twenty-five of whom were field hands. He removed from Kentucky to Missouri when I was quite young, and settled thirty or forty miles above St. Charles, on the Missouri, where, in addition to his practice as a physician, he carried on milling, merchandizing and farming. He had a large farm, the principal productions of which were tobacco and hemp. The slave cabins were situated on the back part of the farm, with the house of the overseer, whose name was Grove Cook, in their midst. He had the entire charge of the farm, and having no family, was allowed a woman to keep house for him, whose business it was to deal out the provisions for the hands.

A woman was also kept at the quarters to do the cooking for the field hands, who were summoned to their unrequited toil every morning at four o'clock, by the ringing of a bell, hung on a post near the house of the overseer. They were allowed half an hour to eat their breakfast, and get to the field. At half past four a horn was blown by the overseer, which was his signal to commence work; and every one that was not on the spot at the time, had to receive ten lashes from the negro-whip, with which the overseer always went armed. The handle was about three feet long, with the butt-end filled with lead, and the lash, six or seven feet in length, made of cow-hide, with platted wire on the end of it. This whip was put in requisition very frequently and freely, and a small offence on the part of a slave furnished an occasion for its use. During the time that Mr. Cook was overseer, I was a house servant—a situation preferable to that of a field hand, as I was better fed, better clothed, and not obliged to rise at the ringing of the bell, but about half an hour after. I have often laid and heard the crack of the whip, and the screams of the slave. My mother was a field hand, and one morning was ten or fifteen minutes behind the others in getting into the field. As soon as she reached the spot where they were at work, the overseer commenced whipping her. She cried, "Oh! pray—Oh! pray—Oh! Pray"—these are generally the words of slaves, when imploring mercy at the hands of their oppressors. I heard her voice, and knew it, and jumped out of my bunk, and went to the door. Though the field was some distance from the house, I could hear every crack of the whip, and every groan and cry of my poor mother. I remained at the door, not daring to venture any further. The cold chills ran over me, and I wept aloud. After giving her ten lashes, the sound of the whip ceased, and I returned to my bed, and found no consolation but in my tears. Experience has taught me that nothing can be more heart-rending than for one to see a dear and beloved mother or sister tortured, and to hear their cries, and not be able to render them assistance. But such is the position which an American slave occupies.

From *Narrative of William Brown, a Fugitive Slave*, Boston: Anti-Slavery Society.

My master, being a politician, soon found those who were ready to put him into office, for the favors he could render them; and a few years after his arrival in Missouri he was elected to a seat in the legislature. In his absence from home everything was left in charge of Mr. Cook, the overseer, and he soon became more tyrannical and cruel. Among the slaves on the plantation was one by the name of Randall. He was a man about six feet high, and well-proportioned, and known as a man of great strength and power. He was considered the most valuable and able-bodied slave on the plantation; but no matter how good or useful a slave may be, he seldom escapes the lash. But it was not so with Randall. He had been on the plantation since my earliest recollection, and I had never known of his being flogged. No thanks were due to the master or overseer for this. I have often heard him declare that no white man should ever whip him—that he would die first.

Cook, from the time that he came upon the plantation, had frequently declared that he could and would flog any nigger that was put into the field to work under him. My master had repeatedly told him not to attempt to whip Randall, but he was determined to try it. As soon as he was left sole dictator, he thought the time had come to put his threats into execution. He soon began to find fault with Randall, and threatened to whip him if he did not do better. One day he gave him a very hard task—more than he could possibly do; and at night, the task not being performed, he told Randall that he should remember him the next morning. On the following morning, after the hands had taken breakfast, Cook called out to Randall, and told him that he intended to whip him, and ordered him to cross his hands and be tied. Randall asked why he wished to whip him. He answered, because he had not finished his task the day before. Randall said that the task was too great, or he should have done it. Cook said it made no difference—he should whip him. Randall stood silent for a moment, and then said, "Mr. Cook, I have always tried to please you since you have been on the plantation, and I find you are determined not to be satisfied with my work, let me do as well as I may. No man has laid hands on me, to whip me, for the last ten years, and, I have long since come to the conclusion not to be whipped by any man living." Cook, finding by Randall's determined look and gestures, that he would resist, called three of the hands from their work, and commanded them to seize Randall, and tie him. The hands stood still;—they knew Randall—and they also knew him to be a powerful man, and were afraid to grapple with him. As soon as Cook had

ordered the men to seize him, Randall turned to them, and said—"Boys, you all know me; you know that I can handle any three of you, and the man that lays hands on me shall die. This white man can't whip me himself, and therefore he has called you to help him." The overseer was unable to prevail upon them to seize and secure Randall, and finally ordered them all to go to their work together.

Nothing was said to Randall by the overseer for more than a week. One morning, however, while the hands were at work in the field, he came into it, accompanied by three friends of his, Thompson, Woodbridge and Jones. They came up to where Randall was at work, and Cook ordered him to leave his work, and go with them to the barn. He refused to go; whereupon he was attacked by the overseer and his companions, when he turned upon them, and laid them, one after another, prostrate on the ground. Woodbridge drew out his pistol, and fired at him, and brought him to the ground by a pistol ball. The others rushed upon him with their clubs, and beat him over the head and face, until they succeeded in tying him. He was then taken to the barn, and tied to a beam. Cook gave him over one hundred lashes with a heavy cowhide, had him washed with salt and water, and left him tied during the day. The next day he was untied, and taken to a blacksmith's shop, and had a ball and chain attached to his leg. He was compelled to labor in the field, and perform the same amount of work that the other hands did. When his master returned home, he was much pleased to find that Randall had been subdued in his absence.

Soon afterwards, my master removed to the city of St. Louis, and purchased a farm four miles from there, which he placed under the charge of an overseer by the name of Friend Haskell. He was a regular Yankee from New England. The Yankees are noted for making the most cruel overseers.

My mother was hired out in the city, and I was also hired out there to Major Freeland, who kept a public house. He was formerly from Virginia, and was a horse-racer, cock-fighter, gambler, and withal an inveterate drunkard. There were ten or twelve servants in the house, and when he was present, it was cut and slash—knock down and drag out. In his fits of anger, he would take up a chair, and throw it at a servant; and in his more rational moments, when he wished to chastise one, he would tie them up in the smoke-house, and whip them; after which, he would cause a fire to be made of tobacco stems, and smoke them. This he called *"Virginia play."*

I complained to my master of the treatment which I received from Major Freeland; but it made no difference. He cared nothing about it, so long as he received the money for my labor. After living with Major Freeland five or six months, I ran away, and went into the woods back of the city; and when night came on, I made my way to my master's farm, but was afraid to be seen, knowing that if Mr. Haskell, the overseer, should discover me, I should be again carried back to Major Freeland; so I kept in the woods. One day, while in the woods, I heard the barking and howling of dogs, and in a short time they came so near that I knew them to be the bloodhounds of Major Benjamin O'Fallon. He kept five or six, to hunt runaway slaves with.

As soon as I was convinced that it was them, I knew there was no chance of escape. I took refuge in the top of a tree, and the hounds were soon at its base, and there remained until the hunters came up in a half or three quarters of an hour afterwards. There were two men with the dogs, who, as soon as they came up, ordered me to descend. I came down, was tied, and taken to St. Louis jail. Major Freeland soon made his appearance, and took me out, and ordered me to follow him, which I did. After we returned home, I was tied up in the smoke-house, and was very severely whipped. After the major had flogged me to his satisfaction, he sent out his son Robert, a young man eighteen or twenty years of age, to see that I was well smoked. He made a fire of tobacco stems, which soon set me to coughing and sneezing. This, Robert told me, was the way his father used to do to his slaves in Virginia. After giving me what they conceived to be a decent smoking, I was untied and again set to work.

Robert Freeland was a "chip of the old block." Though quite young, it was not unfrequently that he came home in a state of intoxication. He is now, I believe, a popular commander of a steamboat on the Mississippi river. Major Freeland soon after failed in business, and I was put on board the steamboat Missouri, which plied between St. Louis and Galena. The commander of the boat was William B. Culver. I remained on her during the sailing season, which was the most pleasant time for me that I had ever experienced. At the close of navigation I was hired to Mr. John Colburn, keeper of the Missouri Hotel. He was from one of the free states; but a more inveterate hater of the negro I do not believe ever walked God's green earth. This hotel was at that time one of the largest in the city, and there were employed in it twenty or thirty servants, mostly slaves.

Mr. Colburn was very abusive, not only to the servants, but to his wife also, who was an excellent woman, and one from whom I never knew a servant to receive a harsh word; but never did I know a kind one to a servant from her husband. Among the slaves employed in the hotel was one by the name of Aaron, who belonged to Mr. John F. Darby, a lawyer. Aaron was the knife-cleaner. One day, one of the knives was put on the table, not as clean as it might have been. Mr. Colburn, for this offence, tied Aaron up in the wood-house, and gave him over fifty lashes on the bare back with a cow-hide, after which, he made me wash him down with rum. This seemed to put him into more agony than the whipping. After being untied he went home to his master, and complained of the treatment which he had received. Mr. Darby would give no heed to anything he had to say, but sent him directly back. Colburn, learning that he had been to his master with complaints, tied him up again, and gave him a more severe whipping than before. The poor fellow's back was literally cut to pieces; so much so, that he was not able to work for ten or twelve days.

There was, also, among the servants, a girl whose master resided in the country. Her name was Patsey. Mr. Colburn tied her up one evening, and whipped her until several of the boarders came out and begged him to desist. The reason for whipping her was this. She was engaged to be married to a man belonging to Major William Christy, who resided four or five miles north of the city. Mr. Colburn had forbid her to see John Christy. The reason of this was said to be the regard which he himself had for Patsey. She went to meeting that evening, and John returned home with her. Mr. Colburn had intended to flog John, if he came within the inclosure; but John knew too well the temper of his rival, and kept at a safe distance:—so he took vengeance on the poor girl. If all the slave-drivers had been called together, I do not think a more cruel man than John Colburn—and he too a northern man—could have been found among them.

While living at the Missouri hotel, a circumstance occurred which caused me great unhappiness. My master sold my mother, and all her children, except myself. They were sold to different persons in the city of St. Louis.

Document 9.12 A Slave's Testimony: Rose Williams

Slave owners paid premium prices to get good "breeders," women who could increase their slave property with the proper incentive. They were willing to use bribes and rewards to get the result they wanted, or use force if the slaves were not willing. This practice stayed vivid in the memories of former slaves. Starting in the 1930s, the New Deal's Federal Writers' Project interviewed former slaves, recording first-hand information about their lives before these people died. This was a necessary balance to all of the one-sided accounts of slavery left by former slave-owners and other White southerners, who in the years after the Civil War whitewashed the horrors of slavery. Despite the advanced age of the former slaves, and the occasional gaps in their memories, these interviews remain the most valuable source of first-hand testimony about slavery. Rose Williams of Texas was 90 years old when interviewed. Why did Rose's master choose a husband for her? What methods did he use to get her to cooperate with reproducing children? Why did she feel obligated to do so?

What I say am de facts. If I's one day old, I's way over 90, and I's born in Bell County, right here in Texas, and am owned by Massa William Black. He owns mammy and pappy, too. Massa Black has a big plantation but he has more niggers dan he need for work on dat place, 'cause he am a nigger trader. He trade and buy and sell all de time.

Massa Black am awful cruel and he whip de cullud folks and works 'em hard and feed dem poorly. We'uns have for rations de cornmeal and milk and 'lasses and some beans and peas and meat once a week. We'uns have to work in de field every day from daylight till dark and on Sunday we'uns do us washin'. Church—Shucks, we'uns don't know what dat mean.

I has de correct memorandum of when de war start. Massa Black sold we'uns right den. Mammy and pappy powerful glad to git sold, and dey and I is put on de block with 'bout ten other niggers. When we'uns gits te de tradin' block, dere lots of white folks dere what come to look us over. One man shows de intres' in pappy. Him named Hawkins. He talk to pappy and pappy talk to him and say, "Dem my woman and chiles. Please buy all of us and have mercy on we'uns." Massa Hawkins say, "Dat gal am a likely lookin' nigger, she am portly and strong, but three am more dan I wants, I guesses."

De sale start and 'fore long pappy a put on de block. Massa Hawkins wins de bid for pappy and when mammy am put on de block, he wins de bid for her. Den dere am three or four other niggers sold befo' my time comes. Den Massa Black calls me to de block and de auction man say, "What am I offer for

dis portly, strong young wench. She's never been 'bused and will make de good breeder."

I wants to hear Massa Hawkins bid, but him say nothin'. Two other men am biddin' 'gainst each other and I sho' has de worryment. Dere am tears comin' down my cheeks 'cause I's bein' sold to some man dat would make separation from my mammy. One man bids $500 and de auction man ask, "Do I hear more? She am gwine at $500.00." Den someone say, $525.00 and de auction man say, "She am sold for $525.00 to Massa Hawkins." Am I glad and 'cited! Why, I's quiverin' all over.

Massa Hawkins takes we'uns to his place and it am a nice plantation. Lots better am dat place dan Massa Black's. Dere is 'bout 50 niggers what is growed and lots of chillen. De first thing massa de when we'uns gits home am give we'uns rations and a cabin. You mus' believe dis nigger when I says dem rations a feast for us. Dere plenty meat and tea and coffee and white flour. I's never tasted white flour and coffee and mammy fix some biscuits and coffee. Well, de biscuits was yum, yum, yum to me, but de coffee I doesn't like.

De quarters am purty good. Dere am twelve cabins all made from logs and a table and some benches and bunks for sleepin' and a fireplace for cookin' and de heat. Dere am no floor, jus' de ground.

Massa Hawkins am good to he niggers and not force 'em work too hard. Dere am as much diff'ence 'tween him and old Massa Black in de way of treatment as 'twixt de Lawd and de devil. Massa Hawkins 'lows he niggers have reason'ble parties and go fishin', but

---

From Government Documents Collection at the University of Kansas.

we'uns am never tooken to church and has no books for larnin'. Dere am no edumcation for de niggers.

Dere am one thing Massa Hawkins does to me what I can't shunt from my mind. I knows he don't do it for meanness, but I allus holds it 'gainst him. What he done am force me to live with dat nigger, Rufus, 'gainst my wants.

After I been at he place 'bout a year, de massa come to me and say, "You gwine live with Rufus in dat cabin over yonder. Go fix it for livin'." I's 'bout sixteen year old and has no larnin', and I's jus' igno'-mus chile. I's thought dat him mean for me to tend de cabin for Rufus and some other niggers. Well, dat am start de pestigation for me.

I's took charge of de cabin after work am done and fixes supper. Now, I don't like dat Rufus, 'cause he a bully. He am big and 'cause he so, he think everybody do what him say. We'uns has supper, den I goes here and dere talkin', till I's ready for sleep and den I gits in de bunk. After I's in, dat nigger come and crawl in de bunk with me 'fore I knows it. I says, "What you means, you fool nigger?" He say for me to hush de mouth. "Dis am my bunk too," he say.

"You's teched in de head. Git out," I's told him. and I puts de feet 'gainst him and give him a shove and out he go on de floor 'fore he know what I's doin'. Dat nigger jump up and he mad. He look like de wild bear. He starts for de bunk and I jumps quick for de poker. It am 'bout three feet long and when he comes at me I lets him have it over de head. Did dat nigger stop in he tracks? I's say he did. He looks at me steady for a minute and you's could tell he thinkin' hard. Den he go and set on de bench and say, "Jus wait. You thinks it am smart, but you's am foolish in de head. Dey's gwine larn you somethin'."

"Hush yous big mouth and stay 'way from dis nig-ger, dat all I wants," I say, and jus' sets and hold dat poker in de hand. He jus' sets, lookin' like de bull.

Dere we'uns sets and sets for 'bout an hour and den he go out and I bars de door.

De nex' day I goes to de missy and tells her what Rufus wants and missy say dat am de massa's wishes. She say, "Yous am de portly gal and Rufus am de portly man. De massa wants you-uns fer to bring forth portly chillen."

I's thinkin' 'bout what de missy say, but say to myse'f, "I's not gwine live with dat Rufus." Dat night when him come in de cabin, I grabs de poker and sits on de bench and says, "Git 'way from me, nigger, 'fore I busts yous brains out and stomp on dem." He say nothin' and git out.

De nex' day de massa call me and tell me. "Woman, I's pay big money for you and I's done dat for de cause I wants yous to raise me chillens. I's put yous to live with Rufus for dat purpose. Now, if you doesn't want whippin' at de stake, yous do what I wants."

I thinks 'bout massa buyin' me offen de block and savin' me from bein' sep'rated from my folks and 'bout bein' whipped at de stake. Dere it am. What am I's to do? So I 'cides to do as de massa wish and so I yields.

When we'uns am given freedom, Massa Hawkins tells us we can stay and work for wages or share crop de land. Some stays and some goes. My folks and me stays. We works de land on shares for three years, den moved to other land near by. I stays with my folks till they dies.

If my mem'randum am correct, it am 'bout thirty year since I come to Fort Worth. Here I cooks for white folks till I goes blind 'bout ten year ago.

I never marries, 'cause one 'sperience am 'nough for dis nigger. After what I does for de massa, I's never wants no truck with any man. De Lawd forgive dis cullud woman, but he have to to 'scuse me and look for some others for to 'plenish de earth.

Document 9.13 A Slave's Testimony: Josiah Henson

The most damning charge against slavery was rape. Southern White masters and overseers forced them-selves upon African-American women to satisfy their own lusts or prove their power over the lives of slaves. Some pro-slavery advocates justified rape as protecting virtuous White womanhood by providing a sexual outlet for young White males. Women could not resist for long, nor could their slave husbands fight for them. To strike a White man raping your wife meant death. Children and husbands were forced to stand by and accept this brutality. Psychological injury added to physical abuse. Children born of a slave mother were slaves, and thus the owner increased his property value. The Reverend Josiah Henson recalled what hap-pened to his mother and father while they were all slaves. What is the outcome for his family? Can you think of any ways that Southern whites, male or female, demonstrated respect for slave families?

I was born June 15th, 1789, in Charles County, Maryland, on a farm belonging to Mr. Francis Newman, about a mile from Port Tobacco. My mother was a slave of Dr. Josiah McPherson, but hired to the Mr. Newman to whom my father belonged. The only incident I can remember which occurred while my mother continued on Mr. Newman's farm, was the appearance one day of my father with his head bloody and his back lacerated. He was beside himself with mingled rage and suffering. The explanation I picked up from the conversation of others only partially explained the matter to my mind; but as I grew older I understood it all. It seemed the overseer had sent my mother away from the other field hands to a retired place, and after trying persuasion in vain, had resorted to force to accomplish a brutal purpose. Her screams aroused my father at his distant work, and running up, he found his wife struggling with the man. Furious at the sight, he sprung upon him like a tiger. In a moment the overseer was down, and, mastered by rage, my father would have killed him but for the entreaties of my mother, and the overseer's own promise that nothing should ever be said of the matter. The promise was kept like most promises of the cowardly and debased—as long as the danger lasted.

The laws of state provide means and opportunities for revenge so ample, that miscreants like him never fail to improve them. "A nigger has struck a white man;" that is enough to set a whole county on fire; no question is asked about the provocation. The authorities were soon in pursuit of my father. The fact of the sacrilegious act of lifting a hand against the sacred temple of a white man's body . . . this was all it was necessary to establish. And the penalty followed: one hundred lashes on the bare back, and to have the right ear nailed to the whipping-post, and then severed from the body. For a time my father kept out of the way, hiding in the woods, and at night venturing into some cabin in search of food. But at length the strict watch set baffled all his efforts. His supplies cut off, he was fairly starved out, and compelled by hunger to come back and give himself up.

The day for the execution of the penalty was appointed. The Negroes from the neighboring plantations were summoned, for their moral improvement, to witness the scene. A powerful blacksmith named Hewes laid on the stripes. Fifty were given, during which the cries of my father might be heard a mile, and then a pause ensued. True, he had struck a white man, but as valuable property he must not be damaged. Judicious men felt his pulse. Oh! he could stand the whole. Again and again the thong fell on his lacerated back. His cries grew fainter and fainter, till a feeble groan was the only response to his final blows. His head was then thrust against the post, and his right ear fastened to it with a tack; a swift pass of a knife, and the bleeding member was left sticking to the place. Then came a hurrah from the degraded crowd, and the exclamation, "That's what he's got for striking a white man." A few said, "it's a damned shame;" but the majority regarded it as but a proper tribute to their offended majesty. . . .

Previous to this affair my father, from all I can learn, had been a good-humored and light-hearted man, the ringleader in all fun at corn-huskings and Chrismas buffoonery. His banjo was the life of the farm, and all night long at a merry-making would he play on it while the other Negroes danced. But from this hour he became utterly changed. Sullen, morose, and dogged, nothing could be done with him. The milk of human kindness in his heart was turned to gall. He brooded over his wrongs. No fear or threats of being sold to the far south—the greatest of all terrors to the Maryland slave—would render him tractable. So off he was sent to Alabama. What was his fate neither my mother nor I have ever learned. . . .

For two or three years my mother and her young family of six children had resided on [Dr. McPherson's] estate; and we had been in the main very happy. . . .

Our term of happy union as one family was now, alas! at an end. Mournful as was the Doctor's death to his friends it was a far greater calamity to us. The estate and the slaves must be sold and the proceeds divided among the heirs. We were but property—not a mother, and the children God had given her.

Common as are slave-auctions in the Southern states, and naturally as a slave may look forward to the time when he will be put upon the block, still the full misery of the event—of the scenes which precede and succeed it—is never understood till the actual experience comes. The first sad announcement that the sale is to be; the knowledge that all ties of the past are to be sundered; the frantic terror at the idea of being "sent South;" the almost certainty that one member of a family will be torn from another; the anxious scanning of purchasers' faces; the agony at parting, often forever, with husband, wife, child—these must be seen and felt to be fully understood. Young as I was then, the iron entered into my soul.

From *Uncle Tom's Story of His Life: An Autobiography of the Reverend Josiah Henson.*

The remembrance of breaking up of McPherson's estate is photographed in its minutest features in my mind. The crowd collected around the stand, the huddling group of Negroes, the examination of muscle, teeth, the exhibition of agility, the look of the autioneer, the agony of my mother—I can shut my eyes and see them all.

My brothers and sisters were bid off first, and one by one, while my mother, paralyzed by grief, held me by the hand. Her turn came, and she was bought by Isaac Riley of Montgomery County. Then I was offered to the assembled purchasers. My mother, half distracted by the thought of parting forever from all her children, pushed through the crowd, while the bidding for me was going on, to the spot where Riley was standing. She fell at his feet and clung to his knees, entreating him in tones that a mother only could command, to buy her baby as well as herself, and spare to her one, at least of her little ones. Will it, can it be believed that this man, thus appealed to, was capable not merely of turning a deaf ear to her supplication, but of disengaging himself from her with such violent blows and kicks, as to reduce her to the necessity of creeping out of his reach, and mingling the groan of bodily suffering with the sob of a breaking heart? As she crawled away from the brutal man I heard her sob out, "Oh, Lord Jesus, how long, how long shall I suffer this way!" I must have been then between five and six years old. I seem to see and hear my poor weeping mother now. This was one of my earlist observations of men; an experience which I only shared with thousands of my race, the bitterness of which to any individual who suffers it cannot be diminished by the frequency of its recurrence, while it is dark enought to overshadow the whole after-life with something blacker than a funeral pall.

Document 9.14 Spirituals: Expressions of Present Life and Future Hope

Slaves sang spirituals any time of the day. They were used in churches, but also as field songs, rowing songs, or celebration songs. The songs expressed hopes for a better future, one where they would achieve the equality and opportunities denied to them by slavery in the present world. Some songs suggest that slaves identified with being the chosen people, and that their owners would be denied salvation for their actions. The difference between real Christians and pretenders was their treatment of all God's children. There would be justice in the future, and an affirmation of the slave's status before God. Following are songs recorded by Thomas Wentworth Higginson, who visited former slaves while traveling through the South after the Civil War for *Atlantic Monthly*. What messages do you see in the lyrics? How positive is the future going to be? Considering that most songs were created before freedom came, how accurate were the predictions?

XXXIV. We'll Soon Be Free

"We'll soon be free,
We'll soon be free,
We'll soon be free,
When de Lord will call us home.
My brudder, how long,
My brudder, how long,
My brudder, how long,
'Fore we done sufferin' here?
It won't be long (Thrice.)

'Fore de Lord will call us home.
We'll walk de miry road (Thrice.)
Where pleasure never dies.
We'll walk de golden street (Thrice.)
Where pleasure never dies.
My brudder, how long (Thrice.)
'Fore we done sufferin' here?
We'll soon be free (Thrice.)
When Jesus sets me free.
We'll fight for liberty (Thrice.)
When de Lord will call us home."

From *The Atlantic Monthly*, June 1867.

XXXV. Many Thousand Go

"No more peck o'corn for me,
No more, no more,—
No more peck o'corn for me,
Many tousand go.

"No more driver's lash for me, (Twice.)
No more, &c.

"No more pint o' salt for me, (Twice.)
No more, &c.

"No more hundred lash for me, (Twice.)
No more, &c.

"No more mistress' call for me,
No more, No more,"
No more mistress' call for me,
Many tousand go."

XXXVI. The Driver

"O, de ole nigger-driver!
O, gwine away!
Fust ting my mammy tell me,
O, gwine away!
Tell me 'bout de nigger-driver,
O, gwine away!
Nigger-driver second devil,
O, gwine away!
Best ting for do he driver,
O, gwine away!
Knock he down and spoil he labor,
O, gwine away!"

Chapter 9 Worksheet and Questions

1. You are the 1856 commencement speaker at a prestigious Southern college. The title of your speech is "The Glorious Civilization of the South and Other Benefits of Slavery." List or explain the major points you will make in the speech, which should be a defense of slavery that explains its connections to all facets of Southern society. Use evidence from the documents in this chapter.

    _____

    _____

    _____

    _____

    _____

    _____

    _____

    _____

    _____

2. Your family has owned slaves for many generations. In your view, what is necessary to regulate and control the slaves? Make the argument that the rules, regulations, and physical violence are necessary to "improve" the slaves.

    _____

    _____

    _____

    _____

    _____

    _____

    _____

    _____

3. As a newcomer to the ranks of Abolitionists, you are filled with excitement and an absolute surety that slavery is evil. You are invited to speak on the evils of slavery to the student body at Oberlin College. Explain why slavery is so bad, from the standpoint of a White Northern Abolitionist. What are the most objectionable features that are detailed in the documents?

_____

_____

_____

_____

_____

_____

_____

_____

_____

_____

4. Now assume the role of a slave. Very simply, what is bad about chattel slavery? This should be very personal, because you and your family have been affected by it. How do you refute the claims of the speaker in question #1 that slavery is a benevolent, paternal institution? Use specific examples of what you believe to be wrong with the institution, and why these actions are wrong.

_____

_____

_____

_____

_____

_____

_____

_____

_____

_____

Chapter 10

Manifest Destiny: Noble Mission or Racist Land Grab?

In the mid-eighteenth century, Bishop George Berkeley of England declared, "Westward the course of empire takes its way," and this attitude was adopted by generations of American nationalists. Benjamin Franklin and George Washington often commented about the future American Empire, and participated in activities to promote westward expansion and an increase in wealth. From colonial times, when the settlers gazed in awe at the "far blue mountains" in their way, the American population expanded westward.

Population expansion into new lands occurred at different intervals, but the pressure pushing on the frontier line was always there. The thirteen states of the new nation in 1789 numbered 27 by 1843, and the national domain doubled in size as well. Seemingly unsurpassable natural barriers gave way as transportation improvements and better communication linked distances together. Steamboats, canals, railroads, and telegraphs overcame mountains and rivers. The federal government assisted this westward motion, sending the Corps of Topographical Engineers to observe, collect scientific samples, and map the West. The United States Army created roads, bridged rivers, spent money promoting local economies, and drove away the Native Americans living in many areas. Recessions following financial panics in 1819 and 1837 sent many Americans westward, to evade creditors and start over. Once the recessions ended, even more people moved west, confident of their future prosperity. The desire for land was widespread, with every farmer, artisan, and laborer wanting his own farm and the status accompanying ownership. Land ownership was a sign of success; you were independent, under no one's control. Independence meant virtue as well, and meant you could be a contributing member of the Republic. Land was to nineteenth-century Americans what owning a house or getting a college degree meant to their descendents in the twentieth and twenty-first centuries.

By the 1840s, popular ideology reinforced our natural tendency to expand westward. We always believed that our form of government and our way of life were superior to all others. We mistakenly believed, every time there was a revolution in Europe or a newly independent nation in South America; that they were copying our republican example. Thomas Jefferson declared that our republic was a "standing monument and example" to freedom-loving people across the globe. Our federal republic was the vanguard of civilization, and we made sure everyone knew. Francis Trollope, English visitor and frequent critic of the nineteenth-century American way of life, reported there was a universal opinion that "the American government was the best in the World." We believed in American exceptionalism and our special sense of mission; we believed that our nation was a beacon of liberty for all other countries, here to guide them out of darkness. The United States thus had a moral responsibility to extend the boundaries of freedom, to spread our unique vision of liberty to other lands, to expand blessed republicanism. Create "an empire for liberty," thundered Congressman Stephen Douglas of Illinois. "We are the nation of human progress," claimed newspaperman John L. O'Sullivan. The commonly expressed attitude was that we can lead other nations and peoples to democracy by example or conquest, because it is our duty to regenerate the backwards peoples. It is our **Manifest Destiny**. This 1840s attitude—that continental expansionism was our unique national Manifest Destiny, and proof of national greatness-was always linked to progress. It served to justify our conquest of the North American continent during this decade.

Americans widely supported Manifest Destiny, but disagreed on specific targets or a timetable for expansion. Many Southerners wanted to annex Texas once she declared independence in 1836. John O'Sullivan and many Northerners longed to detach Canada from Great Britain. Canadian rebels raised funds, collected weapons, and received sanctuary in Great Lakes states, and the United States and Great Britain nearly came to blows while determining the boundary of Maine. Oregon was another hot spot for expansion, attracting American farmers after early settlers reported its rich soil and mild climate. Farmers left the Midwest, to escape the frost, the snow, and the flooding rivers. Merchants wanted control of California and the port of San Francisco to tap into the markets of China. Missourians eyed Santa Fe, where trade between American merchants and local citizens along the Santa Fe Trail brought millions of dollars in Spanish/Mexican silver into the United States economy. Some Americans believed Manifest Destiny should be peaceful, that other peoples will see the benefits of republican rule and voluntarily join us. O'Sullivan believed that these lands would be ours by infiltration; that Americans would settle in them and then seek both independence and later annexation to the United States. Other citizens favored forceful conquest of contiguous lands, even if this meant war with Mexico or Great Britain. Generally, western advocates of Manifest Destiny were more combative and less patient than easterners. Wise politicians saw Manifest Destiny as the means to defuse the slavery issue that was threatening both party and national unity. More land meant space for Southerners to expand and diffuse their rapidly growing slave population, while providing opportunities for Northerners to settle traditional family farms.

Americans justified Manifest Destiny in many other ways. Our growing population needed more land to stay ahead of the rapid increases from natural childbirth and immigration. Indiana Congressman Andrew Kennedy called this population increase the "American Multiplication Table," and insisted we needed land to maintain the Jeffersonian ideal of the yeoman farmer. Rampant Anglophobia promoted expansion also. As a nation we obsessed over British plots and threats against our welfare, a natural outcome from two wars for independence against that nation. But we imagined British sponsored conspiracies everywhere. Southerners were terrified that the British would make Texas a free nation, thus threatening slavery in the American South. Northerners sounded alarms over imagined British plots to seize all of Oregon, as well as California. Fears of being hemmed in by the British gave expansionism a new sense of urgency in the 1840s. One of the missions of Colonel Stephen Watts Kearny's 1845 expedition across the Great Plains was to demonstrate to Great Britain our ability to enforce our claim to Oregon. Other advocates claimed we had a duty to make the land fruitful, and the current inhabitants-Native Americans and Mexicans-were not doing so. From our standpoint, since the British were trapping furs in Oregon they were not even fulfilling God's mission to cultivate the earth. This, of course, ignored the numbers of Native Americans who were farmers, but we had always ignored anything that didn't fit into our chosen explanations.

Racism was always present in national justifications for Manifest Destiny. Since land hunger seized the first colonists, Native Americans were deemed inferior. We praised the Mexicans when they first declared independence, convinced they were emulating our republic. Racial prejudices increased with contact between the nations, and as United States' greed for Mexican possessions increased. By the 1840s Americans condemned Mexicans as inferiors because of their mixed-blood racial ancestry, denounced them as intellectually inferior because they did not have public schools, and dismissed them as morally inferior because of their Catholicism. Even the bard of democracy, Walt Whitman, attacked Mexico, declaring "What has miserable, inefficient Mexico-with her superstition, her burlesque upon freedom, her actual tyranny by the few over the many-what has she to do with the great mission to people the new world with a noble race? Be it ours to achieve that mission!" Joel R. Poinsett, our ambassador to Mexico during the Jackson Administration, denounced the Mexican aristocracy as "ignorant and immoral"; the peasants live under the sway of "gross superstition," and the Catholic Church practices a combination of "pagan and Christian rites." We did not view this as racism, but as the inevitable march of history. It was inevitable that inferior races would disappear as the United States expanded, because that always occurred during the march of civilization. The famous painting by John Gast titled "American Progress" demonstrates this idea: as Columbia advances from the developed cities of the United States in the east, barbaric animals and Indians fall back, while farms, schools, technology, and other signs of civilization follow in her footsteps.

The 1840s saw aggressive promotion of continental expansion. Richard Henry Dana's book, *Two Years Before the Mast*, promoted the natural wonders of California to many Americans. John C. Fremont explored the Far West during 1842 and 1843 for the United States Army Corps of Topographical Engineers. His official reports promoted westward settlement by noting water supplies, good pasture, and woods, as well as the best routes west for wagons. Newspaper editors, however, led the way. The creation of the penny press provided freedom from party requirements, allowing them to rely on money from advertisements and circulation, and thus to take positions on issues that the public embraced sooner than politicians. John L. O'Sullivan at *The New York Morning News*, James Gordon Bennett at *The New York Herald*, and Moses Beach at the *New York Sun* all pushed empire-building and America's mission, because this issue sold newspapers. These men hammered home the idea that national expansion was inevitable, overcoming older views that our nation had limits. Earlier leaders believed that a country could grow too large to be governed as a republic; in fact President Monroe as late as 1824 believed all areas west of the Rocky Mountains would be independent sister republics rather than part of the United States.

In the end, the United States took over parts of Oregon, Texas, California, and the new Southwest. Despite calls for war to take possession of the Pacific coast all the way north to Alaska, the Polk administration negotiated a settlement with Great Britain, dividing the Oregon territory along the 49th parallel. Mexico allowed Americans to settle in their northern province called Texas, starting in 1821, but within two years the numbers of legal and illegal "Texians" were outnumbering the native-born Tejanos. By 1835 they outnumbered the Tejanos seven to one. Disagreeing with Mexican authorities over slavery, religion, and free-trade issues, Texas fought for its independence. Tejanos and Texians combined efforts to win this war in 1836.

Did all groups benefit from our superior civilization and government enveloping them? Natives in areas formerly under Mexican control faced new pressures to abandon their lands to incoming Americans, while tribes previously transplanted by the United States government's actions were forced to leave their "guaranteed" lands in Kansas. Western discoveries of gold and silver increased travel and commerce across the plains, causing new problems for the Native Americans living there. Trade routes and hunting grounds were disrupted, and animals they relied upon for food were slaughtered; they themselves were exposed to deadly diseases. These attacks on their lives led to confrontation and conflict with the Army. Manifest Destiny "justified" the destruction of tribal organizations, the theft of lands, confinement to ever-shrinking reservations, and even genocide. Tejanos also suffered, despite risking their lives and fortunes with the Texians during the Texas War for Independence. They were beaten, murdered, deprived of their lands and legal rights, and eventually driven out of Texas altogether. Entire Tejano communities were uprooted from lands they owned for generations, and expelled from the country. Those who remained faced violence and abuse, especially from the Texas Rangers, who officially accepted the task of keeping "Mexicans in their place." Mexican citizens in the newly conquered lands of the new Southwest and California fared poorly. The Treaty of Guadalupe Hidalgo promised they would be "maintained and protected in the free enjoyment of their liberty and property, and secured in the free exercise of religion." But the new Anglo majority quickly attacked the Mexicans, persecuted them for not abandoning their Catholic religion and becoming Protestants. American courts disallowed land titles held for centuries, and discriminatory laws excluded them from many professions, including mining for gold in California. Men were routinely murdered and women abused, and people thrown off lands with no means to provide for themselves, forcing some Mexicans to resist. Social bandits robbed from the rich Americans who stole their lands and gave to newly destitute Mexican poor, becoming heroes to the oppressed minority. Despite similar vigilante actions in New Mexico and Texas, the Mexican citizens of the "best form of government on earth" continued to lose their lands and their guaranteed rights.

How did Manifest Destiny impact Mexico? The Mexican War was one of the great tragedies in its national history, a blow to national morale and a loss of half of the national domain. To this day Mexicans view Manifest Destiny as a graceful way to justify something unjustifiable, and refer to the Mexican War as "the United States Invasion." From their standpoint the secession of Texas was illegal, and the United States' annexation of Texas in 1845 violated the 1828 border treaty between the two nations. In this treaty the United States fully acknowledged Mexico's absolute sovereignty over Texas. Even the start of the Mexican War was a duplicitous trap from the Mexican view. When President Polk ordered General Zachary Taylor's Army south of the Nueces River, he entered an area populated almost entirely by Tejanos. This land between the Rio Grande and Nueces River was never previously considered part of Texas—except by Texas' government after 1836, which also claimed the eastern half of New Mexico as well. Thus, moving elements of the United States Army into this region was not only an invasion of Mexico, but a trap as well. If Mexico defended its land it would be accused of firing the first shots, of being the aggressor who started the war. The "United States Invasion" began, and some historians argue Mexico never recovered. California, New Mexico, and the rest of the new Southwest fell to the United States during the Mexican War of 1846-1848. This war cost the United States treasury over $100 million, and took the lives of 13,000 American and 20,000 Mexican participants.

This was our first foreign war, and it was the first newspaper war. Newspaper correspondents such as George Wilkins Kendall reported events to an eager public, and many troops sent regular dispatches home (e.g., sketches from Captain Tobin's knapsack) to their local papers as well. These reports reinforced popular views of Manifest Destiny. They reflected views that Mexicans were inferior to Americans, that "they have few of the instincts that govern superior races," that they "lack courage and discipline" but their eyes are "cold-blooded and treacherous." After the war, numerous books of poetry and history reminded readers of our Manifest Destiny and the heroic nature of the war.

Considering the Evidence in the Readings

In this chapter you will hear different Americans' beliefs about what Manifest Destiny means, and what this interpretation justifies the United States to do on the North American continent. Closely examine these arguments for what the Americans believe to be obvious truths, and what arguments they believe they must justify. You will also hear from some of the "lucky people" on the receiving end of Manifest Destiny. Compare their views on the benefits of American expansion with the earlier proponents.

Document 10.1 John L. O'Sullivan Proclaims Our Manifest Destiny, July 1845

John L. O'Sullivan was one of the foremost promoters of the doctrine of Manifest Destiny. Born of American parents in Europe in 1813, he received an MA from Columbia College, and was later licensed to practice law in New York. But politics interested him most, and in 1837 at the age of 23 he founded the *United States Magazine and Democratic Review* (and in 1844 co-founded the *New York Morning News* with Samuel Tilden). Officially the *Democratic Review* promoted America's "democratic genius," and as such the journal was both a Democratic Party mouthpiece and an outlet for Hawthorne, Poe, Whittier, Emerson, Whitman, and other major United States writers. Most of all, it was a mouthpiece for O'Sullivan's views that America's mission was to spread democracy across the entire continent, using American institutions and values to add Canada, Oregon, and California to the Union. He coined the phrase "Manifest Destiny" in the following selection from the journal. He was later involved in filibustering activities in Cuba, and was a confidant of both the Polk and Pierce administrations. How does O'Sullivan define Manifest Destiny? What justification does he provide for the annexation of Texas? How does he justify expansion into the rest of Mexico's North American possessions? How would he answer charges that American expansion is solely motivated by greed?

Texas is now ours. Already, before these words are written, her Convention has undoubtedly ratified the acceptance, by her Congress, of our proffered invitation into the Union; and made the requisite changes in her already republican form of constitution to adopt it to its future federal relations. Her star and her stripe may already be said to have taken their place in the glorious blazon of our common nationality; and the sweep of our eagle's wing already includes within its circuit the wide extent of her fair and fertile land. She is no longer to us a mere geographical space—a certain combination of coast, plain, mountain, valley, forest and stream. She is no longer to us a mere country on the map. She comes within the dear and sacred designation of Our Country; no longer a "*pays*," she is a part of "*la patrie*," and that which is at once a sentiment and a virtue, Patriotism, already begins to thrill for her too within the national heart. It is time then that all should cease to treat her as alien, and even adverse—cease to denounce and vilify all and everything connected with her accession—cease to thwart and oppose the remaining steps for its consummation; or where such efforts are felt to be unavailing, at least to embitter the hour of reception by all the most ungracious frowns of aversion and words of unwelcome. There has been enough of all this. It has had its fitting day during the period when, in common with every other possible question of practical policy that can arise, it unfortunately became one of the leading topics of party division, of presidential electioneering. But that period has passed, and with it let its prejudices and its passions, its discords and its denunciations, pass away too. The next session of Congress will see the representatives of the new young State in their places in both our halls of national legislation, side by side with those of the old Thirteen. Let their reception into "the family" be frank, kindly, and cheerful, as befits such an occasion, as comports not less with our own self-respect than patriotic duty towards them. Ill betide those foul birds that delight to file their own nest, and disgust the ear with perpetual discord of ill-omened croak.

Why, were other reasoning wanting, in favor of now elevating this question of the reception of Texas into the Union, out of the lower region of our past party dissensions, up to its proper level of a high and broad nationality, it surely is to be found, found abundantly, in the manner in which other nations have undertaken to intrude themselves into it, between us and the proper parties to the case, in a spirit of hostile interference against us, for the avowed object of thwarting our policy and hampering our power, limiting our greatness and checking the fulfilment of our manifest destiny to overspread the continent allotted by Providence for the free development of our yearly multiplying millions. This we have seen done by England, our old rival and enemy; and by France, strangely coupled with her against us, under the influence of the Anglicism strongly tinging the policy of her present prime minister, Guizot. The zealous activity with which this effort to defeat us was pushed by the representatives of those governments, together with the character of intrigue accompanying it, fully constituted that case of foreign interference, which Mr. Clay himself declared should, and would unite us all in maintaining the common cause of our country against the foreigner and the foe. . . .

It is wholly untrue, and unjust to ourselves, the pretence that the Annexation has been a measure of spoliation, unrightful and unrighteous—of military conquest under forms of peace and law—of territorial aggrandizement at the expense of justice, and justice due by a double sanctity to the weak. This view of the question is wholly unfounded, and has been before so amply refuted in these pages, as well as in a thousand other modes, that we shall not again dwell upon it. The independence of Texas was complete and absolute. It was an independence, not only in fact but of right. No obligation of duty towards Mexico tended in the least degree to restrain our right to effect the desired recovery of the fair province once our own—whatever motives of policy might have prompted a more deferential consideration of her feelings and her pride, as involved in the question. If Texas became peopled with an American population, it was by no contrivance of our government, but on the express invitation of that of Mexico herself; accompanied with such guaranties of State independence, and the maintenance of a federal system analogous to our own, as constituted a compact fully justifying the strongest measures of redress on the part of those afterwards deceived in this guaranty, and sought to be enslaved under the yoke imposed by its violation. She was released, rightfully and absolutely released, from all Mexican allegiance, or duty of cohesion to the Mexican political body, by the acts and fault of Mexico herself, and Mexico alone. There never was a clearer case. It was not revolution; it was

From *United States Magazine and Democratic Review*, July, 1845.

resistance to revolution; and resistance under such circumstances as left independence the necessary resulting state, caused by the abandonment of those with whom her former federal association had existed. What then can be more preposterous than all this clamor by Mexico and the Mexican interest, against Annexation, as a violation of any rights of hers, any duties of ours? . . .

Nor is there any just foundation for the charge that Annexation is a great pro-slavery measure—calculated to increase and perpetuate that institution. Slavery had nothing to do with it. Opinions were and are greatly divided, both at the North and South, as to the influence to be exerted by it on Slavery and the Slave States. That it will tend to facilitate and hasten the disappearance of Slavery from all the northern tier of the present Slave States, cannot surely admit of serious question. The greater value in Texas of the slave labor now employed in those States, must soon produce the effect of draining off that labor southwardly, by the same unvarying law that bids water descend the slope that invites it. Every new Slave State in Texas will make at least one Free State from among those in which that institution now exists—to say nothing of those portions of Texas on which slavery cannot spring and grow—to say nothing of the far more rapid growth of new States in the free West and Northwest, as these fine regions are overspread by the emigration fast flowing over them from Europe, as well as from the Northern and Eastern States of the Union as it exists. On the other hand, it is undeniably much gained for the cause of the eventual voluntary abolition of slavery, that it should have been thus drained off towards the only outlet which appeared to furnish much probability of the ultimate disappearance of the negro race from our borders. The Spanish-Indian-American populations of Mexico, Central America and South America, afford the only receptacle capable of absorbing that race whenever we shall be prepared to slough it off—to emancipate it from slavery, and (simultaneously necessary) to remove it from the midst of our own. Themselves already of mixed and confused blood, and free from the "prejudices" which among us so insuperably forbid the social amalgamation which can alone elevate the Negro race out of a virtually servile degradation even though legally free, the regions occupied by those populations must strongly attract the black race in that direction; and as soon as the destined hour of emancipation shall arrive, will relieve the question of one of its worst difficulties, if not absolutely the greatest.

No—Mr. Clay was right when he declared that Annexation was a question with which slavery had nothing to do. The country which was the subject of Annexation in this case, from its geographical position and relations, happens to be—or rather the portion of it now actually settled, happens to be—a slave country. But a similar process might have taken place in proximity to a different section of our Union; and indeed there is a great deal of Annexation yet to take place, within the life of the present generation, along the whole line of our northern border. Texas has been absorbed into the Union in the inevitable fulfilment of the general law which is rolling our population westward; the connexion of which with that ratio of growth in population which is destined within a hundred years to swell our numbers to the enormous population of *two hundred and fifty millions* (if not more), is too evident to leave us in doubt of the manifest design of Providence in regard to the occupation of this continent. It was disintegrated from Mexico in the natural course of events, by a process perfectly legitimate on its own part, blameless on ours; and in which all the censures due to wrong, perfidy and folly, rest on Mexico alone. And possessed as it was by a population which was in truth but a colonial detachment from our own, and which was still bound by myriad ties of the very heart-strings to its old relations, domestic and political, their incorporation into the Union was not only inevitable, but the most natural, right and proper thing in the world—and it is only astonishing that there should be any among ourselves to say it nay. . . . .

California will, probably, next fall away from the loose adhesion which, in such a country as Mexico, holds a remote province in a slight equivocal kind of dependence on the metropolis. Imbecile and distracted, Mexico never can exert any real governmental authority over such a country. The impotence of the one and the distance of the other, must make the relation one of virtual independence; unless, by stunting the province of all natural growth, and forbidding that immigration which can alone develope its capabilities and fulfil the purposes of its creation, tyranny may retain a military dominion which is no government in the legitimate sense of the term. In the case of California this is now impossible. The Anglo-Saxon foot is already on its borders. Already the advance guard of the irresistible army of Anglo-Saxon emigration has begun to pour down upon it, armed with the plough and the rifle, and marking its trail with schools and colleges, courts and representative halls, mills and meeting-houses. A population will soon be in actual occupation of California, over which it will be idle for Mexico to dream of dominion. They will necessarily become independent. All this without agency of our government, without responsibility of our people—in the natural flow of events, the spontaneous working of principles, and the adaptation of the tendencies and wants of the human race to the elemental circumstances in the midst of which they find themselves placed. And they will have a right to independence—to self-government—to the possession of the homes conquered from the wilderness by their own labors and dangers, sufferings and sacrifices—a better and a truer right than the artificial title of sovereignty in Mexico a thousand miles distant, inheriting from Spain a title good only against those who have none better. Their right to independence will be the natural right of self-government belonging to any community strong enough to maintain it—distinct in position, origin and character, and free from any mutual obligations of membership of a common political body, binding it to others by the duty of loyalty and compact of public faith. This will be their title to independence; and by this title, there can be no doubt that the population now fast streaming down upon California will both assert and maintain that independence. Whether they will then attach themselves to our Union or not, is not to be predicted with any certainty. Unless the projected rail-road across the continent to the Pacific be carried into effect, perhaps they may not; though even in that case, the day is not distant when the Empires of the Atlantic and Pacific would again flow together into one, as soon as their inland border should approach each other. But that great work, colossal as appears the plan on its first suggestion, cannot remain long unbuilt. Its necessity for this very purpose of binding and holding together in its iron clasp our fast settling Pacific region with that of the Mississippi valley—the natural facility of the—the case with which any amount of labor for the construction can be drawn in from the overcrowded populations of Europe, to be paid in the lands made valuable by the progress of the work itself—and its immense utility to the commerce of the world with the whole eastern coast of Asia, alone almost sufficient for the support of such a road— these considerations give assurance that the day cannot be distant which shall witness the conveyance of the representatives from Oregon and California to Washington within less time than a few years ago was devoted to a similar journey by those from Ohio; while the magnetic telegraph will enable the editors of the "San Francisco Union," the "Astoria Evening Post," or the "Nootka Morning News" to set up in type the first half of the President's Inaugural, before the echoes of the latter half shall have died away beneath the lofty porch of the Capitol, as spoken from his lips.

Away, then, with all idle French talk of *balances of power* on the American Continent. There is no growth in Spanish America! Whatever progress of population there may be in the British Canadas, is only for their own early severance of their present colonial relation to the little island three thousand miles across the Atlantic; soon to be followed by Annexation, and destined to swell the still accumulating momentum of our progress. And whosoever may hold the balance, though they should cast into the opposite scale all the bayonets and cannon, not only of France and England, but of Europe entire, how would it kick the beam against the simple solid weight of the two hundred and fifty, or three hundred millions—and American millions—destined to gather beneath the flutter of the stripes and stars, in the fast hastening year of the Lord 1945!

Document 10.2 Senator Thomas Hart Benton Explains the Mission of the Anglo-Saxon Race

Thomas Hart Benton was born in North Carolina, and settled later in Tennessee, where he became a member of legislature, raised a regiment of volunteers, and fought in the War of 1812. He moved to St. Louis, Missouri and established a newspaper. Benton served as United States Senator from 1821 to 1851. He was known as a strong nationalist and determined opponent of nullification. Benton was also a passionate advocate of American expansion and popular sovereignty. He was the father-in-law of John C. Fremont, the "Pathfinder" who charted western trails and participated in the military conquest of California during the Mexican War. Benton strongly supported the annexation of Texas; as did most Missourians, but he personally saw Manifest Destiny as a way to diffuse the slavery issue threatening national unity. Why does Senator Benton believe we are superior to all other nations and races? How does American superiority justify expansion and conquest? Are there limits to where the United States can expand? According to the Senator's speech, how should we treat other nations and races?

Since the dispersion of man upon earth, I know of no human event, past or to come, which promises a greater, and more beneficent change upon earth than the arrival of the van of the Caucasian race (the Celtic-Anglo-Saxon division) upon the border of the sea which washes the shore of the eastern Asia. The Mongolian, or Yellow race, is there, four hundred millions in number, spreading almost to Europe; a race once the foremost of the human family in the arts of civilization, but torpid and stationary for thousands of years. It is a race far above the Ethiopian, or Black—above the Malay, or Brown, (if we must admit five races)—and above the American Indian, or Red; it is a race far above all these, but still, far below the White; and, like all the rest, must receive an impression from the superior race whenever they come in contact. It would seem that the White race alone received the divine command, to subdue and replenish the earth! for it is the only race that has obeyed it—the only one that hunts out new and distant lands, and even a New World, to subdue and replenish. Starting from western Asia, taking Europe for their field, and the Sun for their guide, and leaving the Mongolians behind, they arrived, after many ages, on the shores of the Atlantic, which they lit up with the lights of science and religion, and adorned with the useful and the elegant arts. Three and a half centuries ago, this race, in obedience to the great command, arrived in the New World, and found new lands to subdue and replenish. For a long time it was confined to the border of the new field, (I now mean the Celtic-Anglo-Saxon division;) and even fourscore years ago the philosophic Burke was considered a rash man because he said the English colonists would top the Alleganies, and descend into the valley of the Mississippi, and occupy without parchment if the Crown refused to make grants of land. What was considered a rash declaration eighty years ago, is old history, in our young country, at this day. Thirty years ago I said the same thing of the Rocky Mountains and the Columbia: it was ridiculed then: it is becoming history to-day. The venerable Mr. Macon has often told me that he remembered a line low down in North Carolina, fixed by a royal governor as a boundary between the whites and the Indians: where is that boundary now? The van of the Caucasian now top the Rocky Mountains, and spread down to the shores of the Pacific. In a few years a great population will grow up there, luminous with the accumulated lights of European and American civilization. Their presence in such a position cannot be without its influence upon eastern Asia. The sun of civilization must shine across the sea: socially and commercially, the van of the Caucasians, and the rear of the Mongolians, must intermix. They must talk together, and trade together, and marry together. Commerce is a great civilizer—social intercourse as great—and marriage greater. The White and Yellow races can marry together, as well as eat and trade together. Moral and intellectual superiority will do the rest: the White race will take the ascendant, elevating what is susceptible of improvement—wearing out what is not. The Red race has disappeared from the Atlantic coast: the tribes that resisted civilization, met extinction. This is a cause of lamentation with many. For my part, I cannot murmur at what seems to be the effect of divine law. I cannot repine that this Capitol has replaced the wigwam—this Christian people, replaced the savages—white matrons, the red squaws—and that such men as Washington, Franklin, and Jefferson, have taken the place of Powhattan, Opechonecanough, and other red men, howsoever respectable they may have been as savages. Civilization, or extinction, has been the fate of all people who have found themselves in the track of the advancing Whites, and civilization, always the preference of the Whites, has been pressed as an object, while extinction has followed as a consequence of its resistance. The Black and the Red races have often felt their ameliorating influence. The Yellow race, next to themselves in the scale of mental and moral excellence, and in the beauty of form, once their superiors in the useful and elegant arts, and in learning, and still respectable though stationary; this race cannot fail to receive a new impulse from the approach of the Whites, improved so much since so many ages ago they left the western borders of Asia. The apparition of the van of the Caucasian race, rising upon them in the east after having left them on the west, and after having completed the circumnavigation of the globe, must wake up and rereanimate the torpid body of old Asia. Our position and policy will commend us to their hospitable reception: political considerations will aid the action of social and commercial influences. Pressed upon by the great Powers of Europe—the same that press upon us—they must in our approach hail the advent of friends, not of foes—of benefactors, not of invaders. The moral and

---

From *Congressional Globe,* 29th Congress, 1st Session, May 28, 1846.

intellectual superiority of the White race will do the rest: and thus, the youngest people, and the newest land, will become the reviver and the regenerator of the oldest.

It is in this point of view, and as acting upon the social, political, and religious condition of Asia, and giving a new point of departure to her ancient civilization, that I look upon the settlement of the Columbia river by the van of the Caucasian race as the most momentous human event in the history of man since his dispersion over the face of the earth.

Document 10.3 President Polk Plans for War with Mexico

James K. Polk was the perfect president for an expansion-minded nation. He never doubted that American institutions were superior to all others, or that these institutions and the American people would spread across the North American continent. Polk placed himself at the head of the continental crusade. As early as July 1845 he ordered General Zachary Taylor to move into the disputed border region between the Rio Grande and the Nueces Rivers. Taylor's 4,000-man army eventually marched to the mouth of the Rio Grande in March 1846, and while United States naval vessels blockaded the river, his men built a fort and targeted their cannons across the Rio Grande on the buildings of Matamoros, Mexico. Polk also sent secret orders in July 1845 to Commodore Sloat, commander of the United States Pacific fleet, instructing him to seize San Francisco if a war broke out. By May 8, 1846, the President decided to force the issue with Mexico. President Polk kept a daily diary of White House happenings and meetings, two days of which make up this document. On what grounds is Polk proposing to ask Congress for a declaration of war on the morning of May 9? What happens to change his request to Congress? On what grounds will he demand that Congress declare war?

Saturday, 9th May, 1846. —The Cabinet held a regular meeting today; all the members were present. I brought up the Mexican question, and the question of what was the duty of the administration in the present state of our relations with that country. The subject was very fully discussed. All agreed that if the Mexican forces at Matamoras committed any act of hostility on General Taylor's forces I should immediately send a message to Congress recommending an immediate declaration of war. I stated to the Cabinet that up to this time, as we knew, we had heard of no open act of aggression by the Mexican army, but that the danger was imminent that such acts would be committed. I said that in my opinion we had ample cause of war, and that it was impossible that we could stand in *statu quo*, or that I thought I could remain silent much longer, that I thought it was my duty to send a message to Congress very soon and recommend definite measures. I told them that I thought I ought to make such a message by Tuesday next, that the country was excited and impatient on the subject, and if I failed to do so I would not be doing my duty I then propounded the distinct question to the Cabinet, and took their opinions individually, whether I should make a message to Congress on Tuesday, and whether in that message I should recommend a declaration of war against Mexico. All except the Secretary of the Navy gave their advice in the affirmative. Mr. Bancroft dissented but said if any act of hostility should be committed by the Mexican forces he was then in favour of immediate war. Mr. Buchanan said he would feel better satisfied in his course if the Mexican forces had or should commit any act of hostility, but that as matters stood we had ample cause of war against Mexico, and gave his assent to the measure. . . .

About 6 O'Clock p.m. Gen. R. Jones, the Adjutant-General of the army, called and handed to me dispatches received from General Taylor by the Southern mail which had just arrived, giving information that a part of the Mexican army had crossed the Del Norte and attacked and killed and captured two companies of dragoons of General Taylor's army consisting of 63 officers and men. . . . I immediately

---

From Polk: *The Diary of a President*, Longmans, Green and Company, 1929.

summoned the Cabinet to meet at 7 1/2 O'Clock this evening. The Cabinet accordingly assembled at that hour; all the members present. The subject of the dispatch received this evening from General Taylor, as well as the state of our relations with Mexico, were fully considered. The Cabinet were unanimously of opinion, and it was so agreed, that a message should be sent to Congress on Monday . . . recommending vigorous & prompt measures to enable the Executive to prosecute the war.

Monday, 11th May, 1846.—I refused to see company generally this morning. I carefully revised my message on the Mexican question. . . .

I addressed [notes] to Senators Cass and Benton this morning requesting them to call. Gen. Cass called first. The message was read to him and he highly approved it. Col. Benton called before Gen. Cass left, and I gave him the copy of the message and he retired to an adjoining room and read it. After he had read it I had a conversation with him alone. I found he did not approve it in all its parts. He was willing to vote men and money for defense of our territory, but was not prepared to make aggressive war on Mexico. He disapproved the marching of the army from Corpus Christi to the left bank of the Del Norte, but said he had never said so to the public. I had a full conversation with him, and he left without satisfying me that I could rely on his support . . . further than the mere defence of our territory. I inferred, too, from his conversation that he did not think the territory of the United States extended West of the Nueces River.

At 12 O'Clock I sent my message to Congress. It was a day of great anxiety with me. Between 5 & 6 O'Clock p.m. Mr. Slidell, United States Minister to Mexico, called and informed me that the House of Representatives had passed a bill carrying out the recommendations of the message by a vote of 173 ayes to 14 noes, and that the Senate had adjourned after a debate without coming to a decision.

My private secretary brought me a note from Col. Benton desiring information as to the number of men and amount of money required to defend the country . . . The Secretaries of War and State called a few minutes before 8 O'Clock but before I had consulted the former in relation to Col. Benton's note, Col. Benton came in . . . I told him if the war [was] recognized by Congress, that with a large force on land and sea I thought it could be speedily terminated. Col. Benton said that the Ho. Repts. [House of Representatives] had passed a bill today declaring war in only two hours, and that one and a half hours of that time had been occupied in reading the documents which accompanied my message, and that in his opinion in the nineteenth century war should not be declared without full discussion and much more consideration than had been given to it in the Ho. Repts. Mr. Buchanan then remarked that war already existed by the act of Mexico herself and therefore did not require much deliberation to satisfy all that we ought promptly and vigorously to meet it. Mr. Marcy and Mr. Buchanan discussed the subject for some time with Mr. Benton, but without any change of opinion. . . .

Document 10.4 President Polk's War Message to Congress

The previous document established that President Polk was prepared to declare war as early as May 8, 1846. The following is the complete text of his May 11th war message to Congress. On what grounds does President Polk want Congress to declare war? Who has provoked this war, and how, according to the President? Is this a truthful statement by President Polk? Is he being honest when he says we tried to establish peace with Mexico? What are the weaknesses of his arguments?

To the Senate and House of Representatives:

The existing state of the relations between the United States and Mexico renders it proper that I should bring the subject to the consideration of Congress. In my message at the commencement of your present session the state of these relations; the causes which led to the suspension of diplomatic intercourse between the two countries in March, 1845, and the long-continued and unredressed wrongs and injuries committed by the Mexican Government on citizens of

War message of May 11, 1846.

the United States in their persons and property were briefly set forth.

As the facts and opinions which were then laid before you were care fully considered, I can not better express my present convictions of the condition of affairs up to that time than by referring you to that communication. The strong desire to establish peace with Mexico on liberal and honorable terms, and the readiness of this Government to regulate and adjust our boundary and other causes of difference with that power on such fair and equitable principles as would lead to permanent relations of the most friendly nature, induced me in September last to seek the reopening of diplomatic relations between the two countries. Every measure adopted on our part had for its object the furtherance of these desired results. In communicating to Congress a succinct statement of the injuries which we had suffered from Mexico, and which have been accumulating during a period of more than twenty years, every expression that could tend to inflame the people of Mexico or defeat or delay a pacific result was carefully avoided. An envoy of the United States repaired to Mexico with full powers to adjust every existing difference. But though present on the Mexican soil by agreement between the two Governments, invested with full powers, and bearing evidence of the most friendly dispositions, his mission has been unavailing. The Mexican Government not only refused to receive him or listen to his propositions, but after a long-continued series of menaces have at last invaded our territory and shed the blood of our fellow-citizens on our own soil.

It now becomes my duty to state more in detail the origin, progress, and failure of that mission. In pursuance of the instructions given in September last, an inquiry was made on the 13th of October, 1845, in the most friendly terms, through our consul in Mexico, of the minister for foreign affairs, whether the Mexican Government would receive an envoy from the United States intrusted with full powers to adjust all the questions in dispute between the two Governments, with the assurance that should the answer be in the affirmative such an envoy would be immediately dispatched to Mexico. The Mexican minister on the 15th of October gave an affirmative answer to this inquiry, requesting at the same time that our naval force at Vera Cruz might be withdrawn, lest its continued presence might assume the appearance of menace and coercion pending the negotiations. This force was immediately withdrawn.

On the 10th of November, 1845, Mr. John Slidell, of Louisiana, was commissioned by me as envoy extraordinary and minister plenipotentiary of the United States to Mexico, and was intrusted with full powers to adjust both the questions of the Texas boundary and of indemnification to our citizens. The redress of the wrongs of our citizens naturally and inseparably blended itself with the question of boundary. The settlement of the one question in any correct view of the subject involves that of the other. I could not for a moment entertain the idea that the claims of our much-injured and long-suffering citizens, many of which had existed for more than twenty years, should be postponed or separated from the settlement of the boundary question.

Mr. Slidell arrived at Vera Cruz on the 30th of November, and was courteously received by the authorities of that city. But the Government of General Herrera was then tottering to its fall. The revolutionary party had seized upon the Texas question to effect or hasten its overthrow. Its determination to restore friendly relations with the United States, and to receive our minister to negotiate for the settlement of this question, was violently assailed, and was made the great theme of denunciation against it. The Government of General Herrera, there is good reason to believe, was sincerely desirous to receive our minister; but it yielded to the storm raised by its enemies, and on the 21st of December refused to accredit Mr. Slidell upon the most frivolous pretexts. These are so fully and ably exposed in the note of Mr. Slidell of the 24th of December last to the Mexican minister of foreign relations, herewith transmitted, that I deem it unnecessary to enter into further detail on this portion of the subject. Five days after the date of Mr. Slidell's note General Herrera yielded the Government to General Paredes without a struggle, and on the 30th of December resigned the Presidency. This revolution was accomplished solely by the army, the people having taken little part in the contest; and thus the supreme power in Mexico passed into the hands of a military leader. Determined to leave no effort untried to effect an amicable adjustment with Mexico, I directed Mr. Slidell to present his credentials to the Government of General Paredes and ask to be officially received by him.

There would have been less ground for taking this step had General Paredes come into power by a regular constitutional succession. In that event his administration would have been considered but a mere constitutional continuance of the Government of General Herrera, and the refusal of the latter to receive our minister would have been deemed conclusive unless an intimation had been given by General Paredes of his desire to reverse the decision of his predecessor. But the Government of General Paredes owes its existence to a military revolution, by which the subsisting constitutional authorities had been subverted. The form of government was entirely changed, as well as all the high functionaries by whom it was administered.

Under these circumstances, Mr. Slidell, in obedience to my direction, addressed a note to the Mexican minister of foreign relations, under date of the 1st of March last, asking to be received by that Government in the diplomatic character to which he had been appointed. This minister in his reply, under date of the 12th of March, reiterated the arguments of his predecessor, and in terms that may be considered as giving just grounds of offense to the Government and people of the United States denied the application of Mr. Slidell. Nothing therefore remained for our envoy but to demand his passports and return to his own country.

Thus the Government of Mexico, though solemnly pledged by official acts in October last to receive and accredit an American envoy, violated their plighted faith and refused the offer of a peaceful adjustment of our difficulties. Not only was the offer rejected, but the indignity of its rejection was enhanced by the manifest breach of faith in refusing to admit the envoy who came because they had bound themselves to receive him. Nor can it be said that the offer was fruitless from the want of opportunity of discussing it; our envoy was present on their own soil. Nor can it be ascribed to a want of sufficient powers; our envoy had full powers to adjust every question of difference.

Nor was there room for complaint that our propositions for settlement were unreasonable; permission was not even given our envoy to make any proposition whatever. Nor can it be objected that we, on our part, would not listen to any reasonable terms of their suggestion; the Mexican Government refused all negotiation, and have made no proposition of any kind. In my message at the commencement of the present session I informed you that upon the earnest appeal both of the Congress and convention of Texas I had ordered an efficient military force to take a position between the Nueces and the Del Norte. This had become necessary to meet a threatened invasion of Texas by the Mexican forces, for which extensive military preparations had been made. The invasion was threatened solely because Texas had determined, in accordance with a solemn resolution of the Congress of the United States, to annex herself to our Union, and under these circumstances it was plainly our duty to extend our protection over her citizens and soil.

This force was concentrated at Corpus Christi, and remained there until after I had received such information from Mexico as rendered it probable, if not certain, that the Mexican Government would refuse to receive our envoy. Meantime Texas, by the final action of our Congress, had become an integral part of our Union. The Congress of Texas, by its act of December 19, 1836, had declared the Rio del Norte to be the boundary of that Republic. Its jurisdiction had been extended and exercised beyond the Nueces. The country between that river and the Del Norte had been represented in the Congress and in the convention of Texas, had thus taken part in the act of annexation itself, and is now included within one of our Congressional districts. Our own Congress had, moreover, with great unanimity, by the act approved December 31, 1845, recognized the country beyond the Nueces as a part of our territory by including it within our own revenue system, and a revenue officer to reside within that district has been appointed by and with the advice and consent of the Senate. It became, therefore, of urgent necessity to provide for the defense of that portion of our country. Accordingly, on the 13th of January last instructions were issued to the general in command of these troops to occupy the left bank of the Del Norte. This river, which is the southwestern boundary of the State of Texas, is an exposed frontier. From this quarter invasion was threatened; upon it and in its immediate vicinity, in the judgment of high military experience, are the proper stations for the protecting forces of the Government. In addition to this important consideration, several others occurred to induce this movement. Among these are the facilities afforded by the ports at Brazos Santiago and the mouth of the Del Norte for the reception of supplies by sea, the stronger and more healthful military positions, the convenience for obtaining a ready and a more abundant supply of provisions, water, fuel, and forage, and the advantages which are afforded by the Del Norte in forwarding supplies to such posts as may be established in the interior and upon the Indian frontier.

The movement of the troops to the Del Norte was made by the commanding general under positive instructions to abstain from all aggressive acts toward Mexico or Mexican citizens and to regard the relations between that Republic and the United States as peaceful unless she should declare war or commit acts of hostility indicative of a state of war. He was specially directed to protect private property and respect personal rights.

The Army moved from Corpus Christi on the 11th of March, and on the 28th of that month arrived on the left bank of the Del Norte opposite to Matamoras, where it encamped on a commanding position, which has since been strengthened by the erection of fieldworks. A depot has also been established at Point Isabela, near the Brazos Santiago, 30 miles in rear of the encampment. The selection of his position was necessarily confided to the judgment of the general in command.

The Mexican forces at Matamoras assumed a belligerent attitude, and on the 12th of April General Ampudia, then in command, notified General Taylor to break up his camp within twenty-four hours and to retire beyond the Nueces River, and in the event of his failure to comply with these demands announced that arms, and arms alone, must decide the question. But no open act of hostility was committed until the 14th of April. On that day General Arista, who had succeeded to the command of the Mexican forces, communicated to General Taylor that he considered hostilities commenced and should prosecute them. A party of dragoons of 63 men and officers were on the same day dispatched from the American camp up the Rio del Norte, on its left bank, to ascertain whether the Mexican troops had crossed or were preparing to cross the river, became engaged with a large body of these troops, and after a short affair, in which some 16 were killed and wounded, appear to have been surrounded and compelled to surrender. The grievous wrongs perpetrated by Mexico upon our citizens throughout a long period of years remain unredressed, and solemn treaties pledging her public faith for this redress have been disregarded. A government either unable or unwilling to enforce the execution of such treaties fails to perform one of its plainest duties.

Our commerce with Mexico has been almost annihilated. It was formerly highly beneficial to both nations, but our merchants have been deterred from prosecuting it by the system of outrage and extortion which the Mexican authorities have pursued against them, whilst their appeals through their own Government for indemnity have been made in vain. Our forbearance has gone to such an extreme as to be mistaken in its character. Had we acted with vigor in repelling the insults and redressing the injuries inflicted by Mexico at the commencement, we should doubtless have escaped all the difficulties in which we are now involved.

Instead of this, however, we have been exerting our best efforts to propitiate her good will. Upon the pretext that Texas, a nation as independent as herself, thought proper to unite its destinies with our own she has affected to believe that we have severed her rightful territory, and in official proclamations and manifestoes has repeatedly threatened to make war upon us for the purpose of reconquering Texas. In the meantime we have tried every effort at reconciliation. The cup of forbearance had been exhausted even before the recent information from the frontier of the Del Norte. But now, after reiterated menaces, Mexico has passed the boundary of the United States, has invaded our territory and shed American blood upon the American soil. She has proclaimed that hostilities have commenced, and that the two nations are now at war.

As war exists, and, notwithstanding all our efforts to avoid it, exists by the act of Mexico herself, we are called upon by every consideration of duty and patriotism to vindicate with decision the honor, the rights, and the interests of our country.

Anticipating the possibility of a crisis like that which has arrived, instructions were given in August last, as a precautionary measure against invasion or threatened invasion, authorizing General Taylor, if the emergency required, to accept volunteers, not from Texas only, but from the States of Louisiana, Alabama, Mississippi, Tennessee, and Kentucky, and corresponding letters were addressed to the respective governors of those States. These instructions were repeated, and in January last, soon after the incorporation of Texas into our Union of States, General Taylor was further authorized by the President to make a requisition upon the executive of that State for such of its militia force as may be needed to repel invasion or to secure the country against apprehended invasion. On the 2d day of March he was again reminded, in the event of the approach of any considerable Mexican force, promptly and efficiently to use the authority with which he was clothed to call to him such auxiliary force as he might need. War actually existing and our territory having been invaded, General Taylor, pursuant to authority vested in him by my direction, has called on the governor of Texas for four regiments of State troops, two to be mounted and two to serve on foot, and on the governor of Louisiana for four regiments of infantry to be sent to him as soon as practicable.

In further vindication of our rights and defense of our territory, I involve the prompt action of Congress to recognize the existence of the war, and to place at the disposition of the Executive the means of prosecuting the war with vigor, and thus hastening the restoration of peace. To this end I recommend that authority should be given to call into the public service a large body of volunteers to serve for not less than six or twelve months unless sooner discharged. A volunteer force is beyond question more efficient than any other description of citizen soldiers, and it is not to be doubted that a number far beyond that required would readily rush to the field upon the call of their country. I further recommend that a liberal provision be made for sustaining our entire military force and furnishing it with supplies and munitions of war.

The most energetic and prompt measures and the immediate appearance in arms of a large and overpowering force are recommended to Congress as the most certain and efficient means of bringing the existing collision with Mexico to a speedy and successful termination.

In making these recommendations I deem it proper to declare that it is my anxious desire not only to terminate hostilities speedily, but to bring all matters in dispute between this Government and Mexico to an early and amicable adjustment: and in this view I shall be prepared to renew negotiations whenever Mexico shall be ready to receive propositions or to make propositions of her own . . .

Document 10.5 A Texan Describes Troop Conduct in Mexico

As noted earlier, Americans rushed to volunteer for the fighting. Army regulars complained that the volunteers saw the war as an opportunity to drink, and to rob and kill innocent civilians, and that they resisted both discipline and following orders. There were also reports of cowardice among the volunteers. Volunteer units angrily denied these claims, and claimed they took great care protecting Mexican women from harm. But they did a large share of the fighting, and along with the regulars took part in some of the nastiest fighting—house-to-house resistance in the cities they invaded. New Englander Samuel Chamberlain described the fighting in Monterrey in September 1846. What accounts of the volunteers behavior stand out in the reading?

The Fall of Monterey

At daylight on the morning of the 23rd the column to assault the northern part of the town was formed inside the "Half Moon Battery." They presented a strange and terrific appearance, faces, and clothes all covered with a mixture of mud, mortar, powder and blood, eyes bloodshot, with a hungery savage look which was truly fearful. Their costumes and arms added to the Banditti like effect of the command. There was Rangers dressed in the mountain-man suits of buckskin, in Red shirts, Blue shirts, Mexican leather jackets, and serapas; Louisiana volunteers, each clothed as his fancy dictated, regular Dragoons, Artillery, and Infantry armed with "Kentucky Rifles," double-barrelled shot Guns, Winsor Rifles, Harper's Ferry Muskets, Carbines, Revolvers. Holster Pistols, Sabres, Swords, Axes, and Bowie Knives. A look of determination was on each countenance, as they gazed on the City lying so quiet below. Rumors had reached us of defeat and disaster to our forces that attacked the eastern part of town, that we had met with terrible loss, and that Gen Taylor was even in full retreat for Camargo, leaving us to our Fate. What gave apparrent credence to this rumor, was the quietness that reigned in town and non-appearance of our army toward Walnut Springs. Not a tent or a wagon was in sight. The green, white and red Banner of Mexico floated over the Black Fort, the Cathedral and other places. In the plain to our left near the Rancho San Jeromino we could see a large force of the Enemy's Lancers, and their pickets extended as far as we could see beyond the Citadel. All remained quiet for hours! waiting waiting hungry and savage. Gen. Worth appeared anxious and nervous; he ascended the tower of the Palace, and with his glass scanned the defiant stronghold below. About nine o'cl'k A.M., the nine Pounder captured in Fort Soldado opened on the town, and at ten o'clock a heavy firing that commenced on the eastern side of Monterey informed us that rumor lied! that Taylor was still there! We were organized in two columns, one to take

Samuel Chamberlain, *My Confession: Recollections of a Rogue*, ed. By William Goetzmann [Austin, Texas: Texas State Historical Association, 1965], 92-98.

the right hand street Calle de Monterey under the command of Col. Hays, the other to enter the city to the left by the Calle de Iturbide under Lieut Col. Walker. I was with the latter. Finally the word was given and with a roar like that of wild beasts, the two columns dashed down the hill and entered the city. Our column penetrated as far as the square "Plazuela de la Carne," and then we found ourselves in a hornet's nest; every house was a fort that belched forth a hurricane of ball; the flat roofs surmounted by breastworks of sand bags were covered with soldiers who could pour down a distructive fire in safety; the windows of iron barred "Rejas" were each vomiting forth fire and death. On we went at a run, stung to madness at not being able to retaliate on our hidden foes, we gained a large square, the "Plaza de la Capella," when artillery opened on us with canester! The heavy stone wall of a churchyard was embrasured for their guns, while a scaffold was erected from which infantry were posted who kept up a constant fire. Our men were falling fast, and not a Mexican hit; they were all under cover, our fire was only waisted on their stone walls. I was close to Col. Walker when a column of Mexican Infantry came round the corner of the church and at double quick charged us with the bayonet. We were in a tight fix, not twenty rangers were in the square. Fortuneatly our arms were all loaded and we made every shot tell, but we were compelled to give ground; our men flocked in, and two six P'drs of McCall's Battery came up at a gallop, unlimbered within twenty yard[s] of the Mexican line, and gave them double doses of canister. This proved too much for our brave foes; they gave back and soon run, we close at their heels, and in the rush we captured the church of Santer Maria and the fortified yard. The enemy succeeded in hauling off their guns, their infantry charge was probably made to cover this movement.

We halted under shelter of the walls of the church, and could hear the explosion of firearms and shouts on the street to our right, giving us to understand the resistance that the other column was meeting with. Our wounded were taken care of by surgeons who kept with us, the Mexican's were quietly disposed of by those humane fellows, the Texan Rangers.

Reforming, we dashed around the church, and found the street barracaded, and the same infernal fire was again poured in to us: we rushed over the breastwork, and wild yells charged up the street, men dropping every moment. It would have required Salamanders to withstand the fire that scorch [ed] us on every side. Our run came down to a walk, Our walk to a general seeking of shelter in doors and passages. I

stuck to Walker, who had gained my boyish esteem in speaking a kind and cheerful word to me in the terrible storming of Independence Hill. About a dozen of us with Col. Walker were hugging a door in mighty close, when a volly was fired through it from the inside. Three of our party fell. By order of the Colonel, two men with axes hewed away at the stout oak plank. Another volly was fired, when one of the axemen with a deep curse dropped his axe, a ball had broke the bone of his arm. Walker took his place, and soon the barrier gave way, and we rushed in. Some eight or ten hard looking "hombres" tried to escape through a back way, but they were cut down to a man. No quarter was given. In a back room we found some women and children who were not molested. Pickaxes and Crowbars were sent to us, also some six P'dr shells. A house on the other side of the street was forced and our men were all soon under cover. Our advance was now systematized; one party composed of the best shots ascended to the roof, and now on equal terms renewed the fight. The rest tore holes in the limestone partitions that divided the blocks into houses, then a lighted shell was thrown in, an explosion would follow, when we would rush and we generaly left from two to six dead greassers. We found plenty of eatables and large quantities of wine, and one house was a "Pulque" Fonda, or liquor store. To prevent us from getting drunk the liquor was reported as poisoned, but we were not to be beat in that way; we would make a greasser drink some of each kind, no ill effects appearing, we would imbibe, while the "assayer" would be dispatched by a sabre thrust. When Mexicans were scarce, we used a Dutch artilleryman whose imperfect knowledge of our language prevented him from understanding why we gave him the first drink! and why we watched his countenance with so much anxiety. But the only bad effect it had was to get the Dutchman dead drunk, and the glorious so-so....

We reached a corner house of a block, as usual it was a "corner grocery" full of wine, aquadenta and Mescal. On the opposite side of the street we had to cross, was another of those infernal fortified stone walls, enclosing a house a fort in its self. It was now 3. P.M., all firing had ceased in the eastern part of the town, and from the loud cries of defiance, and increased boldness of our foes, we were satisfied that they had been largely reenforced. Things were getting desperate, the men were all getting crazy drunk and unmanagable. With words of cheer, Walker orderd the door of the Shop to be thrown open and a dash made for the wall. The fire was so blinding that we held our heads down and shut our eyes, "going it blind." One fine young fellow, a Texan named Lockridge, had been with me all day, in this affair he wrapped a Mexican blanket around his head, and Bowieknife in hand led the charge. Our foes met the rush with so heavy a fire that the air seemd to rain balls. Bullets striking on the stone pavements and walls, ricochet and glancing from side to side, as we staggerd on. At least a regiment of infantry came up a side street, poured their fire in our flank, and then charged us with the bayonet. All fought now on his own hook, and fought more like devils, than human beings, with axes, club'd rifles, sabre and Bowieknife. We held them for a moment, then, inch-by-inch we gave ground. My Carbine and Hoster pistol were lost in the Bishop's Palace, and I fought with my sabre alone. I was no doubt badly scarte, but I laid about me in great fury, yelling like a fiend, and when a soldier run on to the point of my weapon, which came out at his back, I considered myself quite a hero. Lockridge, whose huge knife was driping with gore, noticing the act, cried out "Well done honey! nothing like the cold steel for greasers." I had now that tiger thirst for blood that will take possession of a man when engaged in close conflict, a desire to slay, to destroy life, that is a frenzy amounting almost to insanity, making men demons, indifferent alike to danger, wounds and death. I was in this state when a severe blow, dealt by a Mexican on my head with his clubbed musket, brought me to the ground and somewhat cooled my ardour. I with other wounded were dragged in to the "Fonda" in which all that was left of our party retreated, leaving over fifty of our men "toes up" in the street. The door was hastily barred, and a fire opened from the windows on the black devils, who were bayoneting our wounded left in the street. My head was coverd with blood, it was bathed in "muscal" which made it smart as if fire had been put on it, and bound up in a "rebosa."

I soon felt better and full of fight. The cries of our wounded as they were butcherd drove the men perfectly frantic. They howled like wild beasts, such oaths! such fearful imprecations! Walker cried out "My hoses! I have sworn to sleep in the Post office tonight or in hell! Thar is no time to spare, try them again." The door was thrown open, when tremendous explosions of artillery shook the house and the street was swept by a tempest. Canister and bags of musket balls were fired into the ranks of our foes by our two six pounders, one of which had been brought along and mounted on the roof of the house in which we were; the other gun was unlimberd in the street, while a twelve P'dr, with the other column in the "Calle de Monterey" had been mounted on a roof of a tower facing on the "Plazuela de la Carne," and threw shells in to the fortified yard in our front. The enemy fire soon slackened, and we gained their position without further loss. The other column advanced no farther then the church of Sante Maria, where they entrenched and sent us re-enforcements. For four hours until dark, Hell reigned in this part of the city. The air was filled with the roar of artillery, the rattle of musketry, the bursting of shells, the dull heavy blows on doors and walls, the shouts and yells of the Rangers, mingled with cries of children and shrieks of women, made it a scene in which a Demon would delight. House after house we gained, cutting through the longitudinal walls, bursting in to the presence of terrified groups of feamales and children. We must have seemd to them like fiends from another world, our appearence was certainly terrific enough to daunt the boldest, with faces and bare arms encrusted with black blood, hair and beards mattened and stuck full of bits of mortar, garments torn, with a variety of articles found in the houses fastened on their person, weapons all smeared with gore, and all yelling and shouting. What fearful apparitions to meet the gaze of a quite nervous family!

In one house showing unmistakeable sign of wealth, I came upon a group of laides before a crucifix on a small alter situated in an alcove: three were young and quite beautiful, and dressed in pure white, two middle-aged women, their companions, rent the air with their shrill cries. Lockridge who was with me spoke Spanish like a native. He tried to calm them, but they threw themselves on the floor rolling over and over, the younger ones made no outcries but remained with their eyes fixed on the cross. One of the rollers sat up and in Spanish begged us to "spare the Senoreitas, and use them as we wished." This drove us out and Col. Walker placed an old mountain man as a safeguard over them.

In another house lay a mother killed by a random shot, with a little child crying beside her. In every house fearful sights told of the horrors of a town taken by storm! To add to the woe of the defenceless inhabitants, the garison in the Black Fort, finding that we were in possession of the northwestern part of the city, opened with morters, throwing huge bombs high in air that fell in the streets and crashed through houses exploding with great violence. We pushed on, and one hour after dark, Walker with some fifty others gained a lodgement in the Post Office, a high stone building within one hundred yards and overlooking the Grande Plaza. Walker, when a "Meer prisoner," was confined in this house, and the knowledge then acquired, was of great benefit to him now. Among those who staid by Walker was Lockridge and myself, and we ascended to the top of the builden with the gallant Ranger, who had accomplished his oath.

The scene from the roof was magnificent, the rattle of small arms, the shouts and cries of combatants had ceased, darkness had settled over the city and shrouded its scenes of carnage in deep gloom, the dead horses and men laying in the streets looked black and uncanny in the darkness; to the north camp fires mapped out the position of our reserve. Gen. Worth's Head Quarters, the Bishop's Palace, was one blaze of light from the fires built inside. The occasional shout of a drunken stormer or the bray of Donkeys in the Plaza was the only sounds we heard. Silence fell on city and camp. Our wounded were stu-pefied with stimulants and lay unconscious of their pains. This silence was broken by a roar in our rear, and a stream of fire shot up from the "Plaza de la Capella" showing in bold relief the dark towers of the Church of Sante Maria, and rushed over our heads with a strange roaring scream, and burst in the Grande Plaza beyond. Old Maj. Munroe had got his nine inch Morter in position and was trying its range! Another Bomb followed and broke through the roof of the Cathedral, and exploded inside. Tons and tons of ammunition were stored in the Church, and we were not two hundred yards off! The Major only fired these two, but the Black Fort opened and fired at intervals for hours. I made a bed of clothes found in the house, and slept sound until daylight on the 24th.

Document 10.6 A Missouri Volunteer Justifies the War with Mexico

Once Congress declared war in May 1846, President Polk called for volunteers. Some 3,000 Missourians (among 73,000 total Americans) signed up as one-year volunteers. Many more were turned away: in Illinois, 14,000 men competed for 4,000 spots in regiments. Among the Missouri volunteers were Alexander Doniphan and John Taylor Hughes. Hailing from Liberty, Missouri, Doniphan was chosen Colonel of the 1st Regiment of Missouri Mounted Volunteers. He became the second-ranking officer of Colonel Stephen Watts Kearney's "Army of the West" as it marched from Fort Leavenworth to conquer Santa Fe. Colonel Doniphan and his men later marched across northern Mexico, capturing two state capitols, defeating two Mexican forces, and eventually marching 5,500 miles overland. When they returned home, Doniphan's men completed the longest march in United States military history. This remarkable march caught the public's eye because of a book written by one of Doniphan's men, Private John Taylor Hughes. Hughes was teaching school in Liberty when the war broke out. His plan to write a history of the 1st Regiment became *Doniphan's Expedition: Containing an Account of the Conquest of Mexico.* In this brief excerpt from the book's beginning, how does Hughes explain the American rationale for the war? What does he see as the admirable goals of the United States? How does his account compare with Mexican complaints that Doniphan's men desecrated Catholic churches, seized all the food stored by civilians, and cut down all the trees for firewood?

The passage, by the American Congress, of the resolutions of annexation, by which the Republic of Texas was incorporated into the Union as one of the States, having merged her sovereignty into that of our own Government, was the prime cause which led to the recent war with Mexico. However, the more immediate cause of the war may be traced to the occupation, by the American Army, of the strip of disputed territory lying between the Nueces and the Rio Grande. Bigoted and insulting Mexico, always prompt to manifest her hostility toward this Government, sought the earliest plausible pretext for declaring war against the United States. This declaration of war by the Mexican Government (which bore date in Apr., 1846) was

From *Doniphan's Expedition: Containing an Account of the Conquest of Mexico*, Cincinnati: UP James, 1847.

quickly and spiritedly followed by a manifesto from our Congress at Washington, announcing that "a state of war exists between Mexico and the United States." Soon after this counter declaration the Mexicans crossed the Rio Grande, in strong force, headed by the famous generals, Arista and Ampudia. This force, as is well known, was defeated at Palo Alto on the 8th, and at Resaca de la Palma on the 9th of May, 1846, by the troops under command of Maj. Gen. Taylor, and repulsed with great slaughter. The whole Union was soon in a state of intense excitement. Gen. Taylor's recent glorious victories were the constant theme of universal admiration. The war had actually begun, and that, too, in a manner which demanded immediate and decisive action. The United States Congress passed an act, about the middle of May, 1846, authorizing the President to call into the field 50,000 volunteer troops, designed to operate against Mexico at three distinct points, namely, the southern wing or "Army of Occupation," commanded by Maj. Gen. Taylor, to penetrate directly into the heart of the country; the column under Brig. Gen. Wool, or the "Army of the Center," to operate against the city of Chihuahua; and the expedition under the command of Col. (now Brig. Gen.) Kearney, known as the "Army of the West," to direct its march upon the city of Santa Fe. This was the original plan of operation against Mexico. But subsequently the plan was changed; Maj. Gen. Scott, with a well-appointed army, was sent to Vera Cruz; Gen. Wool effected a junction with Gen. Taylor at Saltillo, and Gen. Kearney divided his force into three separate commands; the first he led in person to the distant shores of the Pacific; a detachment of near 1,000 Missouri volunteers, under command of Col. A. W. Doniphan, was ordered to make a descent upon the State of Chihuahua, expecting to join Gen. Wool's division at the capital, while the greater part was left as a garrison at Santa Fe, under command of Col. Sterling Price. The greatest eagerness was manifested by the citizens of the United States to engage in the war; to redress our wrongs; to repel an insulting foe; and to vindicate our national honor and the honor of our oft-insulted flag. The call of the President was promptly responded to; but of the 60,000 volunteers at first authorized to be raised, the services of only about 17,000 were required.

The cruel and inhuman butchery of Col. Fannin and his men, all Americans; the subsequent and indiscriminate murder of all Texans who unfortunately fell into Mexican hands; the repeated acts of cruelty and injustice perpetrated upon the persons and property of American citizens residing in the northern Mexican provinces; the imprisonment of American merchants without the semblance of a trial by jury, and the forcible seizure and confiscation of their goods; the robbing of American travelers and tourists in the Mexican country of their passports and other means of safety, whereby in certain instances they were deprived of their liberty; the forcible detention of American citizens, sometimes in prison and at other times in free custody; the recent blockade of the Mexican ports against the United States trade; the repeated insults offered our national flag; the contemptuous ill-treatment of our ministers, some of whom were spurned with their credentials; the supercilious and menacing air uniformly manifested toward this Government, which with characteristic forbearance and courtesy, has endeavored to maintain a friendly understanding; her hasty and unprovoked declaration of war against the United States; her army's unceremonious passage of the Rio Grande in strong force and with hostile intention; her refusal to pay indemnities; and a complication of less evils, all of which have been perpetrated by the Mexican authorities or by unauthorized Mexican citizens in a manner which clearly evinced the determination on the part of Mexico, to terminate the amicable relations hitherto existing between the two countries are the causes which justify the war. Are not these sufficient? Or should we have forborne until the catalogue of offenses was still deeper dyed with infamous crimes, and until the blood of our brothers, friends, and consanguinity, like that of the murdered Abel, should cry to us from the ground? Who that has the spirit, the feelings, and the pride of an American would willingly see his country submit to such a complication of injury and insult? In truth, the only cause of regret is that the war was not prosecuted with more vigor, energy, and promptitude from the commencement. This, perhaps, would have prevented the effusion of so much blood and the expenditure of so much treasure.

Document 10.7 Commodore Robert F. Stockton Justifies the Conquest of California

Few United States officers played a larger role in the conquest of California than Commodore Robert F. Stockton. Carrying secret orders from President Polk, he replaced Commodore Sloat as commander of the Pacific Fleet on July 23, 1846. Joined two days later by John C. Fremont and his California battalion, they moved south and captured Los Angeles on August 12, 1846. Using Polk's orders to conquer California and then establish a civilian government under his protection, Stockton named himself governor of California. Stockton returned from these conquests to make the following comments at a public dinner in Philadelphia on December 30, 1847. How does the Commodore justify the conquest of California and the defeat of Mexico? What American accomplishments, both before the war and since its inception in California, does he praise? What should future United States actions be?

Annexation, nay acquisition, is not a necessary consequence of conquest—and, therefore, it is not on that account that I would offer my congratulations here to day—oh, no!

I care not for the beautiful fields and healthful skies of California. I care not for her leagues of land and her mines of silver. The glory of the achievements there—if any glory there be, is in the establishment of the first free press, in California—(Great applause)—in having built the first school house in California—in having established religious toleration as well as civil liberty in California—(Tremendous applause)—May the torch grow brighter and brighter, until from Cape Mendocino to Cape St. Lucas, it illumines the dark path of the victim of religious intolerance and political despotism. (Thunders of applause.) . . .

No thoughtful observer of the progress of the U. States, can fail to be impressed with the conviction that we enjoy a degree of happiness and prosperity never heretofore vouchsafed to the nations of mankind. With an unexampled measure of political liberty; unbroken social order, extraordinary growth of the arts and sciences—philanthropic and benevolent institutions, the fair offspring of the christian faith, extending their blessed agency, in all directions—unbounded religious toleration, heaven's best gift; for which our fathers risked and suffered most—with all these rich endowments, do we not indeed present an example of the beneficent care of Providence for which we can find no parallel in the history of man? . . .

But indemnity is not the object of the war. No man here or elsewhere will consent to weigh blood against money. [Great applause.] I do not care who presents the proposition—when it is presented; or to whom it is presented, whig or democrat; no man will weigh blood for money. (Loud applause.) But this is not, I repeat, our condition. Higher and nobler objects present themselves for the attainment of which you must increase your armies in Mexico, *cost what it may.* [Great applause.] Fifty thousand men must go to Mexico. [Renewed applause.]—Let me then state the objects for the attainment of which, in my judgment, this augmentation of our force in Mexico, is required.

Mexico is poor and wretched. Why? Misgovernment—insatiable avarice—unintermitted wrong unsparing cruelty and unbending insolence—these have inflicted their curse on the unhappy country, and made her what she is. But as the darkest hour is that which just precedes the advent of the morning sun, so let us hope that a better and happier day is now about to dawn upon unfortunate Mexico. Be it ours, now to forgive her all her trespasses, and returning good for evil, make her free and happy!—[Enthusiastic applause which lasted several minutes.]

If I were now the sovereign authority, as I was once the viceroy—[laughter]—I would prosecute this war for the express purpose of redeeming Mexico from misrule and civil strife. . . . The priceless boon of civil and religious liberty has been confided to us as trustees—[cheers.]—I would insist, if the war were to

---

From *Niles Weekly National Register*, January 22, 1848.

be prolonged for fifty years, and cost money enough to demand from us each year the half of all that we possess, I would still insist that the inestimable blessings of civil and religious liberty should be guaranteed to Mexico. We must not shrink from the solemn duty. We dare not shrink from it. We cannot lose sight of the great truth that nations are accountable as well as individuals, and that they too must meet the stern responsibilities of their moral character—they too must encounter the penalty of violated law in the more extended sphere adapted to their physical condition. . . .

We have vanquished Mexico. She is prostrate at our feet—we can afford to be magnanimous. Let us act so that we need not fear the strictest scrutiny of the christian and civilized world. I would with a magnanimous and kindly hand gather these wretched people within the fold of republicanism.

Document 10.8 A Mexican View of United States' Manifest Destiny, 1848

Mexico stood in the way of United States' Manifest Destiny. Forced into a war to defend their national boundaries, they eventually lost one half of their nation to the United States, and were understandably critical of aggressive American expansionism. As early as 1837, the Mexican Secretary of War, Jose Maria Tornel y Mendivel, accused the United States of deception and lies in its foreign policy. He declared that the American people naturally "covet, wait, and act" against other nations for the right moment to attack them. He predicted that the loss of Texas would lead to the eventual loss of New Mexico and California. Bernal Diaz del Castillo echoes those observations 11 years later, accusing the United States of duplicity and conspiracy. On March 21, 1846, Mexican President Paredes declared that Mexico would not recognize the American annexation of Texas, would defend its "invaded possessions, and will never, ever allow further conquests." Who are the "evil men and evil parties" criticized here, and whose fault is the Mexican War? According to this selection, what inherently bad traits or cowardly actions by the United States prompted the conflict? Why will Mexico keep fighting? What does the author see as the fate of all groups the United States takes over?

It is difficult to write with sincerity and impartiality about the great events that have been happening here when, aside from the factions which convulse the citizenry and disturb the inner peace of families, these same families find themselves infiltrated by an espionage that aims its fire from within private society, covering itself with a hypocritical mask, which, when it falls, has already produced the ruin of a family. Such is the position in which Mexicans find themselves today. Their natural enemies are the officers and soldiers of the North American army which dominates them through martial law, but also their enemies are the ungrateful foreigners of other nations whose only desire is the gold from our mines. Enemies too are the horde of citizens who have acted as guides to the American army. As legitimate descendants of the ancient Tlaxcalans, they glory in their immorality and maintain the same hatred as did those who aided in the taking of Mexico City while in the service of Hernan Cortés. . . . Such is the position in which he, who now aspires to write this history, finds himself. *Nevertheless*, he will do it, because truth prevails over terrorism and imposture. Truth is for all times; it is from God, and not even the Lord himself can make what really happened cease from having happened. . . .

The complaints of Mexico against the United States before the annexation of Texas are the following:

The introduction of troops from the United States army in the course of Mexico's campaign in Texas. A considerable number of cavalry under General Gaines crossed the Sabine. This was protested by our minister in Washington. The public enlistment and military equipping of troops, which has been done on various occasions in the port city of New

Orleans, in order to invade Mexico through Texas and other points, despite the fact that the United States maintained diplomatic relations with Mexico and the guarantees of treaties of peace and commerce remained in force. This also has been the subject of altercations between the two governments. Mexico has never had the forthrightness to ask of the United States that it lend its assistance against Texas, but Mexico certainly has had the right to demand of the United States that it maintain absolute neutrality. The above mentioned palpable actions demonstrate that the United States has not done so.

As for the recognition of the independence of Texas by other nations, there is nothing unusual in that. The various powers recognize de facto governments, but that in no way takes away from Mexico the right to recover, if it were possible, the territory which it had lost. The independence of Mexico was equally recognized by the European powers and by the United States itself, but nevertheless Spain did not recognize Mexico until a great deal of time had passed, and it made an attempt in the year 1829 to invade Mexico without opposition from any nation.

Now, if Texas were to be considered strong and capable of backing up its declaration of independence, why did it attach itself to the United States? Why did it seek this method to get the United States to come to its support in Mexico? This is just one more proof that Texas cannot be compared to other nations, including the United States, that have declared their independence and by deed have been able to sustain it and triumph.

As for the annexation, the person who is writing this piece was in the United States when these events were happening and was a witness to the fact that the greater part of the press in the northern states clamored strongly against this step, calling those who belonged to the annexation party thieves and usurpers, and setting forth strong and well-founded reasons, which at this point I will not repeat in order to prevent this exposition from becoming too lengthy. If the wise and honorable Henry Clay had attained the seat of the presidency, would the annexation of Texas have come to pass? Certainly not. The bringing in of Texas was the result of the intrigues and machinations of the Loco Foco party, and that which is done by such a farcical group cannot be considered rational or just.

The question of annexation was much debated in the Senate, and only by one vote (I believe that of Mr. Benton) was the measure passed.

In the Texas Convention [which voted for annexation] the majority present consisted of persons from the Southern states, notably partisan, and the newspapers [presumably of the United States] published their names and inveighed against this intrigue.

Thus matters have arrived at the state in which they are now, because evil parties and evil men, of which there are as many in this country as in the United States, have operated according to their partisan tendencies and have not attended to the well-being and justice of both republics. Can you deny this, American citizens, if you are not blind? Will you not confess that Mexico has suffered more than any other nation? The act of annexation was the equivalent of taking away from Mexico a considerable part of its territory, which had, rightly or wrongly, carried on a dispute with Mexico, but in no way can a nation be construed as friendly which has mixed itself in this affair to the point that Mexico has been deprived of its rights. Did not our minister in Washington protest against the annexation? Did he not declare that it would be a hostile act which would merit a declaration of war? Who, then, provoked the war—Mexico which only defended itself and protested, or the United States which became aggressors and scorned Mexico, taking advantage of its weakness and of its internecine agitations.

The administration of General Herrera, which was in fact one of the best that the country has had and that history will in time do justice to, had arranged the affair in a satisfactory manner to the considerable advantage of both Mexico and the United States, because the administration, composed of illustrious people, looked forward to the future, considering questions not only in terms of politics but from the vantage point of humanity as a whole and in particular of this generation of Mexicans whose fate has been to suffer throughout the last thirty years the lashes and calamities of war. The dignity of the government demanded, in effect, that the [American] naval forces withdraw, which in fact they did. Was it the administration of General Herrera that broke its word? Surely not, and the U.S. commissioner [John Slidell] was not received because the administration had changed. In effect, a cowardly general without honor or patriotism [Mariano Paredes] turned his back to the enemy while at the same time proclaiming a war that he had no intention of waging. Thus, like the villain he was, he destroyed the most legitimate and most popular government that Mexico has had. But I ask: Was this a failure on the part of the nation? Can it be blamed for some of this? And I must answer: Did not the nation manifest in all possible ways its displeasure, to the point of overthrowing this intrusive and evil government? Does not that general pine away in exile, one which he imposed upon himself in order to escape the vengeance of the nation?

Up to this point things could still have been arranged through diplomatic channels, and the rights of Mexico could have been guaranteed by a treaty, but the Loco Foco party was absolutely determined that Mexico should not only suffer the loss of its territory but it should bear the shame and humiliation of having its territory torn from it by force of arms. The sending of troops into Mexican territory doomed all moderation, and Mexico was left with no other recourse but to engage in battle. The territory between the Nueces and Rio Grande rivers neither by fact nor by law could have belonged to Texas. Not by fact because it was not populated by Texans. For ten years there existed only one little ranch in Corpus Christi, inhabited by Mr. Kyney and Mr. Aubry [sic], who had served as double agents, having had dealings with the Texans and with various Mexican generals, using them for the purpose of carrying on contraband trade. Nor did this territory belong to Texas by law because all this coast, through a territorial division recognized by all the nation and by the Texas colonists themselves, has belonged to the state of Tamaulipas. Thus, from the point of view of the Mexican government, the occupying of Corpus Christi by troops of the United States amounted to the same thing as if they had occupied the port of Tampico. In every way it was a violation of all treaties, of friendly relations, and of good faith. I wish now that you would judge these events with a Mexican heart and would ask yourself: Which has been the aggressor country? What would your government have done in the controversy with England over the Maine border if that nation had brought in troops, large or small in number? Without any doubt your government would have declared war and would not have entertained any propositions put forth until the armed force had evacuated the territory.

The war began because there was no other course, and Mexico will always be able to present a serene front before the world and maintain its innocence despite whatever misfortunes might befall it. . . .

The events and future prospects of the present war are prejudicial for Mexico, but nonetheless so are they for the United States. Can there be a comparison between the domestic joys of illuminating the streets of the United States on the one hand and on the other of the immense waste of sacrificing peaceful Germans, Irishmen, and native-born Americans who might otherwise be tranquilly at home, enjoying the harvests of the fertile fields of the North? What peace of mind can the United States enjoy while invading and destroying a nation that far from having offended it has clasped it to its bosom as a brother? Could not the Americans have availed themselves, through peaceful means, of the gold and silver of Mexico? Do you believe that the American nation will not lose, even though it triumphs over us completely, in the poor repute that it will have deserved among the nations of Europe?

Mexico finds itself in this contest absolutely alone. Spain was helped by England, and the Duke of Wellington with a powerful army routed the hosts of Napoleon. The United States had General Lafayette and the fleets and armies of France. The most powerful nations of Europe gathered together to defeat Napoleon. Mexico is alone, but that does not matter, nor do the reverses which it has suffered as long as it maintains its constancy. That is what made the United States triumph in its war of independence, and that is what will make us triumph. I imagine that the American army will triumph over Mexico, but what will happen if it cannot find anybody to make peace with?

It is necessary that you keep these considerations in mind and that you be persuaded that Mexico will prefer ruin before treating for peace while enemy forces still remain on Mexican soil.

The lower classes of Mexico generally believe that you are heretics, barbarians, and bloody-minded types. That is an error like the one that persists in the United States where we are judged as being the same as barbarians. The educated people of the Mexican Republic that know your history and have traveled and lived in the North judge the country with a proper impartiality, respect your human and democratic institutions, appreciate the industrious character of the people, and rightfully admire a nation that in a short time has become powerful, but at the same time these Mexicans have become seriously alarmed about the future fate of Mexico as they remember certain tendencies which are proved by events in that nation's history.

Before the Americans began to advance, the French held Louisiana, Canada, and parts of the banks of the Mississippi. The French population, one might say, formed a strip that encircled the coastal area where the American colonies had established themselves.

What has happened to the French race? It has almost totally disappeared and has been supplanted by the English race, invaders by character and ambitious of possessing more territory than they need.

History records that in addition to the sword, gunfire, and the dagger, which they used against the Indians, they practiced the infernal device of introducing smallpox among them.

Did they not send police dogs against the Seminole Indians to destroy them? And finally uproot them from their Florida lands to transplant them on the remote banks of the Missouri?

As a strange anomaly in the freest country in the world, slaves are sold, and the most beautiful women in the world, some of them well educated and amiable, are looked down upon because they are quadroons and are therefore irremediably condemned to dishonor and prostitution.

Does the United States need Texas? Is it not true that fifteen or twenty million more inhabitants could fit into the territory of the Union? Once they have Texas, does not that seem enough? And they still want three more provinces and California? Does not the press of the United States daily vociferate that the country should acquire those territories? They talk to us of peace, and they take California. They talk to us of peace, and they send expeditions to New Mexico and Chihuahua. They talk to us of peace, and the troops of General Taylor, according to his own admission, commit atrocities in the provinces of the north.

Thinking men do not believe the same things as do the lower classes, but they entertain more serious and well-grounded fears and consider the possibility of an interminable and profound war between the races, a war in which Mexico cannot yield without evident danger to its independence. These considerations pose still more obstacles to the peace. . . .

Document 10.9 Mariano Vallejo Relates the Mexican View of the War in California

The United States invaded California from three directions. Led by Governor Pio de Pico, civilians and military resisted the attack, and managed to drive American forces out of Los Angeles, and besieged those holding San Diego. Eventually, forces under John C. Fremont came down from northern California and joined the troops under General Kearny, completing the conquest of California. There is some dispute over the treatment of the Californios. Mariano Vallejo believed that the American presence in California was a good thing at first, and he expected that the economy would flourish. How is he treated by American forces? Does his view of the American presence change, and if so, why?

All during the first week of the month of June various interviews took place between Captain Fremont and his compatriots. What passed between them is not public knowledge, but if the antecedents may be drawn from what followed, it is easy to presume that they were perfecting the plans they thought most appropriate for seizing Alta California and devising the means to come off victorious in their undertaking. That such may have been the object of their frequent meeting is proved by the fact that on the afternoon of June 11th Fremont and his men, without a previous declaration of war and under no other pretext than their own caprice or necessity, seized the three hundred horses (two hundred of which belonged to the Indians emancipated from San Rafael ex-mission, the interests of whom were managed by Timothy Murphy) which on the account and by the order of Commanding General Castro were grazing to the north of the Cosumnes River in charge of Lieutenant Francisco Arce and several soldiers.

This was the first hostile act that Captain Fremont committed against the property of the inhabitants of California, and although the enormity of his conduct is somewhat mitigated by the fact of his having allowed the cowboys to return to San Jose mounted upon the horses, the impartial historian should not for that reason fail to censure in severe terms a soldier who belies his glorious mission and

Mariano Guadalupe Vallejo, translated by Earl R. Hewitt, *Historical and Personal Memoirs Relating to Alya California [Recuerdos Historicaos y Personales Tocante a la Alta California (1875]*, Vol. 5:1845-48, 87-90, 93-98, 101-103, 106, 107.

becomes a leader of thieves. In spite of my desire to palliate as much as I can the conduct of the individuals who participated in the theft of the Indians horses, I cannot but stigmatize them with the anathema which society fulminates against those who without legal right to do so appropriate the property of others.

After distributing the horses as they thought most advantageous to their plans, gentlemen under Captain Fremont's command took the road leading through the Napa Hills to Sonoma and at dawn on the fourteenth of June they surrounded my house located on the plaza at Sonoma. At daybreak they raised the shout of alarm and when I heard it, I looked out of my bedroom window. To my great surprise I made out groups of armed men scattered to the right and left of my residence. The recent arrivals were not in uniform, but were all armed and presented a fierce aspect. Some of them wore on their heads a visorless cap of coyote skin, some a low-crowned plush hat, [and] some a red cotton handkerchief. As for the balance of the clothing of the assaulters of my residence, I shall not attempt to describe it, for I acknowledge that I am incapable of doing the task justice. I suspected that the intruders had intentions harmful not to my [property] interests alone, but to my life and that of the members of my family. I realized that my situation was desperate. My wife advised me to try and flee by the rear door, but I told her that such a step was unworthy and that under no circumstances could I decide to desert my young family at such a critical time. I had my uniform brought, dressed quickly and then ordered the large vestibule door thrown open. The house was immediately filled with armed men. I went with them into the parlor of my residence. I asked them what the trouble was and who was heading the party, but had to repeat that question a second time, because almost all of those who were in the parlor replied at once, "Here we are all heads." When I again asked with whom I should take the matter up, they pointed out William B. Ide who was the eldest of all. I then addressed that gentleman and informed him that I wanted to know to what happy circumstance *I owed the visit of so many individuals.*

In reply he stated that both Captain Merritt and the other gentlemen who were in his company had decided not to continue living any longer under the Mexican government, whose representatives Castro and Pio Pico, did not respect the rights of American citizens living in the *Departamento*; that Castro was every once in a while issuing proclamations treating them all as bandits and, in a desire to put a stop to all these insults, they had decided to declare California independent; that while he held none but sentiments of regard for me, he would be forced to take me prisoner along with all my family.

We were at this point when there appeared in the room *don* Salvador Vallejo, *don* Pepe de la Rosa, Jacob P. Leese, and *don* Victor Prudon, all friends of mine for whom an order of arrest was suggested until it was decided what should be my fate. I thought for a moment that through some sacrifice on my part I might get rid of so many and such little desired guests, but my hopes were frustrated by the unworthy action of the Canadian, Oliver Beaulieu, who, knowing from his own experiences that liquor is an incentive for all kinds of villainous acts, had gone to his house and procured there a barrel full of brandy, which he distributed among the companions of Merritt and Ide. Once under the influence of the liquor, they forgot the chief object of their mission and broke into shouts of "Get the loot, get the loot?"

Fortunately, these seditious cries emitted by Scott, Beaulieu, Sears and others attracted the attention of Doctor Semple who stepped very angrily to the door of the entrance vestibule and by means of a speech of much feeling, in which there were not threats, gave them to understand that he would kill the first man who by committing robbery would cast a blot upon the expedition he had helped organize to advance a political end that, so long as he was alive, he would not allow it to be turned into a looting expedition....

Shortly after Lieutenant Misroons arrival at Sonoma, he endeavored to enter into extra-official relations with William B. Ide and the companions of that impoverished commander, but his advances met with no response, because Ide and the others sheltered under the fateful "Bear Flag" did not leave the barracks, the entrance to which was protected by nine cannon of different calibers that they had taken away from me at dawn on June 14th and which they kept loaded to the muzzle. These were all in charge of their respective gunners (the artillery men did not know their business, for they had been improvised) who never for a single instant relaxed their vigilance over the war materials of which they had been left in charge.

When Lieutnant Misroon had arranged everything as best he could, he left instructions for his subordinate and returned on board the frigate "Portsmouth," where it is to be presumed that he submitted to Captain Montgomery an account of all he had heard and witnessed at Sonoma.

Shortly after Doctor Semple had set out for the Sacramento, *the plaza* at Sonoma was taken in charge by William B. Ide, whom the rest of the force that had invaded my residence had agreed to obey. The number of those who along with William B. Ide remained in charge of the Sonoma garrison was at least fifty. I am aware that various historians have fixed the number at eighteen, but I absolutely know that they are in error. It only remains to determine whether the mistake has been accidental or intentional, for it seems that a hidden but powerful hand has taken great pains to garble all the facts relative to the capture of the Sonoma plaza by the group of adventurers to whom history has given the name of "The Bear Flag Party." I, who was made the chief victim those *patriotic gentlemen* sacrificed upon the altar of their well-laid plans, have no interest whatsoever in bespattering them with mud, nor do I aspire to ennoble myself at the expense of their reputation. All I desire is that the impartial public may know what took place at Sonoma on fateful June 14th, 1846, and that it may, after learning all there is to know in regard to this scandalous violation of law that deprived of liberty those who for years had been making countless sacrifices to redeem from the hands of the barbarous heathen the territory known as the Sonoma Frontier, decide in favor of one or the other of the participants in the events I have just related. All I demand is that the decision arrived at may be upon a basis of fact.

On the fourth day that Mr. Ide was in command at the Sonoma plaza and when he saw that a great number of Americans and foreigners had hurried in to place themselves under his protection, being fearful lest the Californians would attack them on their ranchos should they continue to live scattered over the country, he issued a document in which he set forth the reasons that had impelled him to refuse to recognize the authority of the Mexican government. The original proclamation, which was very brief, merely stated that, since the lives of foreigners were in imminent danger, he had felt it his duty to declare Alta California independent and that, counting as he did upon the definite support and cooperation of the "fighting men" who had rallied around him, he aimed to do all he could to prevent the Californians or the Mexicans from recovering the military post and arms which the valor of his men had seized from them. This is approximately what "Captain" Ide read aloud before the flagpole in the Sonoma *plaza*. I am fully aware that the original proclamation was destroyed and that a few weeks later another was drawn up which, it was said, contained a list of the wrongs which

the Mexican authorities had perpetrated against United States citizens.

After the reading, of the Commander-in-chiefs proclamation, they proceeded with great ceremony to hoist the flag by virtue of which those who had assaulted my home and who had by that time appropriated to themselves two hundred fifty muskets and nine cannon proposed to carry on their campaign.

This flag was nothing more nor less than a strip of white cotton stuff with a red edge and upon the white part, almost in the center, were written the words "California Republic." Also on the white part, almost in the center, there was painted a bear with lowered head. The bear was so badly painted, however, that it looked more like pig than a bear. The material for the flag was furnished, according to some, by Mrs. Elliot; according to others by Mrs. Sears. I also heard it said that Mrs. Grigsby furnished it.

Those who helped to prepare, sew and paint the flag were the following young men: Alexander Todd, Thomas Cowie and Benjamin Duell. The latter was the one who suggested that a star be painted near the mouth of the bear. Of course, both the bear and the star were very badly drawn, but that should not be wondered at, if one takes into consideration the fact that they lacked brushes and suitable colors.

The running up of this queer flag caused much fear to the families of the Californians established in the neighborhood of Sonoma, Petaluma and San Rafael, for they realized that the instigators of the uprising that had disturbed the tranquility of the frontier had made up their minds to rule, come what might, and, as the rumor had been spread far and wide that Ide and his associates had raised the bear flag in order to enjoy complete liberty and not be obliged to render any account of their activities to any civilized governments, the ranchers, who would have remained unperturbed should the American flag have been run up in Sonoma and who would have considered it as the harbinger of a period of progress and enlightenment, seized their machetes and guns and fled to the woods, determined to await a propitious moment for getting rid of the disturbers of the peace. Strange to relate, the first victim that the ranchers sacrificed was the painter of the "Bear Flag," young Thomas Cowie who, along with P. Fowler, was on his way to Fitchs ranch to get one-eyed Moses Carson (brother of the famous explorer Colonel Kit Carson), who was employed as an overseer by Captain Henry Fitch, to give them a half barrel of powder he had locked up in one of the storage closets of his farmhouse. Fowler and Cowie were taken by surprise at the Yulupa Rancho by the party operating under the command of Captains Padilla and Ramon Carrillo, who at the request of the people had assumed direction of the hostilities it had been decided to undertake against "the Bears." Neither of the two extemporaneous commanders thought it right to take the lives of their young captives, upon whom there had been found letters that proved beyond any doubt that Moses Carson and certain others of the Americans employed at the Fitch Ranch were in accord with Ide, Merritt and others of those who had made up their minds to put at end to Mexican domination in California; so they decided to tie them up to a couple of trees while they deliberated as to what should be done with the captives, whose fate was to be decided at the meeting that night to which had been summoned all the ranchers who by their votes had shared in entrusting command of the Californian forces to those wealthy citizens, Padilla and Carrillo. I am of the opinion that the lives of Cowie and Fowler would have been spared, had it not been that a certain Bernardo Garcia, better known under the name of "Three-fingered Jack," taken advantage of the darkness of the night, approached the trees to which the captives were tied and put an end to their existence with his well-sharpened dagger.

After committing the two murders I have just told about, Bernardo Garcia entered the lonely hut in which Padilla, Carrillo and others had met and were discussing as to what disposition should be made of the prisoners. Without waiting for them to ask him any questions, he said to his compatriots, "I thought you here were going to decide to free the prisoners and, as that is not for the good of my country, I got ahead of you and took the lives of the Americans who were tied to the trees."

Those few words, spoken with the greatest of sangfroid by the wickedest man that California had produced up to that time, caused all who heard him to shudder. No one dared to object to what had been done, however, for they knew that such a step would have exposed them to falling under the knife of the dreaded Bernardo Garcia, who for years past had been the terror of the Sonoma frontier.

Equally with the relatives of the unfortunate youths, Cowie and Fowler, I regretted their premature death, for, in spite of the fact that they belonged to a group of audacious men who had torn me from the bosom of my family and done as they pleased with my horses, saddles and arms, I did not consider that the simple fact that they were the bearers of a few letters made them deserving of the supreme penalty. Until that fatal June 21st, neither they nor their companions had shed any Mexican blood and it was not right for the Mexicans to begin a war that could not help but bring very grievous consequences upon them and their families....

When we reached New Helvetia, the Canadian, Alexis, who was heading our escort, gave three knocks upon the main gate with his lance and it was immediately thrown open by Captain Sutter, who, feigning surprise at seeing us as prisoners, led us into his living quarters. He then promised to comply with the orders that Captain Fremont had delivered to him by the mouth of his lieutenant, Alexis, who had said in our presence, "Captain Fremont is turning these gentlemen over to you for you to keep as prisoners behind these walls and upon your own responsibility."

"All right," said Sutter, and without any further ceremony he turned to us and suggested that we accompany him to a large room situated on the second floor where the only furniture was a kind of rude benches. When we were all inside this room, Sutter locked the door and thought no more about us that night.

I leave my readers to imagine how we cursed at finding ourselves locked up in a narrow room and forced to sleep upon the floor without a mattress and without a blanket, even without water with which to quench our burning thirst. There, seated upon a bench, I ran over in my mind all that I had witnessed since that fatal June 14th and I assure you I regretted very much not having accepted the offer of that brave captain of militia, don Cayetano Juarez, had ordered made to me through his brother Vicente Juarez.

On June 14, 1846, Captain Juarez was at his Tulcay hacienda, when he learned that a group of adventurers had assaulted the Sonoma plaza. No sooner did he learn of it than, arming himself, he came to an understanding with Citizens Victorino Altamirano, Antonio Wilson, Vicente and Francisco Juarez, Andres Vaca, Pancho Cibrian and others. He went and took up a position in Portezuelo Pass, where he awaited the reply that was to be brought to him by a brother of his whom he had sent, disguised as a woman to take up a position where I was to pass and ask me if I desired that he (Cayetano Juarez) should make an effort to snatch me from the hands of my guards. I do not recall what it was that caused me to refuse the generous offer of that devoted soldier who had made up his mind to risk his life to procure my freedom. I think that I was influenced above all by the thought I held as to the misfortunes that would inevitably overtake my family, if Captain Juarez and his friends had killed the comrades of those who had remained behind in Sonoma in possession of the plaza and war materials. My repentance came too late, for I was in the hands of a foresworn man, a foreigner who had received many favors from me and mine, [but] who had deliberately forgotten them all and, to cap the climax of [his] infamy, had consented to become my jailor, in order to curry favor with a lot of men who had nothing to their names but an extraordinary dose of boldness, who were not fighting under any recognized flag, and who apparently had no other object than robbery and looting.

After a sleepless night, I greeted the dawn of the new day with enthusiasm, for we were by then beginning to experience the urge of a voracious appetite. Our jailor, however, who had doubtless made up his mind to make us drain the last drop of all which a perverse fate had meted out to us, sent us no food until eleven oclock in the morning, at which time he came and opened the door to permit the entrance of an Indian carrying a jar filled with broth and pieces of meat. He did not send us a spoon, knives and forks, for Captain Sutter no doubt thought that since we had lost our liberty we had also ceased to retain our dignity. Such behavior on the part of a companion in arms (at that time Captain Sutter was still an official of the Mexican Government) could not help but inspire our disgust, for we all recognized the insult that he was inflicting upon us by taking advantage of the circumstances. There are times in life, however, when man should resign himself to suffering every kind of adversity. Doubtless, God had decreed that the month of June, 1846, should be the blackest month of my life.

Four days after our arrival at New Helvetia, Citizen Julio Carrillo appeared at that place. Furnished with a passport issued to him by Lieutenant Misroon, he had undertaken the journey to bring me news of my family. Inasmuch as my jailors did not have any great respect for officials of the United States, they paid no attention to the passport and locked senor Carrillo up in the same room in which I was enjoying Captain Sutters hospitality, along with Victor Prudon, Jacob Leese and Salvador Vallejo. I regretted very much the imprisonment of that friend who, moved by a desire to put an end to my wifes worry, had undertaken the dangerous mission of entering the enemys camp. . . .

Some years ago (in 1868) when I was in Monterey, my friend, David Spence, showed me a book entitled "History of California," written by an author of recognized merit by the name of Franklin Tuthill, and called my attention to that part of the gentlemans narrative where he expresses the assurance that the guerrilla men whom Captain Fremont sent in pursuit of the Californian, Joaquin de la Torre, took nine

field pieces from the latter. I could not help but be surprised when I read such a story, for I know for a fact that Captain de la Torre had only thirty cavalrymen under his command who as their only weapons carried a lance, carbine, saber and pistol. I think that Mr. Tuthill would have done better if, instead of inventing the capture of nine cannon, he had devoted a few lines to describing the vandal-like manner in which the "Bear" soldiers sacked the Olompalí Rancho and maltreated the eighty year old Damaso Rodriguez, alférez retired, whom they beat so badly as to cause his death in the presence of his daughters and granddaughters. Filled with dismay, they gathered into their arms the body of the venerable old man who had fallen as a victim of the thirst for blood that was the prime mover of the guerrilla men headed by Mr. Ford.

I should indeed like to draw a veil over such a black deed, but the inexorable impartiality that is the guiding light of the historian prevents me from passing over a fact that so helps to reveal the true character of the men who on June 14, 1846, assaulted the plaza at Sonoma at a time when its garrison was in the central part of the Departamento busy curbing raids by the barbarous heathen. Let my readers not think that it is my desire to open up wounds that have healed over by now. I am very far from harboring any such thought, for ever since Alta California became a part of the great federation of the United States of North [America], I have spared no effort to establish upon a solid and enduring basis those sentiments of union and concord which are so indispensable for the progress and advancement of all those who dwell in my native land, and, so long as I live, I propose to use all the means at my command to see to it that both races cast a stigma upon the disagreeable events that took place on the Sonoma frontier in 1846. If before I pass on to render an account of my acts to the Supreme Creator, I succeed in being a witness to a reconciliation between victor and vanquished, conquerors and conquered, I shall die with the conviction of not having striven in vain. In bringing this chapter to a close, I will remark that, if the men who hoisted the "Bear Flag" had raised the flag that Washington sanctified by his abnegation and patriotism, there would have been no war on the Sonoma frontier, for all our minds were prepared to give a brotherly embrace to the sons of the Great Republic, whose enterprising spirit had filled us with admiration. Ill-advisedly, however, as some say, or dominated by a desire to rule without let or hindrance, as others say, they placed themselves under the shelter of a flag that pictured a bear, an animal that we took as the emblem of rapine and force. This mistake was the cause of all the trouble, for when the Californians saw parties of men running over their plains and forests under the "Bear Flag," they thought that they were dealing with robbers and took the steps they thought most effective for the protection of their lives and property.

Document 10.10 Texans Drive Juan Seguin Out of His Home

Juan Seguin came from a prominent *Tejano* family that owned land in the San Antonio area. During the 1836 War for Texas Independence, he fought with the American settlers, raising a unit of cavalry to fight alongside the newer residents. After that war he was again elected mayor/alcalde of San Antonio. As the number of Anglos living in the area increased, he found himself under attack by racists wishing to drive all *Tejanos* off their land. Accused of spying for Mexico, he was forced to flee for his life. He returned home briefly after the Mexican War. What does his account say about the treatment of Mexican-American citizens in Texas?

The tokens of esteem, and evidences of trust and confidence, repeatedly bestowed upon me by the Supreme Magistrate, General Rusk, and other dignitaries of the Republic, could not fail to arouse against me much invidious and malignant feeling. The jealousy evinced against me by several officers of the companies recently arrived at San Antonio, from the United States, soon spread amongst the American straggling adventurers, who were already beginning to work their dark intrigues against the native families, whose only crime was, that they owned large tracts of land and desirable property.

John W. Smith, a bitter enemy of several of the richest families of San Antonio, by whom he had been covered with favors, joined the conspiracy which was organized to ruin me.

I will also point out the origin of another enmity which on several occasions, endangered my life. In those evil days, San Antonio was swarming with adventurers from every quarter of the globe. Many a noble heart grasped the sword in the defence of the liberty of Texas, cheerfully pouring out their blood for our cause, and to them everlasting public gratitude is due; but there were also many bad men, fugitives from their country, who found in this land an open field for their criminal designs.

San Antonio claimed then, as it claims now, to be the first city of Texas; it was also the receptacle of the scum of society. My political and social situation

brought me into continual contact with that class of people. At every hour of the day and night, my countrymen ran to me for protection against the assaults or exactions of those adventurers. Sometimes, by persuasion, I prevailed on them to desist; some times, also, force had to be resorted to. How could I have done other wise? Were, not the victims my own countrymen, friends and associates? Could I leave them defenceless, exposed to the assaults of foreigners, who, on the pretext that they were Mexicans, treated them worse than brutes. Sound reason and the dictates, of humanity would, have precluded a different conduct on my part. . . .

1842. After the retreat of the Mexican army under Santa Anna, until Vasquez invasion in 1842, the war between Texas and Mexico ceased to be carried on actively. Although open commercial intercourse did not exist, it was carried on by smuggling, at which the Mexican authorities used to wink, provided it was not carried on too openly, so as to oblige them to notice it, or so extensively as to arouse their avarice.

In the beginning of this year, I was elected Mayor of San Antonio. Two years previously a gunsmith, named Goodman, had taken possession of certain houses situated on the Military Plaza, which were the property of the city. He used to shoe the horses of the volunteers who passed, through San Antonio, and thus accumulated a debt against the Republic, for the

---

Juan Nepomuceno Sequin, *Personal Memoirs of John N. Seguin*, [San Antonio, TX: Ledger Book and Job Office, 1858], 18-27, 29-32.

370   We Are the American People: Our Nation's History Through Its Documents

payment of which he applied to the President to give him possession of the buildings referred to, which had always been known as city property.

The board of Aldermen passed a resolution to the effect, that Goodman should be compelled to leave the premises. Goodman resisted, alleging that the houses had been given to him by the President, in payment for public services. The Board could not, of course, acknowledge in the President any power to dispose of the city property, and consequently directed me to carry the resolution into effect. My compliance with the instructions of the Board caused Goodman to become my most bitter and inveterate enemy in the city.

The term for the mortgage that Messrs. Ogden and Howard held on my property, had run out. In order to raise money and comply with my engagements, I determined to go to Mexico for a drove of sheep. But fearful that this new trip would prove as fatal as the one already alluded to, I wrote to General Vasquez, who was then in command of the Mexican frontier, requesting him to give me a pass. The tenor of Vasquez' answer caused me to apprehend that an expedition was preparing against Texas, for the following month of March.

I called, a session of the Board of Aldermen, (of which the Hon. S. A. Maverick was a member) and laid before them the communication of General Vasquez, stating, that according to my construction of the letter we might soon the approach of the Mexicans.

A few days afterwards, Don Jose Maria Garcia, of Laredo, came to San Antonio; his report was so circumstantial as to preclude all possible doubts as to the near approach of Vasquez to San Antonio. Notice was immediately sent to the Government of the impending danger. In the various meetings held to devise means of defence, I expressed my candid opinion as to the impossibility of defending San Antonio. I observed, that for myself, I was going to the town of Seguin, and advised every one to do the same.

On leaving the city, I passed through a street where some men were making breastworks; I stated to them that I was going to my ranch, and thence to Seguin, in case the Mexican forces should take possession of San Antonio.

From the Nueces river, Vasquez forwarded a proclamation by Arista, to the inhabitants of Texas. I received at my ranch, a bundle of those proclamations, which I transmitted at once to the Corporation of San Antonio.

As soon as Vasquez entered the city, those who had determined upon defending the place, withdrew to Seguin. Amongst them were Dunn and Chevallie, who had succeeded in escaping from the hands of the Mexicans, into which they had fallen while on a reconnoitering expedition on the Medina. The latter told me that Vasquez and his officers stated that I was in favor of the Mexicans; and Chevallie further added that, one day as he was talking with Vasquez, a man named Sanchez, came within sight, whereupon the General observed: "You see that man! Well, Colonel Seguin sent him to me, when he was at Rio Grande. Seguin is with us." He then drew a letter from his pocket, stating that it was from me. Chevallie asked to be allowed to see it, as he knew my handwriting, but the General refused and cut short the interview.

On my return to San Antonio, several persons told me that the Mexican officers had declared that I was in their favor. This rumor, and some threats uttered against me by Goodman, left me but little doubt that my enemies would try to ruin me.

Some of the citizens of San Antonio had taken up arms in favor of the enemy. Judge Hemphill advised me to have them arrested and tried, but as I started out with the party who went in pursuit of the Mexicans, I could not follow his advice.

Having observed that Vasquez gained ground on us, we fell back on the Nueces river. When we came back, to San Antonio, reports were widely spreading about my pretended treason. Captain Manuel Flores, Lieutenant Ambrosio Rodriguez, Matias Curbier, and five or six other Mexicans, dismounted with me to find out the origin of the imposture. I went out with several friends leaving Curbier in my house. I had reached the Main Plaza, when several persons came running to inform me, that some Americans were murdering Curbier. We ran back to the house, where we found poor Curbier covered with blood. On being asked who assaulted him, he answered, that the gunsmith, Goodman, in company with several Americans, had struck him with a rifle. A few minutes afterwards, Goodman returned to my house, with about thirty volunteers, but, observing that we were prepared to meet them, they did not attempt to attack us. We went out of the house and then to Mr. Guilbeau's, who offered me his protection. He went out into the street, pistol in hand, and succeeded in dispersing the mob, which had formed in front of my house. Mr. John Twohig offered me a shelter for that night; on the next morning, I went under disguise to Mr. Van Ness' house; Twohig, who recognised me in the street, warned me to "open my eyes." I remained one day at Mr. Van Ness'; next day General Burleson arrived at San Antonio, commanding a respectable force of volunteers. I presented myself to him asking for a Court of Inquiry; he answered, that there were no grounds for such proceeding. In the evening I went to the camp, and jointly with Colonel Patton, received a commission to forage for provisions in the lower ranchos. I complied with this trust.

I remained hiding from rancho to rancho, for over fifteen days. Every party, of volunteers en route to San Antonio declared, "they wanted to kill Seguin." I could no longer go from farm to farm, and determined to go to my own farm and raise fortifications, &c.

Several of my relatives and friends joined me. Hardly a day elapsed without receiving notice that a party was preparing to attack me, we were constantly kept under arms. Several parties came in sight, but, probably seeing that we were prepared to receive them, refrained from attacking. On the 30th of April, a friend from San Antonio sent me word that Captain Scott, and his company, were coming down by the river, burning the ranchos on their way. The inhabitants of the lower ranchos called on us for aid against Scott. With those in my house, and others to the number of about 100, I started to tend them aid. I proceeded, observing the movements of Scott, from the function of the Medina to Pajaritos. At that place we dispersed and I returned to my wretched life. In those days I could not go to San Antonio without peril of my life.

Matters being in this state, I saw that it was necessary to take some step which would place me in security, and save my family from constant wretchedness. I had to leave Texas, abandon all, for which I had fought and spent my fortune, to become a wanderer. The ingratitude of those, who had assumed to themselves the right of convicting me; their credulity in declaring me a traitor, on mere rumors, when I had to plead, in my favor the loyal patriotism with which I had always served Texas, wounded me deeply.

But, before leaving my country, perhaps for ever, I determined to consult with all those interested in my welfare. I held, a family council. All were in favor of my removing for some time to the interior of Texas. But, to accomplish this, there were some unavoidable obstacles. I could not take one step, from; my ranch, towards the Brazos, without being exposed to the rifle of the first person who might meet me, for, through the whole country, credit had been given to the rumors against; me. To emigrate with my family was impossible, as I was a ruined man, from the time of the invasion of Santa Anna and our flight to Nacogdoches, furthermore, the country of the Brazos was unhealthier than that of Nacogdoches, and what might, we not expect to suffer from disease in a new country, and without friends or means.

Seeing that all these plans were impracticable, I resolved to seek a refuge amongst my enemies, braving all dangers. But before taking this step, I sent in my resignation to the Corporation of San Antonio, as Mayor of the city, stating to them that, unable any longer to suffer the persecutions of some ungrateful Americans, who strove to murder me, I had determined to free my family and friends from their continual misery on my account; and go and live peaceably in Mexico. That for these reasons I resigned my office, with all my privileges and honors as a Texan.

I left Bexar without any engagements towards Texas, my services paid by persecutions, exiled and deprived of my privileges as a Texan citizen. I was in this country a being out of the pale of society, and when she could not protect the rights of her citizens, they seek protection elsewhere. I had been tried by a rabble, condemned without a hearing; and consequently was at liberty to provide for my own safety....

Remarks

After the expeditions of General Woll, I did not return to Texas till the treaty of Guadalupe Hidalgo. During my absence nothing appeared that could stamp me as; a traitor. My enemies had accomplished their object, they had killed me politically in Texas, and the less they spoke of me, the less risk they incurred of being exposed in the infamous means they had used to accomplish my ruin.... The rumor, that I was a traitor, was seized with avidity; by my enemies in San Antonio. Some envied my position, as held by a *Mexican*; others found in me an obstacle to the accomplishment of their villainous plans. The number of land suits which still encumbers the docket of Bexar county would indicate the nature of plans, and any one, who has listened to the evidence elicited in cases of this description, will readily discover the base means adopted to deprive rightful owners of their property....

I have finished my memoirs; I neither have the capacity nor the desire to adorn my acts with literary phrases. I have attempted a short and clear narrative of my public life, in relation to Texas. I give it publicity, without omitting or suppressing anything that I thought of the least interest, and confidently I submit to the public verdict.

Several of those who witnessed the facts which I have related, are still alive and amongst us; they can state whether I have in any way falsified the record.

Document 10.11 Jose Ramirez Condemns American Behavior in Mexico City

After Congress declared war on May 11, 1846, American forces were successful against Mexican opposition. Zachary Taylor's forces crossed the Rio Grande, won a series of battles against larger Mexican forces, and, by September 1846, controlled Matamoros, Monterrey, and most of Northeast Mexico. In February 1847 he defeated General Santa Anna's army at Buena Vista. General Winfield Scott's army captured Veracruz in March 1847, and then fought their way 260 miles to Mexico City, capturing the Mexican capital in September 1847. The behavior of American soldiers was not always outstanding, especially the volunteer units and the Texas Rangers. In February 1847, the Arkansas Frontier Mountain Voluntaries found dozens of civilians hiding in a cave, and proceeded to kill and scalp them before other military units stopped them. The Texas Rangers were sworn to avenge Mexican atrocities from previous years, and bring "Texas vengeance" to Mexico itself. Much to the protests of Regular Army officers, they spread terror across the countryside, indiscriminately killing men, women, and children. In the following selection, Mexican citizen Jose Fernando Ramirez complains about the American occupation of Mexico City. What does he criticize the occupying forces for doing? Whom does he blame for their presence and behavior?

Mexico City, September 30, 1847

My dear friend:

I have not received any word from you to which I can reply, because, since the unfortunate inhabitants of this city are being treated as enemies, there has been no opportunity to get mail in from the outside. Where it is being held heaven only knows. We have hopes that the mail will eventually be permitted to come in, and then I shall know what I have to reply to.

What shall I tell you? Well, to be frank, nothing because this city is no longer the center of political life. According to reports, the center has been transferred to many other centers that will exhaust whatever political life is left to us by our enemy who is oppressing and humiliating us. How I would like to bring home this lesson to certain politicians who have talked incessantly about despotism, etc! Here they would see and get a taste of what it means to live without guarantees! It is all so frightful. I must say that those who have conquered us, brutally savage as they are, have conducted themselves in a manner different from that of European armies belonging to nations that bear the standard of civilization. This does not mean that they do not commit countless excesses every day. But we have here a phenomenon consisting of mingled barbarism and restraint. This

has been the situation for several days, and there is no way to account for it.

Open fighting ceased the third day after the city was occupied; but the undercover struggle goes on, and it is assuming a fearful aspect. The enemy's forces are growing weaker day by day because of assassinations, and it is impossible to discover who the assassins are. Anyone who takes a walk through the streets or goes a short distance away from the center of the city is a dead man. I have been told that a small cemetery has been found in a pulque tavern where deadly liquor was dispensed for the purpose of assuring an increasing number of victims. Seven corpses were discovered inside the establishment, but the tavern keeper could not be found. I am also told that the number of those who have been taken off this way amounts to 300, without counting those dying of sickness and wounds. Five days ago a funeral cortege with the bodies of four officers passed by my residence. The plague has begun to show its signs, and the monuments that those filthy soldiers have scattered along the streets of their quarters unmistakably testify to the fact that dysentery is destroying them. I have never before seen such sodden drunkenness, nor any more scandalous or impudent than the drunkenness that holds these men in its grip. Nor have I ever seen more unrestrained appetites. Every hour of the day, except during the evenings, when they are all drunk, one can find them eating everything they see.

From *Mexico During the War with the United States* by Walter V. Scholes. Reprinted with permission from University of Missouri Press. Copyright © 1970 by Marie Scholes.

The Palace and almost all public buildings have been savagely ransacked and destroyed. I think it only right to say, however, that our disgraceful rabble were the ones who began it all. When the enemy's troops entered the Palace, the doors had already been broken down and the building had been plundered. Three days later the embroidered velvet canopy was sold for four pesos at the Palace entrance. The Government records and other items were sold for two reales. The infamous and eternally accursed Santa Anna abandoned us all, both individuals and property, to the mercy of the enemy and did not leave even one sentinel to defend us.

In Durango you probably know more of what is going on than I do, and you no doubt can see how horrible our future is. I am forwarding to you some documents, two of which I want you to keep as testimony of the iniquitous and shameful rule that the Americans have imposed upon us. The sad thing about all this is that the punishment has been deserved.

Forward the enclosed letters and tell the members of my family that we are all in good health. Do not forget your friend, who holds you in great esteem.

Document 10.12 Another View from Mexico after the War

Mexicans have never shared the American view of this war. Present-day historians such as Ramon Eduardo Ruiz dismiss Manifest Destiny as an excuse, a justification for a war of aggression against Mexico. Carlos Bosch Garcia says this war demonstrates that Americans always believe the ends justify any means. Ramon Alcarez wrote the following selection shortly after the war ended. Are his views similar to those of modern professional historians? On what grounds does he condemn United States' actions against Mexico? Is there anything good to be learned from the Mexican War?

To explain then in a few words the true origin of the war, it is sufficient to say that the insatiable ambition of the United States, favored by our weakness, caused it. But this assertion, however veracious and well founded, requires the confirmation which we will present, along with some former transactions, to the whole world. This evidence will leave no doubt of the correctness of our impressions.

In throwing off the yoke of the mother country, the United States of the North appeared at once as a powerful nation. This was the result of their excellent elementary principles of government established while in colonial subjection. The Republic announced at its birth, that it was called upon to represent an important part in the world of Columbus. Its rapid advancement, its progressive increase, its wonderful territory, the uninterrupted augmentation of its inhabitants, and the formidable power it had gradually acquired, were many proofs of its becoming a colossus, not only for the feeble nations of Spanish America, but even for the old populations of the ancient continent.

The United States did not hope for the assistance of time in their schemes of aggrandizement. From the days of their independence they adopted the project of extending their dominions, and since then, that line of policy has not deviated in the slightest degree. This conduct, nevertheless, was not perceptible to the most enlightened: but reflecting men, who examined events, were not slow in recognising it. Conde de Aranda, from whose perception the ends which the United States had resolved upon were not concealed, made use of some celebrated words. These we shall now produce as a prophecy verified by events. "This nation has been born a pigmy: in the time to come, it will be a giant. and even a colossus, very formidable in these vast-regions. Its first step will be an appropriation of the Floridas to be master of the Gulf of Mexico."

The ambition of the North Americans has not been in conformity with this. They desired from the beginning to extend their dominion in such manner as to become the absolute owners of almost all this continent. In two ways they could accomplish their ruling

---

The Other Side, or Notes for the History of the War between Mexico and the United States, translated by Albert C. Ramsey, 1850.

passion: in one by bringing under their laws and authority all America to the Isthmus of Panama, in another, in opening an overland passage to the Pacific Ocean, and making good harbors to facilitate its navigation. By this plan, establishing in some way an easy communication of a few days between both oceans, no nation could compete with them. England herself might show her strength before yielding the field to her fortunate rival, and the mistress of the commercial world might for a while be delayed in touching the point of greatness to which she aspires.

In the short space of some three quarters of a century events have verified the existence of these schemes and their rapid development. The North American Republic has already absorbed territories pertaining to Great Britain, France, Spain and Mexico. It has employed every means to accomplish this—purchase as well as usurpation, skill as well as force, and nothing has restrained it when treating of territorial acquisition. Louisiana, the Floridas, Oregon, and Texas, have successively fallen into its power . . .

While the United States seemed to be animated by a sincere desire not to break the peace, their acts of hostility manifested very evidently what were their true intentions. Their ships infested our coasts; their troops continued advancing upon our territory, situated at places which under no aspect could be disputed. Thus violence and insult were united: thus at the very time they usurped part of our territory, they offered to us the hand of treachery, to have soon the audacity to say that our obstinacy and arrogance were the real causes of the war.

To explain the occupation of Mexican territory by the troops of General Zachary Taylor, the strange idea occurred to the United States that the limits of Texas extended to the Rio Grande del Norte. This opinion was predicated upon two distinct principles: one, that the Congress of Texas had so declared it in December, in 1836; and another, that the river mentioned had once been the natural line of Louisiana. To state these reasons is equivalent at once to deciding the matter; for no one could defend such palpable absurdities. The first, which this government prizing its intelligence and civilization, supported with refined malice, would have been ridiculous in the mouth of a child. Whom could it convince that the declaration of the Texas Congress bore a legal title for the acquisition of the lands which it appropriated to itself with so little hesitation? If such a principle were recognized, we ought to be grateful to these gentlemen senators. who had the kindness to be satisfied with so little. Why not declare the limits of the rebel

state extended to San Luis, to the capital, to our frontier with Guatemala?

The question is so clear in itself that it would only obscure by delaying to examine it further. We pass then to the other less nonsensical than the former. In the first place to pretend that the limits of Louisiana came to the Rio Grande, it was essential to confound this province with Texas, which never can be tolerated. In the beginning of this article we have already shown the ancient and peaceable possession of Spain over the lands of the latter. Again, this same province, and afterwards State of Texas, *never* had extended its territory to the Rio Grande, being only to the Nueces, in which always had been established the boundary. Lastly, a large part of the territory situated on the other side of the Grande, belonged, without dispute or doubt, to other states of the Republic—to new Mexico, Tamaulipas, Coahuila, and Chihuahua.

Then, after so many and such plain proceedings, is there one impartial man who would not consider the forcible occupation of our territory by the North American arms a shameful usurpation? Then further, this power desired to carry to the extreme the sneer and the jest. When the question had resolved itself into one of force which is the ultima ratio of nations as well as of kings, when it had spread desolation and despair in our populations, when many of our citizens had perished in the contest, the bloody hand of our treacherous neighbors was turned to present the olive of peace. The Secretary of State, Mr. Buchanan, on the 27th of July, 1846, proposed anew, the admission of an Envoy to open negotiations which might lead to the concluding of an honorable peace. The national government answered that it could not decide, and left it to Congress to express its opinion of the subject. Soon to follow up closely the same system of policy, they ordered a commissioner with the army, which invaded us from the east, to cause it to be understood that peace would be made when our opposition ceased. Whom did they hope to deceive with such false appearances? Does not the series of acts which we have mentioned speak louder than this hypocritical language? By that test then, as a question of justice, no one who examines it in good faith can deny our indisputable rights. Among the citizens themselves, of the nation which has made war on us, there have been many who defended the cause of the Mexican Republic. These impartial defenders have not been obscure men, but men of the highest distinction. Mexico has counted on the assistance, ineffectual, unfortunately, but generous and illustrious, of a [Henry] Clay, [John Quincy] Adams, a [Daniel] Webster, a[n Albert] Gallatin; that is to say, on the noblest men, the most appreciated for their virtues, for their talents, and for their services. Their conduct deserves our thanks, and the authors of this work have a true pleasure in paving, in this place, the sincere homage of their gratitude.

Such are the events that abandoned us to a calamitous war; and, in the relation of which, we have endeavored not to distort even a line of the private data consulted, to prove, on every occasion, all and each of our assertions.

From the acts referred to, it has been demonstrated to the very senses, that the real and effective cause of this war that afflicted us was the spirit of aggrandizement of the United States of the North, availing itself of its power to conquer us. Impartial history will some day illustrate for ever the conduct observed by this Republic against all laws, divine and human, in an age that is called one of light. and which is, notwithstanding, the same as the former—one of farce and violence.

Document 10.13 The Treaty of Guadalupe Hidalgo

President Polk appointed the Chief Clerk of the State Department, Nicholas Trist, to negotiate a peace treaty with the Mexican government. Trist and General Scott feuded at first, because the general feared civilian interference might jeopardize his army. They resolved this understanding and Scott helped the envoy get in contact with a moderate Mexican faction after the capture of Mexico City. After prolonged negotiations (and ignoring a recall order from the President), Trist concluded the treaty of Guadalupe Hidalgo on February 2, 1848. The treaty confirmed the obvious results of the war, specifically the United States' title of Texas and control over California and New Mexico. The United States agreed to pay $15 million and take over Mexican debts to American citizens of $3.25 million. Some historians have argued this money was to ease a guilty conscience. The Mexican president claimed it was an indemnity won during treaty negotiations. Although President Polk was furious at Trist's conduct, he accepted the treaty, and the Senate approved it (with minor amendments) on March 10, 1848. Polk signed it into law with great fanfare on July 4, 1848. In the excerpts from the official treaty printed below, what does the United States gain? What does Trist commit the nation to doing to meet our part of the treaty? What rights are guaranteed Mexican citizens now living in the United States because of the Treaty? Do you think we keep these solemn guarantees?

The United States of America and the United Mexican States animated by a sincere desire to put an end to the calamities of the war which unhappily exists between the two Republics and to establish Upon a solid basis relations of peace and friendship, which shall confer reciprocal benefits upon the citizens of both, and assure the concord, harmony, and mutual confidence wherein the two people should live, as good neighbors have for that purpose appointed their respective plenipotentiaries, that is to say: The President of the United States has appointed Nicholas P. Trist, a citizen of the United States, and the President of the Mexican Republic has appointed Don Luis Gonzaga Cuevas, Don Bernardo Couto, and Don Miguel Atristain, citizens of the said Republic; Who,

after a reciprocal communication of their respective full powers, have, under the protection of Almighty God, the author of peace, arranged, agreed upon, and signed the following:

Treaty of Peace, Friendship, Limits, and Settlement between the United States of America and the Mexican Republic.

Article I

There shall be firm and universal peace between the United States of America and the Mexican Republic, and between their respective countries, territories, cities, towns, and people, without exception of places or persons.

Washington DC: Thomas H. Ford Printer, 1860.

Article V

The boundary line between the two Republics shall commence in the Gulf of Mexico, three leagues from land, opposite the mouth of the Rio Grande, otherwise called Rio Bravo del Norte, or Opposite the mouth of its deepest branch, if it should have more than one branch emptying directly into the sea; from thence up the middle of that river, following the deepest channel, where it has more than one, to the point where it strikes the southern boundary of New Mexico; thence, westwardly, along the whole southern boundary of New Mexico (which runs north of the town called Paso) to its western termination; thence, northward, along the western line of New Mexico, until it intersects the first branch of the river Gila; (or if it should not intersect any branch of that river, then to the point on the said line nearest to such branch, and thence in a direct line to the same); thence down the middle of the said branch and of the said river, until it empties into the Rio Colorado; thence across the Rio Colorado, following the division line between Upper and Lower California, to the Pacific Ocean.

The southern and western limits of New Mexico, mentioned in the article, are those laid down in the map entitled "Map of the United Mexican States, as organized and defined by various acts of the Congress of said republic, and constructed according to the best authorities. Revised edition. Published at New York, in 1847, by J. Disturnell," of which map a copy is added to this treaty, bearing the signatures and seals of the undersigned Plenipotentiaries. And, in order to preclude all difficulty in tracing upon the ground the limit separating Upper from Lower California, it is agreed that the said limit shall consist of a straight line drawn from the middle of the Rio Gila, where it unites with the Colorado, to a point on the coast of the Pacific Ocean, distant one marine league due south of the southernmost point of the port of San Diego, according to the plan of said port made in the year 1782 by Don Juan Pantoja, second sailing-master of the Spanish fleet, and published at Madrid in the year 1802, in the atlas to the voyage of the schooners Sutil and Mexicana; of which plan a copy is hereunto added, signed and sealed by the respective Plenipotentiaries.

In order to designate the boundary line with due precision, upon authoritative maps, and to establish upon the ground land-marks which shall show the limits of both republics, as described in the present article, the two Governments shall each appoint a commissioner and a surveyor, who, before the expiration of one year from the date of the exchange of ratifications of this treaty, shall meet at the port of San Diego, and proceed to run and mark the said boundary in its whole course to the mouth of the Rio Bravo del Norte. They shall keep journals and make out plans of their operations; and the result agreed upon by them shall be deemed a part of this treaty, and shall have the same force as if it were inserted therein. The two Governments will amicably agree regarding what may be necessary to these persons, and also as to their respective escorts, should such be necessary.

The boundary line established by this article shall be religiously respected by each of the two republics, and no change shall ever be made therein, except by the express and free consent of both nations, lawfully given by the General Government of each, in conformity with its own constitution.

Article VIII

Mexicans now established in territories previously belonging to Mexico, and which remain for the future within the limits of the United States, as defined by the present treaty, shall be free to continue where they now reside, or to remove at any time to the Mexican Republic, retaining the property which they possess in the said territories, or disposing thereof, and removing the proceeds wherever they please, without their being subjected, on this account, to any contribution, tax, or charge whatever.

Those who shall prefer to remain in the said territories may either retain the title and rights of Mexican citizens, or acquire those of citizens of the United States. But they shall be under the obligation to make their election within one year from the date of the exchange of ratifications of this treaty; and those who shall remain in the said territories after the expiration of that year, without having declared their intention to retain the character of Mexicans, shall be considered to have elected to become citizens of the United States.

In the said territories, property of every kind, now belonging to Mexicans now established there, shall be inviolably respected. The present owners, the heirs of these, and all Mexicans who may hereafter acquire said property by contract, shall enjoy with respect to it guarantees equally ample as if the same belonged to citizens of the United States.

Article IX

The Mexicans who, in the territories aforesaid, shall not preserve the character of citizens of the Mexican Republic, conformably with what is stipulated in the preceding article, shall be incorporated into the Union of the United States, and be admitted at the proper time (to be judged of by the Congress of the United States) to the enjoyment of all the rights of citizens of the United States, according to the principles of the Constitution; and in the mean time, shall be maintained and protected in the free enjoyment of their liberty and property, and secured in the free exercise of their religion without; restriction.

Article X

[Stricken out by the United States Amendments]

Article XI

Considering that a great part of the territories, which, by the present treaty, are to be comprehended for the future within the limits of the United States, is now occupied by savage tribes, who will hereafter be under the exclusive control of the Government of the United States, and whose incursions within the territory of Mexico would be prejudicial in the extreme, it is solemnly agreed that all such incursions shall be forcibly restrained by the Government of the United States whensoever this may be necessary; and that when they cannot be prevented, they shall be punished by the said Government and satisfaction for the same shall be exacted all in the same way, and with equal diligence and energy, as if the same incursions were meditated or committed within its own territory, against its own citizens.

It shall not be lawful, under any pretext whatever, for any inhabitant of the United States to purchase or acquire any Mexican, or any foreigner residing in Mexico, who may have been captured by Indians inhabiting the territory of either of the two republics; nor to purchase or acquire horses, mules, cattle, or property of any kind, stolen within Mexican territory by such Indians.

And in the event of any person or persons, captured within Mexican territory by Indians, being carried into the territory of the United States, the Government of the latter engages and binds itself, in the most solemn manner, so soon as it shall know of such captives being within its territory, and shall be able so to do, through the faithful exercise of its influence and power, to rescue them and return them to

their country, or deliver them to the agent or representative of the Mexican Government. The Mexican authorities will, as far as practicable, give to the Government of the United States notice of such captures; and its agents shall pay the expenses incurred in the maintenance and transmission of the rescued captives; who, in the mean time, shall be treated with the utmost hospitality by the American authorities at the place where they may be. But if the Government of the United States, before receiving such notice from Mexico, should obtain intelligence, through any other channel, of the existence of Mexican captives within its territory, it will proceed forthwith to effect their release and delivery to the Mexican agent, as above stipulated.

For the purpose of giving to these stipulations the fullest possible efficacy, thereby affording the security and redress demanded by their true spirit and intent, the Government of the United States will now and hereafter pass, without unnecessary delay, and always vigilantly enforce, such laws as the nature of the subject may require. And, finally, the sacredness of this obligation shall never be lost sight of by the said Government, when providing for the removal of the Indians from any portion of the said territories, or for its being settled by citizens of the United States; but, on the contrary, special care shall then be taken not to place its Indian occupants under the necessity of seeking new homes, by committing those invasions which the United States have solemnly obliged themselves to restrain.

Article XII

In consideration of the extension acquired by the boundaries of the United States, as defined in the fifth article of the present treaty, the Government of the United States engages to pay to that of the Mexican Republic the sum of fifteen millions of dollars.

Immediately after the treaty shall have been duly ratified by the Government of the Mexican Republic, the sum of three millions of dollars shall be paid to the said Government by that of the United States, at the city of Mexico, in the gold or silver coin of Mexico. The remaining twelve millions of dollars shall be paid at the same place, and in the same coin, in annual installments of three millions of dollars each together with interest on the same at the rate of six per centum per annum. This interest shall begin to run upon the whole sum of twelve millions from the day of the ratification of the present treaty by the Mexican Government and the first of the installments shall be paid at the expiration of one year from the same day. Together with each annual installment, as it falls due, the whole interest accruing on such installment from the beginning shall also be paid.

Article XIII

The United States engage, moreover, to assume and pay to the claimants all the amounts now due them, and those hereafter to become due, by reason of the claims already liquidated and decided against the Mexican Republic, under the conventions between the two republics severally concluded on the eleventh day of April, eighteen hundred and thirty-nine, and on the thirtieth day of January, eighteen hundred and forty-three; so that the Mexican Republic shall be absolutely exempt, for the future, from all expense whatever on account of the said claims.

Article XIV

The United States do furthermore discharge the Mexican Republic from all claims of citizens of the United States, not heretofore decided against the Mexican Government, which may have arisen previously to the date of the signature of this treaty; which discharge shall be final and perpetual, whether the said claims be rejected or be allowed by the board of commissioners provided for in the following article, and whatever shall be the total amount of those allowed.

Article XV

The United States, exonerating Mexico from all demands on account of the claims of their citizens mentioned in the preceding article, and considering them entirely and forever canceled, whatever their amount may be, undertake to make satisfaction for the same, to an amount not exceeding three and one-quarter millions of dollars. To ascertain the validity and amount of those claims, a board of commissioners shall be established by the Government of the United States, whose awards shall be final and conclusive; provided that, in deciding upon the validity of each claim, the board shall be guided and governed by the principles and rules of decision prescribed by the first and fifth articles of the unratified convention, concluded at the city of Mexico on the twentieth day of November, one thousand eight hundred and forty-three; and in no case shall an award be made in favour of any claim not embraced by these principles and rules.

If, in the opinion of the said board of commissioners or of the claimants, any books, records, or documents, in the possession or power of the Government of the Mexican Republic, shall be deemed necessary to the just decision of any claim, the commissioners, or the claimants through them, shall, within such period as Congress may designate, make an application in writing for the same, addressed to the Mexican Minister of Foreign Affairs, to be transmitted by the Secretary of State of the United States; and the Mexican Government engages, at the earliest possible moment after the receipt of such demand, to cause any of the books, records, or documents so specified, which shall be in their possession or power (or authenticated copies or extracts of the same), to be transmitted to the said Secretary of State, who shall immediately deliver them over to the said board of commissioners; provided that no such application shall be made by or at the instance of any claimant, until the facts which it is expected to prove by such books, records, or documents, shall have been stated under oath or affirmation.

Article XVII

The treaty of amity, commerce, and navigation, concluded at the city of Mexico, on the fifth day of April, A. D. 1831, between the United States of America and the United Mexican States, except the additional article, and except so far as the stipulations of the said treaty may be incompatible with any stipulation contained in the present treaty, is hereby revived for the period of eight years from the day of the exchange of ratifications of this treaty, with the same force and virtue as if incorporated therein; it being understood that each of the contracting parties reserves to itself the right, at any time after the said period of eight years shall have expired, to terminate the same by giving one year's notice of such intention to the other party.

Article XXIII

This treaty shall be ratified by the President of the United States of America, by and with the advice and consent of the Senate thereof; and by the President of the Mexican Republic, with the previous approbation of its general Congress; and the ratifications shall be exchanged in the City of Washington, or at the seat of Government of Mexico, in four months from the date of the signature hereof, or sooner if practicable.

In faith whereof we, the respective Plenipotentiaries, have signed this treaty of peace, friendship, limits, and settlement, and have hereunto affixed our seals respectively. Done in quintuplicate, at the city of Guadalupe Hidalgo, on the second day of February, in the year of our Lord one thousand eight hundred and forty-eight.

N. P. TRIST
LUIS P. CUEVAS
BERNARDO COUTO
MIGL. ATRISTAIN

Protocol of Queretaro

In the city of Queretaro on the twenty sixth of the month of May eighteen hundred and forty-eight at a conference between Their Excellencies Nathan Clifford and Ambrose H. Sevier Commissioners of the United States of America, with full powers from their Government to make to the Mexican Republic suitable explanations in regard to the amendments which the Senate and Government of the said United States have made in the treaty of peace, friendship, limits and definitive settlement between the two Republics, signed in Guadalupe Hidalgo, on the second day of February of the present year, and His Excellency Don Luis de la Rosa, Minister of Foreign Affairs of the Republic of Mexico, it was agreed, after adequate conversation respecting the changes alluded to, to record in the present protocol the following explanations which Their aforesaid Excellencies the Commissioners gave in the name of their Government and in fulfillment of the Commission conferred upon them near the Mexican Republic.

First.

The American Government by suppressing the IXth article of the Treaty of Guadalupe and substituting the III article of the Treaty of Louisiana did not intend to diminish in any way what was agreed upon by the aforesaid article IXth in favor of the inhabitants of the territories ceded by Mexico. Its understanding that all of that agreement is contained in the IIId article of the Treaty of Louisiana. In consequence, all the privileges and guarantees, civil, political and religious, which would have been possessed by the inhabitants of the ceded territories, if the IXth article of the Treaty had been retained, will be enjoyed by them without any difference under the article which has been substituted.

Second.

The American Government, by suppressing the Xth article of the Treaty of Guadalupe did not in any way intend to annul the grants of lands made by Mexico in the ceded territories. These grants, notwithstanding the suppression of the article of the Treaty, preserve the legal value which they may possess; and the grantees may cause their legitimate titles to be acknowledged before the American tribunals.

Conformably to the law of the United States, legitimate titles to every description of property personal and real, existing in the ceded territories, are those which were legitimate titles under the American law in California and New Mexico up to the 13th of May 1846, and in Texas up to the 2d March 1836.

Chapter 10 Worksheet and Questions

1. The first selections in this chapter expose you to advocates of United States expansion, promoters of our Manifest Destiny. How do they define Manifest Destiny? What justifications do they provide for expansion? Be sure to use the documents, and note which writer advocates each point.

_____

_____

_____

_____

_____

_____

_____

_____

2. Now take all of the proposed benefits American expansionism provides and compare them with the results. What benefits are there for the United States? What benefits are there for other people whom we force to accept our way of life? How different are the claims from the reality? Once again, use specific examples from the documents.

_____

_____

_____

_____

_____

_____

_____

_____

3. How do the Mexican authors in this chapter view Manifest Destiny and the claims made by its promoters? What do they see as the real motivations and "virtues" of the United States? What is the impact on their people and their nation, according to the documents? One of the common accusations against Manifest Destiny is that it is nothing more than a way to ease our conscience, a way to justify blatant and brutal wars of aggression against weaker neighbors. Is this really a case of the "ends justifying the means"?

_____

_____

_____

_____

_____

_____

_____

_____

_____

4. The United States claimed, in this war as in all wars, that we entered for noble purposes. Our troops were not after the traditional spoils of war, but were there to promote freedom and democracy. Using the authors from both sides of the Mexican War, discuss the conduct and goals of the United States participants in the war. Does reality match the claims?

_____

_____

_____

_____

_____

_____

_____

_____

_____

Angry Ideas, Intemperate Actions, and Bloodshed:
The Causes of the United States' Civil War

Victory by arms over Mexico encouraged trade and settlement in the newly acquired lands, far beyond the early connections of the Santa Fe trade. The discovery of gold further breeched the former frontier line, and prompted tens of thousands to cross the prairies and Great Plains. The lush grasses and rich land these travelers described summoned yet another wave of more permanent settlers. Open access to western lands also resurrected earlier disputes over how the lands should be settled. Northerners and Southerners disagreed over which social, economic, and cultural systems should dominate the West. Should the western lands be slave or free?

Each section of the nation firmly believed in its fundamental rights to settle the western lands, and believed that domination of these lands was the only way to assure their destiny and preserve their way of life. Northerners proclaimed the virtues of republican free labor and individual opportunity. They called themselves defenders of the Jeffersonian ideal of the yeoman farmer who was the backbone of the republic, and claimed that the rights of individual white male citizens were more important than any group. Family farms could not compete economically with slave labor, and if you eliminated the areas open to family farming you would cause the demise of virtuous yeoman farmer, and thus bring about the end of the republic. The South, whose growing siege mentality during the nineteenth century made them distrust the rest of the nation, defended its version of states' rights and the sanctity of personal property in slaves. Southerners knew that slavery entwined their entire economy and culture; they utilized a new aggressive version of the states' rights argument to demand expanding the peculiar institution. States' rights no longer simply meant restricting the powers of the national government. Now it meant that state citizens had the absolute right to take their private property, that is, slaves, into any federal territory without restriction. Extremists on both sides were more visible each year, their arguments attracting increased attention as passionate concerns for the future of their own way of life increased.

What options did the nation have? John C. Calhoun espoused his revised states' rights argument, proclaiming that Southerners had the right to take their slave property anywhere they chose, that any restrictions on the expansion of slavery were an attack on the South, and that the South might have to secede to preserve its way of life. Despite the fact that he supported the Missouri Compromise in 1820, he now argued that it or any other federal attempt to regulate or exclude slavery in the territories was unconstitutional. Other Southerners complained that they had a right to territories that Southerners died for, and banning their "social institutions" from these areas implied Southern inferiority. Northern extremists claimed that the Wilmot Proviso, banning slavery in the new lands seized during the Mexican War, was the only way to preserve the Jeffersonian dream of a nation of yeoman farmers. Some Northerners believed this was a fair protection for Northern needs, after the tariff reductions of 1846 hurt industry. Some abolitionists suggested war or disunion would be the only salvation for the North. The Wilmot Proviso quickly became a litmus test of sectional loyalty for many people. Moderates in both regions saw other alternatives, including extending the Missouri Compromise Line out to the Pacific, or using the idea of popular sovereignty. This concept called for the people in the territories to decide if they wanted slavery. None of these options was the perfect solution, but all were in play during the key events and government actions of the 1850s.

Facing threats of secession and a virtual government shutdown over the issue of slavery expansion, the Compromise of 1850 temporarily restored calm to the United States. Unionists and merchants celebrated with mass rallies and parties across the nation. This compromise resolved the issue of admitting California and all its gold as a free state, but also postponed resolving the issue of slavery in the rest of the Southwest, relying on popular sovereignty to determine the fate of the issue sometime in the future. As a sop to the North, the slave trade was abolished in the national capital, but not slavery itself. The South received the new Fugitive Slave Law, which caused the greatest challenge to national harmony over the next few years. Northerners referred to this law as the "Bloodhound Bill," because it denied accused runaways any legal protections, and used federal officials to help catch slaves. Accused African Americans could not testify in their own behalf, and a signed affidavit from their former owner (or "John Doe" warrant) was considered ample evidence to condemn them to slavery. Local white officials and citizens could be ordered against their will to assist in catching runaways, and faced fines or prison if they refused. The law also weighted the pay of slave commissioners, who were paid twice as much if they determined the accused were runaways rather than if they declared them free. Northerners saw this as evidence that the Slavocracy was perverting the legal system for their own ends. Thousands of free Northern African Americans, their lives now at risk, fled to Canada. Nevertheless, much of the furor over this issue faded after a year or so and most Northerners accepted the rule as the law of the land—until 1854. Southern extremists believed the Compromise of 1850 gave up too much. Control of the Senate passed to the North with California's admission as a free state, and the advance of slavery to the Pacific Ocean was stalled.

If they could not have land to the west, then Southerners wanted expansion of slavery to the south. During the 1850s Southerners launched a number of filibustering expeditions to seize control of Cuba and parts of Mexico or Central America by force. The plan was to conquer these lands, bring them into the United States, and let slavery thrive. Of course, armed invasions of other nations are illegal, and while the military was officially ordered to stop the filibusters, the pro-Southern national government let them go to commit crimes in other nations. When the armed invasions did not work, and only got United States citizens tried and executed in foreign lands, the government attempted to buy Cuba from Spain. Other Southern extremists called for re-opening the international slave trade. To many Northerners all of these actions suggested a Southern plot, to corrupt the government and threaten the republic, just to expand slavery.

The temporary national calm evaporated with the Kansas- Nebraska Act of 1854. This act organized two territories out of the remaining Louisiana Purchase lands: the Kansas Territory and the Nebraska Territory. Senator Stephen Douglas and other advocates of Manifest Destiny wanted this region organized to promote settlement and assist in the building of a continental railroad. A group of Southern congressmen, led by the influential Senator David Atchison of Missouri, held up the measure until it specifically repealed the Missouri Compromise Line banning slavery in these areas. To Southern moderates, this was a better option than secession. To Stephen Douglas and other Northern advocates of popular sovereignty, this didn't matter, because Northern settlers would surely outnumber Southerners. But this bill angered many people in the North, who saw it as sectional betrayal by Douglas and other Northern congressmen supporting it, as a Southern attack on the North's future, or even a Slave Power attack on the laws of God and man. The Northern Democratic Party split over the bill, and the Republican Party was born, rallying those who wished to ban the expansion of slavery.

Bleeding Kansas is the other result of this act. Prior to the act's passage, several Southern politicians voiced the opinion they would rather see the Kansas-Nebraska region "sink in hell" than become a free-soil region. Missourians rushed into Kansas, led by United States Senator David Atchison, who saw this land as their own private birthright. Many Missourians felt desperate to conquer Kansas, fearful that slavery would end in Missouri if their state were surrounded by Free states on three sides. Letters went out recruiting Southerners from other states to help in Kansas. Atchison warned that if the South lost Kansas, it meant the end of slavery not only in Missouri, but in Texas, Arkansas, and everywhere else. If they won in Kansas, they could carry slavery to the Pacific Ocean. Atchison and other leaders planned to use any means to control Kansas, including illegal voting, intimidation, theft, and murder. He organized early invasions of "border ruffians" to insure pro-slavery election results, and planned the elimination of all Northern sympathizers from Kansas. Senator William Seward of New York issued a call to arms for the North, declaring "We will engage in competition for the virgin soil of Kansas, and God give the victory to the side which is stronger in numbers as in right." Most of the free-soil advocates entering Kansas came from nearby states, but the small bands sent west by the New England Emigrant Aid Society attracted the most attention because of their strong anti-slavery stance. Arguments over the future of Kansas quickly escalated into fights with fists, knives, and guns. Both sides raided across the border, attacked their neighbors, and committed acts of violence. Many of the Missouri border ruffians and the Kansas jayhawkers had no real interest in the struggle over slavery, but were men drawn to crime and gun violence, using the struggle as an excuse to rob and murder. The violence culminated in 1856 with the attack on Lawrence, Kansas by a force of Missourians that left much of the town in ruins. They burned buildings, destroyed anti-slavery newspapers, and raised a blood-red banner inscribed "Southern Rights" on one side, and "South Carolina" on the other. Newspapers across the North publicized the attack with banner headlines reading "Freedom Bloodily Subdued" and "Triumph of the Border Ruffians."

The disagreement between sections increased with each harsh word uttered in Congress, and with each act of violence in Kansas. Senator Charles Sumner's "Crime Against Kansas" speech (which you shall read in this chapter) outraged both Northern and Southern senators. But when Congressman Preston Brooks of South Carolina beat Sumner with a cane until he collapsed in a heap on the Senate floor, and then was received back home with a brass band and dozens of replacement canes, Northerners were convinced of the arrogance and lawlessness of Southerners. This violence was more than matched when John Brown, seeking revenge for the attacks on Lawrence and Sumner, dragged five men from their cabins in Kansas and hacked them to death with broadswords. The Supreme Court could not resolve the issue in the *Dred Scott* decision, and changing presidents also failed to reconcile the nation.

Before the *Dred Scott* decision, Southerners increasingly asserted that Congress did not have the power to prohibit slavery from federal lands, even though they had agreed to these restrictions in the Northwest Ordinances of 1878 and the Missouri Compromise. After the Supreme Court's ruling, they claimed that only the people of a sovereign state could rule on slavery. Acts of violence continued in Kansas for the rest of the decade, and spread to the east with John Brown's attack on Harpers Ferry, Virginia in 1859. Brown's wild plans to seize weapons from the armory, his use of white and black operatives, and his plan to arm slaves and incite insurrections, were, to Southerners, the natural outcome of Republican and abolitionist ideology. Ever distrustful of the national government, South Carolina used Lincoln's election in 1860 as the excuse to break up the Union in December 1860. Southern extremists could only accept the national union on their own terms, which meant control of some part of the national government. To them, the election of Lincoln meant the more populous North now controlled the government, and the South could not stop attacks on slavery. The Civil War began four months later, on April 12, 1861.

Historians still disagree over the exact cause of the war. Some argue that it was an "irrepressible conflict," inevitable because the two sections of the nation were so different in economics and lifestyles. Others argue the war was very "repressible," but extremists, agitators, and bad politicians on both sides let the nation blunder into the worst war in our history. Another school of historians argues that the political system broke down. Instead of compromising, which is the heart of our system, the 1850s politicians lacked either the ability or desire to do what was right. Perhaps the Civil War was a constitutional crisis, with both sides willing to fight to protect their view of the Constitution or maintain law and order in society. Every one of these explanations involves slavery, because slavery was at the heart of Southern distinctiveness, at the heart of differences in lifestyles and economy, and at the heart of the Southern states' rights argument.

Considering the Evidence in the Readings

These documents all present the views of participants in the events of the 1850s. What issues are they most concerned about? Do you consider them to be extremists? When you have finished reading the documents, be prepared to make an argument about why the war came.

Document 11.1 Georgia Draws a Line in the Sand

The tortuous issue of slavery in the territories nearly wrecked the United States during the years 1849-1850. Paranoia about slavery's continued existence, once dominant only in South Carolina, was now rampant in Mississippi and Alabama as well. Moderates across the nation celebrated when the Compromise of 1850 temporarily resolved the issue, but the threat to national unity was obvious to everyone. Moderate Whigs and Democrats believed abolitionist fanatics were attacking the Southern way of life, and warned their Northern counterparts against letting the fanatics push events too far. Increasingly, Southerners accepted Calhoun's ideas of absolute Southern righteousness, justifiable secession from the Union, and total Southern blamelessness for the problems facing the nation. These ideas, and others, are reflected in this anonymous Georgian's warning to the North in 1850. According to this author, who is to blame for all of the recent troubles and growing national crisis? What future problems for the North and for important Southern institutions does this author believe the Founding Fathers foresaw? What three actions does he warn Northern foes of slavery (and Northerners in general) against taking? Is this Georgian willing to compromise at all in order to preserve the nation?

We have fallen upon times of profound and startling interest. In our day the crisis of trial to our free government has approached imminently near . . . Effort after effort has been made to set aside the Constitution, because it was too stringent a bridle upon selfish prejudice and ambition. But its inherent strength, grounded upon the good sense and sound principle of our people, has so far repelled triumphantly such insidious assaults. In our time these assaults have been directed from a position peculiarly dangerous. The fervor of religious zeal, the ardor of philanthropy, have been artfully enlisted in a most unholy crusade against the citadel of our confidence. To meet a band of enemies battling for wrong under the banner of right has been difficult. . . . Fanaticism and error, honest but dangerous, have existed on the subject of slavery ever since the foundation of our government,—error not confined to one section or one side of the question. Where these exist, the material is ready for the hand of the selfish and designing. In themselves aiming at the right, they are the ready tools of the most egregious wrong. . . . It is useless to disguise that the existence of our Union has been by recent events greatly endangered. It is folly to deny that a few more sessions of Congress like the last, and the Republic, freighted with earth's most glorious hopes, is for ever lost. The arena of public events has disclosed this state of danger. We have seen those bodies composed of the representatives of the Church, wherein discord and fear, we should think, could find no room, torn asunder by the operation of this cause. We have seen the two great parties, cemented by strong bonds, riven into fragments by the detonation of this bomb. We have seen the Congress of the United States spending month after month in the most vituperative and inflammatory debate upon this all-absorbing theme. We have witnessed public meetings composed of Northern men, of those who pride themselves upon adherence to law and order, advocating theft, arson, and Murder Omens grave and serious, these. But there are others, to Northern men almost unknown, which to southern hearts are even more alarming. They are to be found in the condition of Southern feeling upon this subject. But a few years ago not a man in the South dared to avow himself in favor of Disunion. It was looked upon as the synonyme of treachery, and no man dared to avow it. Now, how different is the fact. South Carolina is not only ready, but anxious for the conflict. Her people almost unanimously look upon the Union as a tyranny, whose yoke they would gladly throw off. Her children turn with brow and word of defiance to those whom they consider their oppressors. Mississippi and Alabama partake of the same feeling. In others of the Southern States there prevails less bitterness and more calmness. But in all is the conviction fixed and fastened, that Disunion, aye, even war, is to be preferred to the horrible consequences of an

From *The Union in Crisis* 1850–1877.

interference with slavery among them. Georgia has called a Convention of her people. The action of that body was not difficult to foresee. They will not dissolve this Union, although many of her sons openly avow that thus only can her wrongs be redressed. She will remain in the confederacy, with the hope of obtaining thereunder her rights. But she well knows that but a step or two more taken, and she must defend those rights at all hazards. She will forgive, if possible, forget, the past. But she warns those who have attacked her privileges, that in defence of them we will band together to resist any encroachments. She presents to them the simple alternative, "We will have our rights in this Union, or out of it. You must elect which you prefer." But we, and we only, who have lived amongst her people, who were born and reared upon her soil, know how great has been the struggle in the minds of her sons between an almost superstitious veneration for this Union, and bitter sense of wrong and injury. None else can know how stern is the determination of her people that these wrongs and injuries must cease now and for ever,— cease, quietly and voluntarily if possible, but if not, then terminate in the night of violence and bloodshed. This is the feeling general, nay, unanimous in the South. . . .

In a government where sectional interests and feelings may come into conflict, the sole security for permanence and peace is to be found in a Constitution whose provisions are inviolable. . . . Every State, before entering into that compact, stood in a position of independence. Ere yielding that independence, it was only proper that provision should be made to protect the interests of those which would inevitably be the weaker in that confederacy. In a portion of those independent States a peculiar and most important institution had grown up. It had entwined its tendrils around every interest of the country where it existed,—had become essential to its prosperity. With the foundation of the institution the ancestors of those now warmest to denounce it were identified. Southerners saw that its abolition, nay, even its modification by other hands than their own, might plunge them into all the horrors of a new and more terrible "servile war." While cognizant of all this, they could see the vast interest which posterity might have in this matter; how the North would grow daily in numerical superiority over the South; how slaves would become in process of time the chief source of the wealth of their descendants, and how complex and important would be their relations to society. They also saw how the seeds of fanaticism would grow, how sectional jealousy would increase, how these germs would ripen into animosity. No wonder that they trembled at the prospect—that they demanded protection. Fortunately they had to do with statesmen of enlarged and salutary views. Those Northern men who at that day represented their States could not only perceive how reasonable it was that slavery at the South should be guaranteed in the new government, but also its immense advantages to their own constituency. Intent upon the formation of a great empire, which should embody the principles for which they had fought, they were not willing to yield so great a destiny to the demand of a false and baseless philanthropy. They well knew that those who lived under the institution were not responsible for its foundation; and they saw that its roots were so deeply imbedded, that to tear it away must bring the life-blood from the heart of the new confederacy. They acted wisely, and embodied in the Constitution all that the South could ask. But two Constitutional provisions are necessary to secure Southern rights upon this important question,—the recognition of slavery where the people choose it, and the remedy for fugitive slaves. By the first, foreign interference is prevented, and the whole control and direction of the subject left where it belongs, in the hands of those who only are qualified to understand and to direct it. By the other, is avoided a series of border intestine broils, with which the existence of a Union would have soon become incompatible. We hold that the Constitution of the Union does recognize slavery where it exists. But with the progress of time a spirit has arisen and grown strong, which refuses to make this recognition. True, no effort has as yet been made to attack this principle by abolishing slavery in our midst; but every nerve has been strained to exclude slavery from territories which are the common property of both North and South. Men have allowed the plain dictates of reason to be clouded and obscured by the flimsiest sophistry. A large portion of our States have adopted and allow slavery. The entire country becomes possessed of new territory, to the acquisition of which these slave States contribute mainly. The South admits the right of this new territory to choose for itself whether slavery shall or shall not exist there. But the North insists, that while the territory was partly acquired by Southern men, is partly owned by Southern men, that they shall be excluded from its soil,—that they shall not carry their property into their own land—land which is theirs by the right of purchase. Thus it is rendered, if these views are carried out, simply impossible for any new State representing the Southern interest ever to come into the Union. The equilibrium which alone can preserve the Constitution is utterly destroyed.

And to do this, flagrant violations of the plainest rules of right and wrong are committed. It is said, "You may become the inhabitant of this territory; nay, it is yours, we cannot forbid it; but your property must be left behind." Amounting in effect to the declaration, You may pay out your money to buy land, you may pour out your blood to conquer it, but it is ours; and over it shall be extended only our peculiar customs, our industry, our population: yours have no part nor lot in the matter. Men who would tamely submit to so palpable a usurpation, to so great a wrong, were unworthy to be freemen. Yet such was the famous "Wilmot Proviso." Nor was the course of the North in regard to the provision for the recapture of fugitive slaves less open to objection. Without this provision no Constitution could ever have been formed. Without it now every reasonable Southern man would acquiesce in the necessity of Disunion. We consented, for the sake of our great object, to accept a Constitutional guarantee. Of this Northern men have been well aware; yet the conduct of many of them has been a series of efforts to avoid fulfilling a plain, simple provision of the Constitution. Until the last session, Congress has allowed this provision to remain practically a dead letter. But even the few efforts which have been made to carry into effect its object have met resistance. Legislatures have passed laws with the avowed intention of preventing the execution of this clause of the Constitution, where every member had taken upon his conscience an oath to defend and carry out that Constitution. Judicial officers have forgotten the supreme law of the land, and been carried away by the rush of prejudices. Again in this important matter was the South outraged, her rights denied her.

During the last session of Congress it became evident that no further inroads upon the constitutional rights of the South could be permitted. Then, when the Union was endangered, statesmen of enlarged sentiments came forward to preserve it. The history of that struggle need not be written. It is fresh in the minds of all. Suffice it to say, that the Patriotism of the country rallied against its Radicalism. The conflict was severe; for against the Constitution were leagued the enthusiasts of the North and the ultras of the South. But there is sometimes a principle of strength in governments as in men, which is only developed by circumstances of danger and trial. So in our government has been found to exist a tenacity heretofore sufficient to resist all forces striving to draw it asunder. Our citizens are thinking, reflecting men, and they have seen the disadvantages which are inevitable upon a dissolution of the Union. A majority of them have therefore always rallied to its support. So now,

after every effort to warp and pervert its principles, the Constitution prevailed. The Congress acknowledged *both* the great sanctions which are essential to cement together the Union. It admitted, in the Utah and New-Mexico bills, that it had not the right to exclude slaves from territory common to the whole country, but that its adoption or prohibition depended soley upon the will of the people; and it provided a stringent and effective law for the recapture of fugitive slaves. The action of Congress in both these particulars was based on true principle—a determination to abide by the Constitution. The question now simply is, Will this action be sustained? For the South we answer unhesitatingly, Yes! There are doubtless many amongst us who demand more than they have obtained. The misfortune is also that they have asked more than they had any right to expect. Various motives have urged on these men of ultra sentiments. Some have been animated by a spirit of resentment against the North, which we conceive to be unjust, unless that section of the Union sustains what we hope is but a small and unthinking portion of their population. Others have deemed that a separation would advance the interests of the South; while others have but striven to produce a commotion, in the hope that they would be thrown to the surface in the agitation which must ensue. These men have claimed more than the South obtained by the legislation of the last Congress. Having failed to secure it, they now strive to make that legislation the signal for resistance. Such, we think, is not the sentiment of a majority of the Southern people. The most moderate indeed deem the admission of California to have been irregular, and are pained at much that preceded that admission. But they look upon those irregularities as not affecting the great question which arises upon her application, viz., the right of the people of a State to decide for themselves as to the existence of slavery amongst them. A great majority of the Southern people are satisfied that the people of California do not wish slavery. They contend that they have a right to the institution wherever the municipal law sanctions it. This they hold to be their right under the Constitution. The inference is irresistible that the same right of choice is preserved to others, and that slavery shall not go into territories where the inhabitants desire to exclude it. They therefore submit to the admission of California, notwithstanding the irregularities attending it, because they think that substantially the intent of the people was carried out. And this great test they are willing to abide by, whether it works woe or weal. But with other parts of the legislation of Congress we have better reason to be satisfied. Comprehending a surrender of the Wilmot Proviso, and an energetic law for the recovery of fugitive slaves, it includes all that is necessary to secure the rights of the South. But will the North abide by this just and equitable termination of the matter? Will she be content with the advantages which she will necessarily enjoy in the natural course of events; or will she open this wise and just settlement, and introduce again into the national councils the demons of distraction and terror?

Much of the evil that has threatened has arisen, not from actual assaults upon the vested privileges of the South, but from attacks upon the feelings of her people. As a whole, no people are more sensitive than those of the South, more quick to resent insult and injury. They are placed in a most peculiar position. Born long after slavery had become rooted in their country, they have no option but to sustain it. Even those most anxious to abolish it advance no feasible mode of accomplishing their end. The Southern man well knows it to be utterly impracticable. He sees its many advantages, and he only can feel its peculiar importance to himself. Yet he is doomed to see attack after attack made upon this institution by men who understand nothing whatever of its nature, and who are ignorant of, or indifferent to, the terrible consequences which may follow the intermeddling with its existence. He must be content to hear every term of reproach lavished upon him, as a human taskmaster, by those whose forefathers established the slave trade for gain, and who themselves gladly draw their wealth from the pockets of the much abused slave-owner. Nay, he sees publications filled with onslaughts the most ungenerous, and often untrue, upon his whole community. Southern men were fast becoming tired of vituperation, often obviously hypocritical, and always unjust and impertment. This it was and is yet—this spirit of indignation which more than aught else endangers the Union. Men cannot and ought not to remain calmly indifferent while others seek to deprive them of their rights, and to awake in their midst a spirit which may prove fatal to all they hold most dear. The passage of the Compromise Bills acted like balm upon the wounded feelings of the South. The action of Northern men was essential to procure the success of those measures; and the purest and ablest amongst them came manfully forward to sustain Southern rights. By their assistance those rights were obtained. To a great extent the irritation in Southern minds had subsided. The Southern heart has warmed towards Webster, and Cass, and Dickinson, and Elliott. We have felt at length that those who seek to destroy us are but a faction, and that we

believe neither numerous nor reputable, amongst our Northern brethren. Shall this state of feeling continue? The North must decide. It were idle to deny that the compromises of the last session will not remain unattacked in either section of the Union. But at the South, as we have indicated, they will be sustained. At the North the issue must mainly be fought. The vituperation and howling of enthusiasts we are prepared to expect, but we are beginning to learn how little must their ravings be considered as an exponent of true public feeling at the North.

The question is, Will the North remain content with the so-called Compromise Bills, or will her people persist in attempts to violate the Constitution? The issue must be fought north of the Potomac. And upon its result depends the existence of the Union. Already have the destroyers, defeated but not discouraged, raised the banner of revolt. The South regards them but little, confiding in the patriotism of the North to deprive these madmen of the power to do evil. But if this hope shall prove fallacious; if again a Northern party shall attempt to make the Government the arbiter of the existence of slavery, and to use their numerical power to exclude it, or shall endeavor to throw obstacles in the way of the slave-owner seeking to recover the fugitive, the knell of this Republic will have struck. It is time this matter should be comprehended. The people at the North have now a fair, dear field for the contest. It is not ours to interfere. Themselves must decide whether they prefer Disunion to a confederacy with slave States. They have before them every aid to arrive at a decision. But that decision must be made, and will in all probability be final. If a majority of the people of the North shall see fit to deny us the privileges with which we came into the Union, it will remain for us to seek our rights in independence. But ere we are forced to this alternative, it were well for Northern men to reflect on the path before them. The justice and propriety of slavery we do not intend to discuss. But it is, to one intimately acquainted with its workings, surprising to see the glaring misrepresentations which are common in regard to the slave. But we do not conceive the question which Northern men have to argue with themselves just now is as to the morality or propriety of slavery. If they do not wish it amongst themselves, we do not desire it should exist there. They are welcome to exclude it, and welcome to all the satisfaction to which its exclusion may entitle them. Most dearly if it exists not amongst them, they are not responsible for its grievous sin. The question is, whether it behooves them to sacrifice the Union in a crusade against what they are pleased to consider an abomination amongst their neighbors. The first view of the matter which strikes the mind of every sensible man who thinks at all upon the subject, is the utter hopelessness of the task. It matters not who is responsible for the introduction of slavery; practically its continuation is, as the entire South believe, inevitable. It is identified with the pecuniary, social, and personal interests of the South. But even were it not so, yet no feasible plan for its abolition has ever been offered. All suggestions for its present extinction terminate in anarchy and blood. With the terrible certainty that its abolition must terminate in the most fearful danger to themselves and all whom they love and cherish, can it be doubted that the men of the South will resist, even to the last extremity, any and all interference with this their peculiar institution? The same spirit which fought at King's Mountain, which struggled with Marion in the swamps of Santee, which conquered at San Jacinto and Chapultepec, will disdain submission. It is worse than idle then to persist in striving to accomplish an impossibility. The fearful risk which threatens our country, the dangers which are so apparent, are all to be incurred in the prosecution of a purpose utterly and hopelessly unfeasible. And for this is to be perilled the existence of the Constitution—the hopes of freemen. "Alas!" may we not exclaim, "what inexplicable madness!"

Our Union is but the symbol of Constitutional freedom. Like all symbols which are sanctified by time-hallowed memories, it is dear in itself. The South will be the last to forget the sacred recollections which are entwined alike around the hearts of the inhabitants of every portion of this wide country. Nor are her children insensible to the still more vast and general blessings which that Union dispenses to all mankind. Well do they love liberty, and well do they know that the hopes of its wisest votaries throughout the earth are centered on the success of our Republic. Deeply indeed would we mourn over the failure of the experiment which embodies the noblest principle. But it can never be presumed that the cause of freedom would be advanced by the yielding of one section of the Union to the tyranny of another. The eagle which at the head of the legions of Publicola was the banner of Roman liberty, floated before the army which crossed the Rubicon. The cross which Paul and Peter preached as the sign of meekness, humility and love, became the eidolon of Dominican persecution. It is not impossible that the stars and stripes may likewise be desecrated. The Union, without a living, vital Constitution, is but a vain and empty name. Nay, more, it is but a body powerless for good, strong for evil.

Its destruction is inevitable unless the original guarantees are respected and maintained. Of its consequences to the cause of human freedom, of the frightful intestine wars which must follow, of the hatred which will be sown between brethren, of the terrible effects of a people combating against enemies abroad and a race in bondage at home, it is not our purpose to speak. These thoughts must have occurred often to the mind of every man who is not blinded by the most narrow bigotry. But there are two views of the disasters attendant upon a dissolution, which it behooves Northern men well to think upon. In the first place, let them reflect, it will most seriously interfere with their pecuniary interests. Men of wisdom and experience at the South have sometimes doubted whether a dissolution of this Union would not be an advantage. But of its effect upon the pecuniary affairs of the North there can be no doubt. Let the South be stirred to a pitch of animosity sufficient to cause a dissolution; let Northern manufactures, Northern shipping, be put upon the same footing with those of France and England, and what would be the result? Can they sustain the burden? Those who are most interested well know not. But let not Northern men be deceived. Those amongst them familiar with the details of business, well know that we, the Southern States, with every power to become independent, have been content to share with the North our abundance, to contribute to her wealth and strength. But let us be driven to separate; let us be forced to withdraw our household gods from a Union no longer existing for our protection; let Northern men occupy the position of open, avowed enemies;—they will be looked upon with hatred and aversion. They will in vain look to us for support. We will be separated as widely, as effectively to all practical purposes, as though between us flowed a gulf of fire "measureless to man." No Northern man can fail to see the result of such a state of things; to be incurred, too, for the accomplishment of an object demonstrably Utopian. It seems impossible that the shrewd, sagacious men of the North, seeing and understanding the result, can be compelled to submit to what will prove ruinous to them through the violence of fanatic zeal. The struggle is for them. But again: The efforts of Northern men to interfere with slavery are unfortunate for their unhappy beneficiaries. If we are let alone, it will be our pride and our pleasure to increase the benefits and diminish the disadvantages of their situation; but if we are to be summoned, by those whose object and endeavor it is to poison the minds of those whose opportunities for evil are necessarily so fearful, to destroy our main dependence, nay, perchance to endanger our lives, most severely will these ill-judged efforts react upon the condition of the slave. He has been to us an object of attachment and sympathy. We have sustained and protected him, and in sickness and old age have extended to him every comfort. Nay, many of us have found amongst these humble beings friends whose devotion shames that of others far above them. Happy and contented, he has passed through life, throwing upon his master the entire load of life's cares and sorrows, desiring in his own condition no change. But if into these minds brooding and most dangerous thoughts are to be instilled; if a domestic traitor is to be implanted in every family; if we are to guard alike against the subtraction of this most valuable source of subsistence, and the dangers of their own passions, so savage when roused, we shall be compelled to introduce into our polity elements never before known,—to watch stringently, to restrict closely, to punish severely. The kind familiarity of the master will be gone, and in its place will be substituted the suspicious eye and stern hand of caution

and severity. This is the change which is to be produced by the machinations of those who claim to be the peculiar friends of the slave,—men whom nothing will convince of the madness of their career, save a Union rent unto fragments amidst the wild waves of a bloody convulsion. Alas! that in this age such fanaticism should not be met by the united execrations of every patriot—nay, of every philosopher.

With this matter we of the South have but little more to do. Some of us are, as has been already said, ready for the utmost. Others, we fondly believe a majority, are willing to forget the wrongs of the past and to hope for the future. But let the North refuse to abide by our rights, and the cry, which will go up from the hearts of the whole Southern people, will be, "Let us go out from among them." Meanwhile the battle rages at the North. The din of the conflict is borne to our ears. How it will end we may not know. We can but offer up heart-felt prayers for the success of those who battle for the Union and the Constitution.

Document 11.2 A Southerner's Viewpoint of the Kansas Situation, 1856–1857

Determined to make Kansas a slave state, Missourians crossed the border to vote illegally in elections, and actively recruited settlers from other Southern states. Senator David Atchison wrote to a friend in Georgia, "Let your young men come forth to Missouri and Kansas. Let them come well armed.... We must have the support of the South. We are fighting the battles of the South...." Coming to Kansas in armed parties or as individuals, many Southerners vowed to join Missouri in using any means fair or foul to make Kansas a slave state. But some Southerners came to Kansas for the traditional reasons Americans moved to a new territory--to start over and prosper. Axalla John Hoole came to Kansas in April 1856 with his new bride. He took an active part in Kansas politics, was chosen probate judge by the pro-slavery party, and remained in Kansas for two years. In his letters back home, what issues and concerns does Hoole mention besides the struggle over slavery? According to Hoole, who or what is causing all of the problems in Kansas? What are his views on blacks, slavery, and everyone who rejects slavery?

Douglas City, K. T., Apl. 27th., 1856

My Dear Brother

. . . I am still boarding at the above mentioned place with Mr. Elison and paying $3 a week apiece for myself and wife, but I have sent to Missouri for provisions which I expect here in a day or two, when I will

go to housekeeping. I have two houses which I can rent, one of which we are occupying to sleep in. It is about a hundred yards from Mr. Elison's, where I eat. I commenced working at the carpenter's trade last Monday—I tried to get a school, but failed to get one worth my notice, so I concluded on the whole it was best for me to get at something else, and as a trade pays better than anything else, I went at the

From *Kansas Historical Quarterly*, February, 1934.

carpenter's. The man I am working with is giving from $1.75 to $2.25 a day, but could not tell me what he would give me, but said that we would not fall out about the price, until he could determine what I was worth. I intended to have made him set a price yesterday, but it rained so that I could not go to work. Tomorrow we will come to an understanding. I shall stand out for $2 a day, as I think that I am worth that, at the rate of everything else here. I have a long walk every day to and from my work, about two & a half miles. My work is in Lecompton, the capital, above Douglas.

I have no fun here. Game is scarce. Mr. Elison's son killed a pelican in the river yesterday morning. I went out late in the evening and killed two squirrels, which is the first thing of any kind I have killed since I have been here. They catch cat-fish in the river here that weigh from 10 to 100 lbs., but I have not seen any yet, A man caught one yesterday morning that weighed 20 lbs.

I still don't like this country, and I don't care how soon it is admitted as a state. The Governor sent the sheriff to take some men in Lawrence last Saturday (yesterday week) and the Lawrenceites rescued the prisoner from him. The sheriff came and reported to the Governor, who sent him back with four other men, but they also failed. The Governor then sent a dispatch to the fort for some soldiers; they came on Tuesday, and with the sheriff went to Lawrence on Wednesday and succeeded in taking six prisoners, but as they had not the most important one, they concluded that they would stay there all night. In the night the sheriff (Jones) with two or three other men went out of the tent to get some water, and while drawing it, the sheriff was shot at, the ball passing through his pantaloons behind his leg.

A man can earn from $2 to $2.50 per day, but he will have to spend it to live on. Board and everything else is very high. Board is from $3 to $5.50 per week, no washing at that, coarse fare . . . and have to lie on a comfort or blanket on the floor; there are but few beds in the country as yet. Lumber is from $2.50 to $4 per hundred feet and very inferior. I worked at carpenter's trade for $1.75 a day. For a man to come here to farm it would require from $500 to $1000 to commence—and then pay the government price for it when it comes on the market.

There is no game but a few squirrels, and they are scarce, and no fish of any account. One of my neighbors caught a catfish that weighed 20 or 25 lbs., but I did not see it. All provisions are high, except milk and butter. Flour, $12 a barrel, bacon 8 1/2 to 12 cents, molasses 80 cents per gallon, coffee 16 2/3 cents lb.,

salt 3 1/2 cents lb., so you will have to spend all you make to live on. No scouring is done for want of water. When it rains your feet are stuck so full of mud you can scarcely walk.

The place where I am living is called Douglas City. It has only 5 or 6 houses in it, and they are log houses. It is laid out for a town in lots, and is the place selected for the state university. It is a prettier place than Lecompton where they are building the State House, which is only 2 miles above this place on the river. Timber is more plentiful at Douglas than at Lecompton, and a better landing for boats, when they should run on this river. One has gone to Fort Riley, 100 miles above here. Kansas River is broad but shallow, full of sand bars which makes navigation difficult. Lawrence is the headquarters of the Abolitionists of this Territory.

Yours truly,
A. J. Hoole.

Douglas, K.T., May 18th, 1856

My dearly Beloved Sister,

. . . I rec'd a letter from Mr. Cooper . . . which was dated four days before yours. They had both been written nearly a month before I got them, which I attribute to their being directed to Lawrence. I had left the place, but when I left it I gave the P.M. my name with directions to forward my letters to Lecompton, but he neglected to do so until I wrote to him . . .

The seed of sweet potatoes is almost lost in this Ter. & also in Mo. & other northwestern states. You did not tell me whether you had moved into the new house or not. Do tell me whenever you write to me all such news as that. . . .

You say the Negroes don't forget me in their prayers. Thank them a thousand times for me, and beg them always to remember me when they render up their petitions to Him who rules and governs all things. I feel that I need the prayers of everyone. Tell Stin when he writes to tell me about everybody, everything, dogs, hogs, cows, horses, and chickens and everything—leave nothing out, for anything from Old Darlington will interest me.

And now dear sister, I suppose you would like for me to tell you something of myself, &c. Well, I have been working at carpenters trade for three weeks, until last Thursday when the man I was working for got out of lumber and had no work for coarse workmen like me, so he discharged all of us except those who could do fine work. I was getting $1.75 per day. I made lacking 25 cts. of $30 in what time I worked. But you may depend upon it, I earned every cent I got, for I had to walk about three miles, work eleven hours, and then walk back at night. I was, you may say, exercising fifteen hours of the hardest kind every day. Sometimes I felt like I would give out before I could get home at night. I was sick Friday and Saturday a week ago, and so lost two days, which I attribute to overworking. I was also unwell yesterday and the day before, but if I had had anything to do, I believe I should have worked. I engaged to work for a man near me, but I hear he is bad pay and I believe I will back out. Betsie has been unwell for two or three days, and I fear that she is worse off than she pretends she is. She said she was a good deal better when she first got up this morning, but just as I commenced writing this, she came in and lay down and said she felt worse again.

We are living to ourselves and considering the house, very pleasantly. Betsie cooks, but we hire a Negroe to do our washing at $2 a month. Betsie is a first rate cook. We have meal, flour, bacon (ham shoulder and sides) lard, butter, molasses, sugar, coffee, besides milk (butter milk and sweet milk) as much as we want, whenever we go after it. So you can guess whether we have enough to eat or not.

I pay $2 a month for house rent, but I think that it is cheaper to live to ourselves and keep house than to board out, for the lowest we can board at is $3 a week apiece, and I am certain it is much more pleasant.

Major Beaufort [sic] has arrived in the territory with 4 or 500 men. Beaufort himself is now at Mr. Ellison's, my nearest neighbor. I have not seen him yet, but I heard that he intended to call on me. Colonel Treadwell who came with him was at Mr. Ellison's one night last week. I called on him. He is a very gentlemanly man; he is a brother-in-law of Bertram. I felt like I had met an old friend when I met him. We talked very little though for we had little time that night. The next day he came to where I was working at Lecompton, but did not stay long with me as I expect he thought he was hindering me from my work.

I wrote a long letter to Warley yesterday, which I expect he will publish in the *Flag*. If he does not, you must get Stin or Mr. Cooper to get it from him and read it as I have written a good deal to him which I would have written to you, if I had not thought that you would learn it all. It is mostly on political matters. While I am writing, guns are firing in the camps of the different companies of soldiers who are gathering to attack Lawrence. Sunday, as I expect it is, they are firing in every direction. I expect before you get this Lawrence will be burnt to the ground. I may not know when it will be attacked, but if I do, I expect to go—although I don't think they will show any fight, though they are preparing. But I hear they are very much frightened and have sent to the governor for protection, but he sent word to them that they did not consider him governor and would not submit to the laws, so he would leave them to their fate. But all of this you will see more fully in the letter I have written to Warley, so I will now close this. Do write soon and often to me . . .

Your affectionate Brother, Axalla.

Document 11.3 Pro-Slavery Newspaper Advocates Violence to Win Kansas

Southerners swarmed into eastern Kansas in 1855 and made the towns of Leavenworth and Atchison pro-slavery strongholds. The *Atchison Kansas Squatter Sovereign* was a violently pro-slavery newspaper. Operated by Dr. John Stringfellow and his brother Benjamin, this newspaper regularly denounced all Northern settlers as "barbarians," advised pro-slavery Kansans to vote with a "Bowie knife and revolver," and told its readers to exterminate all "scoundrels" tainted with "free-soilism." Kansas was not a place for Southern recruits whose conscience did not allow them to violate laws. The Stringfellows did more than write editorials. They also participated in lynchings, beatings of free-soilers, and raids across the territory. The following are excerpts from a number of their editorials. Note how any suggestion of moderation, or support for those advocating peaceful or legal methods, is treated.

"Rally! Rally! Forbearance has now ceased to be a virtue; thereupon we call upon every proslavery man in the land to rally to the rescue. The war has again commenced, and the abolitionists have commenced it. Proslavery men, law and order men, strike for your altars! Strike for your firesides! Strike for your rights! Avenge the blood of your brothers who have been cowardly assailed but have bravely fallen in defence of southern institutions. Sound the bugles of war over the length and bredth of the land, and leave not an abolitionist in the territory to relate their treacherous and contaminating deeds. Strike your piercing rifle-balls and your glittering steel to their black and poisonous hearts! Let the war cry never cease in Kansas again.

"Now we will be equally candid . . . for every Negro stolen we will hang ten abolitionists, for it will take at least that many to get one Negro off. So gentlemen Negro thieves, you can commence the war as soon as you choose.

"War to the knife and knife to the hilt . . . Let the watchword be extermination, total and complete."

Document 11.4 Another Pro-Slavery Newspaper Expresses Its Views

The *Leavenworth Kansas Weekly Herald* also advocated extreme Southern activism. This paper suggested that the abolitionist hordes coming to Kansas could either accept Southern institutions (i.e., slavery), leave Kansas as fast as possible, or be buried there. Its editors championed Missourians' voting in Kansas' elections (using force if necessary) to make sure Kansas became a slave state. It claimed all Northern settlers were abolitionist mercenaries, the worst dregs of Northern society, paupers, and convicts sent to ruin Kansas for Southerners. Angered when free-soilers fought back and answered violence with violence, the *Weekly Herald* supported cleansing Leavenworth of all citizens with a different point of view. For days, mobs roamed through the city, hunting down suspected free-staters, driving them from their homes and hiding places. Lucky persons took sanctuary in Fort Leavenworth, but scores, including elderly women, mothers with babies, and the sick, were driven onto steamboats and forced to leave town without any possessions, food, or shelter. This was all done in the name of Southern justice, and supported by the *Weekly Herald*, which advocated "no quarter" to the enemy. Below is their own account of the mob's attack on two brothers who were tarred and feathered a year earlier but remained in their home in Leavenworth.

"I found the street jammed with armed citizens and Missourians, and a Colonel Moore harangueing them . . . When his speech ended Captain Frederick Emory's horse company road off to search free state houses, and disarm the men; they first went to the house of Jerrold Phillips where a number of free state men boarded . . . Phillips, supposing he was to be driven out of house and home, resolved not to submit to the indignity, and bravely took the initiative himself. Standing boldly out on the veranda of his house, when the ruffians drew up in front of it, he fired upon them, killing two of their number. They instantly directed a volley of bullets at him and the house, and Phillips fell pierced in a dozen places, the door casing being literally riddled with the leaden storm. He expired almost instantly in the presence of his wife and another lady. His brother, who was with him, had his arm so badly broken with bullets, that he was compelled to submit to an amputation."

From *Squatter Sovereign* 1/22/1856 and 1/27/1856.
Weekly Herald, July 26, 1856.

Document 11.5 Border Ruffian or Kansas Ranger?: A Southerner in Kansas, 1855-1856

R.H. Williams traveled west to make his fortune, and brought both slaves and investment capital with him. He set up a freighting business between Fort Leavenworth and Fort Riley, shot buffalo for food, and made money by renting out his slaves and investing in land. Although more moderate than many Southerners in Kansas, he was drawn into the struggle over the territory's future. Williams joined a group known as the Kansas Rangers, created to enforce the laws passed by the illegally elected Lecompton Legislature, and to violently discourage free-soil supporters from settling in the territory. The Lecompton Legislature and pro-slavery officials routinely recruited Missourians to enforce laws in Kansas, because of their pro-slavery views. The original "Kansas" territorial militia, created to protect the territory and help officials enforce the law, was entirely made up of Missourians! Many of the "Border Ruffians" served in the militia as well as in various extra-legal organizations. The following is an excerpt from Williams' account of his life in Kansas. Some of his facts are wrong (i.e. Sheriff Jones was NOT shot dead by free-soilers), but he relates the First Sack of Lawrence in May 1856, and also explains the personal nature of the struggle. What does Williams explain as the causes of the struggle in Kansas? Why does he support the Southern cause? What proof does he present that the violence exceeded the bounds of the pro-slavery versus free-soil struggle, and became a matter of personal revenge or violence for violence's sake?

Though by the latter end of February the ice on the river had broken up, no boats were running, or could run, for several weeks. I therefore determined to wait no longer, but to ride to Fort Leavenworth on the Missouri, a distance of 450 miles.

Leaving my niggers with their masters, who treated them well, I mounted a fine young horse I had bought, and set off, one bitterly cold morning, on my long and solitary journey. Roads there were none, except near the widely scattered farms, and then they were more like a series of half-thawed mudholes.

The country was very different from the Virginian forestlands I knew so well, but the people were the same kindly, hospitable folks, making the weary traveller welcome to the best they had, and seldom accepting payment for their entertainment. So I journeyed on, getting over about thirty-five miles a day on an average, and nothing worth recording occurred till Independence, an important town and Indian trading-post on the frontier of Missouri, was reached. There I found the place crowded with Missourians and a goodly sprinkling of men from the Southern States, all full of excitement over the burning question whether the Territory of Kansas, recently opened up for settlement, should be Slave or Free.

The Free State party in the North, managed and worked from Faneuil Hall, Boston, had been sending up men and arms, and had occupied positions defended by light artillery. The Missourians were crossing the river, and volunteers from all the Southern States were marching up to the conflict, which might break out at any moment.

In this scene of seething unrest and wild passion, a stranger was naturally regarded with suspicion until he declared his sympathies. Mine were strongly on the side of the South, and, as soon as I made this known, I was heartily welcomed amongst the "Border Ruffians," as the pro-Slavery party was nicknamed by the Free Staters.

Strong pro-slavery man as I was, I saw a sight, as I rode out of the town next morning, that opened my eyes to the cruelty and barbarity of the "Institution." A slave-dealer was there, with his drove of niggers, collected for the Southern market, and in it was one who had been sold as a desperate character. Just as I started, the unfortunate creature had broken loose, and passed close by me in his frantic rush for the woods near by. After him came his master and some other men, shouting to him to stop. But he was running for life and liberty, and held on in desperation.

From *With the Border Ruffians*, published by University of Nebraska Press.

He was rapidly nearing the covert when the master raised his rifle, fired, and the fugitive fell dead in his tracks. It was a brutal deed, done by a brute, but the law sanctioned it. It was almost as much as my life was worth to remonstrate; so I held my tongue and rode on, sickened and disgusted with this, to me, new aspect of slavery.

That night I put up with "Johnny Cake," the head chief of the Delaware Indians in Kansas, on the Delaware reserve. He was a tame Indian, spoke English well, and was a member of the Methodist Church. He treated me very well, and was most hospitable; but what I chiefly remember of my visit is that my host gave us a long and very extraordinary grace before and after the corn bread and bacon.

Late the next evening I reached Leavenworth City, and, at a wooden shanty dignified with the name of hotel, got taken in.

The "city" was on the Delaware reserve, and was not open for settlement; indeed the U.S. Government had warned all squatters off it by proclamation, under heavy penalties. But these were "paper penalties" only, i.e., never enforced, and were treated as non-existent; especially as it was known that nearly the whole of the reserve would be thrown open in the fall.

In 1855 the "city," now a great centre of the rich wheat-growing district in which it stands, consisted of a few frame buildings, two or three small stores, and the "hotel" I put up at. *The Leavenworth Democrat* represented the majesty of the "Fourth Estate," and was edited printed, and published in a small shanty under a big cottonwood-tree by Major Euston, an out-and-out Southerner, and a typical specimen of the South-western fighting editor. He was the quickest man with his six-shooter I ever saw, even in a country where it behoved every one to be on the alert.

The little place was full of gamblers, as all frontier settlements were in those days.

Their "boss sportsman" was a certain A. B. Miller, who had run up a shanty with a showily fitted-out bar and rooms for the accommodation of the fraternity. There roulette, pharo, and poker were going on from midday all through the night, and large sums changed hands. Now and then some unlucky gambler would end his miseries in the mighty Missouri, and many another was shot in the saloon itself during the constant night rows.

In those early days there was no law in the city, not even a Vigilance Committee, and the sporting fraternity, holding all together, and being well armed, ruled without question. They were a "Sound on the goose," or in other words, strong pro-slavery men,

and their misdeeds notwithstanding, were in a measure popular with the rest of the community.

In face of all these drawbacks, and the prevailing ruffianism, I soon made up my mind to risk my fortunes in the Territory. With a man named Moses Young from Kentucky, a carpenter and contractor, I entered into a sort of partnership, with the object of buying up likely "lots" and building thereon shanties for the new arrivals who kept pouring in.

If I only had had the prescience to foresee what that new country would so rapidly grow to, I might now be a millionaire, simply by buying up, and *holding on to,* town lots.

As soon as I had made this agreement with Young, I left my horse and other belongings with him and set off for St. Louis to fetch my darkies, and my cash and Manor. The soft breath of spring was in the air, spring that comes so suddenly and so sweetly in the Southwestern States of the Union, and my six days' trip down the river was delightful. Ten days I spent in St. Louis, and then started back with my "chattels," my dog, and my capital of $2,000, as well as a wagon and harness for a team I had bought as a spec.

The boat was crowded with pro-slavery men, and some few Free Staters; but the latter kept very quiet. At Leavenworth the Levee was crowded by the whole population, who had turned out to see that our boat had brought no arms for the Free Staters.

Young had found me room in a boarding-house started in my absence, and we marched there in great state, followed by the darkies; and their possession gave me quite a status in the city! The landlady of the house at once hired my girl Ann at $20 a month, and the two boys were as quickly taken for $25 each, and their keep. So I had an income of $70 a month, more than enough for my modest wants, and felt quite independent.

Presently I bought another horse and, with my new wagon, began carrying, at good paying rates. Then Moses Young and I bought a lot and built a Californian frame house, in which to live ourselves and board our hands, with stabling behind it for our horses. Moreover we dug a garden, and planted it; the only one, I think, in all the city.

* * *

Meanwhile the political excitement had day by day been growing more intense, and now was at fever heat.

Quietly and calmly looking back on the situation in the United States, one sees quite clearly that the struggle for supremacy between North and South, of which the fighting in Kansas was only the prelude, had to be decided sooner or later. Further, it is also plain that the two sections were so diametrically opposed to each other in political ideas that they must have fought it out before a peaceful *modus vivendi* could be arrived at. Negro slavery was not the cause of the war, but only one of many causes; nor did the North enter on the struggle with the object of freeing the negro.

The South, broadly speaking, was a landed aristocracy, whilst the North was trading and commercial.

Since the establishment of the Republic, the South, with its comparatively sparse white population, had, by the voting power given by its negroes (though these of course had no votes themselves), ruled the wealthy and rapidly growing Northern States, and the yoke had at last become intolerable.

In Kansas the South fought for the right to add to the number of Slave States, which was its only hope of retaining supremacy in the Union; the North to restrict slavery within the limits fixed by the agreement arrived at in 1820.

***

Now in 1854, just before I arrived on the scene of strife, the South attempted to apply the principle of "squatter sovereignty" to the vast territories of Kansas and Nebraska, lying north of the 36°30' line. This was manifestly a breach of the Missouri Compromise, and the North was up in arms at once.

This is a long digression from my story; but it seemed necessary to explain, as shortly as possible, the cause of the bitter strife in which I played a humble part.

The Southerners then, whether they had law and right on their side or not, were determined to establish "squatter sovereignty" in Kansas, and to carry the vote for slavery. The Northerners were equally determined they should not succeed.

South Carolina, Missouri, and Texas especially, raised war funds and organised companies.

Henry Ward Beecher, the moving spirit of Faneuil Hall, Boston, and his Abolitionist associates, with any amount of capital behind them, poured men and arms into the territory, regardless of expense.

The Government at Washington, controlled by the Southern Democrats, preserved a benevolent neutrality for the Southerners' cause, and did not interfere until compelled to do so by the frightful state of anarchy which eventually prevailed.

To stop the influx of men and arms from the North into Leavenworth, which was the only easily accessible port of entry for them, a "minute com-pany," so called from its brief period of service, was formed to search every boat, more especially for arms. I joined this company directly after my return from Fort Riley, and I remember we seized a great number of rifles; some of them Sharp's breech-loaders, two of which were given to me.

Now the elections for the Territorial Legislature came on, and, considered as elections, were of course a farce. In many places the Missourians and other Southerners seized the polls, and crammed the ballot-boxes. In others the "Free Soilers" did the same. The result was that two Legislatures were elected; the pro-Slavery one making its capital at Lecompton, and the Free State one at Topeka.

The rival parties met at the polls and elsewhere, and many lives were lost in the fights that took place. The excitable Southerners' blood was nearly at boiling-point, when Sheriff Jones, elected by them, was shot dead by a "Free Soiler," in the execution of his duty.

Fully resolved to throw in my lot with the South, I now joined a company of mounted Rangers, raised by A. B. Miller, who, though a professional gambler, had the reputation of a plucky fighting man, and was at once elected orderly sergeant myself. No oath of enlistment was taken, but there was no fear of desertion or insubordination, since death would have been the penalty for either crime.

Our company was the best mounted and equipped in the Southern force, and, as soon as we were mustered, moved into camp at Salt Creek, about three miles from Leavenworth City, where about eight hundred Missouri and Southern volunteers were assembled.

Our commander was "General" Davy Atchison, a well-known and influential character in those parts. When I met him, and served under him, he was about fifty-five years of age, and one of the most popular men in his section of the country; in fact, a typical Western politician. A lawyer by profession, he was also a planter, and large slave-owner; consequently thoroughly "Sound on the goose." At this time he was U.S. Senator for the State of Missouri, and had been Vice-President of the United States. As an Indian fighter and hunter he had made himself a great reputation.

With a somewhat rough exterior, he was really a kindly man, and, being "hail-fellow-well-met" with all his supporters, was, as I have said, extremely popular.

Miller introduced me to the "General" soon after I joined the camp. He invited us into his tent, and ordered drinks forthwith. Youngster that I was, the old fellow received me without any "side" or standoffishness, so that I felt on a friendly footing at once, and, like the rest of his followers, would have gone anywhere with him.

Life in camp was pleasant enough at first, for our "General" didn't go in for much drill, possibly because he didn't know much about it himself, and our principal duty was to keep watch and ward over the river and stop all passing steamboats to search them for Free Soilers and their arms. Those that did not stop when ordered were promptly brought to by a field battery we had posted on the river, commanding the passage. All suspected Free Staters were taken out and kept under guard, and of course all their arms were confiscated.

Our excuse for this rather high-handed proceeding was that "The Massachusetts Emigrants' Aid Society," with great resources at its back, was pouring men and arms into Kansas, with the avowed object of conquering and dominating the Territory, by fair means or foul, for the Free State party.

Our first apparently important movement was now made on Lawrence, the Northern headquarters, which was protected by considerable earthworks and held by a force of some two thousand men under Robinson, the "Free State" governor, and other leaders of the party.

I may say at once that, though we did a deal of marching and counter-marching, and though on several occasions a general engagement between the opposing forces seemed imminent, it never came to a pitched battle; and all the many lives that were lost in this miserable border fighting, were lost in small affairs between scouting parties and outposts. Many men too, on either side, were killed in this way to pay out old scores and gratify private spite and revenge.

So one fine morning we "Border Ruffians," as the enemy called us, struck camp and marched out some fifteen hundred strong, with two 6-pr. field-pieces, to attack Lawrence, my company acting as the advance guard. We halted the first night near Lecompton, our capital, my company being on picket duty, spread out fan-like some two miles round the camp. Next morning Governor Shannon, our own party's governor, paid us a visit of inspection, and was pleased to express his high approval of our discipline and workmanlike appearance.

I can't say much for our discipline myself, but there is no doubt we were a fighting lot, if only the Northerners had given us the chance of proving it.

The morning after the inspection we marched on Lawrence, where we expected a sharp fight, which we were fully confident of winning. My company acted again as the advance guard, and when,

about midday, we reached Mount Oread, a strongly fortified position, on which several guns were mounted, covering the approach to the town, great was our surprise to find it had been evacuated. As soon as our general received the report, he ordered our company to make a wide circuit round the town, to seize the fords of the Kansas River and hold the road leading east.

Then he moved the rest of his force to within half a mile of the town, formed square on the open prairie, and sent in a flag of truce, demanding an unconditional surrender of the place. To the no small disgust of the "Border Ruffians," Governor Robinson, without further parley, threw up the sponge, and meekly surrendered the town and the 2,500 men it contained.

No doubt his men were not very keen on fighting, being the riff-raff of the Northern towns enlisted by the Emigrants' Aid Society, and most of them quite unused to bear arms of any kind. Many of them bolted for the Kansas River ford and the Eastern road; and we of Miller's company took quite three times our own number of these valiant warriors prisoners. I well remember how scared the poor wretches were! I am glad to say that the prisoners' lives were spared, all but two, and they were hanged by the Provost Marshal for horse-stealing, the penalty for which was invariably death, in that Western country, even in ordinary times.

Though the prisoners were spared, I regret to say the town was not, for Atchison's men got completely out of hand, battered down the "Free State Hotel," and sacked most of the houses. It was a terrible scene of orgy, and I was very glad when, about midnight, we of Miller's company were ordered off to Lecompton to report the day's doings to Governor Shannon. There we were kept several days, scouring the country for Free Soilers, and impressing arms, horses, and corn.

In these operations we occupied Topeka, the pro-Slavery capital, and had a brush with a body of Northerners, under Jim Lane, in which we lost two men killed and six wounded.

Next, at "Lone Jack," we had a skirmish with Captain John Brown's men, but the firing was at long range and no harm was done, for the Free Staters soon retired, and we were not strong enough to follow them up.

On the march, the day after this, to Stranger Creek, and whilst scouting ahead of the company with two other men, I came on the bodies of two young men lying close together, both shot through the head. The murdered men, for it was brutal murder and nothing else, were dressed like Yankee mechanics, and apparently had been done to death the previous night.

I had heard that one of our scouting parties had taken some prisoners,—but that they had escaped; and now it was plain what had been done by some of our ruffians. That night I told Miller that I would be no party to such disgraceful villainy, and that if any more of it went on I would quit the company, for I had no mind to fight with murderers, or with a rope round my neck. He made light of the whole affair; said the other side had done just the same, and that for his part he did not mean to ask for, or give, quarter.

Document 11.6 Julia Louise Lovejoy Remembers 1850s Kansas

The Reverend Charles H. Lovejoy and his wife Julia were sent to Kansas by the Methodist Episcopal Church conference in November 1855. Originally sent to the Fort Riley mission, they lived in various locations of eastern Kansas, even spending two years in Lawrence at the height of the border wars. Julia kept up a steady correspondence with eastern newspapers, relating crop problems, high prices, illnesses, and the mission work. Her letters sought donations for the settlers of Kansas, and support for the church mission, but also reported on the struggle between pro-slavery and free-soil forces. While her letters did not often deliberately distort the events of the years in order to raise eastern tempers (as the letters of her peer, Sara Robinson, intended to do), she and her husband did embrace abolitionism. Her husband was cousin of Elijah Lovejoy, the abolitionist editor murdered by a pro-slavery crowd in Alton, Illinois. According to some accounts, her published letters caught the attention of the Missouri Border Ruffians, and they attempted to murder both Lovejoys to silence them. What pro-slavery, Missouri Border Ruffian outrages does Julia relate to the newspapers? According to the author, what crimes do they commit? Can you describe the other issues and problems confronting the Lovejoys and other settlers in frontier Kansas?

LAWRENCE, KANSAS TERRITORY
September 5th, 1856

MR. EDITOR—I am not able to sit up but a few moments, having had a severe attack of bilious intermittent fever, and my husband sick with bilious fever at the same time, and our nurse, who kindly proffered his aid, being an old gentleman upwards of 70, crippled with rheumatism. Altogether, in these "dark days" of crime, we have had a sorry time of it, as every hour almost, of our sickness, some startling intelligence of new murders and depredations saluted our acutely nervous senses. Thanks to an ever watchful Providence, we are both nonconvalescent.

Our hearts sicken at the atrocities perpetrated daily upon the innocent and unoffending.—Ossawattamie has been laid in ashes, every house burned, and four of our men killed.—The gallant Brown, while searching after his saddle, was shot dead in the street. Fifty Ossawattamie families shelterless, are now living in their wagons in the woods, endeavoring to escape these fiends in human form—heaven and Elijah's ravens to feed them! This was a beautiful town, about the size, I think, of Lawrence. Judge Wakefield's house and four of his neighbor's were burnt night before last. The ruffians have burnt every Free State man's house in Leavenworth, pressed the men into their service, at the peril of their lives, driven the women and children, with just the clothes on their backs, into the boats and sent them down the River. Children with no parents to take care of them, were pushed into the boat and sent off too! Our men have driven their army twice this week, at the North, between here and Lecompton, and near Black Jack, between this place and Westport. At Black Jack the two armies were drawn up in line of battle, a ravine separating them, but after viewing our brave fellows, they concluded that running was the better part of valor, and took to their heels, and put spurs to their horses, as though Lucifer was hard after them, and

---

From Kansas Historical Quarterly 3, no. 1, February 1934 by Colonel A. J. Hoole, CSA.

entered Westport, (as we learned by a lady who came in the stage yesterday from thence) and told the people that "Lane had 10,000 men, and was coming down to destroy the place," and they went to fortifying the town. Lane had about four hundred men with him, all told, and they, 'tis said, numbered five to his one! What brave fellows these ruffians are when they are not sucking whiskey!

Our men took a lot of teams, etc., yesterday, they had arrived within a few miles of Lawrence, and were coming to burn the place. A company met them, and fired once, when every man fled to Lecompton. Not one house have our people burnt here, only the forts that were taken honorably in war—but *they* are burning houses, stealing, murdering and abusing the prisoners they take, by chaining some, threatening to scalp others and in every way make them miserable, whilst *our* prisoners are treated as guests. Two seated on their carpeted floors in their nicely furnished room, told a friend of mine who visited them yesterday, "that when they left Platte City to come here to fight, the ladies told them not to come back without bringing some Yankee scalps!" They said "for the future they should pursue a different course."

The people of Westport have great cause for alarm, for the ghosts of murdered victims, we have no doubt, are haunting the place and ere long their blood will be avenged! Our men have gone over the river to help the Delaware Indians today. The Ruffians are stealing their horses, and committing other depredations amongst them, burning one of their houses and an Indian boy with it—this will arouse their ire, and they are a powerful tribe. Now these fellows will find they have got somebody besides Yankees to fight! The Sacs that passed through here, we hardly think will *dare* to fight us, because they will lose their lands by doing so. A scout is now watching on Oread Mount, a few rods from my window, in the direction of Lecompton.

All our men and teams were taken that went to Leavenworth to get us something to eat; when not one sack of flour could be got in town, three men sent down the river, two killed and the teams kept. A lady drove up to Lecompton, and told them "she wanted eleven sacks of flour for the troops." They mistrusted nothing as she, I think, had been cooking for the troops with Mrs. Robinson. She got her flour, carried it to Governor Robinson's tent, and in due time it came safely here, but the troops will hardly grow fat upon it! What is *this* to feed so great a multitude? I cannot write half the enormities practiced here—I must cease or bring on a reaction of my disease.

If any of our friends feel a disposition to contribute their mite to aid those who are periling their lives and their *all* for the sake of freedom, it will be very thankfully received. Our losses by border ruffianism fall more heavily now in these times of scarcity for food.—Money cannot be sent safely—but a check on any good Bank, St. Louis, Chicago or any other, would answer just as well, let the sum be ever so small.

JULIA LOUISA LOVEJOY

LAWRENCE, KAN. TERRITORY
September 19, 1856

MR. EDITOR:—There have been times in life's history, when under circumstances like those that surround us this moment it would have been impossible for us to have written or even composed our nerves sufficiently to follow one continuous train of thought, but we have of late been so accustomed to murder and bloodshed under the most appalling forms, we can write at the cannon's mouth with men weltering in their gore, hard by, as we do this morning.

The "signs of the times" betoken peace and quiet for our little city, at least for a time, after such perils, by day and by night, as we have been through, as had well-nigh worn us out, with incessant excitement, and watching—our men became lax in keeping their scouts on the lookout. Lane and his men had gone to Grasshopper Creek—others had returned to Topeka, as our new government [Gov. John W. Geary] had been here and promised to stand by us, etc.

Yesterday morning, while the people were attending worship, messengers came in telling us that the ruffian army, 3000 strong, was at Franklin, and soon the smoke of burning houses at Franklin told us their whereabouts. Our men set to work at once to prepare for defense, as best they could, immediately despatching a messenger to the Government and U. S. troops at Lecompton, twelve miles distant, and soon every favorable position was occupied, and though 100 of our Sharpe's rifles were out of town, and our men were short of ammunition, they were told to divide their cartridges with their neighbor till ALL WAS GONE then take to their bayonets, and those who had none, to use their pitchforks, as they were liberally distributed from the stores where they were kept for sale. I tell you, Mr. Editor, our men fight like tigers, as the sequel proves, and has proved in all their battles, for their blood for weeks has been at the BOILING POINT. Soon Mt. Oread, was bristling with bayonets, and cannon peering through every port hole or along the summit in our new fort, that looms up high on Mt. Oread, a monument of the industry of our army during their leisure last week.

At this stage a dense volume of black smoke told us our steam saw and grist mill, where we have been getting our unbolted flour to feed the hungry multitude, was on fire at Franklin, and about 4 o'clock in the afternoon the advanced guard of the enemy, 100 strong, headed by Sheriff Jones, galloped boldly toward the town, followed by the main body with their bloody flag floating in the breeze. 'Twas a sight sublime to see our boys, only eighty strong, headed by the gallant Captain Walker, gallop out to meet them, and then wheel and turn towards town, as though running from such overwhelming numbers, to decoy them as near as possible, and they in full chase, when our boys turned, spread out to cover as much space as possible, and then poured a volley of balls into them—the Missourians returned the fire and then retreated into a ravine behind a cornfield to screen themselves as much as possible. Our men returned to town, and about twenty-five horsemen and fifty footmen marched out onto a high rolling prairie, and drew themselves up in a line of battle—a few shots were exchanged, when our men marched upon them, and they wheeled and fled like frightened sheep, when our men followed hard on their heels, firing as they went, killing three or four, and thus on and on they flew as in a race for life, some two miles toward Franklin till they reached their camp, when our men turned back toward town. Had they known our weakness, as the troops had not arrived, we should now probably have been murdered, and our city laid in ashes! [George W.] Dietz[l]er, just escaped from prison, shot six times, and he says "he knows they must have taken effect." Not a man of our company had his hair singed! Two of our boys about the same time shot two of their scouts in a hand-to-hand contest, as they had cocked their guns twice to shoot our boys—when the firing commenced, as our house stands a little out of town, in a direct line from Mt. Oread fort and the enemy, expecting our dwelling to be demolished by cannon balls, though built of stone, I caught my darling babe [Irving] (now a year old) from the bed, burning with fever, from which he has been suffering two weeks, moaning as he went, and though just recovering from the same fever myself and with hardly strength to walk, I rushed to a place of safety out of town as fast as my feeble limbs could carry me until I had walked about two miles; and as I passed from one house to another, in my flight 'twas almost amusing, notwithstanding the awful crisis before us to see the ruling passion strong in such an hour. Here was one arraying herself in a nice dress to

secure it from destruction, another seizing a watch or some other valuable to carry with them, and sir, I did clutch hold of a bowie-knife I espied in one house, a lady friend wished me to take, but as I was rapidly making my weary way, now through bushes and ravines and up difficult steeps, I was afraid I would give my own person an unlucky thrust and was right glad to get rid of it. The scene that met our gaze beggars description—women and children fleeing on every hand to a place of safety—men running to secure the best place to fight—cattle as though aware danger was near huddling together—smoke rolling up in clouds from Franklin, nearly four miles distant—the "smoke and flash" of our well directed rifles, all produced a daguerreotype that will never fade from memory's vision.

Tuesday [Monday], September 15.—Our government and troops arrived yesterday and hastened down to meet the enemy and turn them back as they hove into sight with their blood-red flag waving, bent on our destruction. They have contented themselves during the night in getting all the herds [from our free-state settlers] and horses they could find in that vast bottom, stretching between here and Franklin, and our cow we suppose among the rest, and what we shall do in these deplorable times heaven only knows. Will not some of the friends of freedom help replace our lost homes, and cow, and these other losses by ruffian hands that have brought devastation and ruin to our homes? Last night two or three young ladies came running into town crying bitterly, daughters of our good brother Anderson, having run four miles from Franklin along a bypath through the timber, bareheaded, dragging along little children by the hand. Their house had been burned and their good, gray-haired mother in Israel shot at, and they feared their brother's wife, the mother of a little family, had been murdered. Think of this, my sisters in New Hampshire, pure-minded intelligent ladies fleeing from fiends in human form whose brutal lust is infinitely more to be dreaded than death itself.

Last night, about sunset, about two hundred approached the town of Lawrence with three white flags waving ([Ex-Sen. David R.] Atchison was in this gang), they were permitted to come to the foot of Mt. Oread, when the U. S. troops met them and planted their cannon so as to blow them to atoms if they made any attempt to attack us, as they threatened to do, and this morning they left for Lecompton followed by the other portion of the army that stopped at Franklin for the night watched there by a detachment of troops. The government thinks it is policy to let them pass on to Lecompton unmolested. They had just left

Lawrence this morning before the troops followed them and shot a Mr. Buffum, one of our men, for trying to rescue his horses they were stealing. Oh, how our men ached to fight them this morning and last night as they came from Franklin, where they had ruined so many of our people and turned homeless on to the prairie, but the government, for good reasons, would not permit it. He gives the free state men universal satisfaction, but we are told the ruffians tried to assassinate him at Franklin! It looks ominous to us, after coming upon us to destroy us, so large a force should be permitted to concentrate at Lecompton—for our own part, for the first time in all this commotion unless help speedily comes and our governor gets a stronger force, we have no doubt that our doom is sealed! To-day is a trying time for our faith. My husband, by excitement and exposure, has brought on a relapse of bilious fever, from which he has just recovered—my babe is growing worse, his fever is raging dreadfully to-day, and we have but a few dollars left for any emergency. A few months ago prosperity smiled upon us, but war has fallen heavily upon us and now we shall be left single-handed and alone from all our friends to peril our all for freedom and our New England friends stand aloof? We have not received the first dollar from any source to help sustain our losses, and do not expect to, as all are in trouble here, unless our friends in the East help us a little, and hundreds are worse off than we having no house to shelter them. We have good "claims," but who will buy a "claim" in this territory when war is determined to sweep us all out?

JULIA LOUISA LOVEJOY

LAWRENCE, K. T., JAN. 5, 1857.

BROTHER ROSE:—We have long designed to write to you from this far-off land, for your little sheet, you have so kindly forwarded to our address, but duties of no ordinary character have prevented until now. In our heart, we wish you, and all our dear Green Mountain friends "a happy New Year." It is doubtless known to you and your readers, from letters written for different Eastern papers, that one year and nine months ago, we left our home among the Granite Hills, and took up the line of march for Kansas—*the* spot that we used to point out in our school-girl days, on Morse's old yellow covered Atlas, as "the Great American Desert, inhabited by buffalo, and roving tribes of Indians,"—*this* spot *we* have found, an Eden naturally, a garden in very deed, into which Satan, in the garb of Border Ruffianism, has stealthily crept, and the blood of our murdered

brethren cries to Heaven, to avenge their tragic death! Sir, the graves of butchered victims, that "sleep the sleep that knows no waking," on the plains of Kansas, will never be counted up, until the "sea shall deliver up its dead." Only a *tithe* of the robbery and murder of Free State men, unoffending citizens, has ever reached the public prints. It has been our lot, to live through the entire "reign of terror" and the horrors of the scenes, through which we passed, *have not been*, and we think *cannot* be exaggerated! Take for instance weeks previous to the last memorable invasion of the 14th of September, when almost every man you met was armed with deadly weapons, on which he slept at night, to be ready at a moment's warning, not knowing but in dead of night, his house might be fired, and his family butchered before his eyes, by cut-throat assassins! The never-to be-forgotten 14th of September, was ushered in, and as it was God's holy day, our people assembled in their tent, the usual place of worship, and anticipated a day of quiet, after such stirring scenes, through which they had passed, that had entirely broken up religious meetings. When the services were nearly finished for the forenoon, Dr. Still of South Kansas District, came in hot haste, and told the people that "*the prairies near the Wakarusa were swarming with armed men.*" Who wonders that prayers went up to the Great Deliverer for help, in this extremity? For, far as human view could scan, none but Daniel's God could deliver, as Lawrence was entirely evacuated by our brave troops, who had gone too far to be recalled, and not 200 fighting men could be rallied to face 3000 incarnate fiends, spurred on by the whiskey-demon to burn every house in this devoted town, and to destroy the whole Abolition crew! Even children "*over six months must be murdered,*" as the Rev. Mr. Bird, a Congregationalist minister, a prisoner in their camp, affirms they told him was agreed upon, as their blood would be tainted with abolitionism! What good old Quaker, of the Democratic stamp, on the shores of old Champlain, would not *fight* under such circumstances, that their pure-minded wives and daughters should not be robbed of the brightest jewel in their coronet, and their sons slain in cold blood? Ah! me thinks old broad-brim, of the *straightest jacket*, would exclaim in such *an hour*, to such a ruffian-horde, "if thou so greatly *desirest* to *smell* powder, thou shalt surely be gratified to the full!"—Lawrence at that time, was the rendezvous of clergymen, of every order in the Territory, who had fled from their several charges here for protection, and every minister who *could* procure a rifle was *armed with one*. Said my good husband, scarcely recovered from fever, "*never did* I feel like *fighting*, until I saw that army coming upon us." He stood on the brow of the hill, just back of our dwelling, when the advanced guard of the Missourians, two hundred strong, and our brave boys, just sixty in number, came in collision, and with heart uplifted, prayed to the God of Heaven, to *smite* our enemies.

Never until that awful hour, did I see man meet his fellow man in mortal combat. Whilst fleeing from our house, as I did *three times* in twenty-four hours, with my child in my arms, to prevent being shot by cannon balls, I was in full view of the battle. 'Twas a sight sublime, to witness the *bravery* of our boys, in pouring volley after volley of Sharpe's rifles in their ranks, while they confusedly huddled together, to prevent being hit, *cowards to the last*, as they have always proved *themselves to be*. Heaven *miraculously*, it has seemed to us, interposed, and we were saved that time.

One item we wish to lay before your readers, Mr. Editor, with regard to the suffering and destitution of the people in the Territory this Winter. Our position has brought us into close proximity with *such* an amount of suffering as we cannot describe with pen. Families suffering in poor floorless cabins, for food and clothing. What *has been* distributed has gladdened many a heart—but where *one* garment has *been given* away to cover shivering limbs, one hundred *more* is *needed* to supply the demand. Where *one* sack of flour has *been sent*, one hundred are *wanted* to keep the people from *suffering*, if not from perishing for food.—Large sums of money sent to Kansas for the *needy, have never been received by them*. The *fault rests somewhere*, and the *poor* must suffer in consequence. O that our friends in the East would select some one *known* to have the fear of God and the day of retribution, before his eyes, and confide to him some of the funds, or send *direct to the individuals*, whom you wish to help, if money, a "check" on any good Western Bank, if clothing, put the *name of the individual*, who is to receive them, or to the care of *some* man *known* to be *reliable*, on *the box*, or barrel, and direct to the care of W. F. Arny, Chicago, that every poor soul may receive what is sent them by their friends.

Yours, respectfully,
Julia Louisa Lovejoy.

Lawrence, K.T., Jan. 22, 1857.

Messrs. Editors:—You have doubtless on this (with eyes almost protruding from their sockets with wonder and astonishment) read our Governor's late message, that has set the slave-ocrats at Lecompton, and the fire-eaters from Missouri, attending that famous convocation, the bogus Legislature, now in session at that place, to raving and cursing like madmen; and if their threats are carried into execution, Kansas will soon be minus of a Governor, and His Excellency might well envy the fate of poor "Kirwan," of papal notoriety, who has, by the Holy Father, been thoroughly and *throughout* cursed with "bell, book and candle," in soul and in body, in life, and doomed to the fires of purgatory *evermore*! We deprecate his fate, but have little doubt notwithstanding, that he will yet live to write the "history of Kansas and border-ruffianism run mad!" Could you, friend Fogg, for a few moments steal away from your quiet sanctum, and find yourself in our little city, you might imagine yourself at once jostled by the crowds in Broadway, N. Y., or on one of the *quays* of Boston. Such crowds are thronging the streets, and such briskness in business-matters, on every hand; or like Don Quixote, rub your eyes and wonder how long you had been napping. Hear the hammer of the auctioneer, whilst with stentorian lungs he crieth lustily, those ominous words, on which, perchance, hangs the destiny of some gaping wight, who, with distended jaws and arms ensconced to the elbows, in those huge pockets, eyes the auctioneer, as ever and anon recur those fatal words, that, like a death-knell to his hopes, fall upon his ear, "*Going, going, GONE!*" What an *airth*, cries Mrs. Partington, have them Lawrence folks to vendue off, when they are freezing and starving? Why, madam, we have all kinds of furniture direct from St. Louis, of the most expensive manufacture, of mahogany and black walnut, crockery and house—furnishing goods of almost any kind you want; for, know you, though there is an unparalelled state of suffering with the *unsupplied poor*, speculators are here with their money this winter, from different parts of the Union, and such a mania for "city stock" in the different localities in this Territory, is seldom seen, save in the "Great West," where cities spring up by magic. Lots here are four times the value they were a few weeks since. A friend sold four "shares" of Manhattan "stock" for forty dollars; the same "shares" are now worth four hundred dollars! In Wyandot, Quindaro, Ham[p]den, Columbus and some other places, speculators are clearing their thousands, and still property is rapidly rising.— Claims in the vicinity of Lawrence are held very high, some as high as $5000, and speculators foreseeing the unprecedented tide of emigration that will set in upon Kansas, when Spring opens, have got ahead, and almost daily arrivals show the increase of population, and still there is room!

Did those sturdy, hard-working farmers, that are the pride and glory of the old Granite State, know the *advantages* of a farm in Kansas, 10,000 would be missing at the polls next March, and would be en route for this inviting country. Ah! Sirs; if we were not already here, we would get aboard the first steamer, (even though we could procure no other than a deck-passage, and be under the necessity of travelling incognito, Reeder-like) that leaves the wharves of St. Louis bound for Kansas! What, though we have lived for months in a cabin, without floors or windows, where the rain has stood in pools on the bed. What harm has accrued, though the snakes, as large as an old-fashioned chair post have been so very friendly as to crawl through the interstices of our cabin, to see what we Yankees were about—a rap on the head has soon rendered them perfectly harmless, and taught them never again, uninvited, to intrude upon strangers. What though a huge rattlesnake was found, when the cover was removed, snugly coiled up under my bed, where I had slept sweetly a few hours before, and still another, with beautiful vest, peering with sparkling eyes from a cupboard, suspended over my bed, where my babe lay sleeping, not dreaming he was so noiselessly watched by such an intruder, who had unseen glided to his hiding-place.

Do we not still retain our identity, tho' we have lived on "cornbread and bacon," until the very sight of a four-legged rooter would almost give us "spasms"?

One of these days, we design to give the little folks in New Hampshire some wonderful stories of hair-breadth escapes from a wildcat, fearful, and yet ludicrous, in which we were concerned. If they will wait patiently, the story shall be forth-coming.

We would like, with trumpet-voice, to tell the ladies of Acworth and Manchester, N. H., in behalf of the suffering poor, whose wants can now be supplied from their liberality, how glad the arrival of boxes of clothing from those places have made our hearts.

When Mr. Arney left here to return East, he found that scores who had applied for clothing, and there was *none* for them, must suffer unless help came from some source.—On his way down the Missouri river, he found boxes lodged on account of navigation closing up. These boxes, with commendable zeal, he has found means to send here, and last night Mr. Lovejoy, who devotes himself without charge, almost entirely to relieving the poor, came home from town, where the goods are deposited, and with glistening eye drew from his pocket papers he found in the boxes—two in the Manchester boxes from Mrs. Chapin, President of the M.A.S. A thousand blessings on your head, my dear Mrs. Chapin, and those noble ladies who *pulled* their very bonnets from their heads, as *good*, if not indeed quite, as new! *We* have not seen them, but our husband being judge, they are *very* nice and *very* beautiful. Only think, Mr. Editor, a whole box of bonnets from Manchester! Now look at that big box of boots and shoes from the same place. Now dive into that long-legged boot, and see what you will *fish* up! Try again; there is *another* and still *another* pair of those nice socks, and yarn enough to darn them when they come to mending. And the shoes are stuffed with the same timely articles! We don't wonder you involuntarily ejaculate, "Heaven bless the kind donors!" How many frost-bitten feet will now be made comfortable.

You may think us unpardonably foolish, Sir, but anything that comes from our own State is doubly dear to us, and how earnestly we craved one of those New Hampshire bonnets we dare not tell here. Mr. L., who now has charge of these goods, has an invariable rule, "the greatest sufferers first supplied." Who, think you, sir, sends the most and best goods to Kansas to supply the needy? The stingy yankees! Who is aiding Kansas in every respect more than all others put together? The stingy yankees! Ah, sir, we glory in yankee*ism* and yankee "*isms*." Boxes of goods have been opened in our presence, the worth of the contents of which would not pay the freight, but they were not sent by stingy yankees. We have now an overcoat sent to our "care," for one of the "heroes" in the Territory, which, by the way, is a great curiosity, and were it not for robbing the poor man, we would vote that it should be sacredly preserved for the benefit of posterity, and its history enrolled amongst the "archives" of the Territory. We have concluded it could not have been made in the year one, for the flood must have swept off every vestige that pertained to the giant race, but are very sure it was made before we had a being! Here comes out knitting work, just begun, needles and all—here a little Misses' sack, half done, with the needle sticking in, just where busy fingers dropped the work into the box—here a hank of thread and there a roll of patches, put in by some careful hand.

More anon,
JULIA LOUISA LOVEJOY.

MR. EDITOR:—. . . How full of change is life! More than two years ago, we found ourselves suddenly removed from a dear little cottage nestled on the green hills of New England, to a floorless, windowless cabin, on a vast expanse, where but one other of like stamp with our own appeared, to break the monotony of the view, as far as vision could stretch on either hand. There the untaught savage, almost in a state of nudity, painted and decorated in the most hideous style, shocked us with his repeated intrusions, until we learned not to fear his approach; there the rattlesnake and copperhead, with various others of the serpent species, intruded upon the sanctity of "our home." In that lone spot, almost on the "limits" of civilized life, the angel of mercy laid a beautiful boy in our *cradle*, to repair the breach made by the destroyer in the "household band."

But time passes on, and we find another home, built by our hands. Satan, in the garb of border ruffianism, invades our "beautiful country," and threatens a total extermination of all who will not bow down to the slave power. Men and women *stand erect* and cry, "we will not yield." Then are let loose the "dogs of war"; Atchison and Stringfellow, with others of like spirits, are lying in every hamlet, and their infuriated *yell* is heard along the creeks and rivers; bye and bye, a murderous crew, exceeded only in rage by the "spirits lost" in the infernal pit, urged on by the whiskey-demon, come as formally announced, to "wipe us out." The smoke of burning houses herald their approach; anon, their "bloody flag" heaves in view, surrounded by thousands whose blood-thirsty souls are clamoring for our death—in hot haste the foremost, scarcely able to restrain their impetuosity, as elated with the thought that now the hour so long desired had come, and the last "stronghold" of "abolitionism" *must* give way before the force of such overpowering numbers. The well-sped bullet soon checked their ardor, and told them that a more than "Spartan band" awaited their approach. In full view of the mortal combat we fled from our home, and twice again in 24 hours did we seek a refuge in a place of safety!

The wheel of time rolls on, and so does the wheel of *itinerancy*, until by our system we find a *"new home"*; and shall *we* be permitted to follow the example of Rev. G. E. Chapman, in the last Herald that has yet reached us, and attempt a description of our "surprise," for be assured we have them in this new Conference as well as on the elder ones, though of a different character. And you will not be "surprised"

when *we read* of the many sweet "surprises" that our dear New England friends are making their good pastors, that we are tempted to wish some at least of the "broken fragments" might roll this way to "surprise" them whose entire salary barely exceeds those "donation surprises." Be it known to you who occupy comfortable parsonages in New England, that there is but one parsonage in this whole Territory, as far as we have learned, and the preacher must find a shelter for his family where he can! Behold then, that invalid preacher, who has been contending for months with "ague and fever," listening almost breathlessly as his appointment is read off to a distant place where there is no house of any kind for the preacher to live in. An iron constitution is at last broken down by incessant toil and the inroads of disease! his family must go ten miles in an opposite direction, and he must find a place to lay his aching head where he can.

And now follow the family as they wend their weary way beneath a scorching sun to another home. With oxen duly equipped, attached to a huge baggage wagon, the wife mounts to her elevated seat and begins her toilsome journey! A "wee bit" of space only is allotted to her comfort, for the household goods must occupy all but just room for her to sit, without changing her position in the least for rest—the "goods" towering over her head from a dizzy height, and threatening an avalanche if any of the fixings should give way, a basket of potatoes to rest her feet upon—in *her arms*, a child not quite two years old; in one hand an umbrella to screen her throbbing head from the oppressive heat of the sun, and in the other a bundle of sundries that could find no place secure from falling overboard, from the rocking to and fro of the ponderous vehicle. In due time the journey was completed, with no special misfortune save the premature death of Miss Biddy, who needed no coroner's inquest to prove that she died for want of room, hard pressed for quarters. On our arrival we, too, opened a "suspicious looking box," as did Bro. Chapman, and to our "surprise," found our nice loaf of "corn bread" all broken into fragments by the jolting of the wagon; nevertheless, it served as a choice bit to the hungry baby; and the gentle cow, that we had purposely left unmilked for the day, furnished a wholesome repast for our sharpened appetites.

The preacher must not look for "stopping places" only as he turns his jaded beasts to graze, and lounge in his wagon the while.

For the "surprise" of some of the city preachers' wives, we should like to introduce them to our cabin on the day of our arrival; sick at heart, and almost murmuring at our hard lot, till faith and hope revised and triumphed. Two young men, who knew nothing of the "sublime mysteries" of housekeeping, had been keeping "bachelor lodge"; and to our "surprise," not a spot from the rude shelves of loose boards laid on pins, driven into the logs, to the nethermost nook, but what demanded instant attention from the newly arrived before the place was put to rights—no friendly stranger to lend us a helping hand or bathe our feverish temples, or prepare us a meal, that we might find a moment's respite. This, my dear sisters, is only an outline of "Kansas life" amongst Methodist preachers, and we should be agreeably "surprised" if any of you would give us a call at our little cabin, for the string of our wooden latch is literally out day and night; and although the door turns on big wooden hinges, in primitive style, it will creak as cordial a welcome to you as those with bell or knocker.

You are aware, Sir, that Palmyra is the seat of our projected University, named in honor of Bishop [O. C.] Baker, who was the first M. E. Bishop who attended the *first* session of Kansas and Nebraska Conference. A lovelier site cannot be found. It is to be built on an eminence, overlooking a vast expense on either hand as far away as the eye can stretch, and a more enchanting panorama, we think, the sun never shone upon.

There is more timber here than in any other part of the Territory we have yet seen, and it lies *high* on hills or ridges, and not along the margin of creeks and rivers, as elsewhere. Our Eastern friends may not be aware of the historic incidents connected with Palmyra, though they have doubtless read of the far-famed "Palmyra battle," where the enemy by strata-gem were so wonderfully defeated by a mere handful of brave boys. In this same battle the enemy took a number of Free State men that they had heretofore taken prisoners, and among the number was Rev. Mr. Moore, Methodist preacher from Iowa; and in the heat of the battle formed a rampart of their bodies, so that when *our* men fired the balls would pierce *these* prisoners FIRST, who were *bound* and could not escape! Among the heroes of the day in our ranks, was Bro. Moore's own son, who continued to "blaze away," little thinking his venerable father was exposed to every *bullet* from his rifle. By a singular providence not a hair of one of the prisoners was singed! They had previously taunted him, by drawing their hand significantly across his bald head and say-ing, "your scalp would not bring much," there was so little hair on his head.

Near the cabin is the grave of the man, who was killed by the falling of a stone from the Free State

Hotel, at the time of its destruction. The poor wretch, with his comrades, was so intent on tearing the building down, he did not perceive the stone that, as with an invisable hand, smote him to the earth, and in a moment he was before his Judge; he left a family of five children. Please say to our friends that our address will be still Lawrence, as heretofore.

Respectfully,
JULIA LOUISA LOVEJOY.

Palmyra, K. T., Dec. 2d, 1857.

MESSRS. EDITORS: This ill-fated territory has been the theatre of so many cold-blooded murders, or "deaths by violence," that the record of them has ceased to produce but very little excitement, save in a limited circle, where they occur; but when the "old-est settler," (aside from the Kaw Indians) has been assassinated, by sundry blows, "well laid on"—when he, who for more than a score of years, has held *undisputed* possession, of the region around the junc-tion of the Big Blue and Kaw Rivers, has been ruth-lessly beaten to death; deserves it not, more than a passing notice?

Dr. S. Whitehorn, of Manhattan, with no "malice aforethought," save what he bears to the particular genus, (not genus homo,) has had the audacity, not only to slay, but thrust his lifeless victim, into a glass jar, filled with alcohol, to preserve the trophy of his victory, to grace his cabinet! The culprit met his doom, sans ceremony, as he was in the very act of stealthily crawling under a neighbor's house, whether for purposes of burglary, or intent on getting a good supper, (as they with all other fastidious epicures, have some favorite dish) our deponent saith not. The species are extremely fond of certain four-legged ani-mals, that infest the cabins of the "settlers," where a plentiful supply of the feline species, is an indispensa-ble desideratum; and the feats of agility, they have performed after a night's meal, in dropping from "above" on to beds, to the horror of the occupants, we have not time to tell. John Smith now occupies the first cabin, built in the "Great bend" of the Blue, of which the writer was the sole mistress for many a lonely day.

You are aware, sirs, there is a certain ubiquity attached to this name—this same veritable being awoke one morning from his bachelor slumbers, and found one of the same "kith and kin" of him whose fate we are now recording, stretched at full length across his "light stand," with a mouse in his distended jaws! But we digress from our tale of truth. Dr. W. who by the way, has quite a taste for antiquarian "relics," carefully scanning his victim, found a certain appendage which was unmistakable proof that, for twenty three years, in a Summer's sun, he had basked near the sunny slope of "old Bluemont." Dear reader among the Granite hills, did you ever see a mammoth rattlesnake?

But we want to say a few things with regard to matters politically, in this our adopted home. As much as we *once hated* the idea of women politicians, no true woman who has been cradled among the liberty loving people of New Hampshire, who has from infancy to womanhood, inhaled the zephyrs that fanned the noble brow of a Stark, could be in Kansas, and *see* what we have *seen* and *feel* what we have *felt*, and not wax enthusiastically zealous for universal freedom. Of all the shameful "crises" that has been basely forced upon us as a people, the crisis that matters have now assumed, seems to us the most hateful; and after all we have passed through from the tender mercies of slave democracy, if this bantling of a Constitution fraudulently conceived in whisky-fuddled brains, and ushered into being amid the bristling bayonets of U. S. soldiery to guard it from an outraged people—we repeat: if a government, under that miserable slave code is *forced* upon this struggling people, war is inevitable, and ere its death shriek shall die away along the Kaw valley, the people will be in arms from the nethermost settlement on the Republican fork, to Eldorado, two hundred miles away, in the far S. W. And Sirs: believe me, when this awful crisis comes, there will be found more than one "Joan of Arc" in point of moral courage, that will fearlessly stand for the right.

Tell us not, the heroines of the revolution have never found successful imitators, in "daring deeds" of courage in the present generation of fragile women! We can lead you to the homes of our sex in Kansas, where two lone women mounted their ponies, and in dead of night expecting to meet a detachment of the enemy at every leap of their horses, galloped eight miles to Hickory point, where they had heard the booming of cannon all day, to learn the fate of loved ones, in the battle. The one had a husband, and the other a son. Now let a yankee woman imagine she sees them with their horses at the top of their speed,

their cape bonnets streaming in the wind as "ever and anon" they turn their anxious eyes homeward, to see if their dwelling was in flames, as the threat had often been made, and only saved by the intrepid courage of their daughter, who is a Hoosier, and looked to us, with her brawny arms and big bare feet, with a profusion of jewelry pendant from the ears, as though she might strike terror, even into the heart of a "border ruffian." The husband and father was from home most of the time, in skirmishes with the enemy, and several times, did a party of armed ruffians order the family to leave the house that they might fire the premises, and as there was a group of children, they did not want to roast them alive. This girl would confront them in the door way, and always succeeded in keeping them at bay. There are thrilling incidents connected with "Kansas affairs" that ought to be treasured up for the benefit of the future historian.

What think our democratic friends in New Hampshire now about Walker's promises? The Oxford *fraud* is but a *tithe* of the *fraud* practiced here; and how much longer, suppose ye, will christian men and women—unflinch[ing] advocates for temperance and moral purity—descendants of the pilgrims of Plymouth Rock, submit to be *governed* and *trodden* upon by blear-eyed, whisky-bloated debauchees, who forsooth, before the final "pack up" for head-quarters, might find it convenient to wind up with a grand finale. The fact as reported to us, will be recorded doubtless by an abler pen than we can wield. What the next act in this drama will be, time can alone determine.

Let prayer to the God of heaven go up unceasingly from pious hearts, in behalf of this people, and if war is forced upon us, by Buchanan and Co., who are leagued with the South, let brave hearts, from the Granite hills, respond to the call of their insulted brethren in Kansas, and whole regiments of "*Invincibles*," throng the thorough-fares that lead in this direction. Ere this reaches you, there will be rejoicing or wailing among the sons and daughters of New England sires in this fair land. Heaven defend the right.

JULIA LOUISA LOVEJOY.

Document 11.7 Southern "Justice": The First Sack of Lawrence Remembered

O.E. Leonard moved from Vermont to Kansas in 1855. By 1856 at the age of 26 he was already the commander of a regiment of Free State horsemen. He later served as judge, Lieutenant Colonel of the 1st Kansas Volunteer Infantry during the Civil War, and Superintendent of Haskell Indian Institute, and was a newspaper editor. His account of the raid on and ransacking of Lawrence is one of the milder accounts. More survivors provided greater detail of the robberies, property destruction, and violent injustices committed against Lawrence by pro-slavery Sheriff Jones and his Missouri militia "deputies." Government officials such as Senator Atchison were present during this action, yet did nothing to prevent what happened. Why do the pro-slavery forces invade Kansas and attack Lawrence? On what grounds do they destroy parts of the city and steal private property? What other offenses are they guilty of?

Lawrence, K.T
May 23rd, 1856

Dear Friend:

Tired and worn I can only write you briefly to assure you of my safety after the fearful disaster to which this unfortunate town has been subjected, rumors of which will undoubtedly reach you in advance of this.

I cannot enter into a detailed account now but will give you a sketch of the scene, which unparrelled as it is in the history of this country. I am well aware it will excite much feeling and indignation. Since the shooting of Jones, which proved to be no serious affair, as he has again assumed the duties of "Sheriff of Douglas County" and the attempt to arrest Gov. Reeder, the United States Marshall, and Shannon, have been diligently engaged in assembling a posse of recent emigrants from the South, alias Missouri, for the "enforcement of the laws." For days they were encamped (several hundred of them) in this vacinity engaged in robery of every degree, attended with some sacrifice of life. After renewed threats on their part and every possible effort on our part to avert the impending catastrophe (not that we were AFRAID OF THEM but that we were anxious to avoid a collision, and further to show the world that we have no disposition to thwart the action of the U.S. Authorities).

Day before yesterday, May 21st, **let the day be remembered in the days to come,** as the scene of the grossest outrage ever perpetrated under the cover of war.

At day break a large force were in possession of a heighth that commands the town, which during the forenoon was augmented to some six or eight hundred in number, armed with U.S. Arms furnished by Shannon. On the banners were inscribed "Slavery for Kansas" and such like insults.

Our citizens, for we had no others in town, having refused to accept the assistance of nearly 1000 men, proffered us from different parts of the Territory, determined to make no show of resistance to the U.S. Authorities, and thus give the lie to the base slanders of our disloyalty.

ABOUT NOON THE Marshall came into town and made some arrests without disturbance. Returning to the camp the Marshall informed the mob that his business was done. Sheriff Jones was in command. Whereupon said Jones marched into town and demanded the surrender of all arms, public and private, in town. Not waiting for a reply he ordered the forces marched into town. D. R. Atchison made a speech. Four cannons were planted in the principal street and the "Sack" commenced.

The Free State Hotel and the printing plant having been "indicted" as "nuisances" by Judge Lecompton, were made the first subject of their vengeance. The former was first battered with guns, that failing an attempt was made to blow it up, with like success. It was then fired. It cost twenty thousand dollars and was just finished. Both presses were thrown into the

Kansas River. Every house in town was plundered and women and children driven off.

I cannot enlarge further as I am entirely exhausted. We do not dispair of success, indeed we are more confident than ever. We are making arrangements to redress our own wrongs. I have this day been commissioned to an important task, which when performed I am thinking of paying a hasty visit to the States, perhaps to Vermont.

O.E.L.

Document 11.8 Charles Sumner Denounces the "Crime Against Kansas"

Senator Charles Sumner was a Boston-born and Harvard-educated lawyer known for his powerful oratory and scorn for those who disagreed with his views. During the 1840s he actively supported everything from prison and school reforms to disarmament, before joining the anti-slavery movement. A member of the Free Soil party in 1848, he replaced the legendary Daniel Webster in the United States Senate, after Webster's support of the Compromise of 1850 and the Fugitive Slave Act upset Massachusetts voters. Sumner blamed the "Slave Power" for the violence in Kansas. Violating both Senate customs and rules of conduct, Sumner sharply denounced both the pro-slavery forces trying to seize Kansas and his Senate colleagues who supported those efforts. His personal attacks on Senator Andrew Butler of South Carolina led to Butler's nephew, Congressman Preston Brooks, assaulting him with a cane. This attack caused injuries severe enough to require three years of convalescence, and led to Sumner's eternal hatred of the South. Who is the intended audience for Sumner's speech? Is he trying to convince the South to change its ways? What crimes does he accuse the South and their supporters of? According to the author, why does the South no longer support the ideas of majority rule and popular sovereignty?

Mr. President,—You are now called to redress a great wrong. Seldom in the history of nations is such a question presented. Tariffs, army bills, navy bills, land bills, are important, and justly occupy your care—but these all belong to the course of ordinary legislation. . . . Far otherwise is it with the eminent question now before you, involving, as it does, Liberty in a broad Territory, and also involving the peace of the whole country, with our good name in history forevermore. . . .

The wickedness which I now begin to expose is immeasurably aggravated by the motive which prompted it. Not in any common lust for power did this uncommon tragedy have its origin. It is the rape of a virgin Territory, compelling it to the hateful embrace of Slavery; and it may be clearly traced to a depraved desire for a new Slave State, hideous offspring of such a crime, in the hope of adding to the power of Slavery in the National Government. Yes, Sir, when the whole world alike . . . is rising up to condemn this wrong . . . here in our Republic, *force*—ay, Sir, FORCE—is openly employed in compelling Kansas to this pollution, and all for the sake of political power. . . .

Before entering upon the argument, I must say something of a general character, particularly in response to what has fallen from Senators who have raised themselves to eminence on this floor in championship of human wrong: I mean the Senator from South Carolina [Mr. Butler]. . . . The Senator from South Carolina had read many books of chivalry, and believes himself a chivalrous knight, with sentiments of honor and courage. Of course he has chosen a mistress to whom he has made his vows, and who, though ugly to others, is always lovely to him,—though polluted in the sight of the world, is chaste in his sight: I mean the harlot Slavery. For her his tongue is always profuse with words. Let her be impeached in character, or any proposition be made to shut her out from the extension of her wantonness, and no extravagance of manner or hardihood of assertion is then too great for this Senator . . .

I undertake, in the first place, to expose the CRIME AGAINST KANSAS, in origin and extent. . . . The debate [over the Kansas-Nebraska bill], which convulsed Congress, stirred the whole country. From all sides attention was directed upon Kansas,

---

From *Charles Summer: His Complete Works*, Boston: Lee & Shepard, 1900.

which at once became the favorite goal of emigration. The bill loudly declares that its object is "to leave the people perfectly free to form and regulate their domestic institutions in their own way"; and its supporters everywhere challenge the determination of the question between Freedom and Slavery by a competition of emigration. . . . The populous North, stung by sense of outrage, and inspired by a noble cause, are pouring into the debatable land, and promise soon to establish a supremacy of Freedom.

Then was conceived the consummation of the Crime against Kansas. What could not be accomplished peaceably was to be accomplished forcibly . . . The violence, for some time threatened, broke forth on the 29th of November, 1854, at the first election of a Delegate to Congress, when companies from Missouri, amounting to upwards of one thousand, crossed into Kansas, and with force and arms proceeded to vote for . . . the candidate of Slavery. . . . Five . . . times and more have these invaders entered Kansas in armed array, and thus five . . . times and more have they trampled upon the organic law of the Territory. These extraordinary expeditions are simply the extraordinary witnesses to successive, uninterrupted violence. . . . Border incursions, which in barbarous ages or barbarous lands fretted and harried an exposed people, are here renewed, with this peculiarity, that our border robbers do not simply levy blackmail and drive off a few cattle . . . they commit a succession of deeds in which . . . . the whole Territory is enslaved.

Private griefs mingle their poignancy with public wrongs. I do not dwell on the anxieties of families exposed to sudden assault, and lying down to rest with the alarms of war ringing in the ears, not knowing that another day may be spared to them. . . . Our souls are wrung by individual instances. . . .

Thus was the Crime consummated. Slavery stands erect, clanking its chains on the Territory of Kansas, surrounded by a code of death, and trampling upon all cherished liberties . . . Emerging from all the blackness of this Crime . . . I come now to the APOLOGIES which the Crime has found. . . .

With regret I come again upon the Senator from South Carolina [Butler. His speech slurred by a stroke, Butler had interjected critical comments on more than thirty occasions while Sumner spoke] who, omnipresent in this debate, overflows with rage at the simple suggestion that Kansas has applied for admission as a State, and, with incoherent phrase, discharges the loose expectoration of his speech, now upon her representative, and then upon her people. . . . [I] is against the [free-soil majority in] . . . Kansas that sensibilities of the Senator are particularly aroused. . . .

The contest, which, beginning in Kansas, reaches us will be transferred soon from Congress to that broader stage, where every citizen is not only spectator, but actor, and to their judgment I confidently turn. To the people, about to exercise the electoral franchise, in choosing a Chief Magistrate of the Republic, I appeal, to vindicate the electoral franchise in Kansas. Let the ballot-box of the Union . . . protect the ballot-box in that Territory.

Document 11.9 *Dred Scott v. Sanford*: The United States Supreme Court Rewrites Legal History

In his 1857 Inaugural Address, President James Buchanan downplayed the importance of the national government or the people of a territory deciding whether or not slavery was welcome. In his words, "it is a judicial question, which legitimately belongs to the Supreme Court of the United States, before whom it is now pending, and will…be speedily and finally settled." Two days later, Chief Justice Roger Brooke Taney announced the Court's decision in the *Dred Scott* case. Taney was an old Jacksonian, one of the creators of the Democratic Party along with Martin Van Buren. He was a slave-owning Marylander who hated the Republican Party as a threat to all things he held dear. To Taney, this case provided the opportunity to resolve the issue over slavery's expansion and to eliminate the Republican Party at the same time. The *Dred Scott* case began when his Missouri owner took Scott, a black slave, first to Illinois (a free state) and then to the Wisconsin Territory where the Missouri Compromise of 1820 forbade slavery. Taken back to Missouri, Scott sued for his freedom, claiming he was freed when taken places where slavery did not exist. The Missouri courts rejected his appeals, and the case eventually made it to the Supreme Court of the United States. The Court faced two major questions. First, was Scott a citizen of Missouri or of the United States? If not a U.S. citizen, he could not bring suit and the case could not be heard, Second, was he set free by going into the free territory of Wisconsin, and did the United States government have the power to restrict slavery by laws such as the Missouri Compromise? As you read the excerpts from Taney's decision, determine on what grounds he decides Scott is not a citizen and thus has no right to sue. How does he claim that the Missouri Compromise and all other prohibitions of slavery's expansion are unconstitutional? Are there any apparent limits to the rights of Southern Democratic slaveowners? Do Northerners who want some land reserved for themselves have any rights by this decision?

The question is simply this: Can a negro, whose ancestors were imported into this country, and sold as slaves, become a member of the political community formed and brought into existence by the Constitution of the United States, and as such become entitled to all the rights, and privileges, and immunities, guarantied by that instrument to the citizen? One of which rights is the privilege of suing in a court of the United States in the cases specified in the Constitution.

It will be observed, that the plea applies to that class of persons only whose ancestors were negroes of the African race, and imported into this country, and sold and held as slaves. The only matter in issue before the court, therefore, is, whether the descendants of such slaves, when they shall be emancipated, or who are born of parents who had become free before their birth, are citizens of a State, in the sense in which the word citizen is used in the Constitution of the United States. And this being the only matter in dispute on the pleadings, the court must be understood as speaking in this opinion of that class only, that is, of those persons who are the descendants of Africans who were imported into this country, and sold as slaves.

The situation of this population was altogether unlike that of the Indian race. The latter, it is true, formed no part of the colonial communities, and never amalgamated with them in social connections or in government. But although they were uncivilized, they were yet a free and independent people, associated together in nations or tribes, and governed by their own laws. Many of these political communities were situated in territories to which the white race claimed the ultimate right of dominion. But that claim was acknowledged to be subject to the right of the Indians to occupy it as long as they thought proper, and neither the English nor colonial Governments claimed or exercised any dominion over the tribe or nation by whom it was occupied, nor claimed the right to the possession of the territory, until the tribe or nation consented to cede it. These Indian Governments were regarded and treated as foreign Governments, as much so as if an ocean had separated the red man from the white; and their freedom has constantly been acknowledged, from the time of the first emigration to the English colonies to the present day, by the different Governments which succeeded each other. Treaties have been negotiated with them, and their alliance sought for in war; and the people who compose these Indian political communities have always been treated as foreigners not living under our Government. It is true that the course of events has brought the Indian tribes within the limits of the United States under subjection to the white race; and it has been found necessary, for their sake as well as our own, to regard them as in a state of pupilage, and to legislate to a certain extent over them and the territory they occupy. But they may, without doubt, like the subjects of any other foreign Government, be naturalized by the authority of Congress, and become citizens of a State, and of the United States; and if an individual should leave his nation or tribe, and take up his abode among the white population, he would be entitled to all the rights and privileges which would belong to an emigrant from any other foreign people.

We proceed to examine the case as presented by the pleadings.

The words "people of the United States" and "citizens" are synonymous terms, and mean the same thing. They both describe the political body who, according to our republican institutions, form the sovereignty, and who hold the power and conduct the Government through their representatives. They are what we familiarly call the "sovereign people," and every citizen is one of this people, and a constituent member of this sovereignty. The question before us is, whether the class of persons described in the plea in abatement compose a portion of this people, and are constituent members of this sovereignty? We think they are not, and that they are not included, and were not intended to be included, under the word

---

U.S. Supreme Court, *Dred Scott v. Sanford*, 1857.

"citizens" in the Constitution, and can therefore claim none of the rights and privileges which that instrument provides for and secures to citizens of the United States. On the contrary, they were at that time considered as a subordinate and inferior class of beings, who had been subjugated by the dominant race, and, whether emancipated or not, yet remained subject to their authority, and had no rights or privileges but such as those who held the power and the Government might choose to grant them.

***

The question then arises, whether the provisions of the Constitution, in relation to the personal rights and privileges to which the citizen of a State should be entitled, embraced the negro African race, at that time in this country, or who might afterwards be imported, who had then or should afterwards be made free in any State; and to put it in the power of a single State to make him a citizen of the United States, and endue him with the full rights of citizenship in every other State without their consent? Does the Constitution of the United States act upon him whenever he shall be made free under the laws of a State, and raised there to the rank of a citizen, and immediately cloth him with all the privileges of a citizen in every other State, and in its own courts?

The court thinks the affirmative of these propositions cannot be maintained. And if it cannot, the plaintiff in error could not be a citizen of the State of Missouri, within the meaning of the Constitution of the United States, and, consequently, was not entitled to sue in its courts.

***

It becomes necessary, therefore, to determine who were citizens of the several States when the Constitution was adopted. And in order to do this, we must recur to the Governments and institutions of the thirteen colonies, when they separated from Great Britain and formed new sovereignties, and took their places in the family of independent nations. We must inquire who, at that time, were recognized as the people or citizens of a State, whose rights and liberties had been outraged by the English Government; and who declared their independence, and assumed the powers of Government to defend their rights by force of arms.

In the opinion of the court, the legislation and histories of the times, and the language used in the Declaration of Independence, show, that neither the class of persons who had been imported as slaves, nor their descendants, whether they had become free or not, were then acknowledged as a part of the people, nor intended to be included in the general words used in that memorable instrument.

It is difficult at this day to realize the state of public opinion in relation to that unfortunate race, which prevailed in the civilized and enlightened portions of the world at the time of the Declaration of Independence, and when the Constitution of the United States was framed and adopted. But the public history of every European nation displays it in a manner too plain to be mistaken.

They had for more than a century before been regarded as beings of an inferior order, and altogether unfit to associate with the white race, either in social or political relations; and so far inferior, that they had no rights which the white man was bound to respect; and that the negro might justly and lawfully be reduced to slavery for his benefit. He was bought and sold, and treated as an ordinary article of merchandise and traffic, whenever a profit could be made by it. This opinion was at that time fixed and universal in the civilized portion of the white race. It was regarded as an axiom in morals as well as in politics, which no one thought of disputing, or supposed to be open to dispute; and men in every grade and position in society daily and habitually acted upon it in their private pursuits, as well as in matters of public concern, without doubting for a moment the correctness of this opinion.

***

The case, as he himself states it, on the record brought here by his writ of error, is this:

The plaintiff was a negro slave, belonging to Dr. Emerson, who was a surgeon in the army of the United States. In the year 1834, he took the plaintiff from the State of Missouri to the military post at Rock Island, in the State of Illinois, and held him there as a slave until the month of April or May, 1836. At the time last mentioned, said Dr. Emerson removed the plaintiff from said military post at Rock Island to the military post at Fort Snelling, situate on the west bank of the Mississippi river, in the Territory known as Upper Louisiana, acquired by the United States of France, and situate north of the latitude of thirty-six degrees thirty minutes north, and north of the State of Missouri. Said Dr. Emerson held the plaintiff in slavery at said Fort Snelling, from said last-mentioned date until the year 1838.

In the year 1835, Harriet, who is named in the second count of the plaintiff s declaration, who was the negro slave of Major Taliaferro, who belonged to the army of the United States.

In that year, 1835, said Major Taliaferro took said Harriet to said Fort Snelling, a military post, situated as hereinbefore stated, and kept her there as a slave until the year 1836, and then sold and delivered her as a slave, at said Fort Snelling, unto the said Dr. Emerson hereinbefore named. Said Dr. Emerson held said Harriet in slavery at said Fort Snelling until the year 1838.

In the year 1836, the plaintiff and Harriet intermarried, at Fort Snelling, with the consent of Dr. Emerson, who then claimed to be their master and owner. Eliza and Lizzie, named in the third count of the plaintiff s declaration, are the fruit of that marriage. Eliza is about fourteen years old, and was born on board the steamboat Gipsey, north of the north line of the State of Missouri, and upon the river Mississippi. Lizzie is about seven years old, and was born in the State of Missouri, at the military post called Jefferson Barracks.

In the year 1838, said Dr. Emerson removed the plaintiff and said Harriet, and their said daughter Eliza, from said Fort Snelling to the State of Missouri, where they have ever since resided.

Before the commencement of this suit, said Dr. Emerson sold and conveyed the plaintiff, and Harriet, Eliza, and Lizzie, to the defendant, as slaves, and the defendant has ever since claimed to hold them, and each of them, as slaves.

In considering this part of the controversy, two questions arise: 1. Was he, together with his family, free in Missouri by reason of the stay in the territory of the United States hereinbefore mentioned? And 2. If they were not, is Scott himself free by reason of his removal to Rock Island, in the State of Illinois, as stated in the above admissions?

We proceed to examine the first question.

The act of Congress, upon which the plaintiff relies, declares that slavery and involuntary servitude, except as a punishment for crime, shall be forever prohibited in all that part of the territory ceded by France, under the name of Louisiana, which lies north of thirty-six degrees thirty minutes north latitude, and not included within the limits of Missouri. And the difficulty which meets us at the threshold of this part of the inquiry is, whether Congress was authorized to pass this law under any of the powers granted to it by the Constitution; for if the authority is not given by that instrument, it is the duty of this court to declare it void and inoperative, and incapable of conferring freedom upon any one who is held as a slave under the laws of any one of the States.

The counsel for the plaintiff has laid much stress upon that article in the Constitution which confers on Congress the power "to dispose of and make all needful rules and regulations respecting the territory or other property belonging to the United States;" but, in the judgement of the court, that provision had no bearing on the present controversy, and the power there given, whatever it may be, is confined, and was intended to be confined, to the territory which at that time belonged to, or was claimed by, the United States, and was within their boundaries as settled by the treaty with Great Britain, and can have no influence upon a territory afterwards acquired from a foreign Government. It was a special provision for a known and particular territory, and to meet a present emergency, and nothing more.

***

The language used in the clause, the arrangement and combination of the powers, and the somewhat unusual phraseology it uses, when it speaks of the political power to be exercised in the government of the territory, all indicate the design and meaning of the clause to be such as we have mentioned. It does not speak of any territory, nor of Territories, but uses language which, according to its legitimate meaning, points to a particular thing. The power is given in relation only to the territory of the United States— that is, to a territory then in existence, and then known or claimed as the territory of the United States. It begins its enumeration of powers by that of disposing, in other words, making sale of the lands, or raising money from them, which, as we have already said, was the main object to the cession, and which is accordingly the first thing provided for in the article. It then gives the power which was necessarily associated with the disposition and sale of the lands—that is, the power of making needful rules and regulations respecting the territory. And whatever construction may now be given to these words, every one, we think, must admit that they are not the words usually employed by statesmen in giving supreme power of legislation. They are certainly very unlike the words used in the power granted to legislate over territory which the new Government might afterwards itself obtain by cession from a State, either for its seat of Government, of for forts, magazines, arsenals, dock yards, and other needful buildings.

And the same power of making needful rules respecting the territory is, in precisely the same language, applied to the other property belonging to the United States—associating the power over the territory in this respect with the power over movable or personal property—that is, the ships, arms, and munitions of war, which then belonged in common to the

State sovereignties. And it will hardly be said, that this power, in relation to the last-mentioned objects, was deemed necessary to be thus specially given to the new Government, in order to authorize it to make needful rules and regulations respecting the ships it might itself build, or arms and munitions of war it might itself manufacture or provide for the public service.

No one, it is believed, would think a moment of deriving the power of Congress to make needful rules and regulations in relation to property of this kind from this clause of the Constitution. Nor can it, upon any fair construction, be applied to any property but that which the new Government was about to receive from the confederated States. And if this be true as to this property, it must be equally true and limited as to the territory, which is so carefully and precisely coupled with it—and like it referred to as property in the power granted. The concluding words of the clause appear to render this construction irresistible; for, after the provisions we have mentioned, it proceeds to say, "that nothing in the Constitution shall be so construed as to prejudice any claims of the United States, or of any particular State."

***

The words "needful rules and regulations" would seem, also, to have been cautiously used for some definite object. They are not the words usually employed by statesmen, when they mean to give the powers of sovereignty, or to establish a Government, or to authorize its establishment. Thus, in the law to renew and keep alive the ordinance of 1787, and to reestablish the Government, the title of the law is: "An act to provide for the government of the territory northwest of the river Ohio." And in the Constitution, when granting the power to legislate over the territory that may be selected for the seat of Government independently of a State, it does not say Congress shall have power "to make all needful rules and regulations respecting the territory;" but it declares that "Congress shall have power to exercise exclusive legislation in all cases whatsoever over such District (not exceeding ten miles square) as may, by cession of particular States and the acceptance of Congress, become the seat of the Government of the United States."

The words "rules and regulations" are usually employed in the Constitution in speaking of some particular specified power which it means to confer on the Government, and not, as we have seen, when granting general powers of legislation. As, for example, in the particular power to Congress "to make

rules for the Government and regulation of the land and naval forces, or the particular and specific power to regulate commerce;" "to establish an uniform rule of naturalization;" "to coin money and regulate the value thereof." And to construe the words of which we are speaking as a general and unlimited grant of sovereignty over territories which the Government might afterwards acquire, is to use them in a sense and for a purpose for which they were not used in any other part of the instrument. But if confined to a particular Territory, in which a Government and laws had already been established, but which would require some alterations to adapt it to the new Government, the words are peculiarly applicable and appropriate for that purpose.

The necessity of this special provision in relation to property and the rights or property held in common by the confederated States, is illustrated by the first clause of the sixth article. This clause provides that "all debts, contracts, and engagements entered into before the adoption of this Constitution, shall be as valid against the United States under this Government as under the Confederation." This provision, like the one under consideration, was indispensable if the new Constitution was adopted. The new Government was not a mere change in a dynasty, or in a form of government, leaving the nation or sovereignty the same, and clothed with all the rights, and bound by all the obligations of the preceding one. But, when the present United States came into existence under the new Government, it was a new political body, a new nation, then for the first time taking its place in the family of nations. It took nothing by succession from the Confederation. It had no right, as its successor, to any property or rights of property which it had acquired, and was not liable for any of its obligations. It was evidently viewed in this light by the framers of the Constitution. And as the several States would cease to exist in their former confederated character upon the adoption of the Constitution, and could not, in that character, again assemble together, special provisions were indispensable to transfer to the new Government the property and rights which at that time they held in common; and at the same time to authorize it to lay taxes and appropriate money to pay the common debt which they had contracted; and this power could only be given to it by special provisions in the Constitution. The clause in relation to the territory and other property of the United States provided for the first, and the clause last quoted provided for the other. They have no connection with the general powers and rights of sovereignty delegated to the new Government, and can neither enlarge nor diminish them. They were inserted to meet a present emergency, and not to regulate its powers as a Government.

Indeed, a similar provision was deemed necessary, in relation to treaties made by the Confederation; and when in the clause next succeeding the one of which we have last spoken, it is declared that treaties shall be the supreme law of the land, care is taken to include, by express words, the treaties made by the confederated States. The language is: "and all treaties made, or which shall be made, under the authority of the United States, shall be the supreme law of the land."

Whether, therefore, we take the particular clause in question, by itself, or in connection with the other provisions of the Constitution, we think it clear, that it applies only to the particular territory of which we have spoken, and cannot, by any just rule of interpretation, be extended to territory which the new Government might afterwards obtain from a foreign nation. Consequently, the power which Congress may have lawfully exercised in this Territory, while it remained under a Territorial Government, and which may have been sanctioned by judicial decision, can furnish no justification and no argument to support a similar exercise of power over territory afterwards acquired by the Federal Government. We put aside, therefore, any argument, drawn from precedents, showing the extent of the power which the General Government exercised over slavery in this Territory, as altogether inapplicable to the case before us.

This brings us to examine by what provision of the Constitution the present Federal Government, under its delegated and restricted powers, is authorized to acquire territory outside of the original limits of the United States, and what powers it may exercise therein over the person or property of a citizen of the United States, while it remains a Territory, and until it shall be admitted as one of the States of the Union.

There is certainly no power given by the Constitution to the Federal Government to establish or maintain colonies bordering on the United States or at a distance, to be ruled and governed at its own pleasure; nor to enlarge its territorial limits in any way, except by the admission of new States. That power is plainly given; and if a new State is admitted, it needs no further legislation by Congress, because the Constitution itself defines the relative rights and powers, and duties of the State, and the citizens of the State, and the Federal Government. But no power is given to acquire a Territory to be held and governed permanently in that character.

And indeed the power exercised by Congress to acquire territory and establish a Government there, according to its own unlimited discretion, was viewed with great jealousy by the leading statesmen of the day. And in the Federalist, (No. 38,) written by Mr. Madison, he speaks of the acquisition of the Northwestern Territory by the Confederated States, by the cession from Virginia, and the establishment of a Government there, as an exercise of power not warranted by the Articles of Confederation, and dangerous to the liberties of the people. And he urges the adoption of the Constitution as a security and safeguard against such an exercise of power.

We do not mean, however, to question the power of Congress in this respect. The power to expand the territory of the United States by the admission of new States is plainly given; and in the construction of this power by all the departments of the Government, it has been held to authorize the acquisition of territory, not fit for admission at the time, but to be admitted as soon as its population and situation would entitle it to admission. It is acquired to become a State, and not to be held as a colony and governed by Congress with absolute authority; and as the propriety of admitting a new State is committed to the sound discretion of Congress, the power to acquire territory for that purpose, to be held by the United States until it is in a suitable condition to become a State upon an equal footing with the other States, must rest upon the same discretion. It is a question for the political department of the Government, and not the judicial; and whatever the political department of the Government shall recognize as within the limits of the United States, the judicial department is also bound to recognize, and to administer in it the laws of the United States, so far as they apply, and to maintain in the Territory the authority and rights of the Government, and also the personal rights and rights of property of individual citizens, as secured by the Constitution. All we mean to say on this point is, that, as there is no express regulation in the Constitution defining the power which the General Government may exercise over the person or property of a citizen in a Territory thus acquired, the court must necessarily look to the provisions and principles of the Constitution, and its distribution of powers, for the rules and principles by which its decision must be governed.

Taking this rule to guide us, it may be safely assumed that citizens of the United States who migrate to a Territory belonging to the people of the United States, cannot be ruled as mere colonists, dependent upon the will of the General Government, and to be governed by any laws it may think proper to impose. The principle upon which our Governments rest, and upon which alone they continue to exist, is the union of States, sovereign and independent within their own limits in their internal and domestic concerns, and bound together as one people by a General Government, possessing certain enumerated and restricted powers, delegated to it by the people of the several States, and exercising supreme authority within the scope of the powers granted to it, throughout the dominion of the United States. A power, therefore, in the General Government to obtain and hold colonies and dependent territories, over which they might legislate without restriction, would be inconsistent with its own existence in its present form. Whatever it acquires, it acquires for the benefit of the people of the several states who created it. It is their trustee acting for them, and charged with the duty of promoting the interests of the whole people of the Union in the exercise of the powers specifically granted.

At the time when the Territory in question was obtained by cession from France, it contained no population fit to be associated together and admitted as a State; and it therefore was absolutely necessary to hold possession of it, as a Territory belonging to the United States, until it was settled and inhabited by a civilized community capable of self-government, and in a condition to be admitted to equal terms with the other States as a member of the Union. But, as we have before said, it was acquired by the General Government, as the representative and trustee of the people of the United States, and it must therefore be held in that character for their common and equal benefit; for it was the people of the several States, acting through their agent and representative, the Federal Government, who in fact acquired the Territory in question, and the Government holds it for their common use until it shall be associated with the other States as a member of the Union.

But until that time arrives, it is undoubtedly necessary that some Government should be established, in order to organize society, and to protect the inhabitants in their persons and property; and as the people of the United States could act in this matter only through the Government which represented them, and through which they spoke and acted when the Territory was obtained, it was not only within the scope of its powers, but it was its duty to pass such laws and establish such a Government as would enable those by whose authority they acted to reap the advantages anticipated from its acquisition, and to gather there a population which would enable it to assume the position to which it was destined among the States of the Union. The power to acquire necessarily carries with it the power to preserve and apply to the purposes for which it was acquired. The form of government to be established necessarily rested in the discretion of Congress. It was their duty to establish the one that would be best suited for the protection and security of the citizens of the United States, and other inhabitants who might be authorized to take up their abode there, and that must always depend upon the existing condition of the Territory, as to the number and character of its inhabitants, and their situation in the Territory. In some cases a Government, consisting of persons appointed by the Federal Government, would best serve the interests of the Territory, when the inhabitants were few and scattered, and new to one another. In other instances, it would be more advisable to commit the powers of self-government to the people who had settled in the Territory, as being the most competent to determine what was best for their own interests. But some form of civil authority would be absolutely necessary to organize and preserve civilized society, and prepare it to become a State; and what is the best form must always depend on the condition of the Territory at the time, and the choice of the mode must depend upon the exercise of a discretionary power by Congress, acting within the scope of its constitutional authority, and not infringing upon the rights of person or rights of property of the citizen who might go there to reside, or for any other lawful purpose. It was acquired by the exercise of this discretion, and it must be held and governed in like manner, until it is fitted to be a State.

But the power of Congress over the person or property of a citizen can never be a mere discretionary power under our Constitution and form of Government. The powers of the Government and the rights and privileges of the citizen are regulated and plainly defined by the Constitution itself. And when the Territory becomes a part of the United States, the Federal Government enters into possession in the character impressed upon it by those who created it. It enters upon it with its powers over the citizen strictly defined, and limited by the Constitution, from which it derives its own existence, and by virtue of which alone it continues to exist and act as a Government and sovereignty. It has no power of any kind beyond it; and it cannot, when it enters a Territory of the United States, put off its character, and assume discretionary or despotic powers which the Constitution has denied to it. It cannot create for itself a new character separated from the citizens of the United States, and the duties it owes them under of the

United States, the Government and the citizen both enter it under the authority of the Constitution, with their respective rights defined and marked out; and the Federal Government can exercise no power over his person or property, beyond what that instrument confers, nor lawfully deny any right which it has reserved.

A reference to a few of the provisions of the Constitution will illustrate this proposition.

For example, no one, we presume, will contend that Congress can make any law in a Territory respecting that establishment of religion, or the free exercise thereof, or abridging the freedom of speech or of the press, or the right of the people of the Territory peaceably to assemble, and to petition the Government for the redress of grievances.

Nor can Congress deny to the people the right to keep and bear arms, nor the right to trial by jury, nor compel any one to be a witness against himself in a criminal proceeding.

These powers, and others, in relation to rights of person, which it is not necessary here to enumerate, are, in express and positive terms, denied to the General Government; and the rights of private property have been guarded with equal care. Thus the rights of property are united with the rights of person, and placed on the same ground by the fifth amendment to the Constitution, which provides that no person shall be deprived of life, liberty, and property, without due process of law. And an act of Congress which deprives a citizen of the United States of his liberty or property, merely because he came himself or brought his property into a particular Territory of the United States, and who had committed no offence against the laws, could hardly be dignified with the name of due process of law.

So, too, it will hardly be contended that Congress could by law quarter a soldier in a house in a Territory without the consent of the owner, in time of peace; nor in time of war, but in a manner prescribed by law. Nor could they by law forfeit the property of a citizen in a Territory who was convicted of treason, for a longer period than the life of the person convicted; nor take private property for public use without just compensation.

The powers over person and property of which we speak are not only not granted to Congress, but are in express terms denied, and they are forbidden to exercise them. And this prohibition is not confined to the States, but the words are general, and extend to the whole territory over which the Constitution gives it power to legislate, including those portions of it remaining under Territorial Government, as well as

that covered by States. It is a total absence of power everywhere within the dominion of the United States, and places the citizens of a Territory, so far as these rights are concerned, on the same footing with citizens of the States, and guards them as firmly and plainly against any inroads which the General Government might attempt, under the plea of implied or incidental powers. And if Congress itself cannot do this—if it is beyond the powers conferred on the Federal Government—it will be admitted, we presume, that it could not authorize a Territorial Government to exercise them. It could confer no power on any local Government, established by its authority, to violate the provisions of the Constitution.

It seems, however, to be supposed, that there is a difference between property in a slave and other property, and that different rules may be applied to it in expounding the Constitution of the United States. And the laws and usages of nations, and the writing of eminent jurists upon the relation of master and slave and their mutual rights and duties, and the powers which Governments may exercise over it, have been dwelt upon in the argument.

But in considering the question before us, it must be borne in mind that there is no law of nations standing between the people of the United States and their Government, and interfering with their relation to each other. The powers of the Government, and the rights of the citizen under it, are positive and practical regulations plainly written down. The people of the United States have delegated to it certain enumerated powers, and forbidden it to exercise others. It has no power over the person or property of a citizen but what the citizens of the United States have granted. And no laws or usages of other nations, or reasoning of statesmen or jurists upon the relations of master and slave, can enlarge the powers of the Government, or take from the citizens the rights they have reserved. And if the Constitution recognizes the right of property of the master in a slave, and makes no distinction between that description of property and other property owned by a citizen, no tribunal, acting under the authority of the United States, whether it be legislative, executive, or judicial, has a right to draw such a distinction, or deny to it the benefit of the provisions and guarantees which have been provided for the protection of private property against the encroachments of the Government.

Now, as we have already said in an earlier part of this opinion, upon a different point, the right of property in a slave is distinctly and expressly affirmed in the Constitution. The right to traffic in it, like an ordinary article of merchandise and property, was guarantied to the citizens of the United States, in every State that might desire it, for twenty years. And the Government in express terms is pledged to protect it in all future time, if the slave escapes from his owner. This is done in plain words—too plain to be misunderstood. And no word can be found in the Constitution which gives Congress a greater power over slave property, or which entitles property of that kind to less protection than property of any other description. The only power conferred is the power coupled with the duty of guarding and protecting the owner in his rights.

Upon these considerations, it is the opinion of the court that the act of Congress which prohibited a citizen from holding and owning property of this kind in the territory of the United States north of the line therein mentioned, is not warranted by the Constitution, and is therefore void; and that neither Dred Scott himself, nor any of his family, were made free by being carried into this territory; even if they had been carried there by the owner, with the intention of becoming a permanent resident.

Document 11.10 Northern Reactions to the *Dred Scott* Decision

The Northern response to the *Dred Scott* decision was not what Buchanan and Taney hoped for. The Republican Party did not disappear, and the dispute over slavery's expansion did not go away. Northern legal experts (and most constitutional scholars since) accused Taney of deliberately distorting both the law and United States history to reach his decision. Outrage increased when news leaked that President Buchanan had unethically lobbied the Pennsylvanian on the Supreme Court to vote with the Southern majority, to prevent the impression of a strictly sectional vote on the case. Republican officials played the race card, hinting that if the Supreme Court ruled that the national government and residents of territories could not prohibit slavery, next it would open the doors for slavery to move north into the Free states. The following is a newspaper editorial from the *Chicago Tribune*, denouncing the court decision. What power or influence was really behind the decision, according to the editorial? On what grounds is this decision denounced? Faced with such misbehavior on the Supreme Court, how does the newspaper suggest Northern citizens respond?

We must confess we are shocked at the violence and servility of the Judicial Revolution caused by the decision of the Supreme Court of the United States. We scarcely know how to express our detestation of its inhuman dicta, or to fathom the wicked consequences which may flow from it. The blood of the early day—of the times that tried mens souls—was all healthful and strong, and lived, or was shed, for Liberty as freely as water. That is now changed *legally*. This decision has sapped the constitution of its glorious and distinctive features, and seeks to pervert it into a barbarous and unchristian channel.

Jefferson feared this Supreme Court, and foretold its usurpation of the legislative power of the Federal Government. His prophecy is now reality. The terrible evil he dreaded is upon us.

To say or suppose, that a Free People can respect or will obey a decision so fraught with disastrous consequences to the People and their Liberties, is to dream of impossibilities. No power can take away their rights. They will permit no power to abridge them. No servility of Judges or of Presidents, no servility of Congresses can taint their spirit or subdue it. The contest has come, and in that contest, the Supreme Court, we are sorry to say, will be shorn of its moral power—will lose that prestige, that authority, which instinctively insures respect and commands obedience. By its own bad act it has impaired its organization. Fortunate will it be, if that act does not destroy its utility. . . .

That there has been for long years a conspiracy against Freedom in this Republic, and that certain

Chicago Tribune, March 12, 1857.

members of the Supreme Court were engaged in it, we do not doubt. How this has happened, or why, it is needless to discuss now. It is enough to know, that a continued residence at Washington—the breathing in of its central and polluted atmosphere makes, or tends to make, those in authority, at once obedient and servile to the ruling dynasty, and callous to the purer and higher instincts and principles of the people. The Judiciary has proven no exception. We would, therefore, apply the remedy which JEFFER-SON urged, and JACKSON recommended—decentralization. Strip the President of every power which the people can exercise. Let every office which they are able to fill, be filled by them. Confide into their hands the election of the Judges of the United States, and thus infuse into these Judges a knowledge of their interests, a spirit and a purposeful kindred with theirs, an independence of the Executive worthy of them.

Document 11.11 John Brown Addresses a Virginia Court and the Nation

John Brown's life was one of failures. His leather tanning business failed in Ohio and Pennsylvania. His attempt at sheep farming was unsuccessful also. He lost his first wife and four infant children to early deaths. But he viewed his problems "small things" when compared to the great evil stalking the nation, and that was the existence of slavery. He helped slaves escape, hiding them at his farm and ferrying them northward along the Underground Railroad. But Brown gained national attention when he moved to Kansas in 1856 to battle slavery and its advocates. In response to the first sack of Lawrence, Brown and his followers dragged five pro-slavery advocates out of their homes along Pottawatomie Creek and hacked them to death with swords. He fought the "holy" war in Kansas even after one of his sons was killed, because he believed he was God's chosen instrument to fight slavery, justifying any actions he took. Going back east, he raised money from prominent abolitionists to support a phase of the war against slavery. He would lead an armed band into the South, where they would seize the weapons from the Federal Arsenal in Harper's Ferry, Virginia. With these weapons they would arm slaves and lead them in an uprising against their owners across the South. But Brown and his men were caught at Harper's Ferry, and Virginia state authorities tried Brown for treason. Convicted, he was sentenced to be hanged on December 2, 1859. The following comments are his last speech to the court. What indictments does Brown make of Southern society and the nation as a whole? How does he justify his actions, and what charges does he deny?

I have, may it please the Court, a few words to say.

In the first place, I deny everything but what I have all along admitted,—the design on my part to free the slaves. I intended certainly to have made a clean thing of that matter, as I did last winter, when I went into Missouri and there took slaves without the snapping of a gun either side, moved them through the country, and finally left them in Canada. I designed to have done the same thing again, on a larger scale. That was all I intended. I never did intend murder, or treason, or the destruction of property, or to excite or incite slaves to rebellion, or to make insurrection.

I have another objection: and that is, it is unjust that I should suffer such a penalty. Had I interfered in the manner which I admit, and which I admit has been fairly proved (for I admire the truthfulness and candor of the greater portion of the witnesses who have testified in this case),—had I so interfered in behalf of the rich, the powerful, the intelligent, the so-called great, or in behalf of any of their friends, either father, mother, brother, sister, wife, or children, or any of that class, and suffered and sacrificed what I have in this interference, it would have been all right; and every man in this court would have deemed it an act worthy of reward rather than punishment.

This court acknowledges, as I suppose, the validity of the law of God. I see a book kissed here which I suppose to be the Bible, or at least the New Testament. That teaches me that all things whatsoever I

From *The Life and Letters of John Brown: Liberator of Kansas and Martyr of Virginia*, Boston: Roberts Brothers, 1885.

would that men should do to me, I should do even so to them. It teaches me, further, to "remember them that are in bonds, as bound with them." I endeavored to act up to that instruction. I say, I am yet too young to understand that God is any respecter of persons. I believe that to have interfered as I have done—as I have always freely admitted I have done—in behalf of His despised poor, was not wrong, but right. Now, if it is deemed necessary that I should forfeit my life for the furtherance of the ends of justice, and mingle my blood further with the blood of my children and with the blood of millions in this slave country whose rights are disregarded by wicked, cruel, and unjust enactments, I submit; so let it be done!

Let me say one word further.

I feel entirely satisfied with the treatment I have received on my trial. Considering all the circumstances, it has been more generous than I expected. But I feel no consciousness of guilt. I have stated from the first what was my intention, and what was not. I never had any design against the life of any person, nor any disposition to commit treason, or excite slaves to rebel, or make any general insurrection. I never encouraged any man to do so, but always discouraged any idea of that kind.

Let me say, also, a word in regard to the statements made by some of those connected with me. I hear it has been stated by some of them that I have induced them to join me. But the contrary is true. I do not say this to injure them but as regretting their weakness. There is not one of them but joined me of his own accord, and the greater part of them at their own expense. A number of them I never saw, and never had a word of conversation with, till the day they came to me; and that was for the purpose I have stated.

Now I have done.

Document 11.12 South Carolina Secedes and Breaks Up the Union

Southern paranoia about the federal government increased from the 1820s onward. By the 1850s, Southern extremists preached that the only safeguard for their region was to have a friend in the White House, either an actual Southerner or a "doughface" Northerner they could control. The election of Republican Abraham Lincoln ended this control. Elected with all Northern votes (since the Republican Party was not allowed on Southern ballots) with a pledge to prevent slavery's expansion, he seemed to threaten the South. Despite his well-known views that slavery could not be touched in the South where it existed, the fact that he was elected legally and constitutionally, and the fact that Democrats still controlled both Congress and the Supreme Court, Southern extremists declared that his election alone marked the beginning of a governmental war against slavery. South Carolina's special convention voted 169-0 on December 20, 1860 to leave the Union. They were followed by the other six states in the Deep South over the next month and a half. The following is the justification South Carolina provided for breaking up the national Union. What are the major complaints they lodge against the North as justifications for secession? What legal justifications do they provide for their actions?

Declaration of Causes Which Induced the Secession of South Carolina.

The people of the State of South Carolina in Convention assembled, on the 2d day of April, A. D. 1832, declared that the frequent violations of the Constitution of the United States by the Federal Government, and its encroachments upon the reserved rights of the States, fully justified this State in their withdrawal from the Federal Union; but in deference to the opinions and wishes of the other Slaveholding States, she forbore at that time to exercise this right. Since that time these encroachments have continued to increase, and further forbearance ceases to be a virtue.

From *The Rebellion Record: A Diary of American Events and Documents, Narratives, Illustrations and Incidents,* New York: G.P. Putnam, 1862.

And now the State of South Carolina having resumed her separate and equal place among nations, deems it due to herself, to the remaining United States of America, and to the nations of the world, that she should declare the immediate causes which have led to this act. . . .

[Here follows a review of the history of the formation of the American union from the late colonial period, through the Revolution, and then to the adoption of the Constitution.]

By this Constitution, certain duties were imposed upon the several States, and the exercise of certain of their powers was restrained, which necessarily impelled their continued existence as sovereign states. But, to remove all doubt, an amendment was added, which declared that the powers not delegated to the United States by the Constitution, nor prohibited by it to the States, are reserved to the States respectively, or to the people. On the 23d May, 1788, South Carolina, by a Convention of her people, passed an ordinance assenting to this Constitution, and afterwards altered her own Constitution to conform herself to the obligations she had undertaken.

Thus was established, by compact between the States, a Government with defined objects and powers, limited to the express words of the grant. This limitation left the whole remaining mass of power subject to the clause reserving it to the States or the people, and rendered unnecessary any specification of reserved rights. We hold that the Government thus established is subject to the two great principles asserted in the Declaration of Independence; and we hold further, that the mode of its formation subjects it to a third fundamental principle, namely, the law of compact. We maintain that in every compact between two or more parties, the obligation is mutual; that the failure of one of the contracting parties to perform a material part of the agreement, entirely releases the obligation of the other, and that, where no arbiter is provided, each party is remitted to his own judgment to determine the fact of failure, with all its consequences.

In the present case, that fact is established with certainty. We assert that fourteen of the States have deliberately refused for years past to fulfil their constitutional obligations, and we refer to their own statutes for the proof.

The Constitution of the United States, in its fourth Article, provides as follows:

"No person held to service or labor in one State under the laws thereof, escaping into another, shall, in consequence of any law or regulation therein, be discharged from such service or labor, but shall be delivered up, on claim of the party to whom such service or labor may be due."

This stipulation was so material to the compact that without it that compact would not have been made. The greater number of the contracting parties held slaves, and they had previously evinced their estimate of the value of such a stipulation by making it a condition in the Ordinance for the government of the territory ceded by Virginia, which obligations, and the laws of the General Government, have ceased to effect the objects of the Constitution. The States of Maine, New Hampshire, Vermont. Massachusetts, Connecticut, Rhode Island, New York, Pennsylvania, Illinois, Indiana, Michigan, Wisconsin, and Iowa, have enacted laws which either nullify the acts of Congress, or render useless any attempt to execute them. In many of these States the fugitive is discharged from the service of labor claimed, and in none of them has the State Government complied with the stipulation made in the Constitution. The State of New Jersey, at an early day, passed a law in conformity with her constitutional obligation; but the current of Anti-Slavery feeling has led her more recently to enact laws which render inoperative the remedies provided by her own laws and by the laws of Congress. In the State of New York even the right of transit for a slave has been denied by her tribunals; and the States of Ohio and Iowa have refused to surrender to justice fugitives charged with murder, and with inciting servile insurrection in the State of Virginia. Thus the constitutional compact has been deliberately broken and disregarded by the non-slaveholding States; and the consequence follows that South Carolina is released from her obligation.

The ends for which this Constitution was framed are declared by itself to be "to form a more perfect union, to establish justice, insure domestic tranquillity, provide for the common defence, promote the general welfare, and secure the blessings of liberty to ourselves and our posterity."

These ends it endeavored to accomplish by a Federal Government, in which each State was recognized as an equal, and had separate control over its own institutions. The right of property in slaves was recognized by giving to free persons distinct political rights; by giving them the right to represent, and burdening them with direct taxes for, three-fifths of their slaves; by authorizing the importation of slaves for twenty years; and by stipulating for the rendition of fugitives from labor.

We affirm that these ends for which this Government was instituted have been defeated, and the Government itself has been destructive of them by the action of the non-slaveholding States. Those States have assumed the right of deciding upon the propriety of our domestic institutions; and have denied the rights of property established in fifteen of the States and recognized by the Constitution; they have denounced as sinful the institution of Slavery; they have permitted the open establishment among them of societies, whose avowed object is to disturb the peace of and eloin the property of the citizens of other States. They have encouraged and assisted thousands of our slaves to leave their homes; and those who remain, have been incited by emissaries, books, and pictures, to servile insurrection.

For twenty-five years this agitation has been steadily increasing, until it has now secured to its aid the power of the common Government. Observing the forms of the Constitution, a sectional party has found within that article establishing the Executive Department, the means of subverting the Constitution itself. A geographical line has been drawn across the Union, and all the States north of that line have united in the election of a man to the high office of President of the United States whose opinions and purposes are hostile to Slavery. He is to be intrusted with the administration of the common Government, because he has declared that that "Government cannot endure permanently half slave, half free," and that the public mind must rest in the belief that Slavery is in the course of ultimate extinction.

This sectional combination for the subversion of the Constitution has been aided, in some of the States, by elevating to citizenship persons who, by the supreme law of the land, are incapable of becoming citizens, and their votes have been used to inaugurate a new policy, hostile to the South, and destructive of its peace and safety.

On the 4th of March next this party will take possession of the Government. It has announced that the South shall be excluded from the common territory, that the judicial tribunal shall be made sectional, and that a war must be waged against Slavery until it shall cease throughout the United States.

The guarantees of the Constitution will then no longer exist; the equal rights of the States will be lost. The Slaveholding States will no longer have the power of self-government, or self-protection, and the Federal Government will have become their enemy.

Sectional interest and animosity will deepen the irritation; and all hope of remedy is rendered vain, by the fact that the public opinion at the North has invested a great political error with the sanctions of a more erroneous religious belief.

We, therefore, the people of South Carolina, by our delegates in Convention assembled, appealing to the Supreme Judge of the world for the rectitude of our intentions, have solemnly declared that the Union heretofore existing between this State and the other States of North America is dissolved, and that the State of South Carolina has resumed her position among the nations of the world, as separate and independent state, with full power to levy war, conclude peace, contract alliances, establish commerce, and to do all other acts and things which independent States may of right do.

Chapter 11 Worksheet and Questions

1. The documents in this chapter suggest that the extension of slavery into Kansas became a burning issue across the nation after 1854. Using the words of participants in the struggle over Kansas, as well as those who stayed away but supported one side or the other, explain why the struggle for Kansas was important enough to kill over. Are there other issues at stake in Kansas as well? Focus on Kansas and its participants in your answer.

    _____

    _____

    _____

    _____

    _____

    _____

    _____

    _____

2. You see yourself as a Southern "patriot," increasingly angry with the North during the decade of the 1850s. Using the arguments presented in the documents, explain why the Civil War begins in 1861. Be sure to explain in your Southern interpretation the events in Kansas, Washington D.C., and elsewhere. Make sure you include both underlying causes and specific events that precipitated conflict. Use the words of fellow Southerners in your answer.

    _____

    _____

    _____

    _____

    _____

    _____

    _____

    _____

3. Now assume the role of a Northern patriot who opposes the expansion of slavery into the western territories. Using the documents, trace the development of sectional conflict during the 1850s right up to South Carolina's secession. What underlying causes and specific events caused the Civil War? Who or what is to blame for the decade's troubles?

_____

_____

_____

_____

_____

_____

_____

_____

_____

4. Describe John Brown and his views. How would he explain the events of the 1850s? How would Southerners describe him? What does he do that they find most objectionable? If John Brown is a "Northern extremist," then who have you encountered in this chapter who is a "Southern extremist," and what makes him so?

_____

_____

_____

_____

_____

_____

_____

_____

_____

Chapter 12

"Gone to See the Elephant": Why Soldiers Fought the Civil War

Politicians and agitators held center stage before the Civil War began and in the first crazed days after the firing on Fort Sumter. Abolitionists talked about freeing the slaves, but most Northerners (and later soldiers) were not abolitionists; they disliked both the abolitionists and slaves, and saw both as trouble. Speakers talked about preserving the Northern way of life and thus guaranteeing America's Manifest Destiny. To Northerners, this meant keeping the western lands open to settlement by yeoman family farmers, the backbone of the nation since before the American Revolution. This also meant keeping slavery out, since free farms could not compete with slave-operated plantations. Other orators caught the public's attention with warnings about the "Slave Power Conspiracy," the threat that the Southern slaveowners (or slavocracy) would do anything to keep their slaves. "Anything" meant they were willing to corrupt the legal system, pervert the national government and the Constitution to their own use, take away the rights of Northern whites, and even kill Northerners to keep their power over black slaves. The murder of abolitionist editor Elijah Lovejoy, the criminal and murderous activities of the border ruffians in Kansas, Justice Taney's decision in the *Dred Scott* case, and secession—all appeared to prove the Southerners' willingness to undermine republican institutions and liberties for their own evil purposes. They would even destroy the republic established by the Founding Fathers, the last, best hope on earth. The slavocracy must be stopped!

Once the Civil War began, Northern rhetoric changed slightly. "Rally 'round the flag boys," because the South physically *attacked the nation* when it fired on the flag at Fort Sumter. This was no longer just an exchange of nasty rhetoric, but an actual call to arms. There were long speeches about duty, proclaiming every patriotic man must join up and fight for national honor. The Union and our unique Constitutional form of government must be preserved; we owe that to the Founding Fathers. Northern belief in the sanctity of the national union became an act of faith. The Union was not just the legacy of the Founding Fathers and the American Revolution; it represented all of the moral and political principles that made us different from every other nation on earth. Speakers also talked about heroism, and not just being heroic like the Founding Fathers. They suggested that secession was just another Southern bluff; confront them with a determined national army and they would fold up and the rebellion would end. The South had threatened secession before to gain Northern concessions—remember the Missouri Compromise of 1820, the Nullification Crisis of the 1830s, and the Compromise of 1850? In a nation of poker players, calling their bluff seemed the right thing to do.

Southern agitators and politicians had their own inflammatory rhetoric that carried over from the 1850s into the epic struggle. For years Rhett, Yancy, and others warned that the South must escape from a tyrannical central government, that the national government would (or at least could) be used to take away slavery. The South must secede to preserve its unique way of life, especially preserving slavery and white supremacy. These speakers repeatedly called for preserving Southern states' rights during the 1850s. But this was no longer just the ideal—that a state government possessed certain powers not granted to the national government. To Southern extremists this meant the right of a state to protect its citizens' rights to own slave property, and to take that property wherever they chose, and that Southerners' rights were more important than the rights of Northern citizens.

These arguments continued once the war began, even after the Southern government became larger and more tyrannical than the federal government ever had. The Reverend B.M. Palmer of New Orleans told soldiers they fought in a holy war, "a war of civilization against a ruthless barbarian which would dishonor the dark ages." Wartime orators spoke of the need for patriotism, of duty to the Southern "cause," and the need to preserve their view of the republic created by the Founding Fathers. Southern orators spoke of heroism and volunteering, insisting that Northerners could not fight and would turn and run the first time a Southern army appeared. Besides, if Northerners hated Southerners as much as they seemed to, they surely would not fight to keep the South in the Union. Senator James Chesnut of South Carolina offered to drink all the blood shed in the cause, while Robert Barnwell Rhett, editor of the *Charleston Mercury*, said he would eat the bodies of all men slain because of disunion. Such rhetoric misled the soldiers as well: John C. Reed of Georgia shaved the morning he joined the 8th Georgia Regiment and swore he would never shave again until the South was independent. He still had his beard in 1888.

For both North and South, soldiers were sent off to fight and die with extensive ritual and pomp. Volunteers signed up with friends from their hometown and region, and would stay together in a hometown company until attrition forced them to merge with another unit. Soldiers represented home, family, community, and nation; their units were presented flags made by the women of their hometowns. Defense of the flag meant defense of families and homes, defense of the honor and reputation of their communities; politicians expended a great deal of rhetoric when the flags were presented. The community stayed in touch with "their boys" throughout the war, making the conflict and casualties personal. Homefolk sent and received letters, and sent local reporters to write articles about their boys; civilian politicians made a point of visiting the troops at the front.

But did all of these political appeals, or the justifications presented by fanatics on both sides, motivate the soldiers to fight? Growing up in rural America, as most soldiers had, the greatest excitement when the circus came to town was "seeing the elephant," an excitement they could anticipate but never really know until facing it. They likewise anticipated combat and the thrill of battle, which they had heard about for years, but never experienced. They grew up with stories about the Founding Fathers, Lexington, and Concord, and other examples of bravery. This would be a chance to prove their own manhood, a chance to prove they are worthy descendents of the Founding Fathers.

But what keeps these men fighting as the deaths mount to record numbers, after they discover the misfortunes of camp life, while they are stalked by disease, loneliness, and starvation? Both sides face desertion problems as the war progresses, but most men stay in the armies. Why do they stay, even after they have "seen the elephant" and know war means killing rather than excitement? Why do they persist through illness, wounds, and bad leadership, and then voluntarily re-enlist? The image of the Minutemen was powerful on both sides. The yeoman farmer who abandons his plow in time of need, risks his life for the nation, and then returns to his farm when the crisis is over—this was an image Americans were raised on since Revolutionary days. Civic rituals such as celebrating the Fourth of July and national remembrances passed these ideas along, as did books like Mason Weems's *The Life of Washington*. This book and others reinforced the idea that all common Americans could be heroes, that their love of liberty prepared them for any martial contest. Such images reinforced the idea that each generation of American men needed to prove themselves worthy of the Founding Fathers, who risked everything to create the nation.

Excitement at the prospect of combat fueled early Southern enlistments as well. Colleges closed as entire classes left to enlist; the adventure of army life had to be more exciting than classes. Elite families formed local units, expecting the lower classes to follow their lead into service, as they did in local society. Most Southern soldiers were family farmers, and patriotism for their new country prompted their enlistment. They saw themselves as defenders of the Founding Fathers legacy, repeating the fight of the colonies versus the British Empire. More often they saw the war as a defense of hearth and home from an invader. This meant they were resisting tyranny and subjugation, because invaders always tyrannized a conquered people. This was a classic struggle of liberty versus tyranny. Many Southerners opposed secession and disliked slavery, but objected more to the idea of the North telling them how to run their own lives.

A fight for liberty did not mean liberty for slaves, of course. Racism was very strong, and this connected to concerns for Southern life if the North should win. Soldiers feared that a Northern victory meant slave insurrections, the destruction of slavery, and with it all future prosperity. Southerners feared that the "Yankees" would impose racial equality on the South, and many soldiers declared they were "not willing to see the South governed by a Negro." Others fought for honor and duty. To stay home was cowardly; it meant dishonoring oneself, one's family, and the community.

Simple patriotism filled Northern soldiers at the start of the war as well. Young men defied the wishes of their parents and wives to enlist, because "all true patriots must support their government." Elisha Hunt Rhodes had to obtain his widowed mother's permission to enlist at age 19. Another 14-year-old wrote "16" on a sheet of paper, stuck it in the bottom of his boot, and then, when the recruiting officer asked him if he was "over 16," he could answer yes, and enlist. Many saw themselves defending the republic of the Founding Fathers, preventing the dismemberment and destruction of the Union they created back in 1776. This was not just a defense of constitutional government—it was preservation of law and order. If the highest law in the land could not be upheld, how could governments enforce laws at other levels? Allowing secession to go unchallenged invited anarchy across the United States, and that threatened homes and families. Most of the yeoman farmers who filled the ranks of the armies agreed with President Lincoln that the United States was the "last, best hope" in a world of kings and tyrants. The spread of liberty across the world would collapse if the United States died, and kings/aristocrats would return in triumph. But freedom and liberty can only be protected and promoted with a strong Union. Some soldiers feared that if the South won, her tyrants would come north and enslave soldiers' wives and children. Most Northern soldiers were *not* fighting to free the slaves. They turned on slavery not out of concern for African Americans, but to weaken the slavocracy threatening their liberties and the Union. Finally, Northern soldiers also fought for honor and duty, because they also represented family, community, and nation.

By the end of the Civil War over 179,000 African Americans served in the Union army, and another 18,000 in the navy. The Sable Arm symbolized the triumph of the Union and the idea of equality. Some 33,000 volunteers came from the Free states. More than half of the remaining volunteers came from the slave states of Kentucky, Tennessee, Louisiana, and Mississippi. At first they were used for fatigue duty, digging trenches, burying the dead, and helping in hospitals. Eventually they were employed as combat units. For African Americans, this was a war for freedom as much as a war for the Union. Sometimes this meant personal freedom, for slaves who enlisted gained their freedom, and in some border states gained freedom for their families as well at the war's end. This possibility encouraged Missouri's blacks to enlist at a rate twice the proportion of black men in the state, even though they often had to escape to Kansas to join up. Freedom also meant the chance to liberate slaves in Southern states, to settle old scores with slaveholders. African American soldiers confronted the men who whipped them, raped their wives and sisters, and sold their parents to new masters in the Deep South.

Regimental schools meant education for some units. The very act of armed blacks fighting for the nation and their rights spread confidence through the rest of the African American community, a confidence carried over into Reconstruction. Most of all, African American soldiers understood that the freedom of all black people depended on Union victory, which motivated them even more. So they enlisted, even though they were often assigned the most menial and degrading tasks, even though they faced harsher punishments than white soldiers, even though they were denied chances to be commissioned officers, and even though they were paid at a lower rate than white soldiers. They faced the ongoing racial hostility of white America, although it slowly dissipated in the army after they proved themselves in combat. At Port Hudson, Battery Wagner, and hundreds of other locations, they proved their worth as combat troops.

Considering the Evidence in the Readings

Noted Civil War historian James McPherson declared that the men who fought in the American Civil War composed "the most literate armies in history to that time." Over 90,000 letters passed through Washington D.C. on a daily basis during the war. You will read the first-hand accounts of soldiers from both North and South, written at different times during the Civil War. Some are written in the flush of excitement immediately after the war began, before the reality of the bloodiest conflict in national history sank in. Others are written after years of fighting, victories, and defeats. Determine why the soldiers are still fighting, whether they are wrapped up in the pre-war political rhetoric or if they have their own reasons for fighting. You should also understand that soldiers in camp have other concerns than discussing reasons for the conflict.

Document 12.1 Patriotic Sentiments from a Michigan Volunteer

What is courage? Is it the ability to blank out the horrors of battle around you, to stand and face the fire of lines of soldiers opposite? Is it some animal instinct that some people have? Does courage come from a commitment to country, comrades, home, family, or some god? Does it follow from a good leader? Courage and duty were important themes to many soldiers. The Second Michigan Volunteers were known as the "Wolverine Brigade." Originally recruited as three-month volunteers in the heady days following Fort Sumter, they were mustered into service for three years. Led by Mexican War veteran Israel B. Richardson, the regiment gained a reputation for excellence during the Civil War. Philo H. Gallup of Pokagon, Michigan joined Company E as a 21-year-old private. His letters home provide an insight into the army life of this regiment. The writer's pride in his regiment, in being from Michigan, and in fighting for the cause of the Union are all evident in the letters. Note how he proudly explains how the Michigan troops do not suffer complainers and deserters, but are all ready to do their duty. Gallup was killed near Williamsburg, Virginia in May 1862. According to the author, why do men from Michigan join up to fight for the Union? How do they feel about soldiers who complain about army life? To whom do the Michigan soldiers compare themselves?

Detroit May 8th 1861

Dear sir

i take my pencil in my hand to let you now that i am well and i hope that i shall find you enjoying the same helth i have simply to say that if anybody had cause to complain it would be our men camping as we did three days and three nights in Niles and marching the forth night to Detroit to be on duty by the time required by battalion order No. 1 we arrived at cantonment Blair at 1 1/2 o clock in the morning and not finding the quraters fitted up like the aster [Astor] house we went to work to do what we were able it is the duty of a soldier or a citisan who stands up for his country not to Complain if he cannot hav the acommodation he lieves behind and if there should be any one who complains he had better pack his knapsack and gow home to his mother but i am certain there is no man in the whole regiment who would go or who has complained they evidently know more about our history than citsan did the revolutionary patriots in valley forge complain they had to march in the snow with there bare feet and to stand the cold twenty degrees below zero without blankets and meny times without camp fires did the armey complain when our beloved washington crossed the delaware and fought the battle of trenton they had to march in snow and mud and fight the hessians besieds and they did it in good stile too this patriotic feeling is yet in the men who form the seond regiment and of wich our men are in fact there is no suffering here in any we are all soldiers and as such we will show our fathers and mothers wifes sisters brothers and sweethearts that we are contented if can but go where a fight is in prospect we are well provided with the fat of the land and if the rain of heaven falls on us and makes our grond a little mudy we will be the last to complain

Yours Please show this to Father

Please right ameadiatly Direct your letters in Car of captain Robert Bretchsnider Co E second

Philo H Gallup
A Member of the
Coler Compney
E No 1 second regment

Letter, May 8, 1861.

Document 12.2 Why a Recent Immigrant Fights in the 9th Illinois Volunteer Infantry

Nearly one-half million foreign-born men joined the Union Army during the Civil War. Some were already citizens, others were not but hoped service would provide automatic citizenship. Most joined to demonstrate their support for the ideal of the nation—their dedication to the principles of liberty. Over 200,000 Germans joined the army, proud not only to serve the Union but to fight under German-born leaders ("I fights mit Siegal"). Thomas Barnett of Alton, Illinois was born in England and became a naturalized citizen in 1858. When the Civil War broke out, Barnett and thousands of other recent immigrants rallied to the flag of their adopted country. He joined the Alton Guards as a private in April 1861, and this unit was combined with nine other companies to form the 9th Illinois Volunteer Infantry. Although they signed up for only three months, almost the entire regiment re-enlisted for a full three years. Barnett wrote letters that provide perspectives on camp life, marching, and the war in general. According to Barnett, why are the Alton Guards fighting in this war? Does he demonstrate the same state and community pride as the Michigan volunteers? What does he eagerly look forward to?

APRIL 27, 1861, CAMP YATES,
SPRINGFIELD, ILLINOIS

Dear friend I address these few lines to you hopeing you are well which I am happy to say it leaves me at present Thank God Dear friend we are all in good cheer and we feel as if we had the courage of a Lion and we are willing to fight for that Glorious flag of our Union which those young Ladies made the a present company of it untill we wade in the enemy's blood up to our necks and if we ever get a chance to get a pop at Jef Davis we will take his head and put it to the top of our flag Staf tell the young Ladies of Alton that we will fight for our flag as long as there is a man left and if there is not a man left to return the flag; the young Ladies will have the reason to be proud that the Alton Guards fought nobly for its defence Dear friend we have the finest lot of men that

Ill can afford there is from 3 to 4000 men here and it is a great sight to see all the different companys drilling togather we drill 6 hours per day and we get along first rate Dear friend, I hear there is great excitement in alton and, I think you was pretty sharp to get possesion of the saint Louis arms and there is a regiment leave here this morning for alton to take care the St Louis roudies don't take them from you Dear friend give my kind regards to all my friends and accept the same your self from your sincere friend T Barnett Tell Robert Jonson that our company was reduced to 64 men besides officer and . . . . Johnson . . . . Walters Pat Hughs and lot of others was refused but they have joind another Company and they will be enrolld for the 4th regeiment alton Yeagers and alton Gaurds is enrolled for the 3rd regeiment and we expect orders to leave every minute write by return of Post.

Document 12.3 William S. Stewart, Missouri Unionist, Speaks Out

The border states of Maryland, Kentucky, Tennessee and Missouri were badly split by the Civil War. While many Missourians joined Confederate forces, a majority of patriotic Missourians remained loyal to the Union and fought to preserve the nation. Missouri Unionists were convinced that force was justified to preserve the nation, and that force was necessary in Missouri to prevent secession. St. Louis Unionists were sure that Nathaniel Lyon kept the state in the Union when he captured the state militia at Camp Jackson, a disloyal militia armed and trained by a secessionist governor. This is certainly the view of William S.

Stewart, who was born and educated in Indiana but was practicing law in St. Louis when the war broke out. He was among the first to volunteer in April 1861, joining what became the 1st Regiment of Missouri Volunteers. Stewart served until April 1864, resigning with the rank of Captain. Three of his letters to family members are included here. Note that his loyalty and enthusiasm for the Union cause do not wear out after the first months of excitement. How does Stewart feel about the rebellious states? On what grounds should the rebellion be defeated? What evils do the Southern conspirators bring to the nation?

St. Louis, Mo.
February 10, 1861

Dear Father and Mother,

The two weeks period having arrived for writing to you, I write, though I have nothing to say. It is today a warm, but a wet disagreeable Sunday. I have been in my room nearly all day reading and shall go to church tonight if it shall quit raining. My health is still quite good. I think it was never better than it has been since my visit home. Times are still hard and money scarce. For some two or three months past the most of us have considered that we were doing well if we could collect money enough to pay expenses. We have enough work to do, but the difficulty is to get money when there is none. I believe I have not heard from Frank since I last wrote to you. I am looking every day for a letter from him. Nor have I answered John B's last letter. I must write to him soon, probably this week. I don't want you all to be scared about Civil War. I think all will be well shortly. The rulers and parties of our Country had become so wicked and corrupt, that it was necessary that strong remedies should be used to purify it. The sin of slavery had become so domestical and defended, and the custom of public plunder had become so bold and defiant that it was impossible to bring about a reform, without producing great convulsions. In less than six months the entire North will be enjoying peace and quiet, and the rebellious States will be bitterly repenting their haste and folly. So don't any of you be alarmed as many of the nervous are here.

I wrote to Conklin some few weeks ago, but I have no answer yet from him. I would like to hear how you are all getting along at home. Of course you have plenty to eat and wear which if it is accompanied with good health, is very good for these times. In Kansas at the present time there are thousands of families that are now suffering, and I know it to be true that if the present supplies which have been going into that country for two or three months past, should be stopped, thousands would soon starve to death, and even in this city which is now supposed to be full of provisions, I often see destitute families that are starving for bread. When I see and hear and think of all these miseries I often think how thankless most of us are, who have plenty to eat and to wear. I would like to see you all this winter, but of course I shall not before next summer.

Give my respects to all of the friends and relatives.

Respectfully
Your Son,
William

St. Louis, Mo.
April 7, 1861

Dear Father and Mother,

. . . I was sorry to learn from John Bartlow's letter that Jonathan had lost his horse. I would rather loose [sic] anything myself than to see Jonathan loose it, for he always takes the blues over it. As for me I always expect misfortunes as the inevitable incidents of this life and therefore am never disappointed when they come and during these hard times if a man has plenty to eat and to wear, he ought to rejoice instead of complain.

We have hard times here still with a prospect of still harder times and more than that, a prospect of "Civil War." Rumors of war are rife from the city of Washington, Charleston and Montgomery. And when it does come we will have warm times in St. Louis. We

---

From *Missouri Historical Review*, 61, by Harvey L. Carter and Norma L. Peterson, editors. Reprinted by permission.

have [a] disunion Governor who is trying to force Missouri out of the Union. And as St. Louis is the greatest barrier in the way he is doing all he can to get our city under the rule of traitors. There is a large Flag of the Southern Confederacy floating in our midst now, and to attempt to take it down would cause a bloody time and yet the great majority of our city and State are for the Union. The State officers are all traitors and will try to take the advantage of us. If war does come you may rest assured that I will not desert or dishonor the glorious old flag of the Union. I don't know what your hopes or fears are about the country. Here the country is the whole theme, and everybody has taken sides either for or against us. I'm glad that Lincoln and his cabinet first tried peace measures and now that they have failed, I'm glad that he has adopted a vigorous policy. He cannot now be charged with rashness or precipitation. The South has rejected all propositions for peace, and now must submit to war for the sake of peace. We of the Border Slave State[s] will suffer most from Civil strife, but can't now see how it can be otherwise. But I'll say no more about war now, as of course it cannot interest you much where you are in perfect security from the worst that can come. If matters go favorably I shall visit home again in August. John B. represents Conklin's and Merrills all well, and the folks generally. I am quite well, and am making my way through the pressure of hard times as well as could be expected. Money is a scarce article, and the prospect is now that it will be scarcer before the crisis is past. Tell John Bartlow that I wrote to him today. It will be but a short time till corn planting. I would like to be in the country a couple of weeks this spring. I will keep you posted about our political and military affairs here.

Your Son Respectfully
Will S. Stewart

Camp Fremont
Cape Girardeau, Mo.,
September 6, 1861

Dear Father and Mother,

I wrote to you last from this place I believe, and to Jonathan while on my way to St. Louis about two weeks ago. I don't know what more I have to say, than I said then. I am still quite well and ready to defend our old Flag. Since I wrote to you I have been made Captain of Company "K," of our Rifle Regiment and have as good a set of boys as you ever saw. I never

have the slightest trouble with them, and they declare that they will fight till they die, for me. They are the best drilled Company in the Regiment and what is more, I did the drilling all myself. But enough of this. We have great times in Missouri now, worse than Virginia. However, the Battle at Springfield, was such a crippler to the 23,000 rebels, that they have not yet been able to make a stand, and now Ben McCullough is retreating South. The heat of the war is now near us in the southeast of the State. But our forces are so admirably arranged under Fremont that we begin to be afraid that the rebels will be scared off before we get a shot at them although they have about 17,000 men and we about 10,000. The won't fight unless they have four times our number as at Springfield. And I thank God that in Missouri he has given us courage and ability to meet and conquer four times our numbers, whilst we fight for the blessings bought by the blood and treasure of our Father's [sic]. But I can't write on this subject without stirring up my feelings. Here we have had savage barbarity enough on the part of the Rebels to make us desperate. I have read all the annals of indian atrocity and savage butchery, from the Revolution down to the present time, but none of them can compare with the fiendish, demoniac and hellish butcheries of the secessionists of Missouri, upon innocent grayhaired old men, and any body else who would not join them in their plunders and murders. Do you blame me then for vowing in my heart to fight them to the bitter and bloody end. We now have authority to shoot every man that we catch fighting against us, the same that Benedict Arnold would have been shot, had be been shot, and *we intend to shoot them mark that.*

Yesterday I received a letter from Jno. Bartlow and it was the first time I had heard from home for more than two months. You may imagine how glad I was to receive it. And yet it pained to read that there were men in Franklin County who openly sympathized with the traitors, and that too while the Union men in the border States are suffering and fighting to sustain the government that has given position and affluence and protection to these black hearted traitors of Franklin County.

I have authority now from the Government to arrest and cite to trial every rebel sympathizer and if they be found guilty to have them shot. When I go to Franklin County I shall carry the same authority with me, and as sure as I live, I shall exercise it there, even if it be upon those who were once my best friends. When I shall visit home I cannot yet tell, but as soon as we get the rebels cleaned out of Missouri I think I can spare a week,—and under the Proclamation of

General Fremont we will soon give the rebels a bloody cleaning out. I hope you are all well at home yet and loyal to your country. Tell Jno. Bartlow that I will soon write to him. I have some photographs of myself taken which I will send home as soon as convenient. Give my respects to all my friends who are not enemies of my country. I can love my enemies, but the Lord commanded me to love the enemies of my country. Give me your best wishes and warmest prayers, and if I never see you again, but fall while fighting for the blessed heritage of our fathers, all will be well.

Your affectionate Son.
Will

Document 12.4 Sullivan Ballou Expresses Love for Family and Nation

More than 10 percent of the population of New England enlisted in the Union Army. In some communities, over 55 percent of the adult males joined the army, so that the very existence of towns hung on the communications between soldiers and their home towns. Most soldiers wrote home to their wives or other family members. Many spoke of an obligation to their wives and children, that having inherited an entire nation they must pass the same onto their children and future generations. Among the most poignant letters are those written by Major Sullivan Ballou of the 2nd Rhode Island Volunteers. Ballou was a 32-year-old Providence lawyer and former Speaker of the Rhode Island House of Representatives. He and his wife Sarah planned to build a life around their sons, Edgar and Willie. His passionate letters demonstrate his love for his family and pride in his state regiment, and provide insights into the meaning of the Union. Once again we see a soldier determined to save our national Manifest Destiny, to save from treason and rebellion the republic established by the Founding Fathers. A week after writing the second letter, Major Sullivan Ballou was killed at the First Battle of Bull Run. In these letters, what does Ballou talk about besides the war? How does he compare his love for Sarah with his love for country? Is he afraid of making the ultimate sacrifice to save the nation and our form of government?

Camp Sprague [Washington, D.C.]
Sunday June 23rd/61

My dear Sarah,

I wrote to you very hurriedly & confusedly yesterday soon after our arrival; and feel again as tho I wanted to write you a little more. We are encamped in Paradise. There certainly never was a more beautiful spot. It is an oak grove—the trees all tall and large and the ground free from shrubs. The space we occupy is about half the size of the camp at home and while the sun is pouring down its oppressive heat outside, we are as cool and comfortable as you could wish. While the first regiment is encamped close beside us in booths or sheds and rather cramped for room and oftentimes go outside on the ground to sleep, we are all cool and our white tents in the green woods look more inviting than anything else. Our baggage waggons stand close behind our row of tents—one just at the back door of my tent to which my good horse "Jennie" is tied night & day. My man sleeps in the baggage waggon and I occupy my tent alone much to my delight—he is a kind good natured fellow & I like him much. He now begins to understand his duties & will fill them I have no doubt. Last night I slept in my tent for the first time, & I slept well: have not caught cold and my catarrh continues better. Last night the moon was full I believe & if you could have seen it shining through our trees & glistening on our white tents you would have said it was the most beautiful sight you ever saw. When I went to bed I lay a long time looking up to see the shadows of the leaves and branches painted on my tent & at last

From Rhode Island Historical Society Library.

went to sleep thinking of my loved wife & my little boys. This morning Bishop Clarke preached to us about half an hour, and spoke with his usual force & eloquence. . . . We are about two miles from Washington; & from the hill where the first Regt. are encamped the city & all its buildings can be seen. Tomorrow afternoon at 3 P.M. we are to march down to the White house to be reviewed by the President & Gen. Scott. What is to be done with us I know not. . . .

The first regiment are in splendid health—they are brown and stout as you can imagine. On their return from Harpers ferry they marched 32 miles in 17 hours & feel very proud of it. Our Regiment are all well—among the whole 1000 there is scarcely an ail. You need not think I have put a shining face on, to cheer you up; I really have not exagerated our agreeable situation. At the same time do not harbor the thought that I fail to think of my loved ones at home—they are always in my heart and scarcely ever absent from my mind. I have just begun to realize that though I am here with 2000 men I am yet alone. I am far away from you Sarah & my beautiful boys—and it seems strange to me that I have never prized you as I ought—however much I may have loved you. I yearn to see you now so much, when I know I cannot, that all the love I have heretofore poured out for you seems insignificant. When I could go home every day & see you all, I did not think to weigh you in the scales with my affection; but now I think day by day what a trio I have, far away in my home.

When shall I hear from you: perhaps you are writing me today. I hope so—& that you will write me long letters full of all the little incidents of your daily life & that of the children. Be of good cheer & bear our present separation like the noble christian woman that you are. I already look forward to the time when I shall come home to you safe & well & I pray God I may find you & my dear children all well & rejoiced to see me. I wish you would go out & see my mother often & comfort her. I cannot write her many letters unless I lessen the number to you—& that I do not wish to do—so you must see her and tell her all the news from me. You must not wait for letters from me, dear Sarah but write me as often as you can find a few moments to spare for I shall look for your letters now with as much impatience as I used to when a lover's ardor fired me almost to desperation.

. . . There is a rumor to night that the rebels will attack our lines on Arlington Heights to *night* & that the 1st Regiment has marching orders—but there are so many rumors of the same kind that nobody takes any notice of it. I doubt the rumor & rather believe that there will be no general battle for some time. It will be very unwise to put *our* regiment into the field on account of our bad arms. We shall probably be furnished with rifles & we must be drilled with them some time before the men can use them well. . . .

. . . Goodbye my dear Sarah & believe me

Yours affectionately
Sullivan.

The Adjutant here is a fine flute player & has his flute with him & good music. When you learn of some one coming *directly here* send my Ivory topped flute by him.

July 14th 1861
Camp Clark Washington

My very dear Sarah

The indications are very strong that we shall move in a few days—perhaps tomorrow. Lest I should not be able to write to you again, I feel impelled to write a few lines that may fall under your eye when I shall be no more. Our movement may be one of a few days duration and full of pleasure, and it may be one of severe conflict and death to me. "Not my will, but thine O God be done." If it is necessary that I should fall on the battle field for my country, I am ready. I have no misgivings about, or lack of confidence in the cause in which I am engaged, & my courage does not halt or falter. I know how strongly American civilization now leans on the triumph of the government, & how great a debt we owe to those who went before us through the blood and sufferings of the Revolution, & I am willing, perfectly willing—to lay down all my joys in this life to help maintain this government & to pay that debt. But, my dear wife, when I know that with my own joys, I lay down nearly all of yours, & replace them in this life with cares & sorrows, when after having eaten for long years the bitter fruits of orphanage my self, I must offer it as the only sustenance to my dear little children, is it mean or dishonorable that while the banner of my purpose floats calmly & proudly in the breeze, underneath, my unbounded love for you, my darling wife & children should struggle in fierce, though useless contest with my love of Country. I cannot describe to you my feelings on this calm summer Sabbath night, when thousands now are sleeping around me, many of them enjoying, perhaps the last sleep before that of death, while I am suspicious that death is creeping around me with his Fatal dart, as I sit communing with God, my country and thee. I have sought most closely and diligently & often in my heart for a wrong motive in thus hazarding the happiness of all those I love and I could find none. A pure love of my country and of the principles I have so often advocated before the people. Another name of honor that I love more than I fear death, has called upon me, & I have obeyed.

Sarah, my love for you is deathless: it seems to bind me with mighty cables that nothing but misfortune could break; and yet my love of Country comes over me like a strong wind & bears me irresistibly on with all those charms to the battle field. The memories of all the blissful moments I have spent with you come creeping over me, & I feel most grateful to God & to you that I have enjoyed them so long, and how hard it is for me to give them up & burn to ashes the hopes of future years. Where God willing, we might still have lived and loved together, & seen our sons grown up to honorable manhood around us. I have, I know but few & small claims upon Divine Providence—but something whispers to me perhaps it is the wafted prayer of my little Edgar, that I shall return to my loved ones unharmed. If I do not, my dear Sarah never forget how much I loved you, and when my last breath escapes me—on the battle field—it will whisper your name. Forgive my many faults, and the many pains I have caused you. How thoughtless how foolish I have oftentimes been. How

gladly would I wash out with my tears every little spot upon your happiness, & struggle with all the misfortunes of this world to shield you & your children from harm. But I cannot. I must watch you from the spirit land, and hover near you—while you buffet the storms with your precious freight, and wait with patience till we meet to part no more. But, O Sarah! if the dead can come back to this earth & flit unseen around those they loved, I shall always be near you. In the gladdest days & in the darkest night, amidst your happiest scenes, and gloomiest hours, *always—* always, and if there be a soft breeze upon your cheek it shall be my breath; or the cool air fans your throbbing temples; it shall be my spirit passing by.

Sarah, do not mourn me dead, think I am gone and wait for thee, for we shall meet again. As for my little boys—they will grow up as I have done, and never know a father's love or care. Little Willie is too young to remember me long—and my blue-eyed Edgar—will keep my frolics with him among the dim memories of his childhood.

Sarah, I have unbounded confidence in your maternal care, & your development of their characters, and feel that God will bless you in your holy work. Tell my two mothers I call God's blessing upon them. O Sarah; come to me, and lead thither my children.

Sullivan

Document 12.5 "Sharing the Incommunicable Experience of War"

Patriots from every social class joined the Union army to save the nation from destruction. These volunteers believed that the only way to preserve law and order, as well as maintain individual rights, was to uphold the government. The 20th Regiment of Massachusetts Volunteers became known as the Harvard Regiment, because it contained so many recent graduates. Among the wealthy patriots was Oliver Wendell Holmes Jr., who was commissioned a lieutenant in July 1861. Holmes did not have to serve; as with most Harvard graduates, family wealth and influence could have kept him safely at home. These volunteers heard the call of honor and duty. Holmes was a prodigious writer, and his volumes of letters and diary entries provide a glimpse of a soldier faced with all the horrors of war. Seriously wounded three times, Holmes never considered abandoning the cause of the Union. To him this war was personal, and after the war he repeatedly spoke at veterans' gatherings and monument dedications to make sure that the sacrifices of his generation, the men "touched by fire," were never forgotten. Holmes offered up his life to the principle of duty—the duty of all citizens to loyally sustain their government. His letter here was written while recovering from his first wound. Why is Holmes still ready to do his duty, even after the "butchery" of good soldiers at Fredericksburg? What does he see as the hope for the future of civilization?

Dec. 20, 62.
[Falmouth, Va.]

My Dear Governor

After the inspiration of a night which would have been rather a nipper in your furnace-warmed house with double glass, passed here with a couple of blankets in one of the tents wh. I suppose Gen. Halleck (whom may the Lord confound) would enumerate among the "luxuries" of the Army of the Potomac—I sit down to give you the benefit of my cheerfulness—I always read now the D. Advertiser religiously as well as other papers—and I was glad to see that cheerful sheet didn't regard the late attempt in the light of a reverse—It *was* an infamous butchery in a ridiculous attempt—in wh. I've no doubt our loss doubled or tripled that of the Rebs. However that's neither here nor there—I've just been reading Mr. Motley's letters to Billy Seward. What a noble manly high-toned writer he is—I always thought his letters to you were more thoroughly what a man should write than almost any I ever saw—I never I believe have shown, as you seemed to hint, any wavering in my belief in the right of our cause—it is my disbelief in our success by arms in wh. I differ from you & him—I think in that matter I have better chances of judging than you—and I believe I represent the conviction of the army—& not the least of the most intelligent part of it.—The successes of wh. you spoke were to be anticipated as necessary if we entered into the struggle—But I see no farther progress—I don't think either of you realize the unity or the determination of the South. I think you are hopeful because (excuse me) you are ignorant. But if it is true that we represent civ-

ilization wh. is in its nature, as well as slavery, diffusive & aggressive, and if civn & progress are the better things why they will conquer in the long run, we may be sure, and will stand a better chance in their proper province—peace—than in war, the brother of slavery—brother—it is slavery's parent, child and sustainer at once—At any rate dear Father don't, because I say these things imply or think that I am the meaner for saying them—I, am, to be sure, heartily tired and half worn out body and mind by this life, but I believe I am as ready as ever to do my duty—But it is maddening to see men put in over us & motions forced by popular clamor when the army is only willing to trust its life & reputation to one man—

Please send me by mail 6 of the best kind of photogs of me—(the 2/3 lengths—they are stunners—I think I'd rather play my game with that dummy than in person)—I want to give them to some of the officers—By Ged (the vowel is an E) the Regt did behave gloriously in the late *rumpi*. I feel a sort of dispassionate pride combined with my regret at my own absence—Isn't this a bully kind of a letter? I shall get Patten to direct it so that you may think it a bill—

The groaning board calls me—in fact it howls—"To dinner" A bully dinner today—beefsteak (fried) beans (stewed—baked unknown) & rice—Hyah!

Dinner's over—the beefsteak was broiled on the coals not fried and for the 1st time for 2 weeks I've eaten my belly full and any animal food to speak of—10 to 1 it makes me sick—

My love to all—Oh—please send me also by mail—books go cheap—Cairnes' book—Amer. Ed

Your Aff. Son
O W Holmes, Jr.

Document 12.6 A New Orleans Black Soldier Explains the War

African-American soldiers often fought for different motives, or from a different sense of duty, from their white counterparts. For them the destruction of slavery was tightly linked to a Northern victory and the preservation of the Union. Black soldiers overcame difficulties that white soldiers never faced, including discrimination in pay. The Militia Act of 1862 authorized paying white privates $13 per month, but only $10 to "persons of African descent." These troops faced racism in many ways, including officers who were sure blacks could not fight, or believed that it was better to have them die so that white soldiers could live. African-American soldiers were unsure of their support among the civilian population as well, since many Northern states still prohibited black voting or integrated schools. These are some of the issues raised by the following letter from an anonymous "Colored Man" in New Orleans. The First Louisiana Regiment was composed of free blacks from New Orleans, and was originally commanded by black officers. Why is saving

Letter dated December 20, 1862.

the Union not enough, according to the writer? Who are the two masters of the colored population, and how are they different? What makes it difficult for African Americans to fully support the goals of the Union?

[New Orleans, La. September? 1863]

***

it is retten that a man can not Serve two master But it Seems that the Collored population has got two a rebel master and a union master   the both want our Servises   one wants us to make Cotton and Sugar And the Sell it and keep the money   the union masters wants us to fight the battles under white officers and the injoy both money and the union   black Soldiers And white officers will not play togeathe much longer   the Constitution is if any man rebells against those united States his property Shall be confescated and Slaves declared and henceforth Set free forever when theire is a insurection or rebllion against these united States the Constitution gives the president of the united States full power to arm as many soldiers of African decent as he deems nescesisary to Surpress the Rebellion and officers Should be black or white According to their abillitys   the Collored man Should guard Stations Garison forts and mand vessels according to his Compasitys

A well regulated militia being necessary to the cecurity of a free State the right of the people to keep and Bear arms Shall not be infringed

we are to Support the Constitution but no religious test Shall ever be required as a qualification to Any office or public trust under the united States the excitement of the wars is mostly keep up from the Churches   the Say god is fighting the battle but it is the people   But the will find that god fought our battle once   the way to have peace is to distroy the enemy   As long as theire is a Slave their will be rebles Against the Government of the united States So we must look out our white officers may be union men but Slave holders at heart   the Are allways on hand when theire is money but Look out for them in the battle feild   liberty is what we want and nothing Shorter

our Southern friend tells that the are fighting for negros and will have them   our union friends Says

the are not fighting to free the negroes   we are fighting for the union and free navigation of the Mississippi river   very well let the white fight for what the want and we negroes fight for what we want   there are three things to fight for and two races of people divided into three Classes   one wants negro Slaves the other the union the other Liberty   So liberty must take the day nothing Shorter   we are the Blackest and the bravest race   the president Says there is a wide Difference Between the black Race and the white race   But we Say that white corn and yellow will mix by the taussels but the black and white Race must mix by the roots as the are so well mixed and has no tausels—freedom and liberty is the word with the Collered people

***

Sure the Southern men Says the are not fighting for money the are fighting for negros   the northern men Say the did not com South to free the negroes but to Save the union   very well for that much what is the colored men fighting for   if the makes us free we are happy to hear it And when we are free men and a people we will fight for our rights and liberty   we care nothing about the union   we heave been in it Slaves over two hundred And fifty years we have made the contry and So far Saved the union and if we heave to fight for our rights let us fight under Colored officers for we are the men that will kill the Enemies of the Government

***

now is the united States government and constitution free or a local Government   if it is free let us colored population muster in to ams and garison forts guard Station and mand vessels and then we will know wheather we are free people or not   then we will know wheather you want to make brest works of us or not or make us fools or not   I heard one of most Ables and distingush lawiers Say that the Colored population was all free and Had as much liberty

---

From *Freedom's Soldiers: The Black Military Experience in the Civil War*. Reprinted with the permission of Cambridge University Press.

in the union as he had   in four or five days after I went to him to get him to atend Some buiness for me he Said to me Are you free or Slave   Sir Said i am free By your own speeches   was you born free   no Sir Said i   we have been made fools of from the time Butlers fleet landed hear but I have remained At my old Stand and will untill i See what i am dowing

I know very well that the white union men cannot put down the rebeles for them that was not rebles Soon will be   i am Sory that I am not able to write good   may the union forever Stand with peace and liberty to All good people

HD   A Colored man

Document 12.7 The Meaning of the War from the 54th Massachusetts

The 54th Massachusetts Infantry was organized in March 1863, composed primarily of free blacks from northern states. One of the first black units organized, it was an object of great interest and speculation over its battle-worthiness. These issues were all settled when it led the controversial assault on Battery Wagner, crossing open ground under heavy fire and capturing part of the fort for an hour. Because the Union commander failed to follow up and support their attack, the unit suffered almost 50 percent casualties in the attack, including its white commander, Colonel Robert Gould Shaw. The following letter is from Meunommie L. Maimi of Connecticut, who transferred into the 54th after they were organized. According to Maimi, why does he fight? What does he believe this war will decide? Why are the slaveholders his enemies?

Buckingham Legion, Co. I 20th Regt., C.V.
Camp near Stafford C. H.

March 1863

My Dear Wife:

When I wrote you the last letter I was quite sick, and did not know as I should ever be able to write you again; but I am better now and write to relieve your mind, in case you might worry too much about me. When I wrote my last letter, I did not expect to write another; but some good news which I received and the kind usage of a few friends, who came to my hut and did what was needed for me, have saved you your husband, and I am enabled to write again. There is one thing your selfish love for your husband has made you forget, and that is, that he is naturally a soldier, and in time of war, and particularly in times like the present, a good soldier has something else to do besides enjoying himself at home with his family. I shall come, if permitted to go home, but as soon as my health will admit I will return to duty.

Do you know or think what the end of this war is to decide? It is to decide whether we are to have freedom to all or slavery to all. If the Southern Confederacy succeeds, then you may bid farewell to all liberty thereafter and either be driven to a foreign land or held in slavery here. If our government succeeds, then your and our race will be free. The government has torn down the only barrier that existed against us as a people. When slavery passes away, the prejudices that belonged to it must follow. The government calls for the colored man's help and, if he is not a fool, he will give it. . . .

[Slaveholders] are my enemies, my flag's enemies, the flag I was born under, have suffered so much under—the enemies to God and our government. It is they who have struck down the flag which so long has defended their institutions before they left our Union. It has by them been cast to the earth and trampled under foot, because it professed to be the flag of liberty and freedom, although it was only liberty for the white man. . . . They tore that flag from its staff and in its place put their rebel rag, and swore by it that freedom should die. But they shall find that it cannot die, that its black sons as well as its

From *Weekly Anglo-African*, April 18, 1863.

loyal white sons are faithful, and will shed the last drop of blood in defense of the starry banner that is to be the emblem of freedom to all, whether black or white. . . .

I do not blame you altogether for what you said about returning home, as it was cowardly in me to complain to you of . . . bad usage. I forgive you, as it was prompted by your too-selfish love for your husband. But I want you to remember hereafter that you *are* a soldier's wife, a warrior's bride—one who has not a single drop of cowardly blood in his veins, and who will not desert his flag, or country, or his brother in bonds, not even for his dearly beloved wife, the friend of his bosom. Ponder this well; take the right sense of it and be proud that you have such a man for a husband. What is money but trash? And is trash to be compared to a country's and my own liberty? If the goverment gets so poor, before the war ends, that it cannot pay but $10 per month and no bounties, I will take that and fight on. That will buy bread for you and my poor old grandmother. If I return at all, let me come back to your arms a free man, of a free country and a free flag, and my brothers free, or else let me rest in death on the battlefield, with my face to the slaveholders, a continual reproach and curse unto him as long as the world shall stand or a slaveholder breathe. This from your soldier-husband.

M. L. Maimi

Document 12.8 An Early Southern View of the Civil War

As in the North, many more Southern volunteers came forward at the start of the war than the Confederate government could accept. Southern soldiers were just as passionate in their views about the war as the Northern writers already covered. Before the first large battles took place, many were just as optimistic about a quick victory, believing the myth that one Southerner could outfight ten Yankees. The following letter was written from training camps in Virginia before the First Battle of Bull Run. Thomas Rowland was born in Detroit, Michigan but was raised in Fairfax, Virginia by his "mother's people" after his father died. He was a cadet at West Point when Virginia seceded from the Union, whereupon he resigned and joined the Provisional Army of Virginia. He was serving in the Engineering Corps of the Confederate Army when he wrote this letter. According to Rowland, why are the men in his camp ready to fight? Do they view themselves responsible for destroying the Union?

HD. QUARTERS, CAVALRY CAMP,
ASHLAND, VA.,
May 15, 1861.

I am writing from the Adjutant's office of the Cavalry Camp, which is now my office, so my letter is dated accordingly. I have been appointed by Col. Ewell Adjutant of the Cavalry Camp, which now comprises six companies. It is soon to be increased by four more, making a full regiment. I have no uniform and no sabre yet and do not like to get one until I am sure that I will be able to pay for it *myself*. I conduct Dress Parade in my grey pants and blue coat, and borrow a sabre from some one on the sick list. If we should receive marching orders, I can probably obtain a horse and a sabre in this way and march with the regiment.

These cavalry troops are the finest soldiers I have ever seen anywhere and bring with them fine horses. They are mostly gentlemen, and both mentally and physically capable. I have just been out taking a snack with the Hanover Dragoons. They all cook their own rations, of course, but this morning one of them had received a special supply of pies and buttermilk from home. The ordinary ration is bread, pork, and beef, if it can be had. The officers all board at the hotel, which is kept in real old Virginia style, good country fare, and legions of little negro waiters always on hand.

From *William and Mary Quarterly*, January 1913.

The troops all keep in good health and good spirits. They are ready to fight, and the more reflecting ones ready to make peace, if those Yankees will keep their feet off the soil of the Old Dominion. You would be surprised to see what men we have in the ranks, cool headed farmers, and men of property and family, men who will give all they have and devote their lives to the cause of their native State. Men who were opposed to secession have taken arms to maintain the right to secede, recognizing the action of Virginia as the guide of their action. Troops arrive in Richmond continually from different parts of this State and from the South. If the Yankees wish it we will fight them, and by the help of God and a righteous cause *we'll whip them*. I am very busy at present, attending to my own duties, and instructing the uninitiated. Having been at West Point, I have the advantage in tactics, but I expect they can all beat me in riding.

Ashland is really a very pretty place, in spite of the poorness of the soil. It takes its name from its locality, being only about four miles from the birthplace of Henry Clay. The cottage in which he was born and the mill to which he used to ride upon a bag of corn are still standing. The birthplace of Patrick is also in this county; two noble Henrys who if they were now living, would speak and fight for Dixie's Land. I have quite a pleasant time here, many pleasant officers and warm-hearted Virginians among these cavalry companies. My captain was a member of the Convention.

I wish you would send me the *Alexandria Gazette*, whenever you can; I like to hear all that is going on at home, and I cannot get it here, though it is quite a popular paper at present in Richmond. I sent the *Dispatch* this morning containing an excellent article about Gen. Butler. I wish I could hear you sing "Dixie's Land" this evening. Our bugler plays it quite well, but he doesn't play those words that you sing to it.

CAVALRY CAMP, ASHLAND, VA,
June 14th, 1861.

I was so well satisfied to hear that you were safely out of Fairfax Co. and on your way to "Eastern View," that I have been culpably slow in offering my congratulations. I suppose you know that Uncle Robert [Genl Robert H. Chilton] has been in command here for several weeks, but having been appointed Asst. Adj. Gen. with the rank of Lt. Col. in the Confederate Army has returned to Richmond. Capt. Field who was the Instructor in Cavalry tactics at West Point, is stationed here in the same capacity. Three of my West Point friends passed here yesterday on their way to Richmond, Cadets Rice, Campbell, and Patterson, one from Kentucky, the others from Missouri and Arkansas. They were in the first class, and I suppose, graduated before they resigned.

I made application a few days ago for a commission in the Confederate Army. The civilized world from all quarters are beginning to condemn this war of subjugation against the South. The *London Times* compares it to England's war upon the American Colonies and suggests a similar result. The State Senate of Ohio has declared its intention of furnishing no more men to carry on a war of invasion and insurrection against the South. I shall not be surprised if we yet gained the victory without fighting a single battle, though we are ready to fight as many as Lincoln's army are willing to venture. Tyranny cannot prosper in the Nineteenth Century, either from kings or republics. "*Sic Semper Tyrannis.*" I saw yesterday copied from a Georgia paper a proposition to call our Southern Republic the "Confederate States of Virginia."

Document 12.9 Why a Louisiana Man Fights So Far from Home in Virginia

Most of the soldiers joining the Confederate armies did not own slaves. Whatever the rhetoric of Southern extremists before, and Southern politicians during, the Civil War, slavery was not the foremost concern of these family farmers. They fought to protect their homes from a Northern invasion. Defense of hearth and family from rapacious invaders is one of the most commonly used themes in war anywhere. George M. Lee of Union Parish, Louisiana served in the Confederate army along with three of his brothers. George enlisted for one year in Company A, 6th Louisiana Volunteer Infantry on June 4, 1861 at Camp Moore, Louisiana. His unit was sent to Virginia later in 1861. He re-enlisted at Camp Carondelet, Virginia but died of pneumonia on February 19, 1862. His letter is addressed to his brother-in-law, Jordan Taylor Jr. What is the attitude of the men in Lee's camp? What concerns do they have about army life? How does Lee explain the Louisiana viewpoint of the war, and why his family is fighting?

George M. Lee to Jordan G. Taylor, Jr.

Camp Lay Va. August 26th 1861
J.G. Taylor Farmerville La

Dear Jordan, I received Jeff's letter this morning under date of Aug. 18th, which I was more than glad to receive. I write this in reply to Jeffs letter. I would write to him, but I suppose from what he wrote me, that he is in Camp Moore: if he is let me know in your next letter. Wm has returned from *Richmond* with his goods, and has very near sold out; he will go to their again in a few days to buy another stock. This letter leaves us both in fine health. I am as fat as pork & crackers with a hard bed to sleep on can make any one. Were you to see my Ambrotype now you would hardly recognize it. My hair long & disheveled and my face is as brown as a gingercake.

I have no war news to write you. Every thing is quiet so far as I know. But should any thing turn up we are ready cut and dried for the fight. It is getting very cool up here. We want two blankets to sleep under. If their is any boys their who want to join our company, tell them to come on, we will take them in.

If I could get a furlough to go home & see all my relatives & sweetheart once more, I would then be willing to stay until our independence is acknowledged, or die with her noble sons in the struggle for liberty. I would like to write you a full history of the little incidents of Camp life had I the time & opportunity for I know you would be amused at them & no doubt say that they were tales of fiction. We have only received one months pay since we were mustered into the service, have received no clothing only what we have bought with our own money, but will receive a regimental uniform in a few days. Tell *Mother* I wish she would cook me a real good country dinner & send it to me by mail, a good peach cobler for instance it would go down faster than rain. Jord, you cant imagine the inconveniences & vicissitudes that a soldier has to undergo but in a cause like this of ours we should sacrifice all the comforts & necessaries of life, & offer our bodies a living sacrifice if necessary at the alter of our common Country. Jord, these are my sentiments & were at the time, that the boys were disbanded at Camp Moore. Some perhaps censured me for not going home with the other boys from Camp Moore, but to-day I am proud that I was one who in that trying day counted not the loss of the comforts & pleasures of this life but consulted & enlisted in the service of the glorious Southern Confederacy. Jord, our cause is a glorious & holy one and I for one am willing that my bones shall bleach the sarced [sacred] soil of Virginia in driving the envading host of tyrants from our soil. It is after tattoo & I must blow out my candle. Give my love to all the family & tell them though I be in a distant land the chords of kindred affection bind them near to me & I hope that the time will soon come when I shall be allowed to return to them all a free man, their to spend the remainder of my days among them enjoying the fruits of my present Vicissitudes. Tell Sis to be certain & write & give me all the news she has. Some of you can write as often as once a week, without any inconvenience. Give my love to all enquiring friends & especially the girls.

Your Brother in Law
G. M. Lee

Document 12.10 Cynicism Grows with the War: A Mississippi Veteran Speaks

The Confederate Guards, officially known as Company G of the 17th Mississippi Regiment, were mustered into service at Holly Springs. Two-thirds of the original 150 members were farmers, another 20 were students, and the rest came from a variety of mechanical and professional careers. Few owned any slaves. Robert Augustus Moore's family owned a few slaves when he enlisted. He was the seventh of ten children of Austin E. and Elizabeth Reeves Moore.

Private Moore kept a wartime diary, recording news about camp activities and bad food, evaluating regimental officers, commenting on illnesses, combat, and pretty women who caught his eye. As with most Civil

---

From *Louisiana Historical Quarterly* Volume 26, 1943 by Frank E. Vandiver, editor. Copyright © by Louisiana Historical Society. Reprinted by permission.

War soldiers, his concerns often centered on staying warm and dry and getting enough food to eat. He was proud of the sacrifices his company made, commenting that his comrades died as "true Mississippians." When the war began he was filled with optimism and patriotism, but became discouraged as the tide turned against the South. Moore stayed loyal to the Southern cause, and died at the battle of Chickamauga on September 20, 1863. How does Moore view the North and its soldiers? How are his views as a seasoned soldier different from the pre-war rhetoric by political extremists? How does he compare what he believes their reasons for fighting are to his own? Why does he believe [hope] the South will prevail?

Wednesday, Jan. 1st, 1862, camp near Swan's.

Mason & Slidell left Fort Warren to-day. This day commences a New Year & the first one of our beloved republic. A lovely day indeed it has been a real Indian summer day. After taking a retrospect of the past year, I think we have cause to be proud of our success in driving from our soil the ruthless invader who is seeking to reduce us to abject slavery. I think ere another anniversary of this day, the North will have been taught a lesson not to be forgotten. We have already achieved many brilliant victories. May this prove a happy year to our country and to all mankind. Took dinner in the country at Mr. Brown's. Passed the day very pleasantly.

Tuesday, Dec. 30th, 1862, camp near Fredericksburg.

The weather has turned some cooler. Have had battallion drill this evening. The boys have had a camp dance to-night. Fighting at Vicksburg & an engagement is expected at Murfreesboro soon.

Wednesday, Dec. 31st, 1862, camp near Fredericksburg.

To-day closes the year 1862 & it has been an eventful one in the history of our country. At the beginning of the year it looked as if our enemies would by the strength of numbers, overrun our whole country but by heroic endurance, hard fighting & the favor of a just God, we have successfully resisted their every attempt at subjugation. Cousin Bob Hardy has reached camp, having been absent, wounded, since Sept. 17th. Snowing a little to-night. The Christmas holidays have been very dull with us.

Thursday, Jan. 1st, 1863, on picket in Fredericksburg.

The old year is gone; its volume is closed; its history is completed; its record written up, sealed up, & laid away in the archives of eternity to be reproduced only when the judgement is set & the books are opened. To-day begins a new year. May but few of its weeks elapse ere we hear the joyful sound for which we so long & then return to home & friends. The greatest curse that can befall a land is upon our beloved South now. But we trust for success for our cause in the God of Battles. We have had evidences that He is on our side & I hope for more signal display of His power in our behalf. Oh! that peace would once more assume her gentle sway. That the son might return to his mother, husband to wife, brother to sister and lover to beloved. Came down on the river this evening for picket. This has been a beautiful day.

Document 12.11 Letters to North Carolina Talk about the Civil War

Volunteers joined the Confederate armies from all over the South. Just as in the North, the swelling of patriotism and the idea of duty were never limited to one area or group of people. All soldiers faced death and had to deal with it. Death came in many forms: from the enemy in battle, from your own army after court martial for desertion, or most often from nameless, faceless disease. Lack of a balanced diet, poor water, and fatigue led to many illnesses, with bowel complaints and deaths being the most common. Even 620,000 deaths did not make the shock any less when the person who died was someone you knew. The following letters came from different family members, written at different times during the war. The prospects for the South were different at the time each letter was written. How do the views of the war and the primary concerns of these writers change over the years? What faces of death do the following writers encounter in Lee's Army, and how do they respond? How do they view the Civil War, and what is ultimately at stake?

To Allen Brown from J B Gordon, his brother,—Camp Beauregard, Va., Aug 1861.

My Dear Brother: I returned from Raleigh yesterday and found two letters from home, one making many anxious inquiries after you, and yours of the 18th inst., all of which was a source of much pleasure and gratification until the Richmond papers came and Col Baker was reading an account of the battle near Springfield, Mo., and among those mentioned and killed Oh—how shall I tell you the name of our dear Brother, Capt H T Brown was in that list. It was to me my dear Brother the most terrible shock I ever experienced; to think he has fallen by the hands of an invading foe on the plains of Missouri far from home and kindred, and God alone knows where his remains may now be. We should my dear Brother bear it with that fortitude and firmness that becomes soldiers engaged in the cause of liberty; but it really seems impossible to reconcile one self to the belief that we shall never again behold that manly form imbued with all the impulses of a noble and generous heart whose many virtues and high toned bearing won him the esteem and high regard of all who knew him. He was so universally a favorite in the family. I fear to hear the effect of the news upon our aged and afflicted parents. I cant as yet have the heart to communicate it to them. . . . I have written to Mr Craig in Richmond to ascertain all the facts about the matter he can, and to write to me. I think Allen you should go home, you have been absent three months, your father and mother are extremely anxious to see you. If you are not necessarily required to remain with your company for ten days, ask Col Stokes for a furlough. If you do get off, stop by Richmond and call on Mr Burton Craig who boards at the American Hotel. If a fight is in prospect soon, you should remain, otherwise stop and see me as you go,—at Ridgeway which is 5 miles above Warrenton, Va.

As ever, your affectionate brother, J B Gordon.

To Allen Brown, CSA, in Virginia.

PS

After writing this letter I concluded to come to Richmond and ascertain more definitely the truth of our beloved brother's death. Oh! do I regret to say that the account is too true. I have learned no particulars, but have telegraphed to Little Rock to find out more if possible. I met Mr Thompson today, member of Congress from VanBuren. He knew Tom very well and says the report is undoubtedly true. I met Col Stokes who seems much distressed to hear about it. He will get a furlough from Gen Holmes for you to go home for 10 days at least.

J B G

Camp 27th NC Infty, near Hanover Jct., Va., Sept 19, 1863.

My dear Aunt Rob:. . . . I have been on another miserable Court Martial this week—which had kept me quite busy, and very much confined. It is certainly the most unpleasant, as well as most tiresome duties I ever had to perform as a soldier. Just imagine one, having to sit from one day's end to another just as a juryman in a country court, trying men for their lives—for commiting crimes—which they have been persuaded to, by W. W. Holden and Co., who are the ones, that would give me pleasure to hang, without a trial. I cannot help feeling for the poor wretches, who have been thus deluded, and have forfeited their lives; but nevertheless it is a duty which we owe ourselves, our country, and the noble and gallant men who are doing their duty in this struggle, to take steps to put a stop to the wholesale desertion, with death. There are a great many of them being shot, both in, and out of the Army, and I say let the good work go on, for such men are of no service to God, nor man, and are a curse to the Army and the country. They get no sympathy in the Army, but I am sorry to believe

---

From letters August and September, 1863.

that they are too much countenanced at home, or they would not be so fond of going there. It is awful to think of the countless numbers of good men, who have been sacrificed in this terrible war, and the large number who are yet to go, but we had better all go the same way, and leave the women and children free, than suffer the wretches who are trying to enslave us, to accomplish their ends. I prefer death to Yankee rule, but I am full of confidence as to our ultimate success, for I know there is a just God overlooking us, who will never suffer the Yankees to carry out their hellish designs, upon us,—besides we have 29 gallant and as invincible Armies, as any nation was ever blessed with. It will be a long time, and we have many severe trials to go through with, before the End of all this. . . . I believe it has been definitely decided that our Brigade does not belong to Ransom's Division, but to the Army of Northern Virginia; at any rate, we get all of our orders from Genl. Lee.

I will go about next week up to Orange Court House to see my brother. I had a letter from him the other day. Had been trying to get a furlough to come to see me, but, as he says a private has rather a poor chance of getting away from camp.

. . . Write to me soon.

Your afft. Nephew. Jos. C. Webb

Document 12.12 The Inner Civil War in East Tennessee

East Tennessee was a pro-Union stronghold in a Confederate state, and thus experienced its own private civil war between neighbors while the larger conflict raged around them. While the guerilla war between neighbors in Missouri is better known, it did not surpass the Tennessee struggle in bitterness. The Unionist majority lived under Confederate occupation, and to protest the suppression of their rights (and to avoid charges of treason) they became guerillas, ambushing Confederate patrols and supply trains. Family and friends turned on each other and the Civil War became justification for murders, lootings, and settling old scores. William Williams Stringfield managed the family farm and doubled as a depot agent for the East Tennessee and Virginia Railroad at Strawberry Plains, Tennessee. He ran for state office as a conditional Unionist in 1861, someone who supported the national government but opposed an invasion by "a horde of abolitionist incendiaries." Lincoln's call for troops to maintain national authority forced Stringfield to enlist in the Confederate Cavalry on July 20, 1861. He kept diaries detailing his inner struggle over the war, agonizing over the loss of friends, the destruction of his family farm, and the hardships forced upon his family. These selections from his diary are from December 1863, which was a disastrous year for the Confederate war effort. What are his major concerns? What is his attitude toward the war after three years of fighting?

Dec. 14 Marble Hall. Marched from Yellow Store to day extremely disagreeable tramps. Mud—mud—mud. We distinctly hear cannon in direction of Beans Station. I never saw weather or roads so bad. We moved out at daylight another 24 hours will bring us face to face with Burnside's Army. Then perhaps I may have to surrender my life upon my country's Alter. I fear not to face the issue, whatever it may be for head, heart, limb and life are with my country. When God, in His infinite mercy, calls me hence I hope to go to a better world. Lets us advance upon them and drive them out.

Dec. 15 Camp near Beans Station. A pretty hard march brought us here. I was in command of rear guard of 200 men. I did not reach camp on the immediately South of Beans Station. Started AM West of Moristown road. Cold has moderated a little. Cannonading distinctly heard in the direction of Rutledge. The fight here yesterday was quite severe. Enemy driven from Morrisburg to 1 mile west of

From *The East Tennessee Historical Society Publications*, No. 56–57, 1984–1985, by Vernon H. Crowe, editor. Copyright © 1986 by The East Tennessee Historical Society. Reprinted by permission.

here. Our loss 14 Killed 50 wounded. Enemies not know. 2 dead and 2 mortally wounded found. They took shelter in the large Hotel and the sharpshooters hurts us much till our cannon riddled the Hotel with shot & shell. The marks of deadly conflict can never be effaced from that and other Buildings near. We are likely to stay here for a day or so. I say go on.

Dec. 16 and 17 Beans Station—We remained quietly for 2 days "All hands and the cooks" are well rested and we are ready to advance upon the retreat-ing foe. I hope that E. Tenn is soon to be redeemed & distingishly. God grant it.

Dec. 18 Beans Station—Still quietly here. I can but give vent to my pent up feelings of disgust and displeasure of the apparent tardiness of our comd. General in not moving on the Enemy. But I hope all is for the best. I hope. As I am not responsible for those delays, I will try to rest easy. But Oh, how I do want the Enemy driven from my home and country.

Document 12.13 Civil War Diary Describes the Experience of War

Thomas J. Key believed in Southern destiny, and committed himself to the region's future long before the Civil War began. Born in Bolivar, Tennessee on June 17, 1831, he grew up in Jacinto, Mississippi. At age 15 he began working for a weekly newspaper in Tuscumbie, Alabama to earn money for college. When the struggle over Kansas erupted, Key was one of 130 Alabamans who went in an armed group to colonize the territory for the South. Settling at Doniphan, Kansas, Key began publishing the *Kansas Constitutionalist,* a militantly pro-slavery newspaper not well received by most of his neighbors. Key and his press were repeatedly assaulted, just like most editors on both sides of the slavery issue in the territory. He also served in the infamous Lecompton Constitutional Convention, which tried to force slavery on the Free State majority. Moving to Arkansas, Key served in the state legislature and voted for secession in 1861. He enlisted as a private on May 1, 1862 in Company G, 15th Regiment Arkansas Infantry. Transferred to Calvert's Battery (Arkansas Light Artillery), he was soon promoted to lieutenant. His battery fought with distinction at Murfreesboro, Chickamauga, and Missionary Ridge. After the war he moved to Corinth, Mississippi and began publishing the *Southern Agriculturalist,* which became one of the most important farm journals in the country. In Key's writings, some of the darker reasons for fighting are voiced. What reasons does he give for fighting the war? Is he prepared to compromise or be generous to his enemies? Why or why not?

April 10th

This being the Sabbath I employed the day as near as possible with reading. Among the articles I perused was one from the New York correspondent of the *London Times,* giving the state of society at the North and discussing miscegenation, the new doctrine which has gained such popularity in Yankeedom since the beginning of the revolution: The sentiments made my heart yearn to sweep from the face of the earth the base and amorous race of Puritans which has so degraded itself and villified and slandered the Southern ladies. As a matter of record and history I dip some extracts, as follows, from a book titled "Miscegenation." . . .

Is it surprising that the Southron, whose veins throb with the proud blood of the Anglo-Saxons, should fight with double daring, fearless of death, when he remembers that if the Yankees subjugate his country his sister, wife, and mother are to be given up to the embraces of their present "dusky male servitors."

September 22nd

While the men are working on the fortifications, I divide my time between superintending and perusing such books as I can obtain. In reading the sketches of French history, I am struck with the

From *Two Soldiers: The Campaign Diaries of Thomas J. Key and Robert J. Campbell.* University of North Carolina Press.

sacredness of the familiar song known as the Marseillaise hymn.

The armistice for the exiling of the women and children of Atlanta expired today. I received a kind letter from Mrs. Octavia Hobbs benevolently extending to me the hospitality of her house during the armistice or in case I should be wounded. Oh, the women of the South are the heroines of the age! May they be rewarded for their self-sacrifice and devotion to our great cause.

September 23rd

The weather is remarkably warm for fall, and showers of rain come as in blooming, cheerful spring. Having completed our breastworks we moved back about half a mile, into the woods and pitched our flies to rest. My ambulance driver, who had been bringing out the exiled women and children from Atlanta, returned today and gave a gloomy story of the demoralization, or rather at the disgusting equalization, of the whites and blacks under Sherman. A trustworthy lady told him that the day before she departed from Atlanta a big black negro man went to one of the most respected young ladies in the city and offered her $10 if she would come to his tent and spend the night with him. The thought of such an occurrence arouses every nerve in my body for vengeance, and I feel like crying: "Raise the black flag and let slip the dogs of war."

May 3rd

The thought of starting a long journey to my home, which I had not seen in fourteen months, and the dear inmates thereof, caused me to throw off my slumbers earlier than usual, and I arose to prepare for the trip. A warm and excellent breakfast, to which I paid my hearty compliments, was soon on the table, and after bidding Mr. Artope's good family farewell, I jumped into the carriage with my host and was soon at the residence of Mr. Burnett where the generous ladies had prepared some delicacies for my refreshment on my long march. I also halted for a moment at the home of Mrs. Green who had liberally made me some clothing and prepared biscuits for me. Although it had been only two months since I was an entire stranger in Macon, I was treated with as much generosity and consideration as if I had been an old neighbor, or almost as a brother. With farewells said, I hastened down to the train where I found that neither the thieves nor the rats had carried away my mule, and having given him his breakfast I left him to do his own kicking for the day.

The train was so heavily loaded that it did not reach Atlanta until 6 o'clock, two hours behind time. Twelve months had elapsed since I was in this city, and as I passed around the piles of ruins I could not realize that I was in the "Gate City." Sherman had literally laid it in ruins, leaving but one block of business houses and a few residences. Where once stood beautiful edifices, nothing now remains except rubbish and naked brick walls. The ladies were banished from their own homes and then their beautiful palaces committed to the flames. Sherman has caused thousands of women to weep over the ashes of their sacred homes, and made ten thousand children cry piteously for bread. Oh, how can the Southern people love the country that endorses such cruel and relentless officers as Sherman? The hatred will linger as long as this generation shall exist, and perhaps longer if not avenged.

Sergeant Burns and I, with my mule, went into the once beautiful park in Atlanta and there made us a small fire and "rented" for the night a room six feet square under a small tree. Since there were so many soldiers on their route home, many of whom doubtless would not be averse to riding, I gave my mule a berth under the same tree and he was polite enough not to intrude on my humble bed. During the night a crowd of soldiers assembled to break open the commissary in the city and take all the rations. What was the result of this ill-advised proposal I did not learn.

May 4th

As soon as it was light we arose from our grassy couch and, having partaken of the rations furnished by my lady friends in Macon, we began the long journey—Sergeant Burns and I riding alternately on my mule. As we passed Atlanta we had a full view of the works thrown up by both the Confederates and the Yankees; also beheld the places where we had fought many days. The railroad was completely wrecked by Sherman for a distance of 45 miles. At noon we halted in the once beautiful town of Marietta, which had been destroyed by the vandals who came under Sherman to burn, consume, and steal. The whole country carries the mark of war. Even the remains of hundreds of horses and mules still rot on the highway and offend the nostrils of the traveler. For the distance of 30 miles from Atlanta scarcely a house is left and all the fencing has been burned. We made a long march this day, traversing forty miles, and at dark halted at Allatoona. Having washed my blistered feet and donned a neat pair of socks, I threw myself on the ground to refresh my weary limbs.

Document 12.14 Mounting Concerns for Confederate Soldiers

As the Civil War continued, *many soldiers worried about their families at home. They received plaintive letters describing hardships at home, sometimes a request to come home long enough to plant one crop of corn or else the family would starve.* William Wakefield Garner enlisted in Company C of the Arkansas Mounted Cavalry (Home Guard) in 1862. Promoted to 1st Lieutenant, he and his unit were attached to General Hindman's forces. He took part in Price's raid into Missouri. Shot through both legs but surviving the war alive, Garner experienced army life in all its extremes. The glory of battle, the boredom, and illnesses of camp life were all his. What observations does he make about the enemy during the war? About soldiers in general? What are his greatest concerns during the war? When he writes home, what does he take time to warn his wife about?

Quitman, Ark. Feby. 3, 1862.

Mrs. Elvira Ellington,
My Dear Sister:

It has become my painful duty to convey to you the sad and painful intelligence of the death of Nelson. He ceased to breathe five minutes after three o'clock, P. M., January, 22nd at Bowling Green, Ky.

His spirit has taken its flight to that bourne from whence no traveler has ever returned. Matt wrote us on the 19th that he was sick, that he had him in a comfortable room. Also wrote on the 21st that he was getting better. The letters came Friday and yesterday (Sunday) to our great surprise and grief. His corpse arrived here at one o'clock and today at one o'clock his remains were paid the last respect that the living can pay the dead. He was burried by the Good Templars with the full honors of the order. Almost every member present, attended by a large collection of people, although the inclemency of the weather forbade. Nearly all in the neighborhood for several miles around were out. I never saw as much weeping at one burrying. Nearly everybody seemed to bear a share of sorrow. The coffin was opened and he looked as natural as if he had not been dead more than twelve hours. The measles splotches showed plainly on his face, did not seem to shrunk but little. In fact I believe looked the most natural corpse I ever saw, not the least smell. He was neatly dressed in black cloth like he was going to church, in a nice walnut coffin, inclosed in a case.

Enclosed is a letter from Capt. Witt and was to have been brought by Matt but he did not get to come. He had gotten a furlough from Gen. Bowen and Gen. Hardee had promised to sign it and when the furlough was presented to him he refused to sign it so Matt got a young man by the name of Oliphant to come with the corpse. Matt wrote to me also but the letter has gotten misplaced or I would send it to you.

I think from what Capt. Witt and Matt write and what Oliphant tells me he was well taken care of during his sickness. Matt writes that he was with him from the hour he was taken and I know that he had many warm friends that would have done anything and all that was in their power, especially the boys that had been living with me so long. They all sent me word that he was well cared for. Buck Manees, Wiley Cargile, Jim Bennett, Gorge Grigg, Bob Mitchell and all the Witt boys and many others that I could mention. He was very popular in his company, well liked by all that knew him. His physisian was considered one of the best in this country. He came here the year I did and has known him every since.

Now sister, don't grieve any more than you can help. Your boy is gone, he has fallen but honor to his name. It was in a good and righteous cause in defending his country from the ravages of a relentless foe. In him we have lost one of our best and brightest youths and to me the next to our own son. I have no relative except my own children that is nearer or dearer to me or that I could mourn their loss more. Also all our family, Henrietta and the girls seem as much distressed as if they had lost a brother. Poor Sally she

---

From *The Arkansas Historical Quarterly*, 2, 1943, with permission.

took it very hard when the corpse came but seems much more reconciled.

Enclosed is a lock of Nelson's hair. He is buried here at Mount Pisgah church yard and as soon as I can get it done I will have his grave properly fixed. I send money back by Oliphant to pay his expenses.

He starts tomorrow to Kentucky.

I am as ever,

Your brother,
W. W. Garner.

I wrote to you by John M. Hicks of our company who if he gets home unmolested, you have got this one. I wrote you from Frederickstown. From there we took up the line of march to Jackson from there to Cape Girardeau. Jackson we found to be an abolition hole ten miles from the Cape. We took up the line of March Saturday 3 o'clock p.m. for Cape Girardeau. Travelled all night, halted 5 miles from the fort Sunday morning and got breakfast. While getting breakfast an old tree burned down and fell on three men: killed Dud Lockard of Captain Christopher's Company, brother of Adam Lockard. He died in a few minutes. Lut. Edwards from Captain Cannon's Company died in a few hours. The third man was James Baley son of old Parson Baley of Greasy Valley, he has gotten about well. We prepared to attack this Fort about 11 o'clock, principally with cannon, although our brigade stormed one fort and took it. We fought them until 3 o'clock. They reinforced heavily and we fell back. Our regiment was dismounted and taken on the field amidst the booming of cannon and bursting of bombs.

I led our Company, of course. While going on the field several shells passed near and through our ranks. One struck poor Stephen Drake, cut away the under part of his right hand; broke the wrist bone and passed across the pit of his stomach. The cut on the stomach is not to the hollow and I hope and think, not fatal. I did not know he was hurt until we got on the field, although he stopped immediately and was carried to the hospital. I stopped and saw him as we came off the field. A man was detailed to stay with him and wait on him. We were taken on the field to support a battery and were placed behind an eminence when the shot and shell passed close over us. Bombs bursting close to us. I saw two or three men wounded and one horse. I was not particularly scared. Our boys faced the music finely. I felt more under the influence of excitement.

We left the battlefield for Jackson and camped about 2 miles south of Jackson. Just after dark the encampment was thrown into a blaze of excitement by the enemy firing into Captain Venable's Camp which by some mismanagement was nearly 1/4 mile from the main encampment. Everything was bustle and confusion. We were ordered to saddle and mount immediately. We lost all our cooking utensils and several of the boys lost all their clothes, arms, etc. Two of Captain Venable's men were killed. From the description given by citizens that buried them—supposed to be F. M. Bradford and one of the Gattons. Twelve are missing, supposed to be captured. Wood Clayton among the missing.

The enemy followed us from Cape Girardeau to St. Francis River, over 100 miles. We fought them every day for 7 days. When we could make a stand they would not attack us, but made their attack while on march. They surprised us once by calvary raid, run into our lines while we had stopped to cook. We worried them considerably. One Brigade stampeded and broke our Company in two. Our boys stuck and rallied and wanted to charge them, but we called back. If I should always feel as I did then I will never suffer from fear. We killed many a Blue Coat and think got but 5 killed. The cannon was kept in our rear and when the Feds ran too near was fired on and leave immediately. We took a decided stand at Bloomfield, stayed on the battlefield 24 hours: lay on our arms all night without fire. Suffice to say we made a speedy and successful retreat: but the trip or raid I look on as a complete failure, done but little less than rob and steal from friend and foe alike. In some instances took the last horse, bushel of corn, lb. of bacon from women and their husbands in our army. Took all the horses on the way. Took mares from young colts. I think the Federals do not do worse than we have done. I do hope we will get out of this command. I almost despise the name of a Missourian. I like our Colonel and think Colonel Bergrage commanding this Brigade is a gentleman: but the Arkansas and Missourians can't get along well together. I have stood this trip very well. I had sore eyes a few days very badly caused for want of sleep and exposure. I did without any sleep, only what I got on my horse for 60 hours. We did without anything to eat except some corn burnt on the cob and 2 small slices of bacon. 39 hours, in fact, we have not had more than 1/2 ration for 8 day. Many times we could get it we had no time to cook it. We bake bread on a board and broil our meat and think we are doing well.

If you hear of an army about to pass, hide all your corn and bacon for they will steal all you have got. * * * Captain Rollow has escaped a hard trip by going home. I have got along with the Company very well considering such a trip. I would write to the Capt. but have not got paper nor time. I look for him in Camp soon. * * * Our boys are in tolerable health. All have fallen off very much. So have our horses. All have sore backs. I reckon we will stop to recruit in Jackson County. * * *

W. W. Garner.
Direct to Newtons Regiment, Berbrages Brigade, Marmadukes Division Write first opportunity.

Camp on Bayou Des Arc, 2 miles north of Des Arc.
August 7th, 1863

* * * there is nothing more gratifying than to receive a letter from you. * * * It seems to light the dull evenings of a soldier's life and everything seems a pleasure to perform in the place of a burden. The health of our Company and Regiment is about as when I last wrote you. We have none that are very sick in Camp. We left John M. Bailey on the other side of White River. When he left us he was able to ride his horse off. He went to one Doctor whose name I have forgotten—an old acquaintance of his. We also left Ross Bianum over there. He is a son of old Billy Bianum. He had the chills very bad. We left a man to wait on him. We left some sick men yesterday between this and Searcy. They were not anxious, of course, to come on. I am happy to learn that * * * our children are going to school and learning fast. * * * should I fall in this war, I want my children to have a good education if they have nothing else left them. * * * I think our wheat made a very poor turnout. It must have got wasted or not—divided right or some mistake about it.

Captain L. R. Venable went home sick a day or two ago. He was complaining of being out of money. I told him to call on you and you would let him have what he wanted. Mr. Stout has not come to the Command and Mr. Witt could not tell anything of him. His time has been out several days.

In regard to Uncle Steve Simpkins notes—I am anxious that they should be paid, for they are debts of honor. At the same time, I don't conceive any justice in my letting him have cotton at the same old prices, as I have to stand the risks thus far and should the war close cotton will be worth 75 or 100% in current money. I want to do what is right and am willing to more than do what I think is really right. Let him have cotton at 20 cents to pay the debt or give one and a half dollars in Confederate money for one dollar on the notes or let him pick my notes over and endorse them and let them go the same as Confederate money. I think the time is now past for the Government to burn and distribute it, and if the Feds should come in the country, have it hauled out and hid in out of the way place or old out of the way house, but be sure to have it covered and put up off the ground. As for general news I have none. The men are deserting from this Regiment. I believe some from all the companies but ours. We have not had a man to desert yet. Some of the companies are getting small. Several of Captain Venable's and several of Captain Christopher's men have deserted. They are becoming tired of the War and disheartened. They have not been paid and the fall of Vicksburg and Port Hudson seems to weigh very heavily on the men and those that are deserting are rather weak on the cause. That is the only fear I have, that our men will become disheartened. It is true our fare is hard and our officers are getting very tight on us, yet that is not sufficient cause for me to forsake my honor, my family and my all. I will stick close and make the best out of it I can.

The Colonel told me he had the money on hand to pay the soldiers. I learn they will pay off all four months wages: privates first and after that, officers, if they have the money. I hope they will soon for I have but $5.00. I have divided with the boys. I hope Captain Rollow will come to Camp soon as I nor Lt. Thompson can't either get leave of absence until he comes. Many of our boys are complaining very much at the Captain being so much from them. He made fine promises when we started out if the men would stick to him he would to them. Now is the time to try men's souls, who will stick or who will shirk. Say to Wib that his resignation got misplaced or lost and on the 24th of July, I wrote out his resignation and took the liberty to assume it myself, got it certified by the Surgeon and approved by the Colonel and I think the Colonel was so urgent and explicit in his approval that I think there is no doubt but it will be received. Witt told me Wib is making preparation to send after salt which I hope he will do promptly and if the Feds should overrun our country put your salt in a good tight barrel; bury it in the ground, out in the orchard or some safe place. I forgot to say that Wib which is precisely 7 months.

I am pleased to know that our boys are paroled and get to come home, poor fellows. I sympathize with and for them for their past suffering and hardships and hope they will receive their reward in due season. * * * I would be very glad to see the boys before they are exchanged for. I tried when we were at Searcy to get 3 or 4 days leave of absence, but could not, on account of the Captain being absent. I intend to come as soon as I can get leave.

Camp in Field 10 Miles N. E. Washington, Ark.
Nov. 21st, 1863.

Your very kind and interesting letters of Oct. 13, and Nov. 8th and 13th came to hand day before yesterday * * * and I do assure you I was one of the proudest fellows in all the Confederate States. * * * I don't think that I would ever tire reading letters from you. I am truly glad to hear that you are well and doing as well as what you are; that you have escaped Jayhawkers and robbers and come off from the Feds as well as you did. I think you acted your part fine in treating them well for it is worse than folly to be cross or to go cutting up on such occasions. It is an old adage and very true that when you get your hand in the lion's mouth the easiest way to get it out is the best. It is very true they used things pretty rough, but no worse than I expected. In fact, not so bad as long as they keep from pilfering the dwelling houses and leave enough to eat, we may think we came off well. I wonder they did not take your horses, but I reckon from what you wrote me, you made yourself known to them as the wife of a Mason which will have a great bearing with all true Masons. I hope, however, that you may not have a similar visitation. But I would by far prefer the regular Feds to the low-flung Militia, for I don't think that ever an honorable man went into such arrangements as they do. I look on them as being cowards, Jayhawkers, and thieves. Generally, as for the Federals they are like our own Army. They have honorable men and gentlemen—men who are serving through pure motives, that are honest in what they do and say; also men that are capable of doing anything that is low-down and mean: for instance, that Major that was out there, in taking that toy flag from that lady, in threatening to burn the house if it was not given up even in the act of demanding it, for if I understand the thing right, it was not made known to them in a boasting manner. I hope however, that will serve as a warning and that more caution will be used in the future in such cases if any more should come up. Caution is said to be the better part of valor and that a still tongue makes a wise head. And in our country overrun and surrounded by enemies we can't be too cautious. I don't give this to you in person for I know that you are reserved and cautious enough;

but others that may be staying or having about the house. I am truly glad that Shelby's men got old Chance and do hope they killed him for such a man is not worthy of living. Any man that will lead an army in his own neighborhood to plunder and steal what little people have to live on, is not fit to live on the face of the earth. Men, too, that never interrupted or harmed him. I would be pleased if old * * * was served in like manner or any other man that would do in like manner, friend or foe.

I am pleased to learn that you were successful in getting leather to do your family. I hope before this you have been able to get their shoes made. I am pleased that you have got your wool carded and succeeded in getting plenty of cotton cards. (I hope you have paid old McClure that pair you borrowed) and admire your courage and business tact in attending to your own affairs * * * You may be sure that I was glad to see Matt. * * * He will go to his command tomorrow and I think I will go with him as I want to see all the boys. The Parole Camp is about 12 or 15 miles from here. I saw Henry and Charley three or four days ago. They heard that there had been a fight at or near your pa's; that the Feds had taken three of your Pa's horses, old Paddy among the rest. Old Paddy got away and came back. They only heard this as a rumor, but it is more than likely it is true. Matt saw a man as he came down who said that James Humphrey had come home on a furlough * * * You need not be surprised to see me back in that country before long. I think there is a probability of being sent back there on a recruiting tour, if our command does not come north of the Arkansas River. I am rather of the opinion that there will soon be an advance made. If matters are as we hear they are don't let it be known that there is a probability of me coming back, for if I come alone I will have to be sly about it.

I am in hopes that you have succeeded in getting the wheat sown on the home place for it would be a pity to let so much land lie idle. I can't conclude without thanking you for the comfortable clothing you sent, especially those nice and excellent gauntlets. I was offered twenty dollars for them in less than five minutes after I got them, but of course money was no inducement for them. The drawers came in good time. * * * This will be taken by Mr. Barbe of Clinton, or Rensonn Rule, son-in-law of old man Johnson, who is discharged and will be sent home shortly.

Chapter 12 Worksheet and Questions

1. You are a white Unionist, and in 1861 you joined the army along with numerous friends from your home town. Looking back on the events of the last four years, explain what issues made you join the army, and why they are so important, important enough to die for. Using the letters in the chapter, explain the views of this soldier. What does he refer to? What national events and ideologies are important to him? What does he have in common with the other soldiers in the chapter?

    _____

    _____

    _____

    _____

    _____

    _____

    _____

    _____

2. You are a black Unionist, and in 1862-1863 you joined the army along with numerous other freemen from your home town. Looking back on the events of the Civil War years, explain what issues made you join the army, and why they are so important, important enough to die for. Using the letters in the chapter, explain the views of this soldier. What does he refer to? What national events and ideologies are important to him? What does he have in common with the other soldiers in the chapter?

    _____

    _____

    _____

    _____

    _____

    _____

    _____

    _____

3. You are a Confederate soldier, and in 1861 you joined the army along with numerous friends from your home county. Looking back on the events of the last four years explain what issues made you join the army, and why are they so important, important enough to die for? Using the letters in the chapter, explain the views of this soldier. What does he refer to, what national events and ideologies are important to him? What does he have in common with the other soldiers in the chapter?

_____

_____

_____

_____

_____

_____

_____

_____

_____

_____

4. It is April 1861, and you are an 18-year-old man. War has broken out and thousands of your country-men are flocking to the colors. Are you going to join them? Why or why not? If you do, which of the reasons given by the authors in this chapter would be yours?

_____

_____

_____

_____

_____

_____

_____

_____

_____

_____

5. The editor of this book argued in the chapter introduction that soldiers did not always fight for the same reasons that extremists and politicians spoke of before and during the war. Do you agree with this argument? If so, use examples of the soldiers' writings to prove the editor's point. If you disagree, use examples to prove the soldiers continued to believe in the recruiting messages of politicians throughout the Civil War years.

_____

_____

_____

_____

_____

_____

_____

_____

_____

_____

Chapter 13

Old South, New South: Reconstruction and Beyond

Few events in United States history are commemorated as much as the Civil War. A trip to Gettysburg or any other battle site reveals statues dedicated to fallen heroes, paid for by friends, relatives, and grateful state governments. During the war itself the American people celebrated heroes marching valiantly off to war, fighting and dying for their ideals. During the horrible conflict, both governments used those ideals to rally the civilian population as well, urging them to make sacrifices as great as the troops at the front. This is the heroic stuff that unifies a nation during wartime, and makes people remember the Civil War and raise monuments to fallen heroes. But where are the monuments to Reconstruction, to the people and leaders who struggled to rebuild the nation and justify the great sacrifices of the late war? Where are the fallen heroes and hard-fought successes of Reconstruction? The fighting was over in 1865. The last Southern armies surrendered and troops from both sides returned home. The Old South was destroyed and four million slaves were free. But what comes next? After the guns fall silent, how do you reunite the nation? Few people agreed in 1865 on the answers to these questions, and historians have disagreed about Reconstruction ever since.

The end of the Civil War in 1865 left three questions to be answered about the South. First, what was going to happen to all of the "traitors," those men who fought in Southern armies or served in the government? Second, what would be the fate of the Southern states? Would they be treated as conquered provinces, or as colonies, or would they be restored to their pre-war status as equals to all Northern states? Third, what will happen to the four million former slaves? What do they receive besides freedom, and what responsibility does the national government have for the people it set free? Attempting to answer these questions during the next 12 years, the national government passed civil rights acts, amended the Constitution three times, and set up agencies such as the Freedman's Bureau. Northerners and Southerners, Republicans and Democrats disagreed over what actions to take, over the proper use of the United States army to act as a national constabulary in the South, and over forcing social change through legislation. Should Southern society be restructured now, collapsing the plantations and making every freedman a landowner, or should free market capitalism direct the economic future of the South? In the end, the South was treated quite mildly compared to the losers in other attempted revolutions. In most western nations the losers would face massive executions, land seizures, and permanent loss of wealth and privileges. Despite myths about Reconstruction, the South was handled with kid gloves.

The last days of the war and the early years of Reconstruction were filled with misery and uncertainty. Eva Jones complained from Georgia that poverty was widespread. Losing slaves meant losing property, and she complained that Yankees and former slaves stole all the food before they left the area. Confederate veterans across the South complained about shortages of beans, corn, and meat. For former slaves, emancipation was both bewildering and dangerous. Some owners took out their frustrations and vengeance for defeat by whipping and killing former slaves. The system that had regulated the freedmen's lives vanished without training them how to survive. Many wandered about in search of family members sold before the war.

Bloody vengeance was not visited upon the traitors/Southern patriots who fought in the Civil War. Despite Union soldiers singing "We'll Hang Jeff Davis from a Sour Apple Tree" as they marched south, he did not die. He went to jail for two years, and came out as a martyr. Robert E. Lee and other military leaders, who had sworn an oath to defend the United States when they were in the antebellum Army, were never tried for treason, nor were they even arrested. If you could not prosecute Robert E. Lee, then the lesser soldiers were safe. The promise of safety, which General Grant included in the surrender terms, made sure of that. Former congressmen and federal judges who had also violated their oaths were safe as well. The only rebel tried and executed was Henry Wirz, Commandant of Andersonville Prison. He was tried for war crimes, not treason.

The popular myth of Reconstruction claimed that Radical Republicans plotted to rule the South through Northern carpetbaggers (criminals) and former slaves, plundering everything of value and terrorizing innocent White Southerners. The former states did go through a formal process to regain their equal status in the American political system. To protect their ownership rights to the land, Southern landowners were forced to swear a loyalty oath to the Union. Radical Republicans were never in charge of the Northern government, and moderate Republicans held off formal action until violent acts and continued signs of treason forced their hand. George Templeton Strong, a conservative New Yorker who never really trusted President Lincoln or the Republican Party, symbolized the moderates and conservatives who gradually accepted harsher treatment of the South. Strong's diary and daily newspapers reported planters who refused to accept the reality of defeat and shot their former slaves for refusing to work. He noted in horror the White mob that killed 48 people in Memphis, most of them families of Black soldiers. Outrage increased with the New Orleans riots, where Whites killed 37 White and Black Unionists. The creation of Black Codes, enforced by Southern militias still wearing confederate grey uniforms, was the final insult.

The Reconstruction Acts of 1867 set up a process for federal control and law enforcement in the South, partial disenfranchisement of former Confederates, and assistance to the freedmen until the conquered states proved their loyalty. The Habeas Corpus Act of 1867 facilitated state citizens' transferring their cases from biased state courts to federal courts. New state constitutions had to ensure Black suffrage and "equal justice." State governments were required to pass the 14th and 15th Amendments, renouncing both secession and the Confederacy's wartime debts, and eliminating the Black Codes restricting the rights of freedmen. During the years that Reconstruction governments controlled Southern states, they increased democracy by opening up most state offices for election, building schools for Blacks and for Whites, stimulating industry, and diversifying the Southern economy. Despite later Southern claims, these governments were controlled by White leaders, who were no more corrupt than the Southern "Redeemer" governments that replaced them, and actually improved the Southern standard of living.

What of the freedmen? Former Confederate General Robert V. Richardson reflected the popular view when he declared, "The emancipated slaves own nothing, because nothing but freedom has been given to them." In the wake of emancipation, many former slaves fled the plantations for towns and cities, where "freedom was free-er." Others took steps (after locating missing family members) to legalize earlier marriages and living arrangements, and by 1870 most Black Southerners were living in traditional two-parent homes. African Americans had their own agenda, which called for political power and economic independence. This meant the right to vote and hold office, and the opportunity to hold land. If not land, they needed the opportunity to earn a decent wage at skilled labor. The former slaves realized, as did their former masters, that the right to vote is easily removed without economic independence. The freedmen collected money and built both churches and schools. The Civil Rights Act of 1866, and the 14th and 15th Amendments, helped achieve the goal of political rights, but economic successes were far fewer. Years after the war ended, many African-American veterans and their dependents were still waiting for the federal government to pay overdue pay and bounties.

Prejudice and resentment fueled continued Southern White resistance to Reconstruction. Anger and bigotry saw insults to White honor with each liberty granted African Americans. Tax increases, used to build schools and fuel economic development, made any corruption in the "carpetbagger" governments seem to be too much. Using a variety of illegal methods, Whites disenfranchised Black voters, segregated public facilities, partially re-enslaved freedmen on the farms and former plantations, and used massive violence to keep them in their "place." By 1877, Southern Whites proclaimed the South was redeemed (meaning they regained control of the state governments); for the rest of the century they systematically eliminated the political and social advances that African Americans had achieved because of the Civil War. Share-cropping and crop-liens, intimidation by the night-riding Ku Klux Klan and other White Leagues, and lynching of any

African American seeking equality led many to question what about the South was actually reconstructed by the beginning of the twentieth century.

Considering the Evidence in the Readings

The documents in this chapter provide first-hand accounts of the South during Reconstruction. As you learn what happened and how people were treated, consider what actions the federal government needs to take to protect the rights of all its citizens. This is what these reports and first-hand testimony are all about: giving the government information so it can act as needed. Be sure to trace the evolution of the South from the end of the war to the twentieth century, and consider how much the region did or did not change.

Document 13.1 An Anonymous Journalist Describes the South in 1866

More than two hundred writers visited the South in the first 15 years after the Civil War. Most worked for Northern newspapers and journals, and were assigned to investigate Southern conditions and report back to their readers. This meant primarily observing the lives of the freedmen and checking on the loyalty of the former Confederates. Some writers hoped for a quick reconciliation between sections, while others expected treason to still be rampant. Whitelaw Reid, who made three separate trips South in 1865 and 1866, reported that former Confederate soldiers accepted the outcome of the war, but civilians who never fought were filled with hatred. He and Sidney Andrews filed reports of White women murdering their former servants, of women teaching their children to hate the North, and of reporters threatened with violence. The following report is from the *Atlantic Monthly* of February 1866. How does the author describe Southern attitudes? Have they accepted the outcome of the war, or the supremacy of the national government? What is the attitude toward the former slaves or Northern soldiers and officials? What action does this writer recommend?

I spent the months of September, October, and November, 1865, in the States of North Carolina, South Carolina, and Georgia. I travelled over more than half the stage and railway routes therein, visited a considerable number of towns and cities in each State, attended the so-called reconstruction conventions at Raleigh, Columbia, and Milledgeville, and had much conversation with many individuals of nearly all classes.

I was generally treated with civility, and occasionally with courteous cordiality. I judge, from the stories told me by various persons, that my reception was, on the whole, something better than that accorded to the majority of Northern men travelling in that section. Yet at one town in South Carolina, when I sought accommodations for two or three days at a boarding-house, I was asked by the woman in charge, "Are you a Yankee or a Southerner?" and when I answered, "Oh, a Yankee, of course," she responded, "No Yankee stops in this house!" and turned her back upon

me and walked off. In another town in the same State I learned that I was the first Yankee who had been allowed to stop at the hotel since the close of the war. In one of the principal towns of Western Carolina, the landlord of the hotel said to a customer, while he was settling his bill, that he would be glad to have him say a good word for the house to any of his friends; "but," added he, "you may tell all d—d Yankees I can git 'long jest as well, if they keep clar' o me"; and when I asked if the Yankees were poor pay, or made him extra trouble, he answered, "I don't want 'em 'round. I ha'n't got no use for 'em nohow." In another town in the same State, a landlord said to me, when I paid my two-days' bill, that "no d—d Yankee" could have a bed in his house. In Georgia, I several times heard the people of my hotel expressing the hope that the passenger-train wouldn't bring any Yankees; and I have good reason for believing that I was quite often compelled to pay an extra price for accommodations because I was known to be from the

---

From *Atlantic Monthly*, February 1866.

North. In one town, several of us, passengers by an evening train, were solicited to go to a certain hotel; but the clerk declined to give me a room, when he learned that I was from Massachusetts, though I secured one after a time through the favor of a travelling acquaintance, who sharply rebuked the landlord.

It cannot be said that freedom of speech has been fully secured in either of these three States. Personally, I have very little cause of complaint, for my role was rather that of a listener than of a talker; but I met many persons who kindly cautioned me, that at such and such places, and in such and such company, it would be advisable to refrain from conversation on certain topics. Among the better class of people, resident in the cities and large towns, I found a fair degree of liberality of sentiment and courtesy of speech; but in travelling off the main railway-lines, and among the average of the population, any man of Northern opinions must use much circumspection of language; while in many counties of South Carolina and Georgia, the life of an avowed Northern radical would hardly be worth a straw but for the presence of the military. In Barnwell and Anderson districts, South Carolina, official records show the murder of over a dozen Union men in the months of August and September; and at Atlanta, a man told me, with a quiet chuckle, that in Carroll County, Georgia, there were "four d—d Yankees shot in the month of October." Any Union man, travelling in either of these two States, must expect to hear many very insulting words; and any Northern man is sure to find his principles despised, his people contemned, and himself subjected to much disagreeable contumely. There is everywhere extreme sensitiveness concerning the negro and his relations; and I neither found nor learned of any village, town, or city in which it would be safe for a man to express freely what are here, in the North, called very moderate views on that subject. Of course the war has not taught its full lesson, till even Mr. Wendell Phillips can go into Georgia and proclaim "The South Victorious."

I often had occasion to notice, both in Georgia and the Carolinas, the wide and pitiful difference between the residents of the cities and large towns and the residents of the country. There is no homogeneity, but everywhere a rigid spirit of caste. The longings of South Carolina are essentially monarchical rather than republican; even the common people have become so debauched in loyalty, that very many of them would readily accept the creation of orders of nobility. In Georgia there is something less of this spirit; but the upper classes continually assert their right to rule, and the middle and lower classes have no ability to free themselves. The whole structure of society is full of separating walls; and it will sadden the heart of any Northern man, who travels in either of these three States, to see how poor, and meagre, and narrow a thing life is to all the country people. Even with the best class of townsfolk it lacks very much of the depth and breadth and fruitfulness of our Northern life, while with these others it is hardly less materialistic than that of their own mules and horses.

Thus, Charleston has much intelligence, and considerable genuine culture; but go twenty miles away, and you are in the land of the barbarians. So, Raleigh is a city in which there is love of beauty, and interest in education; but the common people of the county are at least forty years behind the same class of people in Vermont. Moreover, in Macon are many fine residences, and the city may boast of its gentility and its respect for the nourishing elegancies of life; but a dozen miles out are large neighborhoods not yet half-civilized. The contrast between the inhabitants of the cities and those of the country is hardly less striking than that between the various classes constituting the body of the common people. Going from one county to another is frequently going into a foreign country. Travel continually brings novelty, but with that always came pain. Till all these hateful walls of caste are thrown down, we can have neither intelligent love of liberty, decent respect for justice, nor enlightened devotion to the idea of national unity. "Do men gather grapes of thorns, or figs of thistles?"

It has been the purpose of the ruling class, apparently, to build new barriers between themselves and the common people, rather than tear away any of those already existing. I think no one can understand the actual condition of the mass of whites in Georgia and the Carolinas, except by some daily contact with them. The injustice done to three fourths of them was hardly less than that done to all the blacks. There were two kinds of slavery, and negro slavery was only the more wicked and debasing than white slavery. Nine of every ten white men in South Carolina had almost as little to do with even State affairs as the negroes had. Men talk of plans of reconstruction;— that is the best plan which proposes to do most for the common people. Till civilization has been carried down into the homes and hearts of all classes, we shall have neither regard for humanity nor respect for the rights of the citizen. In many sections of all these States human life is quite as cheap as animal life. What a mental and moral condition does this indicate! Any plan of reconstruction is wrong that does not assure toleration of opinion, and the elevation of the common people to the consciousness that ours is a republican form of government. Whether they are technically in the Union or out of the Union, it is the national duty to deal with these States in such a manner as will most surely exalt the lower and middle classes of their inhabitants. The nation must teach them a knowledge of their own rights, while it also teaches them respect for its rights and the rights of man as man.

Stopping for two or three days in some back county, I was always seeming to have drifted away from the world which held Illinois and Ohio and Massachusetts. The difficulty in keeping connection with our civilization did not so much lie in the fact that the whole structure of daily life is unlike ours, nor in the other fact that I was forced to hear the Union and all loyal men reviled, as in the greater fact that the people are utterly without knowledge. There is everywhere a lack of intellectual activity. Schools, books, newspapers,—why, one may almost say there are none outside the cities and towns. The situation is horrible enough, when the full force of this fact is comprehended; yet there is a still lower deep,—there is small desire, even feeble longing, for schools and books and newspapers. The chief end of man seems to have been "to own a nigger." In the important town of Charlotte, North Carolina, I found a white man who owned the comfortable house in which he lived, who had a wife and three half-grown children, and yet had never taken a newspaper in his life. He thought they were handy for wrapping purposes, but he couldn't see why anybody wanted to bother with the reading of them. He knew some folks spent money for them, but he also knew a many houses where none had ever been seen. In that State I found several persons—whites, and not of the "clay-eater" class, either—who never had been inside a schoolhouse, and who didn't mean to 'low their children to go inside one. In the upper part of South Carolina, I stopped one night at the house of a moderately well-to-do farmer who never had owned any book but a Testament, and that was given to him. When I expressed some surprise at this fact, he assured me that he was as well off as some other people thereabouts. Between Augusta and Milledgeville I rode in a stage-coach in which were two delegates of the Georgia Convention. When I said that I hoped the day would soon come in which school-houses would be as numerous in Georgia as in Massachusetts, one of them answered: "Well, I hope it'll never come,—popular education is all a d—d humbug in my judgment"; whereunto the other responded, "That's my opinion, too." These are exceptional cases, I am

aware, but they truly index the situation of thousands of persons. It is this general ignorance, and this general indifference to knowledge, that make a Southern trip such wearisome work. You can touch the masses with few of the appeals by which we move our own people. There is very little aspiration for larger life; and, more than that, there is almost no opportunity for its attainment. That education is the stairway to a nobler existence is a fact which they either fail to comprehend or to which they are wholly indifferent.

Where there is such a spirit of caste, where the ruling class has a personal interest in fostering prejudice, where the masses are in such an inert condition, where ignorance so generally prevails, where there is so little ambition for improvement, where life is so hard and material in its tone, it is not strange to find much hatred and contempt. Ignorance is generally cruel, and frequently brutal. The political leaders of this people have apparently indoctrinated them with the notion that they are superior to any other class in the country. Hence there is usually very little effort to conceal the prevalent scorn of the Yankee,—this term being applied to the citizen of any Northern State. Any plan of reconstruction, is wrong that tends to leave these old leaders in power. A few of them give fruitful evidence of a change of heart,—by some means save these for the sore and troubled future; but for the others, the men who not only brought on the war, but ruined the mental and moral force of their people before unfurling the banner of rebellion,—for these there should never any more be place or countenance among honest and humane and patriotic people. When the nation gives them life, and a chance for its continuance, it shows all the magnanimity that humanity in such case can afford.

In North Carolina there is a great deal of something that calls itself Unionism; but I know nothing more like the apples of Sodom than most of this North Carolina Unionism. It is a cheat, a Will-o-the-wisp; and any man who trusts it will meet with overthrow. Its quality is shown in a hundred ways. An old farmer came into Raleigh to sell a little corn. I had some talk with him. He claimed that he had been a Union man from the beginning of the war, but he refused to take "greenback money" for his corn. In a town in the western part of the State I found a merchant who prided himself on the fact that he had always prophesied the downfall of the so-called Confederacy and had always desired the success of the Union arms; yet when I asked him why he did not vote in the election for delegates to the Convention, he answered, sneeringly,—"I shall not vote till you take away the military." The State Convention declared by a vote of ninety-four to nineteen that the Secession ordinance had always been null and void; and then faced squarely about, and, before the Presidential instructions were received, impliedly declared, by a vote of fifty-seven to fifty-three, in favor of paying the war debt incurred in supporting that ordinance! This action on these two point exactly exemplifies the quality of North Carolina Unionism. There may be in the seed of loyalty, but woe to him who mistakes the germ for the ripened fruit! In all sections of the State I found abundant hatred of some leading or local Secessionist; but how full of promise for the new era of national life is the Unionism which rests only on this foundation?

In South Carolina there is very little pretence of loyalty. I believe I found less than fifty men who admitted any love for the Union. There is everywhere a passionate devotion to the State, and the common sentiment holds that man guilty of treason who prefers the United States to South Carolina. There is no occasion to wonder at the admiration of the people for Wade Hampton, for he is the very exemplar of their spirit,—of their proud and narrow and domineering spirit. "It is our duty," he says, in his letter of last November, "it is our duty to support the President of the United States so long as he manifests a disposition to restore all our rights as a sovereign State."

That sentence will forever stand as a model of cool arrogance, and yet it is in full accord with the spirit of the South-Carolinians. He continues:— "Above all, let us stand by our State,—all the sacred ties that bind us to her are intensified by her suffering and desolation. . . . It only remains for me, in bidding you farewell, to say, that, whenever the State needs my services, she has only to command, and I shall obey." The war has taught this people only that the physical force of the nation cannot be resisted. They will be obedient to the letter of the law, perhaps, but the whole current of their lives flows in direct antagonism to its spirit.

In Georgia there is something worse than sham Unionism or cold acquiescence in the issue of battle; it is the universally prevalent doctrine of the supremacy of the State. Even in South Carolina a few men stood up against the storm, and now claim credit for faith in dark days. In Georgia that man is hopelessly dead who doubted or faltered. The common sense of all classes pushes the necessity of allegiance to the State into the domain of morals as well as into that of politics; and he who did not "go with the State" in the Rebellion is held to have committed the unpardonable sin. At Macon I met a man who was one of the leading Unionists in the winter of 1860–1861. He told me how he suffered then for his hostility to Secession, and yet he added,—"I should have considered myself forever disgraced, if I hadn't heartily gone with the State, when she decided to fight." And Ben Hill, than whom there are but few more influential men in the State, advises the people after this fashion,— "I would vote for no man who could take the Congressional test-oath, because it is the highest evidence of infidelity to the people of the State." I believe it is the concurrent testimony of all careful travellers in Georgia, that there is everywhere only cold toleration for the idea of national sovereignty, very little hope for the future of the State as a member of the Federal Union, and scarcely any pride in the strength and glory and renown of the United States of America.

Much is said of the hypocrisy of the South. I found but little of it anywhere. The North-Carolinian calls himself a Unionist, but he makes no special pretence of love for the Union. He desires many favors, but he asks them generally on the ground that he hated the Secessionists.

He expects the nation to recognize rare virtue in that hatred, and hopes it may win for his State the restoration of her political rights; but he wears his mask of nationality so lightly that there is no difficulty in removing it. The South-Carolinian demands only something less than he did in the days before the war, but he offers no pleas of Unionism as a guaranty for the future. He rests his case on the assumption that he has fully acquiesced in the results of the war, and he honestly believes that he has so acquiesced. His confidence in South Carolina is so supreme that he fails to see how much the conflict meant. He walks by such light as he has, and cannot yet believe that Destiny has decreed his State a secondary place in the Union. The Georgian began by believing that rebellion in the interest of Slavery was honorable, and the result of the war has not changed his opinion. He is anxious for readmission to fellowship with New York and Pennsylvania and Connecticut, but he supports his application by no claim of community of interest with other States. His spirit is hard and uncompromising; he demands rights, but does not ask favors; and he is confident that Georgia is fully as important to the United States as they are to Georgia.

Complaint is made that the Southern people have recently elected military men to most of their local State offices. We do ourselves a wrong in making this complaint. I found it almost everywhere true in Georgia and the Carolinas the best citizens of to-day are the Confederate soldiers of yesterday. Of course, in many individual cases they are bitter and malignant; but in general the good of the Union, no less than the hope of the South, lies in the bearing of the men who were privates and minor officers in the armies of Lee and Johnston. It may not be pleasant to us to recognize this fact; but I am confident that we shall make sure progress toward securing domestic tranquillity and the general welfare, just in proportion as we act upon it. It should be kept in mind that comparatively few of those who won renown on the field were promoters of rebellion or secession. The original malcontents,—ah! where are they? Some of them at least are beyond interference in earthly affairs; others are in hopeless poverty and chilling neglect; others are struggling to mount once more the wave of popular favor. A few of these last have been successful,—to see that no more of them are so is a national duty. I count it an omen of good, when I find that one who bore himself gallantly as a soldier has received preferment. We cannot afford to quarrel on this ground; for, though their courage was for our wounding, their valor was the valor of Americans. The really bad feature of the situation with respect to the relations of these States to the General Government is, that there is not only very little loyalty in their people, but a great deal of stubborn antagonism, and some deliberate defiance. Further war in the field I do not deem among the possibilities. Be the leaders never so bloodthirsty, the common people have had enough of fighting. The bastard Unionism of North Carolina, the haughty and self-complacent State pride of South Carolina, the arrogant dogmatism and insolent assumption of Georgia,—how shall we build nationality on such foundations? That is the true plan of reconstruction which makes haste very slowly. It does not comport with the character of our Government to exact pledges of any State which are not exacted of all. The one sole needful condition is, that each State establish a republican form of government, whereby all civil rights at least shall be assured in their fullest extent to every citizen. The Union is no Union, unless there is equality of privileges among the States. When Georgia and the Carolinas establish this republican form of government, they will have brought themselves into harmony with the national will, and may justly demand readmission to their former political relations in the Union. Each State has some citizens, who, wiser than the great majority, comprehend the meaning of Southern defeat with praiseworthy insight. Seeing only individuals of this small class, a traveller might honestly conclude that the States were ready for self-government. Let not the nation commit the terrible mistake of acting on this conclusion. These men are the little leaven in the gross body politic of Southern communities. It is no time for passion or bitterness, and it does not become our manhood to do anything for revenge. Let us have peace and kindly feeling; yet, that our peace may be no sham or shallow affair, it is painfully essential that we keep these States awhile within national control, in order to aid the few wise and just men therein who are fighting the great fight with stubborn prejudice and hide-bound custom. Any plan of reconstruction is wrong which accepts forced submission as genuine loyalty, or even as cheerful acquiescence in the national desire and purpose.

Before the war, we heard continually of the love of the master for his slave, and the love of the slave for his master. There was also much talk to the effect that the negro lived in the midst of pleasant surroundings, and had no desire to change his situation. It was asserted that he delighted in a state of dependence, and throve on the universal favor of the whites. Some of this language we conjectured might be extravagant; but to the single fact that there was universal good-will between the two classes every Southern white person bore evidence.

So, too, in my late visit to Georgia and the Carolinas, they generally seemed anxious to convince me that the blacks had behaved well during the war,—had kept at their old tasks, had labored cheerfully and faithfully, had shown no disposition to lawlessness, and had rarely been guilty of acts of violence, even in sections where there were many women and children, and but few white men.

Yet I found everywhere now the most direct antagonism between the two classes. The whites charge generally that the negro is idle, and at the bottom of all local disturbances, and credit him with most of the vices and very few of the virtues of humanity. The negroes charge that the whites are revengeful, and intend to cheat the laboring class at every opportunity, and credit them with neither good purposes nor kindly hearts. This present and positive hostility of each class to the other is a fact that will sorely perplex any Northern man travelling in either of these States. One would say, that, if there had formerly been such pleasant relations between them, there ought now to be mutual sympathy and forbearance, instead of mutual distrust and antagonism. One would say, too, that self-interest, the common interest of capital and labor, ought to keep them in harmony; while the fact is, that this very interest appears to put them in an attitude of partial defiance toward each other. I believe the most charitable traveller must come to the conclusion, that the professed love of the whites for the blacks was mostly a monstrous sham or a downright false pretence. For myself, I judge that it was nothing less than an arrogant humbug.

The negro is no model of virtue or manliness. He loves idleness, he has little conception of right and wrong, and he is improvident to the last degree of childishness. He is a creature,—as some of our own people will do well to keep carefully in mind,—he is a creature just forcibly removed from slavery. The havoc of war has filled his heart with confused longings, and his ears with confused sounds of rights and privileges: it must be the nation's duty, for it cannot be left wholly to his late master, to help him to a clear understanding of these rights and privileges, and also to lay upon him a knowledge of his responsibilities. He is anxious to learn, and is very tractable in respect to minor matters; but we shall need almost infinite patience with him, for he comes very slowly to moral comprehensions.

Going into the States where I went,—and perhaps the fact is true also of the other Southern States,—going into Georgia and the Carolinas, and not keeping in mind the facts of yesterday, any man would almost be justified in concluding that the end and purpose in respect to this poor negro was his extermination. It is proclaimed everywhere that he will not work, that he cannot take care of himself, that he is a nuisance to society, that he lives by stealing, and that he is sure to die in a few months; and, truth to tell, the great body of the people, though one must not say intentionally, are doing all they can to make these assertions true. If it is not said that any considerable number wantonly abuse and outrage him, it must be said that they manifest a barbarous indifference to his fate, which just as surely drives him on to destruction as open cruelty would.

There are some men and a few women—and perhaps the number of these is greater than we of the North generally suppose—who really desire that the negro should now have his full rights as a human being. With the same proportion of this class of persons in a community of Northern constitution, it might be justly concluded that the whole community would soon join or acquiesce in the effort to secure for him at least a fair share of those rights. Unfortunately, however, in these Southern communities the opinion of such persons cannot have such weight as it would in ours. The spirit of caste, of which I have already spoken, is an element figuring largely against them in any contest involving principle,—an element

of whose practical workings we here know very little. The walls between individuals and classes are so high and broad, that the men and women who recognize the negro's rights and privileges as a freeman are almost as far from the masses as we of the North are. Moreover, that any opinion savors of the "Yankee"— in other words, is new to the South—is a fact that even prevents its consideration by the great body of the people. Their inherent antagonism to everything from the North—an antagonism fostered and cunningly cultivated for half a century by the politicians in the interest of Slavery,—is something that no traveller can photograph, that no Northern man can understand, till he sees it with his own eyes, hears it with his own ears, and feels it by his own consciousness. That the full freedom of the negroes would be acknowledged at once is something we had no warrant for expecting. The old masters grant them nothing, except at the requirement of the nation,—as a military and political necessity; and any plan of reconstruction is wrong which proposes at once or in the immediate future to substitute free-will for this necessity.

Three-fourths of the people assume that the negro will not labor, except on compulsion; and the whole struggle between the whites on the one hand and the blacks on the other hand is a struggle for and against compulsion. The negro insists, very blindly perhaps, that he shall be free to come and go as he pleases; the white insists that he shall come and go only at the pleasure of his employer. The whites seem wholly unable to comprehend that freedom for the negro means the same thing as freedom for them. They readily enough admit that the Government has made him free, but appear to believe that they still have the right to exercise over him the old control. It is partly their misfortune, and not wholly their fault, that they cannot understand the national intent, as expressed in the Emancipation Proclamation and the Constitutional Amendment. I did not anywhere find a man who could see that laws should be applicable to all persons alike; and hence even the best men hold that each State must have a negro code. They acknowledge the overthrow of the special servitude of man to man, but seek through these codes to establish the general servitude of man to the commonwealth. I had much talk with intelligent gentlemen in various sections, and particularly with such as I met during the conventions at Columbia and Milledgeville, upon this subject, and found such a state of feeling as warrants little hope that the present generation of negroes will see the day in which their race shall be amenable only to such laws as apply to the whites.

I think the freedmen divide themselves into four classes: one fourth recognizing, very clearly, the necessity of work, and going about it with cheerful diligence and wise forethought; one fourth comprehending that there must be labor, but needing considerable encouragement to follow it steadily; one fourth preferring idleness, but not specially averse to doing some job-work about the towns and cities; and one fourth avoiding labor as much as possible, and living by voluntary charity, persistent begging, or systematic pilfering. It is true, that thousands of the aggregate body of this people appear to have hoped, and perhaps believed, that freedom meant idleness; true too, that thousands are drifting about the country or loafing about the centres of population in a state of vagabondage. Yet of the hundreds with whom I talked, I found less than a score who seemed beyond hope of reformation. It is a cruel slander to say that the race will not work, except on compulsion. I made much inquiry, wherever I went, of great numbers of planters and other employers, and found but a very few cases in which it appeared that they had refused to labor reasonably well, when fairly treated and justly paid. Grudgingly admitted to any of the natural rights of man, despised alike by Unionists and Secessionists, wantonly outraged by many and meanly cheated by more of the old planters, receiving a hundred cuffs for one helping hand and a thousand curses for one kindly word,—they bear themselves toward their former masters very much as white men and women would under the same circumstances. True, by such deportment they unquestionably harm themselves; but consider of how little value life is from their stand-point. They grope in the darkness of this transition period, and rarely find any sure stay for the weary arm and the fainting heart. Their souls are filled with a great, but vague longing for freedom; they battle blindly with fate and circumstance for the unseen and uncomprehended, and seem to find every man's hand raised against them. What wonder that they fill the land with restlessness!

However unfavorable this exhibit of the negroes in respect to labor may appear, it is quite as good as can be made for the whites. I everywhere found a condition of affairs in this regard that astounded me. Idleness, not occupation, seemed the normal state. It is the boast of men and women alike, that they have never done an hour's work. The public mind is thoroughly debauched, and the general conscience is lifeless as the grave. I met hundreds of hale and vigorous young men who unblushingly owned to me that they had not earned a penny since the war closed. Nine tenths of the people must be taught that labor is even not debasing. It was pitiful enough to find so much idleness, but it was more pitiful to observe that it was likely to continue indefinitely. The war will not have borne proper fruit, if our peace does not speedily bring respect for labor, as well as respect for man. When we have secured one of these things, we shall have gone far toward securing the other; and when we have secured both, then indeed shall we have noble cause for glorying in our country,—true warrant for exulting that our flag floats over no slave.

Meantime, while we patiently and helpfully wait for the day in which "All men's good shall Be each man's rule, and Universal Peace Lie like a shaft of light across the land, " there are at least five things for the nation to do: make haste slowly in the work of reconstruction; temper justice with mercy, but see to it that justice is not overborne; keep military control of these lately rebellious States, till they guaranty a republican form of government; scrutinize carefully the personal fitness of the men chosen therefrom as representatives in the Congress of the United States; and sustain therein some agency that shall stand between the whites and the blacks, and aid each class in coming to a proper understanding of its privileges and responsibilities.

Document 13.2 Reports from the Joint Committee on Reconstruction, June 20, 1866

In December 1865, Republicans in Congress voted to create a joint committee of fifteen (nine representatives and six senators) to create national reconstruction policy. Dominated by moderate members of the Republican Party, this committee held hearings and solicited testimony from Freedman's Bureau agents, traveling correspondents, military commanders, and Southern Unionists about growing hostility and violence in the South, violence aimed at undoing the results of the war. Based on the evidence presented, the committee determined that new laws were required to protect Blacks, insure the loyalty of the South, and help the freedmen become productive citizens. The committee also looked into the recent elections in the South, where avowed disunionists and former Confederate leaders were elected to seats in Congress.

To many moderates, Southern behavior suggested that they had not learned any lesson, and that the 360,000 Northern deaths were for nothing. At a time when Blacks were denied chances to vote in the South, and the Southern states had not yet renounced secession, were these elections valid? What justifications or evidence indicate the need for further federal controls and regulation of the South? What steps are suggested by the speakers and the committee?

A claim for the immediate admission of senators and representatives from the socalled Confederate States has been urged, which seems to your committee not to be founded either in reason or in law, and which cannot be passed without comment. Stated in a few words, it amounts to this: That inasmuch as the lately insurgent States had no legal right to separate themselves from the Union, they still retain their positions as States, and consequently the people thereof have a right to immediate representation in Congress without the imposition of any conditions whatever. . . . It has even been contended that until such admission all legislation affecting their interests is, if not unconstitutional, at least unjustifiable and oppressive.

It is believed by your Committee that these propositions are not only wholly untenable, but, if admitted would tend to the destruction of the government.

It must not be forgotten that the people of these States, without justification or excuse, rose in insurrection against the United States. They deliberately abolished their State governments so far as the same connected them politically with the Union. . . . They opened hostilities and levied war against the government. They continued this war for four years with the most determined and malignant spirit. . . . Whether legally and constitutionally or not, they did, in fact, withdraw from the Union and made themselves subjects of another government of their own creation. And they only yielded when they were compelled by utter exhaustion to lay down their arms . . . expressing no regret, except that they had no longer the power to continue the desperate struggle.

It cannot, we think, be denied by any one, having tolerable acquaintance with public law, that the war thus waged was a civil war of the greatest magnitude. The people waging it were necessarily subject to all the rule which, by the law of nations, control a contest of that character, and to all the legitimate consequences following it. One of those consequences was that, within the limits prescribed by humanity, the conquered rebels were at the mercy of the conquerors. That a government thus outraged had a most perfect right to exact indemnity for the injuries done, and security against the recurrence of such outrages in the future, would seem too clear for dispute.

Your committee came to the consideration of the subject referred to them with the most anxious desire to ascertain what was the condition of the people of the States recently in insurrection, and what, if anything, was necessary to be done before restoring them to the full enjoyment of all their original privileges. It was undeniable that the war into which they had plunged the country had materially changed their relations to the people of the loyal States. Slavery had been abolished by constitutional amendment. A large proportion of the population had become, instead of mere chattels, free men and citizens. Through all the past struggle these had remained true and loyal, and had, in large numbers, fought on the side of the Union. It was impossible to abandon them, without securing them their rights as free men and citizens. . . . Hence it became important to inquire what could be done to secure their rights, civil and political. It was evident to your committee that adequate security could only be found in appropriate constitutional provisions. By an original provision of the Constitution, representation is based on the whole number of free persons in each State, and three-fifths of all other persons. When all become free, representation for all necessarily follows. As a consequence the inevitable effect of the rebellion would be to increase the political power of the insurrectionary States, whenever they should be allowed to resume their position as States of the Union. . . . It did not seem just or proper that all the political advantages derived from their becoming free should be confined to their former masters, who had fought against the Union, and withheld from themselves, who had always been loyal. . . . Doubts were entertained whether Congress had power, even under the amended Constitution, to prescribe the qualifications of voters in a State, or could act directly on the subject. It was

---

Report from Joint Committee on Reconstruction, June 20, 1866.

doubtful . . . whether the States would consent to surrender a power they had always exercised, and to which they were attached. As the best if not the only method of surmounting the difficulty, and as eminently just and proper in itself, your committee came to the conclusion that political power should be possessed in all the States exactly in proportion as the right of suffrage should be granted, without distinction of color or race. This it was thought would leave the whole question with the people of each State, holding out to all the advantage of increased political power as an inducement to allow all to participate in its exercise. Such a provision would be in its nature gentle and persuasive, and would lead, it was hoped, at no distant day, to an equal participation of all, without distinction, in all the rights and privileges of citizenship, thus affording a full and adequate protection to all classes of citizens, since all would have, through the ballot-box, the power of self-protection. . . .

With such evidence before them, it is the opinion of your committee

I. That the States lately in rebellion were, at the close of the war, disorganized communities, without civil government, and without constitutions or other forms, by virtue of which political relations could legally exist between them and the federal government.

II. That Congress cannot be expected to recognize as valid the election of representatives from disorganized communities, which, from the very nature of the case, were unable to present their claim to representation under those established and recognized rules, the observance of which has been hitherto required.

III. That Congress would not be justified in admitting such communities to a participation in the government of the country without first providing such constitutional or other guarantees as will tend to secure the civil rights of all citizens of the republic; a just equality of representation; protection against claims founded in rebellion and crime; a temporary restoration of the right of suffrage to those who had not actively participated in the efforts to destroy the Union and overthrow the government, and the exclusion from positions of public trust of, at least, a portion of those whose crimes have proved them to be enemies to the Union, and unworthy of public confidence.

Document 13.3 The Louisiana Black Code, 1865

One action that particularly disturbed Northerners was the passage of "Black Codes" by the Southern legislatures during 1865 and 1866. These codes regulated Black behavior and restricted their rights, segregated public facilities, prohibited interracial marriage, and excluded Blacks from juries—all actions similar to some Northern laws. The overall goal was to keep the former slaves "in their place" and insure they remained a cooperative agricultural labor force, but the Codes essentially reinvented slavery. Blacks would be declared vagrants if they could not produce evidence of employment every year, and then were hired out to planters to pay off the court-imposed fines. Black workers were not allowed to leave plantations without permission of their employer. White courts could decide if underaged Blacks had adequate parental support; then apprentice the young freedmen to their former masters for an undetermined length of time. Consider the sections of the Louisiana Black Code in the following reading. This was one of the milder codes among Southern states. What basic rights are Blacks denied? Is this an attempt to overturn the results of the Civil War? Why would Northern voters and Congressmen see the laws as such, and how would they react after the losses in the Civil War?

Sec. 1. *Be it ordained by the police jury of the parish of St. Landry*, That no negro shall be allowed to pass within the limits of said parish without special permit in writing from his employer. Whoever shall violate this provision shall pay a fine of two dollars and fifty cents, or in default thereof shall be forced to work four days on the public road, or suffer corporeal punishment as provided hereinafter. . . .

Sec. 3. . . . No negro shall be permitted to rent or keep a house within said parish. Any negro violating this provision shall be immediately ejected and compelled to find an employer; and any person who shall rent, or give the use of any house to any negro, in violation of this section, shall pay a fine of five dollars for each offence.

Sec. 4. . . . Every negro is required to be in the regular service of some white person, or former owner, who shall be held responsible for the conduct of said negro. But said employer or former owner may permit said negro to hire his own time by special permission in writing, which permission shall not extend over seven days at any one time. . . .

Sec. 5. . . . No public meeting or congregations of negroes shall be allowed within said parish after sunset; but such public meetings and congregations may be held between the hours of sunrise and sunset, by the special permission in writing of the captain of patrol, within whose beat such meetings shall take place. . . .

Sec. 6. . . . No negro shall be permitted to preach, exhort, or otherwise declaim to congregations of colored people, without a special permission in writing from the president of the police jury. . . .

Sec. 7. . . . No negro who is not in the military service shall be allowed to carry fire-arms, or any kind of weapons, within the parish, without the special written permission of his employers, approved and endorsed by the nearest and most convenient chief of patrol. . . .

Sec. 8. . . . No negro shall sell, barter, or exchange any articles of merchandise or traffic within said parish without the special written permission of his employer, specifying the article of sale, barter or traffic. . . .

Sec. 9. . . . Any negro found drunk within the said parish shall pay a fine of five dollars, or in default thereof work five days on the public road, or suffer corporeal punishment as hereinafter provided.

Sec. 11. . . . It shall be the duty of every citizen to act as a police officer for the detection of offences and the apprehension of offenders, who shall be immediately handed over to the proper captain or chief of patrol.

Document 13.4 African American Citizens Petition the United States Government, 1865

The former slaves realized that they had their freedom, but without federal protection they would not have much else. Vengeful Southern whites could deny them (or take violently from them) food, shelter, and almost every basic right. After finding their lost/sold family members, they needed a way to support them that was free from extortion. Gathering in conventions across the South, African Americans discussed the best way to protect their new freedoms, and many sent petitions to Congress. Most petitions declared the loyalty of the freedmen, reminded the government of their service in the Union army, and described the conditions they faced. The following is a petition from a convention held in Alexandria, Virginia from August 2 to August 5, 1865. What do they warn the national government about? Why do they need protection and aid? What actions do they recommend the national government take? How do their claims and issues compare with the issues raised in the Declaration of Independence in Chapter 4?

We, the undersigned members of a Convention of colored citizens of the State of Virginia, would respectfully represent that, although we have been held as slaves, and denied all recognition as a constituent of your nationality for almost the entire period of the duration of your Government, and that by *your permission* we have been denied either home or country, and deprived of the dearest rights of human nature: yet when you and our immediate oppressors met in deadly conflict upon the field of battle the one to destroy and the other to save your Government and nationality, *we*, with scarce an exception, in our inmost souls espoused your cause, and watched, and prayed, and waited, and labored for your success.

When the contest waxed long, and the result hung doubtfully, you appealed to us for help, and how well we answered is written in the rosters of the two hundred thousand colored troops now enrolled in

Louisiana Black Code, 1865.
Petition from a Convention of Loyal African American Citizens, 1865.

your service; and as to our undying devotion to your cause, let the uniform acclamation of escaped prisoners, *"whenever we saw a black face we felt sure of a friend,"* answer.

Well, the war is over, the rebellion is "put down," and we are *declared* free! Four fifths of our enemies are paroled or amnestied, and the other fifth are being pardoned, and the President has, in his efforts at the reconstruction of the civil government of the States, late in rebellion, left us entirely at the mercy of these subjugated but unconverted rebels, in *everything* save the privilege of bringing us, our wives and little ones, to the auction block. . . . We *know* these men—know them *well*—and we assure you that, with the majority of them, loyalty is only "**lip deep**," and that their professions of loyalty are used as a cover to the cherished design of getting restored to their former relations with the Federal Government, and then, by all sorts of "unfriendly legislation," to render the freedom you have given us more intolerable than the slavery they intended for us.

We warn you in time that our only safety is in keeping them under Governors of the *military persuasion* until you have so amended the Federal Constitution that it will prohibit the States from making any distinction between citizens on account of race or color. In one word, the only salvation for us besides the power of the Government, is in the *possession of the ballot*. Give us this, and we will protect ourselves. . . . But, it is said we are ignorant. Admit it. Yet who denies we *know* a traitor from a loyal man, a gentleman from a rowdy, a friend from an enemy? The twelve thousand colored votes of the State of New York sent Governor Seymour home and Reuben E. Fenton to Albany. Did not they know who to vote for? . . . All we ask is an *equal chance* with the white traitors varnished and japanned with the oath of amnesty. Can you deny us this and still keep faith with us?

We are *"sheep in the midst of wolves,"* and nothing but the military arm of the Government prevents us and all the truly loyal white men from being driven from the land of our birth. Do not then, we beseech you, give to one of these "wayward sisters" the rights they abandoned and forfeited when they rebelled until you have secured our rights by the aforementioned amendment to the Constitution.

Trusting that you will not be deaf to the appeal herein made, nor unmindful of the warnings which the malignity of the rebels are constantly giving you, and that you will rise to the height of being just for the sake of justice, we remain yours for our flag, our country and humanity.

Document 13.5 The *Atlanta News* Calls for the Use of Brute Force to Maintain White Control

Southern Whites resisted Congressional Reconstruction with violence. Violence was epidemic in the South from the late 1860s onward, but by the early 1870s Whites made open appeals to use force. Conservative newspapers, politicians, and ministers all claimed this was the only way to "redeem" the South from Northern and African-American control. The options were "a White man's government or military rule," and they claimed this was a revolution of principle, not a matter of politics. Independent voters who would not follow racial appeals were considered race traitors, spawns of corruption and worse than Blacks. Besides brute force, other methods of intimidation discouraged Black voters and ostracized Whites cooperating with Republican rule, including loss of jobs, shared land, and other livelihoods. Rifle clubs were formed to attack Reconstruction supporters, and the Ku Klux Klan and White Leagues stepped up open attacks on Blacks. These groups proclaimed their goals to be the restoration of honest, White, Christian governments; but many wore their old grey uniforms as they attacked opposition voters. The following is the editorial appeal of a major newspaper, the *Atlanta News*, for increased violence in the cause of redeeming the South. What specific actions does the writer approve or advocate? What justifications does he offer for such extreme measures?

From *Atlanta News*, 1870.

Let there be White Leagues formed in every town, village and hamlet of the South, and let us organize for the great struggle which seems inevitable. If the October elections which are to be held at the North are favorable to the radicals, the time will have arrived for us to prepare for the very worst. The radicalism of the republican party must be met by the radicalism of white men. We have no war to make against the United States Government, but against the republican party our hate must be unquenchable, our war interminable and merciless. Fast fleeting away is the day of wordy protests and idle appeals to the magnanimity of the republican party. By brute force they are endeavoring to force us into acquiescence to their hideous programme. We have submitted long enough to indignities, and it is time to meet brute-force with brute-force. Every Southern State should swarm with White Leagues, and we should stand ready to act the moment Grant signs the civil-rights bill. It will not do to wait till radicalism has fettered us to the car of social equality before we make an effort to resist it. The signing of the bill will be a declaration of war against the southern whites. It is our duty to ourselves, it is our duty to our children, it is our duty to the white race whose prowess subdued the wilderness of this continent, whose civilization filled it with cities and towns and villages, whose mind gave it power and grandeur, and whose labor imparted to it prosperity, and whose love made peace and happiness dwell within its homes, to take the gage of battle the moment it is thrown down. If the white democrats of the North are men, they will not stand idly by and see us borne down by northern radicals and half-barbarous negroes. But no matter what they may do, it is time for us to organize. We have been temporizing long enough. Let northern radicals understand that military supervision of southern elections and the civil-rights bill mean war, that war means bloodshed, and that we are terribly in earnest, and even they, fanatical as they are, may retrace their steps before it is too late.

Document 13.6 Personal Accounts of Ku Klux Klan Attacks

The oldest and best known of all the Southern White supremacist organizations is the Ku Klux Klan (KKK). Originally organized to insure a steady labor supply on postwar plantations, the KKK moved on to other goals. Its night-riding, white-hooded members enforced a code of behavior, "visiting" freed African Americans who acted or spoke "improperly" to Whites. The Klan was determined to maintain White supremacy at all costs. By the 1870s their primary goal was terrorizing Black Republican voters in the South, allowing White Southern Democrats to regain control of the states and end Reconstruction. This terrorist organization utilized whippings, shootings, and psychological terror, and murdered hundreds of voters and elected state officials. Following are three accounts of Klan activity. Note that the KKK attacked field hands, women, and even members of state legislatures. African Americans who owned or rented land were often targets, because they had an independence that threatened White power. What do the following accounts have in common? What response is needed by the federal government to combat these terrorist attacks?

Elias Hill is a remarkable character. He is crippled in both legs and arms, which are shriveled by rheumatism; he cannot walk; cannot help himself, has to be fed and cared for personally by others; was in early life a slave, whose freedom was purchased, his father buying his mother and getting Elias along with her, as a burden of which his master was glad to be rid. Stricken at seven years old with disease, he never was afterward able to walk, and he presents the appearance of a dwarf with the limbs of a child, the body of a man, and a finely developed intellectual head. He learned his letters and to read by calling the school children into the cabin as they passed, and also learned to write. He became a Baptist preacher, and after the war engaged in teaching colored children, and conducted the business correspondence of many of his colored neighbors. He is a man of blameless character, of unusual intelligence, speaks good English, and we put the story of his wrongs in his own language:

Personal Accouts of Ku Klux Klan Attacks, 1870.

"On the night of the 5th of last May, after I had heard a great deal of what they had done in that neighborhood, they [the Ku Klux Klan] came. It was between 12 and 1 o'clock at night when I was awakened and heard the dogs barking, and something walking, very much like horses. . . . At last they came to my brother's door, which is in the same yard, and broke open the door and attacked his wife, and I heard her screaming and mourning. . . . At last I heard them have her in the yard. She was crying and the Ku-Klux were whipping her to make her tell where I lived. . . . Some one then hit my door. It flew open. One ran in the house, and stopping about the middle of the house, which is a small cabin, he turned around, as it seemed to me as I lay there awake, and said, 'Who's here?' Then I knew they would take me, and I answered, 'I am here.' He shouted for joy, as it seemed, 'Here he is! Here he is! We have found him!' and he threw the bedclothes off of me and caught me by one arm, while another man took me by the other and they carried me into the yard between the houses. . . . The first thing they asked me was, 'Who did the burning? Who burned our houses?' —gin-houses, dwelling-houses and such. Some had been burned in the neighborhood. I told them it was not me; I could not burn houses; it was unreasonable to ask me. Then they hit me with their fists, and said I did it, I ordered it. They went on asking me didn't I tell the black men to ravish all the white women. No, I answered them. They struck me again with their fists on my breast, and then they went on. . . .

"They pointed pistols at me all around my head once or twice, as if they were going to shoot me, telling me they were going to kill me; wasn't I ready to die, and willing to die" Didn't I preach? That they came to kill me—all the time pointing pistols at me. . . . One said 'G-d d—n it, hush!' He had a horse-whip, and he told me to pull up my shirt, and he hit me. He told me at every lick, 'Hold up your shirt.' I made a moan every time he cut with the horsewhip. I reckon he struck me eight cuts right on the hip bone; it was almost the only place he could hit my body, my legs are so short—all my limbs drawn up and withered away with pain. . . . They all had disguises on. I then thought they would not kill me. One of them then took a strap, and buckled it around my neck and said, 'Let's take him to the river and drown him . . .'

"They said 'Look here! Will you put a card in the paper next week like June Moore and Sol Hill?' They had been prevailed on to put a card in the paper to renounce all republicanism and never vote. I said, 'If I had the money to pay the expense, I could.' They said I could borrow, and gave me another lick. They

asked me, 'Will you quit preaching?' I told them I did not know. I said that to save my life. They said I must stop the republican paper that was coming to Clay Hill. It has been only a few weeks since it stopped. The republican paper was then coming to me from Charleston. It came to my name. They said I must stop it, quit preaching, and put a card in the newspaper renouncing republicanism, and they would not kill me; but if I did not they would come back the next week and kill me."

Harriet Hernandez

Q: Did the Ku-Klux ever come to your house at any time?

A: Yes, sir; twice.

Q: Go on to the second time. . . .

A: They came in; I was lying in bed. Says he, "Come out here, sir; Come out here, sir!" They took me out of bed; they would not let me get out, but they took me up in their arms and toted me out— me and my daughter Lucy. He struck me on the forehead with a pistol, and here is the scar above my eye now. Says he, "Damn you, fall!" I fell. Says he, "Damn you, get up!" I got up. Says he, "Damn you, get over this fence!" And he kicked me over when I went to get over; and then he went to a brush pile, and they laid us right down there, both together. They laid us down twenty yards apart, I reckon. They had dragged and beat us along. They struck me right on the top of my head, and I thought they had killed me; and I said, "Lord o' mercy, don't, don't kill my child!" He gave me a lick on the head, and it liked to have killed me; I saw stars. He threw my arm over my head so I could not do anything with it for three weeks, and there are great knots on my wrist now.

Q: What did they say this was for?

A: They said, "You can tell your husband that when we see him we are going to kill him."

Q: Did they say why they wanted to kill him?

A: They said, "He voted the radical ticket, didn't he?" I said, "Yes, that very way."

Q: When did your husband get back after this whipping? He was not at home, was he?

A: He was lying out; he couldn't stay at home, bless your soul! . . .

Q: Has he been afraid for any length of time?

A: He has been afraid ever since last October. He has been lying out. He has not laid in the house ten nights since October.

Q: Is that the situation of the colored people down there to any extent?

A: That is the way they all have to do—men and women both.

Q: What are they afraid of?

A: Of being killed or whipped to death.

Q: What has made them afraid?

A: Because men that voted radical tickets they took the spite out on the women when they could get at them.

Q: How many colored people have been whipped in that neighborhood?

A: It is all of them, mighty near.

Testimony of Abram Colby (1872)

On the 29th of October 1869, they broke my door open, took me out of bed, took me to the woods and whipped me three hours or more and left me for dead. They said to me, "Do you think you will ever vote another damned radical ticket?" I said, "I will not tell you a lie." I supposed they would kill me anyhow. I said, "If there was an election tomorrow, I would vote the radical ticket." They set in and whipped me a thousand licks more, with sticks and straps that had buckles on the ends of them.

Q: What is the character of those men who were engaged in whipping you?

A: Some are first-class men in our town. One is a lawyer, one a doctor, and some are farmers. They had their pistols and they took me in my night-clothes and carried me from home. They hit me five thousand blows. I told President Grant the same that I tell you now. They told me to take off my shirt. I said, "I never do that for any man." My drawers fell down about my feet and they took hold of them and tripped me up. Then they pulled my shirt up over my head. They said I had voted for Grant and had carried the Negroes against them. About two days before they whipped me they offered me $5,000 to go with them and said they would pay me $2500 in cash if I would let another man go to the legislature in my place. I told them that I would not do it if they would give me all the county was worth.

The worst thing about the whole matter was this. My mother, wife and daughter were in the room when they came. My little daughter begged them not to carry me away They drew up a gun and actually frightened her to death. She never got over it until she died. That was the part that grieves me the most.

Q: How long before you recovered from the effects of this treatment?

A: I have never got over it yet. They broke something inside of me. I cannot do any work now, though I always made my living before in the barber-shop, hauling wood, &c.

Q: You spoke about being elected to the next legislature?

A: Yes, sir, but they run me off during the election. They swore they would kill me if I staid. The Saturday night before the election I went to church. When I got home they just peppered the house with shot and bullets.

Q: Did you make a general canvas there last fall?

A: No, sir. I was not allowed to. No man can make a free speech in my county. I do not believe it can be done anywhere in Georgia.

Q: You say no man can do it?

A: I mean no Republican, either white or colored.

Document 13.7 General Alfred Terry Testifies about Race Relations in Georgia

General Alfred Terry filed this official report to the Secretary of War in 1869. Many army officers advocated harsh treatment of the South, and were removed from their commands by President Johnson for voicing their opinions. By contrast, General Terry was a moderate in his views, but was increasingly concerned with the growing violence and threat to the freedmen. In this official report he discusses the deteriorating state of race relations, the increased intolerance and attacks by groups such as the KKK, and the overall attitude of the Southern people. What does he propose as a government response? What justifications does Terry give for the use of force by the national government?

I have delayed making the report thus called for until the present time, in order that I might become acquainted with the condition of affairs in Georgia before expressing any opinion in regard to them. Now I have reluctantly come to the conclusion that the situation here demands the interposition of the national government, in order that life and property may be protected, freedom of speech and political action secured, and the rights and liberties of the freedmen maintained. This opinion is based upon complaints made to me, the reports of officers detailed to investigate alleged outrages, and upon the statements of many persons of respectability and high position from different parts of the State, in whose representations I must repose confidence; some of whom have given me information only under the pledge of secrecy, the state of affairs in their section being such that they feared the extreme of personal violence should it become known that they had been in communication with me.

In many parts of the State there is practically no government. The worst of crimes are committed, and no attempt is made to punish those who commit them. Murders have been and are frequent; the abuse in various ways of the blacks is too common to excite notice. There can be no doubt of the existence of numerous insurrectionary organizations known as "Ku-Klux Klans," who, shielded by their disguise, by the secrecy of their movements, and by the terror which they inspire, perpetrate crime with impunity. There is great reason to believe that in some cases local magistrates are in sympathy with the members of these organizations. In many places they are overawed by them and dare not attempt to punish them. To punish such offenders by civil proceedings would be a difficult task, even were magistrates in all cases disposed and had they the courage to do their duty, for the same influences which govern them equally affect juries and witnesses. A conversation which I have had with a wealthy planter, a gentleman of intelligence and education, and a political opponent of the present national administration, will illustrate this difficulty. While deploring the lamentable condition of affairs in the county in which he lives, he frankly admitted to me that, were the most worthless vagabond in the county to be charged with a crime against the person of a republican or a negro, neither he nor any other person of property within the county would dare to refuse to give bail for the offender, nor

would they dare to testify against him, whatever might be their knowledge of his guilt.

That very many of the crimes which have been committed have no political bearing I believe; that some of them were prompted by political animosity, and that most of the numerous outrages upon freedmen result from hostility to the race induced by their enfranchisement, I think cannot be controverted.

The same difficulties which beset the prosecution of criminals are encountered by negroes who seek redress for civil injuries in the local courts. Magistrates dare not do their duty toward them, and instances are not wanting where it has even been beyond the power of a magistrate to protect a negro plaintiff from violence in his own presence while engaged in the trial of his case. I desire it to be understood that in speaking of magistrates I in no degree refer to the judges of the superior courts; they are gentlemen of high character. I have every confidence that they will do their duty fearlessly and impartially, but it is to be observed that even they cannot control grand and petty juries; they cannot compel the former to indict, nor the latter to render unprejudiced verdicts.

The executive of the State would gladly interpose to give to all citizens the protection which is their right, but under the constitution and laws he has power neither to act directly in bringing offenders to justice nor to compel subordinate officers to do their duty. I do not suppose that the great majority of the people of the State, of either race, approve of the commission of these crimes. I believe that not only would they gladly see good order restored, peace and quiet maintained, and the law vindicated; but would lend their aid to secure these ends were they not controlled by their fears. Governed, however, by their apprehensions, and having no confidence that the civil authorities will afford them protection, in many counties they suffer these evils to exist without an effort to abate them, and meekly submit to the rule of the disorderly and criminal minority.

While I have been in command of the department I have endeavored to take no action which could not be justified by the letter of the law, even if Georgia should be held to be restored to its original relations to the general government. I have confined myself to giving support to the civil authorities and

Official Report to the Secretary of War, 1869.

moving detachments of troops into some of the disturbed counties, where their presence would exert a good influence, and where they would be ready to act if properly called upon. I think that some good has in this way been accomplished, but the great evil has by no means been reached. As a department commander I can do no more; for whatever may be the status of Georgia, and whatever may be the powers which an officer assigned to command the third district created by the reconstruction acts would possess, it is only an officer so assigned who could exercise them; they are not vested in me by my assignment to the command of this department. Where, therefore, the civil authorities are in sympathy with or are overawed by those who commit crime, it is manifest that I am powerless. In this connection I respectfully call the special attention of the General commanding the army to the reports in regard to the attempt made in Warren County to secure the arrest and punishment of persons charged with crime, which are this day forwarded. It appears to me that the national honor is pledged to the protection of the loyalists and the freedmen of the South. I am well aware that the protection of persons and property is not ordinarily one of the functions of the national government, but when it is remembered that hostility to the supporters of the government is but a manifestation of hostility to the government itself, and that the prevailing prejudice against the blacks results from their emancipation—the act of the government—it would seem that such protection cannot be denied them if it be within the power of the government to give it. I know of no way in which such protection can be given in Georgia except by the exercise of the powers conferred on military commanders by the reconstruction acts.

Document 13.8 Black Lives during Reconstruction

Not all freedmen were attacked, and life consisted of more than dodging White bullets. During the 1930s the New Deal's Federal Writers' Project sent interviewers out to collect first-hand biographies of the survivors of slavery and Reconstruction. Between 1936 and 1938, interviewers in 17 states recorded the memories of thousands of former slaves. These materials left a record of daily life that went beyond contemporary newspaper accounts. In the two accounts that follow, what do the participants remember most about life? Is the Klan ever too far from their minds? How does the fear of violence compare with fear of discipline during slave days? How does freedom compare with slavery?

Mingo White

Interviewed at Burleson, Alabama
Interviewed by Levi D. Shelby, Jr.
Age when interviewed: 85–90

De day dat we got news dat we was free, Mr. White called us niggers to the house. He said: "You are all free, just as free as I am. Now go and get yourself somewhere to stick your heads."

Just as soon as he say dat, my mammy hollered out: "Dat's 'nough for a yearlin'." She struck out across de field to Mr Lee Osborn's to get a place for me and her to stay. He paid us seventy-five cents a day, fifty cents to her and two bits for me. He gave us our dinner along with de wages. After de crop was gathered for that year, me and my mammy cut and hauled wood for Mr. Osborn. Us left Mr. Osborn dat fall and went to Mr. John Rawlins. Us made a sharecrop with him. Us'd pick two rows of cotton and he'd pick two rows. Us'd pull two rows of corn and he'd pull two rows of corn. He furnished us with rations and a place to stay. Us'd sell our cotton and open corn and pay Mr. John Rawlins for feedin' us. Den we moved with Mr. Hugh Nelson and made a sharecrop with him. We kept movin' and makin' sharecrops till us saved up 'nough money to rent us a place and make a crop for ourselves.

Us did right well at dis until de Ku Klux got so bad, us had to move back with Mr. Nelson for protection. De mens that took us in was Union men. Dey lived here in the South but dey taken us part in de

From *New Deal's Federal Writers' Project.*

slave business. De Ku Klux threat to whip Mr. Nelson, 'cause he took up for de niggers. Heap of nights we would hear of de Ku Klux comin' and leave home. Sometimes us was scared not to go and scared to go away from home.

One day I borrowed a gun from Ed Davis to go squirrel huntin'. When I taken de gun back I didn't unload it like I always been doin'. Dat night de Ku Klux called on Ed to whip him. When dey told him to open de door, he heard one of 'em say, "Shoot him time he gets de door open." "Well," he says to 'em, "Wait till I can light de lamp." Den he got de gun what I had left loaded, got down on his knee and stuck it through a log and pulld de trigger. He hit Newt Dobbs in de stomach and kilt him.

He couldn't stay round Burleson any more, so he come to Mr. Nelson and got 'nough money to get to Pine Bluff, Arkansas. The Ku Klux got bad sure 'nough den and went to killin' niggers and white folks, too.

Charles Davenport

Interviewed at Natchez, Mississippi
Interviewed by Edith Wyatt Moore
Age at interview: About 100

Like all de fool niggers o' dat time I was right smart bit by de freedom bug for awhile. It sounded powerful nice to be told: "You don't have to chop cotton no more. You can throw dat hoe down and go fishin' whensoever de notion strikes you. And you can roam 'round at night and court gals just as late as you please. Ain't no marster gwine to, say to you, 'Charlie, you's got to be back when de clock strikes nine.'"

I was fool 'nough to believe all dat kind o' stuff. But to tell de honest truth, most o' us didn't know ourselfs no better off. Freedom meant us could leave where us'd been born and bred, but it meant, too, dat us had to scratch for us ownselfs. Dem what left de old plantation seemed so all fired glad to get back dat I made up my mind to stay put. I stayed right with my white folks as long as I could.

My white folks talked plain to me. Dey say real sadlike, "Charlie, you's been a dependence, but now you can go if you is so desirous. But if you wants to stay with us you can sharecrop. Dey's a house for you and wood to keep you warm and a mule to work. We ain't got much cash, but dey's de land and you can count on havin' plenty o' victuals. Do just as you please."

When I looked at my marster and knowed he needed me, I pleased to stay. My marster never forced me to do nary thing about it.

Lord! Lord! I knows about de Kloo Kluxes. I knows a-plenty. Dey was sure 'nough devils a-walkin' de earth a-seekin' what dey could devour. Dey larruped de hide off de uppity niggers an' drove de white trash back where dey belonged.

Us niggers didn't have no secret meetin's. All us had was church meetin's in arbors out in de woods. De preachers would exhort us dat us was de chillen o' Israel in de wilderness an' de Lord done sent us to take dis land o' milk and honey. But how us gwine-a take land what's already been took?

I sure ain't never heard about no plantations bein' divided up, neither. I heard a lot o' yaller niggers spoutin' off how dey was gwine-a take over de white folks' land for back wages. Dem bucks just took all dey wages out in talk. 'Cause I ain't never seen no land divided up yet.

In dem days nobody but niggers and "shawl-strap" folks voted. Quality folks didn't have nothin' to do with such truck. If dey hada wanted to de Yankees wouldn'ta let 'em. My old marster didn't vote and if anybody knowed what was what he did. Sense didn't count in dem days. It was powerful ticklish times and I let votin' alone. . . . [O]ne night a bunch o' uppity niggers went to a entertainment in Memorial Hall. Dey dressed deyselfs fit to kill and walked down de aisle and took seats in de very front. But just about time dey got good set down, de curtain dropped and de white folks rose up without a-sayin' a word. Dey marched out de buildin' with dey chins up and left dem niggers a-sittin' in a empty hall.

Dat's de way it happen every time a nigger tried to get too uppity. Dat night after de breakin' up o' dat entertainment, de Kloo Kluxes rode through de land. I heard dey grabbed every nigger what walked down dat aisle, but I ain't heard yet what dey done with 'em.

Document 13.9 Black Land Ownership and Sharecropping in the Postwar South

For most former slaves, freedom meant owning and farming their own land, but this rarely happened in the postwar South. The legendary promises of "forty acres and a mule" for the former slaves never became a reality. Approximately 80 percent of former slaves ended up as sharecroppers on land owned by Whites, sometimes by their former masters. On the plus side, this arrangement provided them more autonomy than slavery did because they worked the land without a slave driver, and they could keep their wives out of the fields if they chose. However, it also bound them to the land and guaranteed perpetual poverty. The property owner provided the land, seed, livestock, and farm implements, as well as credit to live on before harvest. The cropper provided the labor and received half of the crop in return, but then had to pay off his debts—if he ever could. This system also kept the South producing cotton, the closest thing to ready cash they had, even as over-production wore out the soil. The following are accounts of freed African Americans discussing their attempts to make a living through honest labor. What are they able to accomplish? Do they reach any sort of financial independence through their hard work? What obstacles stand in their way?

Henry Blake

After freedom, we worked on shares a while. Then, we rented. When we worked on shares, we couldn't make nothing—just over-alls, and something to eat. Half went to the white man, and you would destroy your half, if you weren't careful. A man that didn't know how to count would always lose. He might lose anyhow. The white folks didn't give no itemized statements. No, you just had to owe so much. No matter how good account you kept, you had to go by their account, and—now, brother, I'm telling you the truth about this—it's been that way for a long time. You had to take the white man's words and notes on everything. Anything you wanted you could get, if you were a good hand. If you didn't make no money, that's all right; they would advance you more. But you better not try to leave and get caught. They'd keep you in debt. They were sharp. Christmas come, you could take up twenty dollars in somethin' to eat and much as you wanted in whiskey. You could buy a gallon of whiskey—anything that kept you a slave. Because he was always right and you were always wrong, if there was a difference. If there was an argument, he would get mad and there would be a shooting take place.

Emanuel Fortune

They will not sell our people any land. They have no disposition to do so. They will sell a lot now and then in a town, but nothing of any importance.

Q: What could you get a pretty good farm for—how much an acre?
A: Generally from $10 to $15 an acre. Very poor people cannot afford that
Q: You can get it if you have the money?
A: They will not sell it in small quantities. I would have bought forty acres if the man would have sold me less than a whole tract. They hold it in that way so that colored people cannot buy it. The lands we cultivate generally are swamp or lowlands.
Q: Is there not plenty of other land to buy?
A: Not that is worth anything. I do not know of any Government land that will raise cotton.

Henry M. Turner

Q: You say that colored men employed in the country have not been able to get anything for their labor. Why is that?
A: During the year there is very little money paid to them and if they want to obtain provisions or

---

From *New Deal's Federal Writers' Project.*

clothing they are given an order on some store. At the end of the year these little bills are collected and however small a quantity of things have been taken, almost always the colored man is brought into debt. That is alleged as a reason why they should be bound to stay with their employers and work out what they say they owe them.

Q: A sort of practical peonage?

A: Yes, sir. Whenever there is fear that the laborer will go to work with someone else the following year, he is apt to come out $25 to $30 in debt and his employer calls upon him to work it out.

There was a bill introduced the other day to make it a penal offense for a laborer to break his contract. For instance, a white man writes out a contract. He reads the contract to the black man and, of course, reads just what he pleases. When the black man takes it to somebody else and gets him to read it, it reads quite differently. Among other things there is a provision in the contract that he must not go to any political gathering or meeting. If he does, he will lose $5 for every day that he is absent, and yet he is to receive only $50 or $75 a year. Every day that he is sick, a dollar or a dollar and a half is to be deducted. The man may want to quit and work for some person else who will pay him better wages.

Q: The effect of the legislation would be to render the laborer practically a slave during the period of his contract?

A: Or else he would be liable to punishment by imprisonment. There is no doubt that they will pass some kind of law to that effect.

Q: With a view to harmonize the relations of labor and capital?

A: Yes, sir, that is the phrase.

Document 13.10 A Texas Shares Contract

Sharecropping contracts usually spelled out clearly what the obligations of both parties were, but greater detail was given to the local sharecropper's duties, including what crops must be produced, number of hours to work each day, extra work required beyond normal, and how debts are to be repaid. Some freedmen worked for wages instead of a share of the crops. The following shares contract provides a typical division of obligations and rewards. What obligations does each side assume? What are the penalties for failing to meet your obligations?

Said _____ of the first part furthermore agrees to furnish the said Freedmen of the second part with good and sufficient quarters, _____ wholesome food, fuel, and such medical treatment as can be rendered by the person superintending the place. Said *J C Mitchell* of the 1st part in consideration of the faithful discharge of the duties assumed by the parties of the second part, does hereby agree to furnish *the freedmen* the necessary tools and implements for the cultivation of the land, and allow said Freedmen *one third* interest in the crops raised on said *plantation* by their labor. It is also mutually agreed that ten hours shall constitute a day's work, and if any labor in excess of ten hours per day is rendered it shall be paid for as extra labor. Said parties of the second part do furthermore agree to do all necessary work on Sundays or at night when it is for the protection of plantation or crops against destruction by storms, floods, fire or frost, provided always that such service shall be paid for as extra labor; extra labor to be paid for at the rate of one day's labor and one-half rations extra for each six hours work. Provided that our employer failing to comply with any part of this agreement, this contract shall be annulled; also provided, that should any of the parties of the second part leave said *plantation* without proper authority, or engage elsewhere, or neglect or refuse to work as herein agreed, they or any part of them so offending shall be liable to be discharged and forfeit all wages due up to that time.

Also Provided, that this Contract shall constitute the first lien upon all crops raised by the labor of said parties of the Second part.

Said J C Mitchell shall have power to make such rules and regulations necessary to the management of the plantation as are not inconsistent with the term of this contract; all lost time to [be] deducted from the one third interest in crop to the freedmen.

Document 13.11 Lynching in the South

After Reconstruction, Southern Whites steadily eroded the rights that Blacks had acquired after the war. Jim Crow laws regulated association between Whites and Blacks, enforced segregation, and restricted Black job opportunities. A strict code of social etiquette was also in place, and Blacks were expected to behave deferentially around Whites at all time. This behavior included removing hats, addressing them as Mister or Ma'am, and bowing—behavior reminiscent of slavery's heyday. To enforce these laws and rules, two types of justice system were in place in the South: formal court systems and lynch mobs. Between 1889 and 1918, there were 2,522 African Americans lynched, 50 of them women. They were hacked to death, burned alive, or hanged. Some form of torture usually preceded death. While Whites claimed that lynching occurred for sexual offenses, most took place because Blacks attempted to vote, argued with a White man, or became economically successful. Following are two examinations of lynching. The first is a report from the *Crisis*, of the lynching of Samuel Petty in Leland, Mississippi in 1914. The second is an article written by Mary Church Terrell of Washington D.C., criticizing the practice. What do the two accounts have in common? Why did lynchings take place, according to White Americans? What are the real causes according to these accounts? Is this law and order, or just racism run amuck?

The news spread like wildfire and in twenty minutes the entire white population was armed and headed for the cabin which was situated about a half mile from the depot, which is in the center of the town. I looked in every direction and could see men and mere boys, some not over 12 years old, carrying rifles, shotguns, pistols and, in fact, every imaginable thing that would shoot. They were acting as though there was an entire army of Negroes to be taken. The man who had killed the officer submitted to arrest by the mob, which by this time numbered about 400. Placing a rope around his neck he was led to the center of the town and in the presence of women and children they proceeded to hold a conference as to the kind of death that should be meted out to him. Some yelled to hang him; some to burn him alive. It was decided in a few minutes. Willing hands brought a large dry goods box, place it in the center of the street, in it was straw on which was poured a tub of oil; then the man was lifted with a rope around his neck and placed in this box head down, and then another tub of oil was poured over him. A man from the crowd deliberately lit a match and set fire to the living man. While in this position the flames shot up at great height. The crowd began to yell as the flames shot upward. In an instant the poor creature managed to lift himself out of the box, a mass of flames. He was fighting the flames with his hands in an effort to shield his face and eyes, and

in this condition attempted to run. The crowd allowed him to run to the length of the rope, which was held by willing hands, until he reached a distance of about twenty feet; then a yell went up from the crowd to shoot. In an instant there were several hundred shots and the creature fell in his tracks. The crowd deliberately walked up to the prostrate form and shot the remainder of their guns into his lifeless body. With the flames still leaping into the air, he was pulled back into the fire that was now roaring with boxes and oil brought out of the different stores by men and boys. Every time they would throw on more oil and boxes the crowd would yell as though they were at a bull fight. Standing about fifty or seventy-five feet from the scene I could actually smell the flesh of the poor man as it was being burned. Not a voice was raised in the defense of the man. No one attempted to hide their identity. I looked into the faces of men whom I knew to be officers of the town lending a willing hand in the burning of this man. No wonder the coroner who held the inquest returned a verdict that the Negro came to his death "at the hands of an enraged mob unknown to the jury," because to get a jury in that town they had to get some who participated in the burning. I can never feel toward the white man as I have felt after seeing what I have attempted to describe. After burning the body into ashes the burned bones and ashes were buried in the edge of

---

From *Crisis*, 1914.

the street in front of a colored barber shop. May God forbid that any other living man will ever see a sight as I witnessed; this is the third Negro who has been killed in this vicinity in the last three weeks. The man burned was named Sam Pettie [sic], known by everybody to be quiet and inoffensive. I write this hoping you may get enough out of what I have tried to describe to tell your great number of readers what we are up against. To mention my name in connection with this would be equivalent to committing suicide.

Mary Church Terrell

Hanging, shooting and burning black men, women and children in the United States have become so common that such occurrences create but little sensation and evoke but slight comment now. . . . In the discussion of this subject, four mistakes are commonly made.

In the first place, it is a great mistake to suppose that rape is the real cause of lynching in the South.

Beginning with the Ku Klux Klan, the negro has been constantly subjected to some form of organized violence ever since he became free. It is easy to prove that rape is simply the pretext and not the cause of lynching. Statistics show that, out of every 100 negroes who are lynched, from 75–85 are not even accused of this crime, and many who are accused of it are innocent. . . .

In the second place, it is a mistake to suppose that the negro's desire for social equality sustains any relation whatsoever to the crime of rape. . . . It is safe to assert that, among the negroes who have been guilty of ravishing white women, not one had been taught that he was the equal of white people or had ever heard of social equality. . . . Negroes who have been educated in Northern institutions of learning with white men and women, and who for that reason might have learned the meaning of social equality and have acquired a taste for the same, neither assault white women nor commit other crimes, as a rule. . . . Strange as it may appear, illiterate negroes, who are the only ones contributing largely to the criminal class, are coddled and caressed by the South. To the educated, cultivated members of the race, they are held up as a bright and shining examples of what a really good negro should be. The dictionary is searched in vain by Southern gentlemen and gentlewomen for words sufficiently ornate and strong to express their admiration for a dear old "mammy" or a faithful old "uncle," who can neither read nor write, and who assure their white friends

they would not if they could. On the other hand, no language is sufficiently caustic, bitter and severe, to express the disgust, hatred and scorn which Southern gentlemen feel for what is called the "New Issue," which, being interpreted, means negroes who aspire to knowledge and culture, and who have acquired a taste for the highest and best things in life. At the door of this "New Issue, " the sins and shortcomings of the whole race are laid. This "New Issue" is beyond hope of redemption, we are told, because somebody, nobody knows who, has taught it to believe in social equality, something, nobody knows what. The alledged fear of social equality has always been used by the South to explain its unchristian treatment of the negro and to excuse its many crimes . . . In the North, which is the only section that accords the negro the scrap of social equality enjoyed by him in the United States, he is rarely accused o rape. The only form of social equality ever attempte between the two races, and practised to any consid erable extent, is that which was originated by th white masters of slave women, and which has bee perpetuated by them and their descendants eve unto the present day. . . . There is no more conne tion between social equality and lynching today th there was between social equality and slavery befo the war, or than there is between social equality a the convict-lease system, or any other form oppression to which the negro has uniformly be subjected in the South.

The third error on the subject of lynching co sists of the widely circulated statement that moral sensibilities of the best negroes in the Uni States are so stunted and dull, and the standard morality among even the leaders of the race is low, that they do not appreciate the enormity heinousness of rape. . . . Only those who densely ignorant of the standards and sentimen the best negroes, or who wish willfully to misre sent and maliciously slander a race already res under burdens greater than it can bear, w accuse its thousands of reputable men and wome sympathizing with rapists, either black or whit of condoning their crime. . . .

What, then is the cause of lynching? At th analysis, it will be discovered that there are jus causes of lynching. In the first place, it is d to race hatred, the hatred of a stronger people toward a weaker who were once held as slaves. In the second place, it is due to the lawlessness so prevalent in the section where nine-tenths of the lynchings occur. . . .

Lynching is the aftermath of slavery. The white men who shoot negroes to death and flay them alive, and the white women who apply flaming torches to their oil-soaked bodies today, are the sons and daughters of women who had but little, if any, compassion on the race when it was enslaved. The men who lynch negroes today are, as a rule, the children of women who sat by their firesides happy and proud in the possession and affection of their own children, while they looked with unpitying eye and adamantine heart upon the anguish of slave mothers whose children had been sold away, when not overtaken by a sadder fate . . . It is impossible to comprehend the cause of the ferocity and barbarity which attend the average lynching-bee, without taking into account the brutalizing effect of slavery upon the people of the section where most of the lynchings occur. . . . It is too much to expect, perhaps, that the children of women who for generations looked upon the hardships and the degradation or their sisters of a darker hue with few if any protests, should have mercy and compassion upon the children of that oppressed race now. But what a tremendous influence for law and order, and what a mighty foe to mob violence Southern white women might be, if they would arise in the purity and power of their womanhood to implore their fathers, husbands and sons no longer to stain their hands with the black man's blood! . . . Whenever Southern white people discuss lynching, they are prone to slander the whole negro race. Not long ago, a Southern writer of great repute declared without qualification or reservation that "the crime of rape is well-nigh wholly confined to the negro race," and insisted that "negroes furnish most of the ravishers. " These assertions are as unjust to the negro as they are unfounded in fact. According to statistics recently published, only one colored male in 100,000 over five years of age was accused of assault upon a white woman in the South in 1902, whereas one male out of every 20,000 over five years of age was charged with rape in Chicago during the same year. If these figures prove anything at all, they show that the men and boys in Chicago are many times more addicted to rape than are the negroes in the South. . . .

But even if the negro's morals were as loose and as lax as some claim them to be, and if his belief in the virtue of women were as slight as we are told, the South has nobody to blame but itself . . . Men do not gather grapes of thorns nor figs of thistles. Throughout their entire period of bondage, colored women were debauched by their masters. From the day they were liberated to the present time, prepossessing young colored girls have been considered the rightful prey of white gentlemen in the South, and they have been protected neither by public sentiment nor by law. In the South, the negro's home is not considered sacred by the superior race. White men are neither punished for invading it, not lynched for violating colored women and girls. . . .

How can lynching be extirpated in the United States? . . . Lynching can never be suppressed in the South, until the masses of ignorant white people in that section are educated and lifted to a higher moral plane. . . . Lynching cannot be suppressed in the South, until all classes of white people who dwell there . . . respect the rights of other human beings, no matter what may be the color of their skin . . . and learn a holy reverence for the law. . . .

Until there is a renaissance or popular belief in the principles of liberty and equality upon which this government was founded, lynching, the Convict-Lease System, the Disfranchisement Acts, the Jim Crow Car Laws, unjust discriminations in the professions and trades and similar atrocities will continue to dishearten and degrade the negro, and stain the fair name of the United States. For there can be no doubt that the greatest obstacle in the way of extirpating lynching is the general attitude of the public mind toward this unspeakable crime. The whole country seems tired of hearing about the black man's woes. The wrongs of the Irish, or the Armenians, of the Romanian and Russian Jews, or the exiles of Russia and of every other oppressed people upon the face of the globe, can arouse the sympathy and fire the indignation of the American public, while they seem to be all but indifferent to the murderous assaults upon the negroes in the South.

Document 13.12 Booker T. Washington: The Atlanta Compromise

What is the best way for African Americans to get ahead? Should they behave in a certain way to please Whites? Should they only train for, or pursue, certain jobs, so they do not challenge White status? Should they seek higher education, or just vocational training? These themes are prominent in the famous speech made by Booker T. Washington in 1895. Washington was born a slave in 1856, earned a living, and paid for his education through a series of menial jobs. His whole life was dedicated to hard work. A guiding force behind the Tuskegee Institute in Alabama, Washington argued that Blacks should learn ba[ ] ills to provide for themselves, and thus earn the respect of Whites. In his Atlanta speech, what doe[ ] say Blacks should do? What should they not push for, as that might offend Whites? How do you think So[ ]rn Whites responded to this speech? Is this a surrender of the rights promised in the 14th and 15th Ame[ ]ents, and won by the blood shed in the Civil War? Why do you think many prominent African-American[ ]ers, such as W.E.B. DuBois, opposed Washington's views?

Mr. President and Gentlemen of the Board of Directors and Citizens:

One-third of the population of the South is of the Negro race. No enterprise seeking the material, civil, or moral welfare of this section can disregard this element of our population and reach the highest success. I but convey to you, Mr. President and Directors, the sentiment of the masses of my race when I say that in no way have the value and manhood of the American Negro been more fittingly and generously recognized than by the managers of this magnificent Exposition at every stage of its progress. It is a recognition that will do more to cement the friendship of the two races than any occurrence since the dawn of our freedom.

Not only this, but the opportunity here afforded will awaken among us a new era of industrial progress. Ignorant and inexperienced, it is not strange that in the first years of our new life we began at the top instead of at the bottom; that a seat in Congress or the state legislature was more sought than real estate or industrial skill; that the political convention or stump speaking had more attractions than starting a dairy farm or truck garden.

A ship lost at sea for many days suddenly sighted a friendly vessel. From the mast of the unfortunate vessel was seen a signal, "Water, water; we die of thirst!" The answer from the friendly vessel at once came back, "Cast down your bucket where you are." A second time the signal, "Water, water; send us water!" ran up from the distressed vessel, and was answered, "Cast down your bucket where you are." And a third and fourth signal for water was answered, "Cast down your bucket where you are." The captain of the distressed vessel, at last heeding the injunction, cast down his bucket, and it came up full of fresh, sparkling water from the mouth of the Amazon River. To those of my race who depend on bettering their condition in a foreign land or who underestimate the importance of cultivating friend[ ] ations with the Southern white man, who is their [ ]-door neighbor, I would say: "Cast down your buc[ ] 'here you are"—cast it down in making friends [ ] very manly way of the people of all races by who[ ] are surrounded.

Cast it down in agriculture, mechanics, [ ] m-merce, in domestic service, and in the prof[ ] ns. And in this connection it is well to bear in mi[ ] at whatever other sins the South may be called to [ ] r, when it comes to business, pure and simple, it is [ ] South that the Negro is given a man's chance i[ ] commercial world, and in nothing is this Expos[ ] more eloquent than in emphasizing this chance. [ ] greatest danger is that in the great leap from sla[ ] to freedom we may overlook the fact that the mas[ ] of us are to live by the productions of our hands, a[ ] fail to keep in mind that we shall prosper in prop[ ] tion as we learn to dignify and glorify commo[ ] labour, and put brains and skill into the commo[ ] occupations of life; shall prosper in proportion as w[ ] learn to draw the line between the superficial and the substantial, the ornamental gewgaws of life and the useful. No race can prosper till it learns that there is as much dignity in tilling a field as in writing a poem. It is at the bottom of life we must begin, and not at the top. Nor should we permit our grievances to overshadow our opportunities.

To those of the white race who look to the incoming of those of foreign birth and strange tongue and habits for the prosperity of the South, were I permitted I would repeat what I say to my own race, "Cast down your bucket where you are." Cast it down among the eight millions of Negroes whose habits you know, whose fidelity and love you have tested in days when to have proved treacherous meant the ruin of your firesides. Cast down your bucket among these people who have, without strikes and labour wars, tilled your fields, cleared your

---

Booker T. Washington, 1895.

forests, builded your railroads and cities, and brought forth treasures from the bowels of the earth, and helped make possible this magnificent representation of the progress of the South. Casting down your bucket among my people, helping and encouraging them as you are doing on these grounds, and to education of head, hand, and heart, you will find that they will buy your surplus land, make blossom the waste places in your fields, and run your factories. While doing this, you can be sure in the future, as in the past, that you and your families will be surrounded by the most patient, faithful, law-abiding, and unresentful people that the world has seen. As we have proved our loyalty to you in the past, in nursing your children, watching by the sick-bed of your mothers and fathers, and often following them with tear-dimmed eyes to their graves, so in the future, in our humble way, we shall stand by you with a devotion that no foreigner can approach, ready to lay down our lives, if need be, in defense of yours, interlacing our industrial, commercial, civil, and religious life with yours in a way that shall make the interests of both races one. In all things that are purely social we can be as separate as the fingers, yet one as the hand in all things essential to mutual progress.

There is no defense or security for any of us except in the highest intelligence and development of all. If anywhere there are efforts tending to curtail the fullest growth of the Negro, let these efforts be turned into stimulating, encouraging, and making him the most useful and intelligent citizen. Effort or means so invested will pay a thousand per cent interest. These efforts will be twice blessed—blessing him that gives and him that takes. There is no escape through law of man or God from the inevitable:

The laws of changeless justice bind Oppressor with oppressed;

And close as sin and suffering joined We march to fate abreast.

Nearly sixteen millions of hands will aid you in pulling the load upward, or they will pull against you the load downward. We shall constitute one-third and more of the ignorance and crime of the South, or one-third [of] its intelligence and progress; we shall contribute one-third to the business and industrial prosperity of the South, or we shall prove a veritable body of death, stagnating, depressing, retarding every effort to advance the body politic.

Gentlemen of the Exposition, as we present to you our humble effort at an exhibition of our progress, you must not expect overmuch. Starting thirty years ago with ownership here and there in a few quilts and pumpkins and chickens (gathered from miscellaneous sources), remember the path that has led from these to the inventions and production of agricultural implements, buggies, steam-engines, newspapers, books, statuary, carving, paintings, the management of drug stores and banks, has not been trodden without contact with thorns and thistles. While we take pride in what we exhibit as a result of our independent efforts, we do not for a moment forget that our part in this exhibition would fall far short of your expectations but for the constant help that has come to our educational life, not only from the Southern states, but especially from Northern philanthropists, who have made their gifts a constant stream of blessing and encouragement.

The wisest among my race understand that the agitation of questions of social equality is the extremest folly, and that progress in the enjoyment of all the privileges that will come to us must be the result of severe and constant struggle rather than of artificial forcing. No race that has anything to contribute to the markets of the world is long in any degree ostracized. It is important and right that all privileges of the law be ours, but it is vastly more important that we be prepared for the exercise of these privileges. The opportunity to earn a dollar in a factory just now is worth infinitely more than the opportunity to spend a dollar in an opera-house.

In conclusion, may I repeat that nothing in thirty years has given us more hope and encouragement, and drawn us so near to you of the white race, as this opportunity offered by the Exposition; and here bending, as it were, over the altar that represents the results of the struggles of your race and mine, both starting practically empty-handed three decades ago, I pledge that in your effort to work out the great and intricate problem which God has laid at the doors of the South, you shall have at all times the patient, sympathetic help of my race; only let this be constantly in mind, that, while from representations in these buildings of the product of field, of forest, of mine, of factory, letters, and art, much good will come, yet far above and beyond material benefits will be that higher good, that, let us pray God, will come, in a blotting out of sectional differences and racial animosities and suspicions, in a determination to administer absolute justice, in a willing obedience among all classes to the mandates of law. This, coupled with our material prosperity, will bring into our beloved South a new heaven and a new earth.